ROAD KILL
in the CLOSET

by
Jan Eliot

Book Four of the Syndicated Cartoon Stone Soup®

FOUR PANEL PRESS
Eugene, Oregon

Published by Four Panel Press, P.O. Box 50032, Eugene, OR 97405.

Stone Soup is distributed by Universal Press Syndicate.

ISBN 0-9674102-3-1

Library of Congress Control Number: 2003106767

A portion of the profits from this book will go to alleviate hunger through our local food bank, Food for Lane County.

For Marion and Ted

Wally
Val
Andy
Gramma
Joan
Max
Biscuit
Holly
Alix

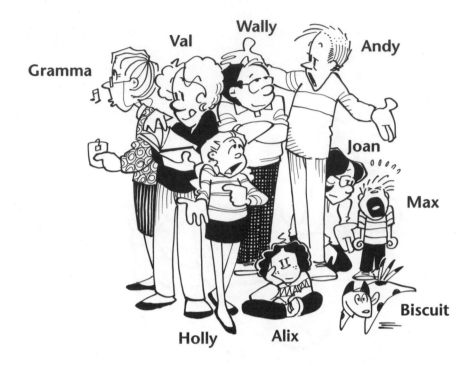

This is the Stone Soup family
...an extended, blended family living in a household where uproar rules.

Joan and **Val**, two sisters, have been sharing a house with their mother and three children. Joan, whose husband went out for milk one night and ended up in the Virgin Islands, struggles with her two year old son **Max**. Val, a widow, juggles drama queen middle-schooler **Holly**, nine-year-old tomboy **Alix**, and a full-time job. **Gramma** lives upstairs and tries, unsuccessfully, to keep her opinions to herself.

In this installment, **Wally**, the nice guy over the fence, has just acquired his 15 year old nephew **Andy** for the summer... and perhaps beyond. Meanwhile, he's got a crush on Joan that won't quit, unless of course **Susan**, the girls basketball coach, gets to him first.

Add **Biscuit**, the "active breed" dog, and get out of the way. **Enjoy!**

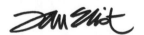

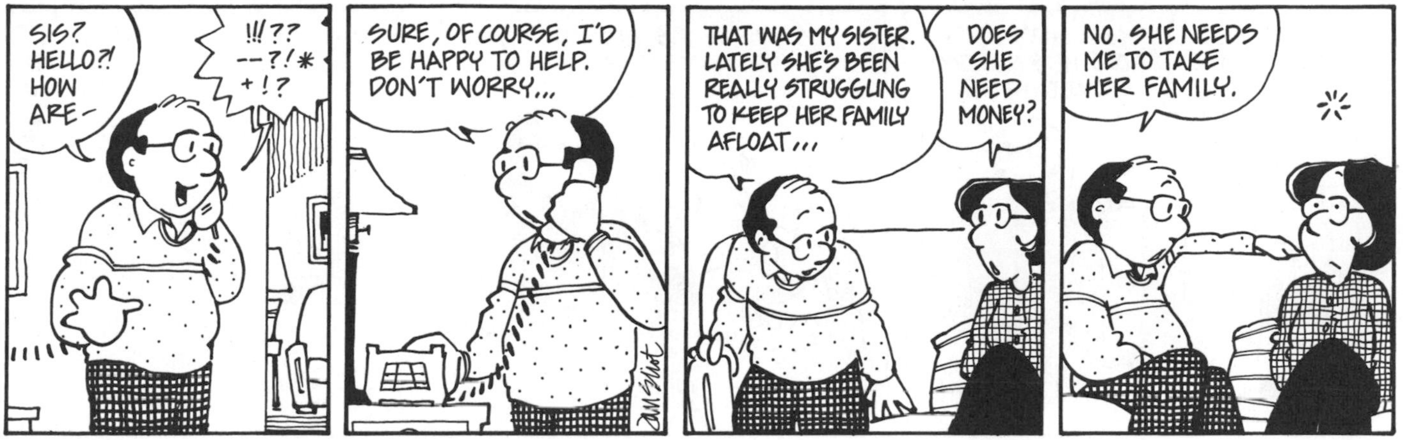
SIS? HELLO?! HOW ARE-
!!!?? --?!* +!?
SURE, OF COURSE, I'D BE HAPPY TO HELP. DON'T WORRY...
THAT WAS MY SISTER. LATELY SHE'S BEEN REALLY STRUGGLING TO KEEP HER FAMILY AFLOAT...
DOES SHE NEED MONEY?
NO. SHE NEEDS ME TO TAKE HER FAMILY.

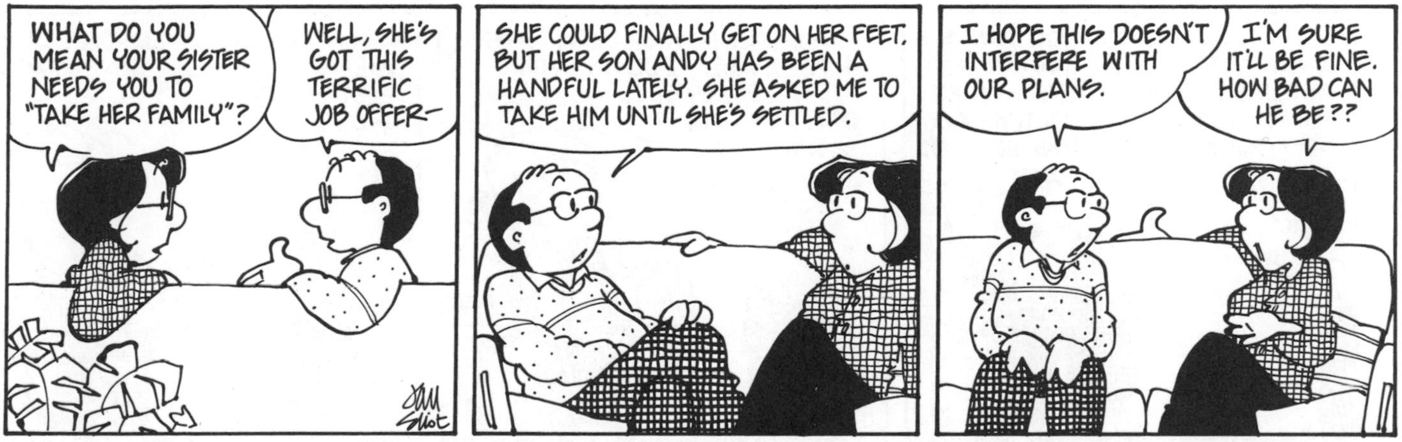
WHAT DO YOU MEAN YOUR SISTER NEEDS YOU TO "TAKE HER FAMILY"?
WELL, SHE'S GOT THIS TERRIFIC JOB OFFER-
SHE COULD FINALLY GET ON HER FEET, BUT HER SON ANDY HAS BEEN A HANDFUL LATELY. SHE ASKED ME TO TAKE HIM UNTIL SHE'S SETTLED.
I HOPE THIS DOESN'T INTERFERE WITH OUR PLANS.
I'M SURE IT'LL BE FINE. HOW BAD CAN HE BE??

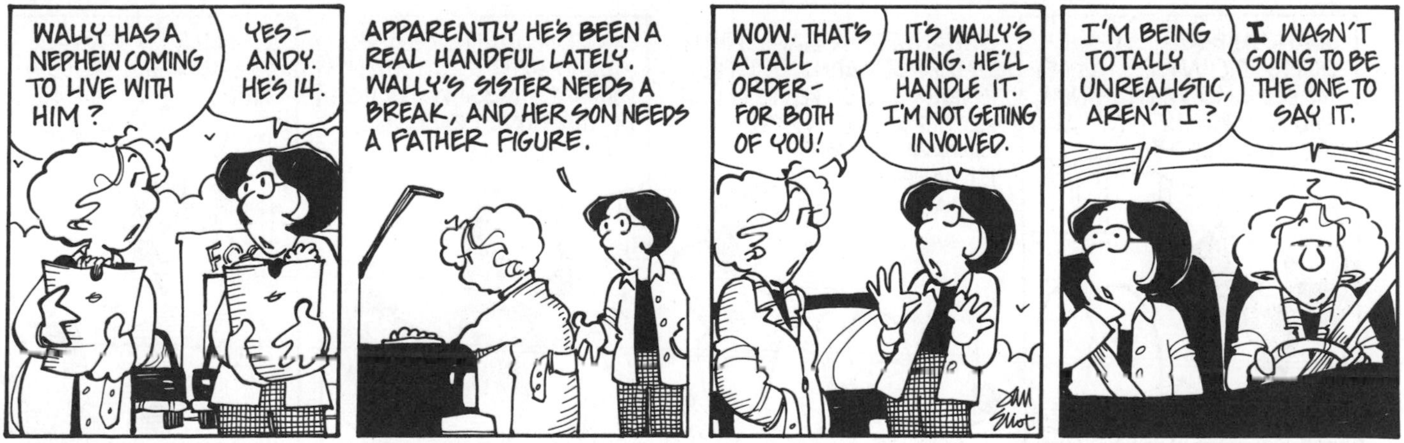
WALLY HAS A NEPHEW COMING TO LIVE WITH HIM?
YES- ANDY. HE'S 14.
APPARENTLY HE'S BEEN A REAL HANDFUL LATELY. WALLY'S SISTER NEEDS A BREAK, AND HER SON NEEDS A FATHER FIGURE.
WOW. THAT'S A TALL ORDER- FOR BOTH OF YOU!
IT'S WALLY'S THING. HE'LL HANDLE IT. I'M NOT GETTING INVOLVED.
I'M BEING TOTALLY UNREALISTIC, AREN'T I?
I WASN'T GOING TO BE THE ONE TO SAY IT.

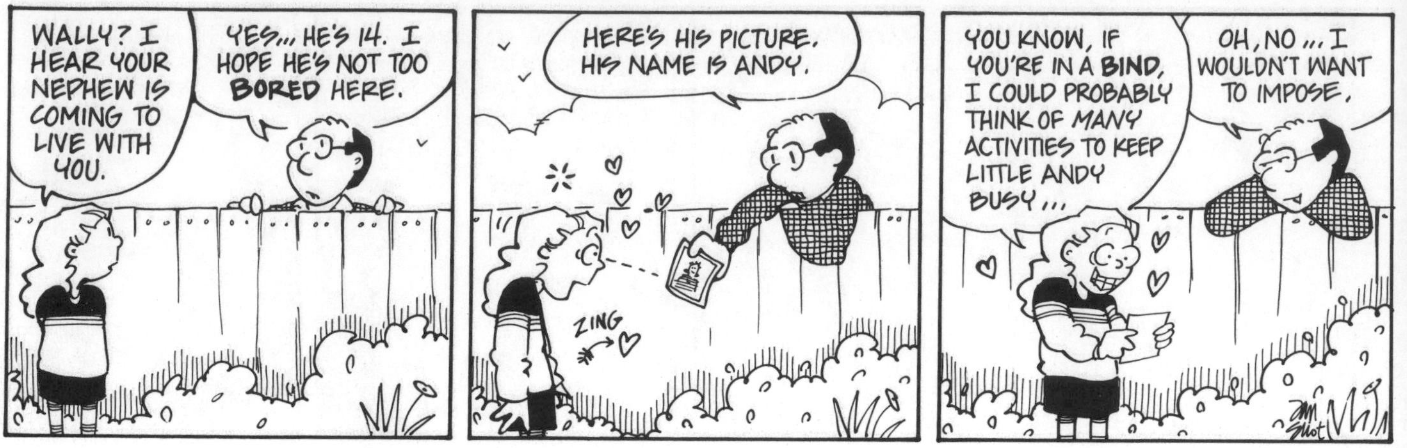
WALLY? I HEAR YOUR NEPHEW IS COMING TO LIVE WITH YOU.
YES... HE'S 14. I HOPE HE'S NOT TOO **BORED** HERE.
HERE'S HIS PICTURE. HIS NAME IS ANDY.
ZING
YOU KNOW, IF YOU'RE IN A **BIND**, I COULD PROBABLY THINK OF *MANY* ACTIVITIES TO KEEP LITTLE ANDY BUSY...
OH, NO... I WOULDN'T WANT TO IMPOSE.

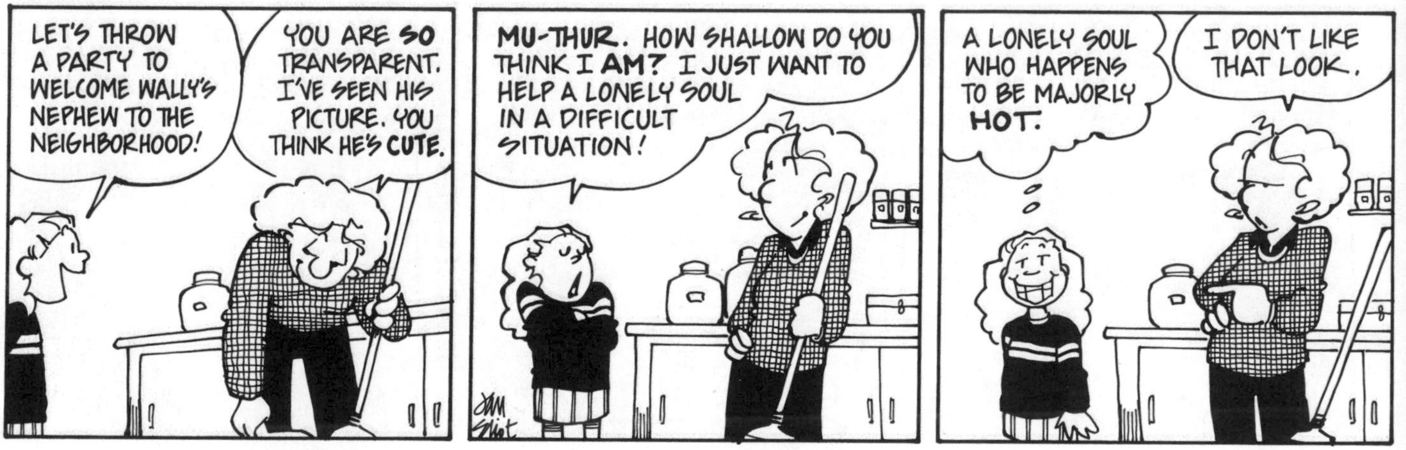
LET'S THROW A PARTY TO WELCOME WALLY'S NEPHEW TO THE NEIGHBORHOOD!
YOU ARE **SO** TRANSPARENT. I'VE SEEN HIS PICTURE. YOU THINK HE'S **CUTE**.
MU-THUR. HOW SHALLOW DO YOU THINK I **AM?** I JUST WANT TO HELP A LONELY SOUL IN A DIFFICULT SITUATION!
A LONELY SOUL WHO HAPPENS TO BE MAJORLY **HOT**.
I DON'T LIKE THAT LOOK.

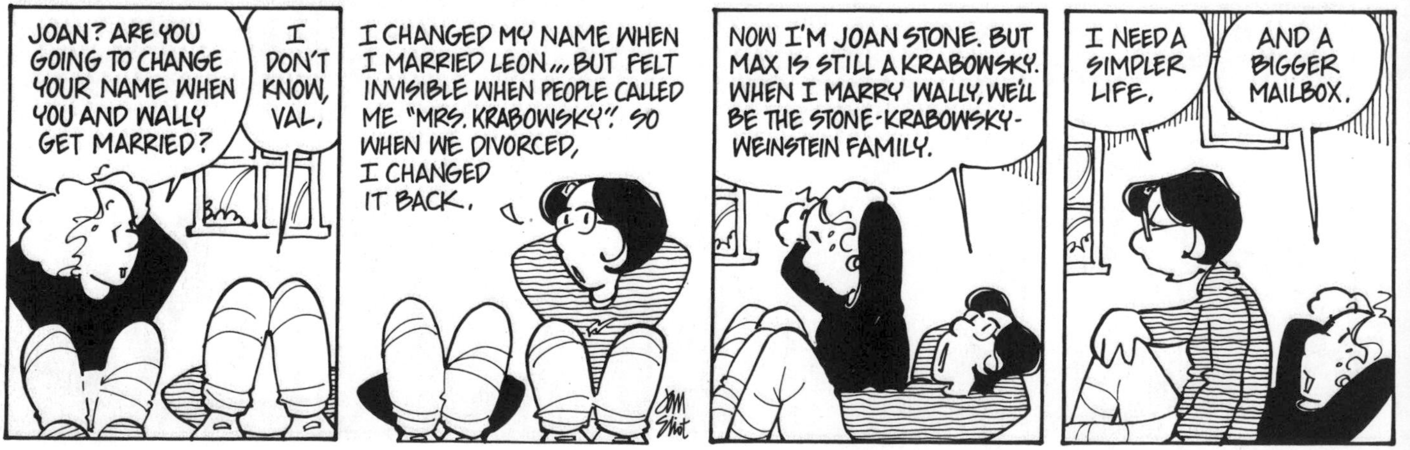
JOAN? ARE YOU GOING TO CHANGE YOUR NAME WHEN YOU AND WALLY GET MARRIED?
I DON'T KNOW, VAL.
I CHANGED MY NAME WHEN I MARRIED LEON... BUT FELT INVISIBLE WHEN PEOPLE CALLED ME "MRS. KRABOWSKY." SO WHEN WE DIVORCED, I CHANGED IT BACK.
NOW I'M JOAN STONE. BUT MAX IS STILL A KRABOWSKY. WHEN I MARRY WALLY, WE'LL BE THE STONE-KRABOWSKY-WEINSTEIN FAMILY.
I NEED A SIMPLER LIFE.
AND A BIGGER MAILBOX.

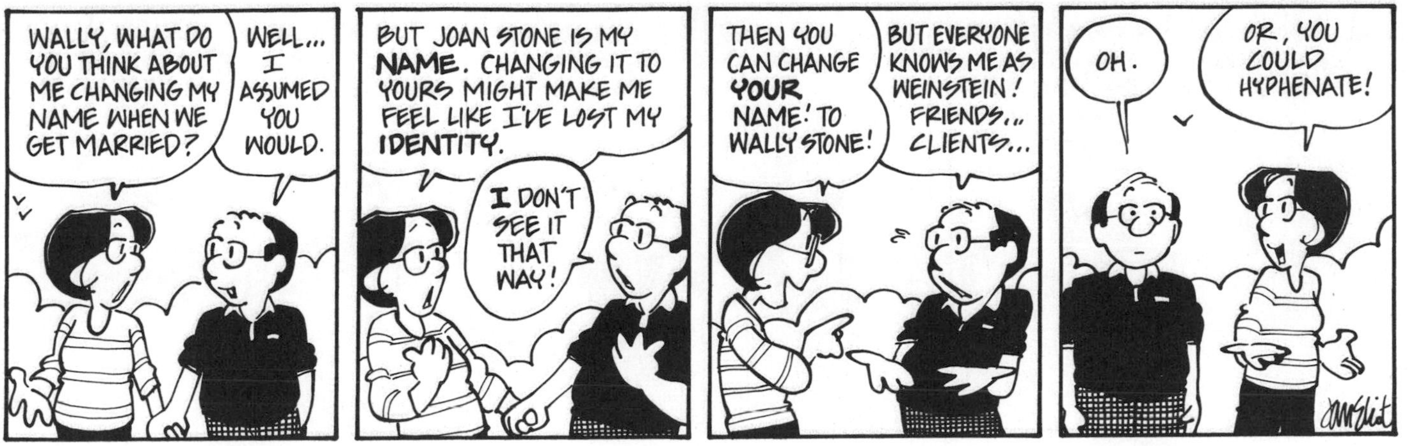
WALLY, WHAT DO YOU THINK ABOUT ME CHANGING MY NAME WHEN WE GET MARRIED?
WELL... I ASSUMED YOU WOULD.
BUT JOAN STONE IS MY **NAME**. CHANGING IT TO YOURS MIGHT MAKE ME FEEL LIKE I'VE LOST MY **IDENTITY**.
I DON'T SEE IT THAT WAY!
THEN YOU CAN CHANGE **YOUR** NAME! TO WALLY STONE!
BUT EVERYONE KNOWS ME AS WEINSTEIN! FRIENDS... CLIENTS...
OH.
OR, YOU COULD HYPHENATE!

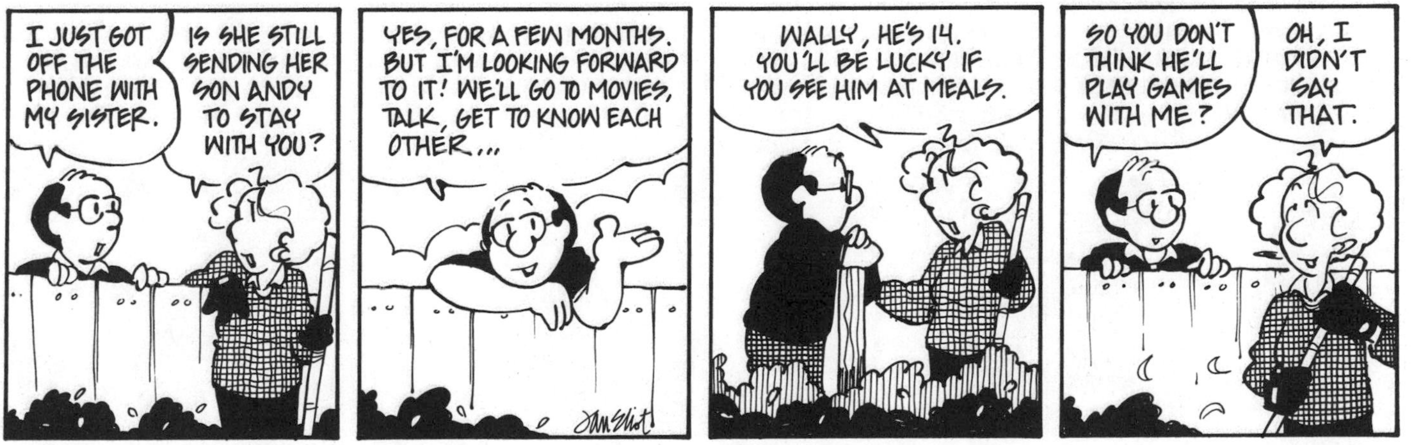
I JUST GOT OFF THE PHONE WITH MY SISTER.
IS SHE STILL SENDING HER SON ANDY TO STAY WITH YOU?
YES, FOR A FEW MONTHS. BUT I'M LOOKING FORWARD TO IT! WE'LL GO TO MOVIES, TALK, GET TO KNOW EACH OTHER...
WALLY, HE'S 14. YOU'LL BE LUCKY IF YOU SEE HIM AT MEALS.
SO YOU DON'T THINK HE'LL PLAY GAMES WITH ME?
OH, I DIDN'T SAY THAT.

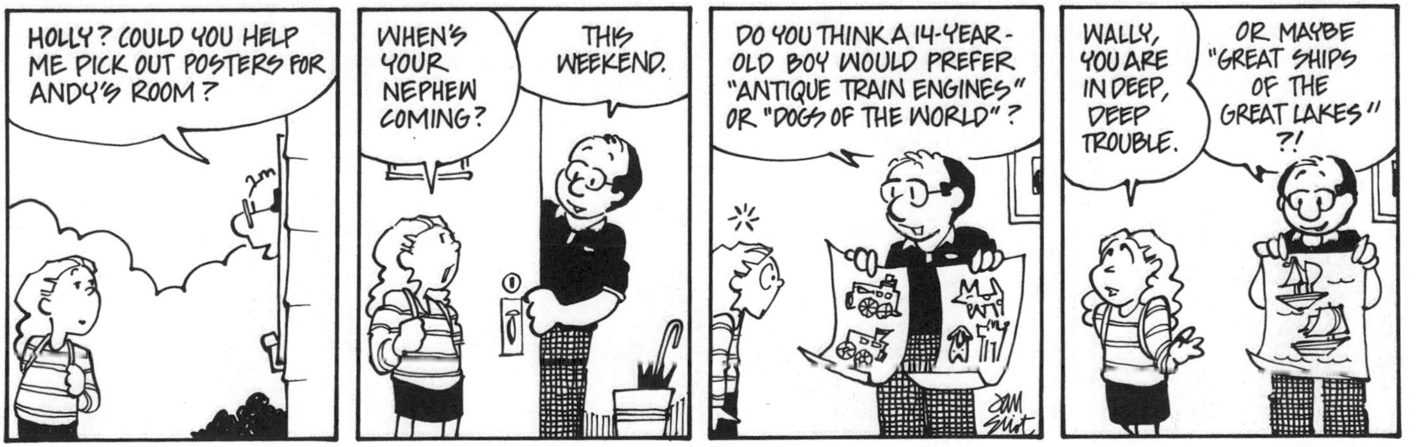
HOLLY? COULD YOU HELP ME PICK OUT POSTERS FOR ANDY'S ROOM?
WHEN'S YOUR NEPHEW COMING?
THIS WEEKEND.
DO YOU THINK A 14-YEAR-OLD BOY WOULD PREFER "ANTIQUE TRAIN ENGINES" OR "DOGS OF THE WORLD"?
WALLY, YOU ARE IN DEEP, DEEP TROUBLE.
OR MAYBE "GREAT SHIPS OF THE GREAT LAKES" ?!

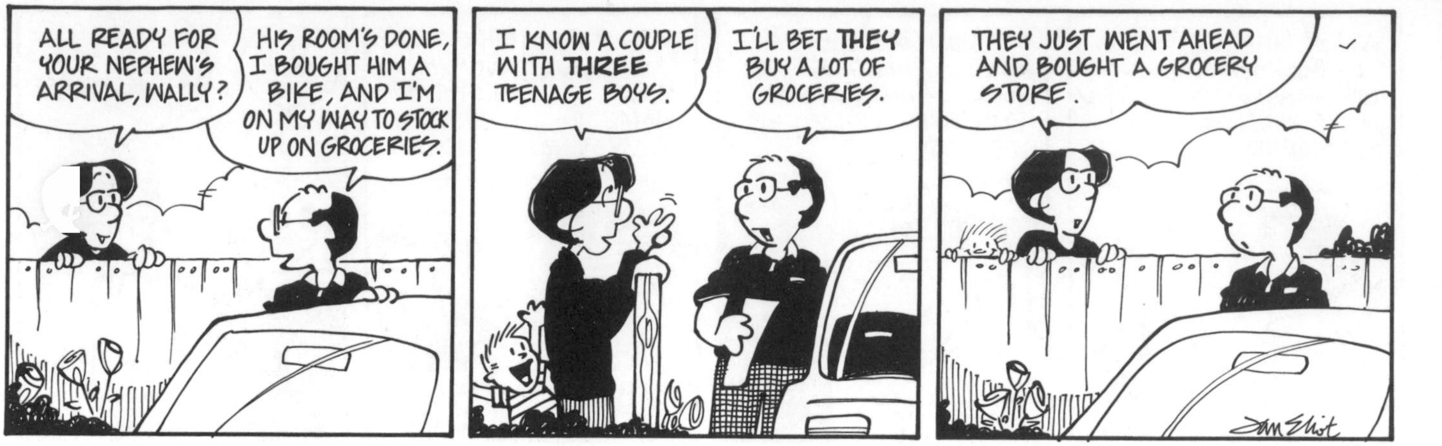
ALL READY FOR YOUR NEPHEW'S ARRIVAL, WALLY?
HIS ROOM'S DONE, I BOUGHT HIM A BIKE, AND I'M ON MY WAY TO STOCK UP ON GROCERIES.
I KNOW A COUPLE WITH **THREE** TEENAGE BOYS.
I'LL BET **THEY** BUY A LOT OF GROCERIES.
THEY JUST WENT AHEAD AND BOUGHT A GROCERY STORE.

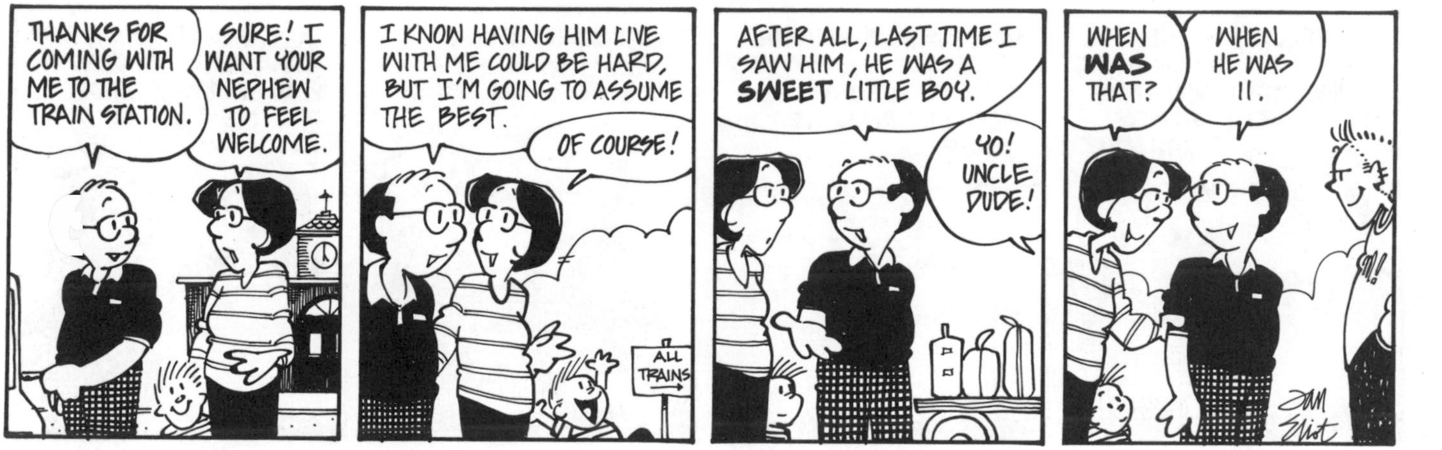
THANKS FOR COMING WITH ME TO THE TRAIN STATION.
SURE! I WANT YOUR NEPHEW TO FEEL WELCOME.
I KNOW HAVING HIM LIVE WITH ME COULD BE HARD, BUT I'M GOING TO ASSUME THE BEST.
OF COURSE!
ALL TRAINS
AFTER ALL, LAST TIME I SAW HIM, HE WAS A **SWEET** LITTLE BOY.
YO! UNCLE DUDE!
WHEN **WAS** THAT?
WHEN HE WAS 11.

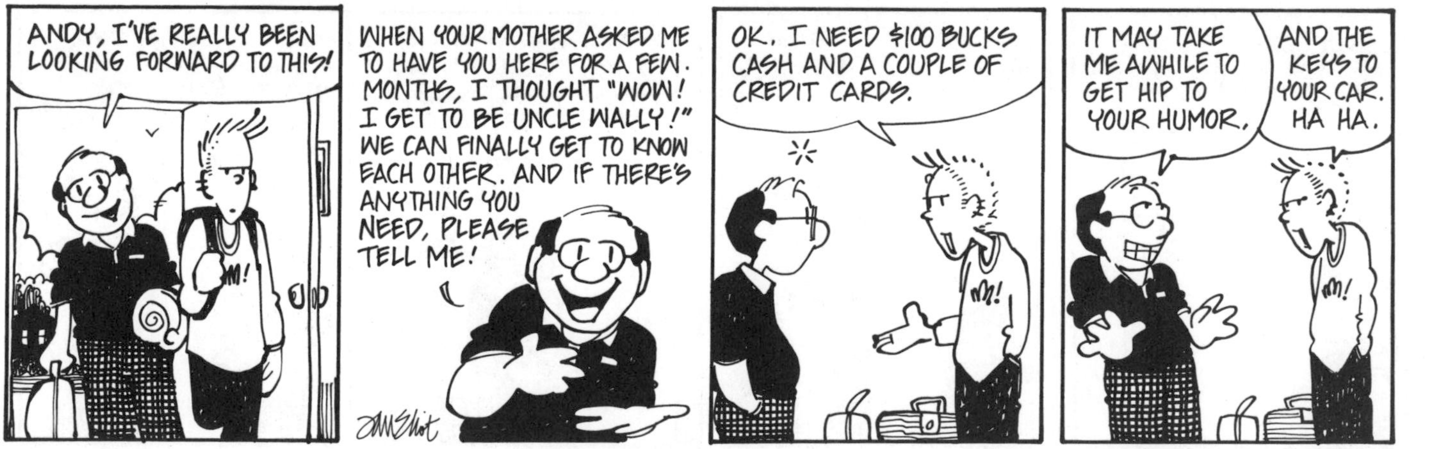
ANDY, I'VE REALLY BEEN LOOKING FORWARD TO THIS!
WHEN YOUR MOTHER ASKED ME TO HAVE YOU HERE FOR A FEW MONTHS, I THOUGHT "WOW! I GET TO BE UNCLE WALLY!" WE CAN FINALLY GET TO KNOW EACH OTHER. AND IF THERE'S ANYTHING YOU NEED, PLEASE TELL ME!
OK. I NEED $100 BUCKS CASH AND A COUPLE OF CREDIT CARDS.
IT MAY TAKE ME AWHILE TO GET HIP TO YOUR HUMOR.
AND THE KEYS TO YOUR CAR. HA HA.

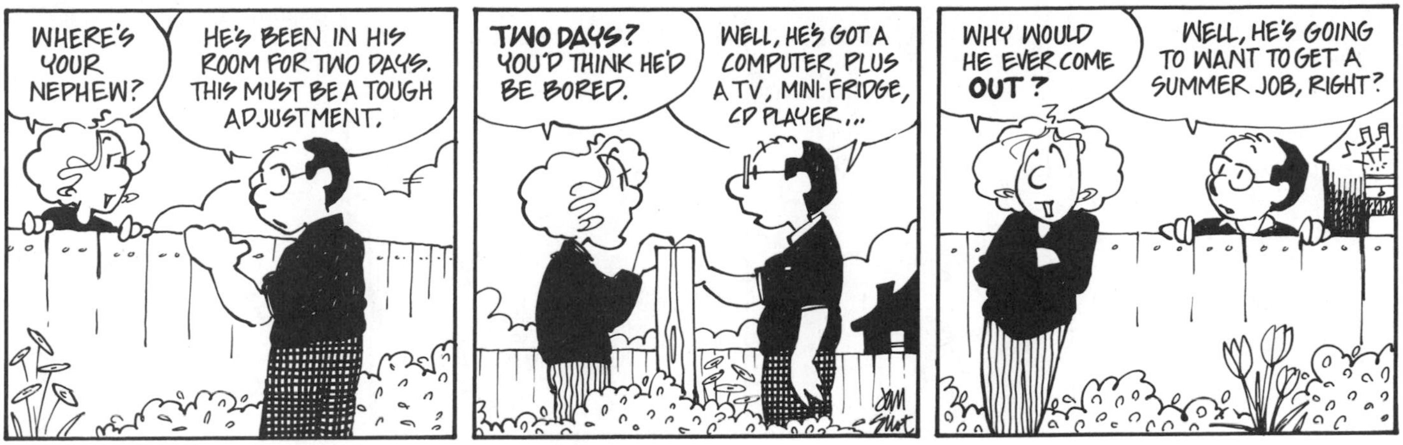
WHERE'S YOUR NEPHEW?
HE'S BEEN IN HIS ROOM FOR TWO DAYS. THIS MUST BE A TOUGH ADJUSTMENT.
TWO DAYS? YOU'D THINK HE'D BE BORED.
WELL, HE'S GOT A COMPUTER, PLUS A TV, MINI-FRIDGE, CD PLAYER...
WHY WOULD HE EVER COME OUT?
WELL, HE'S GOING TO WANT TO GET A SUMMER JOB, RIGHT?

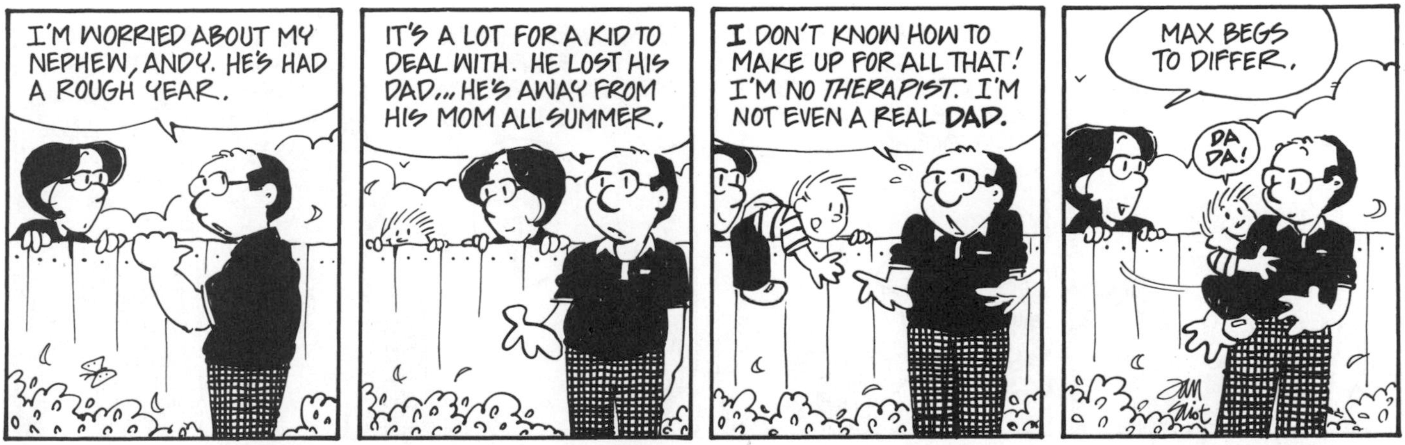
I'M WORRIED ABOUT MY NEPHEW, ANDY. HE'S HAD A ROUGH YEAR.
IT'S A LOT FOR A KID TO DEAL WITH. HE LOST HIS DAD... HE'S AWAY FROM HIS MOM ALL SUMMER.
I DON'T KNOW HOW TO MAKE UP FOR ALL THAT! I'M NO THERAPIST. I'M NOT EVEN A REAL DAD.
MAX BEGS TO DIFFER.
DA DA!

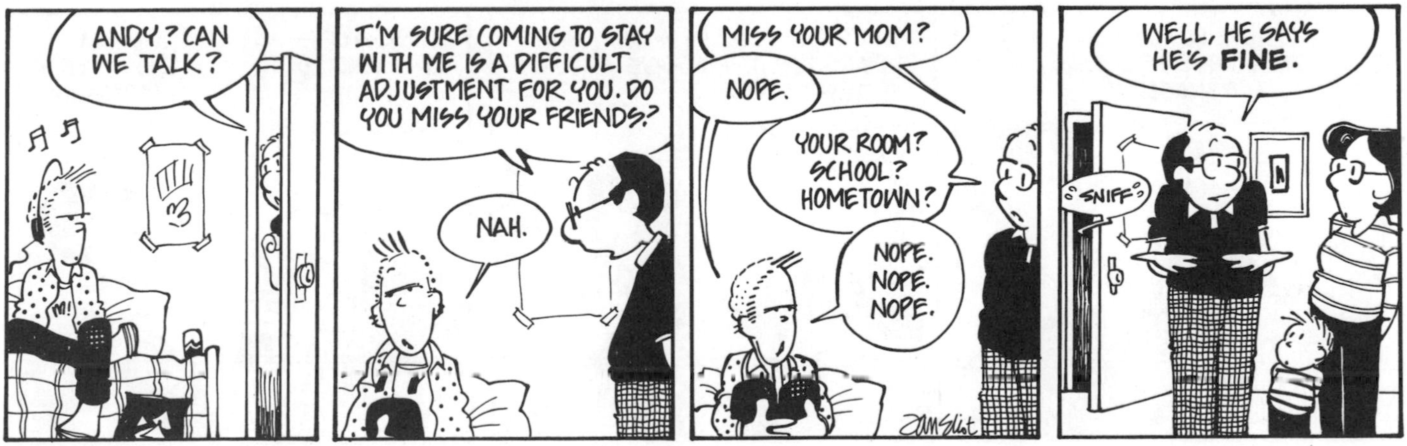
ANDY? CAN WE TALK?
I'M SURE COMING TO STAY WITH ME IS A DIFFICULT ADJUSTMENT FOR YOU. DO YOU MISS YOUR FRIENDS?
NAH.
MISS YOUR MOM?
NOPE.
YOUR ROOM? SCHOOL? HOMETOWN?
NOPE. NOPE. NOPE.
WELL, HE SAYS HE'S FINE.
SNIFF

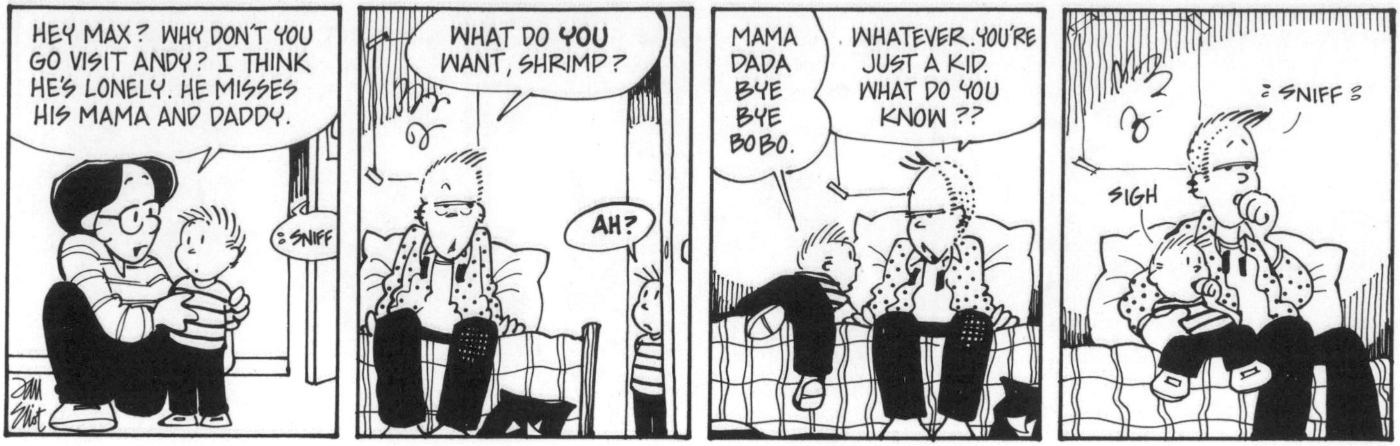
HEY MAX? WHY DON'T YOU GO VISIT ANDY? I THINK HE'S LONELY. HE MISSES HIS MAMA AND DADDY.
SNIFF
WHAT DO YOU WANT, SHRIMP?
AH?
MAMA DADA BYE BYE BOBO.
WHATEVER..YOU'RE JUST A KID. WHAT DO YOU KNOW??
SNIFF
SIGH

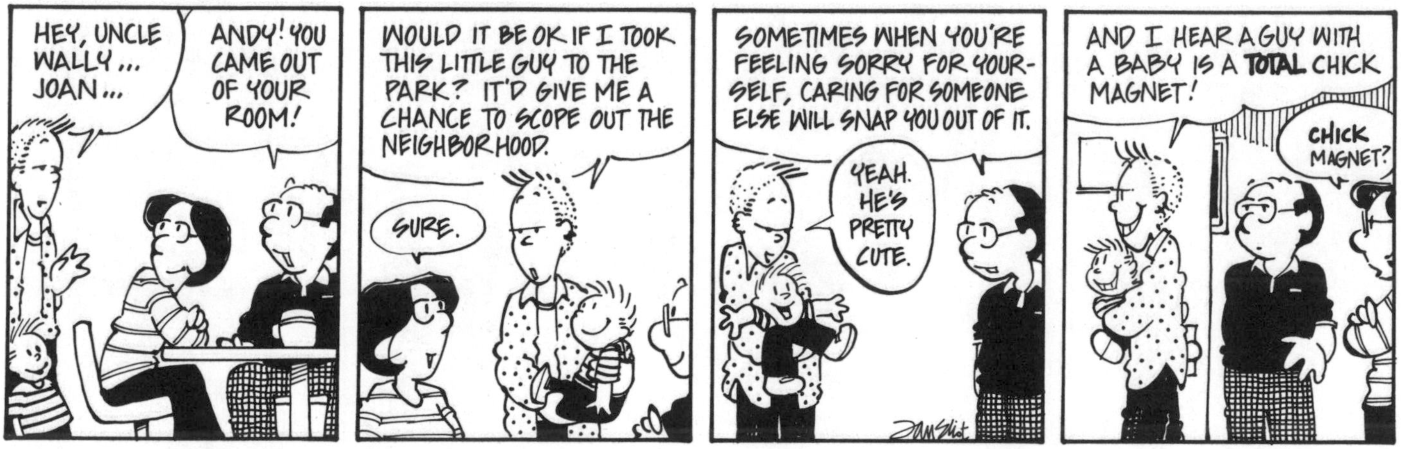
HEY, UNCLE WALLY... JOAN...
ANDY! YOU CAME OUT OF YOUR ROOM!
WOULD IT BE OK IF I TOOK THIS LITTLE GUY TO THE PARK? IT'D GIVE ME A CHANCE TO SCOPE OUT THE NEIGHBORHOOD.
SURE.
SOMETIMES WHEN YOU'RE FEELING SORRY FOR YOURSELF, CARING FOR SOMEONE ELSE WILL SNAP YOU OUT OF IT.
YEAH. HE'S PRETTY CUTE.
AND I HEAR A GUY WITH A BABY IS A TOTAL CHICK MAGNET!
CHICK MAGNET?

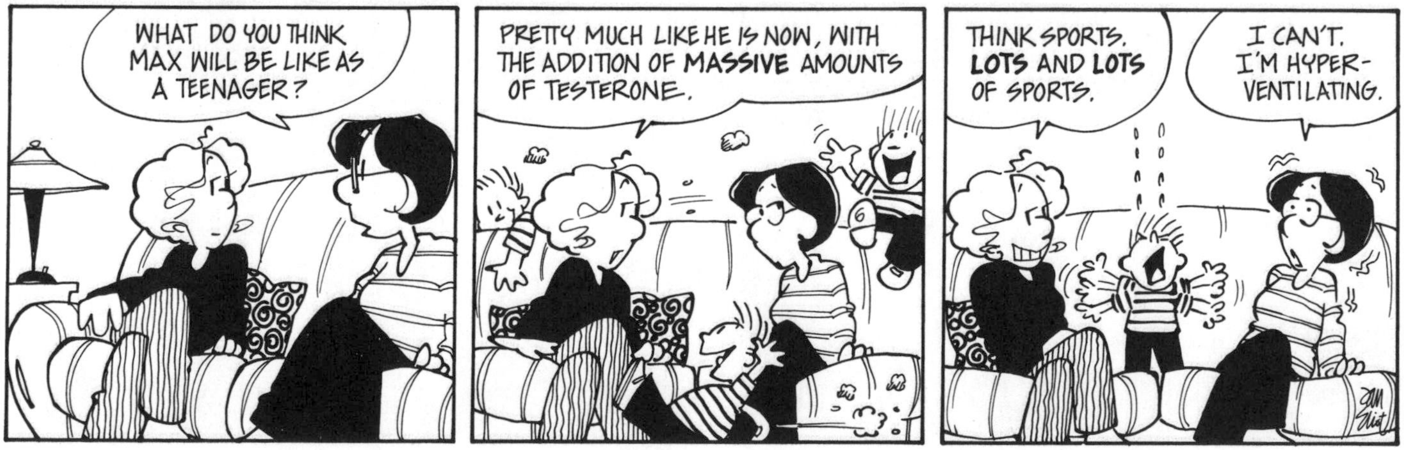
WHAT DO YOU THINK MAX WILL BE LIKE AS A TEENAGER?
PRETTY MUCH LIKE HE IS NOW, WITH THE ADDITION OF MASSIVE AMOUNTS OF TESTERONE.
THINK SPORTS. LOTS AND LOTS OF SPORTS.
I CAN'T. I'M HYPER-VENTILATING.

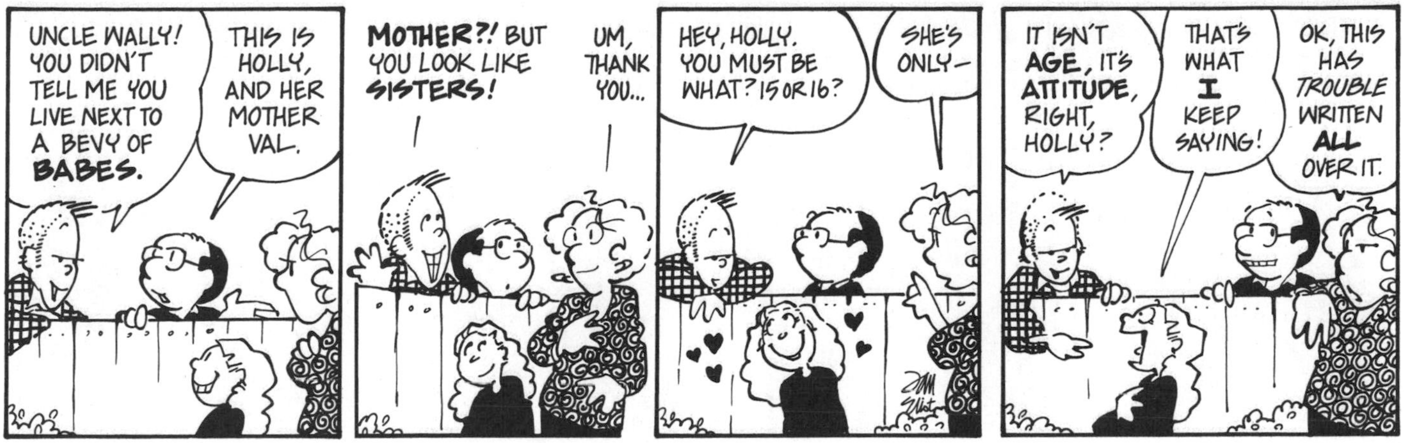
UNCLE WALLY! YOU DIDN'T TELL ME YOU LIVE NEXT TO A BEVY OF BABES.
THIS IS HOLLY, AND HER MOTHER VAL.
MOTHER?! BUT YOU LOOK LIKE SISTERS!
UM, THANK YOU...
HEY, HOLLY. YOU MUST BE WHAT? 15 OR 16?
SHE'S ONLY—
IT ISN'T AGE, IT'S ATTITUDE, RIGHT, HOLLY?
THAT'S WHAT I KEEP SAYING!
OK, THIS HAS TROUBLE WRITTEN ALL OVER IT.

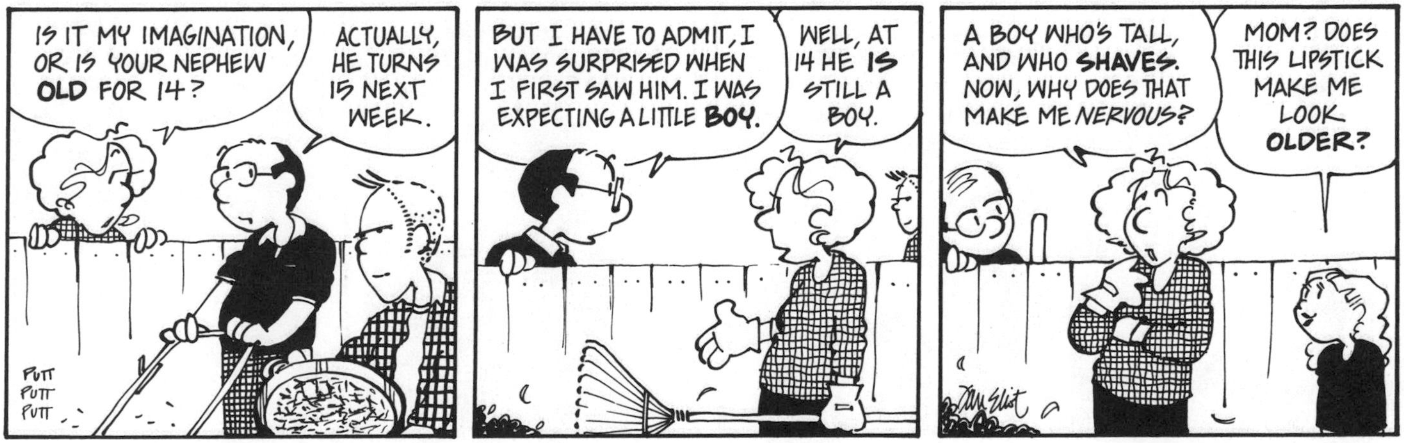
IS IT MY IMAGINATION, OR IS YOUR NEPHEW OLD FOR 14?
ACTUALLY, HE TURNS 15 NEXT WEEK.
PUTT PUTT PUTT
BUT I HAVE TO ADMIT, I WAS SURPRISED WHEN I FIRST SAW HIM. I WAS EXPECTING A LITTLE BOY.
WELL, AT 14 HE IS STILL A BOY.
A BOY WHO'S TALL, AND WHO SHAVES. NOW, WHY DOES THAT MAKE ME NERVOUS?
MOM? DOES THIS LIPSTICK MAKE ME LOOK OLDER?

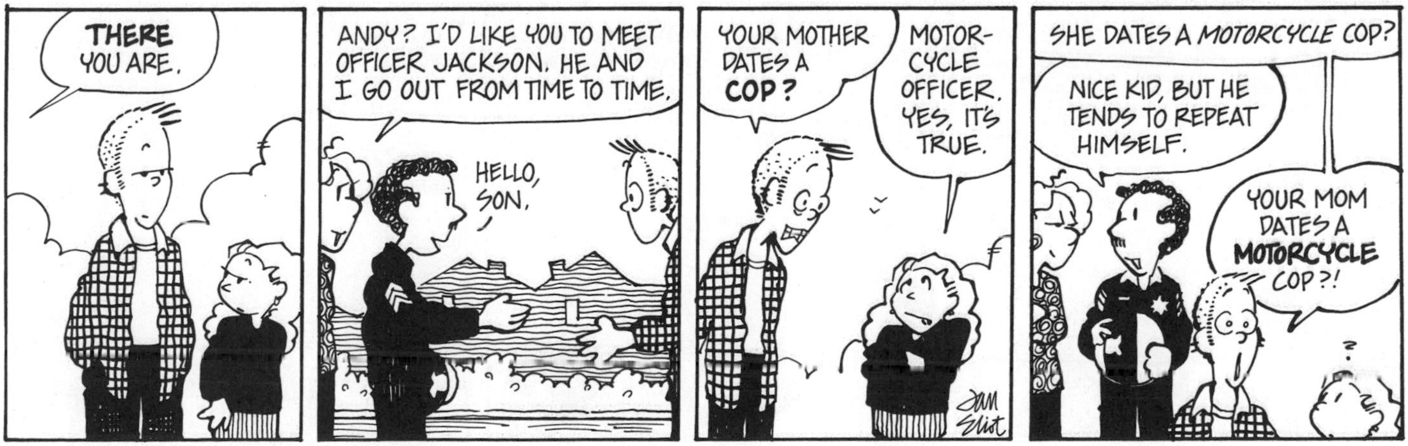
THERE YOU ARE.
ANDY? I'D LIKE YOU TO MEET OFFICER JACKSON. HE AND I GO OUT FROM TIME TO TIME.
HELLO, SON.
YOUR MOTHER DATES A COP?
MOTOR-CYCLE OFFICER. YES, IT'S TRUE.
SHE DATES A MOTORCYCLE COP?
NICE KID, BUT HE TENDS TO REPEAT HIMSELF.
YOUR MOM DATES A MOTORCYCLE COP?!

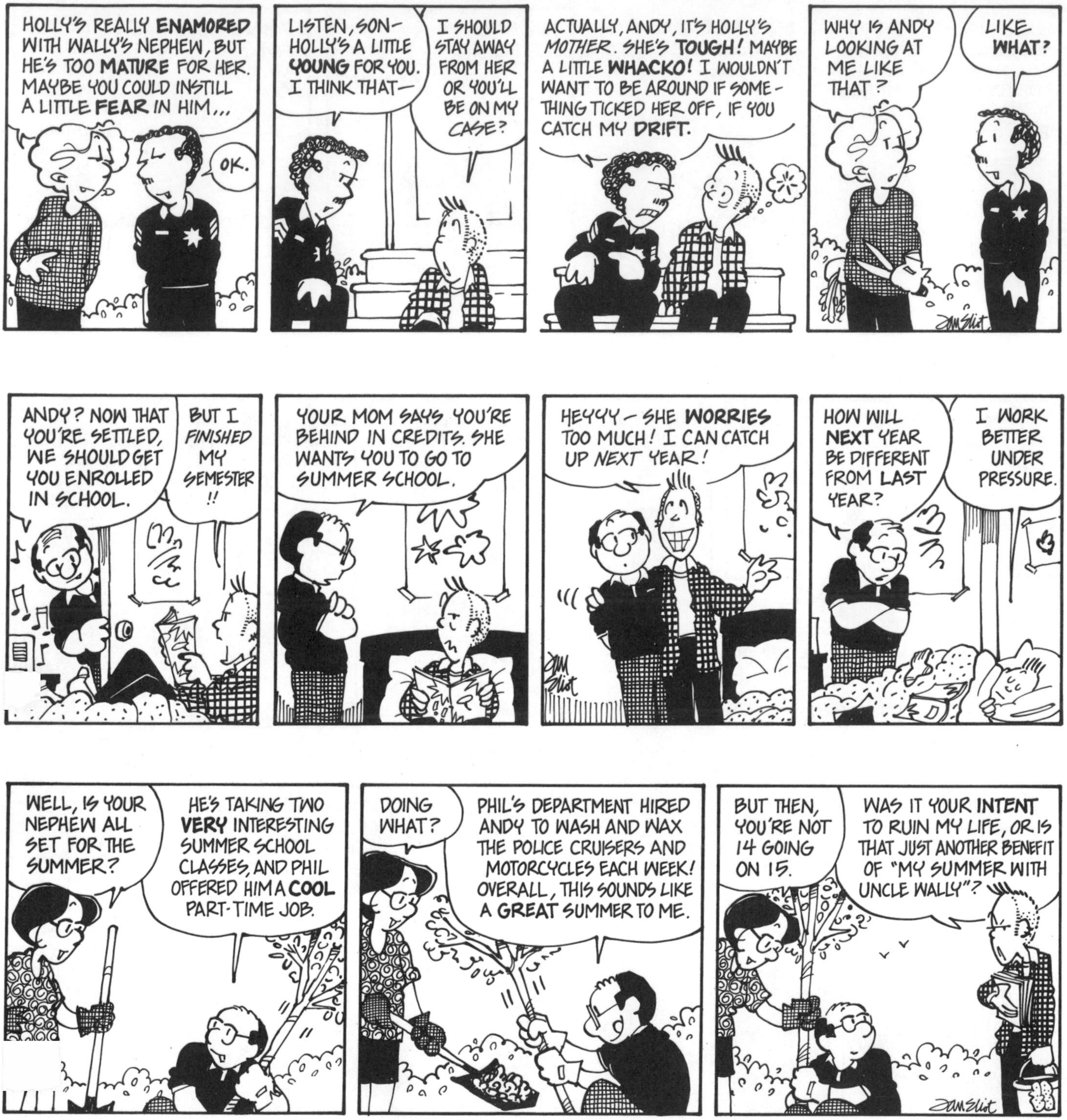
HOLLY'S REALLY ENAMORED WITH WALLY'S NEPHEW, BUT HE'S TOO MATURE FOR HER. MAYBE YOU COULD INSTILL A LITTLE FEAR IN HIM...
OK.
LISTEN, SON– HOLLY'S A LITTLE YOUNG FOR YOU. I THINK THAT–
I SHOULD STAY AWAY FROM HER OR YOU'LL BE ON MY CASE?
ACTUALLY, ANDY, IT'S HOLLY'S MOTHER. SHE'S TOUGH! MAYBE A LITTLE WHACKO! I WOULDN'T WANT TO BE AROUND IF SOMETHING TICKED HER OFF, IF YOU CATCH MY DRIFT.
WHY IS ANDY LOOKING AT ME LIKE THAT?
LIKE WHAT?
ANDY? NOW THAT YOU'RE SETTLED, WE SHOULD GET YOU ENROLLED IN SCHOOL.
BUT I FINISHED MY SEMESTER !!
YOUR MOM SAYS YOU'RE BEHIND IN CREDITS. SHE WANTS YOU TO GO TO SUMMER SCHOOL.
HEYYY – SHE WORRIES TOO MUCH! I CAN CATCH UP NEXT YEAR!
HOW WILL NEXT YEAR BE DIFFERENT FROM LAST YEAR?
I WORK BETTER UNDER PRESSURE.
WELL, IS YOUR NEPHEW ALL SET FOR THE SUMMER?
HE'S TAKING TWO VERY INTERESTING SUMMER SCHOOL CLASSES, AND PHIL OFFERED HIM A COOL PART-TIME JOB.
DOING WHAT?
PHIL'S DEPARTMENT HIRED ANDY TO WASH AND WAX THE POLICE CRUISERS AND MOTORCYCLES EACH WEEK! OVERALL, THIS SOUNDS LIKE A GREAT SUMMER TO ME.
BUT THEN, YOU'RE NOT 14 GOING ON 15.
WAS IT YOUR INTENT TO RUIN MY LIFE, OR IS THAT JUST ANOTHER BENEFIT OF "MY SUMMER WITH UNCLE WALLY"?

Stone Soup

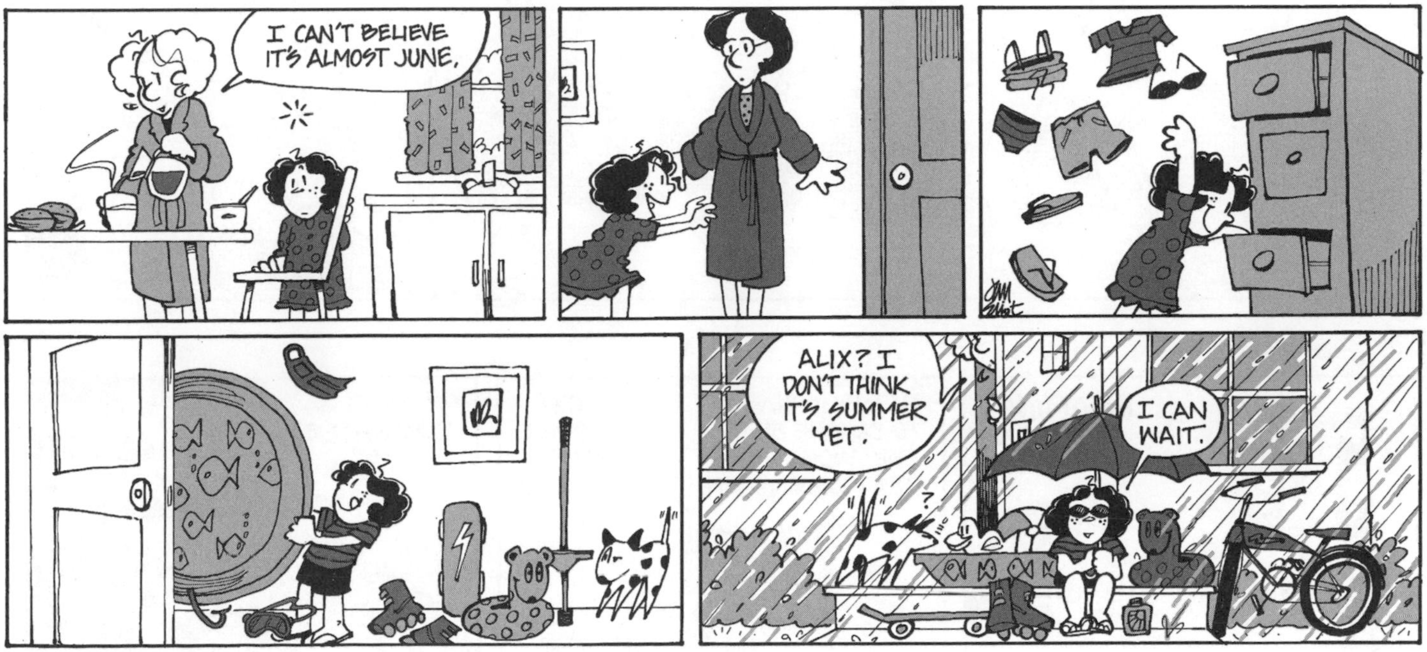
I CAN'T BELIEVE IT'S ALMOST JUNE.
ALIX? I DON'T THINK IT'S SUMMER YET.
I CAN WAIT.

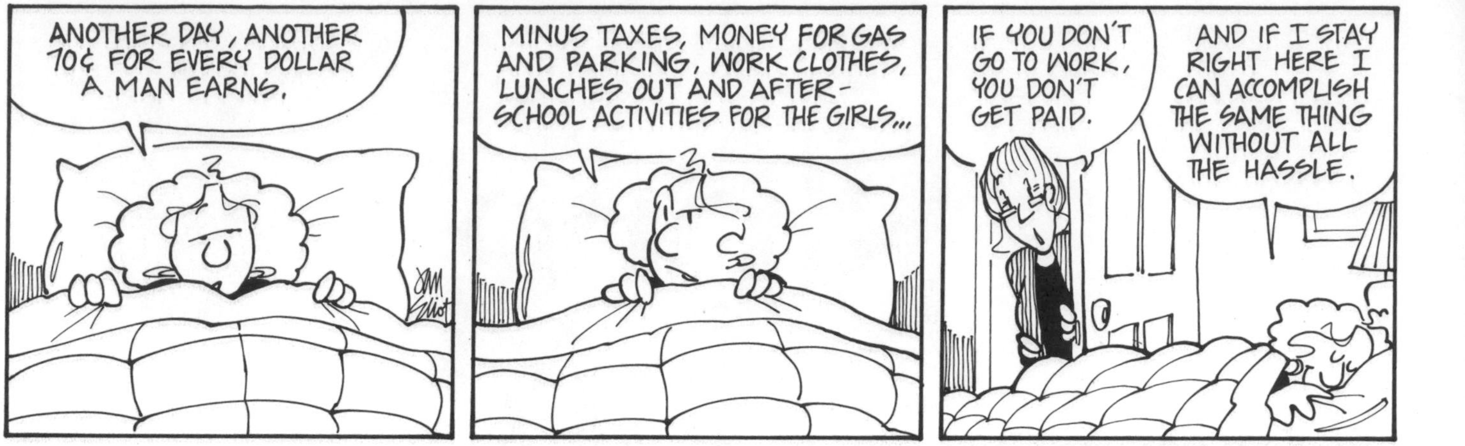
ANOTHER DAY, ANOTHER 70¢ FOR EVERY DOLLAR A MAN EARNS.
MINUS TAXES, MONEY FOR GAS AND PARKING, WORK CLOTHES, LUNCHES OUT AND AFTER-SCHOOL ACTIVITIES FOR THE GIRLS...
IF YOU DON'T GO TO WORK, YOU DON'T GET PAID.
AND IF I STAY RIGHT HERE I CAN ACCOMPLISH THE SAME THING WITHOUT ALL THE HASSLE.

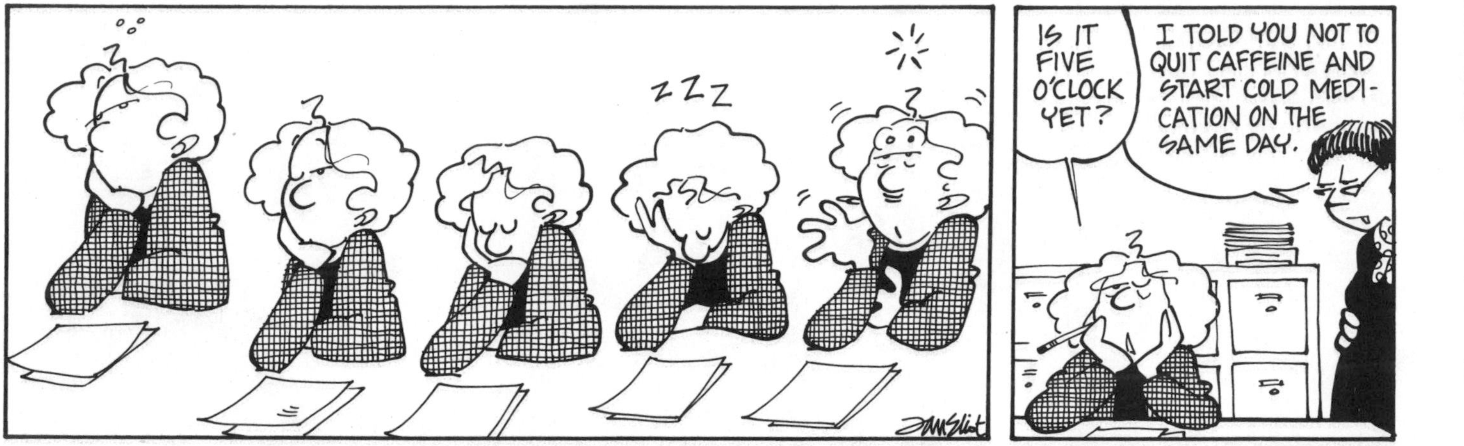
Z Z Z
IS IT FIVE O'CLOCK YET?
I TOLD YOU NOT TO QUIT CAFFEINE AND START COLD MEDICATION ON THE SAME DAY.

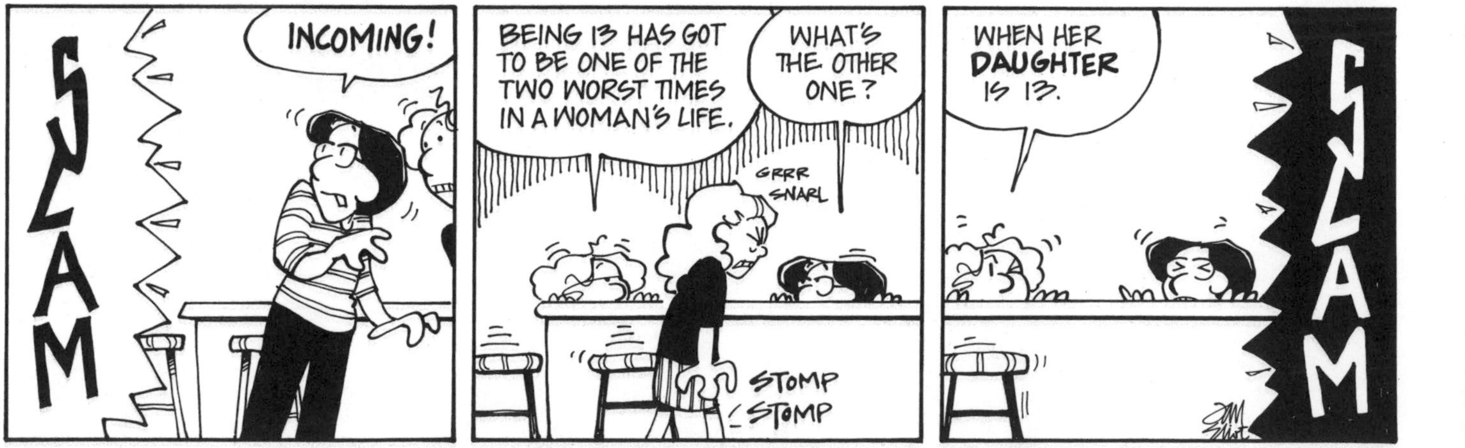
SLAM
INCOMING!
BEING 13 HAS GOT TO BE ONE OF THE TWO WORST TIMES IN A WOMAN'S LIFE.
WHAT'S THE OTHER ONE?
GRRR SNARL
STOMP STOMP
WHEN HER **DAUGHTER** IS 13.
SLAM

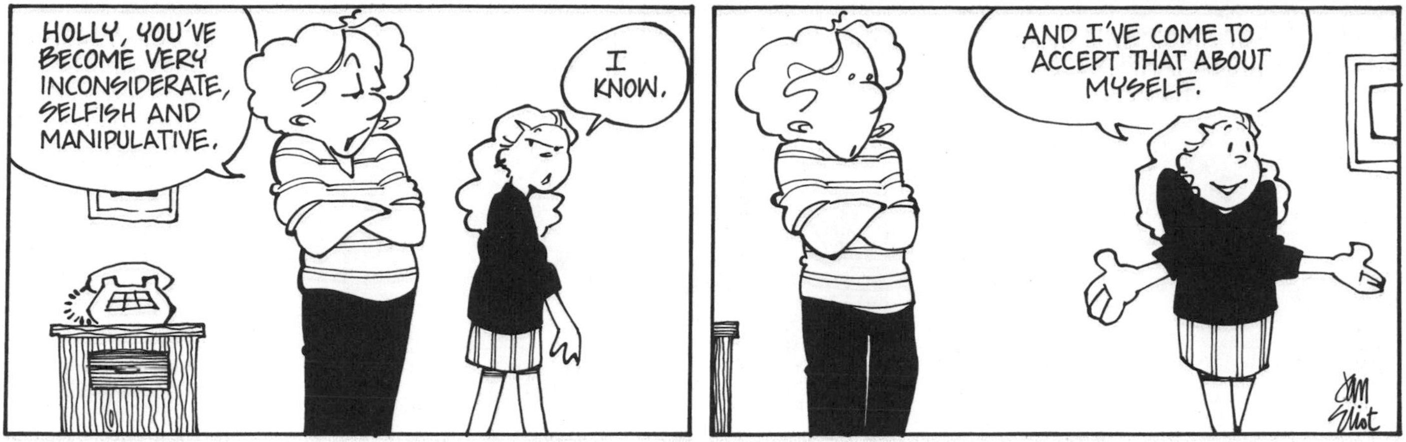
HOLLY, YOU'VE BECOME VERY INCONSIDERATE, SELFISH AND MANIPULATIVE.
I KNOW.
AND I'VE COME TO ACCEPT THAT ABOUT MYSELF.

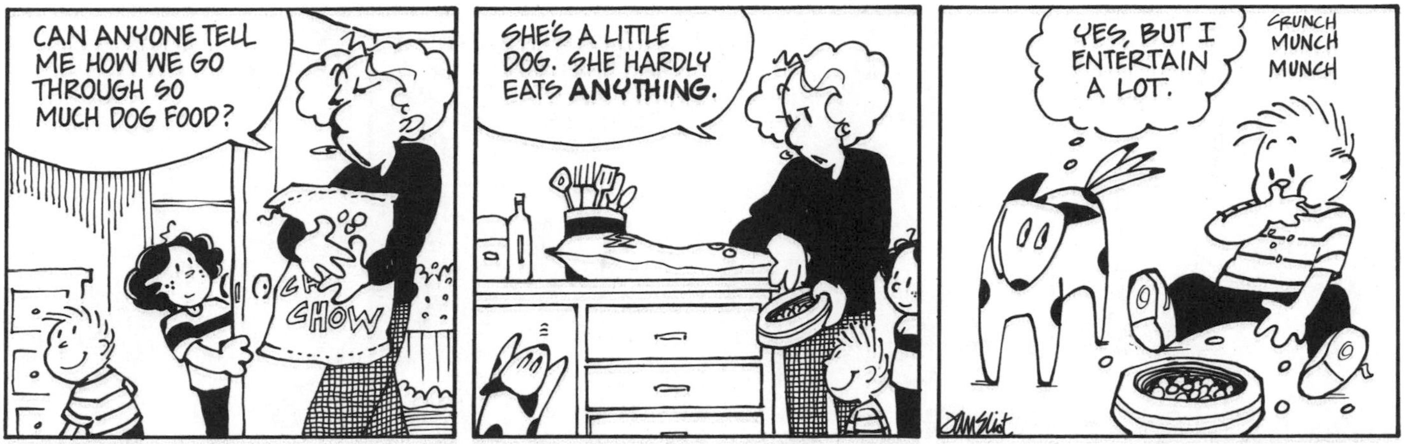
CAN ANYONE TELL ME HOW WE GO THROUGH SO MUCH DOG FOOD?
CHOW
SHE'S A LITTLE DOG. SHE HARDLY EATS **ANYTHING**.
YES, BUT I ENTERTAIN A LOT.
CRUNCH MUNCH MUNCH

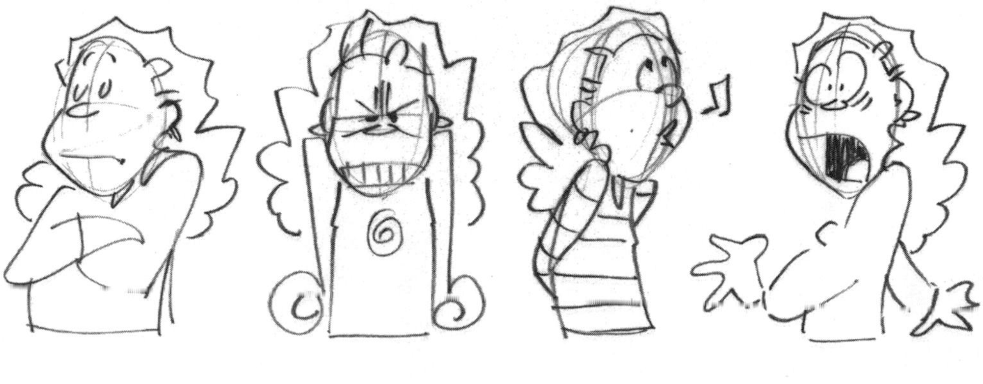

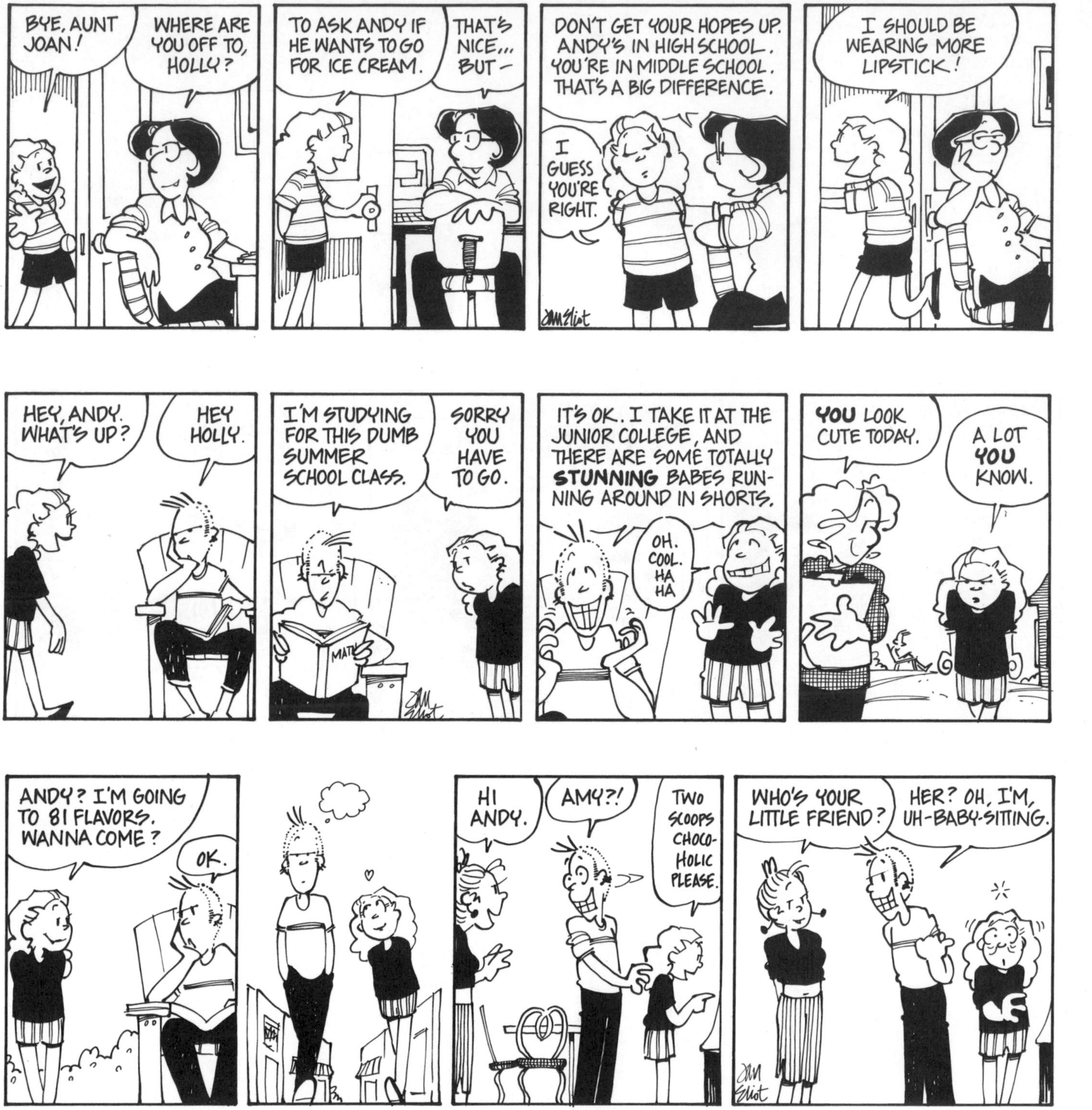

BYE, AUNT JOAN!
WHERE ARE YOU OFF TO, HOLLY?
TO ASK ANDY IF HE WANTS TO GO FOR ICE CREAM.
THAT'S NICE... BUT-
DON'T GET YOUR HOPES UP. ANDY'S IN HIGH SCHOOL. YOU'RE IN MIDDLE SCHOOL. THAT'S A BIG DIFFERENCE.
I GUESS YOU'RE RIGHT.
I SHOULD BE WEARING MORE LIPSTICK!
HEY, ANDY. WHAT'S UP?
HEY HOLLY.
I'M STUDYING FOR THIS DUMB SUMMER SCHOOL CLASS.
SORRY YOU HAVE TO GO.
MATH
IT'S OK. I TAKE IT AT THE JUNIOR COLLEGE, AND THERE ARE SOME TOTALLY **STUNNING** BABES RUNNING AROUND IN SHORTS.
OH. COOL. HA HA
YOU LOOK CUTE TODAY.
A LOT **YOU** KNOW.
ANDY? I'M GOING TO 81 FLAVORS. WANNA COME?
OK.
HI ANDY.
AMY?!
TWO SCOOPS CHOCO-HOLIC PLEASE.
WHO'S YOUR LITTLE FRIEND?
HER? OH, I'M, UH-BABY-SITTING.

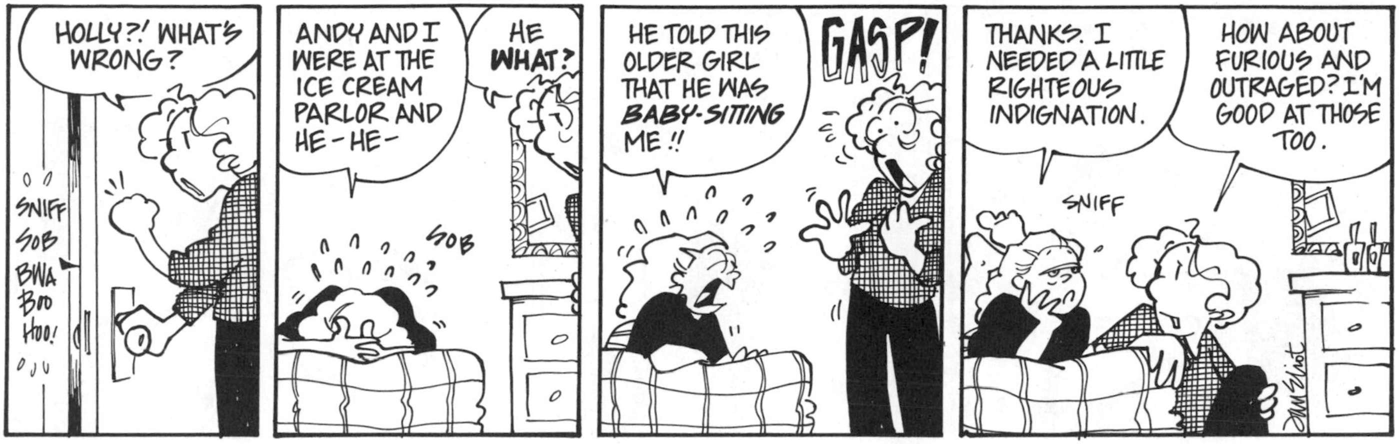
HOLLY?! WHAT'S WRONG?
SNIFF SOB BWA BOO HOO!
ANDY AND I WERE AT THE ICE CREAM PARLOR AND HE - HE -
HE **WHAT?**
SOB
HE TOLD THIS OLDER GIRL THAT HE WAS ***BABY-SITTING*** ME!!
GASP!
THANKS. I NEEDED A LITTLE RIGHTEOUS INDIGNATION.
SNIFF
HOW ABOUT FURIOUS AND OUTRAGED? I'M GOOD AT THOSE TOO.
JAN ELIOT

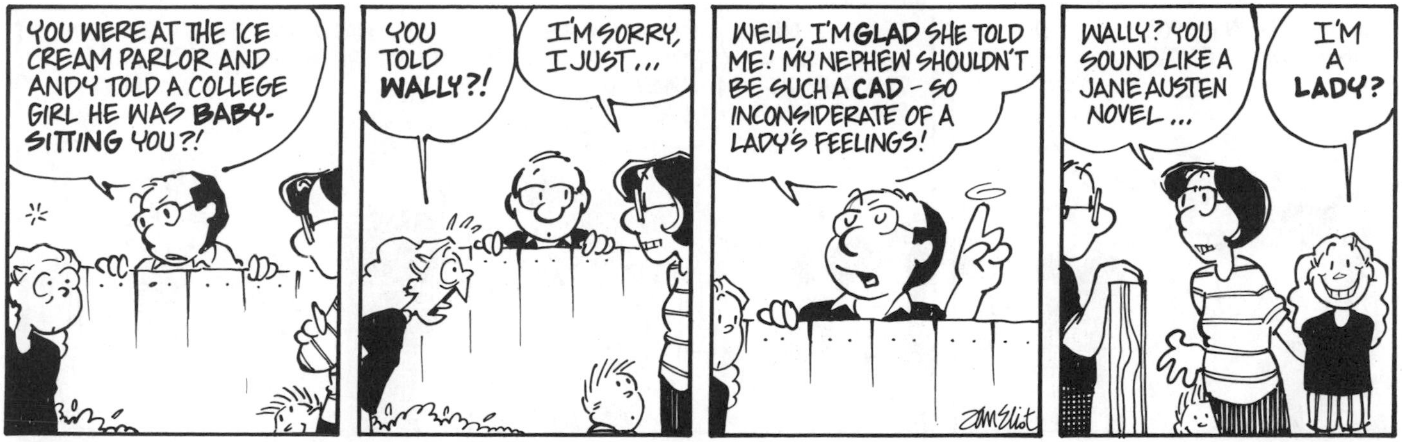
YOU WERE AT THE ICE CREAM PARLOR AND ANDY TOLD A COLLEGE GIRL HE WAS **BABY-SITTING** YOU?!
YOU TOLD **WALLY?!**
I'M SORRY, I JUST...
WELL, I'M **GLAD** SHE TOLD ME! MY NEPHEW SHOULDN'T BE SUCH A **CAD** - SO INCONSIDERATE OF A LADY'S FEELINGS!
JAN ELIOT
WALLY? YOU SOUND LIKE A JANE AUSTEN NOVEL...
I'M A **LADY?**

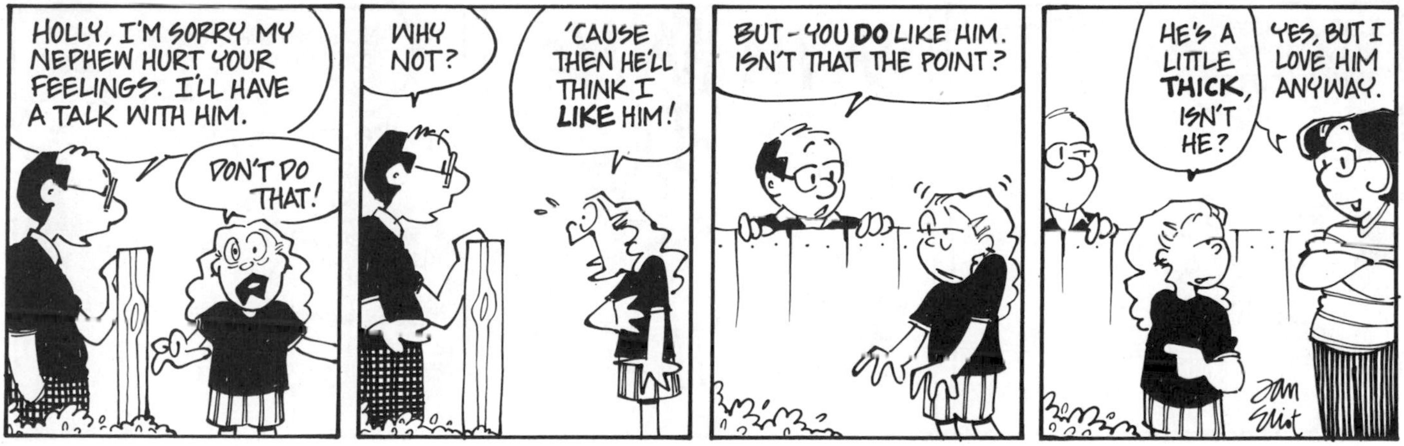
HOLLY, I'M SORRY MY NEPHEW HURT YOUR FEELINGS. I'LL HAVE A TALK WITH HIM.
DON'T DO THAT!
WHY NOT?
'CAUSE THEN HE'LL THINK I **LIKE** HIM!
BUT - YOU **DO** LIKE HIM. ISN'T THAT THE POINT?
HE'S A LITTLE **THICK**, ISN'T HE?
YES, BUT I LOVE HIM ANYWAY.
JAN ELIOT

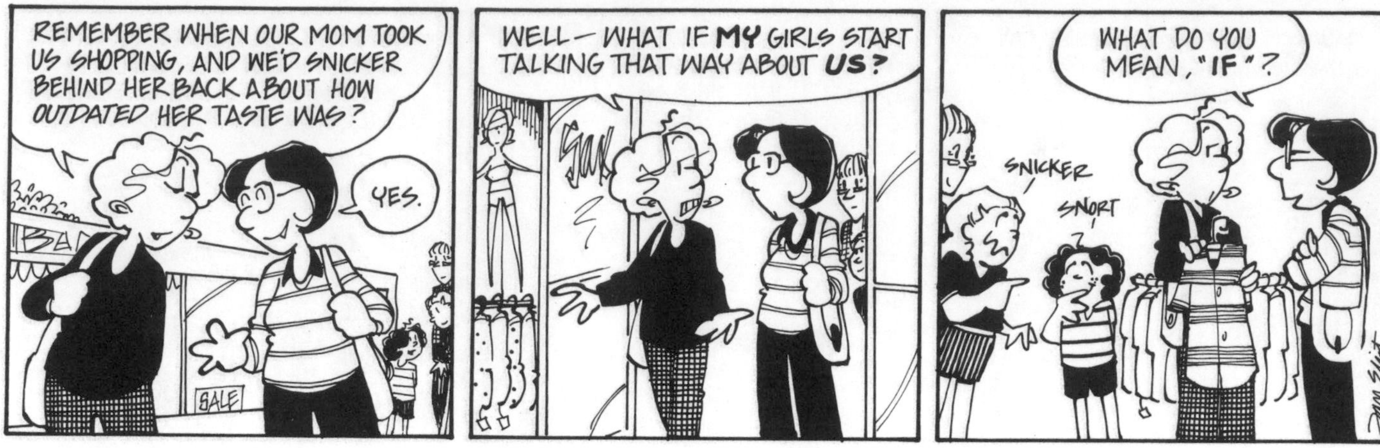
REMEMBER WHEN OUR MOM TOOK US SHOPPING, AND WE'D SNICKER BEHIND HER BACK ABOUT HOW OUTDATED HER TASTE WAS?
YES.
SALE
WELL — WHAT IF **MY** GIRLS START TALKING THAT WAY ABOUT **US**?
WHAT DO YOU MEAN, "**IF**"?
SNICKER
SNORT

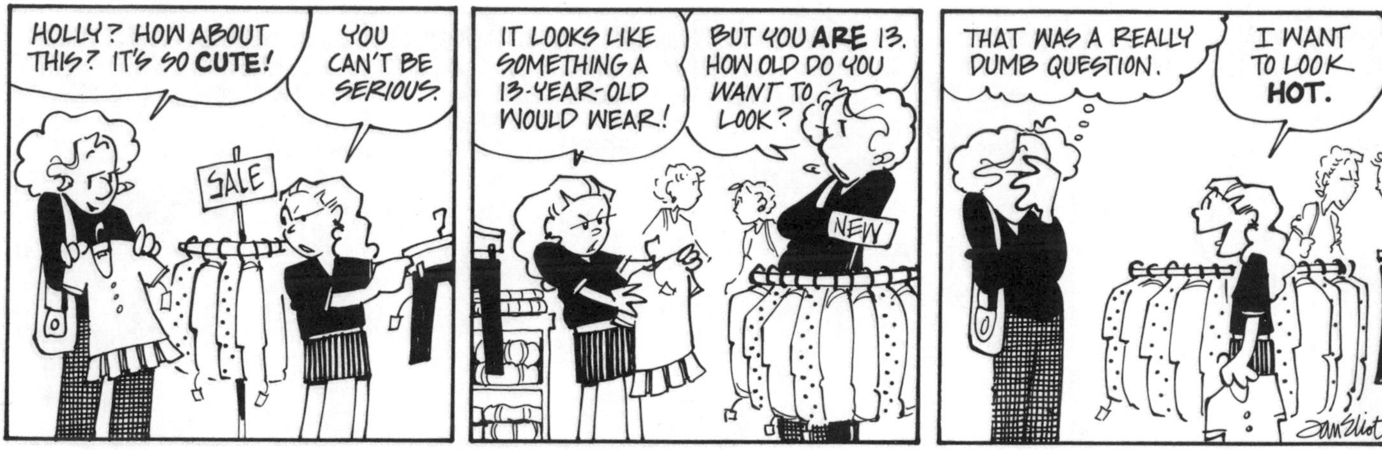
HOLLY? HOW ABOUT THIS? IT'S SO **CUTE**!
YOU CAN'T BE SERIOUS.
SALE
IT LOOKS LIKE SOMETHING A 13-YEAR-OLD WOULD WEAR!
BUT YOU **ARE** 13. HOW OLD DO YOU WANT TO LOOK?
NEW
THAT WAS A REALLY DUMB QUESTION.
I WANT TO LOOK **HOT.**

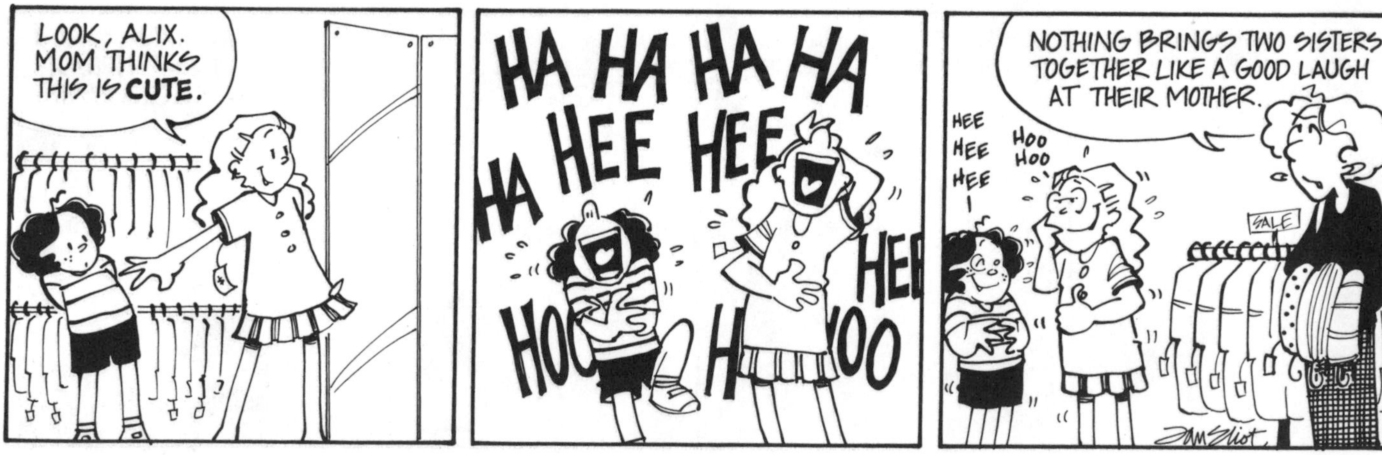
LOOK, ALIX. MOM THINKS THIS IS **CUTE**.
HA HA HA HA
HA HEE HEE
NOTHING BRINGS TWO SISTERS TOGETHER LIKE A GOOD LAUGH AT THEIR MOTHER.
HEE HEE HEE
HOO HOO
SALE

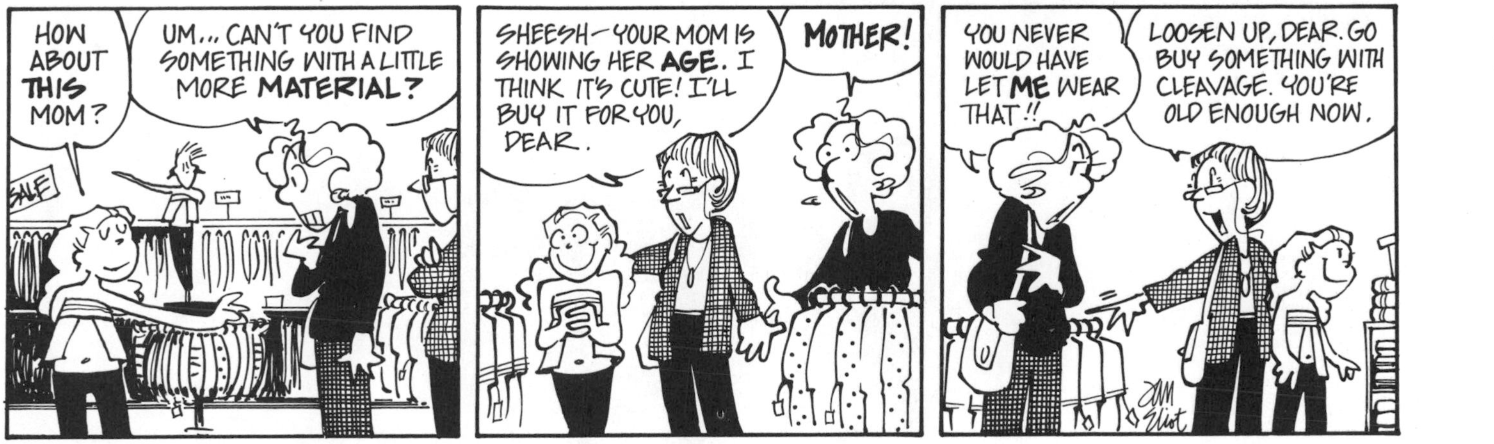
HOW ABOUT **THIS** MOM?
SALE
UM... CAN'T YOU FIND SOMETHING WITH A LITTLE MORE **MATERIAL?**
SHEESH— YOUR MOM IS SHOWING HER **AGE**. I THINK IT'S CUTE! I'LL BUY IT FOR YOU, DEAR.
MOTHER!
YOU NEVER WOULD HAVE LET **ME** WEAR THAT!!
LOOSEN UP, DEAR. GO BUY SOMETHING WITH CLEAVAGE. YOU'RE OLD ENOUGH NOW.

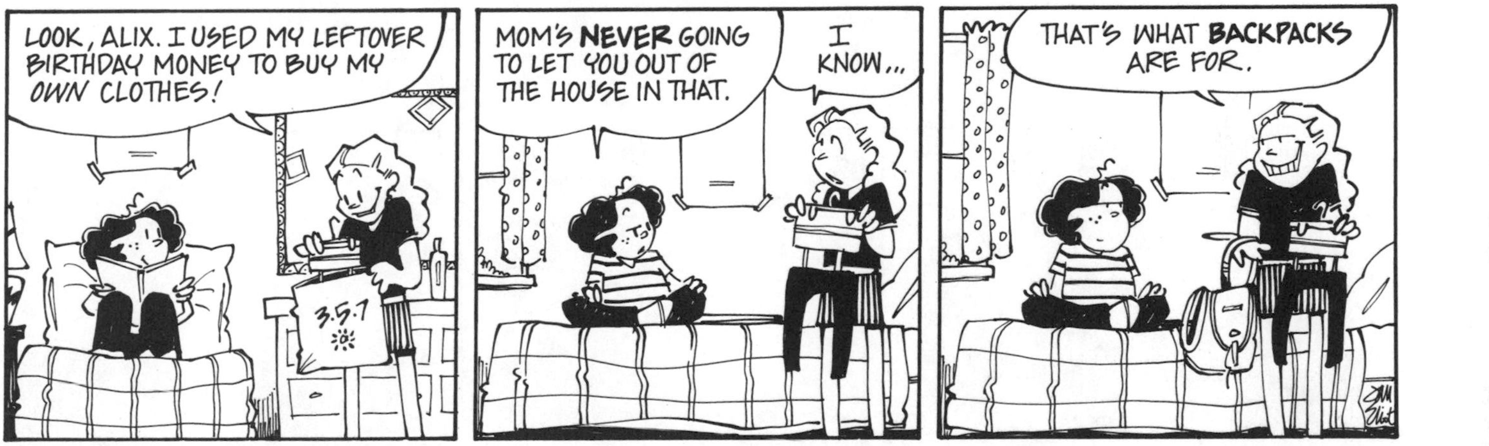
LOOK, ALIX. I USED MY LEFTOVER BIRTHDAY MONEY TO BUY MY *OWN* CLOTHES!
3.5.7
MOM'S **NEVER** GOING TO LET YOU OUT OF THE HOUSE IN THAT.
I KNOW...
THAT'S WHAT **BACKPACKS** ARE FOR.

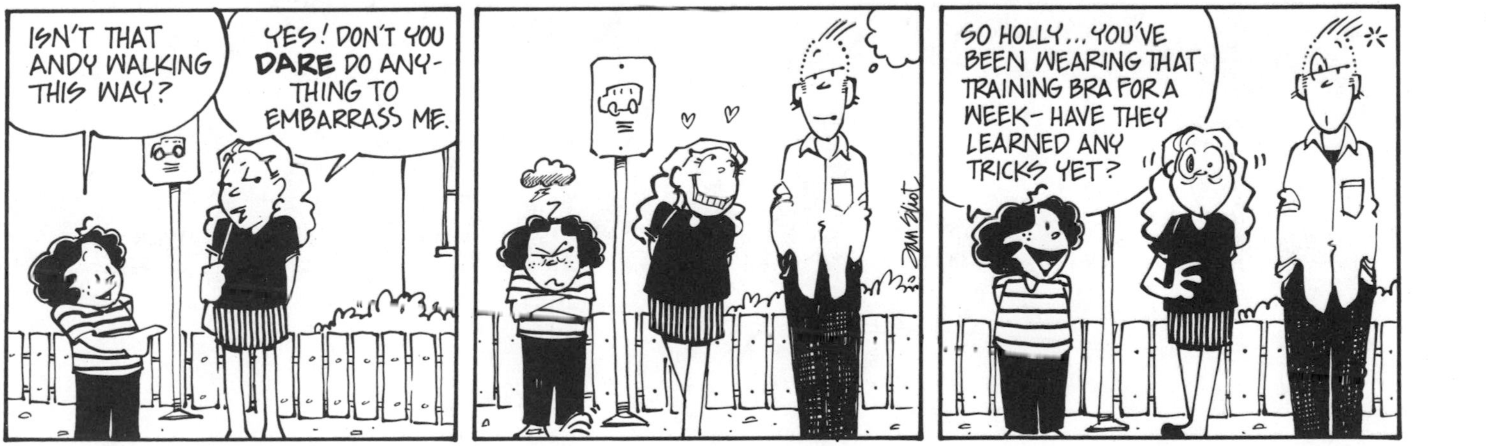
ISN'T THAT ANDY WALKING THIS WAY?
YES! DON'T YOU **DARE** DO ANY-THING TO EMBARRASS ME.
SO HOLLY... YOU'VE BEEN WEARING THAT TRAINING BRA FOR A WEEK— HAVE THEY LEARNED ANY TRICKS YET?

Stone Soup

WOW. WHEN WE GET MARRIED I'LL REALLY BE MAX'S **DAD.** I HOPE I'M UP TO IT.

YOU ARE.

BUT— HE'S GOING TO HAVE SO MANY QUESTIONS! WHAT IF I DON'T HAVE THE **ANSWERS?**

DA?

THAT? THAT'S A BEETLE. HE WON'T HURT YOU.

WELL, **THAT** ONE WAS EASY.

JUST WAIT UNTIL HE ASKS FOR A MOTORCYCLE.

WHAT **KIND** OF MOTORCYCLE?

DA?

THE ANSWER IS **NO.** *BOTH* OF YOU.

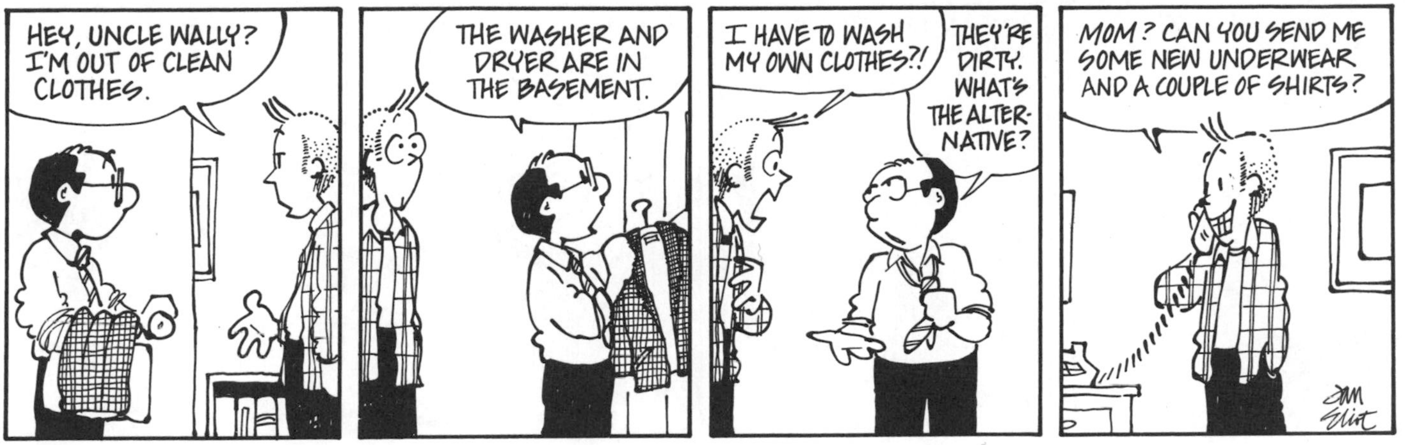
HEY, UNCLE WALLY? I'M OUT OF CLEAN CLOTHES.
THE WASHER AND DRYER ARE IN THE BASEMENT.
I HAVE TO WASH MY OWN CLOTHES?!
THEY'RE DIRTY. WHAT'S THE ALTERNATIVE?
MOM? CAN YOU SEND ME SOME NEW UNDERWEAR AND A COUPLE OF SHIRTS?

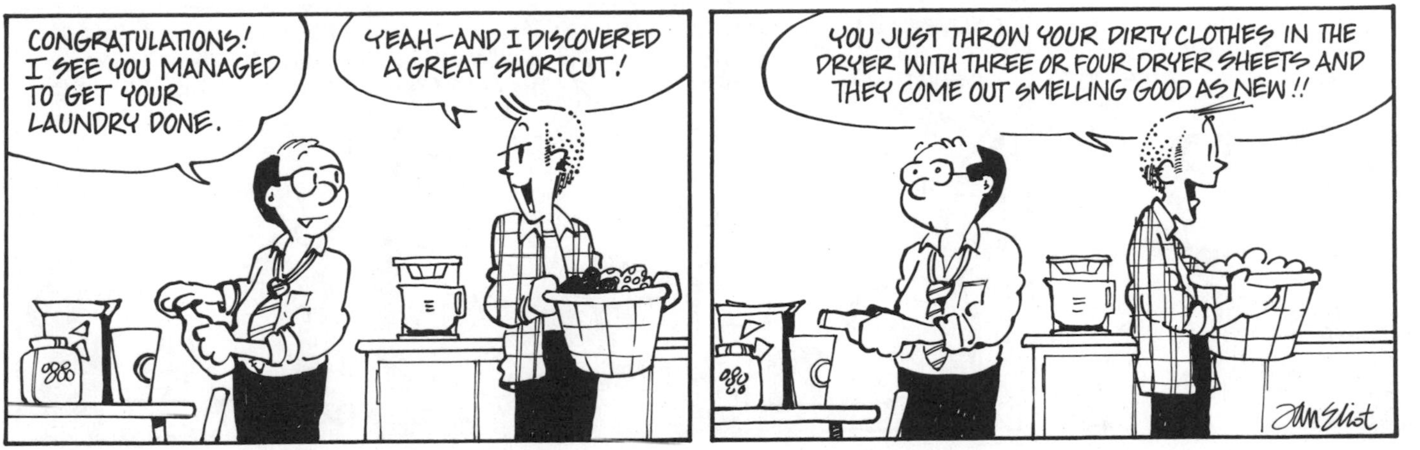
CONGRATULATIONS! I SEE YOU MANAGED TO GET YOUR LAUNDRY DONE.
YEAH—AND I DISCOVERED A GREAT SHORTCUT!
YOU JUST THROW YOUR DIRTY CLOTHES IN THE DRYER WITH THREE OR FOUR DRYER SHEETS AND THEY COME OUT SMELLING GOOD AS NEW!!

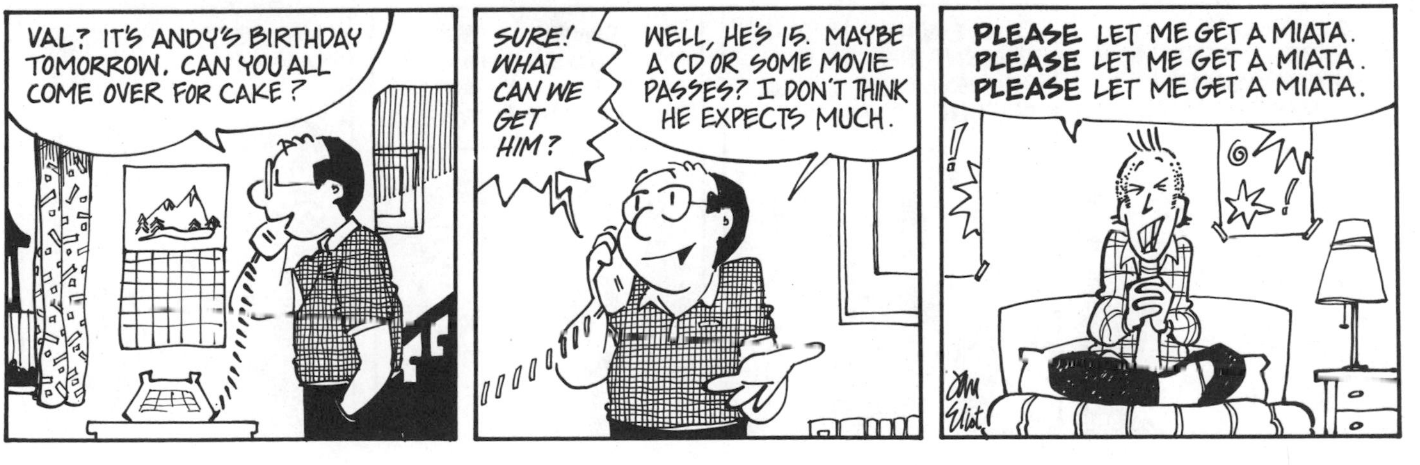
VAL? IT'S ANDY'S BIRTHDAY TOMORROW. CAN YOU ALL COME OVER FOR CAKE?
SURE! WHAT CAN WE GET HIM?
WELL, HE'S 15. MAYBE A CD OR SOME MOVIE PASSES? I DON'T THINK HE EXPECTS MUCH.
PLEASE LET ME GET A MIATA.
PLEASE LET ME GET A MIATA.
PLEASE LET ME GET A MIATA.

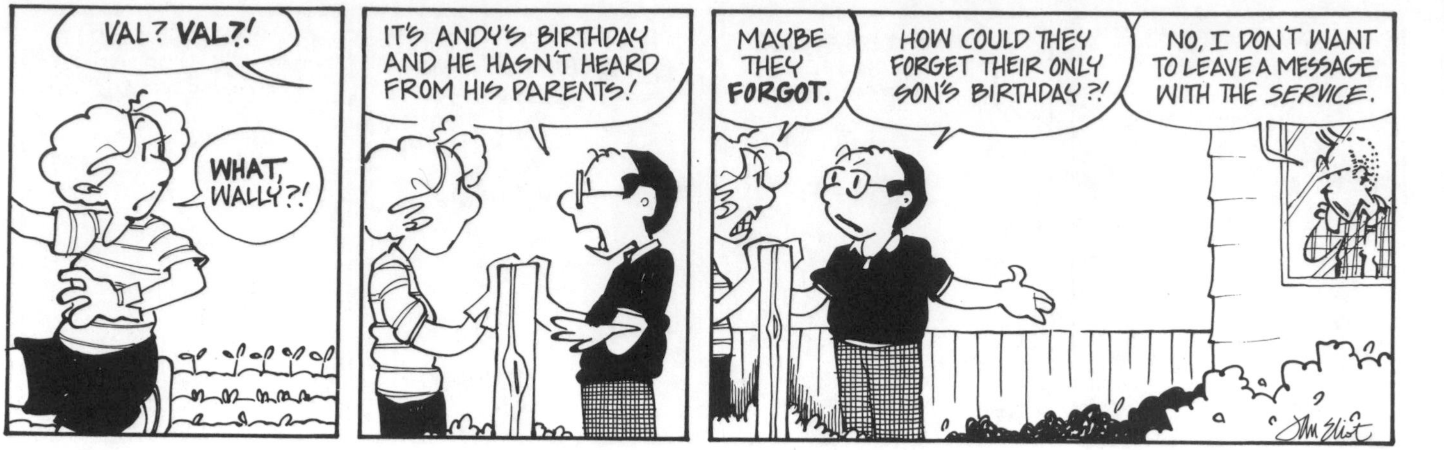
VAL? **VAL?!**
WHAT, WALLY?!
IT'S ANDY'S BIRTHDAY AND HE HASN'T HEARD FROM HIS PARENTS!
MAYBE THEY **FORGOT.**
HOW COULD THEY FORGET THEIR ONLY SON'S BIRTHDAY?!
NO, I DON'T WANT TO LEAVE A MESSAGE WITH THE *SERVICE*.

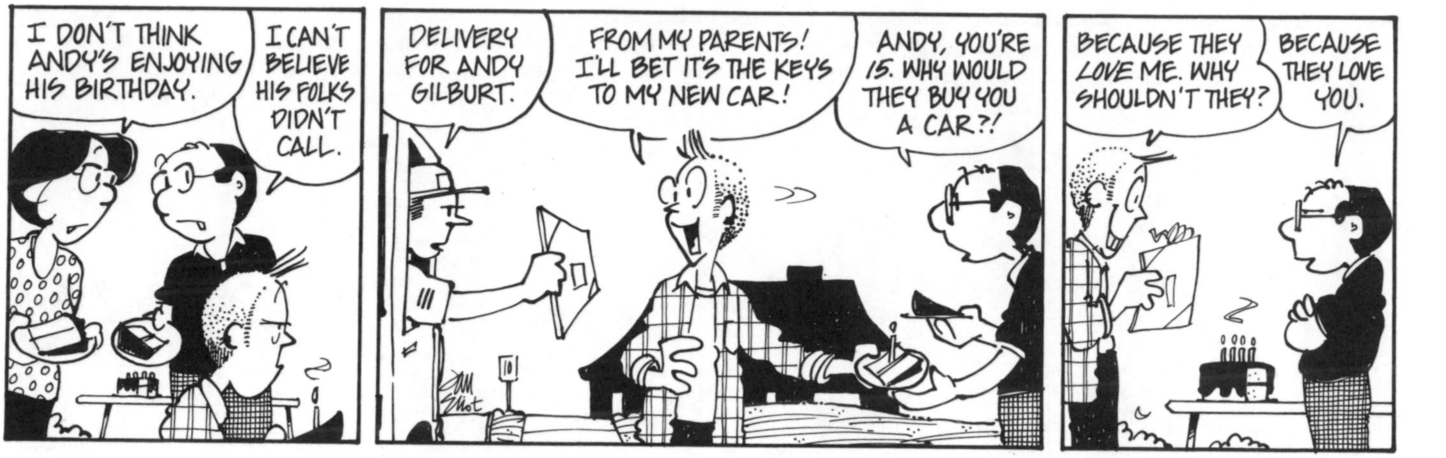
I DON'T THINK ANDY'S ENJOYING HIS BIRTHDAY.
I CAN'T BELIEVE HIS FOLKS DIDN'T CALL.
DELIVERY FOR ANDY GILBURT.
FROM MY PARENTS! I'LL BET IT'S THE KEYS TO MY NEW CAR!
ANDY, YOU'RE *15*. WHY WOULD THEY BUY YOU A CAR?!
BECAUSE THEY *LOVE* ME. WHY SHOULDN'T THEY?
BECAUSE THEY LOVE YOU.

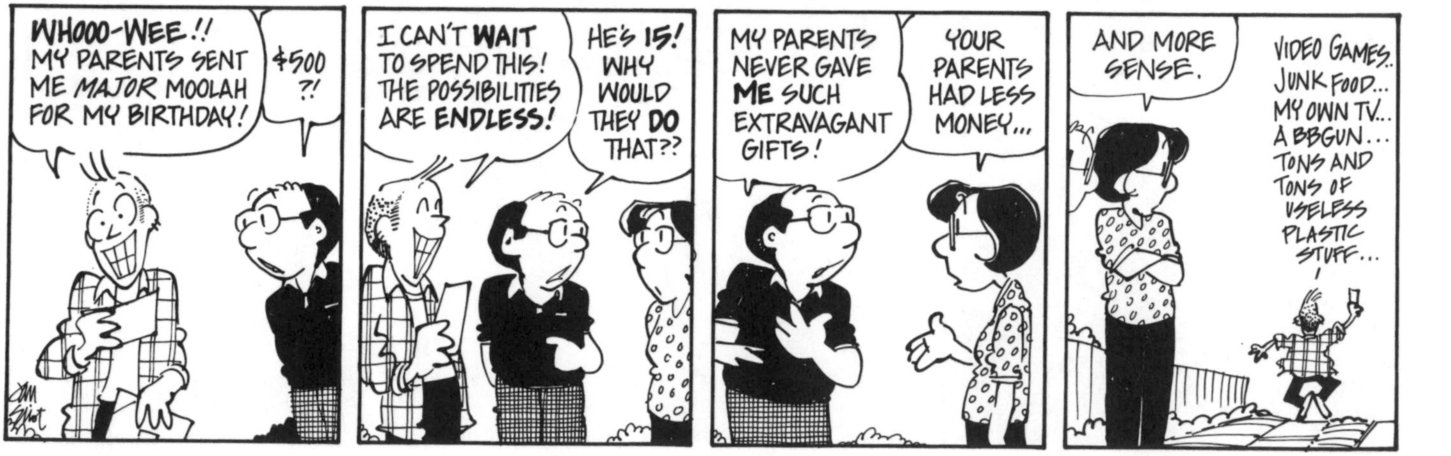
WHOOO-WEE!! MY PARENTS SENT ME *MAJOR* MOOLAH FOR MY BIRTHDAY!
$500 ?!
I CAN'T **WAIT** TO SPEND THIS! THE POSSIBILITIES ARE **ENDLESS!**
HE'S **15! WHY** WOULD THEY **DO** THAT??
MY PARENTS NEVER GAVE **ME** SUCH EXTRAVAGANT GIFTS!
YOUR PARENTS HAD LESS MONEY...
AND MORE SENSE.
VIDEO GAMES... JUNK FOOD... MY OWN TV... A BBGUN... TONS AND TONS OF USELESS PLASTIC STUFF...!

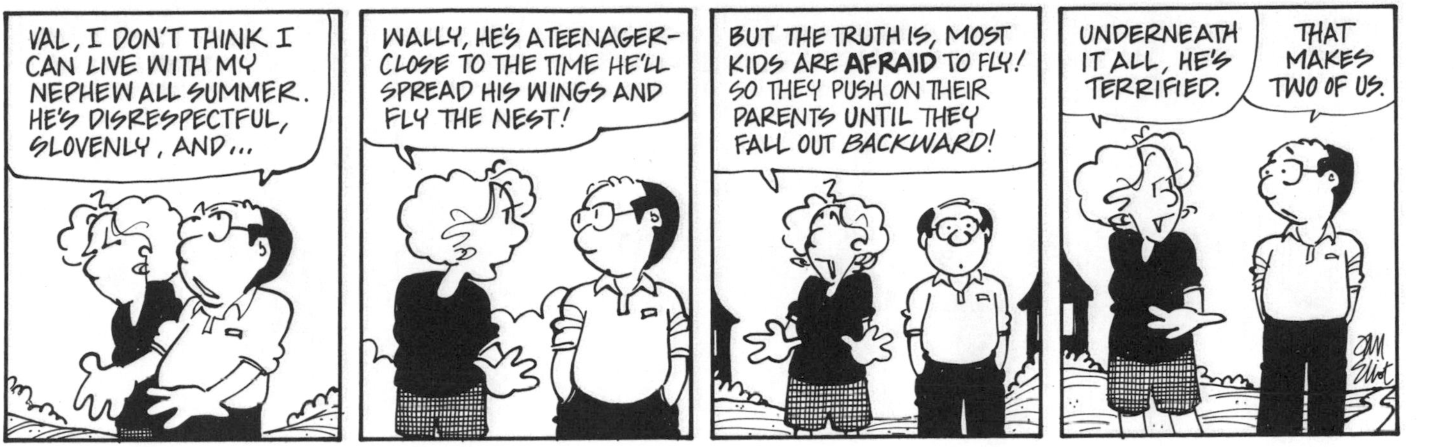
VAL, I DON'T THINK I CAN LIVE WITH MY NEPHEW ALL SUMMER. HE'S DISRESPECTFUL, SLOVENLY, AND...
WALLY, HE'S A TEENAGER- CLOSE TO THE TIME HE'LL SPREAD HIS WINGS AND FLY THE NEST!
BUT THE TRUTH IS, MOST KIDS ARE **AFRAID** TO FLY! SO THEY PUSH ON THEIR PARENTS UNTIL THEY FALL OUT *BACKWARD*!
UNDERNEATH IT ALL, HE'S TERRIFIED.
THAT MAKES TWO OF US.

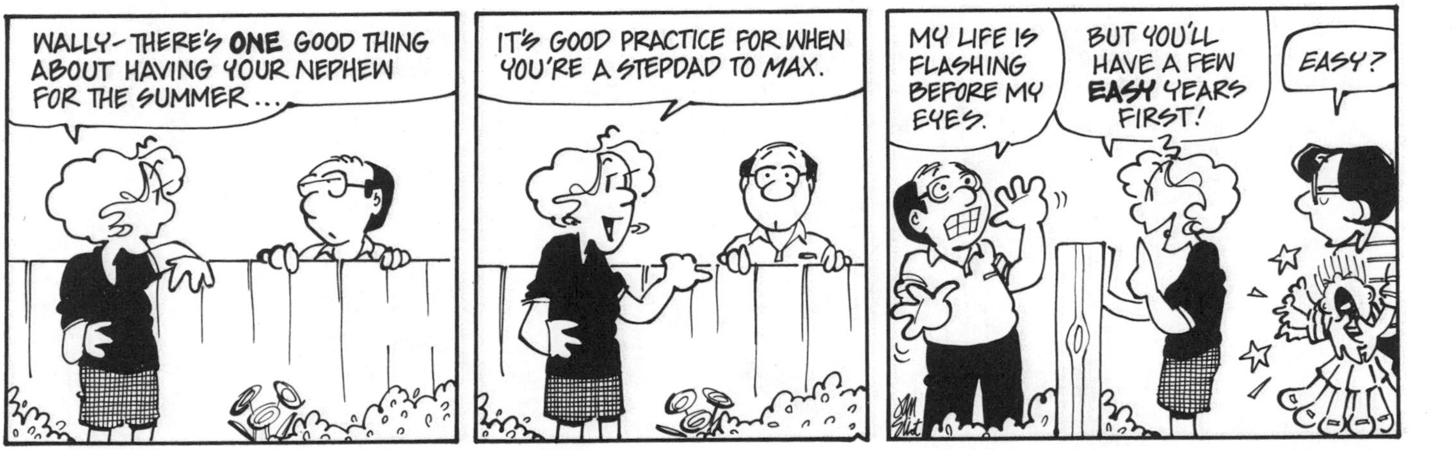
WALLY- THERE'S **ONE** GOOD THING ABOUT HAVING YOUR NEPHEW FOR THE SUMMER....
IT'S GOOD PRACTICE FOR WHEN YOU'RE A STEPDAD TO *MAX*.
MY LIFE IS FLASHING BEFORE MY EYES.
BUT YOU'LL HAVE A FEW **EASY** YEARS FIRST!
EASY?

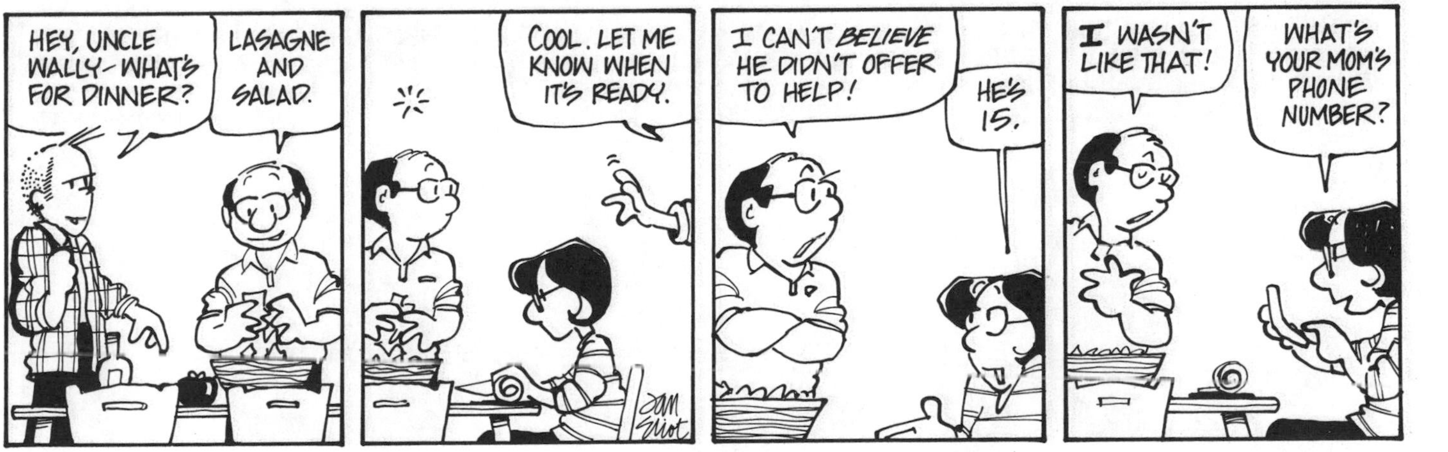
HEY, UNCLE WALLY- WHAT'S FOR DINNER?
LASAGNE AND SALAD.
COOL. LET ME KNOW WHEN IT'S READY.
I CAN'T *BELIEVE* HE DIDN'T OFFER TO HELP!
HE'S 15.
I WASN'T LIKE THAT!
WHAT'S YOUR MOM'S PHONE NUMBER?

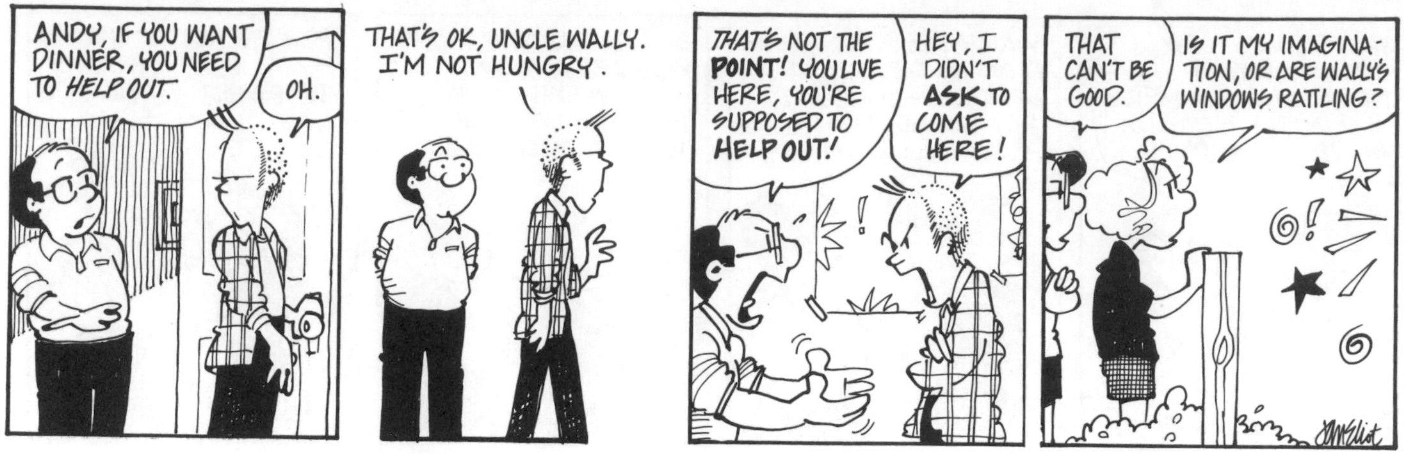
ANDY, IF YOU WANT DINNER, YOU NEED TO HELP OUT.
OH.
THAT'S OK, UNCLE WALLY. I'M NOT HUNGRY.
THAT'S NOT THE POINT! YOU LIVE HERE, YOU'RE SUPPOSED TO HELP OUT!
HEY, I DIDN'T ASK TO COME HERE!
THAT CAN'T BE GOOD.
IS IT MY IMAGINATION, OR ARE WALLY'S WINDOWS RATTLING?

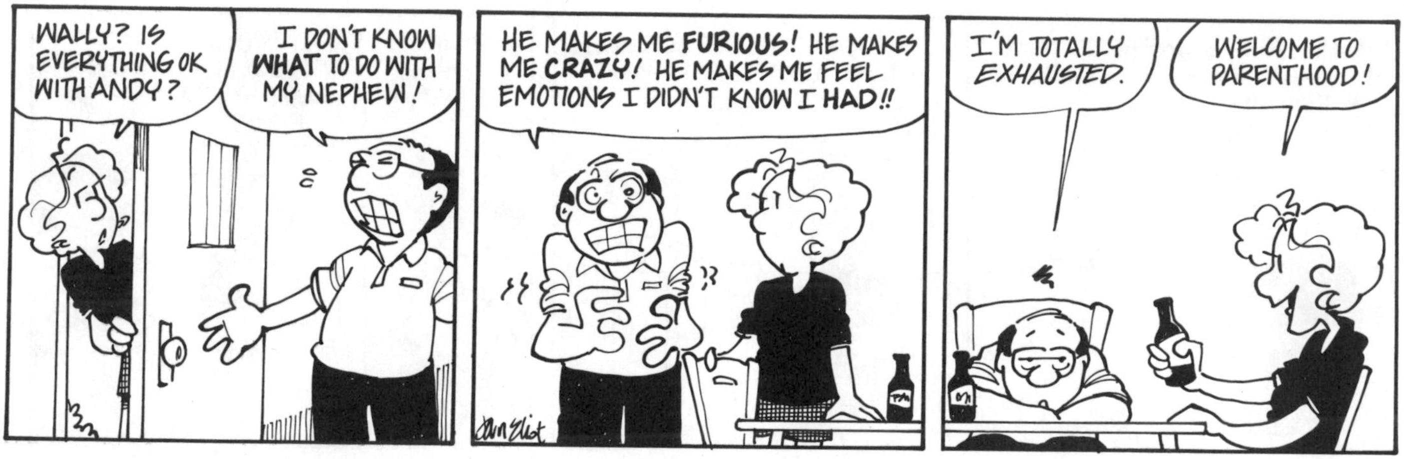
WALLY? IS EVERYTHING OK WITH ANDY?
I DON'T KNOW WHAT TO DO WITH MY NEPHEW!
HE MAKES ME FURIOUS! HE MAKES ME CRAZY! HE MAKES ME FEEL EMOTIONS I DIDN'T KNOW I HAD!!
I'M TOTALLY EXHAUSTED.
WELCOME TO PARENTHOOD!

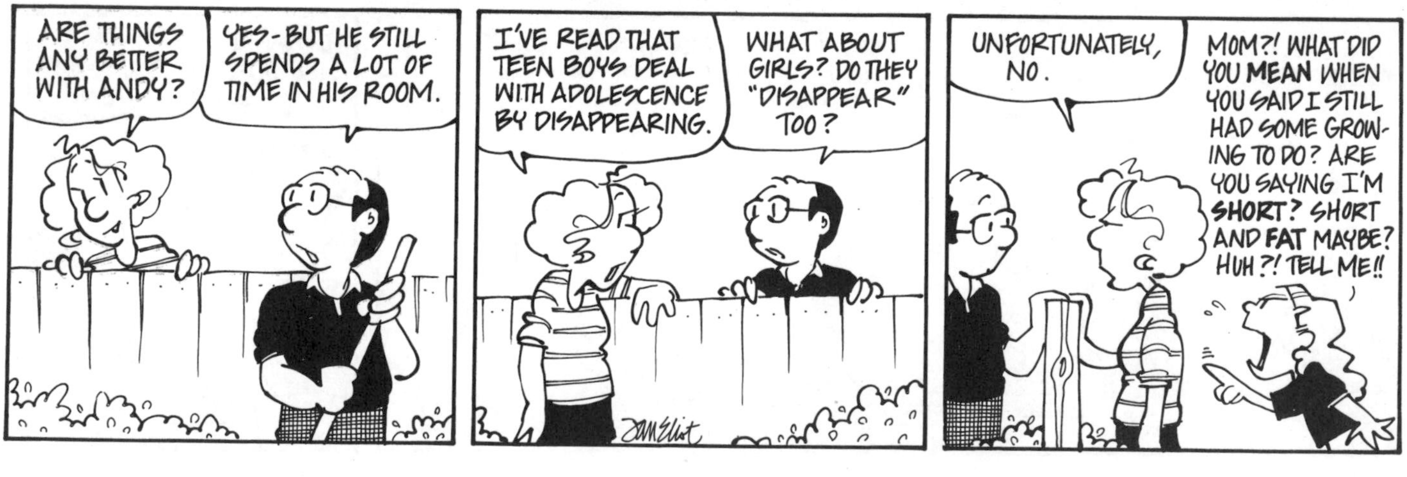
ARE THINGS ANY BETTER WITH ANDY?
YES - BUT HE STILL SPENDS A LOT OF TIME IN HIS ROOM.
I'VE READ THAT TEEN BOYS DEAL WITH ADOLESCENCE BY DISAPPEARING.
WHAT ABOUT GIRLS? DO THEY "DISAPPEAR" TOO?
UNFORTUNATELY, NO.
MOM?! WHAT DID YOU MEAN WHEN YOU SAID I STILL HAD SOME GROWING TO DO? ARE YOU SAYING I'M SHORT? SHORT AND FAT MAYBE? HUH?! TELL ME!!

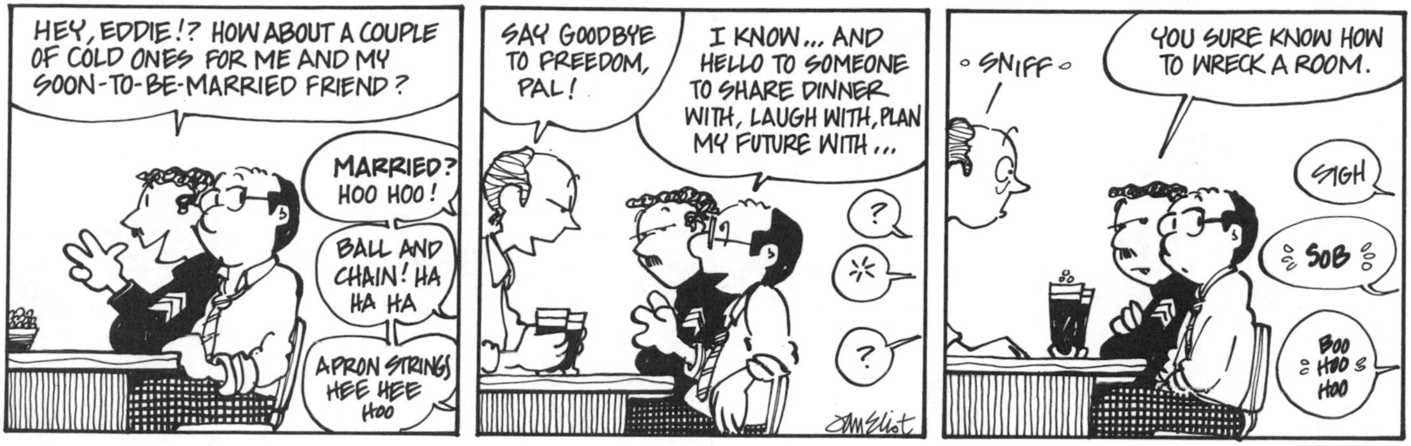
HEY, EDDIE!? HOW ABOUT A COUPLE OF COLD ONES FOR ME AND MY SOON-TO-BE-MARRIED FRIEND?
MARRIED? HOO HOO!
BALL AND CHAIN! HA HA HA
APRON STRINGS HEE HEE HOO
SAY GOODBYE TO FREEDOM, PAL!
I KNOW... AND HELLO TO SOMEONE TO SHARE DINNER WITH, LAUGH WITH, PLAN MY FUTURE WITH...
?
?
SNIFF
YOU SURE KNOW HOW TO WRECK A ROOM.
SIGH
SOB
BOO HOO HOO

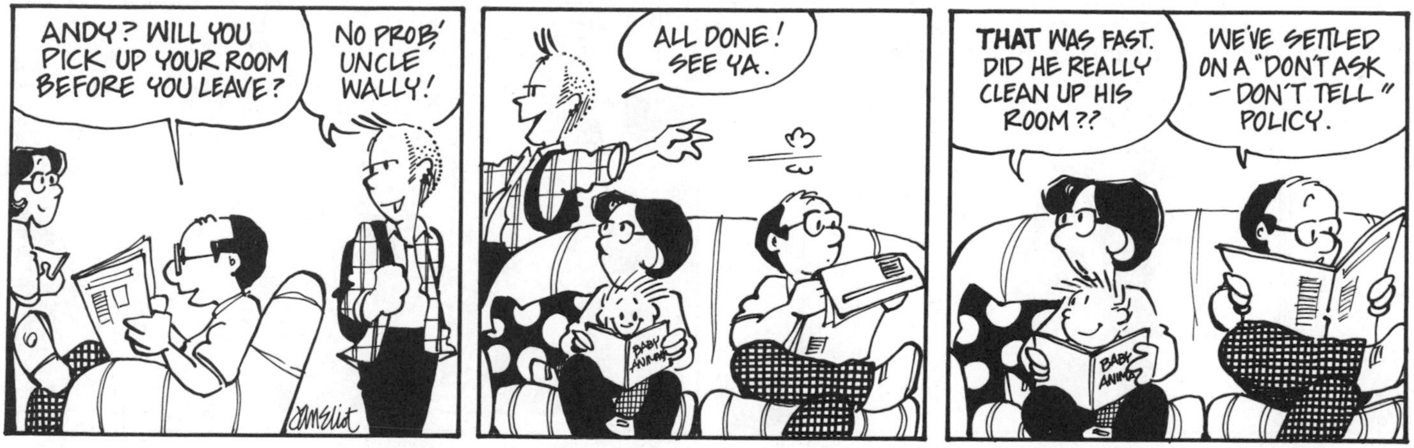
ANDY? WILL YOU PICK UP YOUR ROOM BEFORE YOU LEAVE?
NO PROB' UNCLE WALLY!
ALL DONE! SEE YA.
THAT WAS FAST. DID HE REALLY CLEAN UP HIS ROOM??
WE'VE SETTLED ON A "DON'T ASK — DON'T TELL" POLICY.

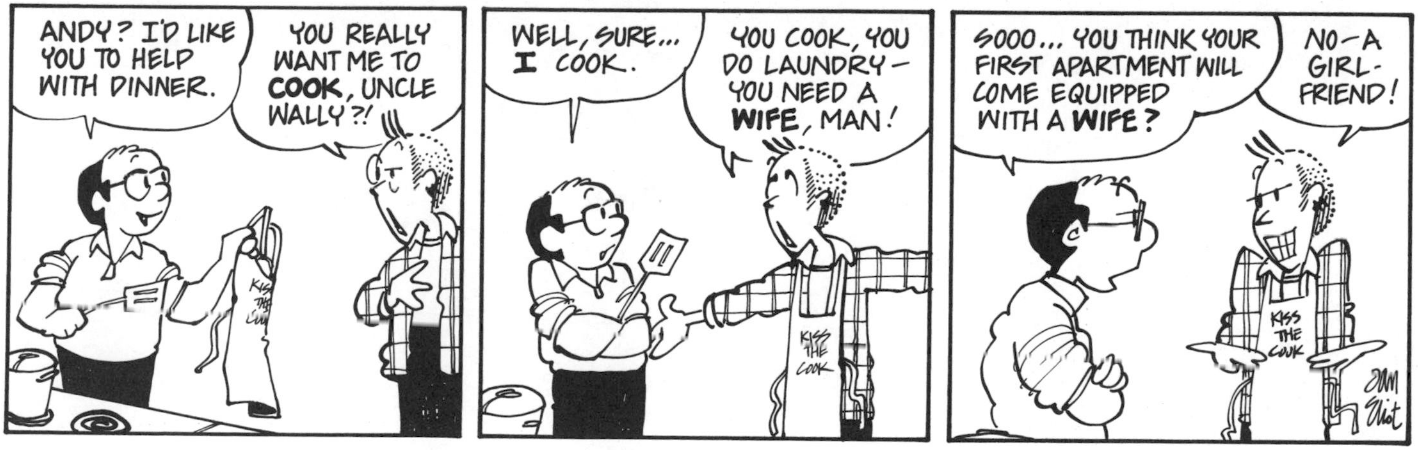
ANDY? I'D LIKE YOU TO HELP WITH DINNER.
YOU REALLY WANT ME TO **COOK**, UNCLE WALLY?!
WELL, SURE... **I** COOK.
YOU COOK, YOU DO LAUNDRY — YOU NEED A **WIFE**, MAN!
SOOO... YOU THINK YOUR FIRST APARTMENT WILL COME EQUIPPED WITH A **WIFE**?
NO — A GIRL-FRIEND!
KISS THE COOK

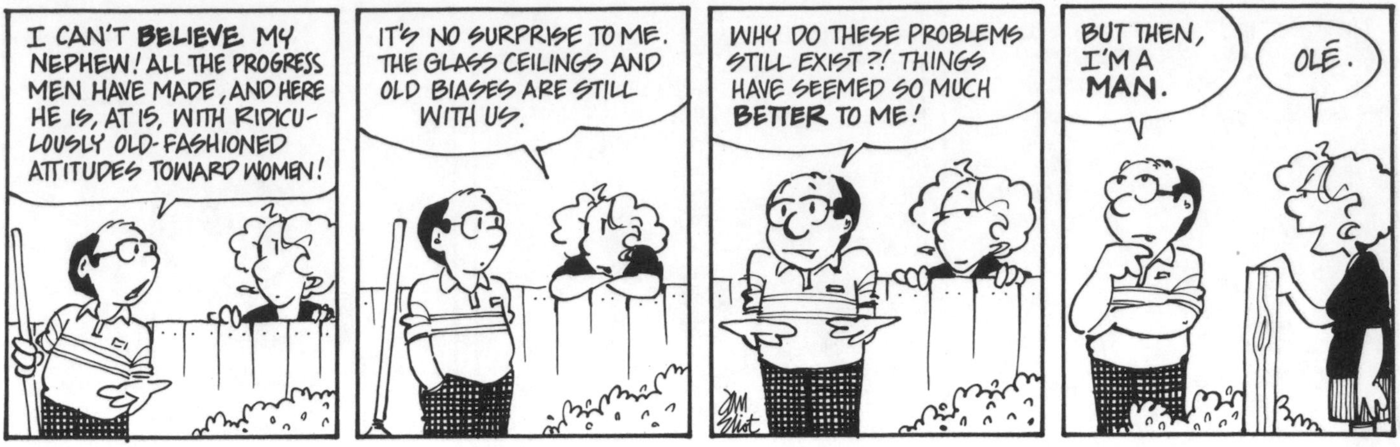
I CAN'T BELIEVE MY NEPHEW! ALL THE PROGRESS MEN HAVE MADE, AND HERE HE IS, AT 15, WITH RIDICULOUSLY OLD-FASHIONED ATTITUDES TOWARD WOMEN!
IT'S NO SURPRISE TO ME. THE GLASS CEILINGS AND OLD BIASES ARE STILL WITH US.
WHY DO THESE PROBLEMS STILL EXIST?! THINGS HAVE SEEMED SO MUCH BETTER TO ME!
BUT THEN, I'M A MAN.
OLÉ.

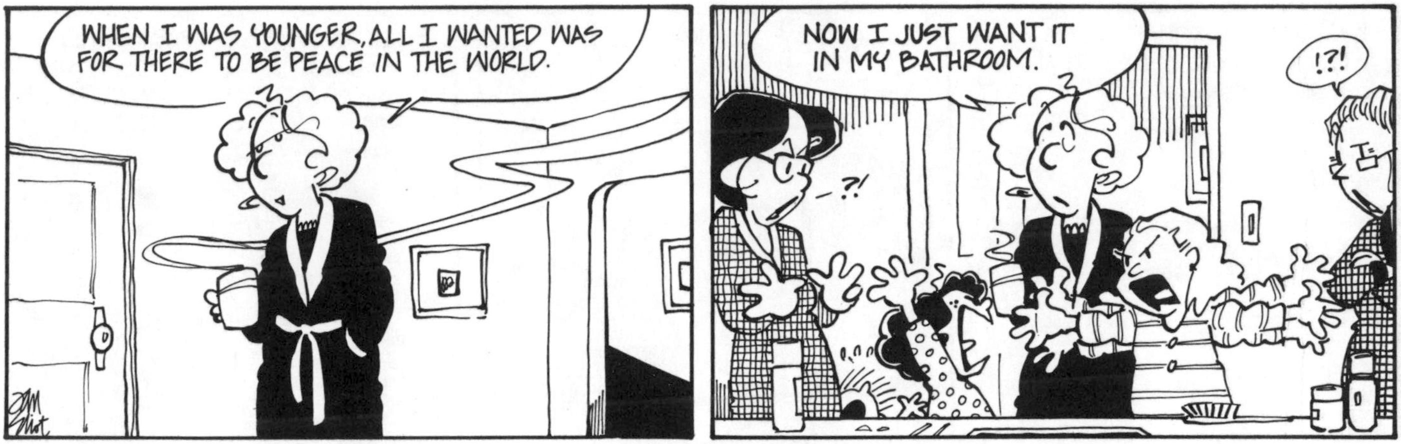
WHEN I WAS YOUNGER, ALL I WANTED WAS FOR THERE TO BE PEACE IN THE WORLD.
NOW I JUST WANT IT IN MY BATHROOM.
!?!
?!

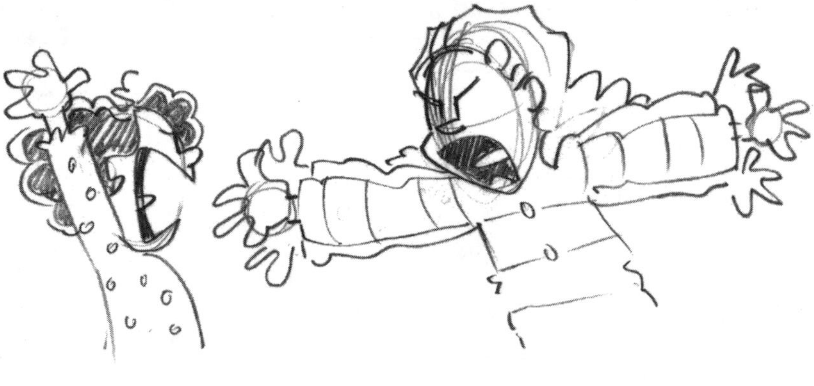

Stone Soup

WOW! IT'S WARM ENOUGH FOR BARE FEET!
WRIGGLE MY TOES IN THE GRASS... SMELL THE SWEET SUMMER BREEZE—
ULP! GAK! I INHALED A BUG! BUG JUICE!
PTOUii PTOUii
GROSS! I STEPPED ON A SLUG! SLUG SLIME!
GROSS
ICKY
ICKY
ICKY
OW! I STEPPED ON A BEE!
BZZZZZZZ
OW! OW OW OW OW
WHOOP!?
EYOW! STICKER BUSHES!
SUMMERTIME, AND THE LIVIN' IS EASY.
SPEAK FOR YOURSELF— AND DIAL 911.

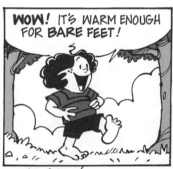

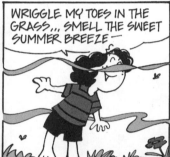

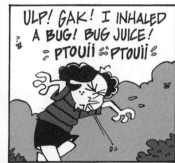

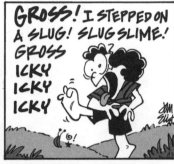

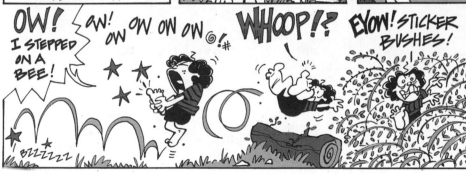

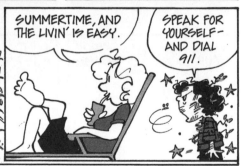

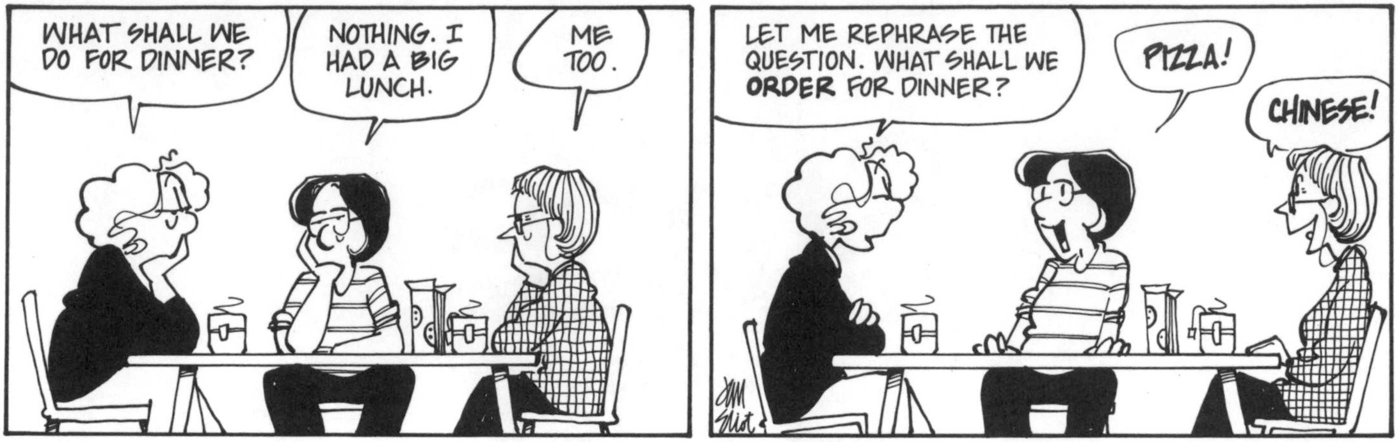
WHAT SHALL WE DO FOR DINNER?
NOTHING. I HAD A BIG LUNCH.
ME TOO.
LET ME REPHRASE THE QUESTION. WHAT SHALL WE ORDER FOR DINNER?
PIZZA!
CHINESE!

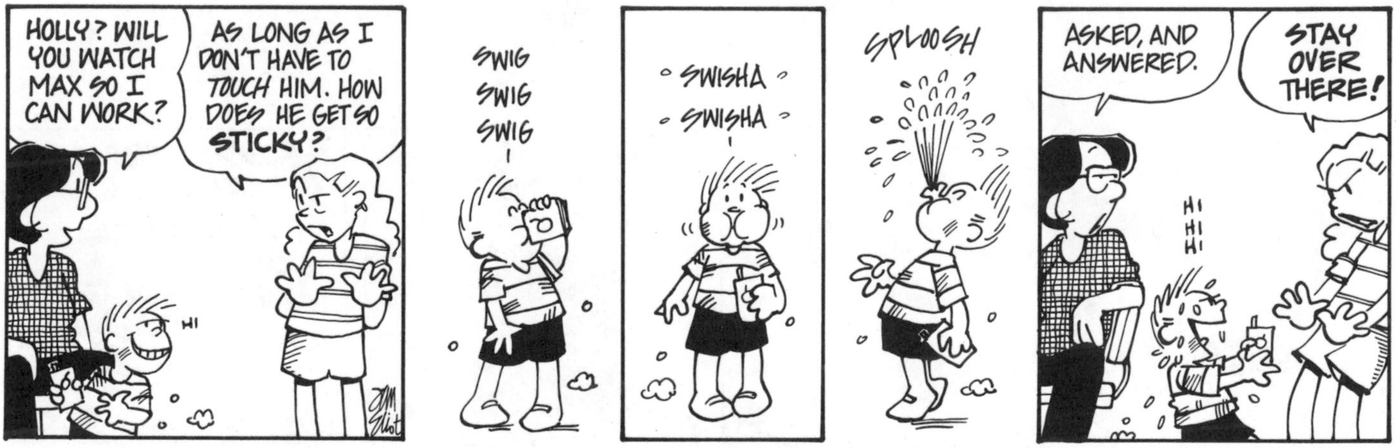
HOLLY? WILL YOU WATCH MAX SO I CAN WORK?
AS LONG AS I DON'T HAVE TO TOUCH HIM. HOW DOES HE GET SO STICKY?
HI
SWIG SWIG SWIG
SWISHA SWISHA
SPLOOSH
ASKED, AND ANSWERED.
STAY OVER THERE!
HI HI HI

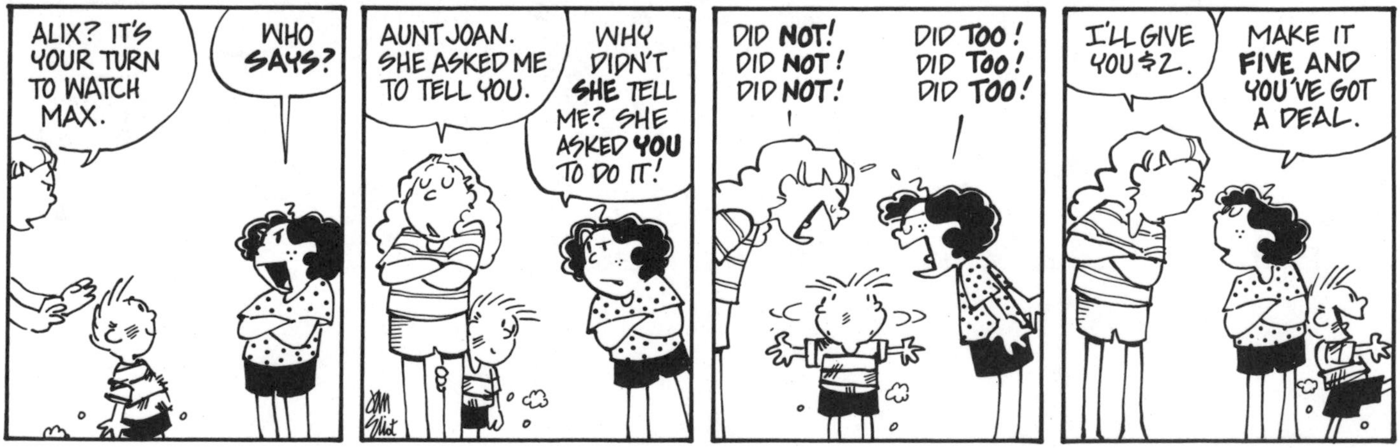
ALIX? IT'S YOUR TURN TO WATCH MAX.
WHO SAYS?
AUNT JOAN. SHE ASKED ME TO TELL YOU.
WHY DIDN'T SHE TELL ME? SHE ASKED YOU TO DO IT!
DID NOT! DID NOT! DID NOT!
DID TOO! DID TOO! DID TOO!
I'LL GIVE YOU $2.
MAKE IT FIVE AND YOU'VE GOT A DEAL.

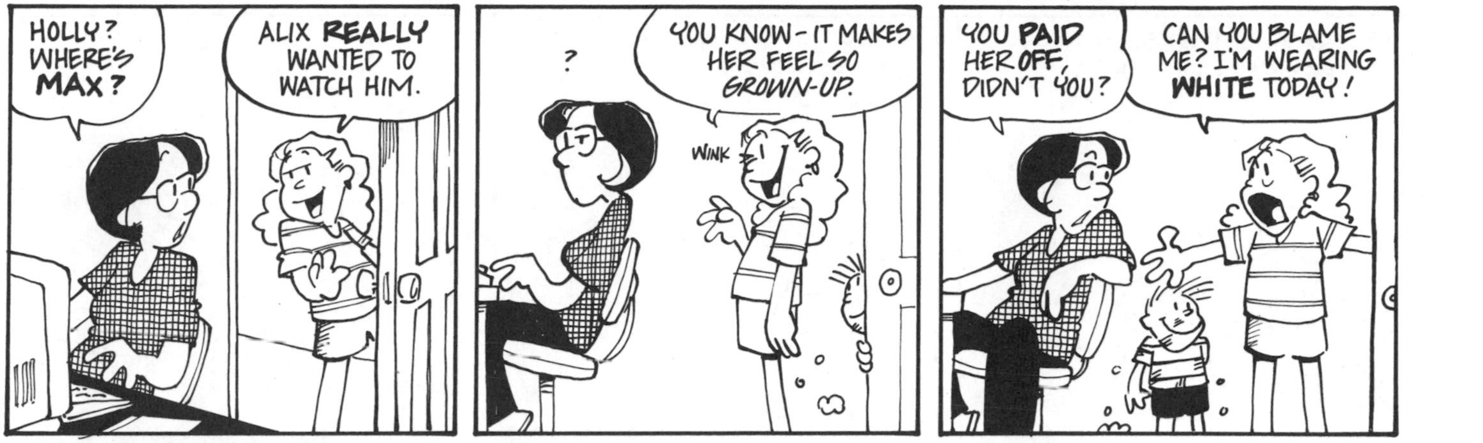
HOLLY? WHERE'S MAX?
ALIX REALLY WANTED TO WATCH HIM.
?
YOU KNOW - IT MAKES HER FEEL SO GROWN-UP.
WINK
YOU PAID HER OFF, DIDN'T YOU?
CAN YOU BLAME ME? I'M WEARING WHITE TODAY!

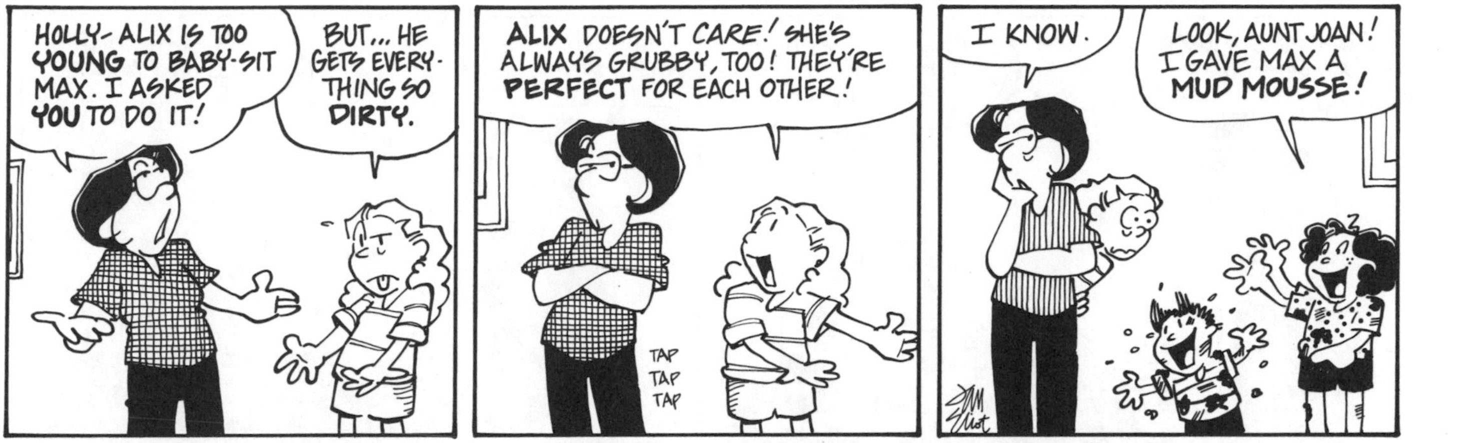
HOLLY- ALIX IS TOO YOUNG TO BABY-SIT MAX. I ASKED YOU TO DO IT!
BUT... HE GETS EVERY-THING SO DIRTY.
ALIX DOESN'T CARE! SHE'S ALWAYS GRUBBY, TOO! THEY'RE PERFECT FOR EACH OTHER!
TAP TAP TAP
I KNOW.
LOOK, AUNT JOAN! I GAVE MAX A MUD MOUSSE!

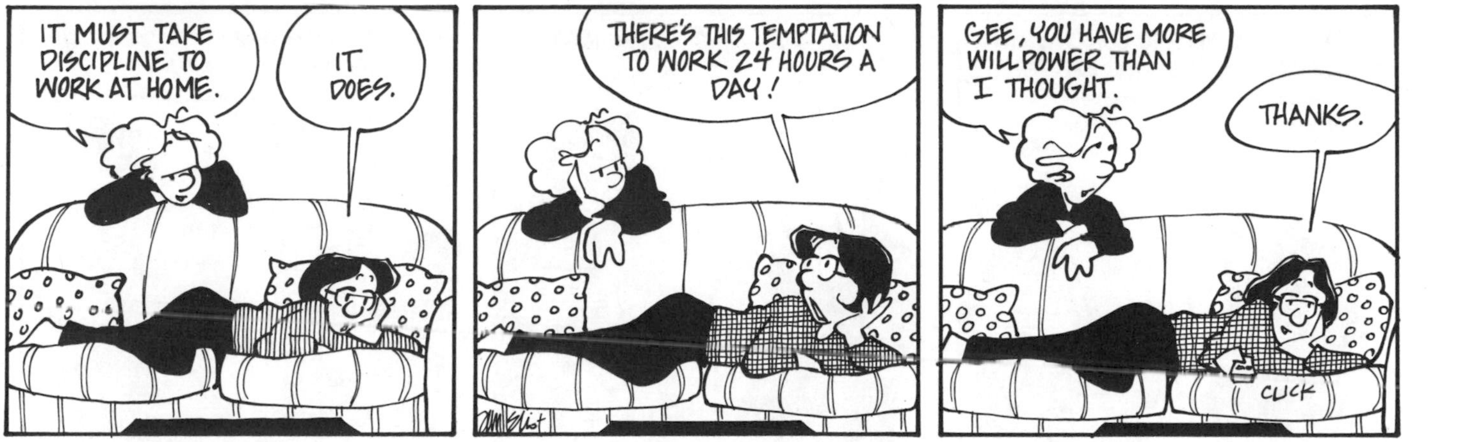
IT MUST TAKE DISCIPLINE TO WORK AT HOME.
IT DOES.
THERE'S THIS TEMPTATION TO WORK 24 HOURS A DAY!
GEE, YOU HAVE MORE WILLPOWER THAN I THOUGHT.
THANKS.
CLICK

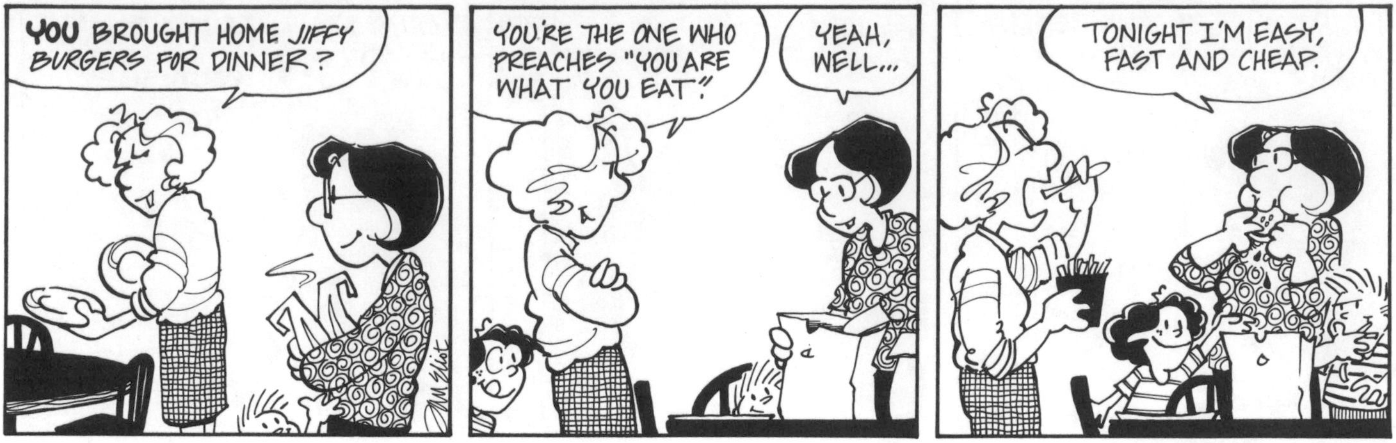
YOU BROUGHT HOME JIFFY BURGERS FOR DINNER?
YOU'RE THE ONE WHO PREACHES "YOU ARE WHAT YOU EAT."
YEAH, WELL...
TONIGHT I'M EASY, FAST AND CHEAP.

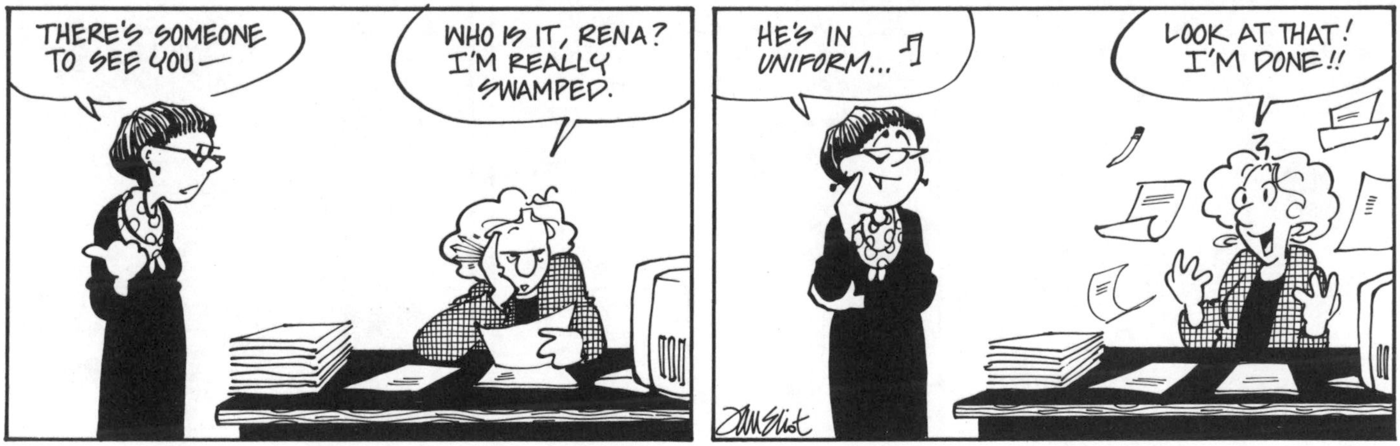
THERE'S SOMEONE TO SEE YOU—
WHO IS IT, RENA? I'M REALLY SWAMPED.
HE'S IN UNIFORM...
LOOK AT THAT! I'M DONE!!

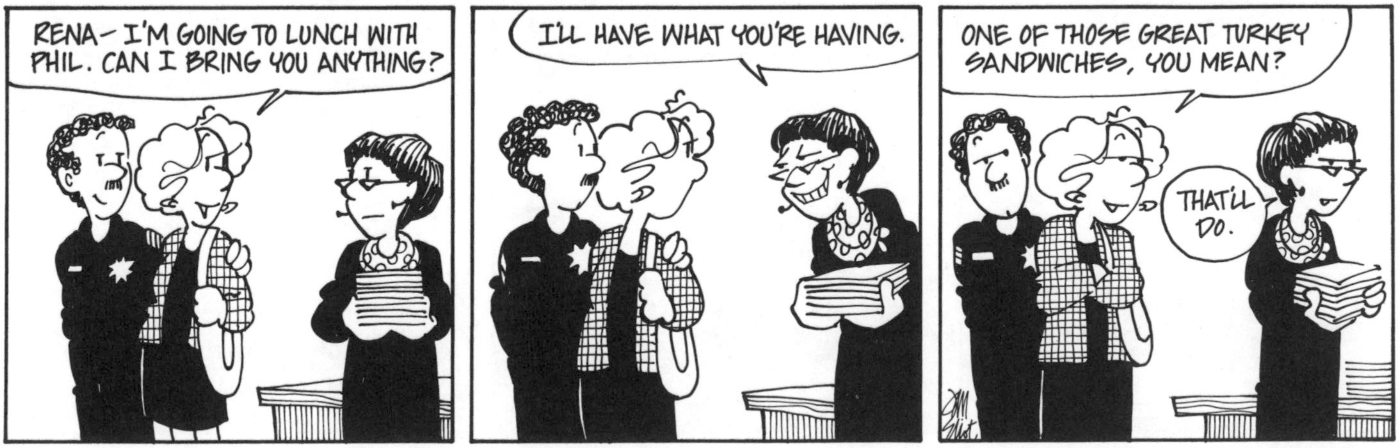
RENA— I'M GOING TO LUNCH WITH PHIL. CAN I BRING YOU ANYTHING?
I'LL HAVE WHAT YOU'RE HAVING.
ONE OF THOSE GREAT TURKEY SANDWICHES, YOU MEAN?
THAT'LL DO.

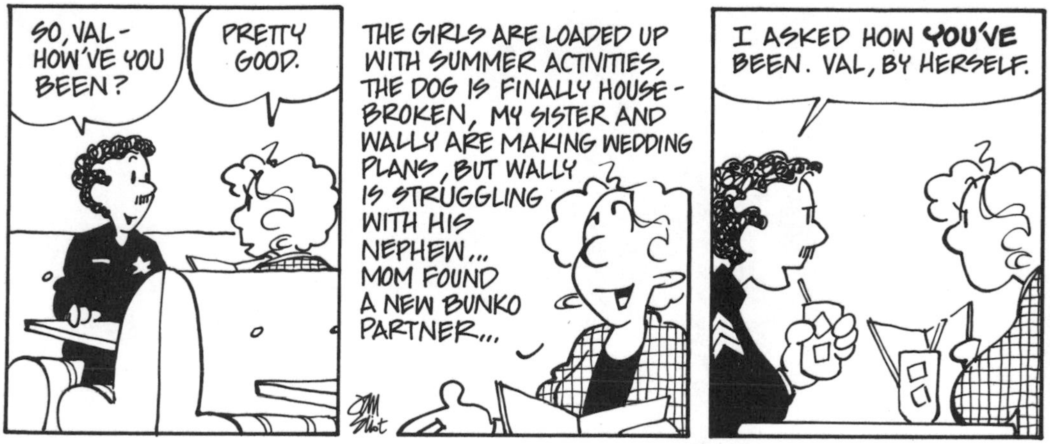
SO, VAL-
HOW'VE YOU BEEN?
PRETTY GOOD.
THE GIRLS ARE LOADED UP WITH SUMMER ACTIVITIES, THE DOG IS FINALLY HOUSE-BROKEN, MY SISTER AND WALLY ARE MAKING WEDDING PLANS, BUT WALLY IS STRUGGLING WITH HIS NEPHEW... MOM FOUND A NEW BUNKO PARTNER...
I ASKED HOW **YOU'VE** BEEN. VAL, BY HERSELF.
I HAVEN'T SEEN "VAL, BY HERSELF" SINCE I HAD A FAMILY. WHAT DOES SHE LOOK LIKE?

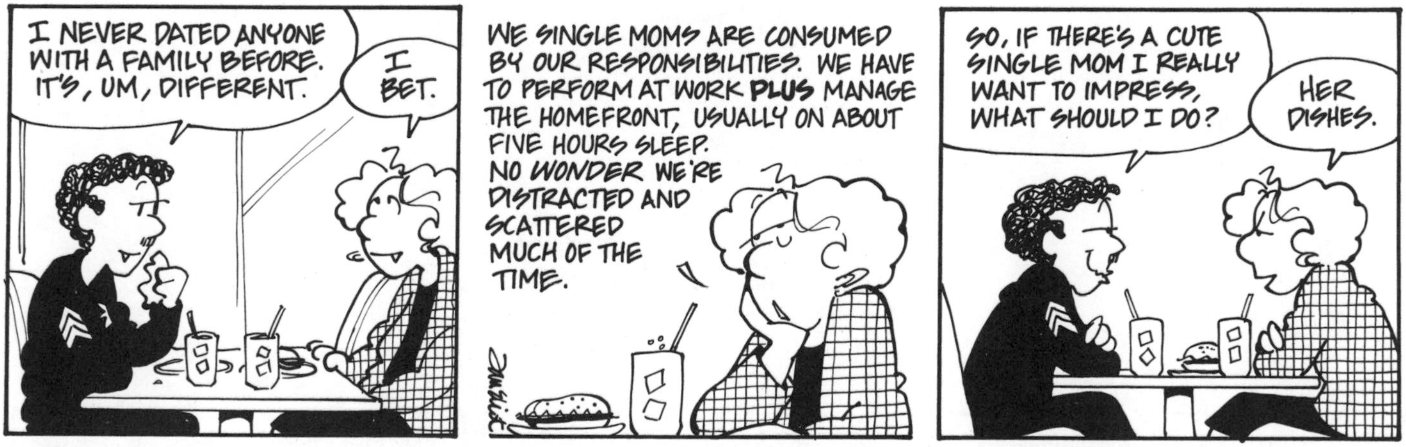
I NEVER DATED ANYONE WITH A FAMILY BEFORE. IT'S, UM, DIFFERENT.
I BET.
WE SINGLE MOMS ARE CONSUMED BY OUR RESPONSIBILITIES. WE HAVE TO PERFORM AT WORK **PLUS** MANAGE THE HOMEFRONT, USUALLY ON ABOUT FIVE HOURS SLEEP.
NO *WONDER* WE'RE DISTRACTED AND SCATTERED MUCH OF THE TIME.
SO, IF THERE'S A CUTE SINGLE MOM I REALLY WANT TO IMPRESS, WHAT SHOULD I DO?
HER DISHES.

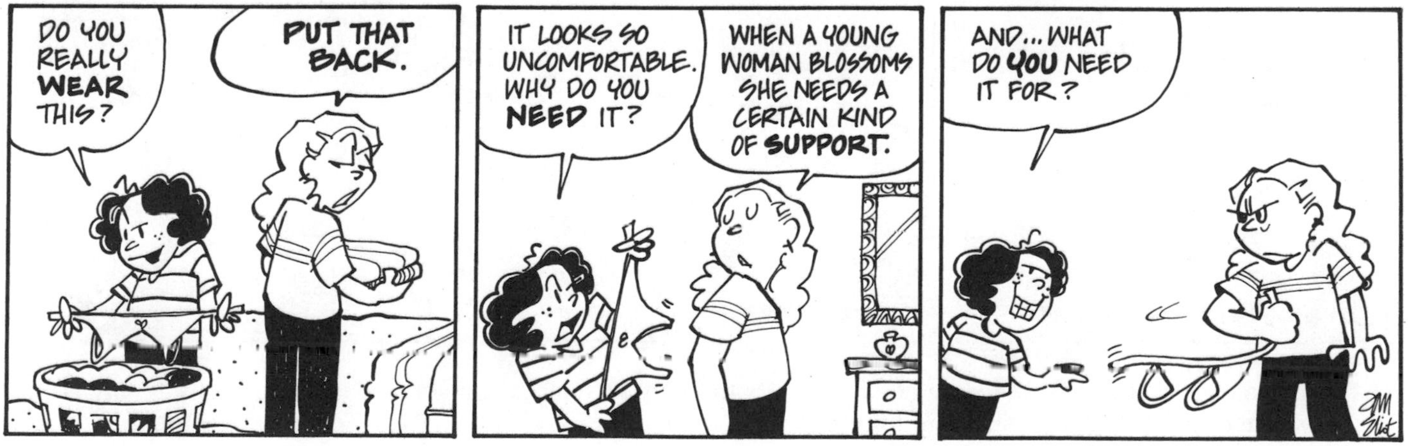
DO YOU REALLY **WEAR** THIS?
PUT THAT BACK.
IT LOOKS SO UNCOMFORTABLE. WHY DO YOU **NEED** IT?
WHEN A YOUNG WOMAN BLOSSOMS SHE NEEDS A CERTAIN KIND OF **SUPPORT**.
AND... WHAT DO **YOU** NEED IT FOR?

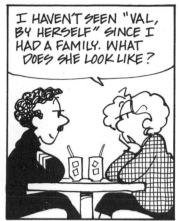

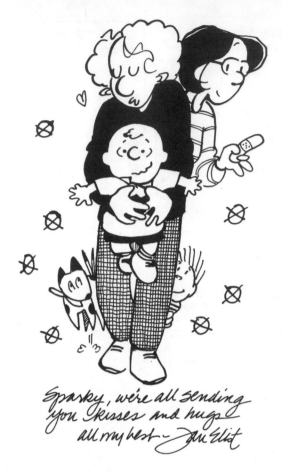

Sparky, we're all sending
you kisses and hugs
all my best - Jan Eliot

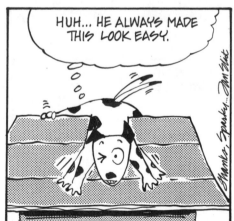

HUH... HE ALWAYS MADE THIS LOOK EASY.
Thanks, Sparky... Jan Eliot
NOW I REALIZE I DON'T KNOW EXACTLY HOW HE DID IT.
IT'S GOING TO BE HARDER THAN WE THOUGHT...
... TO FILL HIS SHOES.
GONE OUT FOR ROOT BEER

When Charles Schulz (Sparky) became ill, cartoonists from all over sent their get well wishes. A tribute day was planned, where cartoonists would honor Schulz in their strips. Unfortunately, he never saw them.

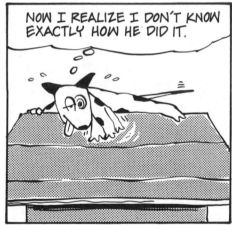

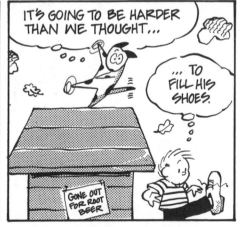

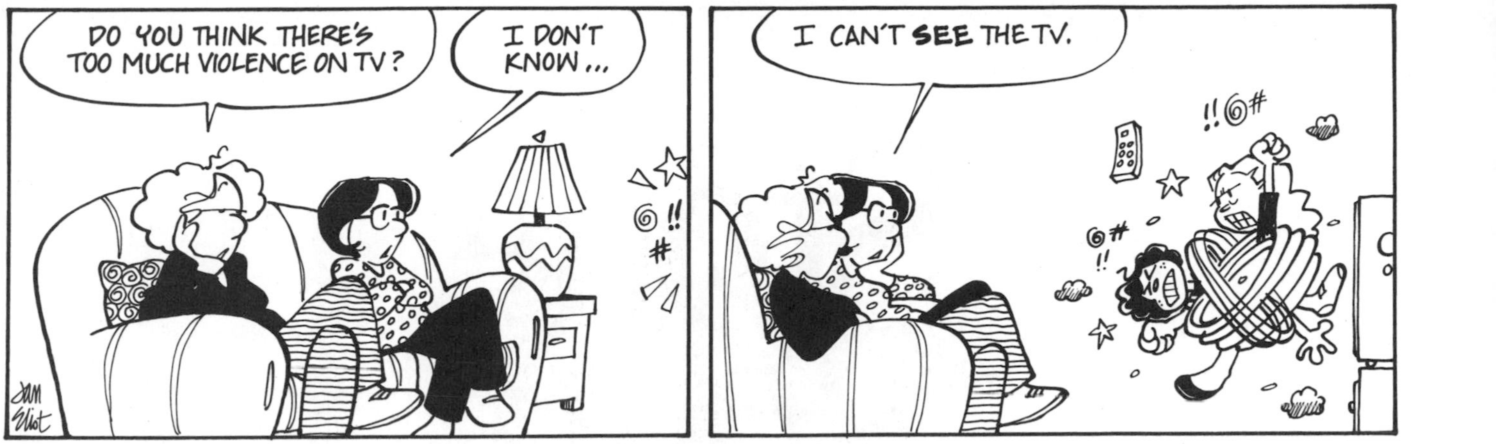
DO YOU THINK THERE'S TOO MUCH VIOLENCE ON TV?
I DON'T KNOW...
I CAN'T **SEE** THE TV.

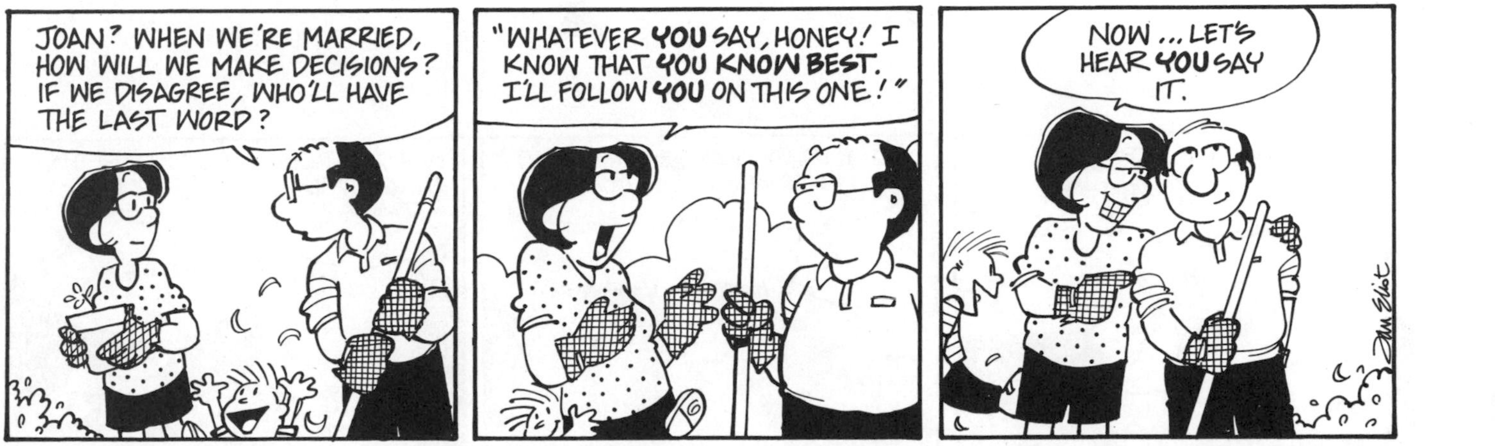
JOAN? WHEN WE'RE MARRIED, HOW WILL WE MAKE DECISIONS? IF WE DISAGREE, WHO'LL HAVE THE LAST WORD?
"WHATEVER **YOU** SAY, HONEY! I KNOW THAT **YOU KNOW BEST**. I'LL FOLLOW **YOU** ON THIS ONE!"
NOW... LET'S HEAR **YOU** SAY IT.

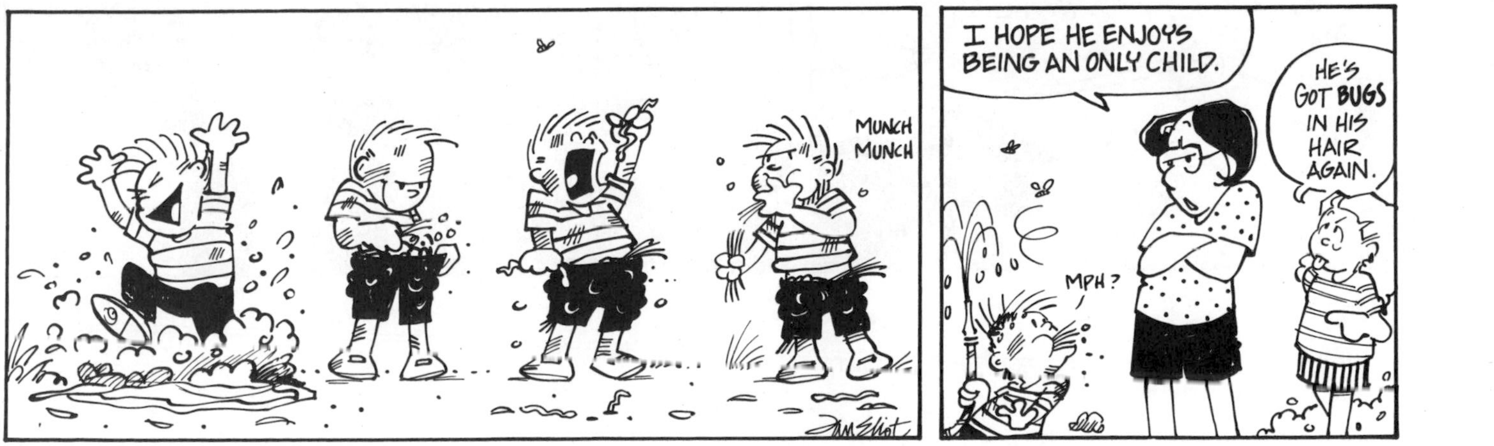
MUNCH MUNCH
I HOPE HE ENJOYS BEING AN ONLY CHILD.
HE'S GOT **BUGS** IN HIS HAIR AGAIN.
MPH?

Stone Soup

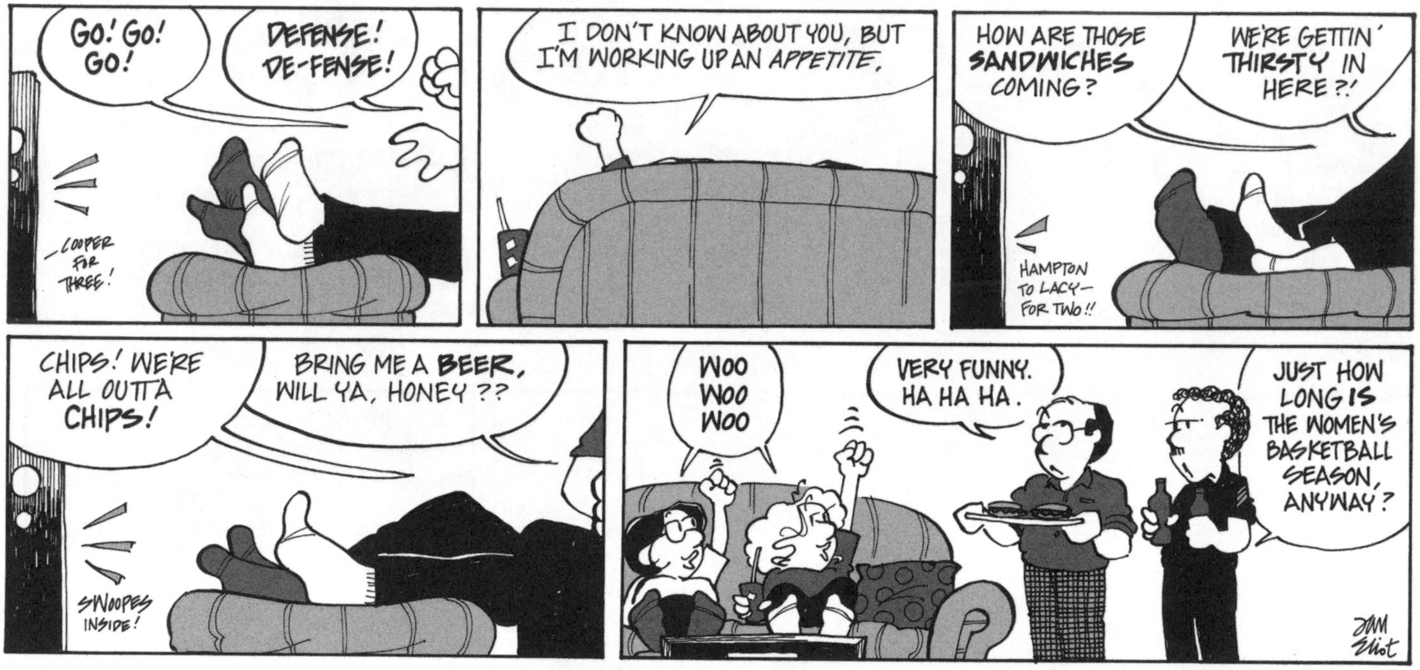
GO! GO! GO!
DEFENSE! DE-FENSE!
—COOPER FOR THREE!
I DON'T KNOW ABOUT YOU, BUT I'M WORKING UP AN APPETITE.
HOW ARE THOSE SANDWICHES COMING?
WE'RE GETTIN' THIRSTY IN HERE?!
HAMPTON TO LACY—FOR TWO!!
CHIPS! WE'RE ALL OUTTA CHIPS!
BRING ME A BEER, WILL YA, HONEY??
SWOOPES INSIDE!
WOO WOO WOO
VERY FUNNY. HA HA HA.
JUST HOW LONG IS THE WOMEN'S BASKETBALL SEASON, ANYWAY?
JAN Eliot

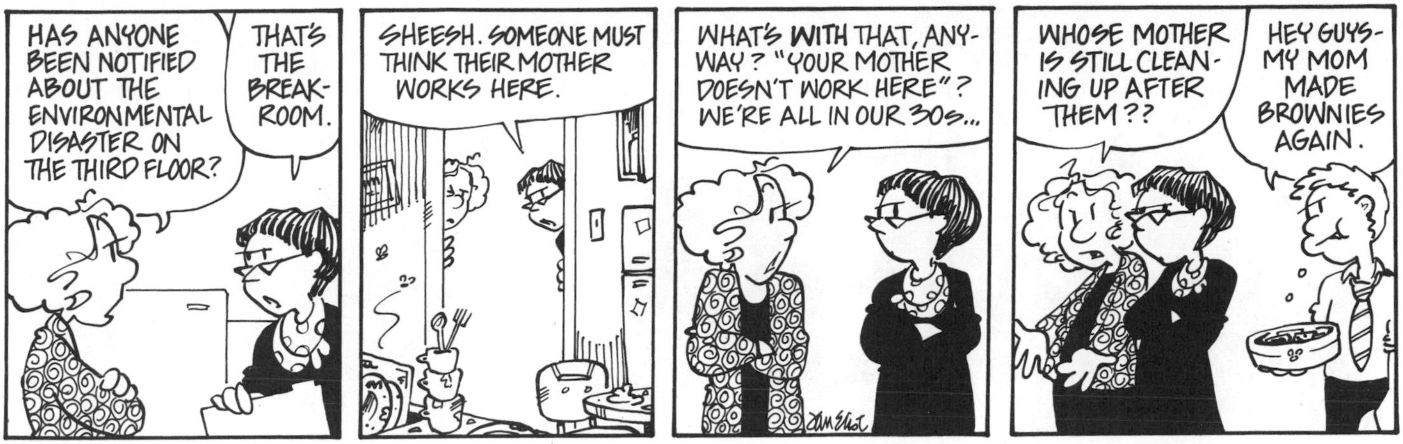
HAS ANYONE BEEN NOTIFIED ABOUT THE ENVIRONMENTAL DISASTER ON THE THIRD FLOOR?
THAT'S THE BREAK-ROOM.
SHEESH. SOMEONE MUST THINK THEIR MOTHER WORKS HERE.
WHAT'S WITH THAT, ANY-WAY? "YOUR MOTHER DOESN'T WORK HERE"? WE'RE ALL IN OUR 30s...
WHOSE MOTHER IS STILL CLEAN-ING UP AFTER THEM??
HEY GUYS- MY MOM MADE BROWNIES AGAIN.

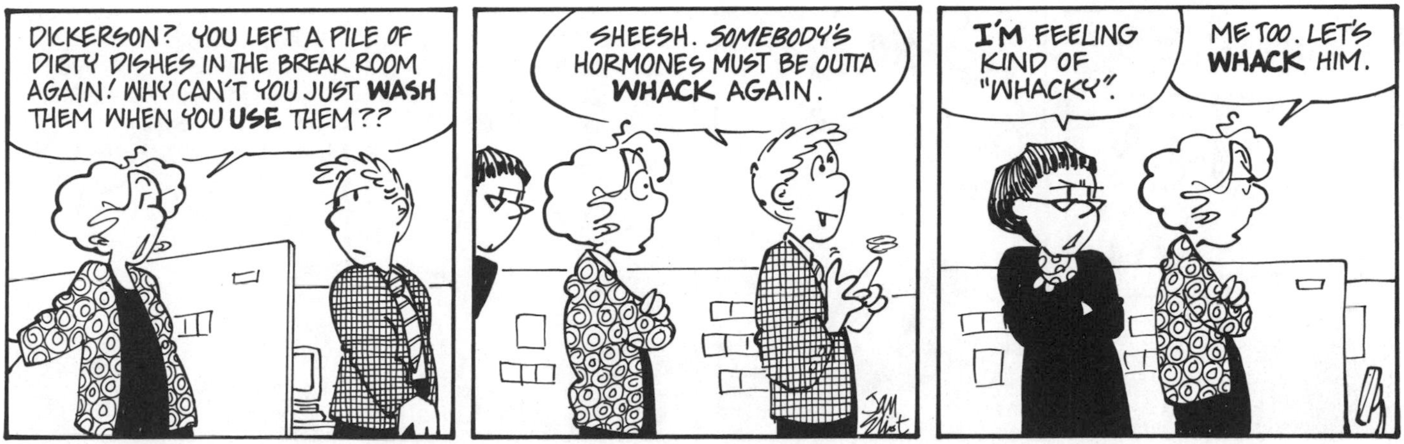
DICKERSON? YOU LEFT A PILE OF DIRTY DISHES IN THE BREAK ROOM AGAIN! WHY CAN'T YOU JUST WASH THEM WHEN YOU USE THEM??
SHEESH. SOMEBODY'S HORMONES MUST BE OUTTA WHACK AGAIN.
I'M FEELING KIND OF "WHACKY".
ME TOO. LET'S WHACK HIM.

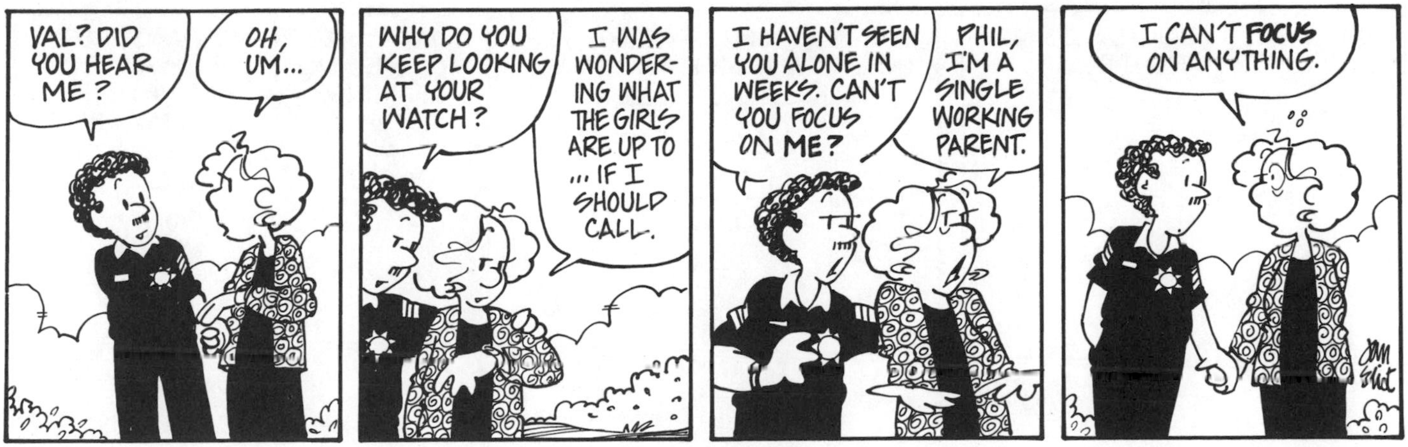
VAL? DID YOU HEAR ME?
OH, UM...
WHY DO YOU KEEP LOOKING AT YOUR WATCH?
I WAS WONDER-ING WHAT THE GIRLS ARE UP TO ... IF I SHOULD CALL.
I HAVEN'T SEEN YOU ALONE IN WEEKS. CAN'T YOU FOCUS ON ME?
PHIL, I'M A SINGLE WORKING PARENT.
I CAN'T FOCUS ON ANYTHING.

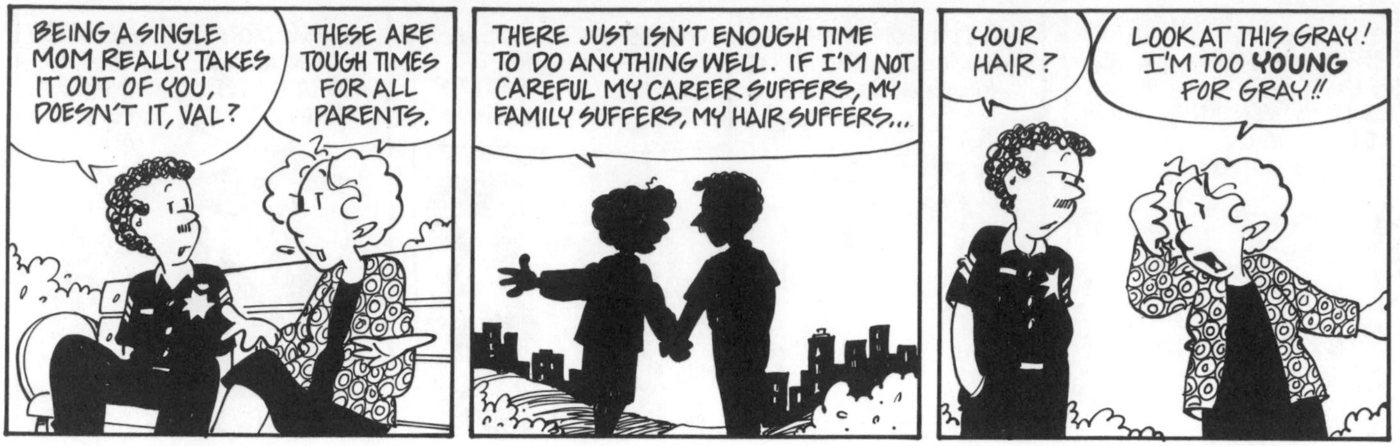
BEING A SINGLE MOM REALLY TAKES IT OUT OF YOU, DOESN'T IT, VAL?
THESE ARE TOUGH TIMES FOR ALL PARENTS.
THERE JUST ISN'T ENOUGH TIME TO DO ANYTHING WELL. IF I'M NOT CAREFUL MY CAREER SUFFERS, MY FAMILY SUFFERS, MY HAIR SUFFERS...
YOUR HAIR?
LOOK AT THIS GRAY! I'M TOO **YOUNG** FOR GRAY!!

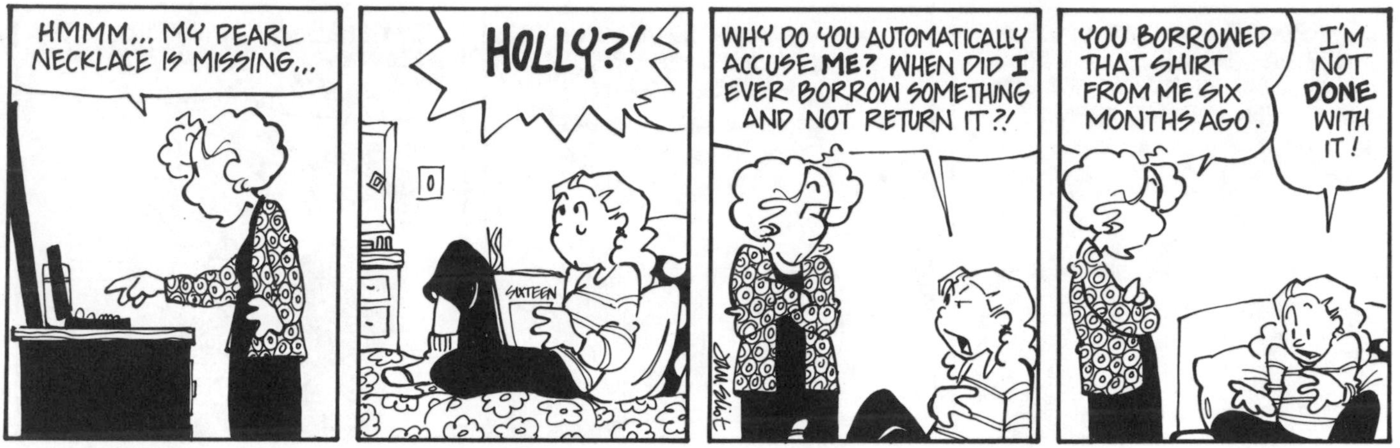
HMMM... MY PEARL NECKLACE IS MISSING...
HOLLY?!
SIXTEEN
WHY DO YOU AUTOMATICALLY ACCUSE **ME**? WHEN DID **I** EVER BORROW SOMETHING AND NOT RETURN IT?!
YOU BORROWED THAT SHIRT FROM ME SIX MONTHS AGO.
I'M NOT **DONE** WITH IT!

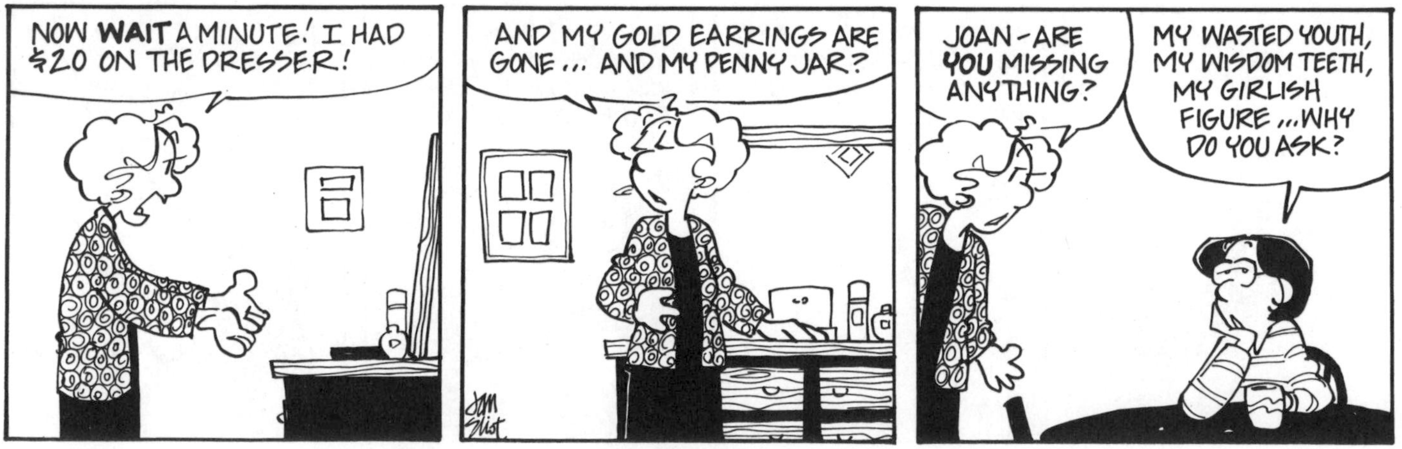
NOW **WAIT** A MINUTE! I HAD $20 ON THE DRESSER!
AND MY GOLD EARRINGS ARE GONE... AND MY PENNY JAR?
JOAN-ARE **YOU** MISSING ANYTHING?
MY WASTED YOUTH, MY WISDOM TEETH, MY GIRLISH FIGURE ...WHY DO YOU ASK?

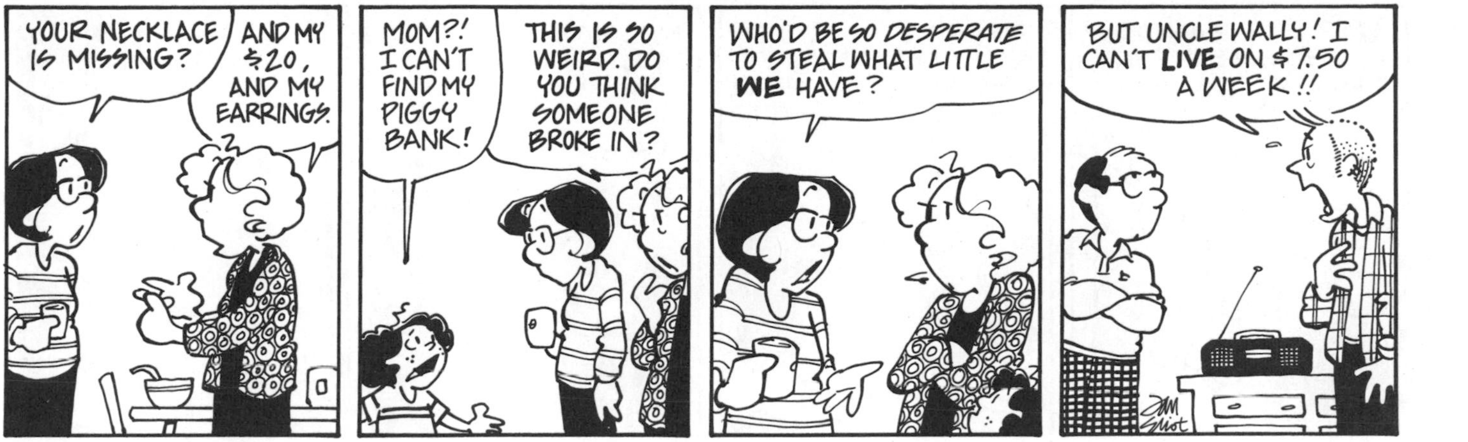
YOUR NECKLACE IS MISSING?
AND MY $20, AND MY EARRINGS.
MOM?! I CAN'T FIND MY PIGGY BANK!
THIS IS SO WEIRD. DO YOU THINK SOMEONE BROKE IN?
WHO'D BE SO *DESPERATE* TO STEAL WHAT LITTLE **WE** HAVE?
BUT UNCLE WALLY! I CAN'T **LIVE** ON $7.50 A WEEK!!

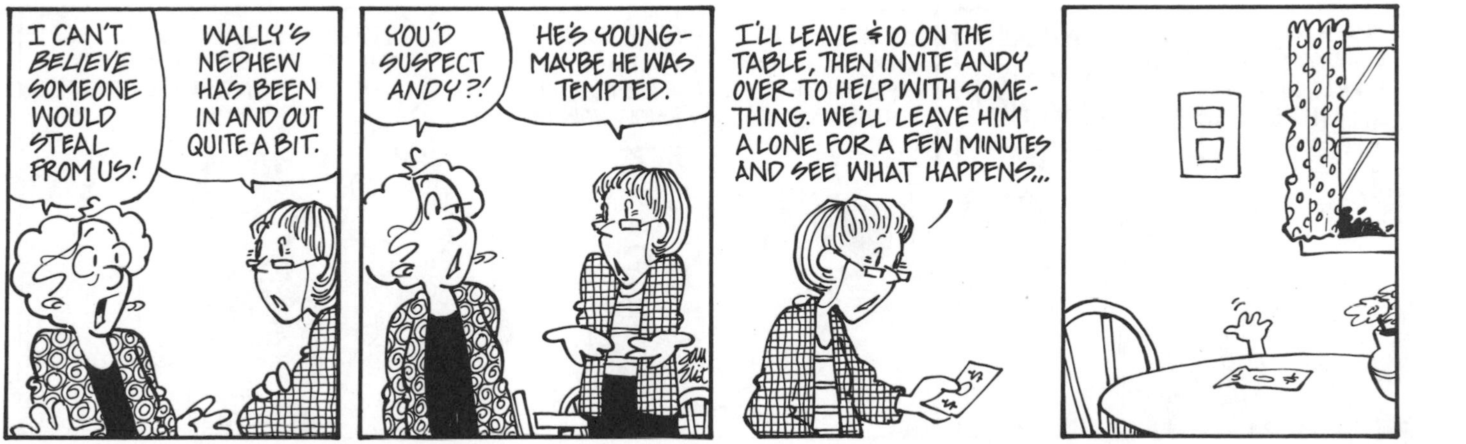
I CAN'T *BELIEVE* SOMEONE WOULD STEAL FROM US!
WALLY'S NEPHEW HAS BEEN IN AND OUT QUITE A BIT.
YOU'D SUSPECT *ANDY*?!
HE'S YOUNG- MAYBE HE WAS TEMPTED.
I'LL LEAVE $10 ON THE TABLE, THEN INVITE ANDY OVER TO HELP WITH SOMETHING. WE'LL LEAVE HIM ALONE FOR A FEW MINUTES AND SEE WHAT HAPPENS...

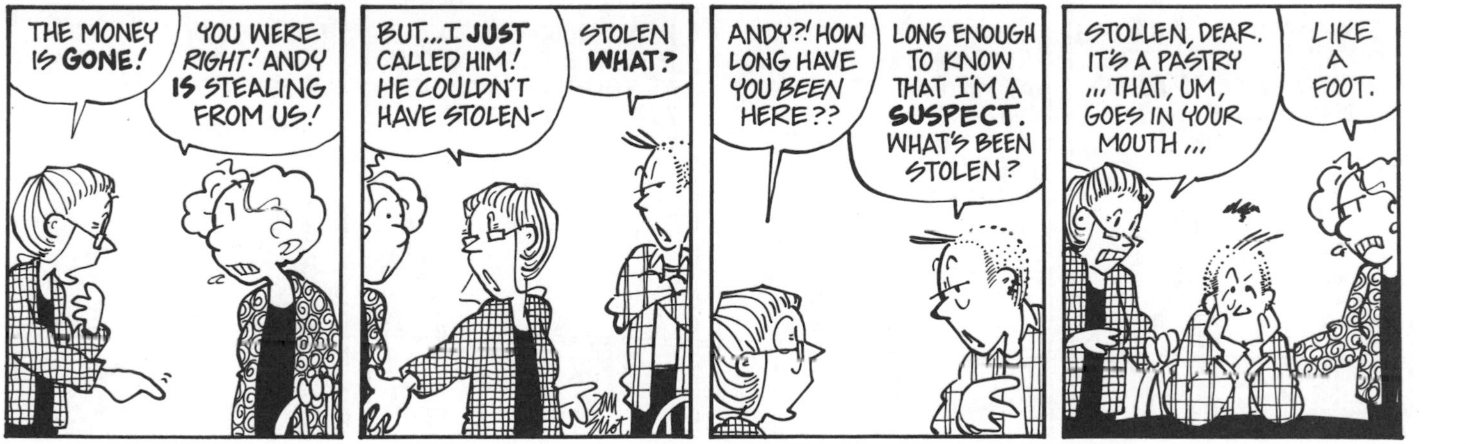
THE MONEY IS **GONE**!
YOU WERE *RIGHT*! ANDY **IS** STEALING FROM US!
BUT... I **JUST** CALLED HIM! HE COULDN'T HAVE STOLEN-
STOLEN **WHAT**?
ANDY?! HOW LONG HAVE YOU *BEEN* HERE??
LONG ENOUGH TO KNOW THAT I'M A **SUSPECT**. WHAT'S BEEN STOLEN?
STOLLEN, DEAR. IT'S A PASTRY ... THAT, UM, GOES IN YOUR MOUTH...
LIKE A FOOT.

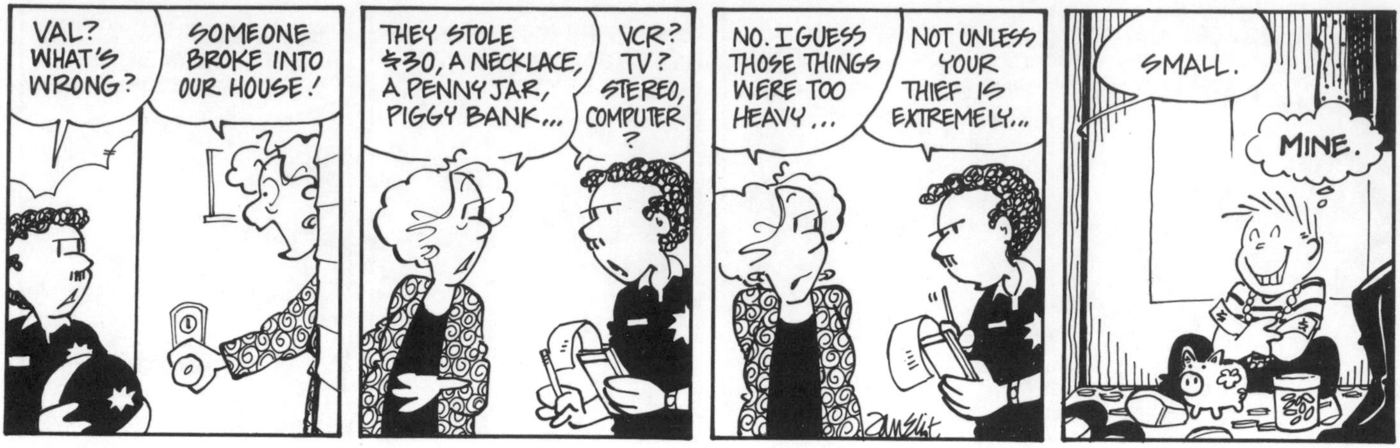
VAL? WHAT'S WRONG?
SOMEONE BROKE INTO OUR HOUSE!
THEY STOLE $30, A NECKLACE, A PENNY JAR, PIGGY BANK...
VCR? TV? STEREO, COMPUTER?
NO. I GUESS THOSE THINGS WERE TOO HEAVY...
NOT UNLESS YOUR THIEF IS EXTREMELY...
SMALL.
MINE.

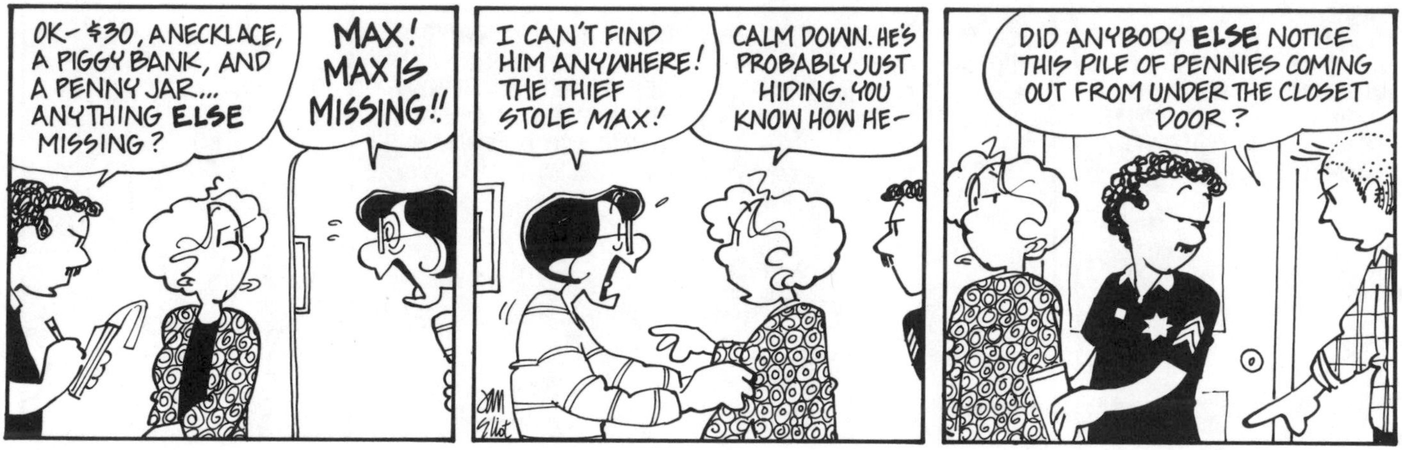
OK- $30, A NECKLACE, A PIGGY BANK, AND A PENNY JAR... ANYTHING ELSE MISSING?
MAX! MAX IS MISSING!!
I CAN'T FIND HIM ANYWHERE! THE THIEF STOLE MAX!
CALM DOWN. HE'S PROBABLY JUST HIDING. YOU KNOW HOW HE-
DID ANYBODY ELSE NOTICE THIS PILE OF PENNIES COMING OUT FROM UNDER THE CLOSET DOOR?

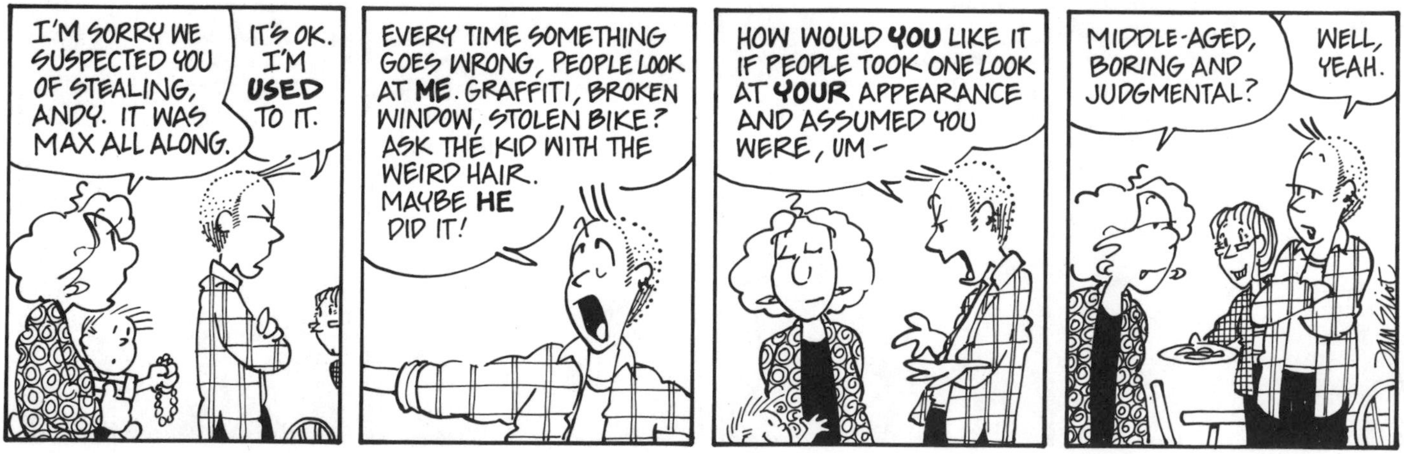
I'M SORRY WE SUSPECTED YOU OF STEALING, ANDY. IT WAS MAX ALL ALONG.
IT'S OK. I'M USED TO IT.
EVERY TIME SOMETHING GOES WRONG, PEOPLE LOOK AT ME. GRAFFITI, BROKEN WINDOW, STOLEN BIKE? ASK THE KID WITH THE WEIRD HAIR. MAYBE HE DID IT!
HOW WOULD YOU LIKE IT IF PEOPLE TOOK ONE LOOK AT YOUR APPEARANCE AND ASSUMED YOU WERE, UM -
MIDDLE-AGED, BORING AND JUDGMENTAL?
WELL, YEAH.

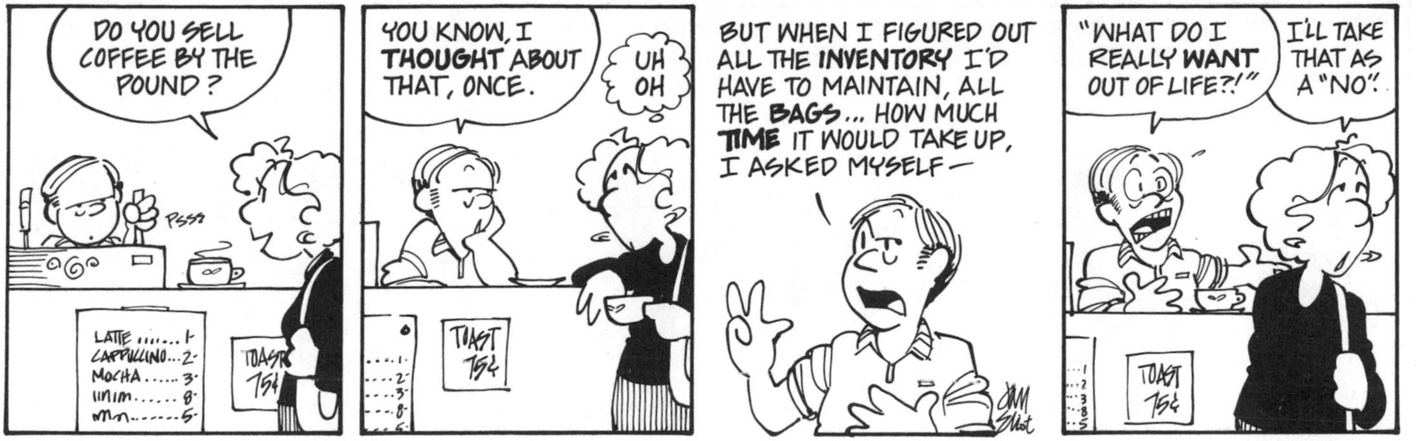
DO YOU SELL COFFEE BY THE POUND?
LATTE 1-
CAPPUCCINO... 2-
MOCHA 3-
TOAST 75¢
YOU KNOW, I **THOUGHT** ABOUT THAT, ONCE.
UH OH
TOAST 75¢
BUT WHEN I FIGURED OUT ALL THE **INVENTORY** I'D HAVE TO MAINTAIN, ALL THE **BAGS**... HOW MUCH **TIME** IT WOULD TAKE UP, I ASKED MYSELF—
"WHAT DO I REALLY **WANT** OUT OF LIFE?!"
I'LL TAKE THAT AS A "NO".
TOAST 75¢

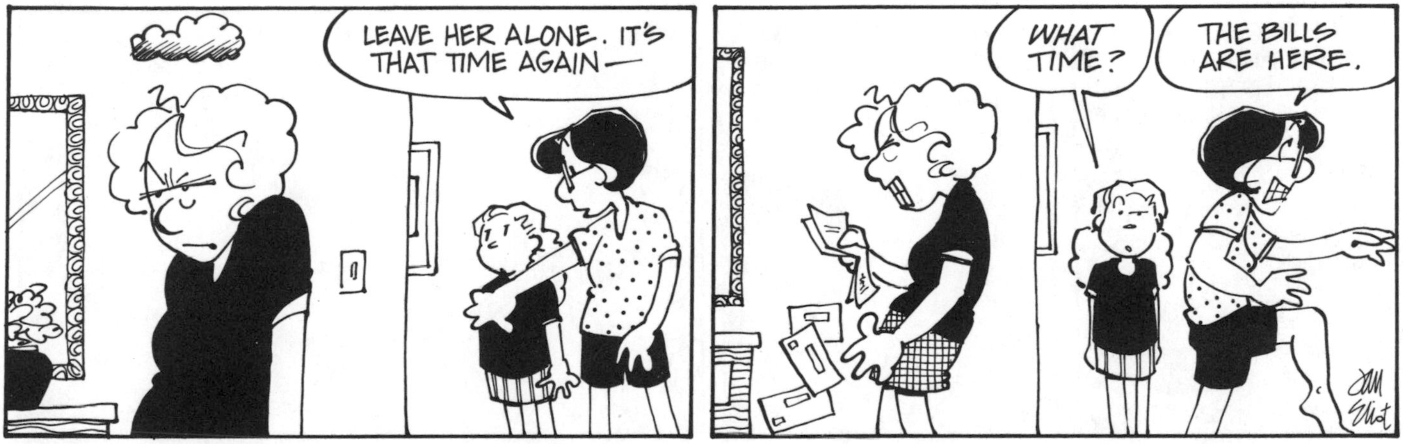
LEAVE HER ALONE. IT'S THAT TIME AGAIN—
WHAT TIME?
THE BILLS ARE HERE.

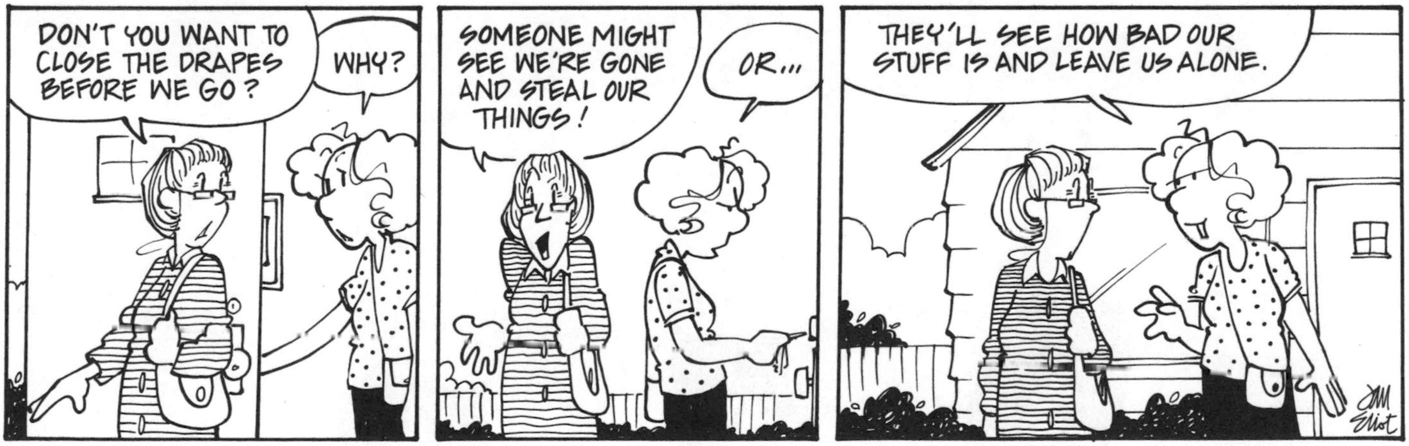
DON'T YOU WANT TO CLOSE THE DRAPES BEFORE WE GO?
WHY?
SOMEONE MIGHT SEE WE'RE GONE AND STEAL OUR THINGS!
OR...
THEY'LL SEE HOW BAD OUR STUFF IS AND LEAVE US ALONE.

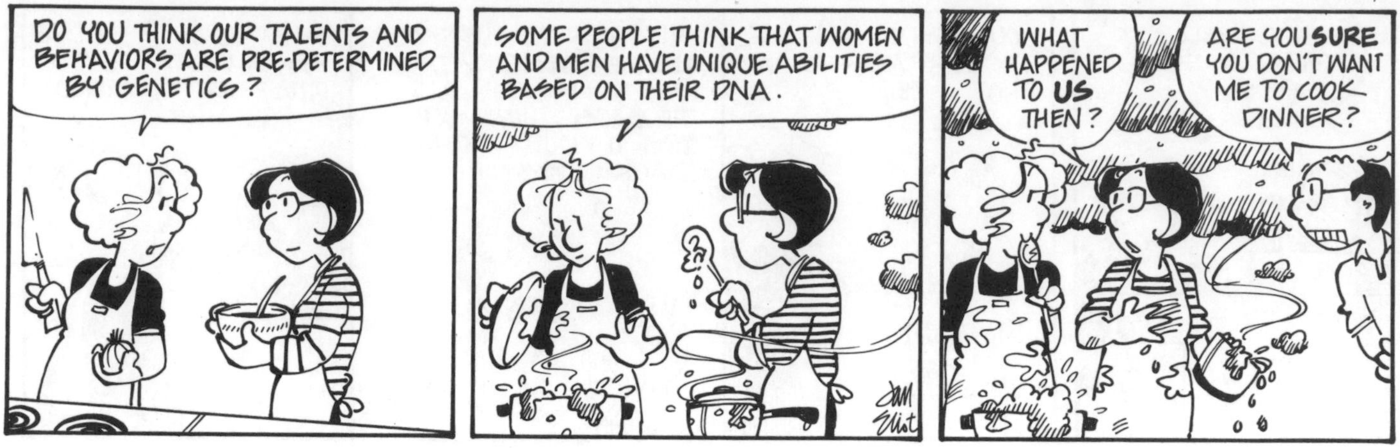
DO YOU THINK OUR TALENTS AND BEHAVIORS ARE PRE-DETERMINED BY GENETICS?
SOME PEOPLE THINK THAT WOMEN AND MEN HAVE UNIQUE ABILITIES BASED ON THEIR DNA.
WHAT HAPPENED TO US THEN?
ARE YOU SURE YOU DON'T WANT ME TO COOK DINNER?

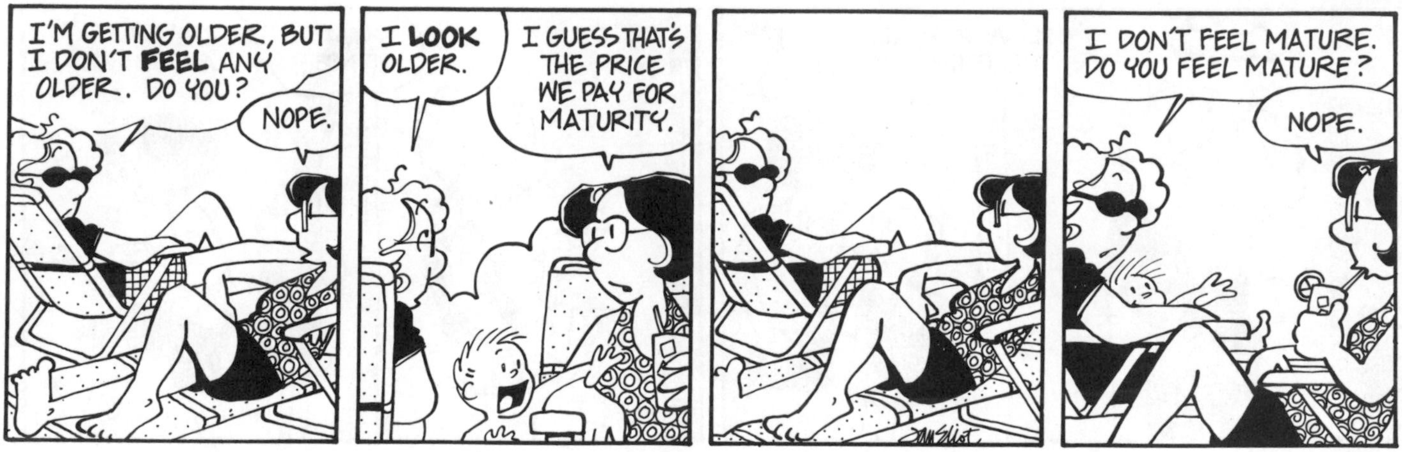
I'M GETTING OLDER, BUT I DON'T FEEL ANY OLDER. DO YOU?
NOPE.
I LOOK OLDER.
I GUESS THAT'S THE PRICE WE PAY FOR MATURITY.
I DON'T FEEL MATURE. DO YOU FEEL MATURE?
NOPE.

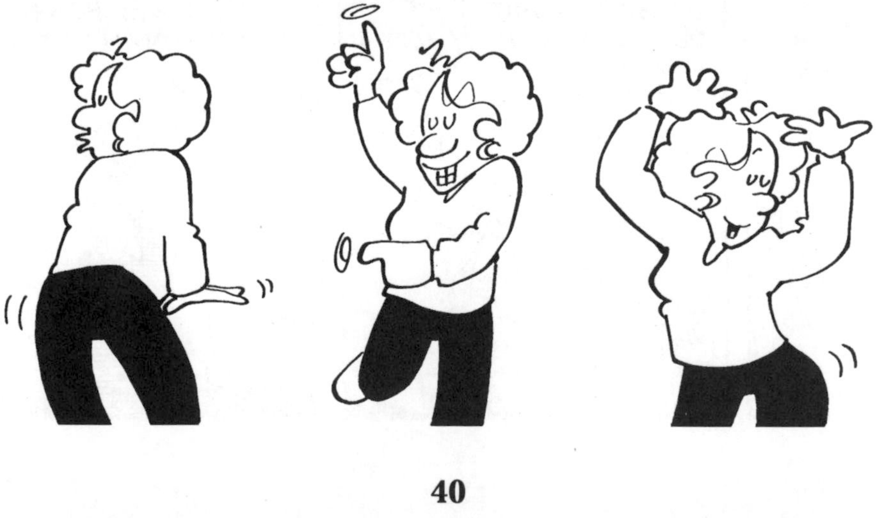

Stone Soup

JOAN? HOW'S WORK TODAY?
HI, WALLY. OK, I GUESS...
I CAN'T GET AS MUCH DONE AS I'D LIKE. I'M ALWAYS A LITTLE BEHIND.
YOU'VE GOT MAIL!
TIKKA TIKKA
I'VE GOT THREE BIG PROJECTS, AND I'M HAVING TROUBLE BALANCING IT ALL. ANY SUGGESTIONS?
M T W TH F S
CLICK
WHRRR
BEEP BEEP BEEP
MAYBE YOU NEED TO LEARN TO DO MORE THAN ONE THING AT A TIME.

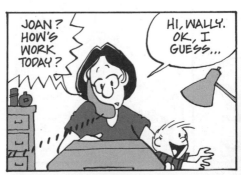

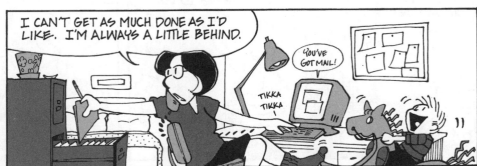

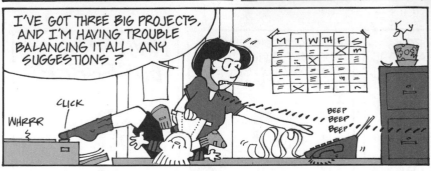

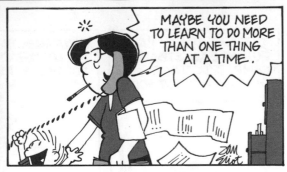

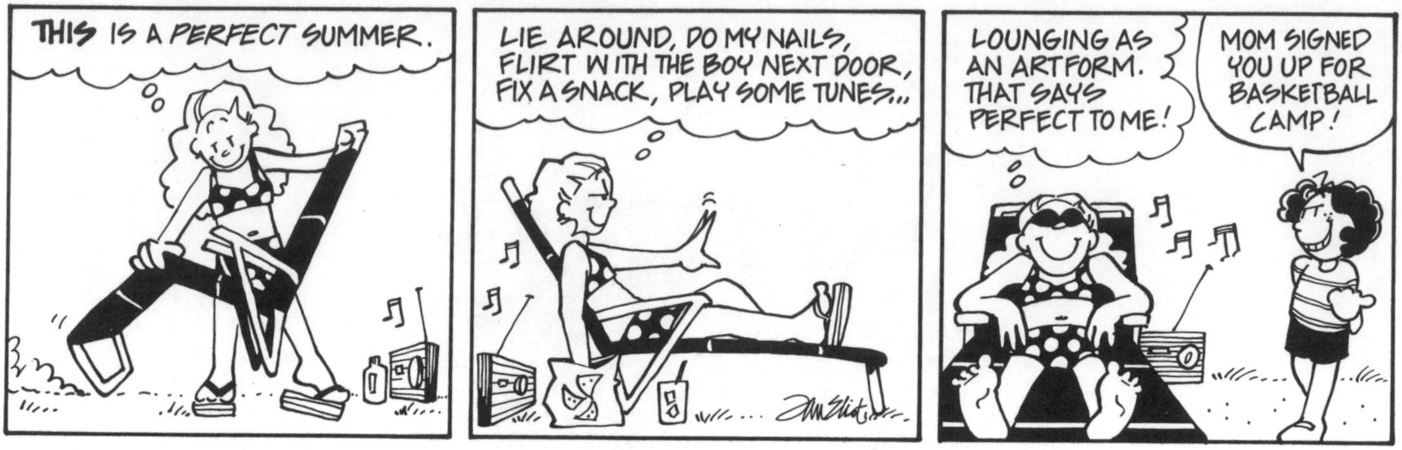
THIS IS A PERFECT SUMMER.
LIE AROUND, DO MY NAILS, FLIRT WITH THE BOY NEXT DOOR, FIX A SNACK, PLAY SOME TUNES...
LOUNGING AS AN ARTFORM. THAT SAYS PERFECT TO ME!
MOM SIGNED YOU UP FOR BASKETBALL CAMP!

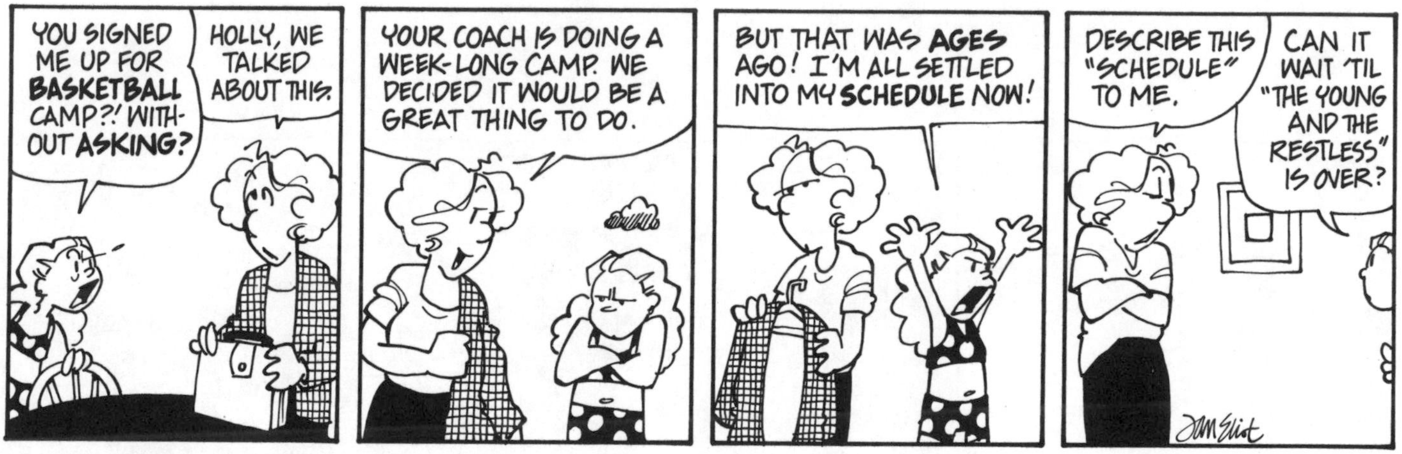
YOU SIGNED ME UP FOR BASKETBALL CAMP?! WITHOUT ASKING?
HOLLY, WE TALKED ABOUT THIS.
YOUR COACH IS DOING A WEEK-LONG CAMP. WE DECIDED IT WOULD BE A GREAT THING TO DO.
BUT THAT WAS AGES AGO! I'M ALL SETTLED INTO MY SCHEDULE NOW!
DESCRIBE THIS "SCHEDULE" TO ME.
CAN IT WAIT 'TIL "THE YOUNG AND THE RESTLESS" IS OVER?

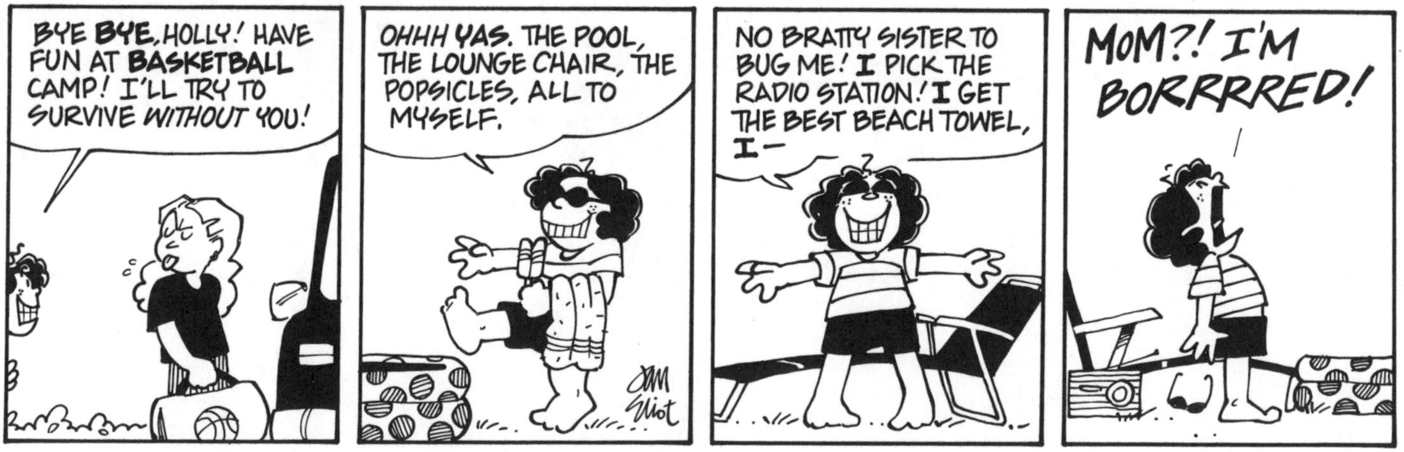
BYE BYE, HOLLY! HAVE FUN AT BASKETBALL CAMP! I'LL TRY TO SURVIVE WITHOUT YOU!
OHHH YAS. THE POOL, THE LOUNGE CHAIR, THE POPSICLES, ALL TO MYSELF.
NO BRATTY SISTER TO BUG ME! I PICK THE RADIO STATION! I GET THE BEST BEACH TOWEL, I–
MOM?! I'M BORRRRED!

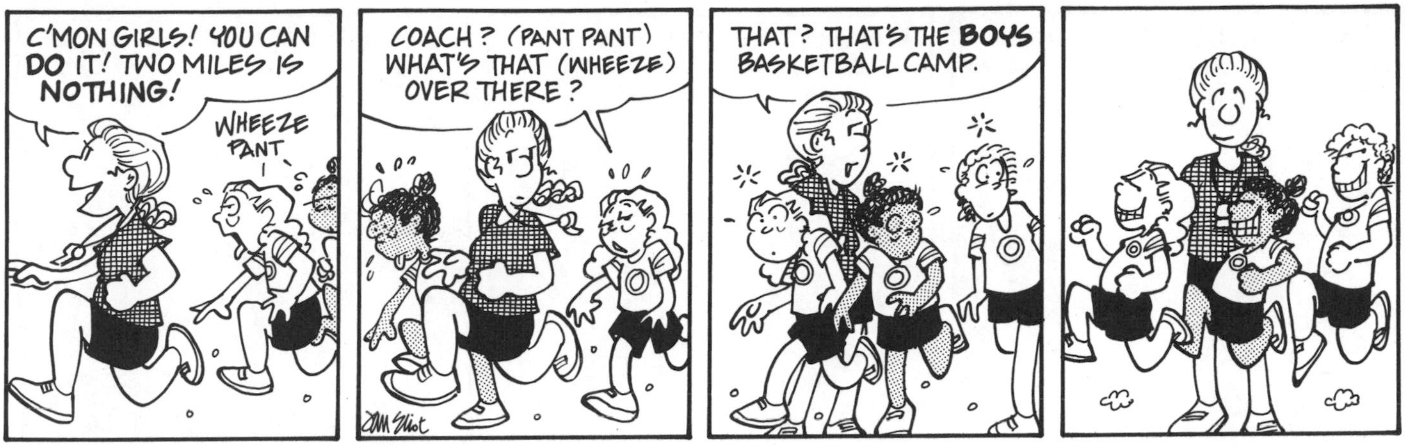
C'MON GIRLS! YOU CAN DO IT! TWO MILES IS NOTHING!
WHEEZE PANT
COACH? (PANT PANT) WHAT'S THAT (WHEEZE) OVER THERE?
THAT? THAT'S THE BOYS BASKETBALL CAMP.

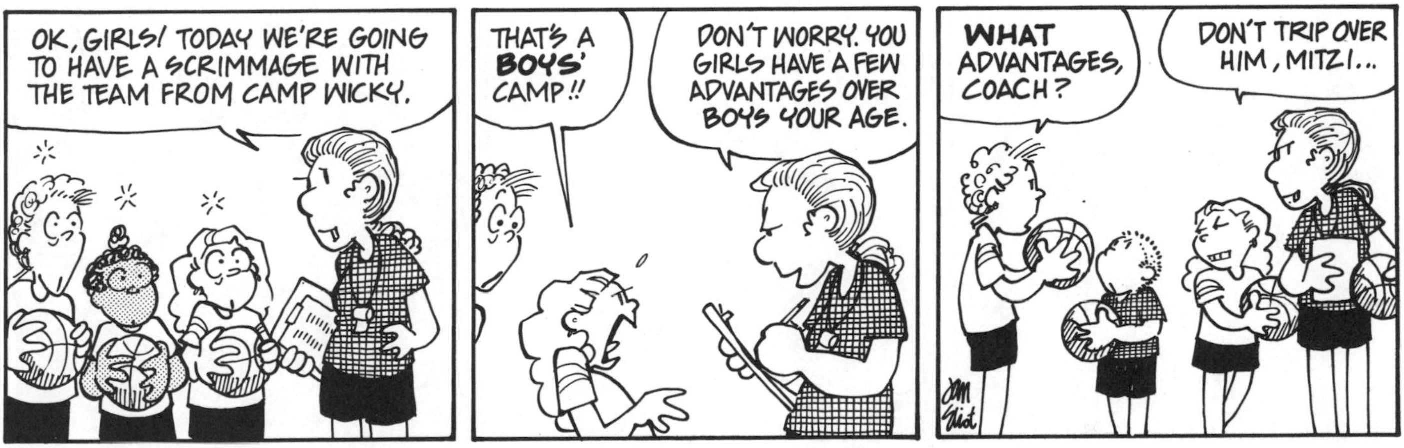
OK, GIRLS! TODAY WE'RE GOING TO HAVE A SCRIMMAGE WITH THE TEAM FROM CAMP WICKY.
THAT'S A BOYS' CAMP!!
DON'T WORRY. YOU GIRLS HAVE A FEW ADVANTAGES OVER BOYS YOUR AGE.
WHAT ADVANTAGES, COACH?
DON'T TRIP OVER HIM, MITZI...

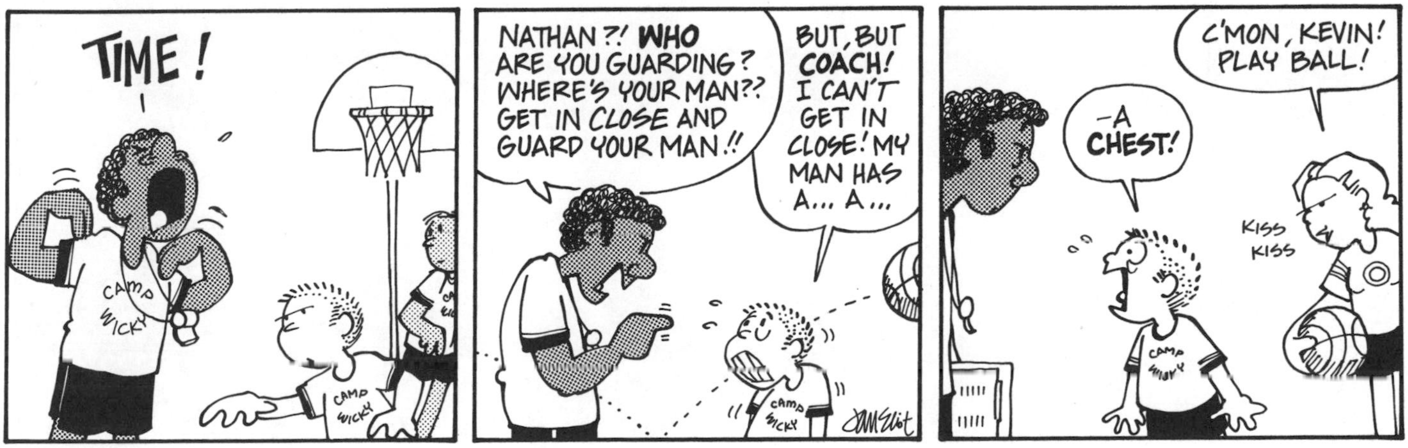
TIME!
CAMP WICKY
NATHAN?! WHO ARE YOU GUARDING? WHERE'S YOUR MAN?? GET IN CLOSE AND GUARD YOUR MAN!!
BUT, BUT COACH! I CAN'T GET IN CLOSE! MY MAN HAS A... A...
-A CHEST!
C'MON, KEVIN! PLAY BALL!
KISS KISS

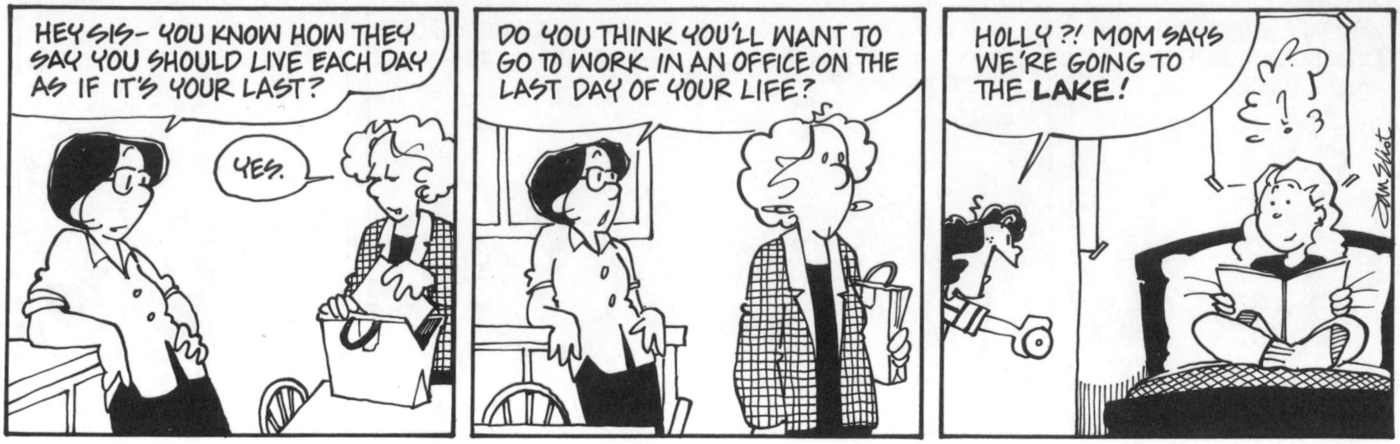
HEY SIS- YOU KNOW HOW THEY SAY YOU SHOULD LIVE EACH DAY AS IF IT'S YOUR LAST?
YES.
DO YOU THINK YOU'LL WANT TO GO TO WORK IN AN OFFICE ON THE LAST DAY OF YOUR LIFE?
HOLLY?! MOM SAYS WE'RE GOING TO THE **LAKE**!

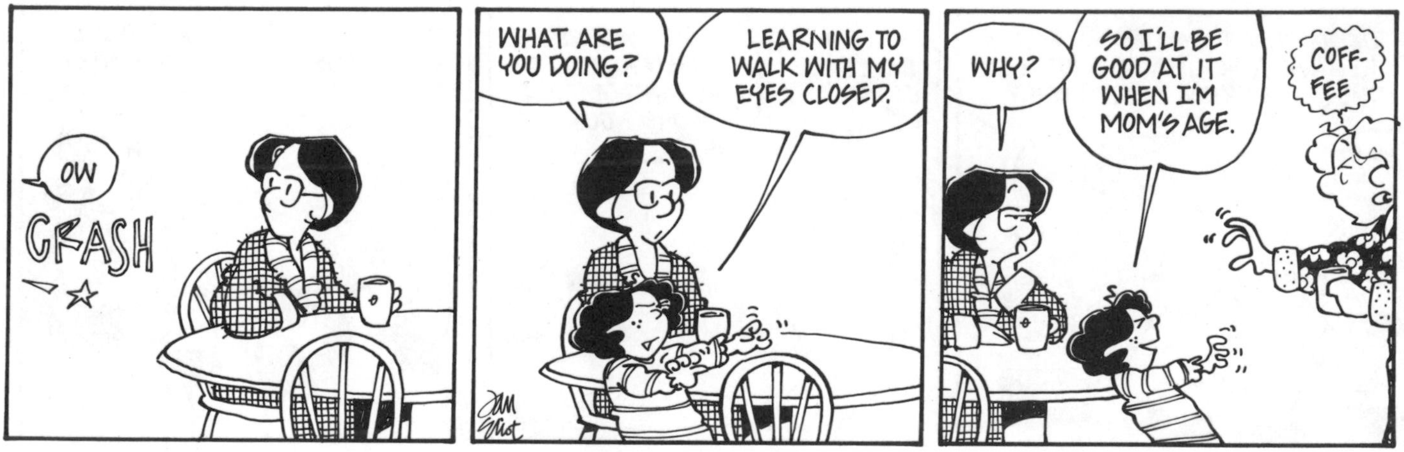
OW
CRASH
WHAT ARE YOU DOING?
LEARNING TO WALK WITH MY EYES CLOSED.
WHY?
SO I'LL BE GOOD AT IT WHEN I'M MOM'S AGE.
COFF-FEE

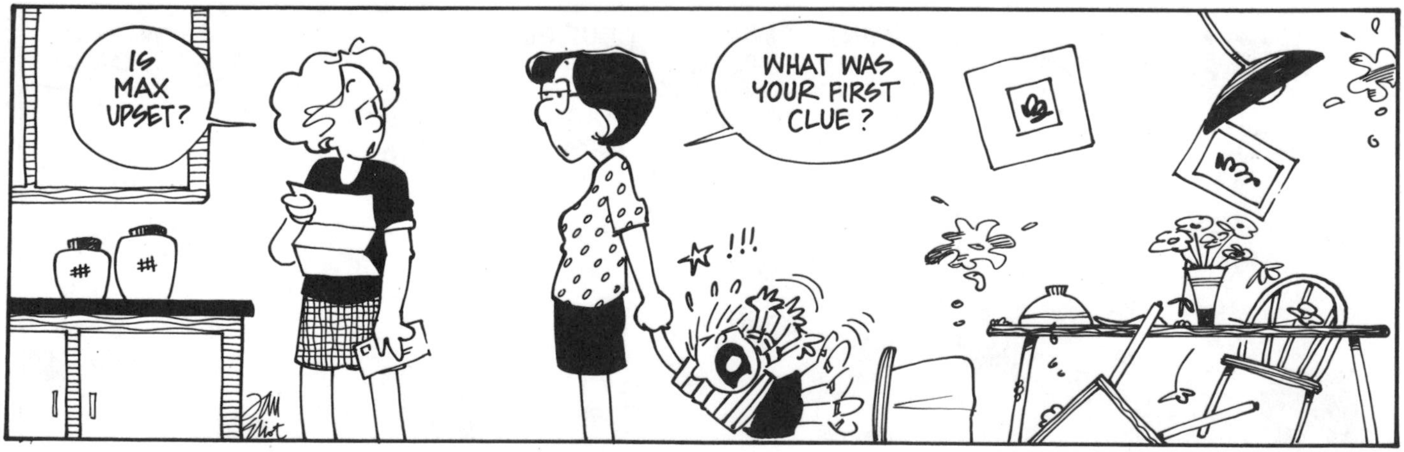
IS MAX UPSET?
WHAT WAS YOUR FIRST CLUE?
!!!

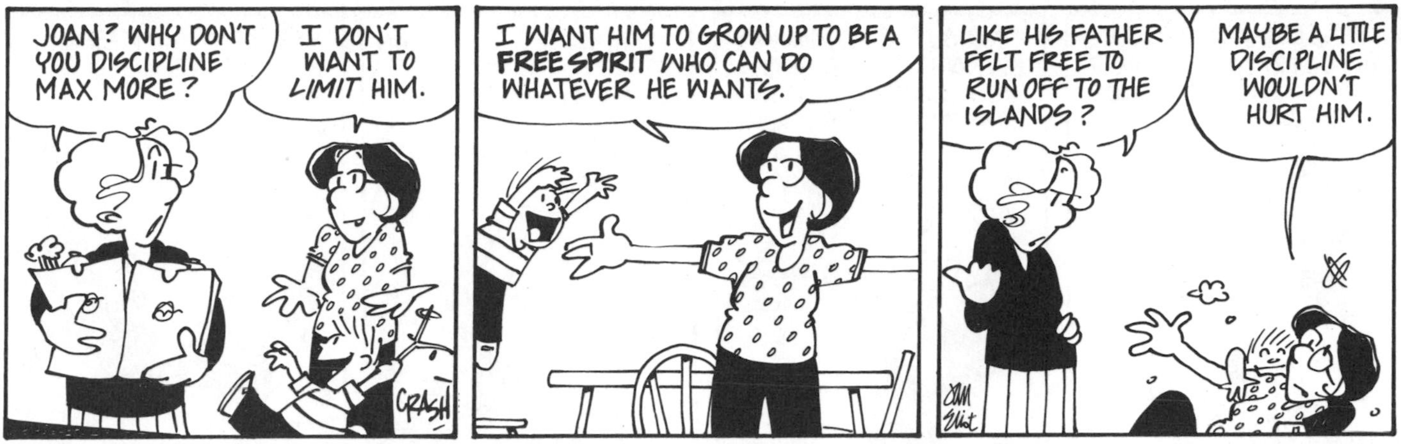
JOAN? WHY DON'T YOU DISCIPLINE MAX MORE?
I DON'T WANT TO *LIMIT* HIM.
CRASH
I WANT HIM TO GROW UP TO BE A **FREE SPIRIT** WHO CAN DO WHATEVER HE WANTS.
LIKE HIS FATHER FELT FREE TO RUN OFF TO THE ISLANDS?
MAYBE A LITTLE DISCIPLINE WOULDN'T HURT HIM.

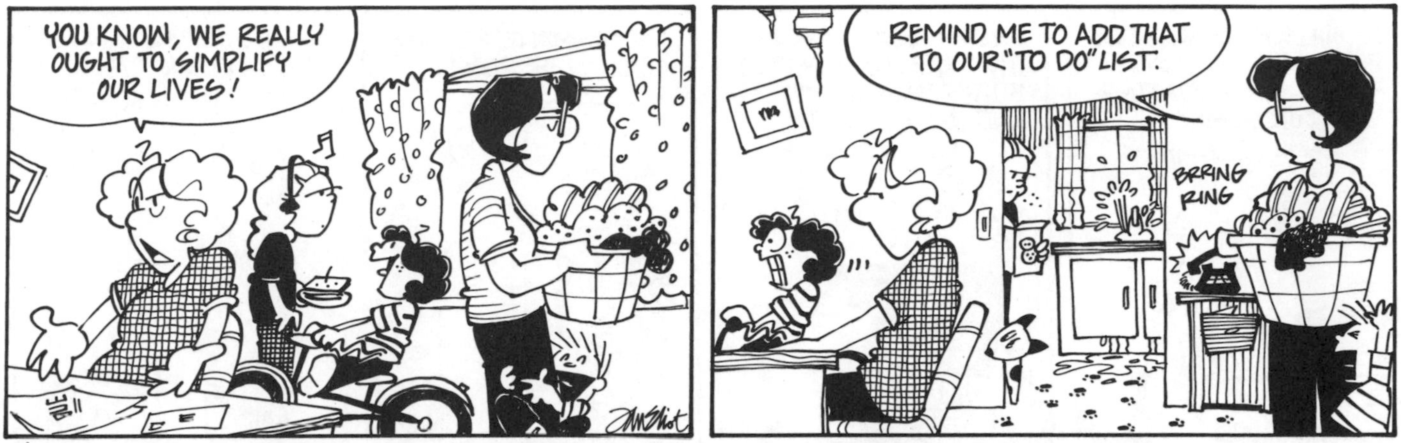
YOU KNOW, WE REALLY OUGHT TO SIMPLIFY OUR LIVES!
REMIND ME TO ADD THAT TO OUR "TO DO" LIST.
BRRING
RING

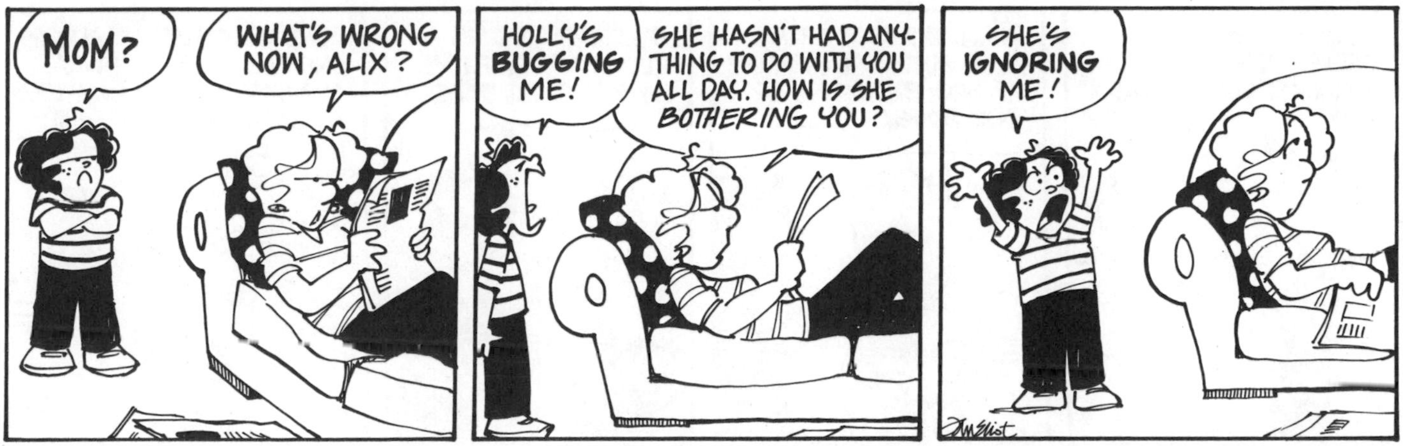
MOM?
WHAT'S WRONG NOW, ALIX?
HOLLY'S **BUGGING** ME!
SHE HASN'T HAD ANY-THING TO DO WITH YOU ALL DAY. HOW IS SHE *BOTHERING* YOU?
SHE'S **IGNORING** ME!

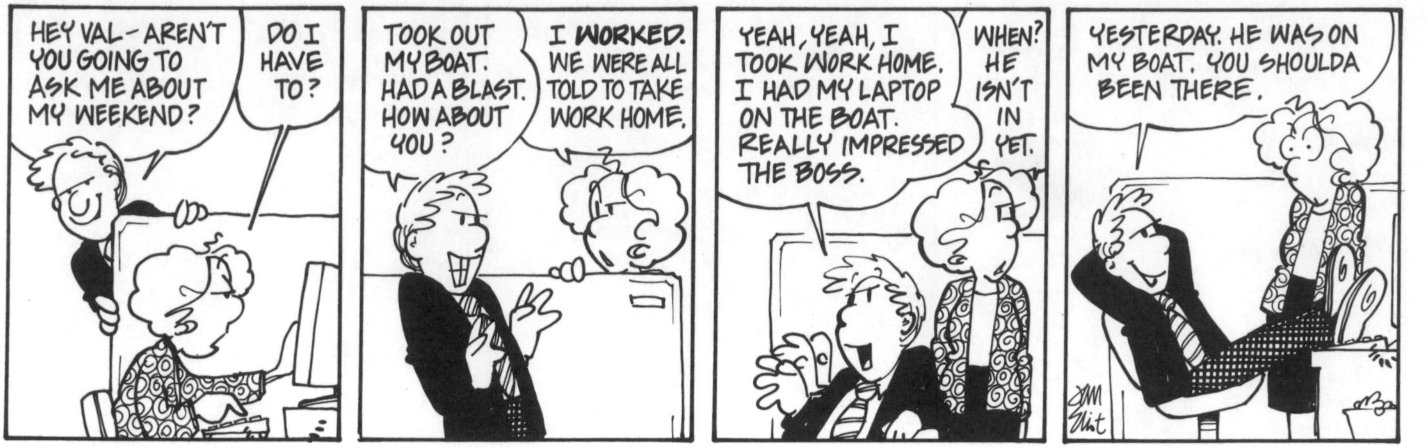
HEY VAL - AREN'T YOU GOING TO ASK ME ABOUT MY WEEKEND?
DO I HAVE TO?
TOOK OUT MY BOAT. HAD A BLAST. HOW ABOUT YOU?
I **WORKED**. WE WERE ALL TOLD TO TAKE WORK HOME.
YEAH, YEAH, I TOOK WORK HOME. I HAD MY LAPTOP ON THE BOAT. REALLY IMPRESSED THE BOSS.
WHEN? HE ISN'T IN YET.
YESTERDAY. HE WAS ON MY BOAT. YOU SHOULDA BEEN THERE.

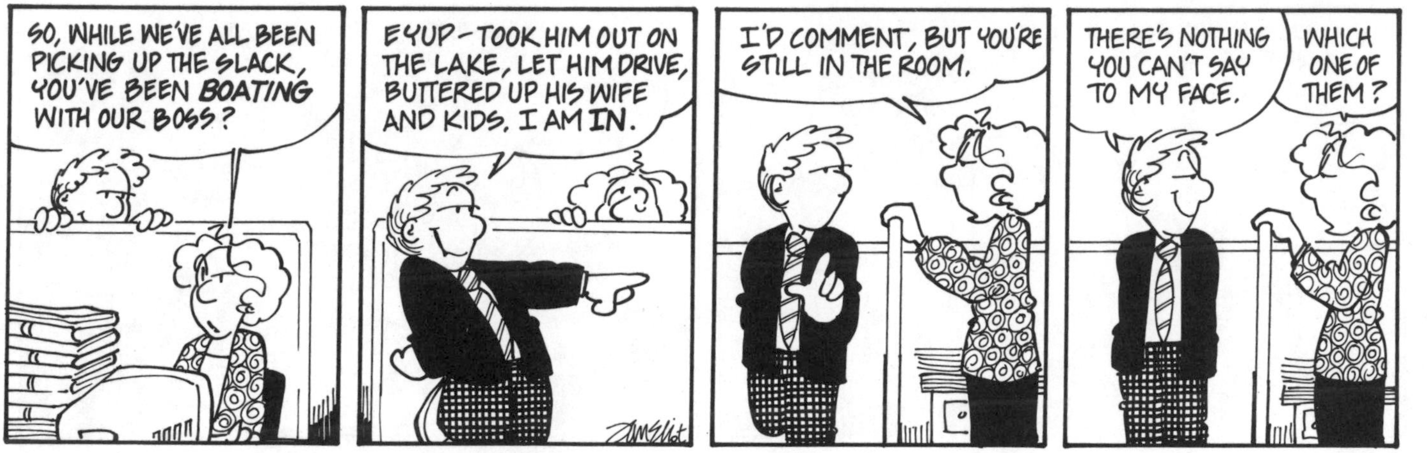
SO, WHILE WE'VE ALL BEEN PICKING UP THE SLACK, YOU'VE BEEN ***BOATING*** WITH OUR BOSS?
EYUP - TOOK HIM OUT ON THE LAKE, LET HIM DRIVE, BUTTERED UP HIS WIFE AND KIDS. I AM **IN**.
I'D COMMENT, BUT YOU'RE STILL IN THE ROOM.
THERE'S NOTHING YOU CAN'T SAY TO MY FACE.
WHICH ONE OF THEM?

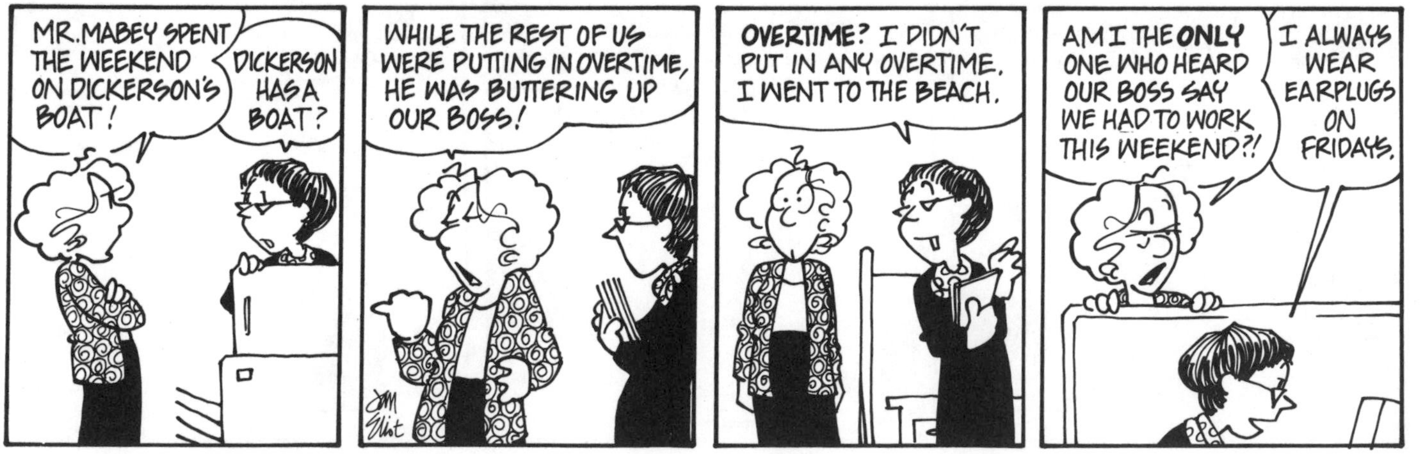
MR. MABEY SPENT THE WEEKEND ON DICKERSON'S BOAT!
DICKERSON HAS A BOAT?
WHILE THE REST OF US WERE PUTTING IN OVERTIME, HE WAS BUTTERING UP OUR BOSS!
OVERTIME? I DIDN'T PUT IN ANY OVERTIME. I WENT TO THE BEACH.
AM I THE **ONLY** ONE WHO HEARD OUR BOSS SAY WE HAD TO WORK THIS WEEKEND?!
I ALWAYS WEAR EARPLUGS ON FRIDAYS.

WHY ARE YOU TWO STILL UP?
WHAT DO YOU MEAN?
IT MUST BE MIDNIGHT. GO TO BED.
IT'S STILL LIGHT OUT!
OUR BEDTIME IS DETERMINED BY HOW TIRED MOM IS, NOT HOW TIRED WE ARE.

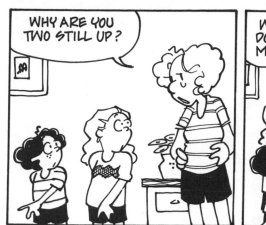

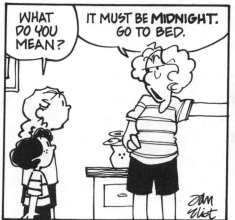

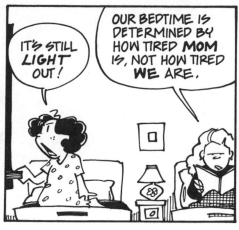

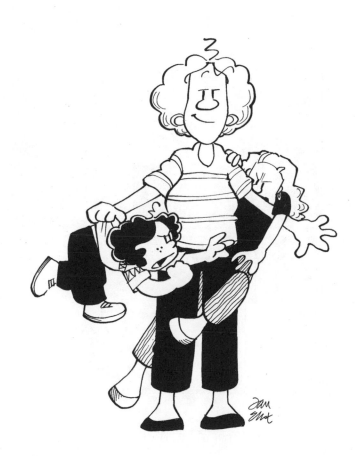

Stone Soup

HEY, ALIX? WHAT DO YOU THINK OF MY NEW SKIRT?
I THINK YOU SHOULD KEEP IT.
YOU THINK IT'S CUTE?
NO, I THINK WHEN YOU'VE GOT A BUTT THE SIZE OF MONTANA, YOU CAN'T BE PICKY.
ALIX, HOW MANY TIMES HAVE I TOLD YOU— "IF YOU CAN'T SAY SOMETHING NICE..."
SNORT HEE HEE
"LEARN TO RUN."

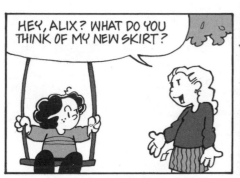

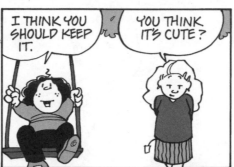

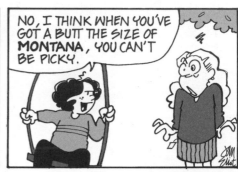

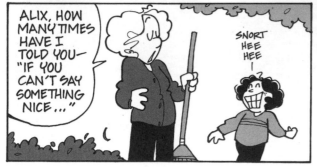

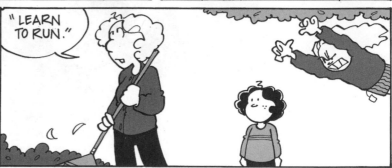

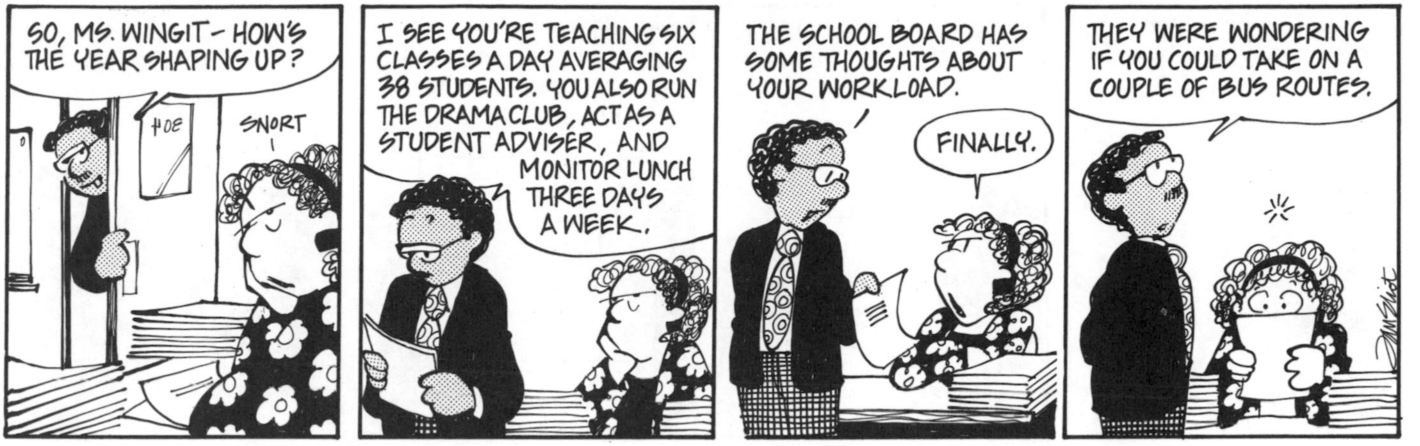
SO, MS. WINGIT - HOW'S THE YEAR SHAPING UP?
SNORT
I SEE YOU'RE TEACHING SIX CLASSES A DAY AVERAGING 38 STUDENTS. YOU ALSO RUN THE DRAMA CLUB, ACT AS A STUDENT ADVISER, AND MONITOR LUNCH THREE DAYS A WEEK.
THE SCHOOL BOARD HAS SOME THOUGHTS ABOUT YOUR WORKLOAD.
FINALLY.
THEY WERE WONDERING IF YOU COULD TAKE ON A COUPLE OF BUS ROUTES.

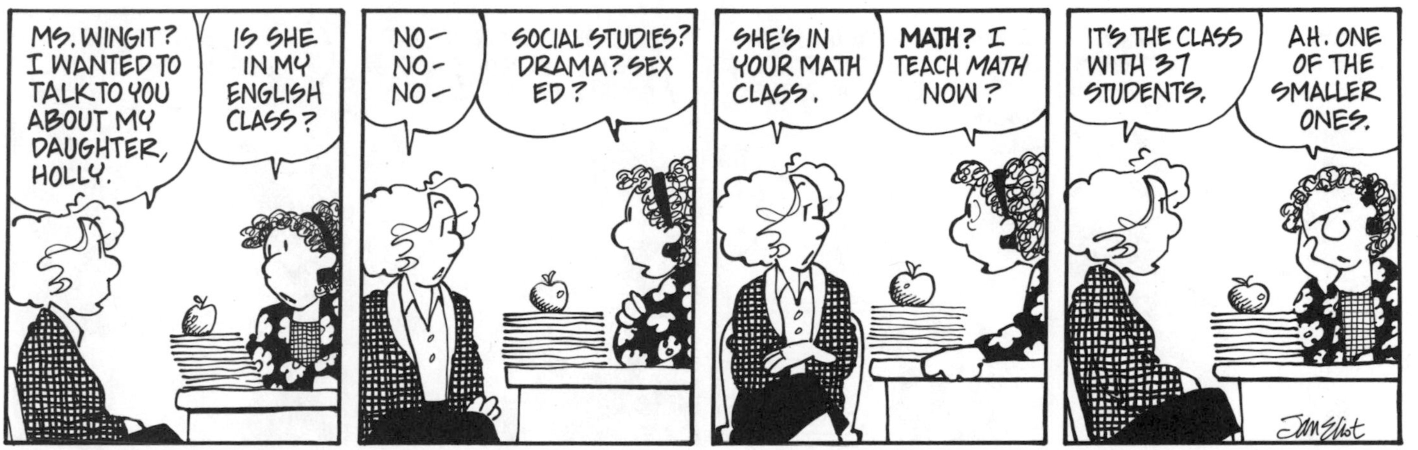
MS. WINGIT? I WANTED TO TALK TO YOU ABOUT MY DAUGHTER, HOLLY.
IS SHE IN MY ENGLISH CLASS?
NO- NO- NO-
SOCIAL STUDIES? DRAMA? SEX ED?
SHE'S IN YOUR MATH CLASS.
MATH? I TEACH *MATH* NOW?
IT'S THE CLASS WITH 37 STUDENTS.
AH. ONE OF THE SMALLER ONES.

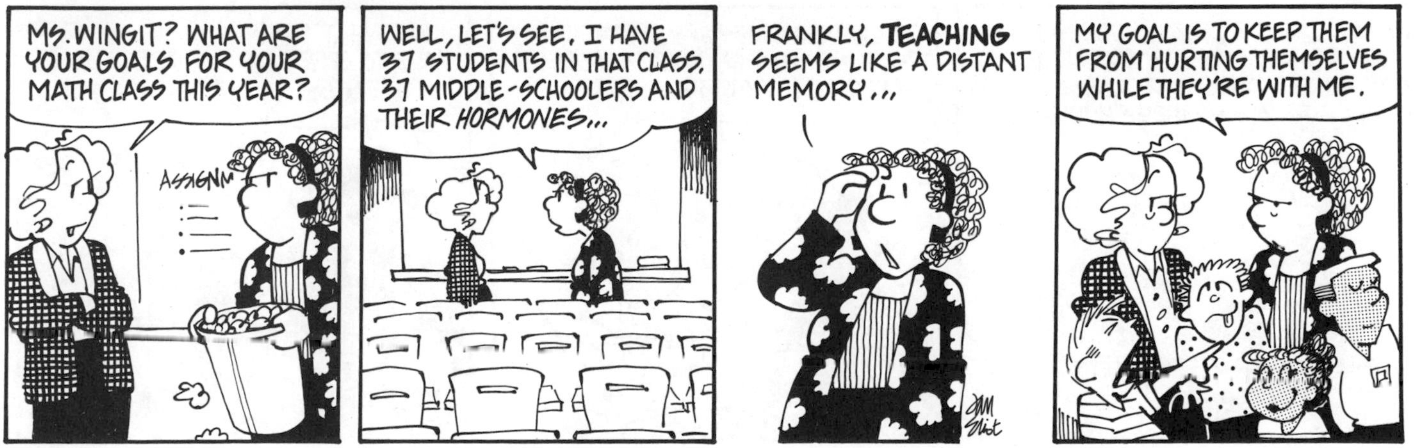
MS. WINGIT? WHAT ARE YOUR GOALS FOR YOUR MATH CLASS THIS YEAR?
WELL, LET'S SEE. I HAVE 37 STUDENTS IN THAT CLASS. 37 MIDDLE-SCHOOLERS AND THEIR *HORMONES*...
FRANKLY, **TEACHING** SEEMS LIKE A DISTANT MEMORY...
MY GOAL IS TO KEEP THEM FROM HURTING THEMSELVES WHILE THEY'RE WITH ME.

MS. WINGIT? WE'VE ADDED BIOLOGY TO YOUR COURSELOAD.

BIOLOGY?! I'VE NEVER TAUGHT THAT! I'VE NEVER EVEN SEEN THE TEXTBOOKS!

OFFICE

ACTUALLY... WE CAN'T AFFORD TEXTBOOKS. BUT YOU TOOK BIOLOGY IN COLLEGE, DIDN'T YOU?

ANY CHANCE YOU STILL HAVE YOUR NOTES?

JMEliot 9-9

ARE YOU THE ENGLISH TEACHER?

AMONG OTHER THINGS.

ASSIGN ME

I ALSO TEACH MATH, SOCIAL STUDIES AND SEX ED. I'M AN ADVISER, I RUN THE DRAMA CLUB...

JAM Eliot

AND NOW THEY WANT ME TO PICK UP BIOLOGY AND A COUPLE OF BUS ROUTES.

YEAH, BUT YOU GET YOUR SUMMERS OFF.

MR. WARNER, THE SCHOOL IS FALLING APART. IT'S IMPOSSIBLE TO TEACH BECAUSE OUR CLASSES ARE TWICE AS BIG AS THEY SHOULD BE.

DON'T RUN

WE HAVE NO LIBRARY. FEW TEXTBOOKS. NO BAND, NO ART CLASSES, FEW CLUBS, NOT MUCH SPORTS.

DON'T RUN

JUST WHAT DO WE HAVE TO OFFER OUR STUDENTS?

DETENTION.

DON'T RUN

JM Eliot.

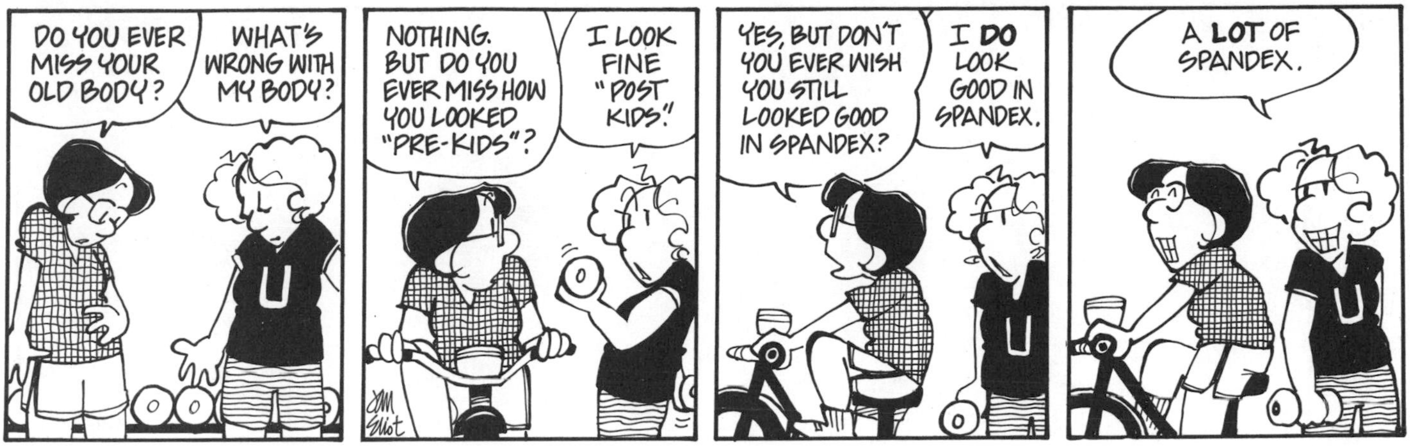
DO YOU EVER MISS YOUR OLD BODY?
WHAT'S WRONG WITH MY BODY?
NOTHING. BUT DO YOU EVER MISS HOW YOU LOOKED "PRE-KIDS"?
I LOOK FINE "POST KIDS."
YES, BUT DON'T YOU EVER WISH YOU STILL LOOKED GOOD IN SPANDEX?
I **DO** LOOK GOOD IN SPANDEX.
A **LOT** OF SPANDEX.

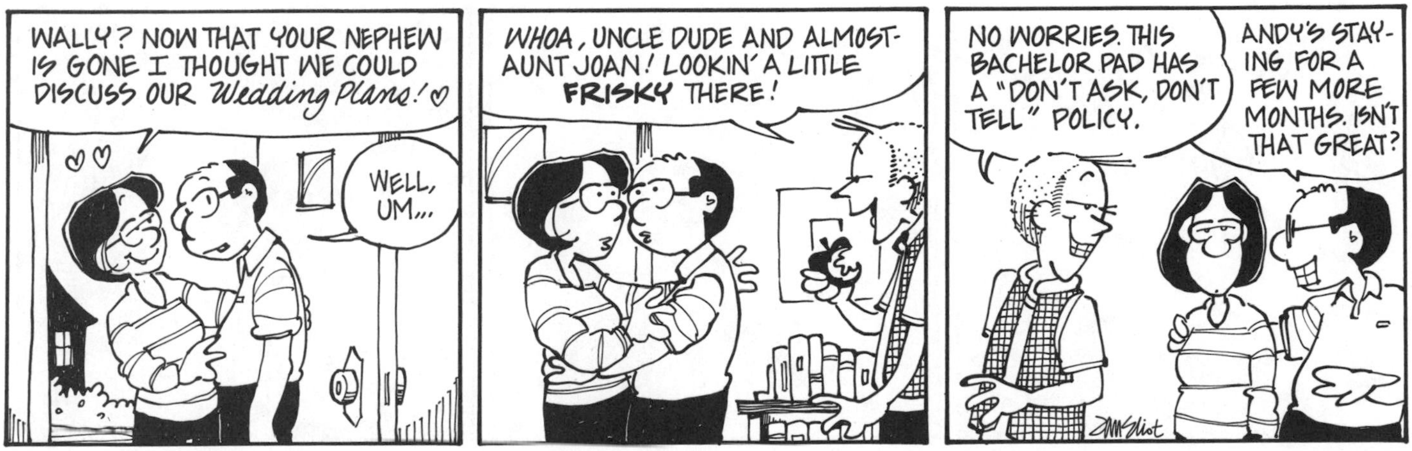
WALLY? NOW THAT YOUR NEPHEW IS GONE I THOUGHT WE COULD DISCUSS OUR *Wedding Plans!* ♡
WELL, UM...
WHOA, UNCLE DUDE AND ALMOST-AUNT JOAN! LOOKIN' A LITTLE **FRISKY** THERE!
NO WORRIES. THIS BACHELOR PAD HAS A "DON'T ASK, DON'T TELL" POLICY.
ANDY'S STAYING FOR A FEW MORE MONTHS. ISN'T THAT GREAT?

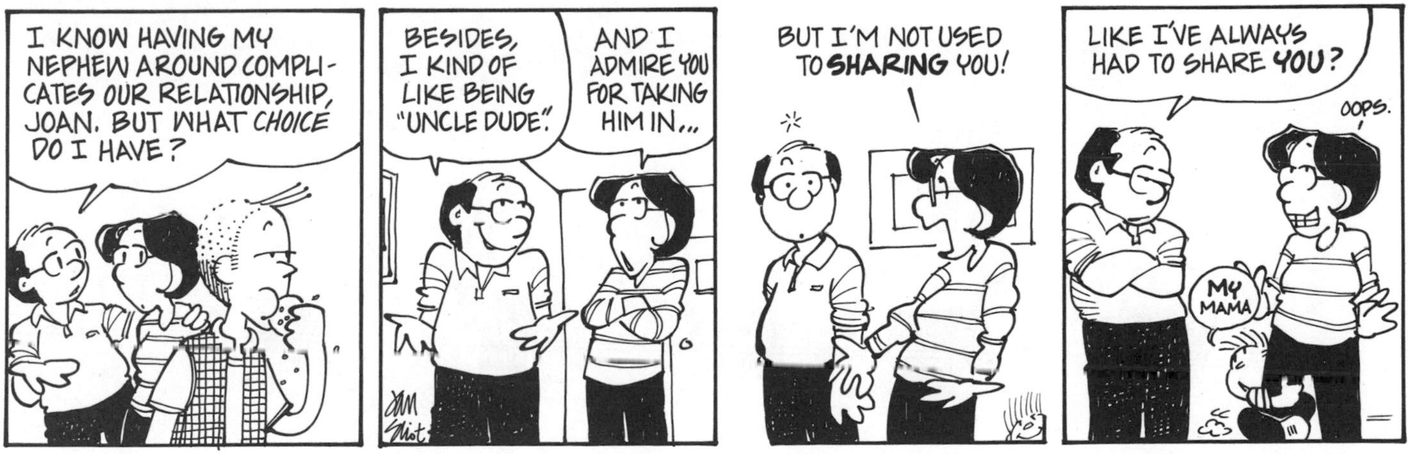
I KNOW HAVING MY NEPHEW AROUND COMPLICATES OUR RELATIONSHIP, JOAN. BUT WHAT *CHOICE* DO I HAVE?
BESIDES, I KIND OF LIKE BEING "UNCLE DUDE."
AND I ADMIRE YOU FOR TAKING HIM IN...
BUT I'M NOT USED TO **SHARING** YOU!
LIKE I'VE ALWAYS HAD TO SHARE **YOU**?
OOPS.
MY MAMA

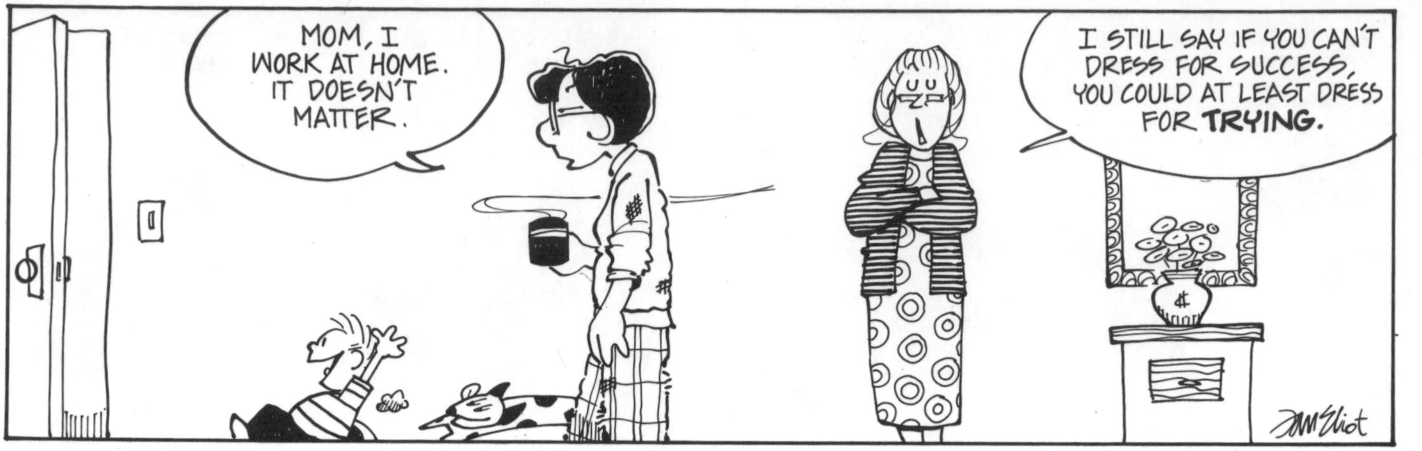
MOM, I WORK AT HOME. IT DOESN'T MATTER.
I STILL SAY IF YOU CAN'T DRESS FOR SUCCESS, YOU COULD AT LEAST DRESS FOR TRYING.

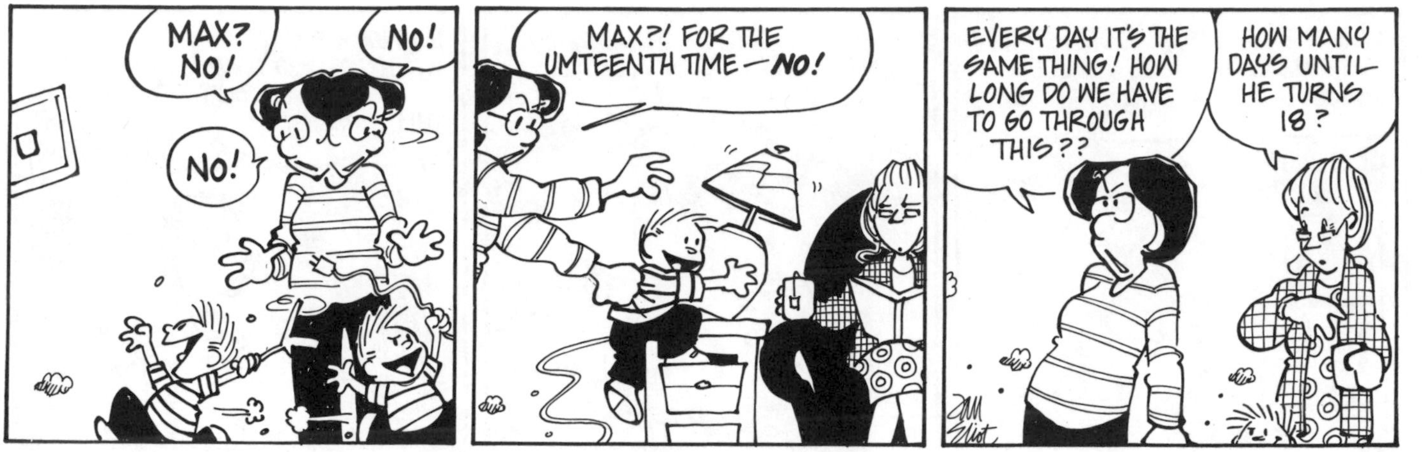
MAX? NO!
NO!
NO!
MAX?! FOR THE UMTEENTH TIME—NO!
EVERY DAY IT'S THE SAME THING! HOW LONG DO WE HAVE TO GO THROUGH THIS??
HOW MANY DAYS UNTIL HE TURNS 18?

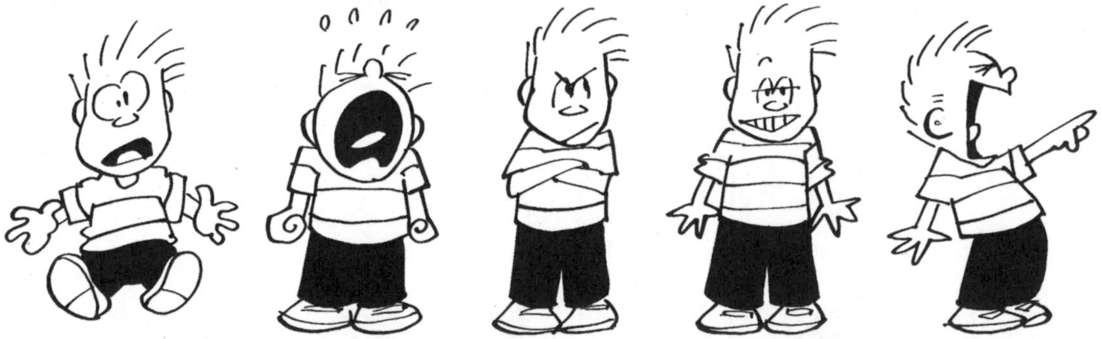

Stone Soup

IT'S **RAINING.** THERE'S NO ONE TO PLAY WITH. WHY CAN'T I WATCH TV??
ALIX, USE YOUR IMAGINATION. YOU'RE CREATIVE ENOUGH TO ENTERTAIN YOURSELF.
TIKKA TIKKA
SCOOT. I HAVE **LOTS** OF WORK TO DO.
TIKKA TIKKA TIKKA TIKKA TIKKA TIKKA
TIK—
BLEEP
DID YOU KNOW THAT THREE HAIR DRYERS ARE ALMOST ENOUGH TO LAUNCH A KITE IN THE HOUSE?

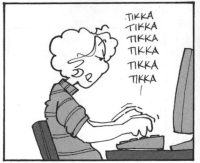

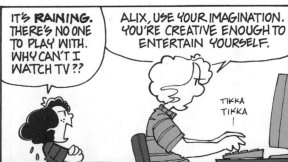

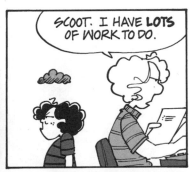

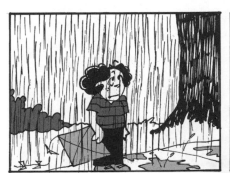

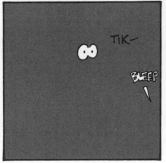

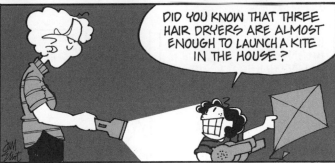

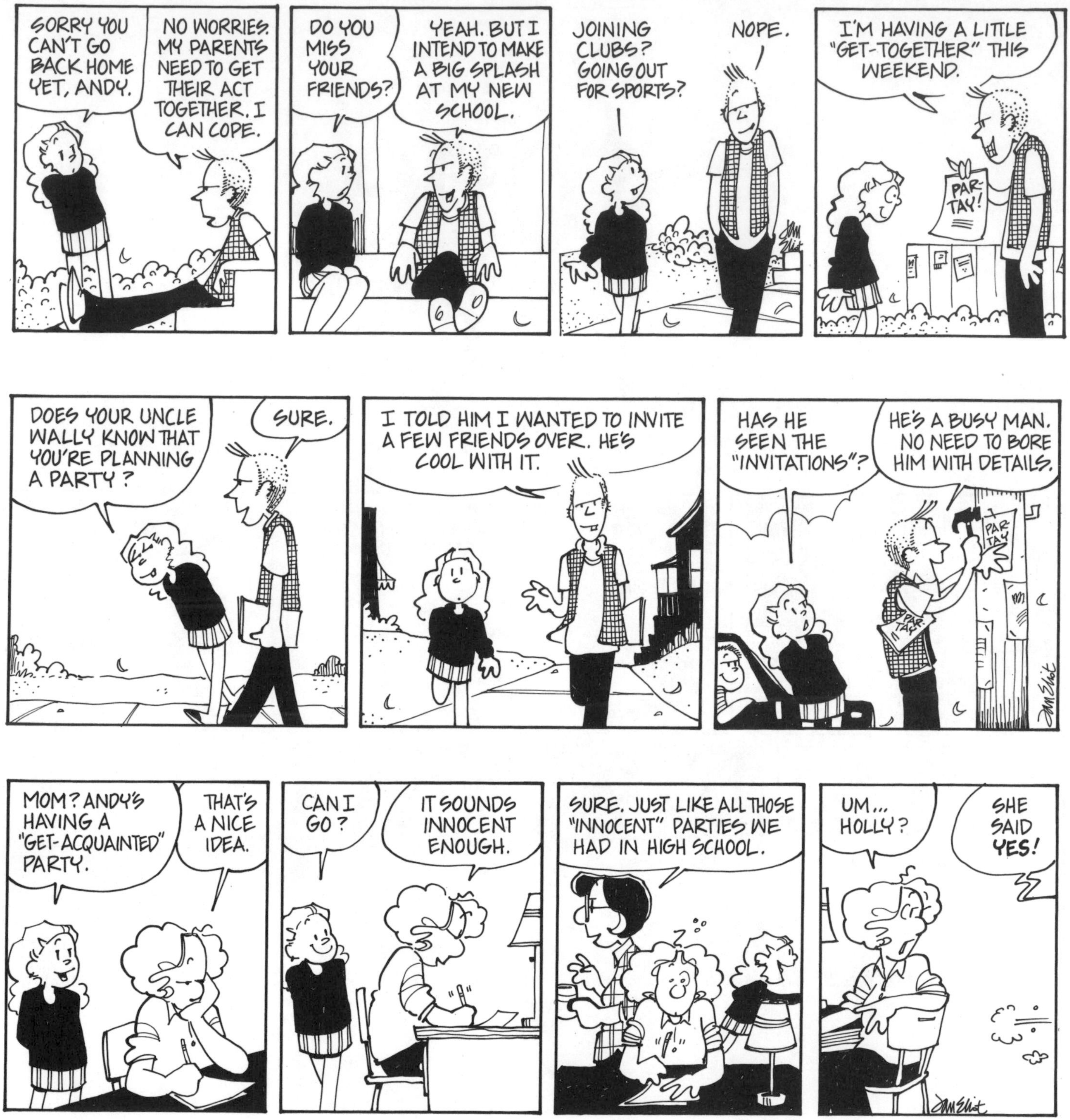
SORRY YOU CAN'T GO BACK HOME YET, ANDY.
NO WORRIES. MY PARENTS NEED TO GET THEIR ACT TOGETHER. I CAN COPE.
DO YOU MISS YOUR FRIENDS?
YEAH. BUT I INTEND TO MAKE A BIG SPLASH AT MY NEW SCHOOL.
JOINING CLUBS? GOING OUT FOR SPORTS?
NOPE.
I'M HAVING A LITTLE "GET-TOGETHER" THIS WEEKEND.
PAR-TAY!
DOES YOUR UNCLE WALLY KNOW THAT YOU'RE PLANNING A PARTY?
SURE.
I TOLD HIM I WANTED TO INVITE A FEW FRIENDS OVER. HE'S COOL WITH IT.
HAS HE SEEN THE "INVITATIONS"?
HE'S A BUSY MAN. NO NEED TO BORE HIM WITH DETAILS.
PAR-TAY
MOM? ANDY'S HAVING A "GET-ACQUAINTED" PARTY.
THAT'S A NICE IDEA.
CAN I GO?
IT SOUNDS INNOCENT ENOUGH.
SURE. JUST LIKE ALL THOSE "INNOCENT" PARTIES WE HAD IN HIGH SCHOOL.
UM... HOLLY?
SHE SAID **YES**!

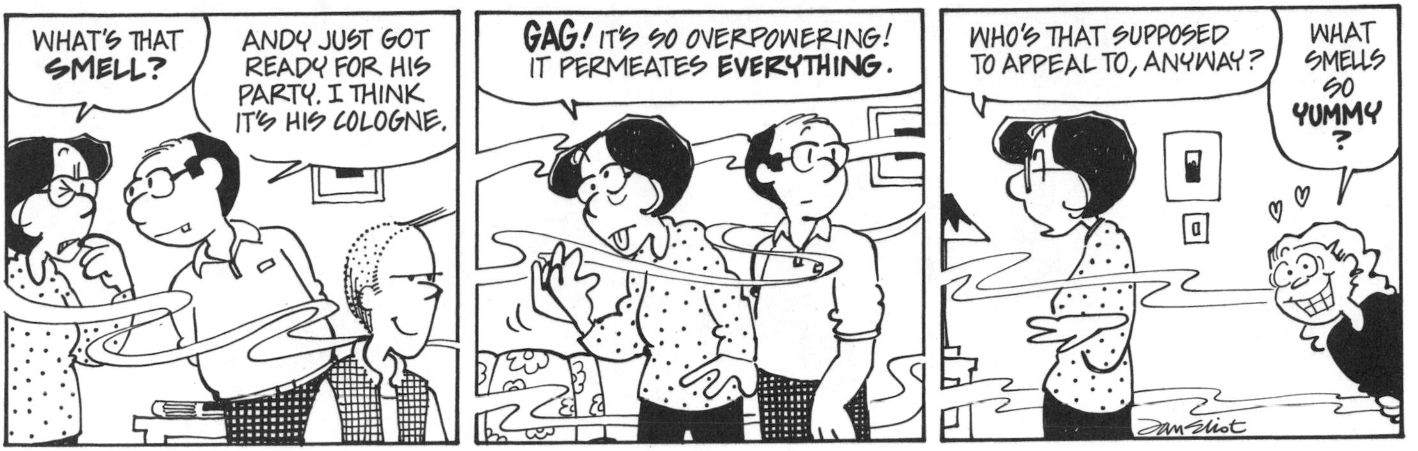
WHAT'S THAT SMELL?
ANDY JUST GOT READY FOR HIS PARTY. I THINK IT'S HIS COLOGNE.
GAG! IT'S SO OVERPOWERING! IT PERMEATES EVERYTHING.
WHO'S THAT SUPPOSED TO APPEAL TO, ANYWAY?
WHAT SMELLS SO YUMMY?

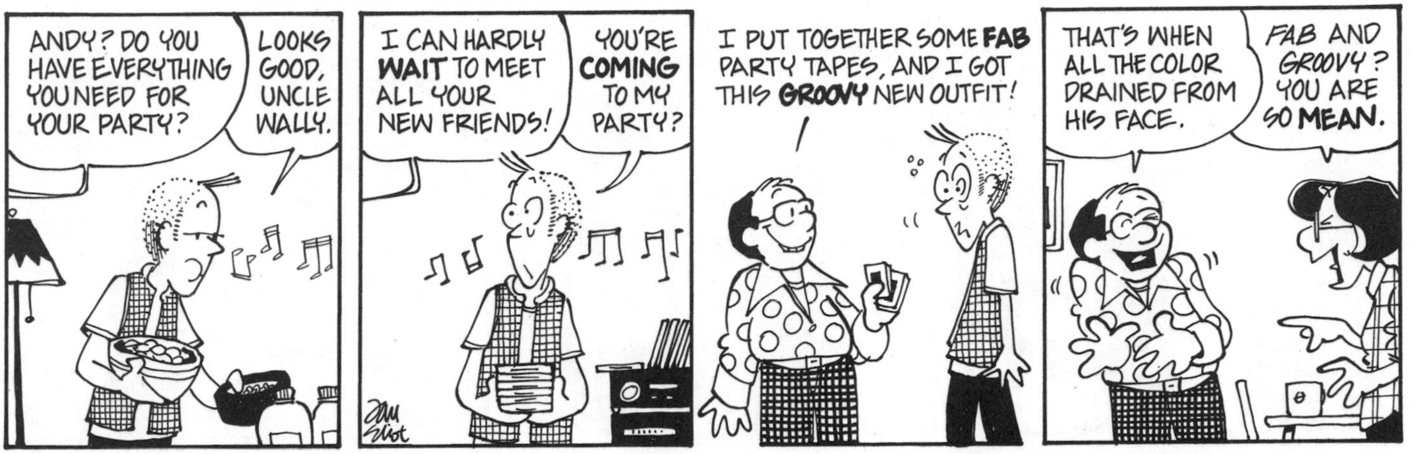
ANDY? DO YOU HAVE EVERYTHING YOU NEED FOR YOUR PARTY?
LOOKS GOOD, UNCLE WALLY.
I CAN HARDLY WAIT TO MEET ALL YOUR NEW FRIENDS!
YOU'RE COMING TO MY PARTY?
I PUT TOGETHER SOME FAB PARTY TAPES, AND I GOT THIS GROOVY NEW OUTFIT!
THAT'S WHEN ALL THE COLOR DRAINED FROM HIS FACE.
FAB AND GROOVY? YOU ARE SO MEAN.

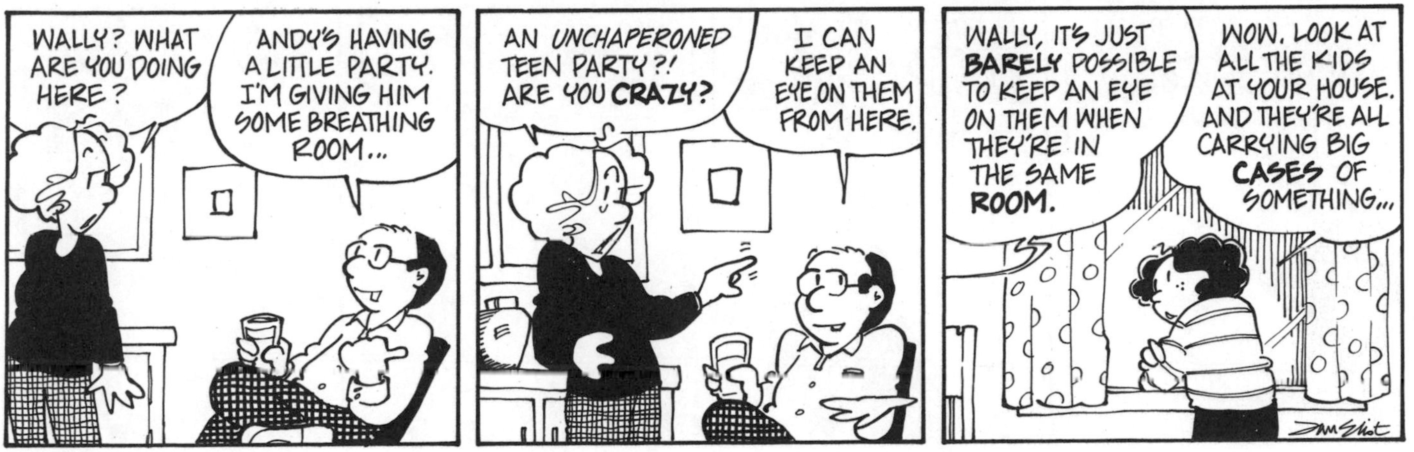
WALLY? WHAT ARE YOU DOING HERE?
ANDY'S HAVING A LITTLE PARTY. I'M GIVING HIM SOME BREATHING ROOM...
AN UNCHAPERONED TEEN PARTY?! ARE YOU CRAZY?
I CAN KEEP AN EYE ON THEM FROM HERE.
WALLY, IT'S JUST BARELY POSSIBLE TO KEEP AN EYE ON THEM WHEN THEY'RE IN THE SAME ROOM.
WOW. LOOK AT ALL THE KIDS AT YOUR HOUSE. AND THEY'RE ALL CARRYING BIG CASES OF SOMETHING...

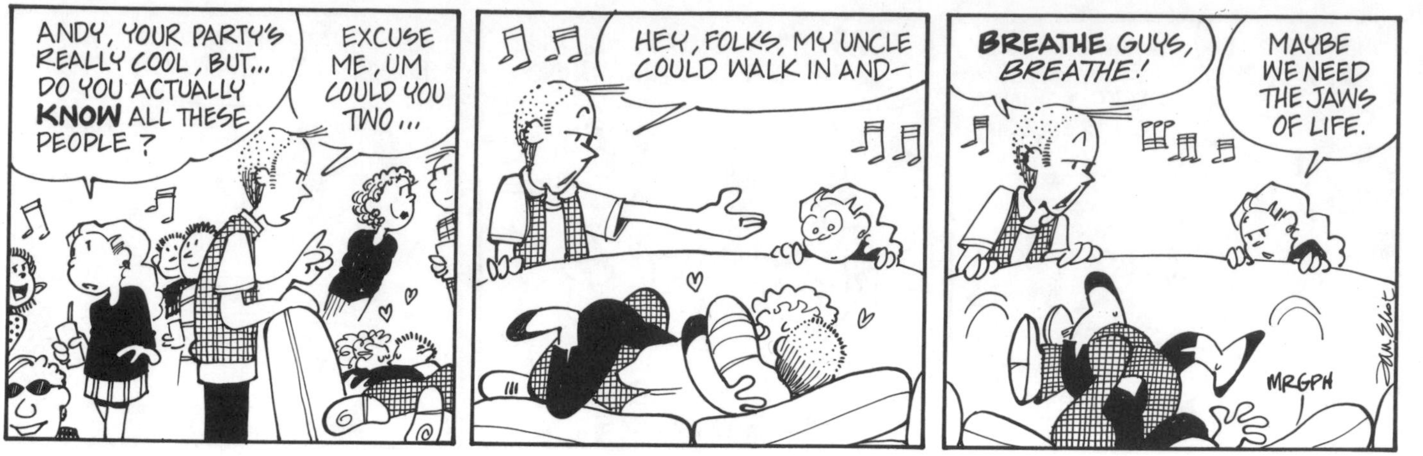
ANDY, YOUR PARTY'S REALLY COOL, BUT... DO YOU ACTUALLY **KNOW** ALL THESE PEOPLE?
EXCUSE ME, UM COULD YOU TWO...
HEY, FOLKS, MY UNCLE COULD WALK IN AND—
BREATHE GUYS, *BREATHE*!
MAYBE WE NEED THE JAWS OF LIFE.
MRGPH

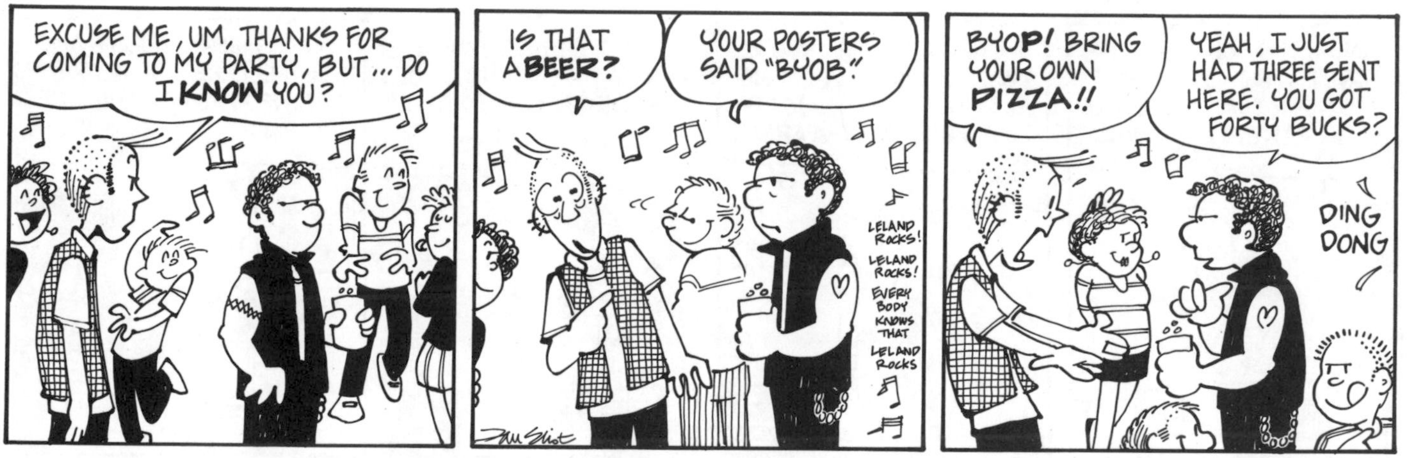
EXCUSE ME, UM, THANKS FOR COMING TO MY PARTY, BUT... DO I **KNOW** YOU?
IS THAT A **BEER?**
YOUR POSTERS SAID "BYOB."
LELAND ROCKS!
LELAND ROCKS!
EVERY BODY KNOWS THAT LELAND ROCKS
BYO**P**! BRING YOUR OWN **PIZZA**!!
YEAH, I JUST HAD THREE SENT HERE. YOU GOT FORTY BUCKS?
DING DONG

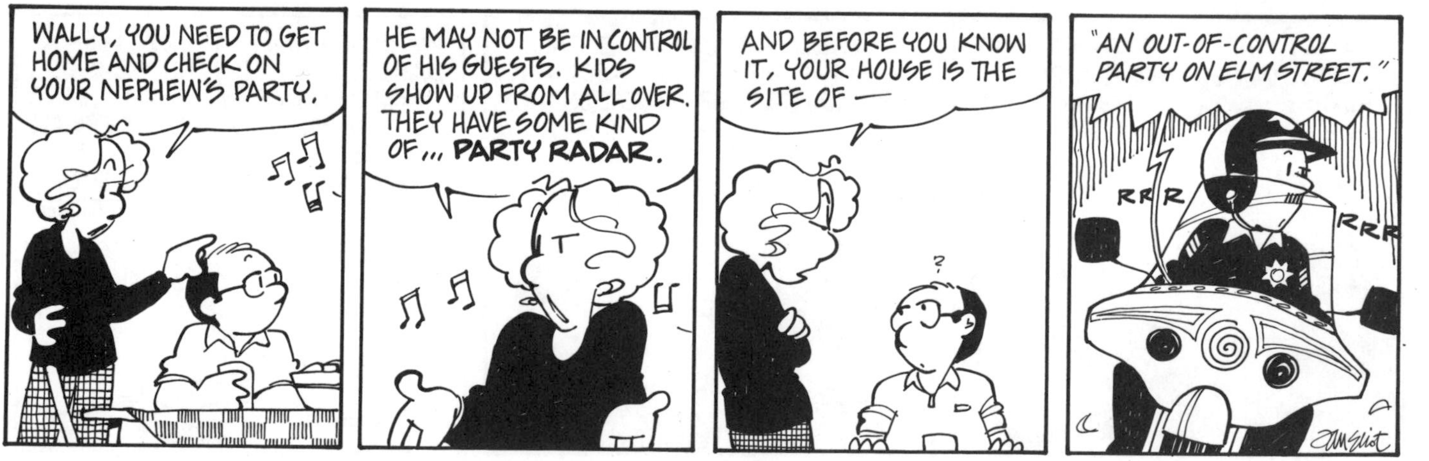
WALLY, YOU NEED TO GET HOME AND CHECK ON YOUR NEPHEW'S PARTY.
HE MAY NOT BE IN CONTROL OF HIS GUESTS. KIDS SHOW UP FROM ALL OVER. THEY HAVE SOME KIND OF... **PARTY RADAR**.
AND BEFORE YOU KNOW IT, YOUR HOUSE IS THE SITE OF—
"AN OUT-OF-CONTROL PARTY ON ELM STREET."
RRR
RRR

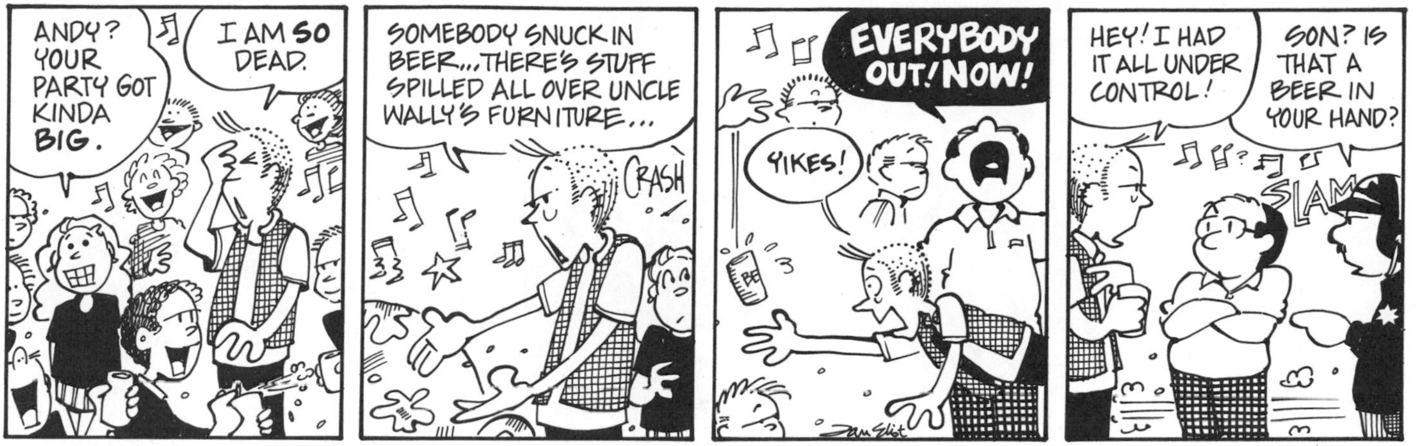
ANDY? YOUR PARTY GOT KINDA **BIG**.
I AM **SO** DEAD.
SOMEBODY SNUCK IN BEER... THERE'S STUFF SPILLED ALL OVER UNCLE WALLY'S FURNITURE...
CRASH
EVERYBODY OUT! NOW!
YIKES!
HEY! I HAD IT ALL UNDER CONTROL!
SON? IS THAT A BEER IN YOUR HAND?
SLAM

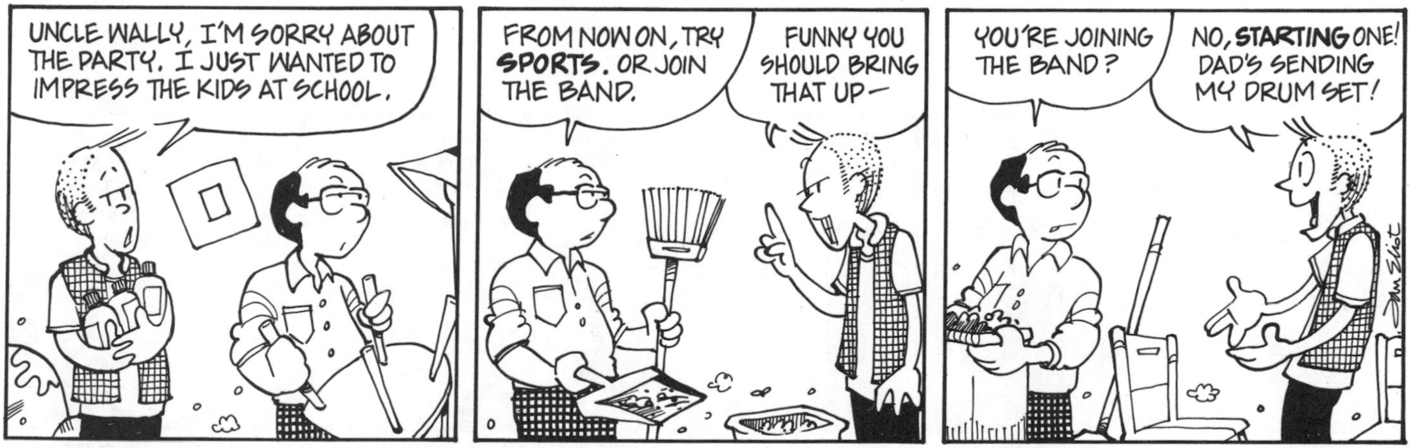
UNCLE WALLY, I'M SORRY ABOUT THE PARTY. I JUST WANTED TO IMPRESS THE KIDS AT SCHOOL.
FROM NOW ON, TRY **SPORTS.** OR JOIN THE BAND.
FUNNY YOU SHOULD BRING THAT UP—
YOU'RE JOINING THE BAND?
NO, **STARTING** ONE! DAD'S SENDING MY DRUM SET!

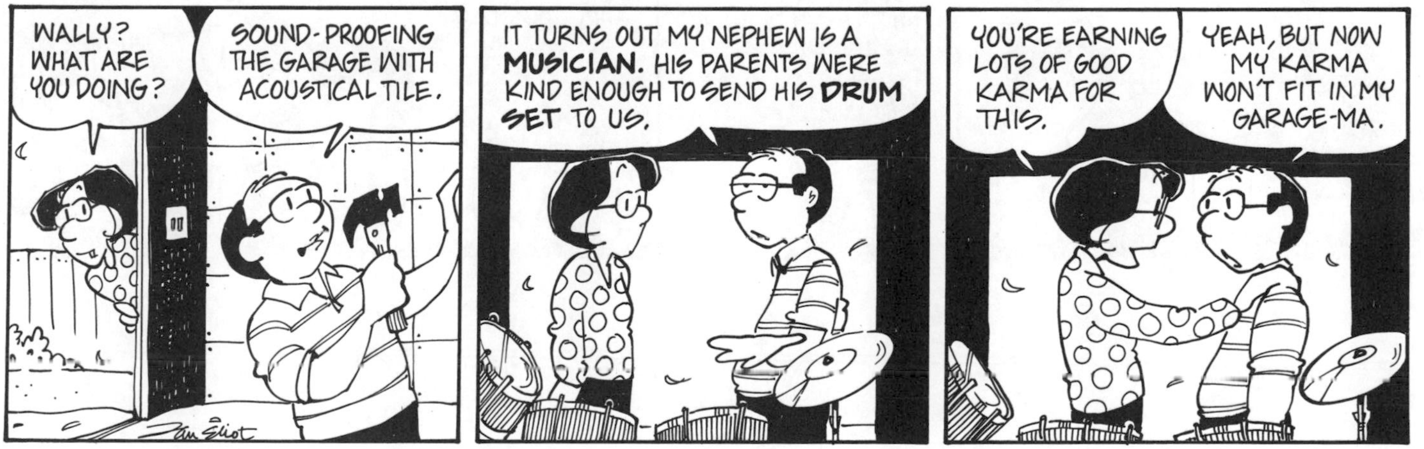
WALLY? WHAT ARE YOU DOING?
SOUND-PROOFING THE GARAGE WITH ACOUSTICAL TILE.
IT TURNS OUT MY NEPHEW IS A **MUSICIAN.** HIS PARENTS WERE KIND ENOUGH TO SEND HIS **DRUM SET** TO US.
YOU'RE EARNING LOTS OF GOOD KARMA FOR THIS.
YEAH, BUT NOW MY KARMA WON'T FIT IN MY GARAGE-MA.

Stone Soup

MY MOM'LL NEVER GO FOR IT. SHE'S GOTTEN SO CONSERVATIVE... TYPICAL MIDDLE-AGE THING...

JOAN? HOW WOULD YOU CLASSIFY US, AGE-WISE?

THIRTY-SOMETHING, I GUESS. WHY?

HOLLY JUST REFERRED TO ME AS "MIDDLE-AGED".

RELAX. YOU CAN'T BE MIDDLE-AGED! I'M ONLY A COUPLE YEARS YOUNGER, SO IF **YOU** WERE MIDDLE-AGED, **I'D** BE—

WHAT'S WITH YOU TWO?

HOLLY THINKS WE'RE MIDDLE-AGED.

OH PLEASE! IF MY DAUGHTERS ARE MIDDLE-AGED, THEN I MUST BE—

WHY'S EVERYBODY SO GLOOMY? IT'S A GORGEOUS DAY!

EASY FOR **YOU** TO SAY, MISS "EVERYTHING'S-STILL-PERKY."

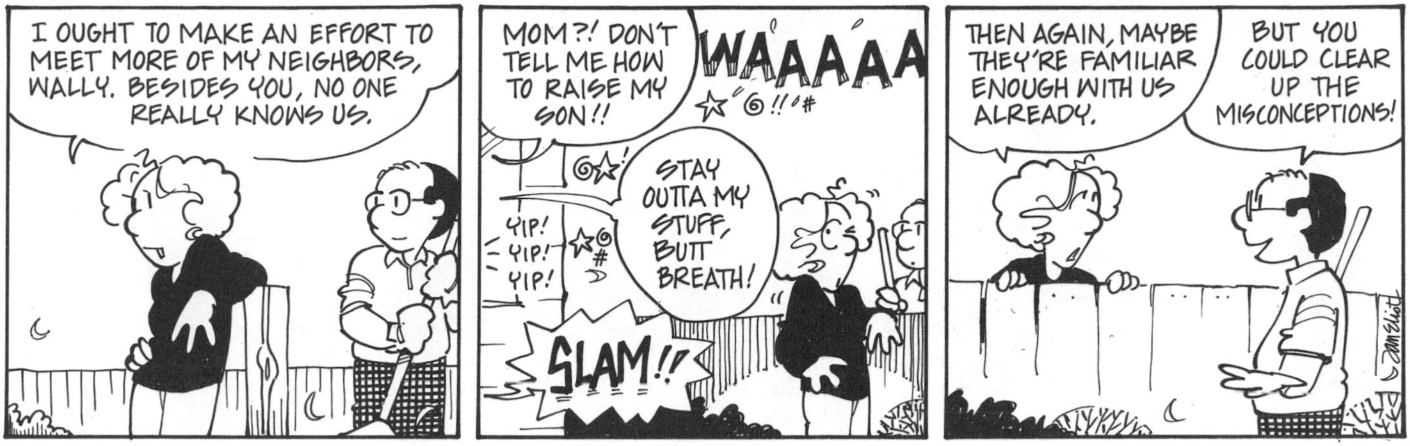
I OUGHT TO MAKE AN EFFORT TO MEET MORE OF MY NEIGHBORS, WALLY. BESIDES YOU, NO ONE REALLY KNOWS US.
MOM?! DON'T TELL ME HOW TO RAISE MY SON!!
WAAAAA
STAY OUTTA MY STUFF, BUTT BREATH!
YIP! YIP! YIP!
SLAM!!
THEN AGAIN, MAYBE THEY'RE FAMILIAR ENOUGH WITH US ALREADY.
BUT YOU COULD CLEAR UP THE MISCONCEPTIONS!

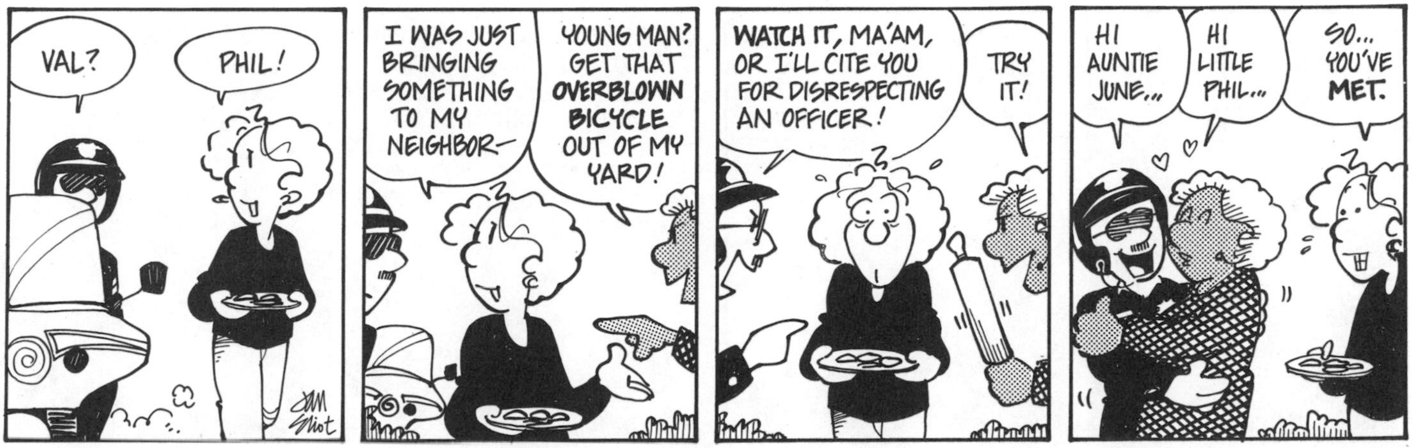
VAL?
PHIL!
I WAS JUST BRINGING SOMETHING TO MY NEIGHBOR—
YOUNG MAN? GET THAT OVERBLOWN BICYCLE OUT OF MY YARD!
WATCH IT, MA'AM, OR I'LL CITE YOU FOR DISRESPECTING AN OFFICER!
TRY IT!
HI AUNTIE JUNE...
HI LITTLE PHIL...
SO... YOU'VE MET.

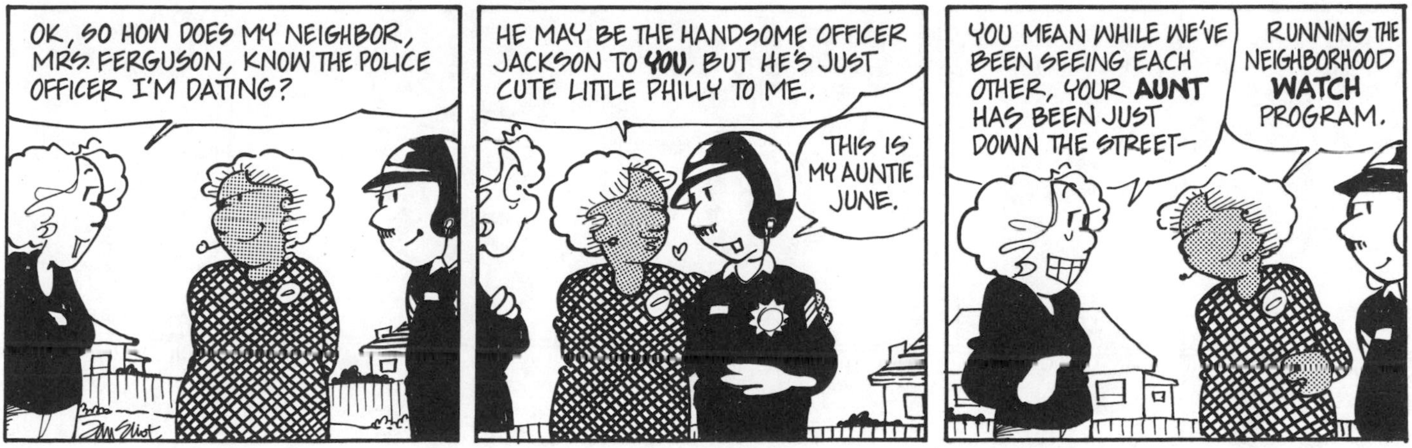
OK, SO HOW DOES MY NEIGHBOR, MRS. FERGUSON, KNOW THE POLICE OFFICER I'M DATING?
HE MAY BE THE HANDSOME OFFICER JACKSON TO YOU, BUT HE'S JUST CUTE LITTLE PHILLY TO ME.
THIS IS MY AUNTIE JUNE.
YOU MEAN WHILE WE'VE BEEN SEEING EACH OTHER, YOUR AUNT HAS BEEN JUST DOWN THE STREET—
RUNNING THE NEIGHBORHOOD WATCH PROGRAM.

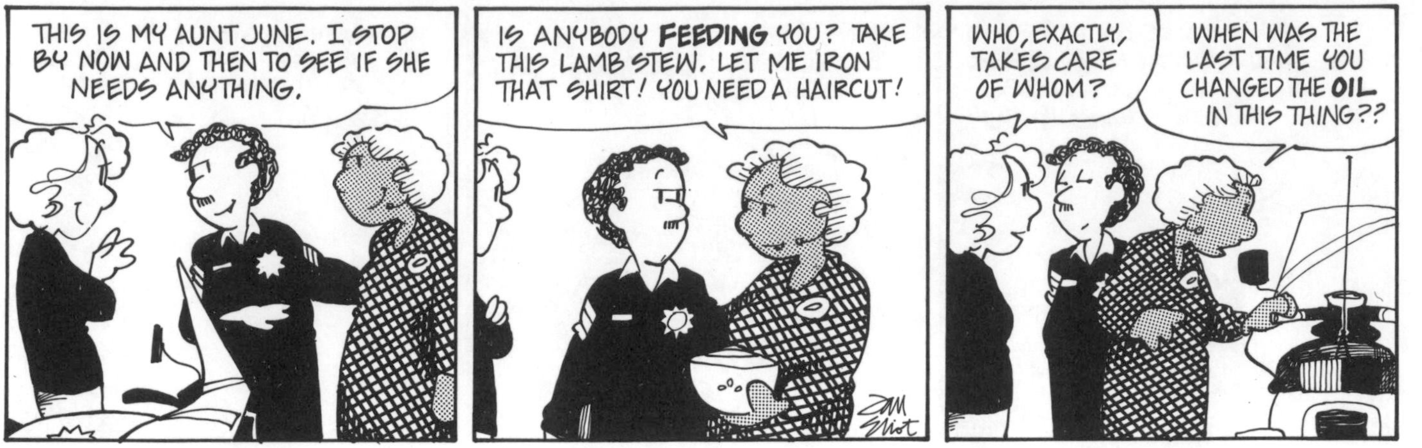
THIS IS MY AUNT JUNE. I STOP BY NOW AND THEN TO SEE IF SHE NEEDS ANYTHING.
IS ANYBODY **FEEDING** YOU? TAKE THIS LAMB STEW. LET ME IRON THAT SHIRT! YOU NEED A HAIRCUT!
WHO, EXACTLY, TAKES CARE OF WHOM?
WHEN WAS THE LAST TIME YOU CHANGED THE **OIL** IN THIS THING??

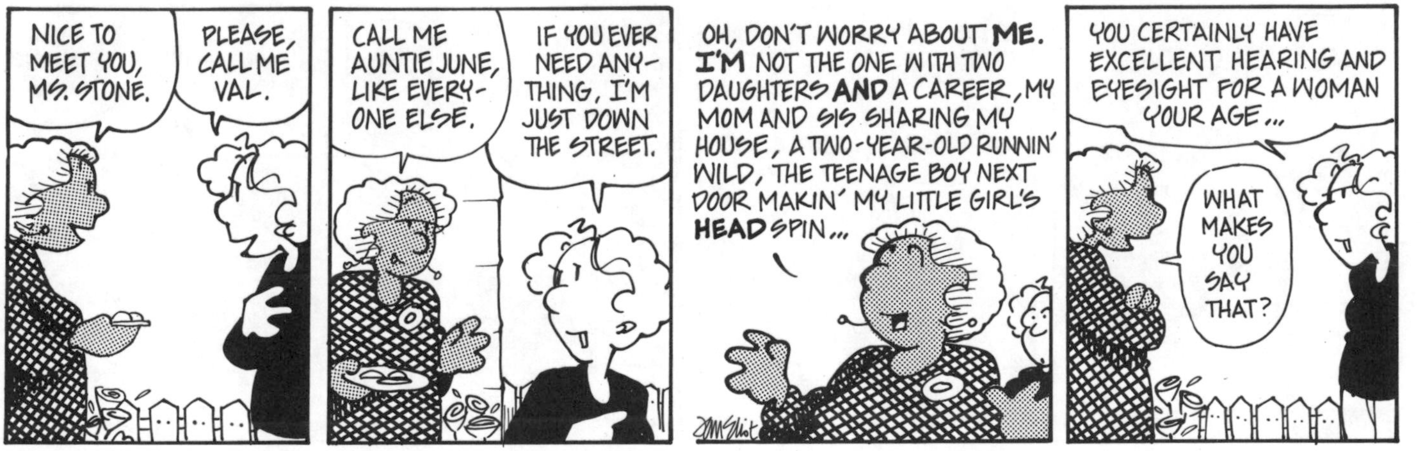
NICE TO MEET YOU, MS. STONE.
PLEASE, CALL ME VAL.
CALL ME AUNTIE JUNE, LIKE EVERY-ONE ELSE.
IF YOU EVER NEED ANY-THING, I'M JUST DOWN THE STREET.
OH, DON'T WORRY ABOUT **ME.** **I'M** NOT THE ONE WITH TWO DAUGHTERS **AND** A CAREER, MY MOM AND SIS SHARING MY HOUSE, A TWO-YEAR-OLD RUNNIN' WILD, THE TEENAGE BOY NEXT DOOR MAKIN' MY LITTLE GIRL'S **HEAD** SPIN...
YOU CERTAINLY HAVE EXCELLENT HEARING AND EYESIGHT FOR A WOMAN YOUR AGE...
WHAT MAKES YOU SAY THAT?

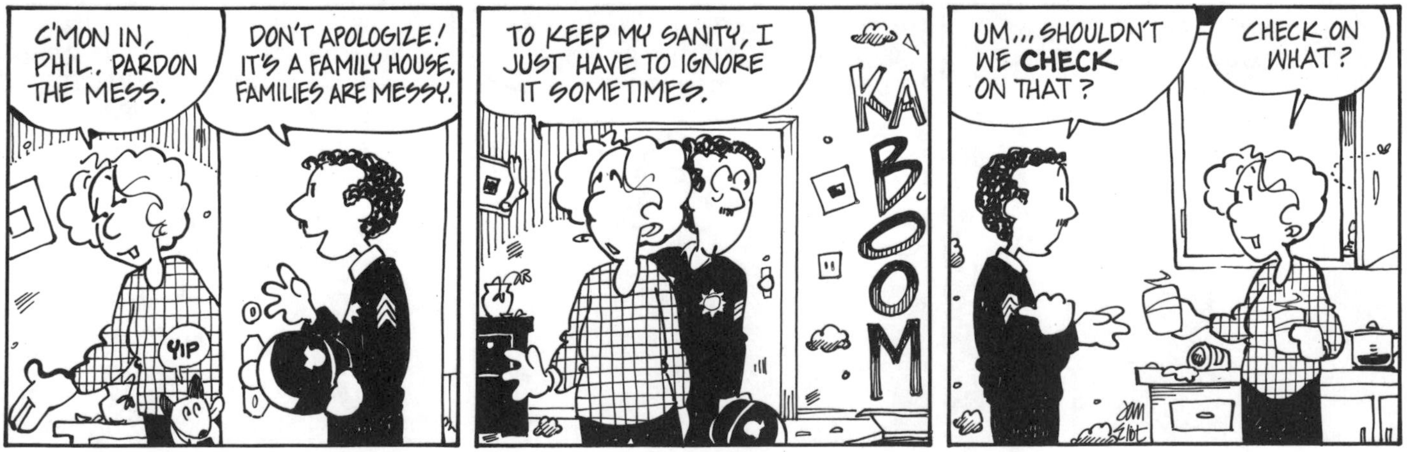
C'MON IN, PHIL. PARDON THE MESS.
DON'T APOLOGIZE! IT'S A FAMILY HOUSE. FAMILIES ARE MESSY.
YIP
TO KEEP MY SANITY, I JUST HAVE TO IGNORE IT SOMETIMES.
KABOOM
UM... SHOULDN'T WE **CHECK** ON THAT?
CHECK ON WHAT?

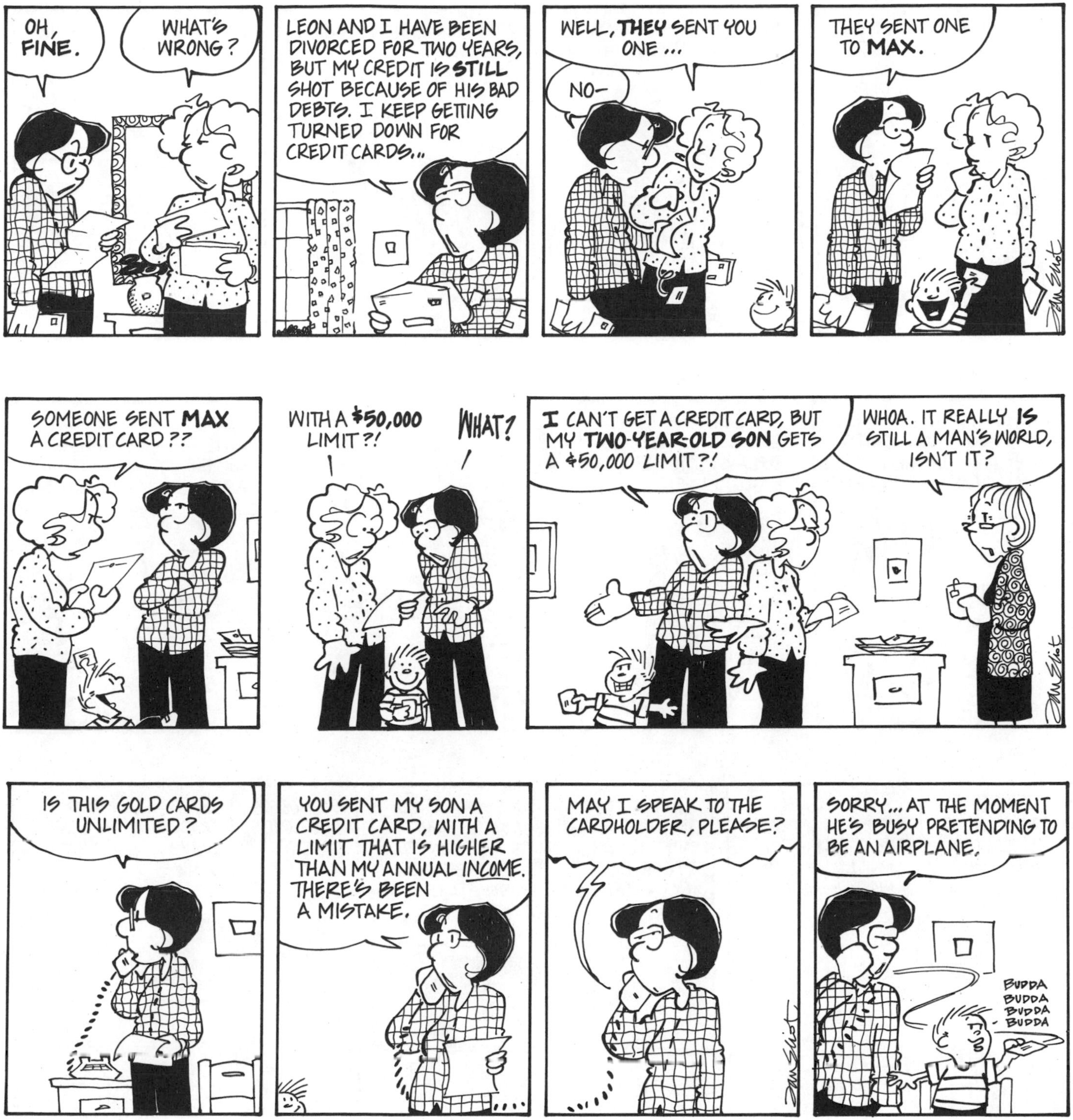
OH, FINE.
WHAT'S WRONG?
LEON AND I HAVE BEEN DIVORCED FOR TWO YEARS, BUT MY CREDIT IS STILL SHOT BECAUSE OF HIS BAD DEBTS. I KEEP GETTING TURNED DOWN FOR CREDIT CARDS...
WELL, THEY SENT YOU ONE ...
NO–
THEY SENT ONE TO MAX.
SOMEONE SENT MAX A CREDIT CARD??
WITH A $50,000 LIMIT?!
WHAT?
I CAN'T GET A CREDIT CARD, BUT MY TWO-YEAR-OLD SON GETS A $50,000 LIMIT?!
WHOA. IT REALLY IS STILL A MAN'S WORLD, ISN'T IT?
IS THIS GOLD CARDS UNLIMITED?
YOU SENT MY SON A CREDIT CARD, WITH A LIMIT THAT IS HIGHER THAN MY ANNUAL INCOME. THERE'S BEEN A MISTAKE.
MAY I SPEAK TO THE CARDHOLDER, PLEASE?
SORRY... AT THE MOMENT HE'S BUSY PRETENDING TO BE AN AIRPLANE.
BUDDA BUDDA BUDDA BUDDA

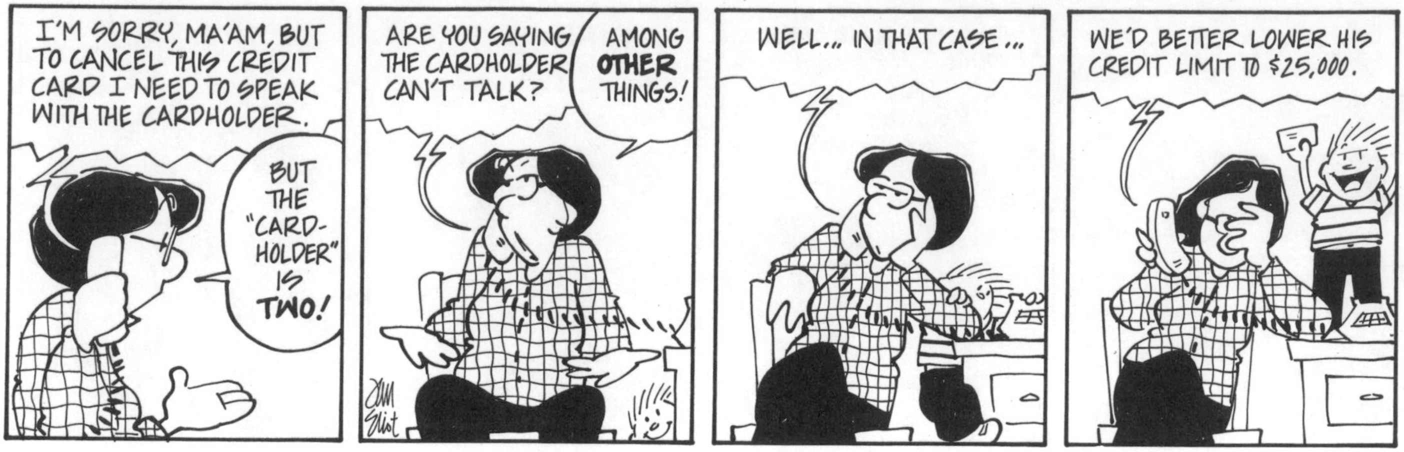
I'M SORRY, MA'AM, BUT TO CANCEL THIS CREDIT CARD I NEED TO SPEAK WITH THE CARDHOLDER.
BUT THE "CARD-HOLDER" IS **TWO**!
ARE YOU SAYING THE CARDHOLDER CAN'T TALK?
AMONG **OTHER** THINGS!
WELL... IN THAT CASE...
WE'D BETTER LOWER HIS CREDIT LIMIT TO $25,000.

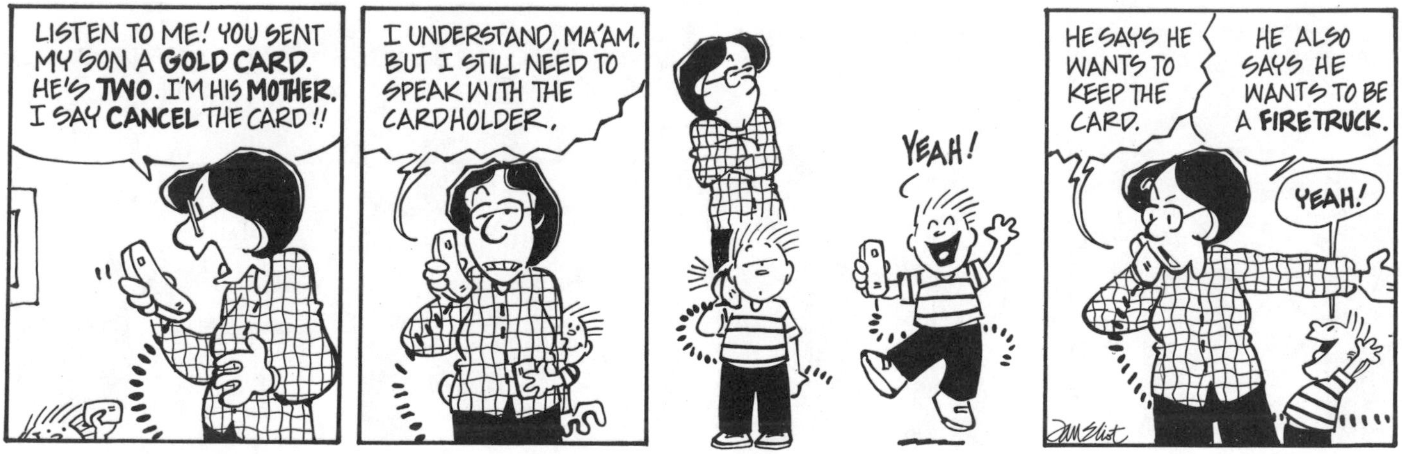
LISTEN TO ME! YOU SENT MY SON A **GOLD CARD**. HE'S **TWO**. I'M HIS **MOTHER**. I SAY **CANCEL** THE CARD!!
I UNDERSTAND, MA'AM, BUT I STILL NEED TO SPEAK WITH THE CARDHOLDER.
YEAH!
HE SAYS HE WANTS TO KEEP THE CARD.
HE ALSO SAYS HE WANTS TO BE A **FIRETRUCK**.
YEAH!

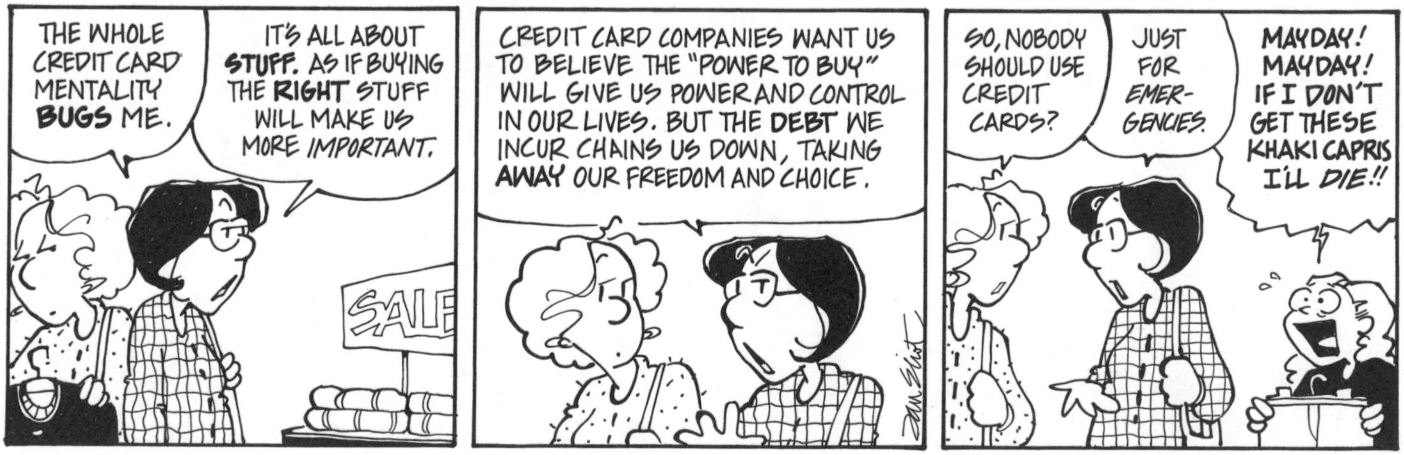
THE WHOLE CREDIT CARD MENTALITY **BUGS** ME.
IT'S ALL ABOUT **STUFF**. AS IF BUYING THE **RIGHT** STUFF WILL MAKE US MORE *IMPORTANT*.
SALE
CREDIT CARD COMPANIES WANT US TO BELIEVE THE "POWER TO BUY" WILL GIVE US POWER AND CONTROL IN OUR LIVES. BUT THE **DEBT** WE INCUR CHAINS US DOWN, TAKING **AWAY** OUR FREEDOM AND CHOICE.
SO, NOBODY SHOULD USE CREDIT CARDS?
JUST FOR *EMER-GENCIES*.
MAYDAY! MAYDAY! IF I DON'T GET THESE KHAKI CAPRIS I'LL *DIE*!!

Stone Soup

AND THAT'S THE NEWS FOR TONIGHT.
IT **IS**?
THAT WASN'T **NEWS!** THAT WAS A 10-MINUTE CRIME REPORT WITH 20 MINUTES OF ADVERTISING.
NOBODY SEEMS VERY CONCERNED ANYMORE ABOUT THE ENVIRONMENT, GLOBAL WARMING, RACE RELATIONS...
PEOPLE LIVE IN A SPIRITUAL VACUUM. WE'RE POORLY EDUCATED. MATERIALISM AND CONSUMERISM RULE THE WORLD!
WHAT DO **YOU** THINK, HOLLY?
I THINK WE SHOULD GO TO THE MALL AND **FORGET** ABOUT IT!

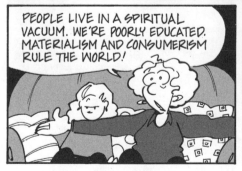

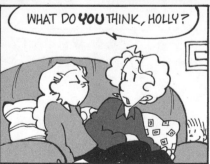

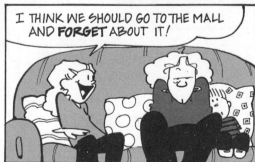

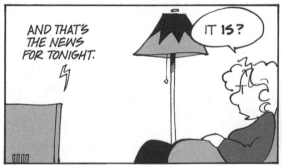

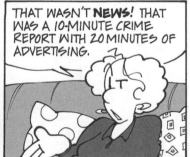

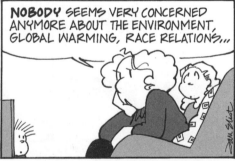

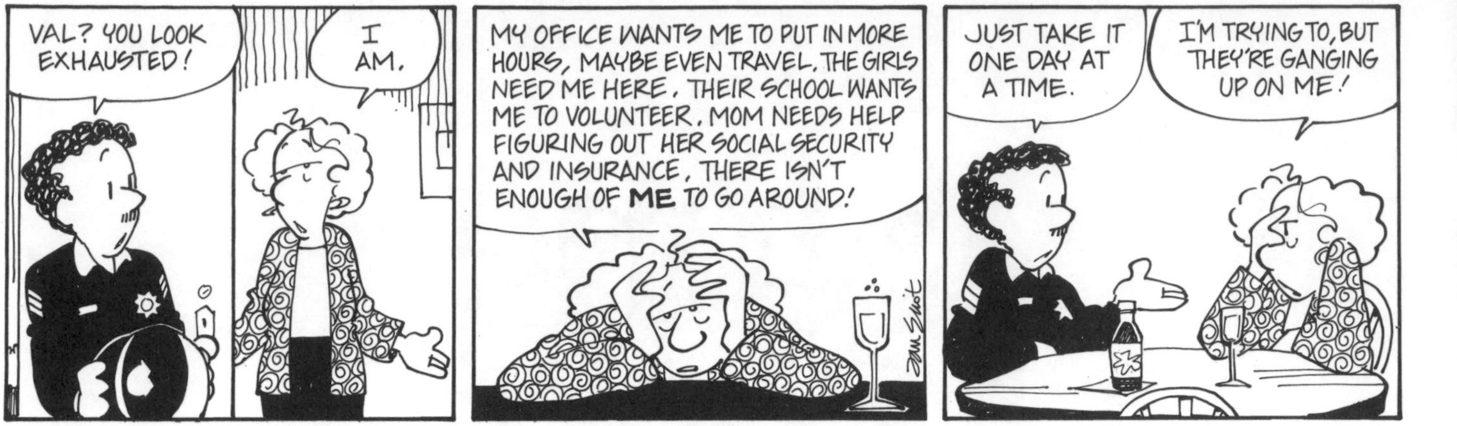
VAL? YOU LOOK EXHAUSTED!
I AM.
MY OFFICE WANTS ME TO PUT IN MORE HOURS, MAYBE EVEN TRAVEL. THE GIRLS NEED ME HERE. THEIR SCHOOL WANTS ME TO VOLUNTEER. MOM NEEDS HELP FIGURING OUT HER SOCIAL SECURITY AND INSURANCE. THERE ISN'T ENOUGH OF **ME** TO GO AROUND!
JUST TAKE IT ONE DAY AT A TIME.
I'M TRYING TO, BUT THEY'RE GANGING UP ON ME!

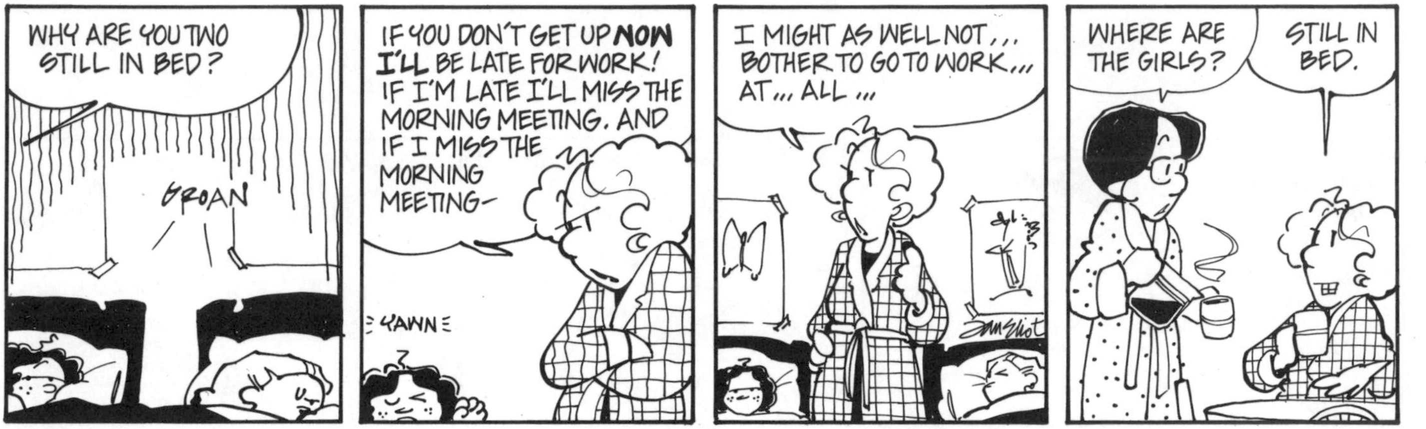
WHY ARE YOU TWO STILL IN BED?
GROAN
IF YOU DON'T GET UP **NOW** **I'LL** BE LATE FOR WORK! IF I'M LATE I'LL MISS THE MORNING MEETING. AND IF I MISS THE MORNING MEETING–
YAWN
I MIGHT AS WELL NOT... BOTHER TO GO TO WORK... AT... ALL...
WHERE ARE THE GIRLS?
STILL IN BED.

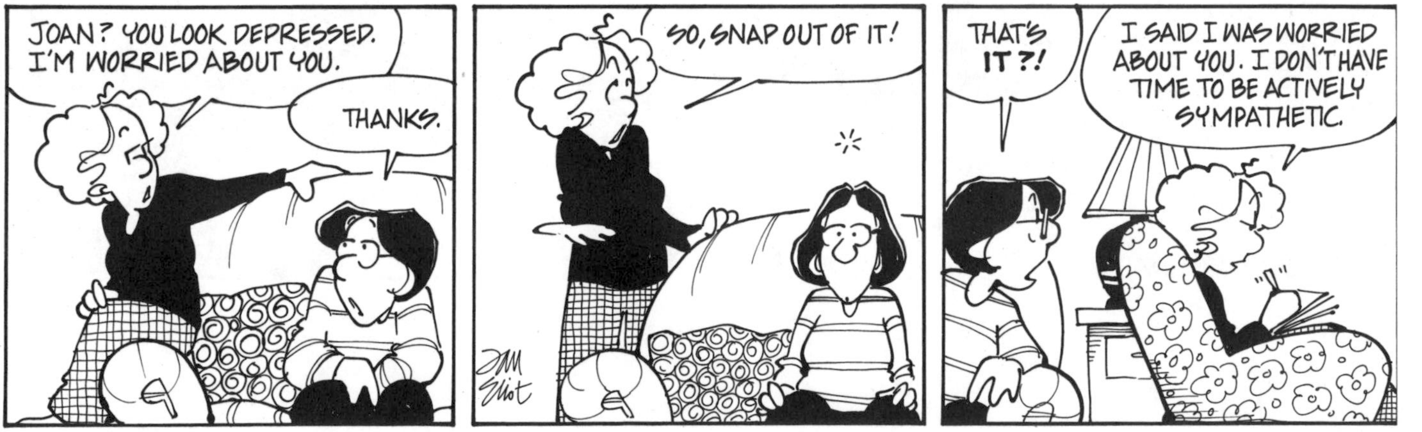
JOAN? YOU LOOK DEPRESSED. I'M WORRIED ABOUT YOU.
THANKS.
SO, SNAP OUT OF IT!
THAT'S **IT?!**
I SAID I WAS WORRIED ABOUT YOU. I DON'T HAVE TIME TO BE ACTIVELY SYMPATHETIC.

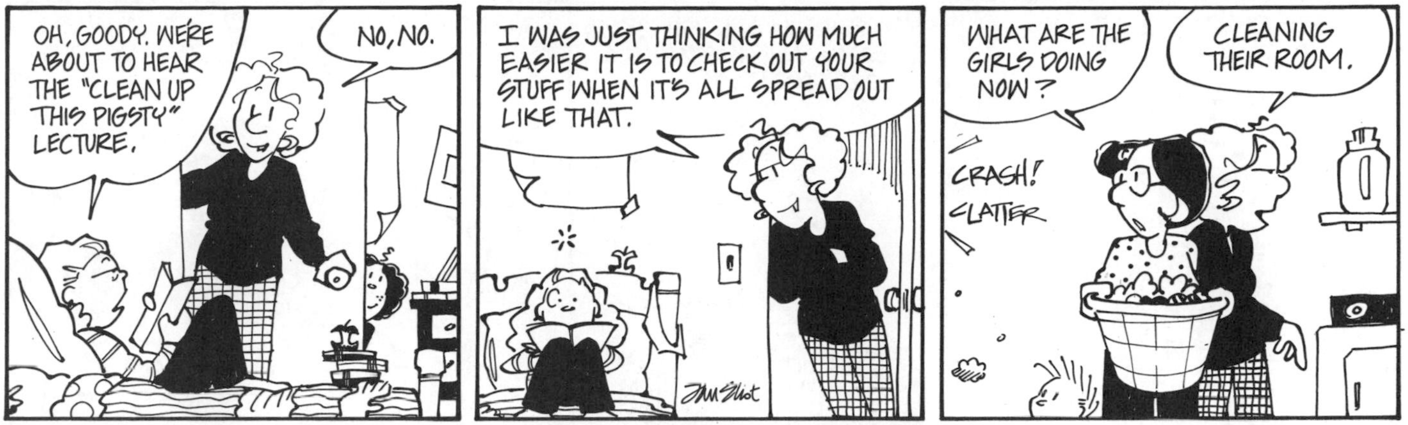
OH, GOODY. WE'RE ABOUT TO HEAR THE "CLEAN UP THIS PIGSTY" LECTURE.
NO, NO.
I WAS JUST THINKING HOW MUCH EASIER IT IS TO CHECK OUT YOUR STUFF WHEN IT'S ALL SPREAD OUT LIKE THAT.
WHAT ARE THE GIRLS DOING NOW?
CLEANING THEIR ROOM.
CRASH!
CLATTER

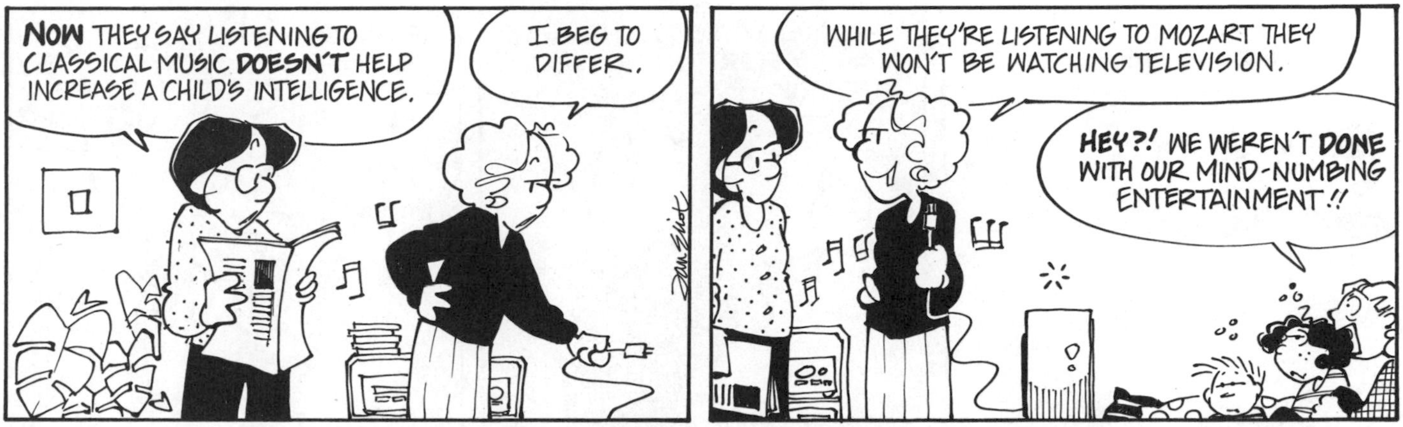
NOW THEY SAY LISTENING TO CLASSICAL MUSIC **DOESN'T** HELP INCREASE A CHILD'S INTELLIGENCE.
I BEG TO DIFFER.
WHILE THEY'RE LISTENING TO MOZART THEY WON'T BE WATCHING TELEVISION.
HEY?! WE WEREN'T **DONE** WITH OUR MIND-NUMBING ENTERTAINMENT!!

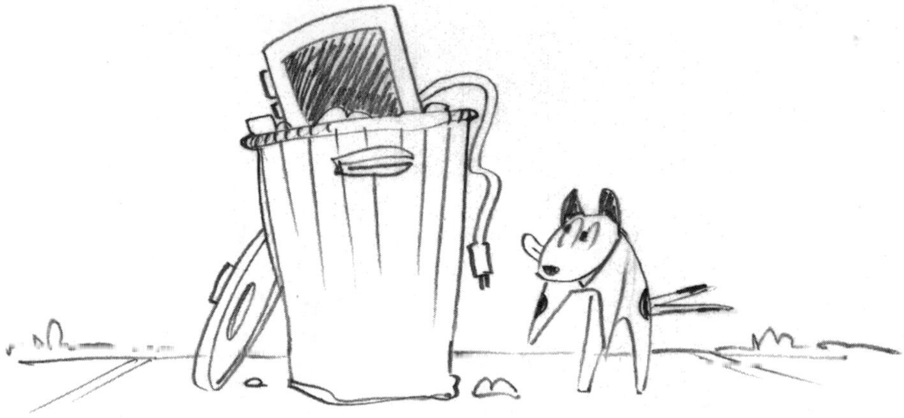

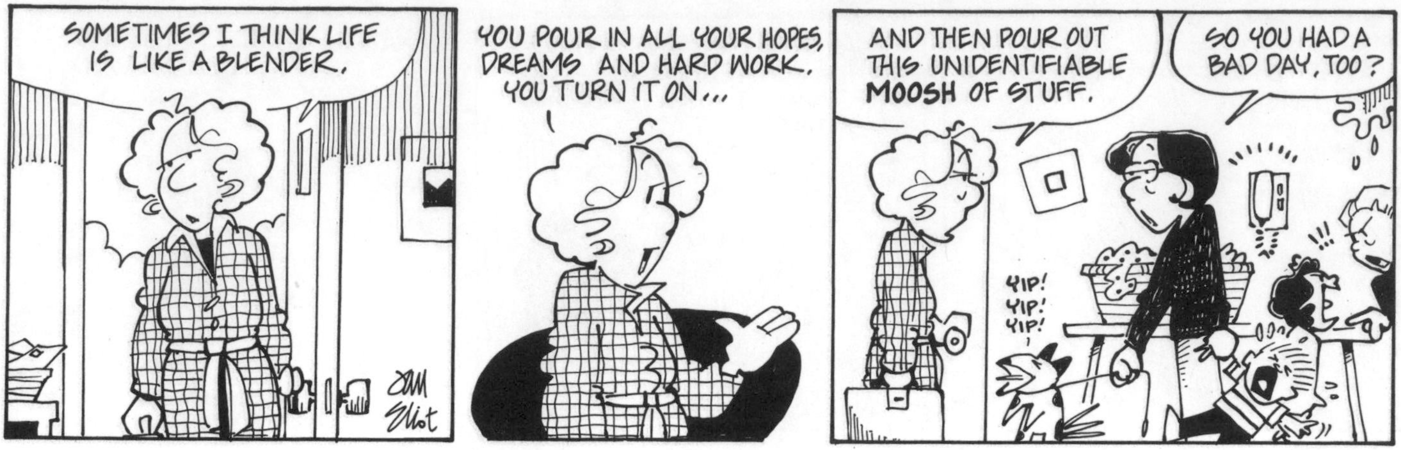
SOMETIMES I THINK LIFE IS LIKE A BLENDER.
YOU POUR IN ALL YOUR HOPES, DREAMS AND HARD WORK. YOU TURN IT ON...
AND THEN POUR OUT THIS UNIDENTIFIABLE MOOSH OF STUFF.
SO YOU HAD A BAD DAY, TOO?
YIP! YIP! YIP!

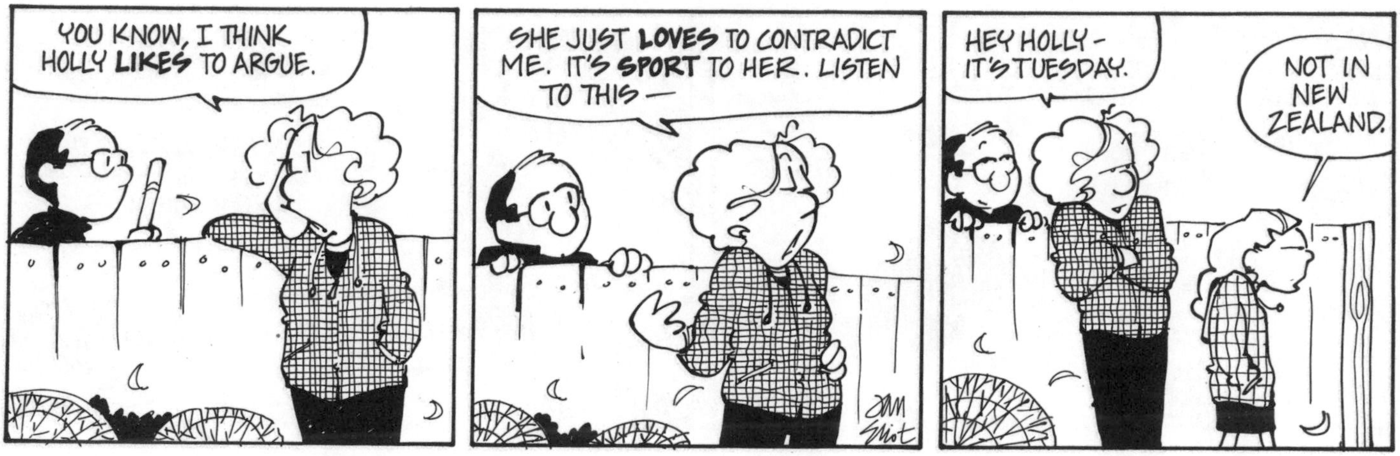
YOU KNOW, I THINK HOLLY LIKES TO ARGUE.
SHE JUST LOVES TO CONTRADICT ME. IT'S SPORT TO HER. LISTEN TO THIS—
HEY HOLLY- IT'S TUESDAY.
NOT IN NEW ZEALAND.

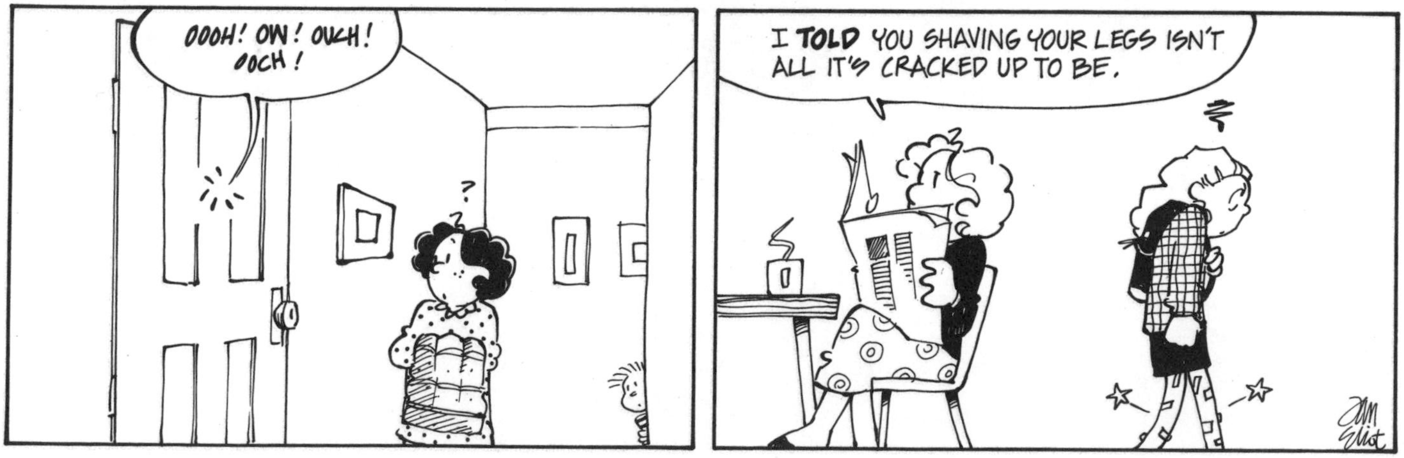
OOOH! OW! OUCH! OOCH!
I TOLD YOU SHAVING YOUR LEGS ISN'T ALL IT'S CRACKED UP TO BE.

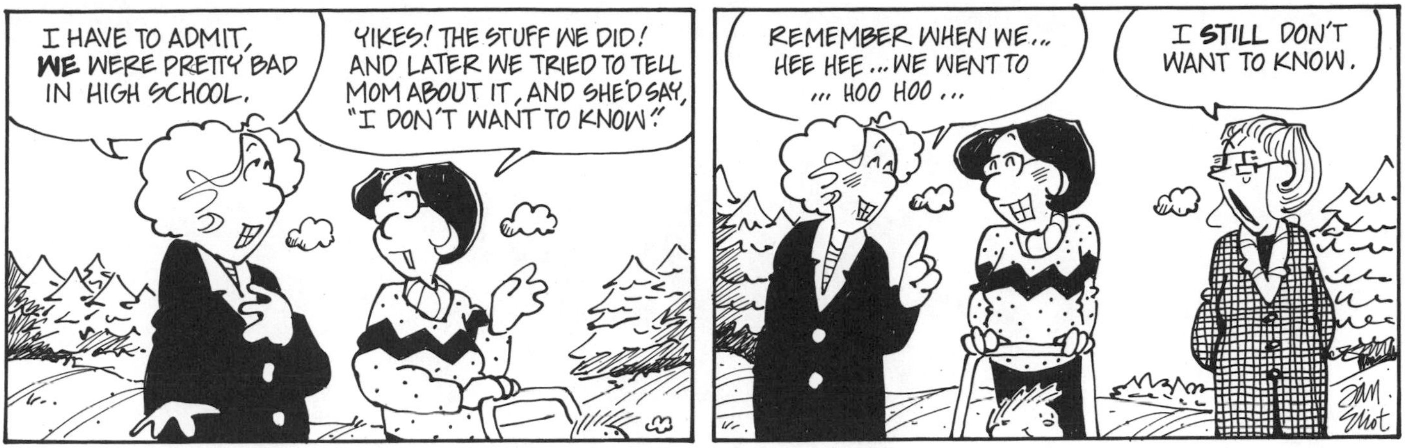
I HAVE TO ADMIT, **WE** WERE PRETTY BAD IN HIGH SCHOOL.
YIKES! THE STUFF WE DID! AND LATER WE TRIED TO TELL MOM ABOUT IT, AND SHE'D SAY, "I DON'T WANT TO KNOW."
REMEMBER WHEN WE... HEE HEE... WE WENT TO ... HOO HOO ...
I **STILL** DON'T WANT TO KNOW.

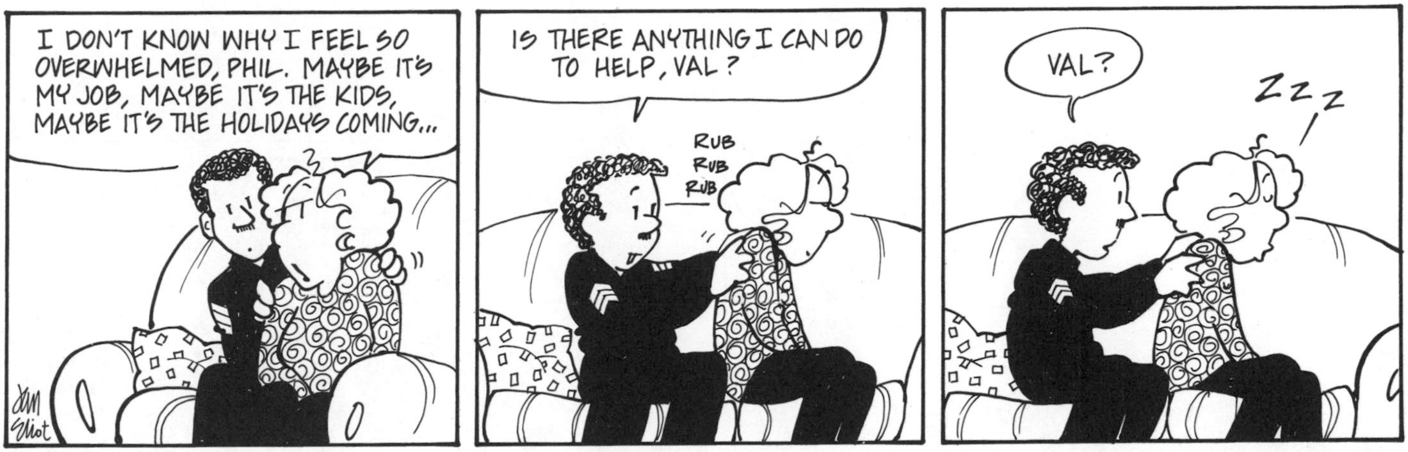
I DON'T KNOW WHY I FEEL SO OVERWHELMED, PHIL. MAYBE IT'S MY JOB, MAYBE IT'S THE KIDS, MAYBE IT'S THE HOLIDAYS COMING...
IS THERE ANYTHING I CAN DO TO HELP, VAL?
RUB RUB RUB
VAL?
Z Z Z

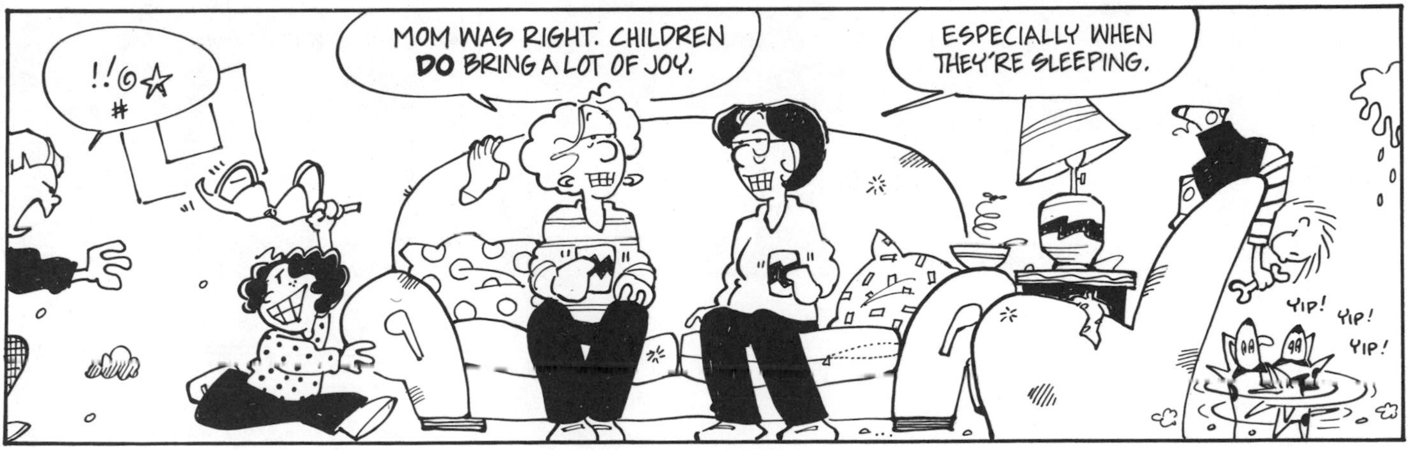
MOM WAS RIGHT. CHILDREN **DO** BRING A LOT OF JOY.
ESPECIALLY WHEN THEY'RE SLEEPING.
YIP! YIP! YIP!

Stone Soup

SHREEE CEEK

YOU ARE SO **GOOD** WITH YOUR SON.

THANK YOU. BUT HE'S NOT ACTUALLY MY SON ...

HE BELONGS TO MY FIANCÉE, JOAN. MAYBE YOU'VE MET HER HERE.

OF COURSE! THIS MUST BE MAX.

I TAKE HIM FOR THE DAY NOW AND THEN. I FIND CHILDREN REALLY *ENERGIZING.*

WALLY? HOW'D YOU END UP WITH ALL THESE KIDS?

I DON'T KNOW, BUT I'M MAKING $20 AN HOUR.

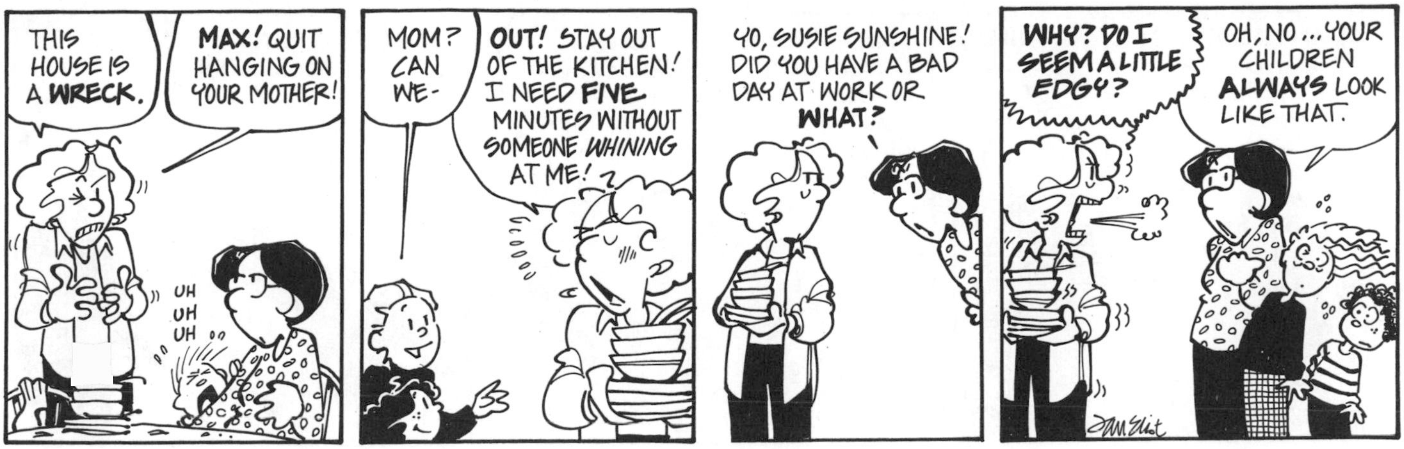
THIS HOUSE IS A **WRECK**.
MAX! QUIT HANGING ON YOUR MOTHER!
UH UH UH
MOM? CAN WE-
OUT! STAY OUT OF THE KITCHEN! I NEED **FIVE** MINUTES WITHOUT SOMEONE *WHINING* AT ME!
YO, SUSIE SUNSHINE! DID YOU HAVE A BAD DAY AT WORK OR **WHAT?**
WHY? DO I SEEM A LITTLE EDGY?
OH, NO... YOUR CHILDREN **ALWAYS** LOOK LIKE THAT.

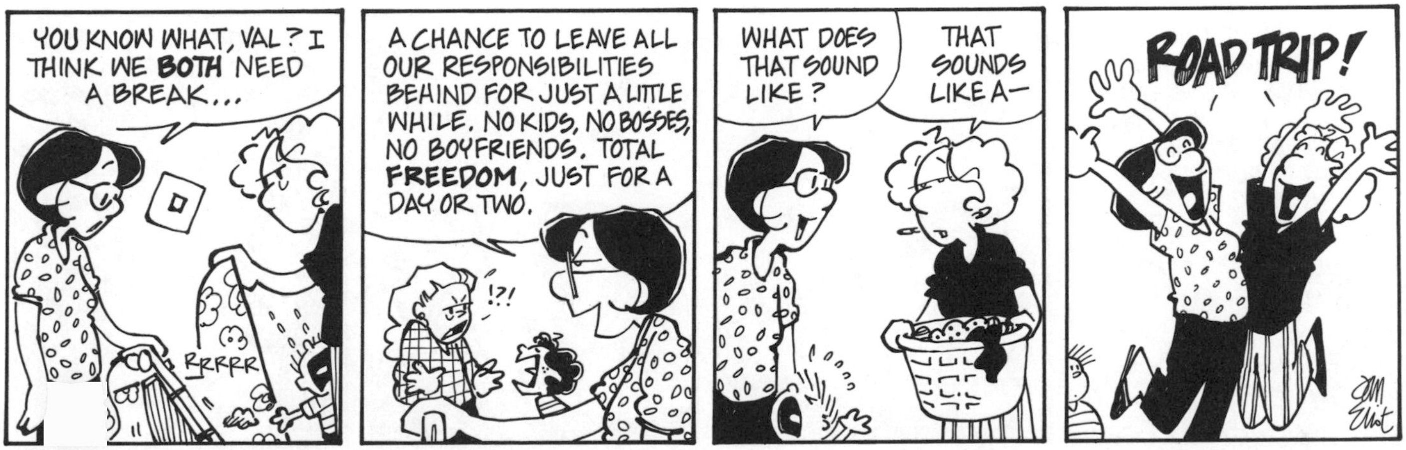
YOU KNOW WHAT, VAL? I THINK WE **BOTH** NEED A BREAK...
RRRRR
A CHANCE TO LEAVE ALL OUR RESPONSIBILITIES BEHIND FOR JUST A LITTLE WHILE. NO KIDS, NO BOSSES, NO BOYFRIENDS. TOTAL **FREEDOM**, JUST FOR A DAY OR TWO.
!?!
WHAT DOES THAT SOUND LIKE?
THAT SOUNDS LIKE A—
ROAD TRIP!

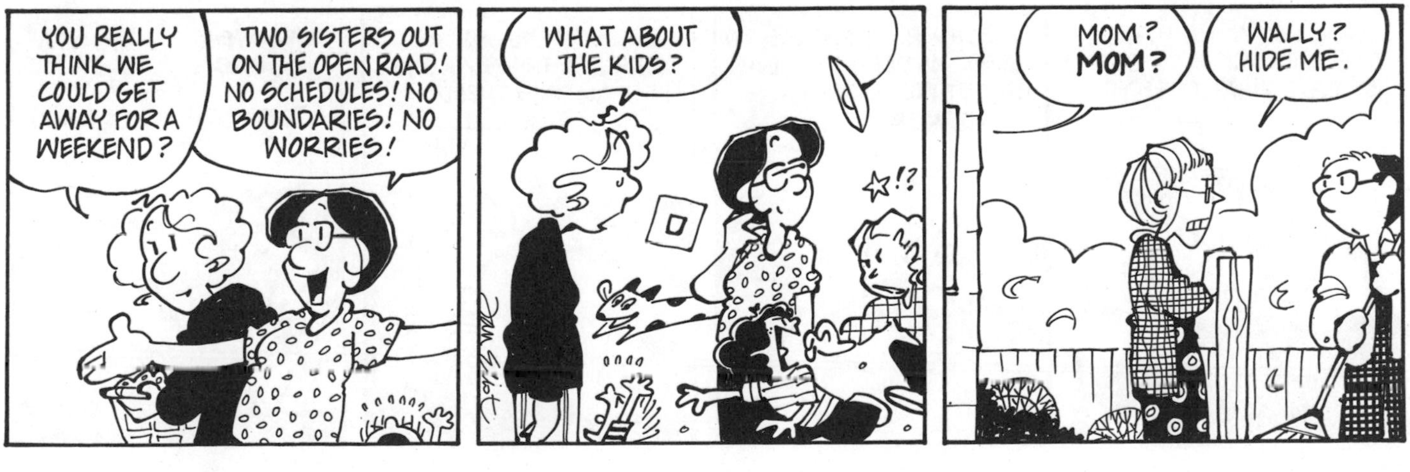
YOU REALLY THINK WE COULD GET AWAY FOR A WEEKEND?
TWO SISTERS OUT ON THE OPEN ROAD! NO SCHEDULES! NO BOUNDARIES! NO WORRIES!
WHAT ABOUT THE KIDS?
MOM? **MOM?**
WALLY? HIDE ME.

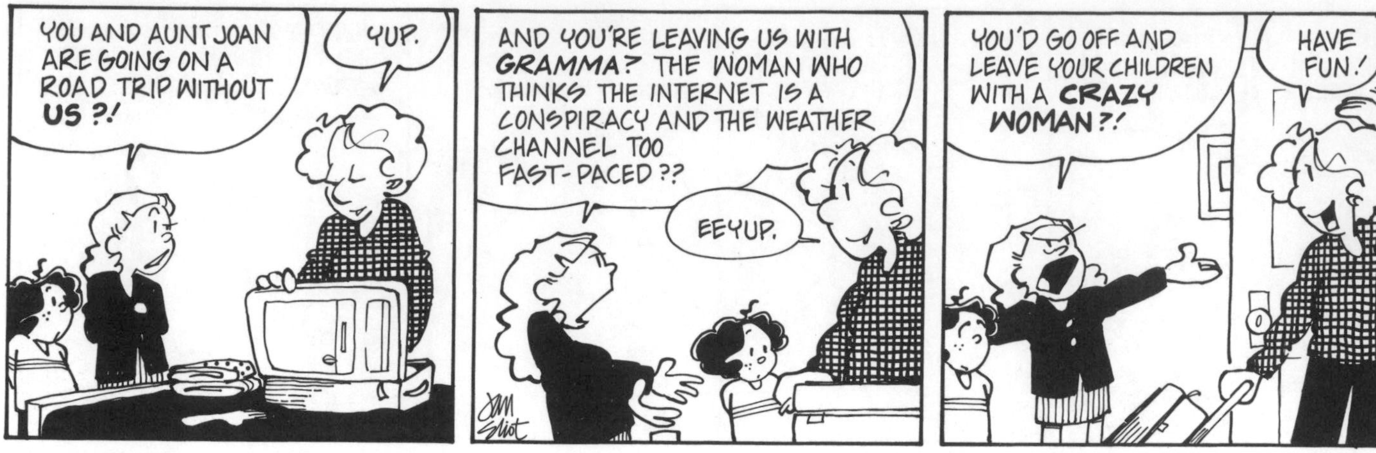
YOU AND AUNT JOAN ARE GOING ON A ROAD TRIP WITHOUT **US** ?!
YUP.
AND YOU'RE LEAVING US WITH **GRAMMA?** THE WOMAN WHO THINKS THE INTERNET IS A CONSPIRACY AND THE WEATHER CHANNEL TOO FAST-PACED ??
EEYUP.
YOU'D GO OFF AND LEAVE YOUR CHILDREN WITH A **CRAZY WOMAN** ?!
HAVE FUN!

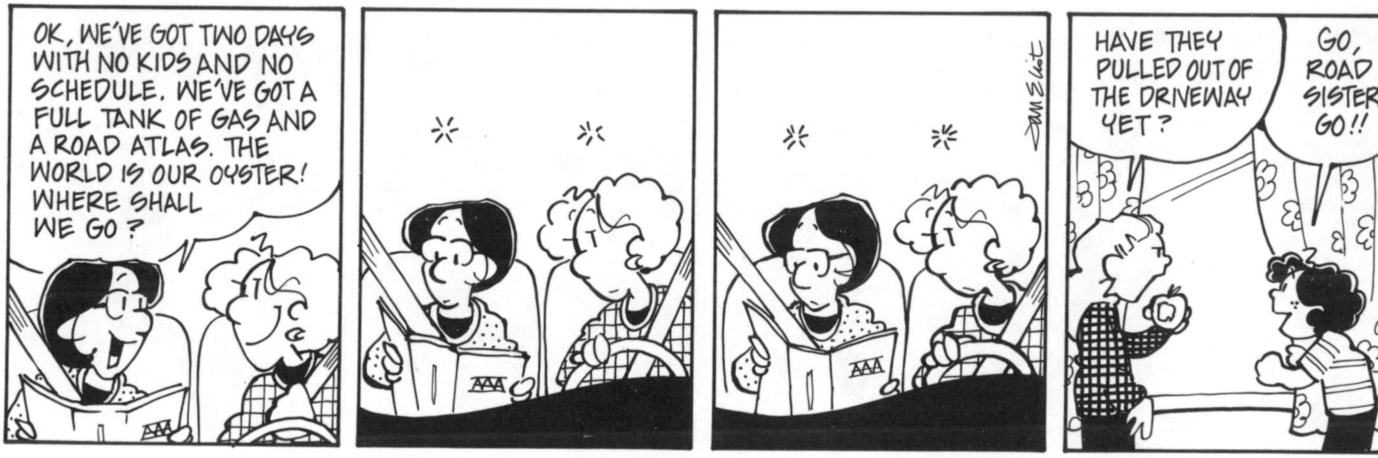
OK, WE'VE GOT TWO DAYS WITH NO KIDS AND NO SCHEDULE. WE'VE GOT A FULL TANK OF GAS AND A ROAD ATLAS. THE WORLD IS OUR OYSTER! WHERE SHALL WE GO ?
AAA
HAVE THEY PULLED OUT OF THE DRIVEWAY YET ?
GO, ROAD SISTERS, GO!!

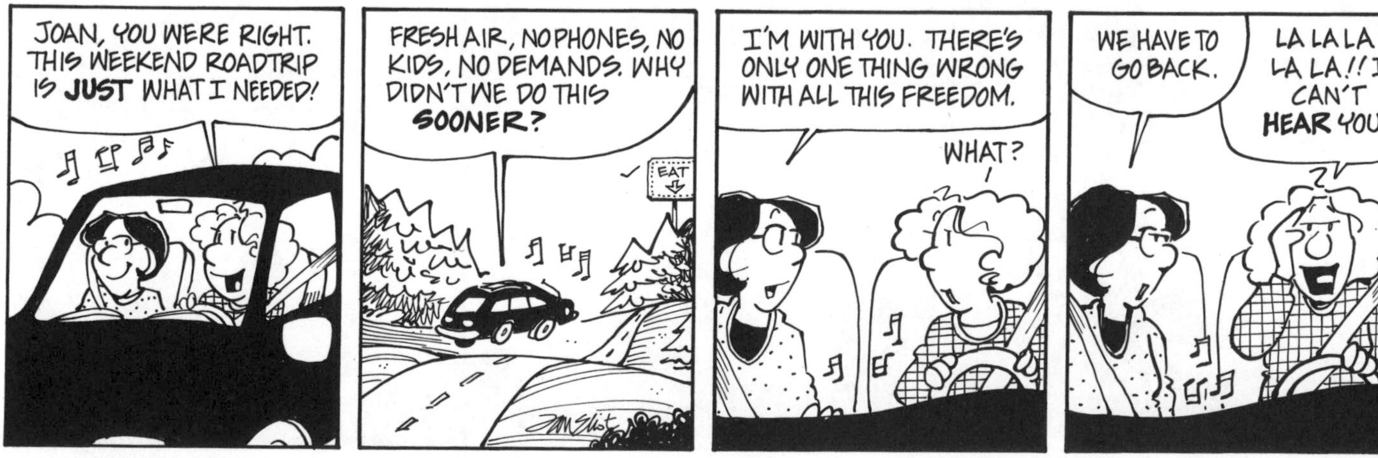
JOAN, YOU WERE RIGHT. THIS WEEKEND ROADTRIP IS **JUST** WHAT I NEEDED!
FRESH AIR, NO PHONES, NO KIDS, NO DEMANDS. WHY DIDN'T WE DO THIS **SOONER?**
EAT
I'M WITH YOU. THERE'S ONLY ONE THING WRONG WITH ALL THIS FREEDOM.
WHAT?
WE HAVE TO GO BACK.
LA LA LA LA LA!! I CAN'T **HEAR** YOU!

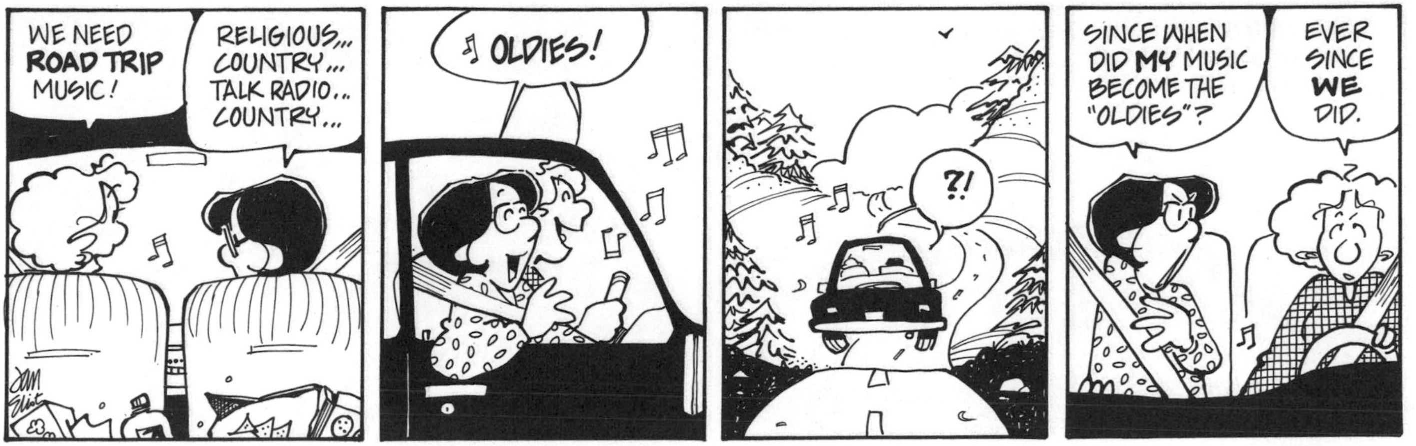
WE NEED **ROAD TRIP** MUSIC!
RELIGIOUS... COUNTRY... TALK RADIO... COUNTRY...
♪ **OLDIES!**
?!
SINCE WHEN DID **MY** MUSIC BECOME THE "OLDIES"?
EVER SINCE **WE** DID.

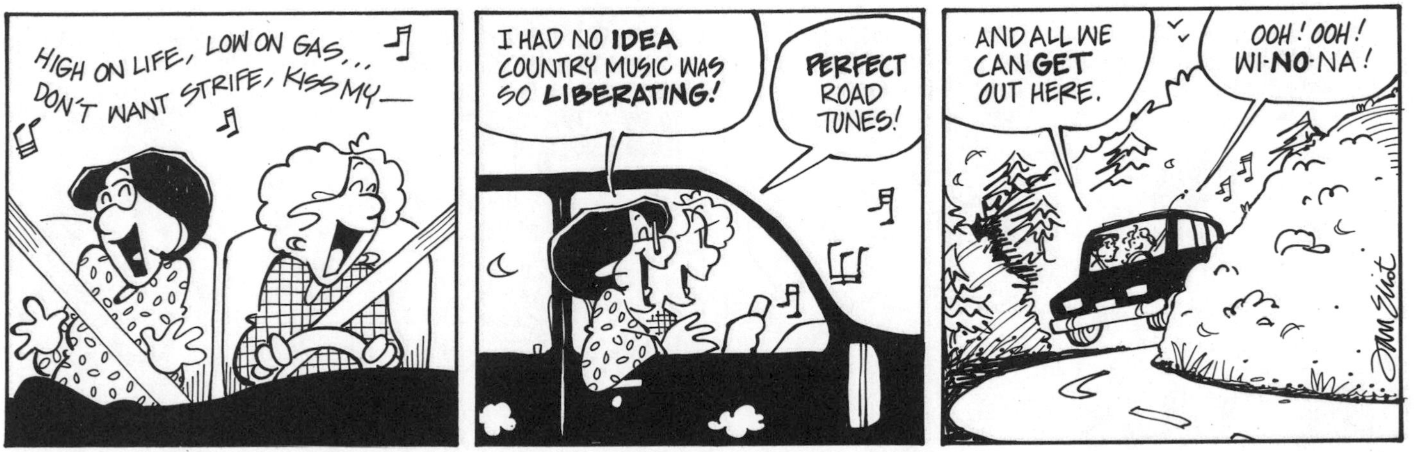
HIGH ON LIFE, LOW ON GAS... DON'T WANT STRIFE, KISS MY—
I HAD NO **IDEA** COUNTRY MUSIC WAS SO **LIBERATING!**
PERFECT ROAD TUNES!
AND ALL WE CAN **GET** OUT HERE.
OOH! OOH! WI-**NO**-NA!

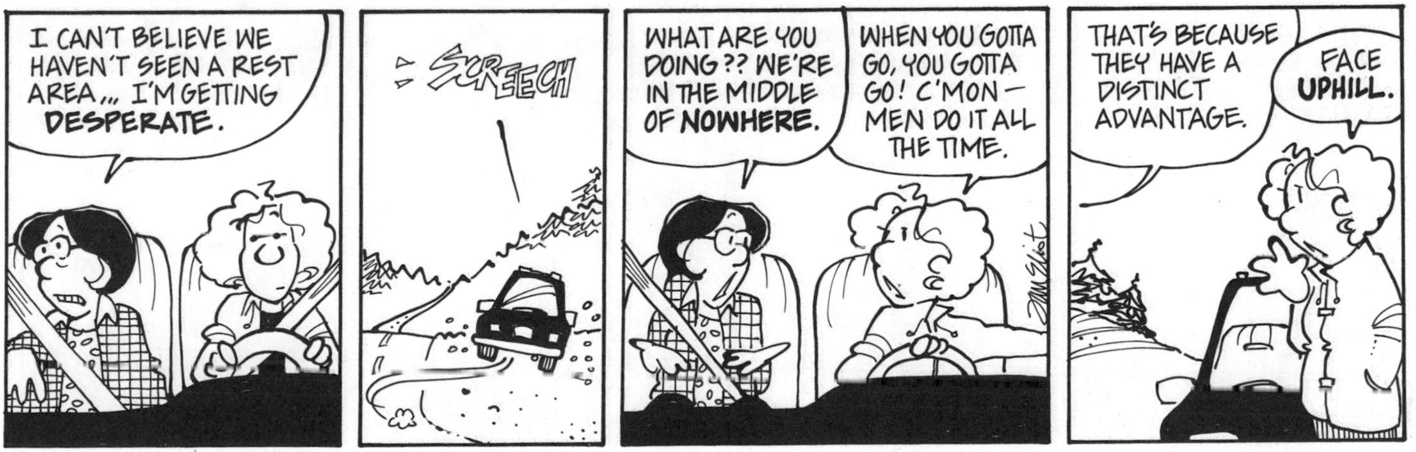
I CAN'T BELIEVE WE HAVEN'T SEEN A REST AREA... I'M GETTING **DESPERATE**.
SCREECH
WHAT ARE YOU DOING?? WE'RE IN THE MIDDLE OF **NOWHERE**.
WHEN YOU GOTTA GO, YOU GOTTA GO! C'MON— MEN DO IT ALL THE TIME.
THAT'S BECAUSE THEY HAVE A DISTINCT ADVANTAGE.
FACE **UPHILL**.

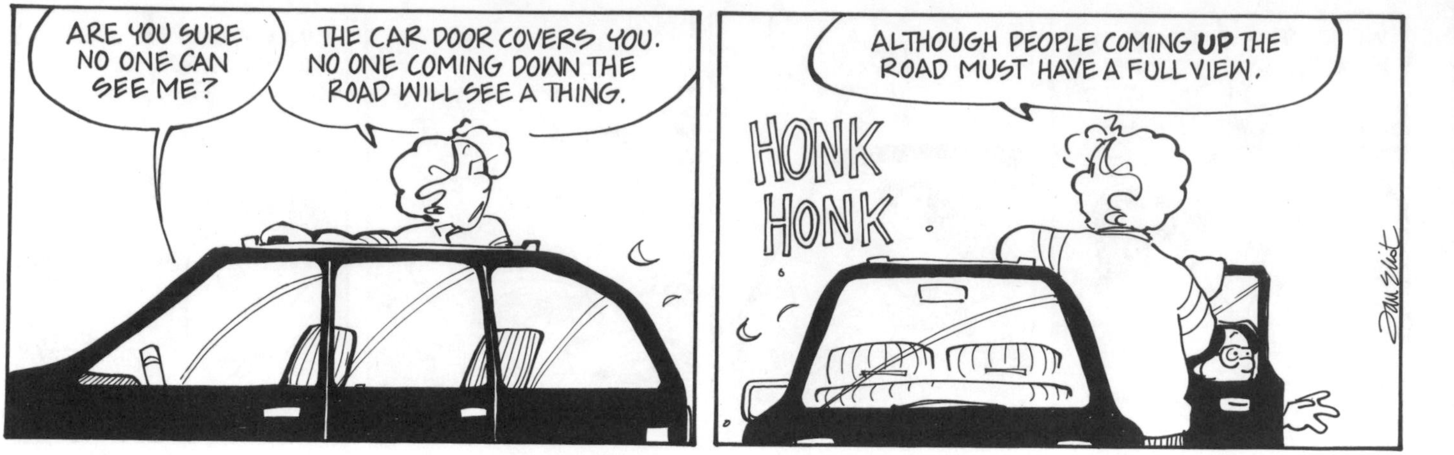
ARE YOU SURE NO ONE CAN SEE ME?
THE CAR DOOR COVERS YOU. NO ONE COMING DOWN THE ROAD WILL SEE A THING.
ALTHOUGH PEOPLE COMING **UP** THE ROAD MUST HAVE A FULL VIEW.
HONK HONK

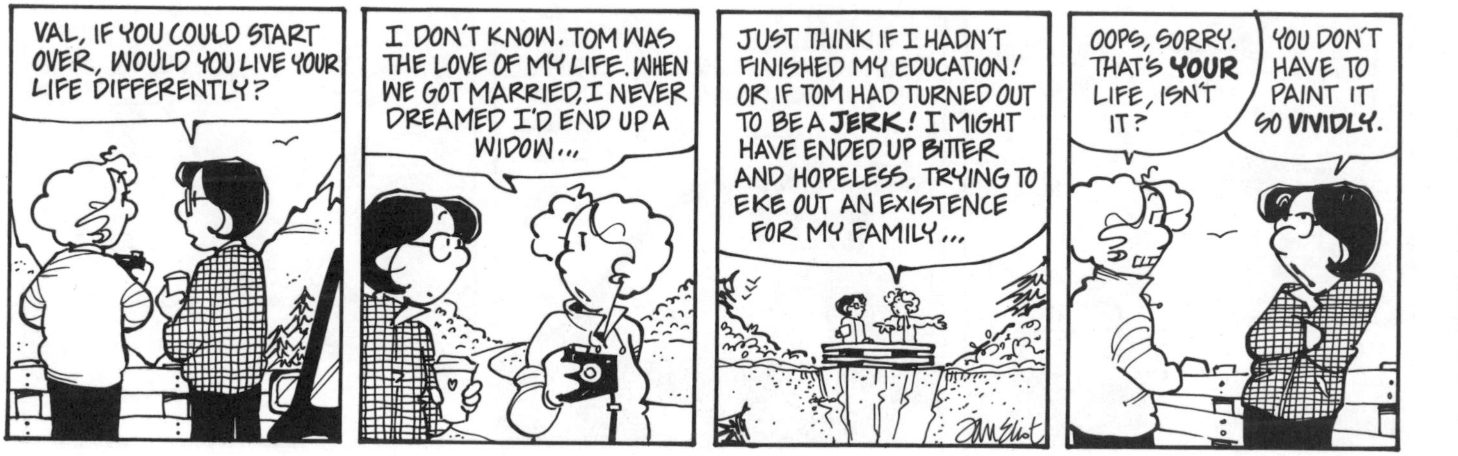
VAL, IF YOU COULD START OVER, WOULD YOU LIVE YOUR LIFE DIFFERENTLY?
I DON'T KNOW. TOM WAS THE LOVE OF MY LIFE. WHEN WE GOT MARRIED, I NEVER DREAMED I'D END UP A WIDOW...
JUST THINK IF I HADN'T FINISHED MY EDUCATION! OR IF TOM HAD TURNED OUT TO BE A **JERK!** I MIGHT HAVE ENDED UP BITTER AND HOPELESS, TRYING TO EKE OUT AN EXISTENCE FOR MY FAMILY...
OOPS, SORRY. THAT'S **YOUR** LIFE, ISN'T IT?
YOU DON'T HAVE TO PAINT IT SO **VIVIDLY**.

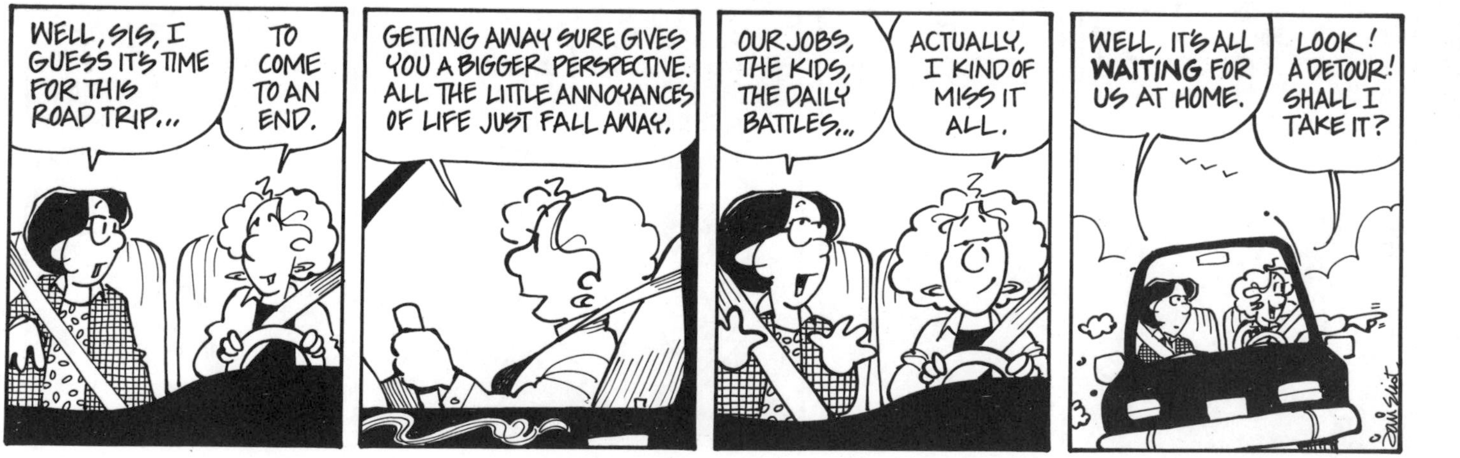
WELL, SIS, I GUESS IT'S TIME FOR THIS ROAD TRIP...
TO COME TO AN END.
GETTING AWAY SURE GIVES YOU A BIGGER PERSPECTIVE. ALL THE LITTLE ANNOYANCES OF LIFE JUST FALL AWAY.
OUR JOBS, THE KIDS, THE DAILY BATTLES...
ACTUALLY, I KIND OF MISS IT ALL.
WELL, IT'S ALL **WAITING** FOR US AT HOME.
LOOK! A DETOUR! SHALL I TAKE IT?

Stone Soup

 I'M BORED!

 HEY MOM?! CAN I PUT ON MY RAINCOAT AND BOOTS AND GO SPLASH IN THE PUDDLES?

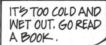 IT'S TOO COLD AND WET OUT. GO READ A BOOK.

 SCREECH!

 STAY OUTTA MY STUFF!!

MAKE ME.

 ALIX?! YOU'RE MAKING A MESS!

 HEE HEE HEE THEY **FELL** FOR IT! I **WON**! I'M **OUTSIDE**! I—

 I NEVER RUN OUT OF WAYS TO MAKE MYSELF MISERABLE...

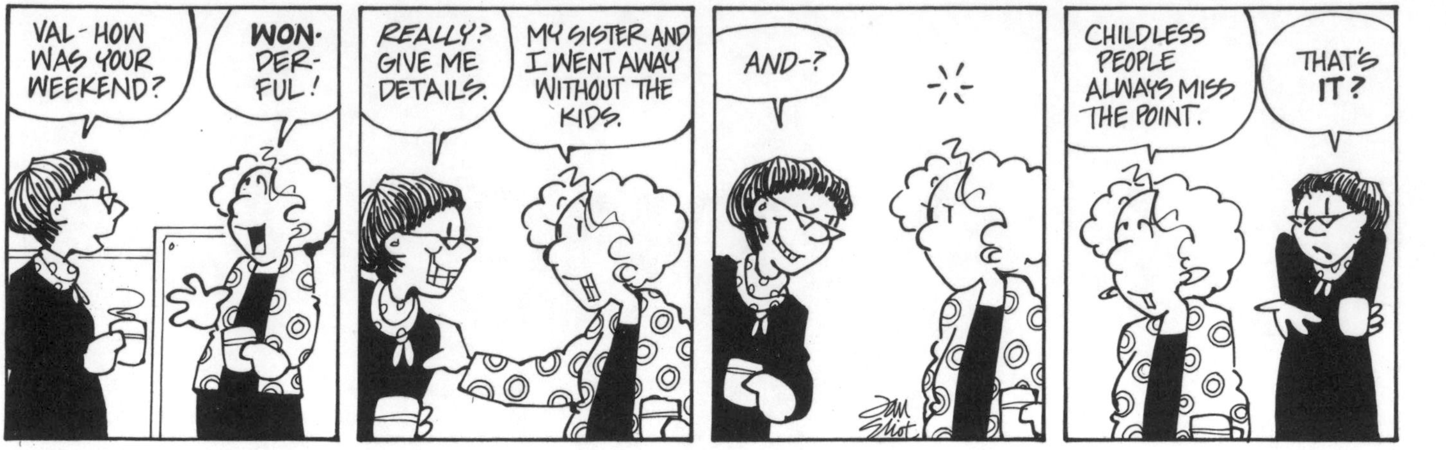
VAL - HOW WAS YOUR WEEKEND?
WON-DER-FUL!
REALLY? GIVE ME DETAILS.
MY SISTER AND I WENT AWAY WITHOUT THE KIDS.
AND-?
CHILDLESS PEOPLE ALWAYS MISS THE POINT.
THAT'S **IT?**

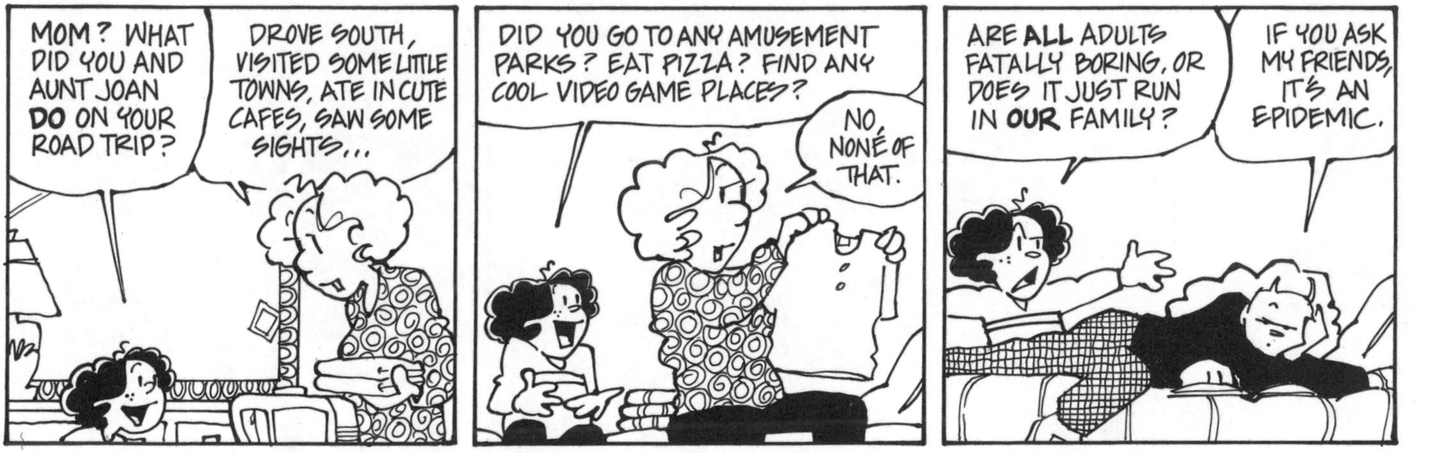
MOM? WHAT DID YOU AND AUNT JOAN **DO** ON YOUR ROAD TRIP?
DROVE SOUTH, VISITED SOME LITTLE TOWNS, ATE IN CUTE CAFES, SAW SOME SIGHTS...
DID YOU GO TO ANY AMUSEMENT PARKS? EAT PIZZA? FIND ANY COOL VIDEO GAME PLACES?
NO, NONE OF THAT.
ARE **ALL** ADULTS FATALLY BORING, OR DOES IT JUST RUN IN **OUR** FAMILY?
IF YOU ASK MY FRIENDS, IT'S AN EPIDEMIC.

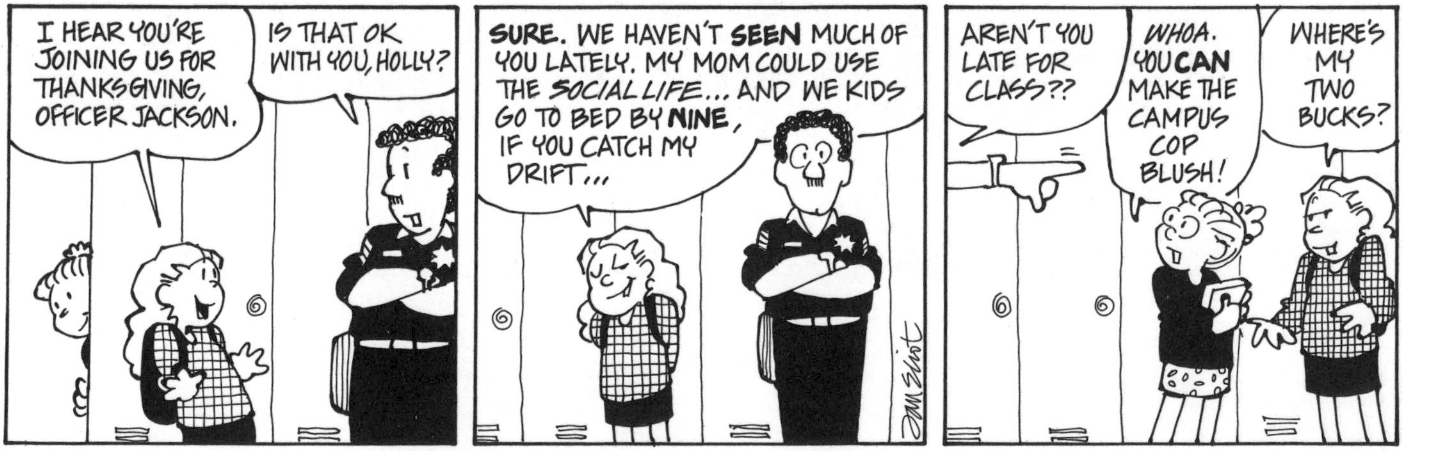
I HEAR YOU'RE JOINING US FOR THANKSGIVING, OFFICER JACKSON.
IS THAT OK WITH YOU, HOLLY?
SURE. WE HAVEN'T **SEEN** MUCH OF YOU LATELY. MY MOM COULD USE THE *SOCIAL LIFE*... AND WE KIDS GO TO BED BY **NINE**, IF YOU CATCH MY DRIFT...
AREN'T YOU LATE FOR CLASS??
WHOA. YOU **CAN** MAKE THE CAMPUS COP BLUSH!
WHERE'S MY TWO BUCKS?

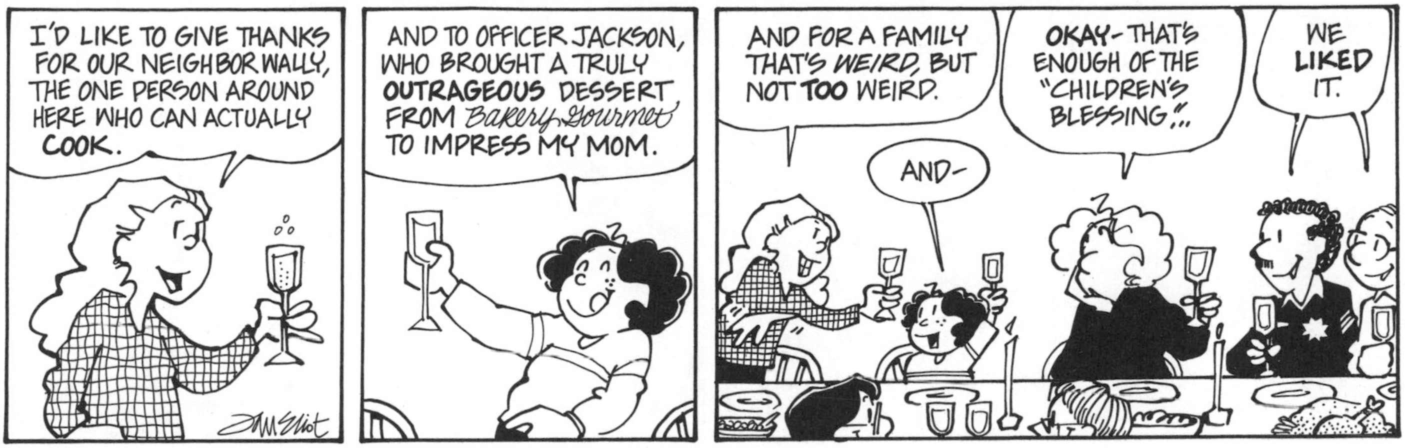
I'D LIKE TO GIVE THANKS FOR OUR NEIGHBOR WALLY, THE ONE PERSON AROUND HERE WHO CAN ACTUALLY **COOK**.
AND TO OFFICER JACKSON, WHO BROUGHT A TRULY **OUTRAGEOUS** DESSERT FROM *Bakery Gourmet* TO IMPRESS MY MOM.
AND FOR A FAMILY THAT'S *WEIRD*, BUT NOT **TOO** WEIRD.
AND-
OKAY- THAT'S ENOUGH OF THE "CHILDREN'S BLESSING"...
WE **LIKED** IT.

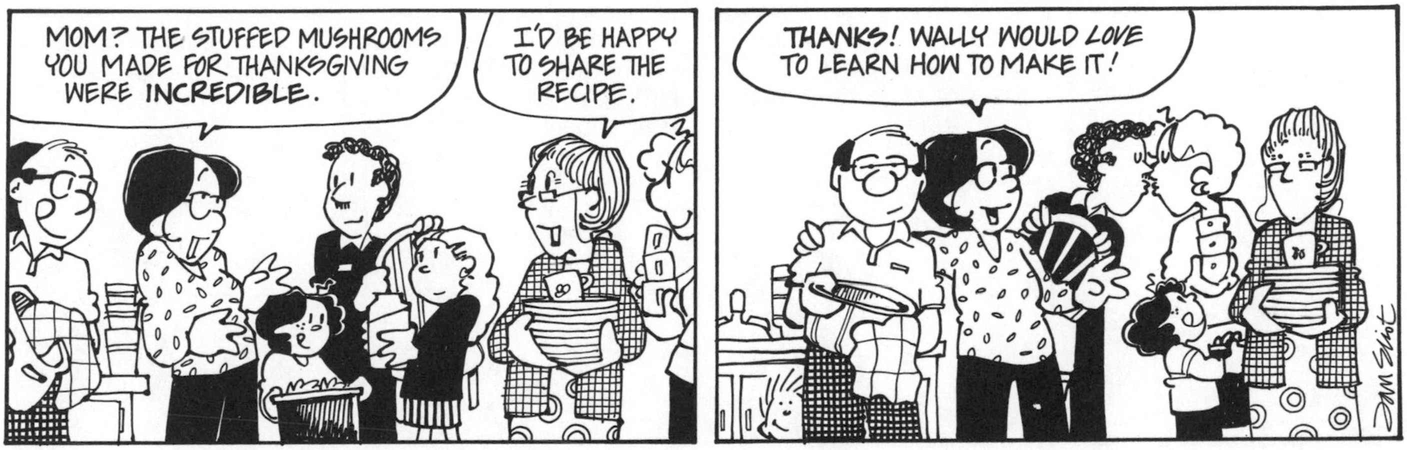
MOM? THE STUFFED MUSHROOMS YOU MADE FOR THANKSGIVING WERE **INCREDIBLE**.
I'D BE HAPPY TO SHARE THE RECIPE.
THANKS! WALLY WOULD *LOVE* TO LEARN HOW TO MAKE IT!

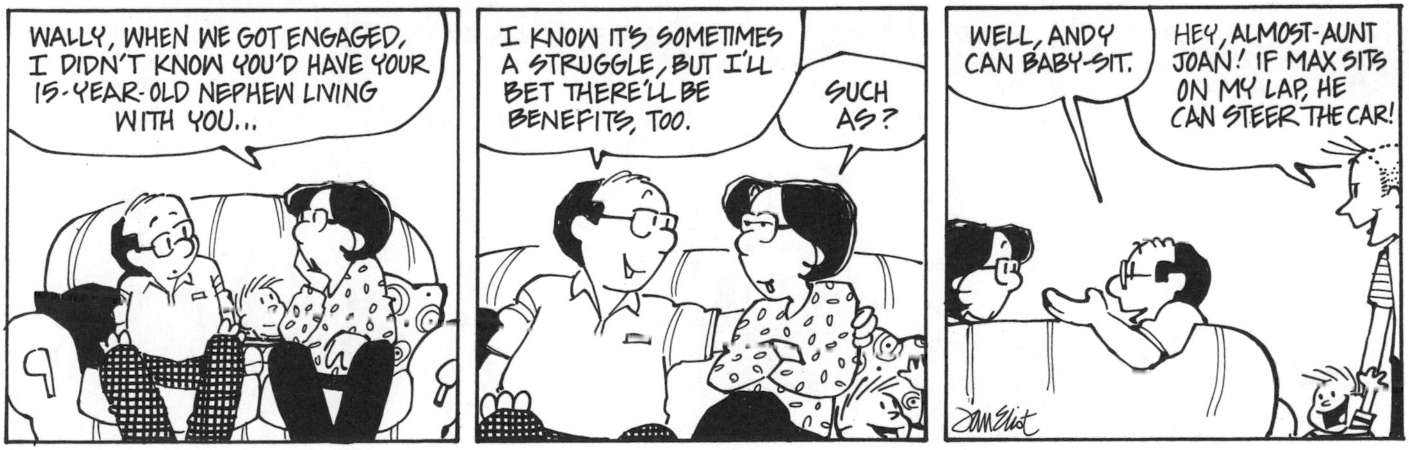
WALLY, WHEN WE GOT ENGAGED, I DIDN'T KNOW YOU'D HAVE YOUR 15-YEAR-OLD NEPHEW LIVING WITH YOU...
I KNOW IT'S SOMETIMES A STRUGGLE, BUT I'LL BET THERE'LL BE BENEFITS, TOO.
SUCH AS?
WELL, ANDY CAN BABY-SIT.
HEY, ALMOST-AUNT JOAN! IF MAX SITS ON MY LAP, HE CAN STEER THE CAR!

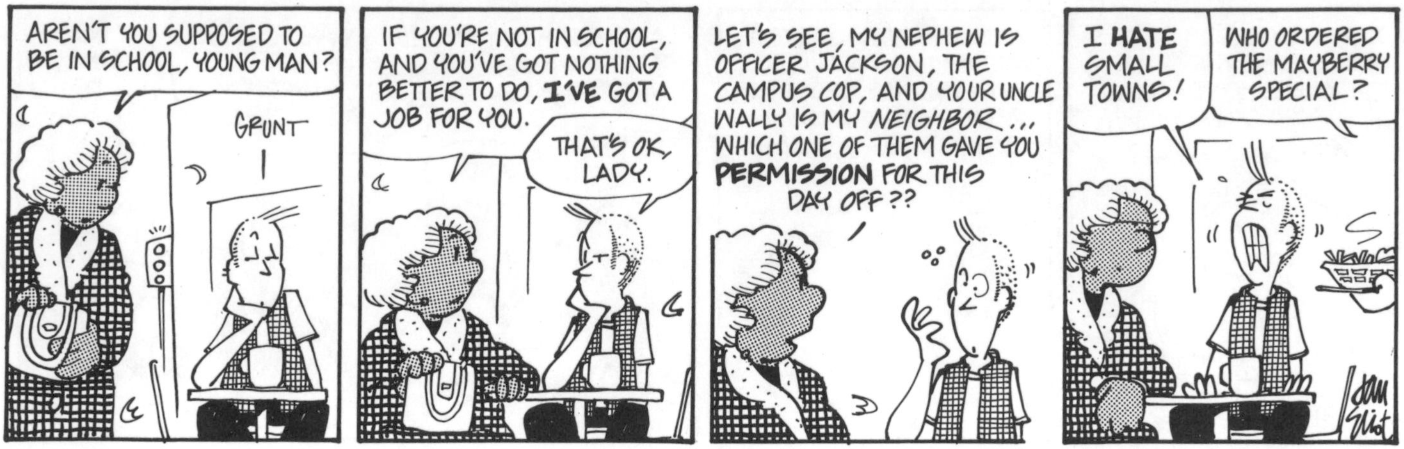
AREN'T YOU SUPPOSED TO BE IN SCHOOL, YOUNG MAN?
GRUNT
IF YOU'RE NOT IN SCHOOL, AND YOU'VE GOT NOTHING BETTER TO DO, **I'VE** GOT A JOB FOR YOU.
THAT'S OK, LADY.
LET'S SEE, MY NEPHEW IS OFFICER JACKSON, THE CAMPUS COP, AND YOUR UNCLE WALLY IS MY *NEIGHBOR*... WHICH ONE OF THEM GAVE YOU **PERMISSION** FOR THIS DAY OFF??
I **HATE** SMALL TOWNS!
WHO ORDERED THE MAYBERRY SPECIAL?

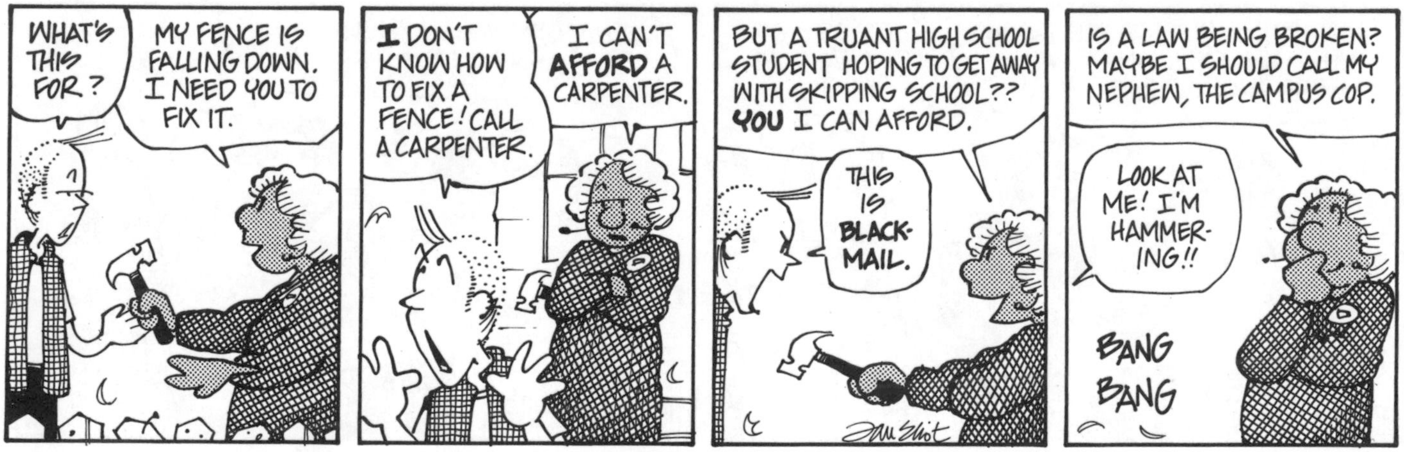
WHAT'S THIS FOR?
MY FENCE IS FALLING DOWN. I NEED YOU TO FIX IT.
I DON'T KNOW HOW TO FIX A FENCE! CALL A CARPENTER.
I CAN'T **AFFORD** A CARPENTER.
BUT A TRUANT HIGH SCHOOL STUDENT HOPING TO GET AWAY WITH SKIPPING SCHOOL?? **YOU** I CAN AFFORD.
THIS IS **BLACKMAIL.**
IS A LAW BEING BROKEN? MAYBE I SHOULD CALL MY NEPHEW, THE CAMPUS COP.
LOOK AT ME! I'M HAMMERING!!
BANG
BANG

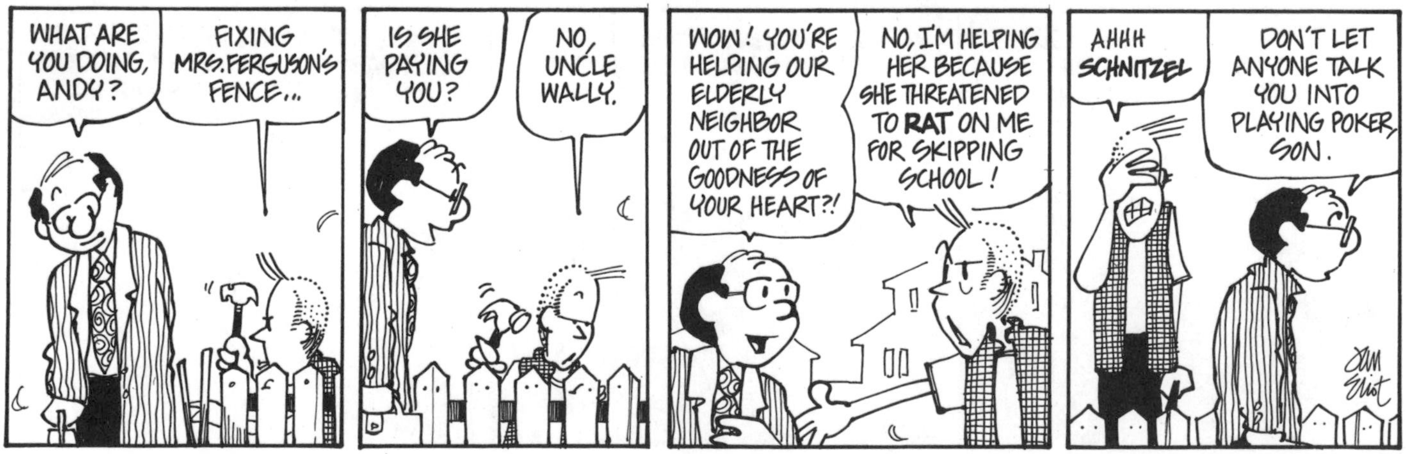
WHAT ARE YOU DOING, ANDY?
FIXING MRS. FERGUSON'S FENCE...
IS SHE PAYING YOU?
NO, UNCLE WALLY.
WOW! YOU'RE HELPING OUR ELDERLY NEIGHBOR OUT OF THE GOODNESS OF YOUR HEART?!
NO, I'M HELPING HER BECAUSE SHE THREATENED TO **RAT** ON ME FOR SKIPPING SCHOOL!
AHHH **SCHNITZEL**
DON'T LET ANYONE TALK YOU INTO PLAYING POKER, SON.

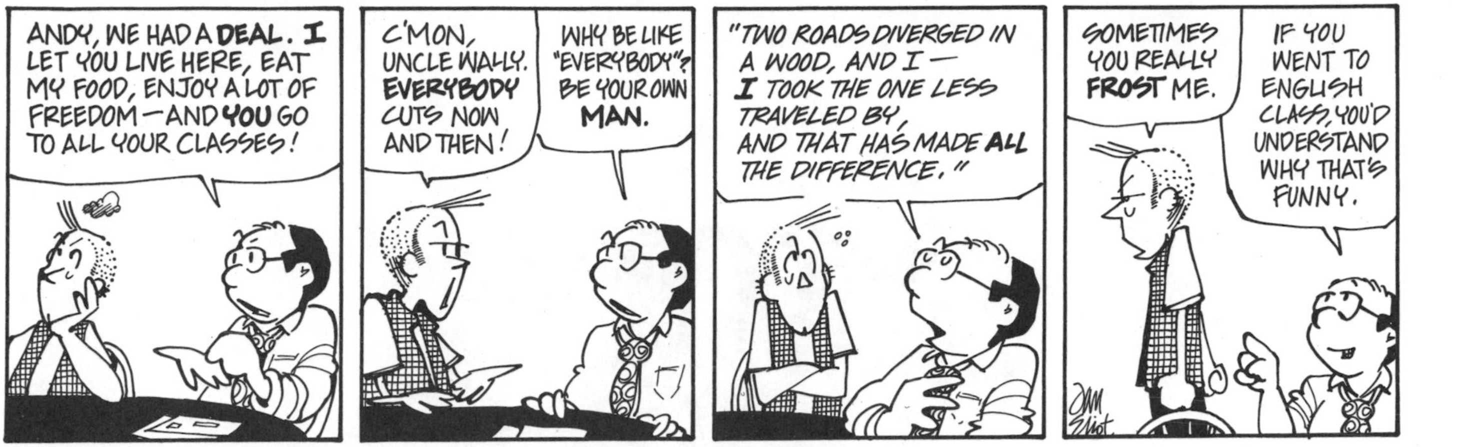
ANDY, WE HAD A DEAL. I LET YOU LIVE HERE, EAT MY FOOD, ENJOY A LOT OF FREEDOM — AND YOU GO TO ALL YOUR CLASSES!
C'MON, UNCLE WALLY. EVERYBODY CUTS NOW AND THEN!
WHY BE LIKE "EVERYBODY"? BE YOUR OWN MAN.
"TWO ROADS DIVERGED IN A WOOD, AND I — I TOOK THE ONE LESS TRAVELED BY, AND THAT HAS MADE ALL THE DIFFERENCE."
SOMETIMES YOU REALLY FROST ME.
IF YOU WENT TO ENGLISH CLASS, YOU'D UNDERSTAND WHY THAT'S FUNNY.

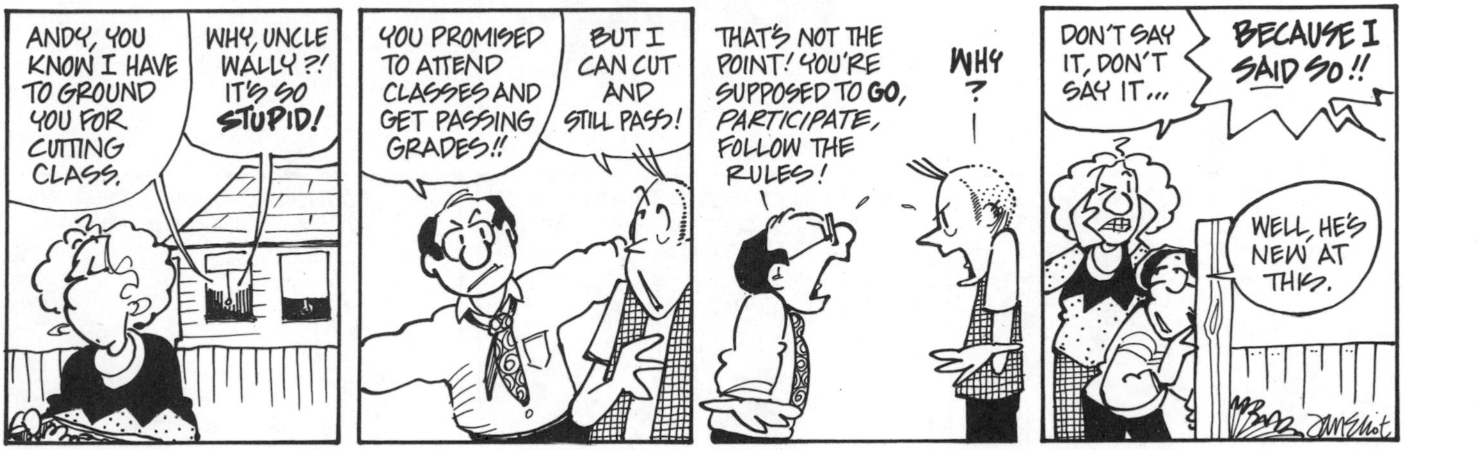
ANDY, YOU KNOW I HAVE TO GROUND YOU FOR CUTTING CLASS.
WHY, UNCLE WALLY?! IT'S SO STUPID!
YOU PROMISED TO ATTEND CLASSES AND GET PASSING GRADES!!
BUT I CAN CUT AND STILL PASS!
THAT'S NOT THE POINT! YOU'RE SUPPOSED TO GO, PARTICIPATE, FOLLOW THE RULES!
WHY?
DON'T SAY IT, DON'T SAY IT...
BECAUSE I SAID SO!!
WELL, HE'S NEW AT THIS.

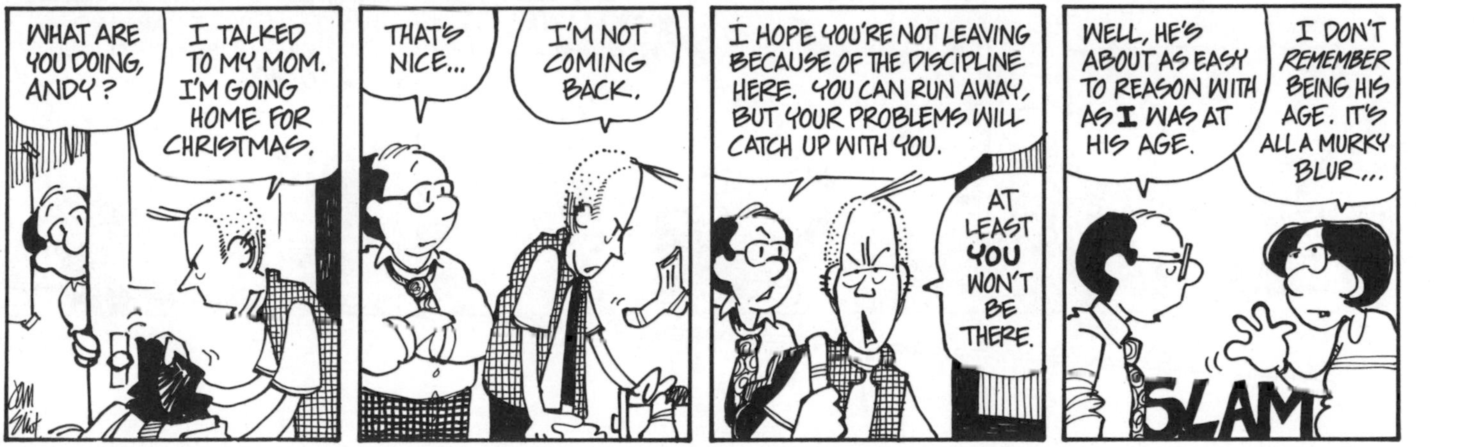
WHAT ARE YOU DOING, ANDY?
I TALKED TO MY MOM. I'M GOING HOME FOR CHRISTMAS.
THAT'S NICE...
I'M NOT COMING BACK.
I HOPE YOU'RE NOT LEAVING BECAUSE OF THE DISCIPLINE HERE. YOU CAN RUN AWAY, BUT YOUR PROBLEMS WILL CATCH UP WITH YOU.
AT LEAST YOU WON'T BE THERE.
WELL, HE'S ABOUT AS EASY TO REASON WITH AS I WAS AT HIS AGE.
I DON'T REMEMBER BEING HIS AGE. IT'S ALL A MURKY BLUR...
SLAM

Stone Soup

HEY *HOLLY*? WHERE'D YOU GET THAT **HAIRDO?** AT THE **BRIDE OF FRANKENSTEIN'S SALON??**
WHOA! THAT IS ONE **DUMPY** OUTFIT! YOU BEEN SHOPPIN' IN YOUR MAMA'S CLOSET AGAIN?!
YES, YOUNG LADY, YOUR PAPER IS DUE **TODAY.** IF IT'S *LATE*, YOU *FAIL*.
BUMP BUMP RUMBLE
JOSTLE
OUTTA MY WAY, DWEEB-BRAIN!
SLAM
HONESTLY, WHAT **HAPPENS** TO KIDS WHEN THEY HIT MIDDLE SCHOOL?

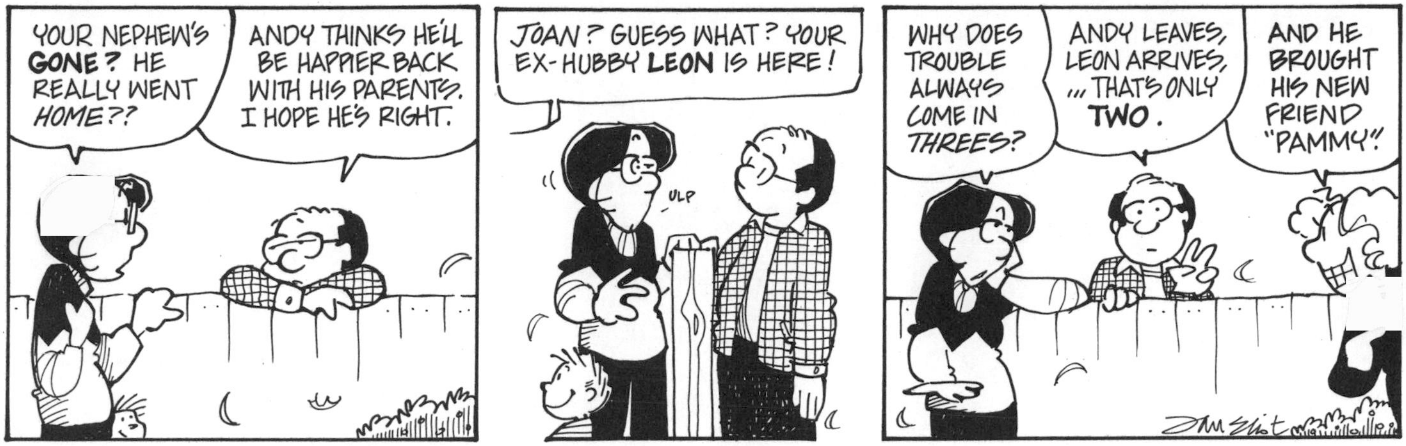
YOUR NEPHEW'S GONE? HE REALLY WENT HOME??
ANDY THINKS HE'LL BE HAPPIER BACK WITH HIS PARENTS. I HOPE HE'S RIGHT.
JOAN? GUESS WHAT? YOUR EX-HUBBY LEON IS HERE!
ULP
WHY DOES TROUBLE ALWAYS COME IN THREES?
ANDY LEAVES, LEON ARRIVES, ... THAT'S ONLY TWO.
AND HE BROUGHT HIS NEW FRIEND "PAMMY"!

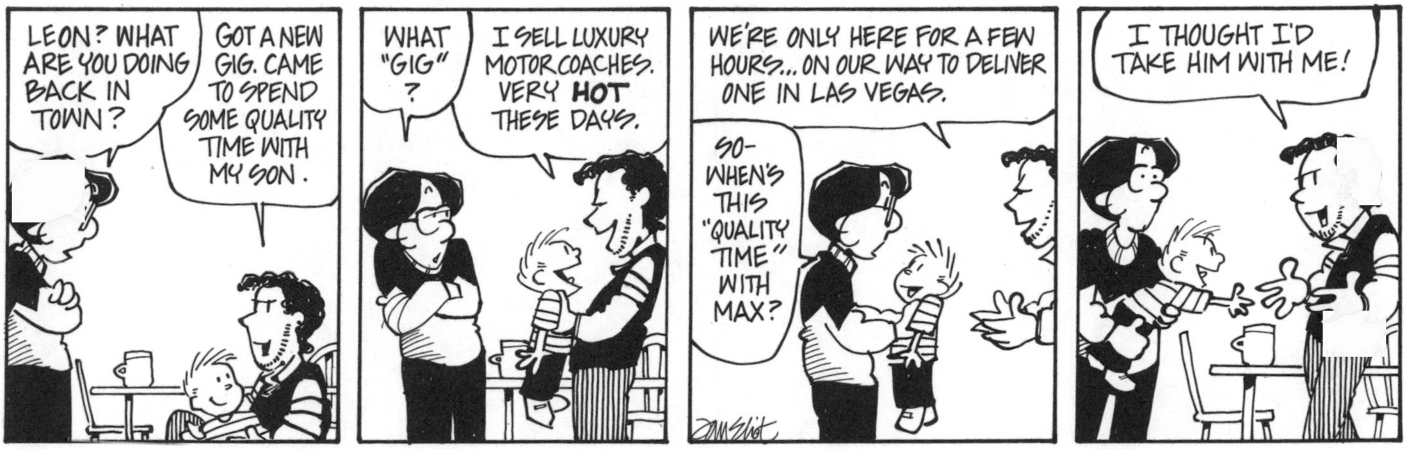
LEON? WHAT ARE YOU DOING BACK IN TOWN?
GOT A NEW GIG. CAME TO SPEND SOME QUALITY TIME WITH MY SON.
WHAT "GIG"?
I SELL LUXURY MOTOR COACHES. VERY HOT THESE DAYS.
WE'RE ONLY HERE FOR A FEW HOURS... ON OUR WAY TO DELIVER ONE IN LAS VEGAS.
SO-WHEN'S THIS "QUALITY TIME" WITH MAX?
I THOUGHT I'D TAKE HIM WITH ME!

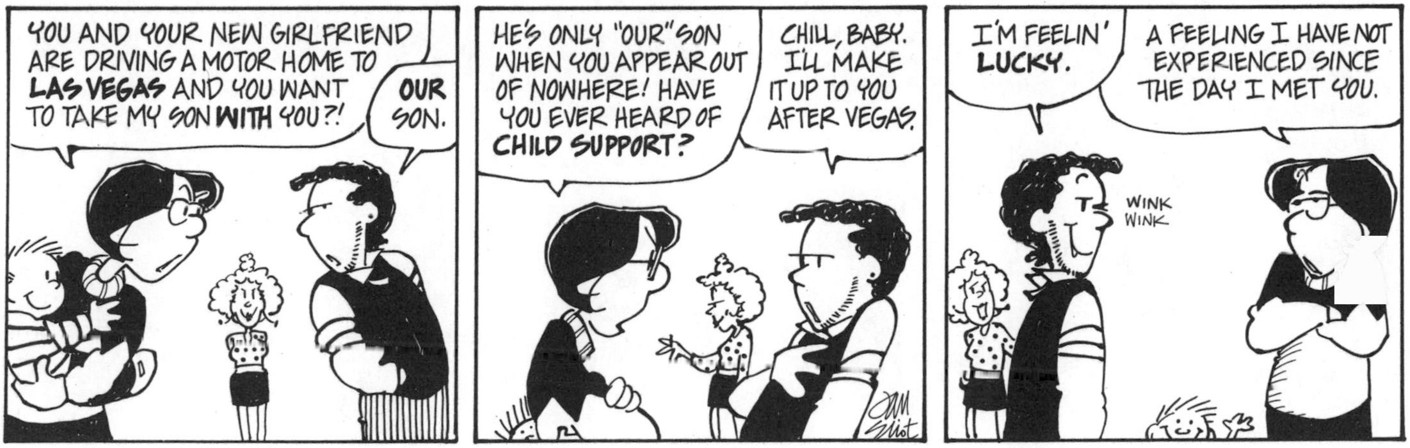
YOU AND YOUR NEW GIRLFRIEND ARE DRIVING A MOTOR HOME TO LAS VEGAS AND YOU WANT TO TAKE MY SON WITH YOU?!
OUR SON.
HE'S ONLY "OUR" SON WHEN YOU APPEAR OUT OF NOWHERE! HAVE YOU EVER HEARD OF CHILD SUPPORT?
CHILL, BABY. I'LL MAKE IT UP TO YOU AFTER VEGAS.
I'M FEELIN' LUCKY.
A FEELING I HAVE NOT EXPERIENCED SINCE THE DAY I MET YOU.
WINK WINK

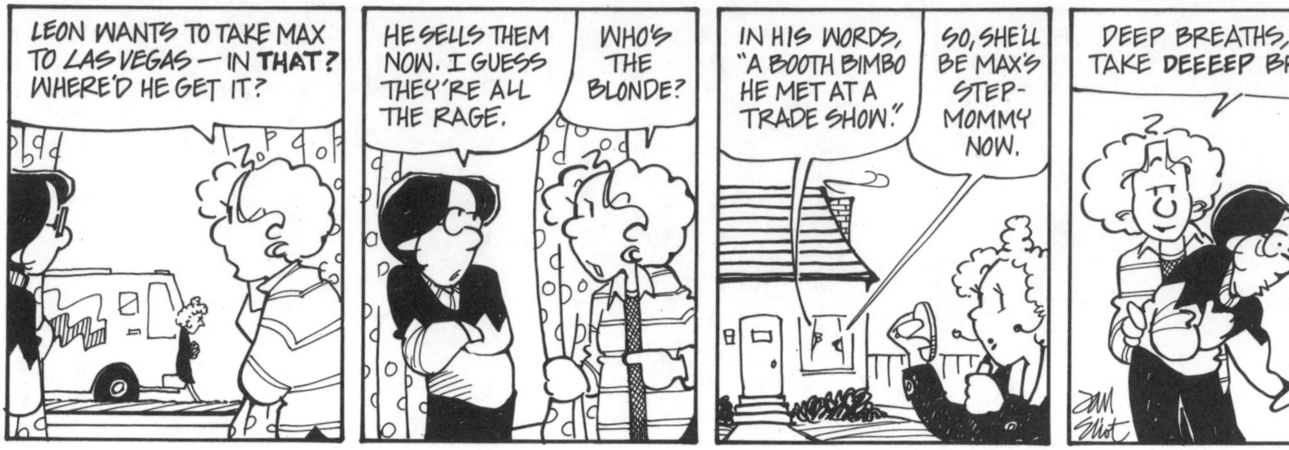
LEON WANTS TO TAKE MAX TO LAS VEGAS — IN THAT? WHERE'D HE GET IT?
HE SELLS THEM NOW. I GUESS THEY'RE ALL THE RAGE.
WHO'S THE BLONDE?
IN HIS WORDS, "A BOOTH BIMBO HE MET AT A TRADE SHOW."
SO, SHE'LL BE MAX'S STEP-MOMMY NOW.
DEEP BREATHS, JOAN. TAKE DEEEEP BREATHS.
GASP
CHOKE
S-S-STEP
M-M-MOMMY ??

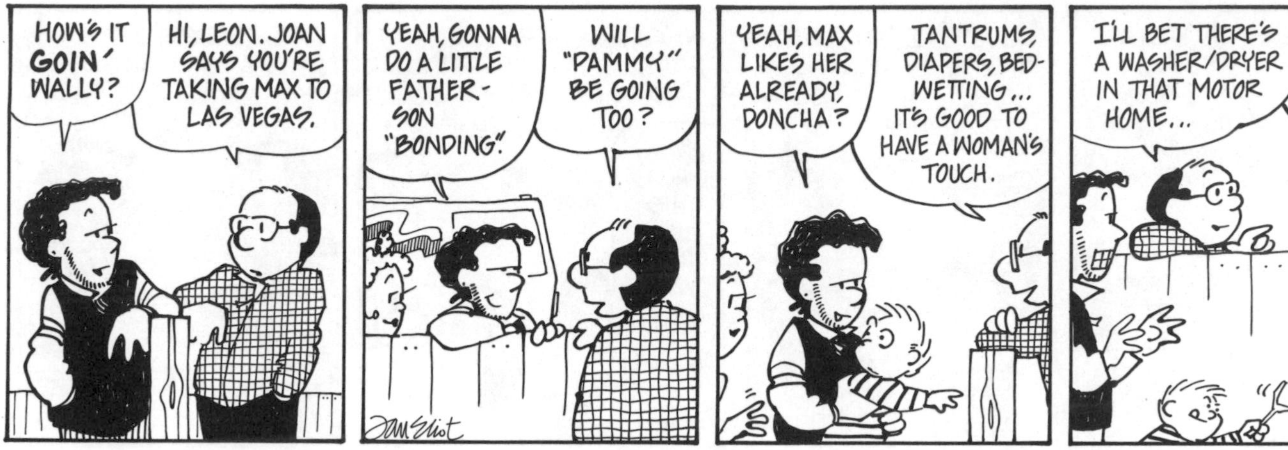
HOW'S IT GOIN' WALLY?
HI, LEON. JOAN SAYS YOU'RE TAKING MAX TO LAS VEGAS.
YEAH, GONNA DO A LITTLE FATHER-SON "BONDING."
WILL "PAMMY" BE GOING TOO?
YEAH, MAX LIKES HER ALREADY, DONCHA?
TANTRUMS, DIAPERS, BED-WETTING... IT'S GOOD TO HAVE A WOMAN'S TOUCH.
I'LL BET THERE'S A WASHER/DRYER IN THAT MOTOR HOME...
LEON?

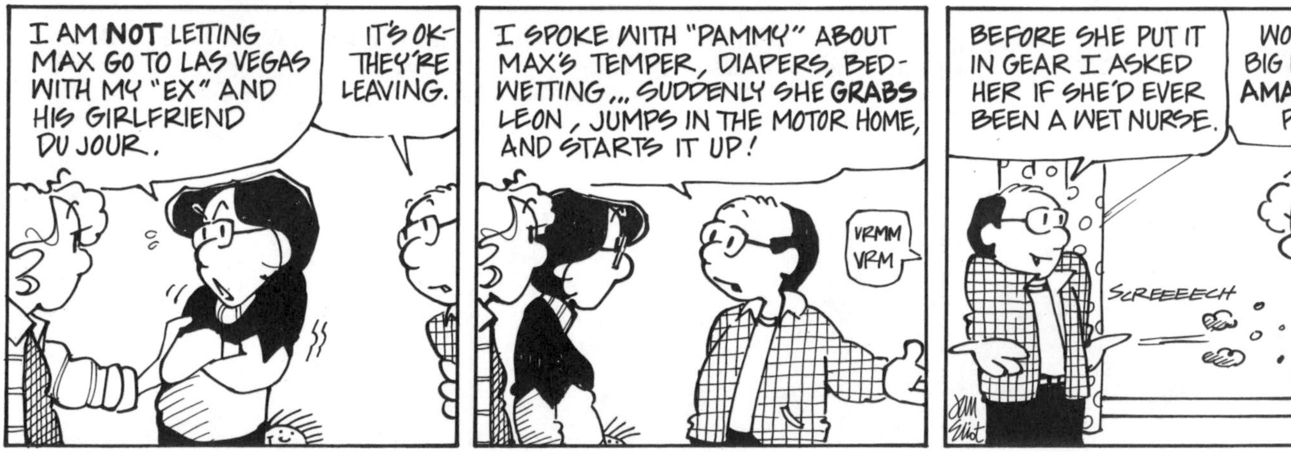
I AM NOT LETTING MAX GO TO LAS VEGAS WITH MY "EX" AND HIS GIRLFRIEND DU JOUR.
IT'S OK-THEY'RE LEAVING.
I SPOKE WITH "PAMMY" ABOUT MAX'S TEMPER, DIAPERS, BED-WETTING... SUDDENLY SHE GRABS LEON, JUMPS IN THE MOTOR HOME, AND STARTS IT UP!
VRMM VRM
BEFORE SHE PUT IT IN GEAR I ASKED HER IF SHE'D EVER BEEN A WET NURSE.
WOW. THOSE BIG RIGS ARE AMAZINGLY PEPPY.
SCREEEECH

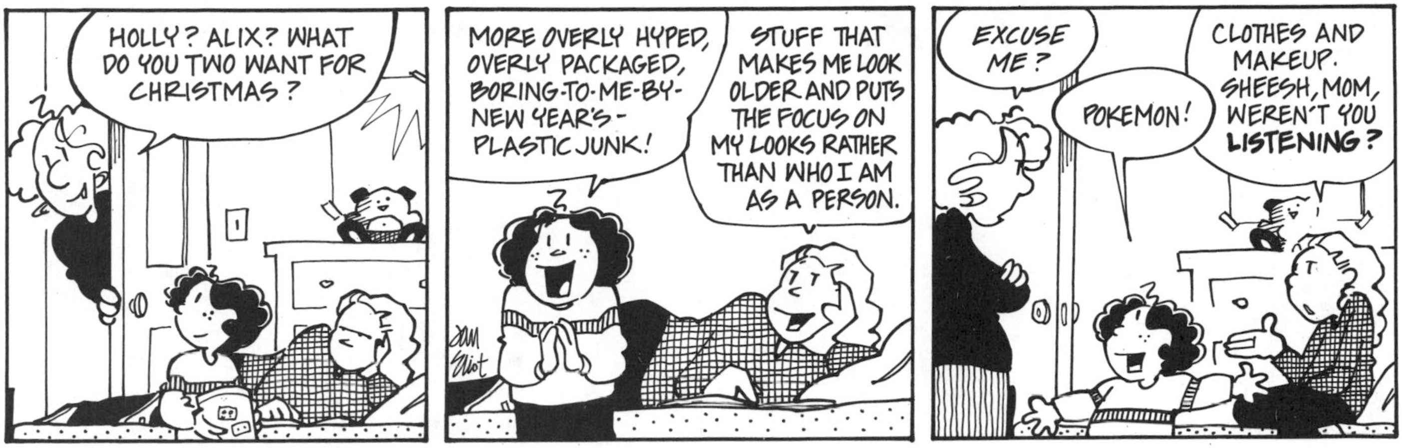
HOLLY? ALIX? WHAT DO YOU TWO WANT FOR CHRISTMAS?
MORE OVERLY HYPED, OVERLY PACKAGED, BORING-TO-ME-BY-NEW YEAR'S-PLASTIC JUNK!
STUFF THAT MAKES ME LOOK OLDER AND PUTS THE FOCUS ON MY LOOKS RATHER THAN WHO I AM AS A PERSON.
EXCUSE ME?
POKEMON!
CLOTHES AND MAKEUP. SHEESH, MOM, WEREN'T YOU **LISTENING?**

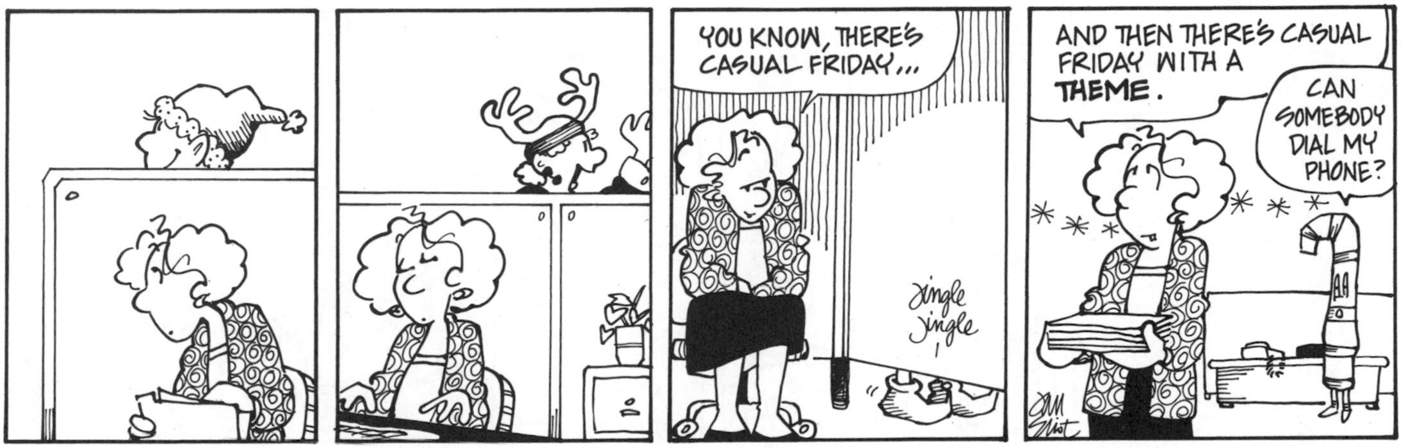
YOU KNOW, THERE'S CASUAL FRIDAY...
jingle jingle
AND THEN THERE'S CASUAL FRIDAY WITH A **THEME**.
CAN SOMEBODY DIAL MY PHONE?

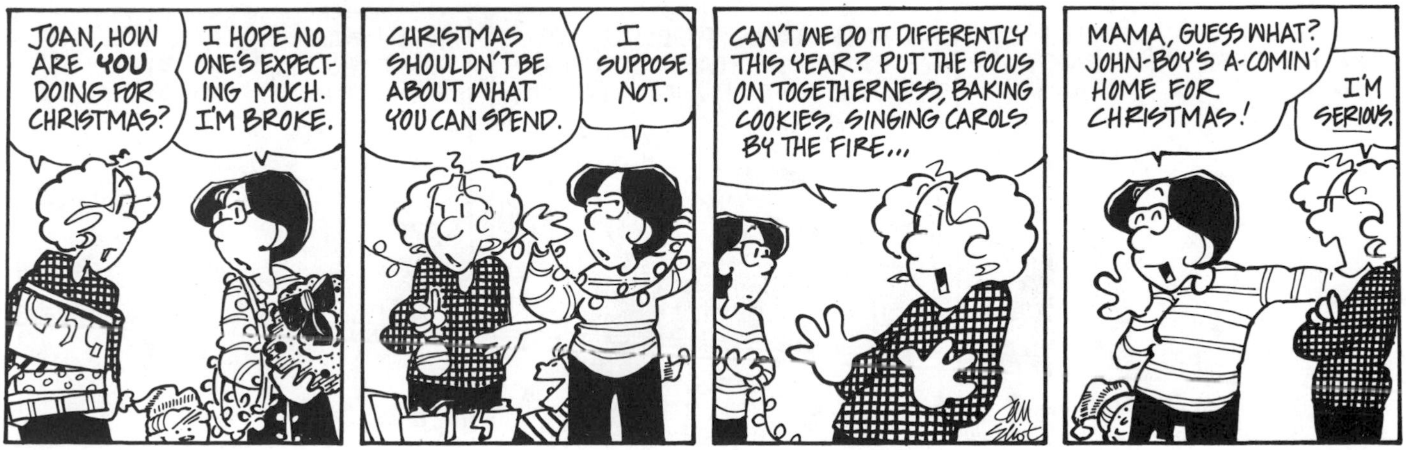
JOAN, HOW ARE **YOU** DOING FOR CHRISTMAS?
I HOPE NO ONE'S EXPECTING MUCH. I'M BROKE.
CHRISTMAS SHOULDN'T BE ABOUT WHAT YOU CAN SPEND.
I SUPPOSE NOT.
CAN'T WE DO IT DIFFERENTLY THIS YEAR? PUT THE FOCUS ON TOGETHERNESS, BAKING COOKIES, SINGING CAROLS BY THE FIRE...
MAMA, GUESS WHAT? JOHN-BOY'S A-COMIN' HOME FOR CHRISTMAS!
I'M SERIOUS.

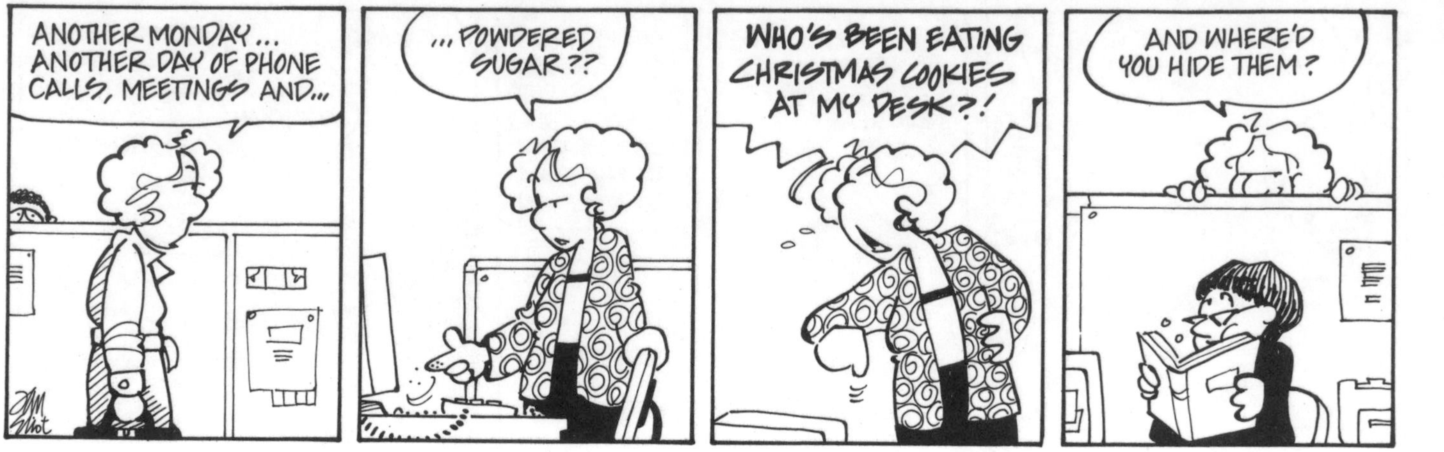
ANOTHER MONDAY... ANOTHER DAY OF PHONE CALLS, MEETINGS AND...
...POWDERED SUGAR??
WHO'S BEEN EATING CHRISTMAS COOKIES AT MY DESK?!
AND WHERE'D YOU HIDE THEM?

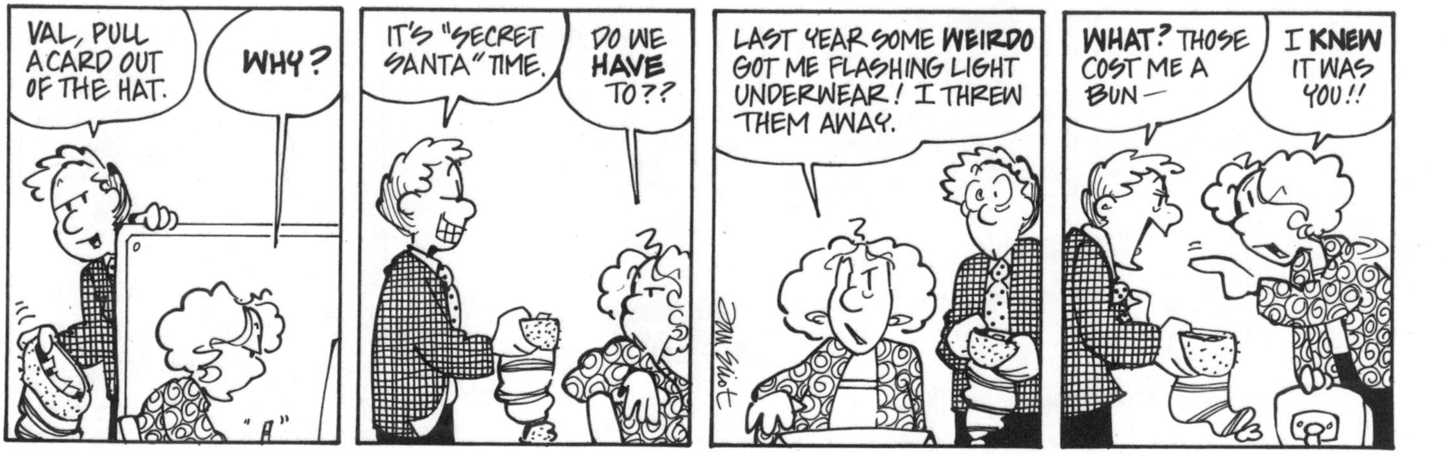
VAL, PULL A CARD OUT OF THE HAT.
WHY?
IT'S "SECRET SANTA" TIME.
DO WE HAVE TO??
LAST YEAR SOME WEIRDO GOT ME FLASHING LIGHT UNDERWEAR! I THREW THEM AWAY.
WHAT? THOSE COST ME A BUN—
I KNEW IT WAS YOU!!

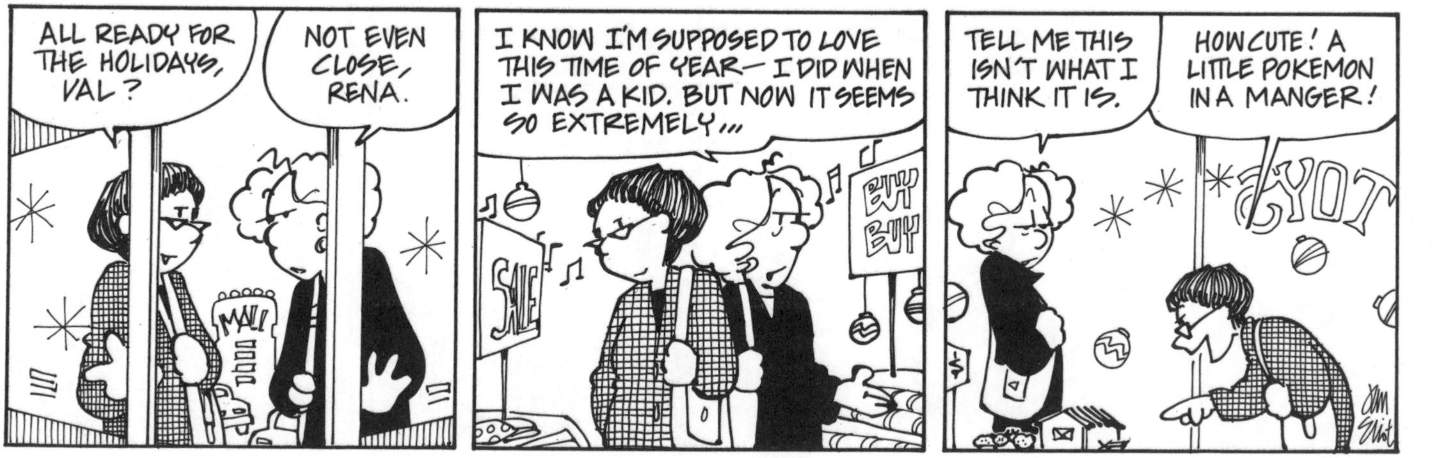
ALL READY FOR THE HOLIDAYS, VAL?
NOT EVEN CLOSE, RENA.
MALL
I KNOW I'M SUPPOSED TO LOVE THIS TIME OF YEAR— I DID WHEN I WAS A KID. BUT NOW IT SEEMS SO EXTREMELY...
SALE
BUY BUY
TELL ME THIS ISN'T WHAT I THINK IT IS.
HOW CUTE! A LITTLE POKEMON IN A MANGER!
TOYS

Stone Soup

"RATS!" "WHAT?"

IT **SNOWED** LAST NIGHT! THE ROADS AND SCHOOLS ARE CLOSED! WE'RE **STUCK** HERE.

BUT I HAVE A **MILLION** ERRANDS TO RUN !!

AND I HAVE **STACKS** OF WORK PILING UP AT THE OFFICE...

NOW WHAT DO WE DO??

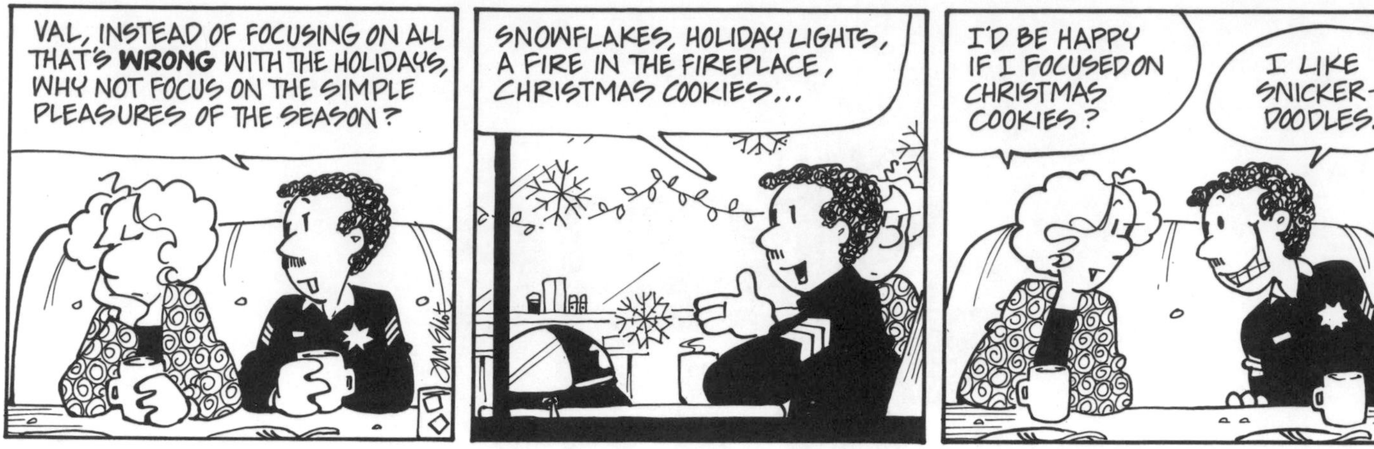
VAL, INSTEAD OF FOCUSING ON ALL THAT'S **WRONG** WITH THE HOLIDAYS, WHY NOT FOCUS ON THE SIMPLE PLEASURES OF THE SEASON?
SNOWFLAKES, HOLIDAY LIGHTS, A FIRE IN THE FIREPLACE, CHRISTMAS COOKIES...
I'D BE HAPPY IF I FOCUSED ON CHRISTMAS COOKIES?
I LIKE SNICKER-DOODLES.

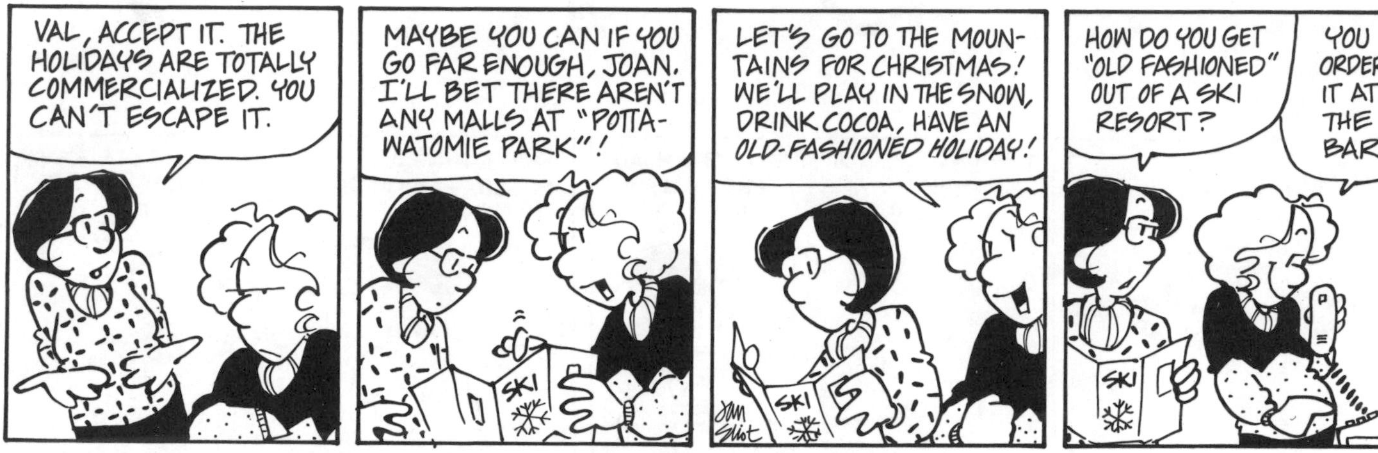
VAL, ACCEPT IT. THE HOLIDAYS ARE TOTALLY COMMERCIALIZED. YOU CAN'T ESCAPE IT.
MAYBE YOU CAN IF YOU GO FAR ENOUGH, JOAN. I'LL BET THERE AREN'T ANY MALLS AT "POTTA-WATOMIE PARK"!
LET'S GO TO THE MOUN-TAINS FOR CHRISTMAS! WE'LL PLAY IN THE SNOW, DRINK COCOA, HAVE AN *OLD-FASHIONED HOLIDAY!*
HOW DO YOU GET "OLD FASHIONED" OUT OF A SKI RESORT?
YOU ORDER IT AT THE BAR.

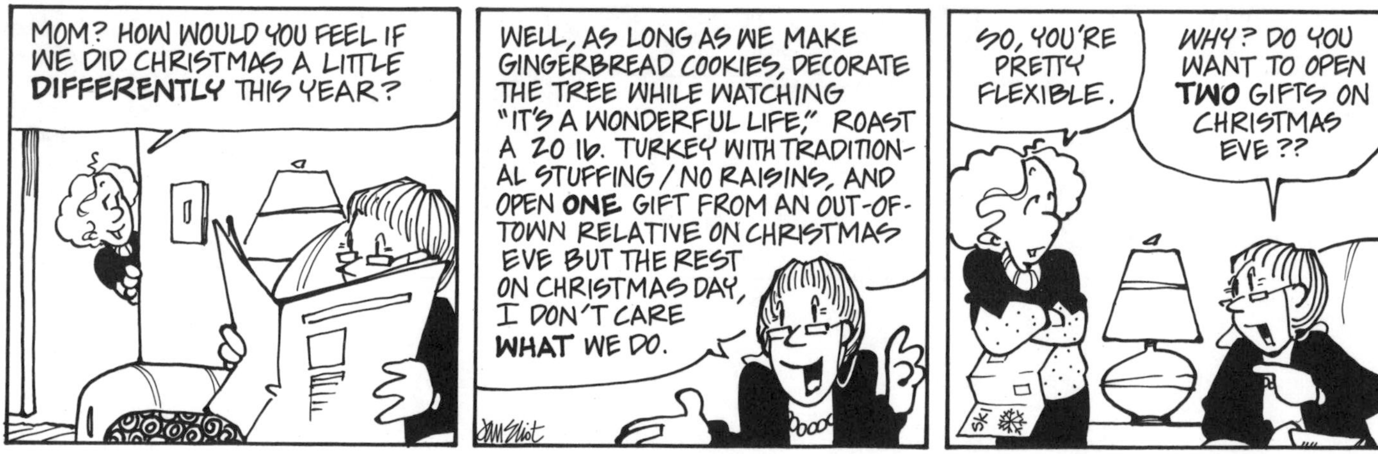
MOM? HOW WOULD YOU FEEL IF WE DID CHRISTMAS A LITTLE **DIFFERENTLY** THIS YEAR?
WELL, AS LONG AS WE MAKE GINGERBREAD COOKIES, DECORATE THE TREE WHILE WATCHING "IT'S A WONDERFUL LIFE," ROAST A 20 lb. TURKEY WITH TRADITION-AL STUFFING / NO RAISINS, AND OPEN **ONE** GIFT FROM AN OUT-OF-TOWN RELATIVE ON CHRISTMAS EVE BUT THE REST ON CHRISTMAS DAY, I DON'T CARE **WHAT** WE DO.
SO, YOU'RE PRETTY FLEXIBLE.
WHY? DO YOU WANT TO OPEN **TWO** GIFTS ON CHRISTMAS EVE??

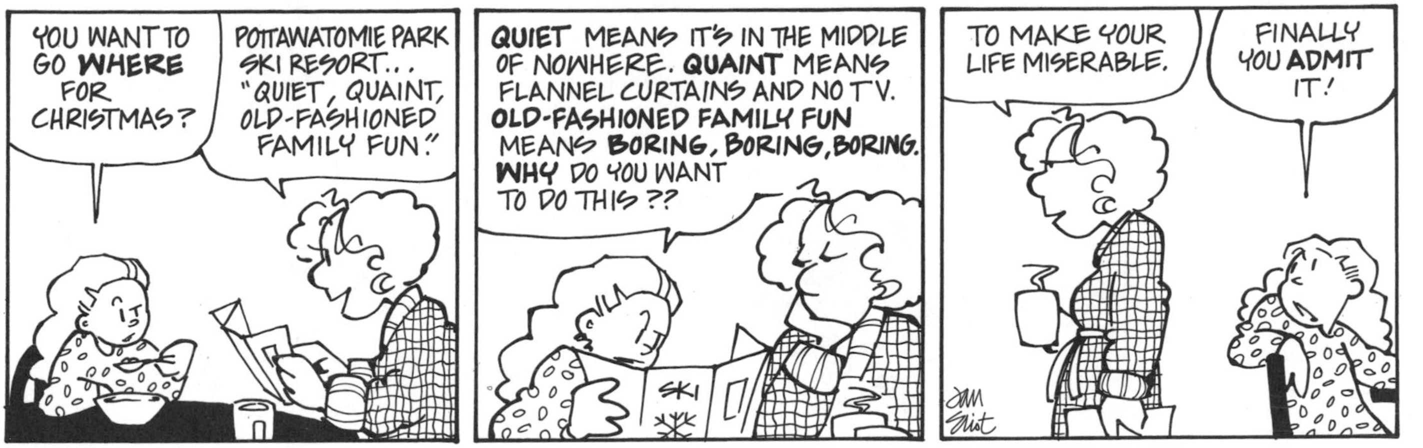
YOU WANT TO GO **WHERE** FOR CHRISTMAS?
POTTAWATOMIE PARK SKI RESORT... "QUIET, QUAINT, OLD-FASHIONED FAMILY FUN."
QUIET MEANS IT'S IN THE MIDDLE OF NOWHERE. **QUAINT** MEANS FLANNEL CURTAINS AND NO T.V. **OLD-FASHIONED FAMILY FUN** MEANS **BORING, BORING, BORING. WHY** DO YOU WANT TO DO THIS??
SKI
TO MAKE YOUR LIFE MISERABLE.
FINALLY YOU **ADMIT** IT!
JAN Eliot

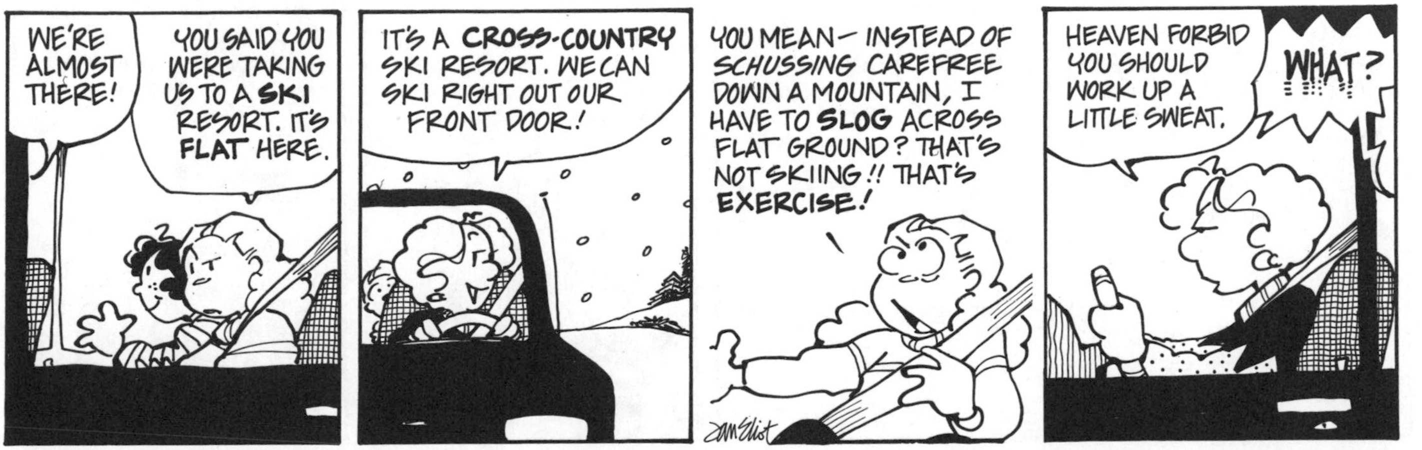
WE'RE ALMOST THERE!
YOU SAID YOU WERE TAKING US TO A **SKI** RESORT. IT'S **FLAT** HERE.
IT'S A **CROSS-COUNTRY** SKI RESORT. WE CAN SKI RIGHT OUT OUR FRONT DOOR!
YOU MEAN— INSTEAD OF *SCHUSSING* CAREFREE DOWN A MOUNTAIN, I HAVE TO **SLOG** ACROSS FLAT GROUND? THAT'S NOT SKIING!! THAT'S **EXERCISE**!
JAN Eliot
HEAVEN FORBID YOU SHOULD WORK UP A LITTLE SWEAT.
WHAT?

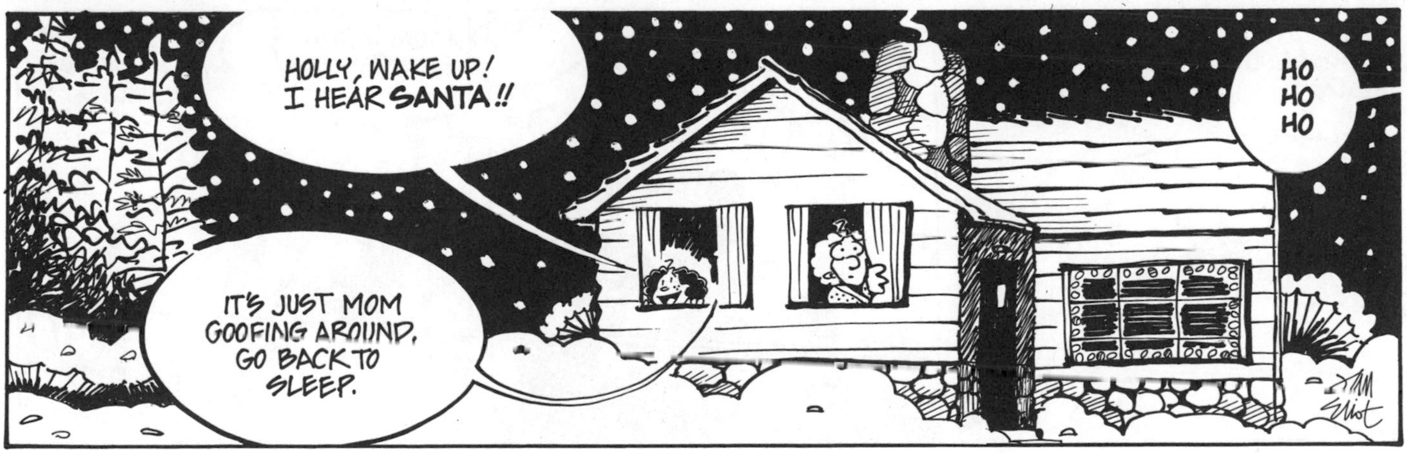
HOLLY, WAKE UP! I HEAR **SANTA**!!
HO HO HO
IT'S JUST MOM GOOFING AROUND. GO BACK TO SLEEP.
JAN Eliot

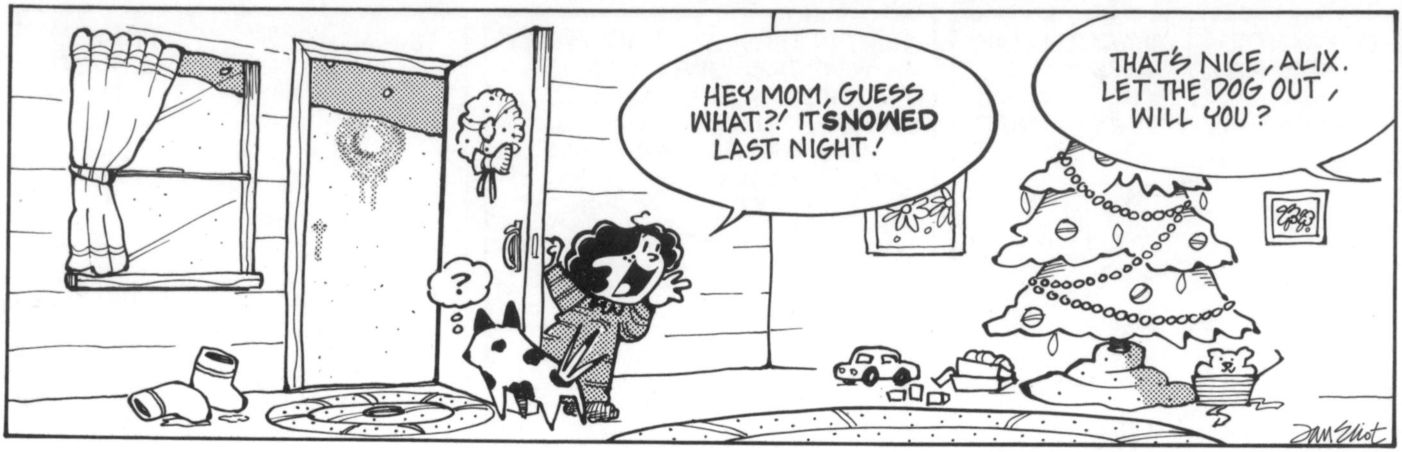
HEY MOM, GUESS WHAT?! IT SNOWED LAST NIGHT!
THAT'S NICE, ALIX. LET THE DOG OUT, WILL YOU?

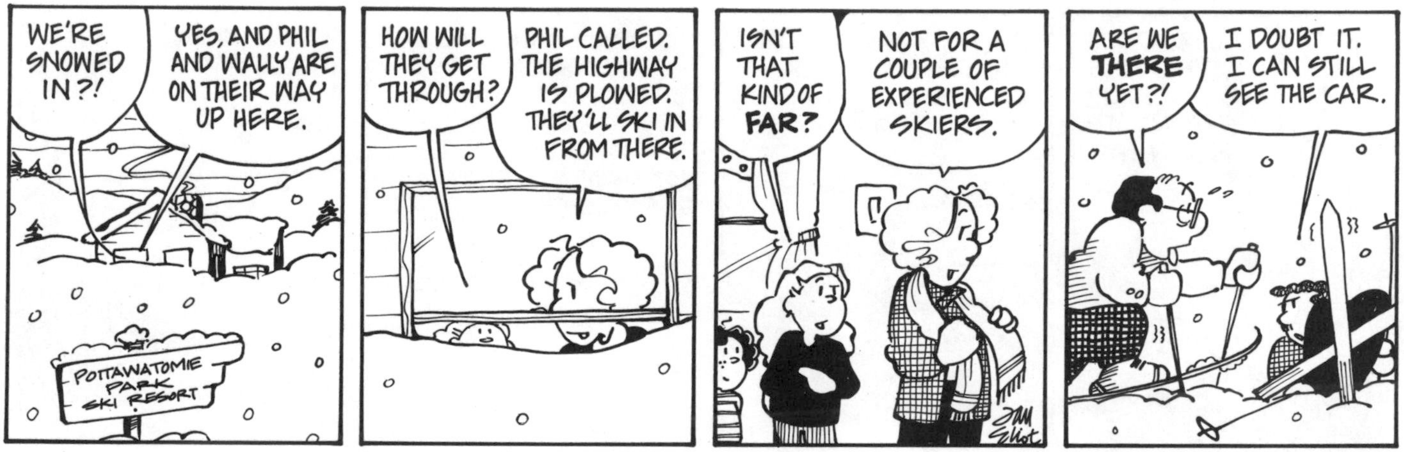
WE'RE SNOWED IN?!
YES, AND PHIL AND WALLY ARE ON THEIR WAY UP HERE.
POTTAWATOMIE PARK SKI RESORT
HOW WILL THEY GET THROUGH?
PHIL CALLED. THE HIGHWAY IS PLOWED. THEY'LL SKI IN FROM THERE.
ISN'T THAT KIND OF FAR?
NOT FOR A COUPLE OF EXPERIENCED SKIERS.
ARE WE THERE YET?!
I DOUBT IT. I CAN STILL SEE THE CAR.

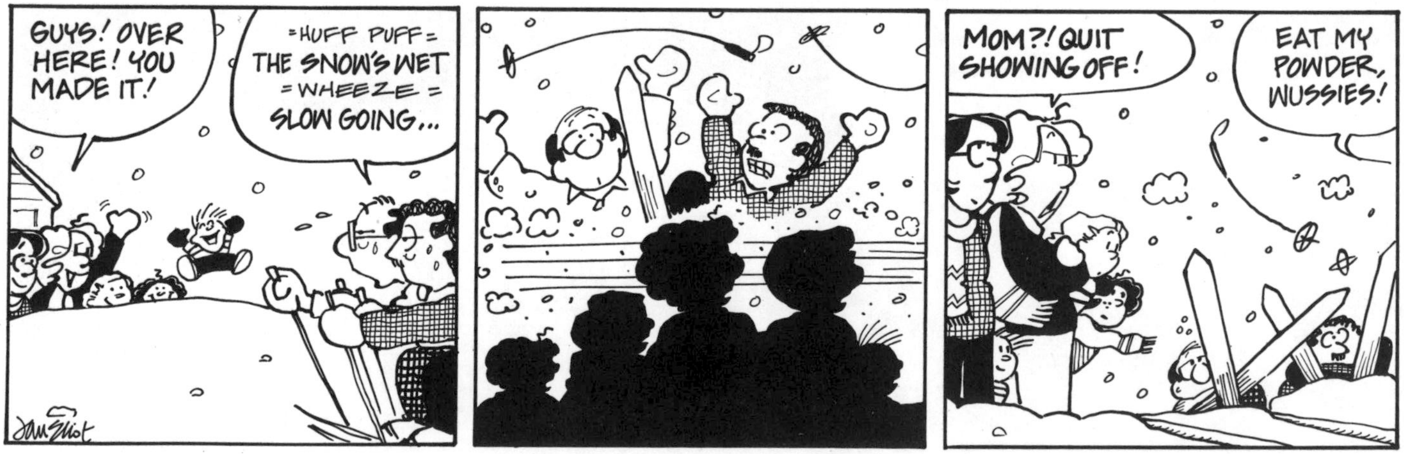
GUYS! OVER HERE! YOU MADE IT!
=HUFF PUFF= THE SNOW'S WET =WHEEZE= SLOW GOING...
MOM?! QUIT SHOWING OFF!
EAT MY POWDER, WUSSIES!

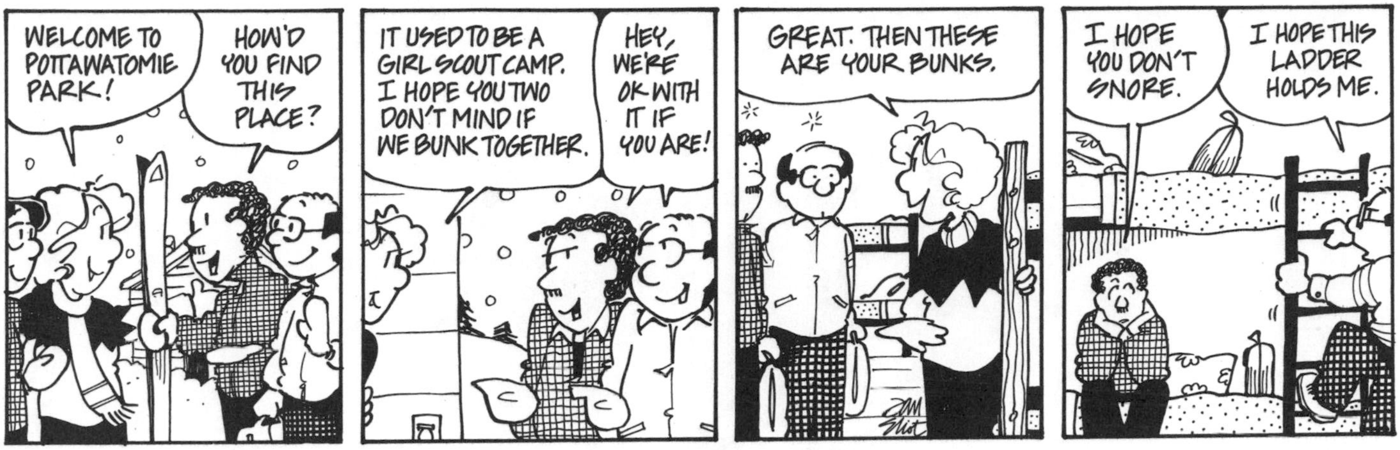
WELCOME TO POTTAWATOMIE PARK!
HOW'D YOU FIND THIS PLACE?
IT USED TO BE A GIRL SCOUT CAMP. I HOPE YOU TWO DON'T MIND IF WE BUNK TOGETHER.
HEY, WE'RE OK WITH IT IF YOU ARE!
GREAT. THEN THESE ARE YOUR BUNKS.
I HOPE YOU DON'T SNORE.
I HOPE THIS LADDER HOLDS ME.

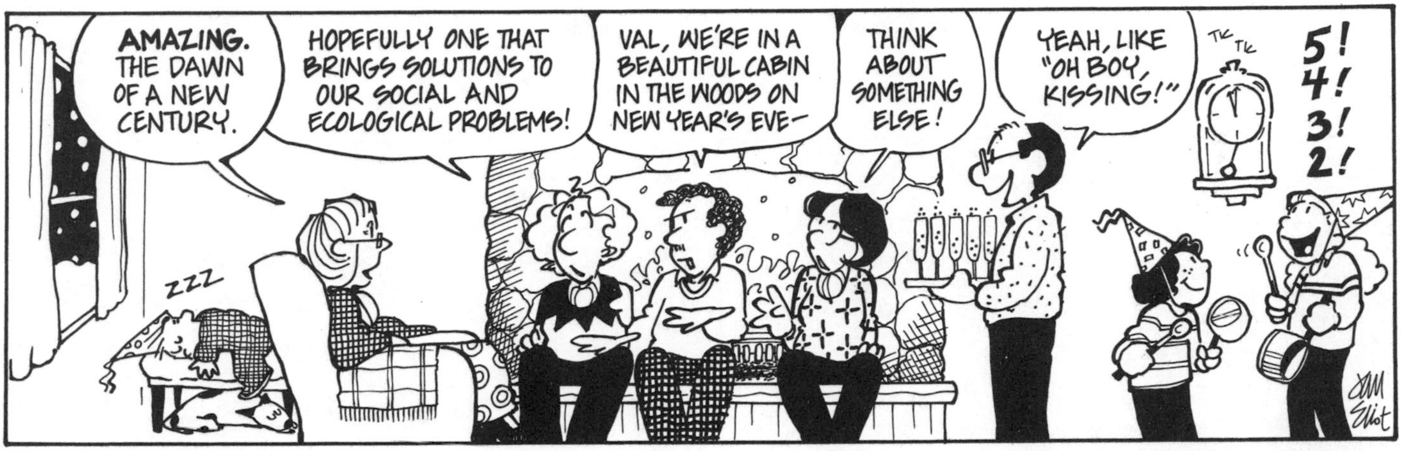
AMAZING. THE DAWN OF A NEW CENTURY.
HOPEFULLY ONE THAT BRINGS SOLUTIONS TO OUR SOCIAL AND ECOLOGICAL PROBLEMS!
VAL, WE'RE IN A BEAUTIFUL CABIN IN THE WOODS ON NEW YEAR'S EVE-
THINK ABOUT SOMETHING ELSE!
YEAH, LIKE "OH BOY, KISSING!"
ZZZ
TK TK
5! 4! 3! 2!

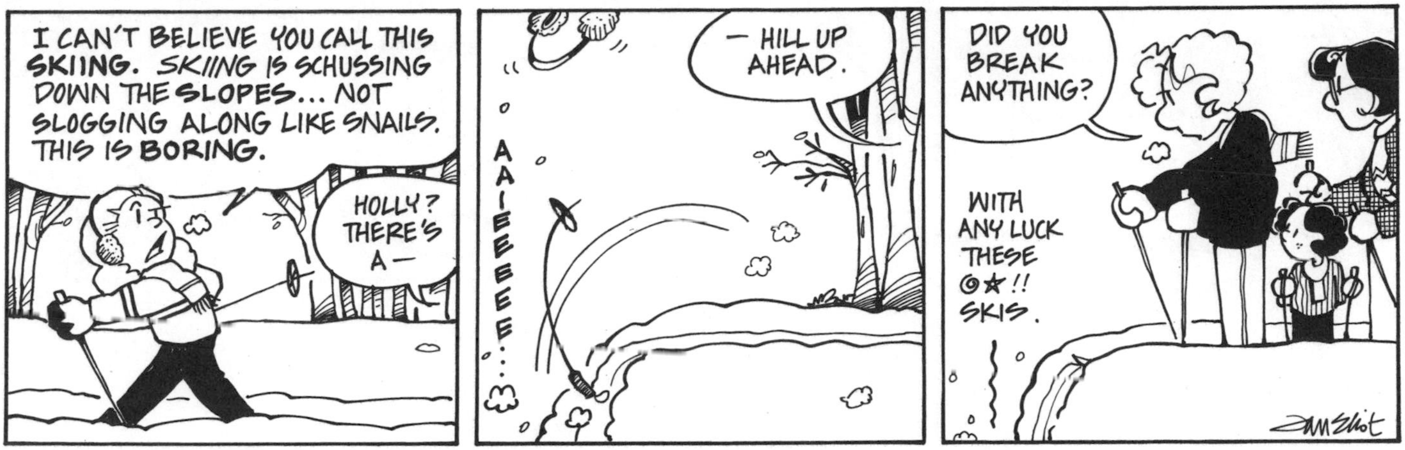
I CAN'T BELIEVE YOU CALL THIS SKIING. SKIING IS SCHUSSING DOWN THE SLOPES... NOT SLOGGING ALONG LIKE SNAILS. THIS IS BORING.
HOLLY? THERE'S A—
— HILL UP AHEAD.
AAIEEEEE...
DID YOU BREAK ANYTHING?
WITH ANY LUCK THESE ◎★!! SKIS.

Stone Soup

ZZZ
DING DONG
RRR
BARK
BARK
BARK
KONK
DING DONG
ALL THAT DOG DOES IS **SLEEP**.

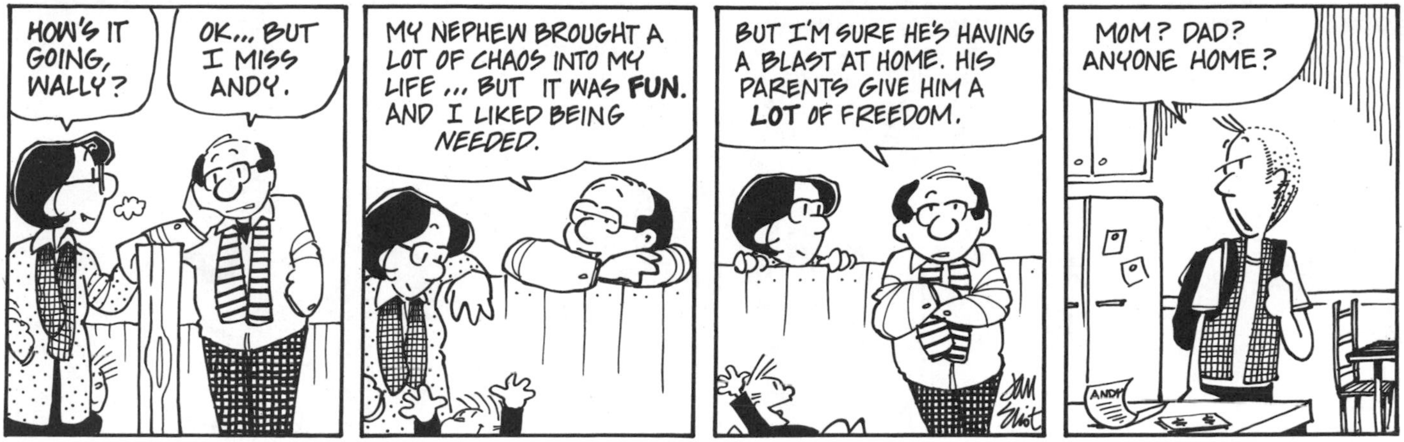
HOW'S IT GOING, WALLY?
OK... BUT I MISS ANDY.
MY NEPHEW BROUGHT A LOT OF CHAOS INTO MY LIFE ... BUT IT WAS **FUN.** AND I LIKED BEING *NEEDED.*
BUT I'M SURE HE'S HAVING A BLAST AT HOME. HIS PARENTS GIVE HIM A **LOT** OF FREEDOM.
MOM? DAD? ANYONE HOME?

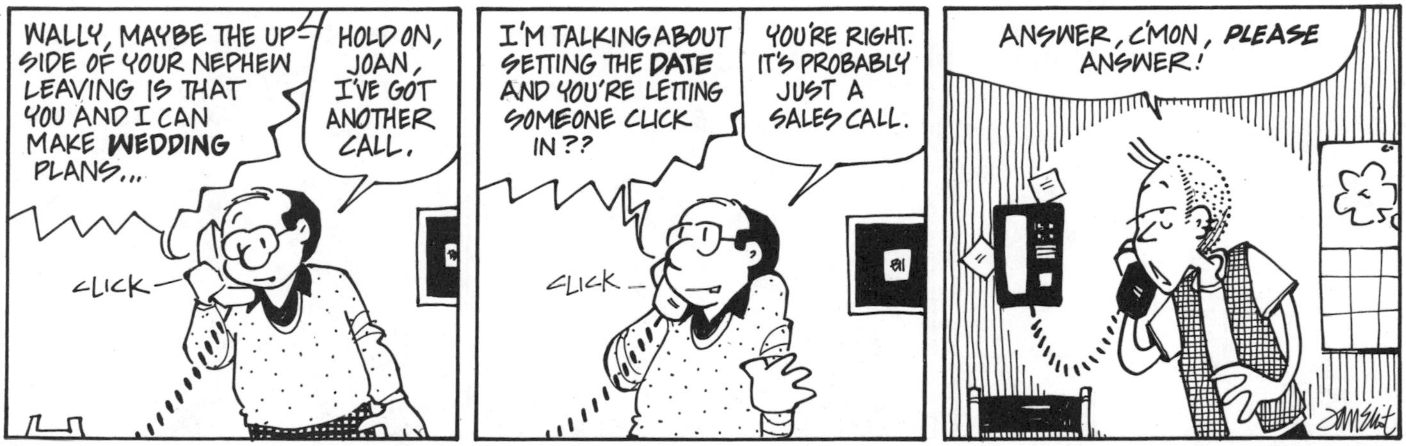
WALLY, MAYBE THE UPSIDE OF YOUR NEPHEW LEAVING IS THAT YOU AND I CAN MAKE **WEDDING** PLANS...
HOLD ON, JOAN, I'VE GOT ANOTHER CALL.
CLICK
I'M TALKING ABOUT SETTING THE **DATE** AND YOU'RE LETTING SOMEONE CLICK IN??
YOU'RE RIGHT. IT'S PROBABLY JUST A SALES CALL.
CLICK
ANSWER, C'MON, ***PLEASE*** ANSWER!

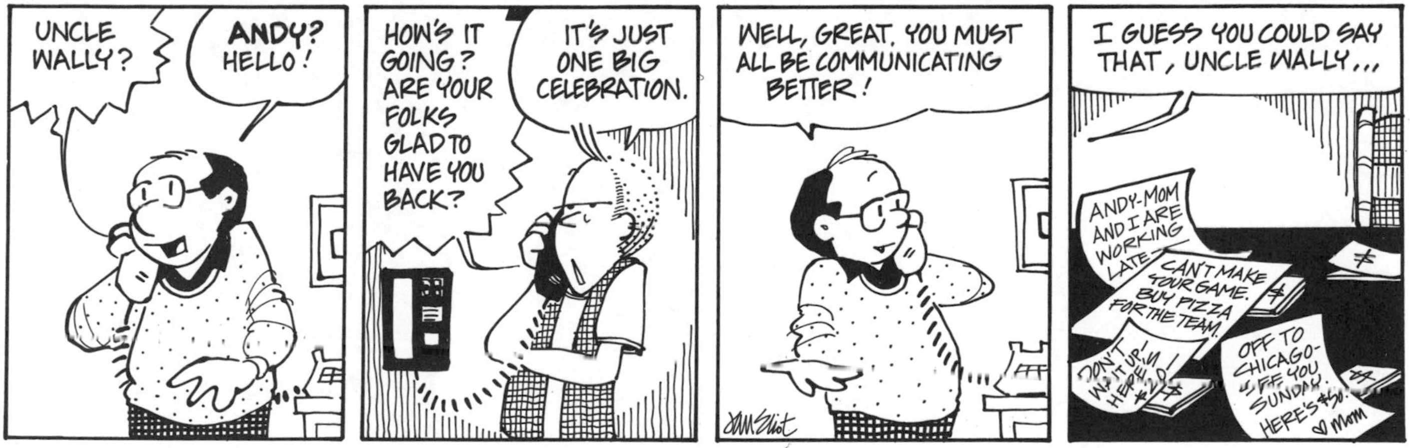
UNCLE WALLY?
ANDY? HELLO!
HOW'S IT GOING? ARE YOUR FOLKS GLAD TO HAVE YOU BACK?
IT'S JUST ONE BIG CELEBRATION.
WELL, GREAT. YOU MUST ALL BE COMMUNICATING BETTER!
I GUESS YOU COULD SAY THAT, UNCLE WALLY...
ANDY-MOM AND I ARE WORKING LATE.
CAN'T MAKE YOUR GAME. BUY PIZZA FOR THE TEAM.
DON'T
OFF TO CHICAGO-
SUNDAY.
HERE'S $50.
♡ MOM

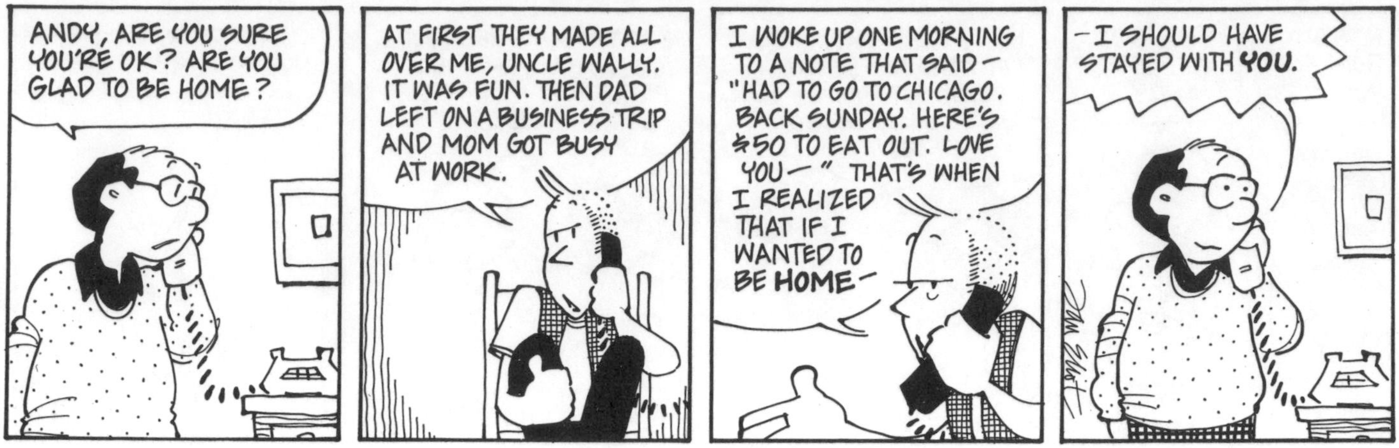
ANDY, ARE YOU SURE YOU'RE OK? ARE YOU GLAD TO BE HOME?
AT FIRST THEY MADE ALL OVER ME, UNCLE WALLY. IT WAS FUN. THEN DAD LEFT ON A BUSINESS TRIP AND MOM GOT BUSY AT WORK.
I WOKE UP ONE MORNING TO A NOTE THAT SAID— "HAD TO GO TO CHICAGO. BACK SUNDAY. HERE'S $50 TO EAT OUT. LOVE YOU—" THAT'S WHEN I REALIZED THAT IF I WANTED TO BE HOME—
—I SHOULD HAVE STAYED WITH YOU.

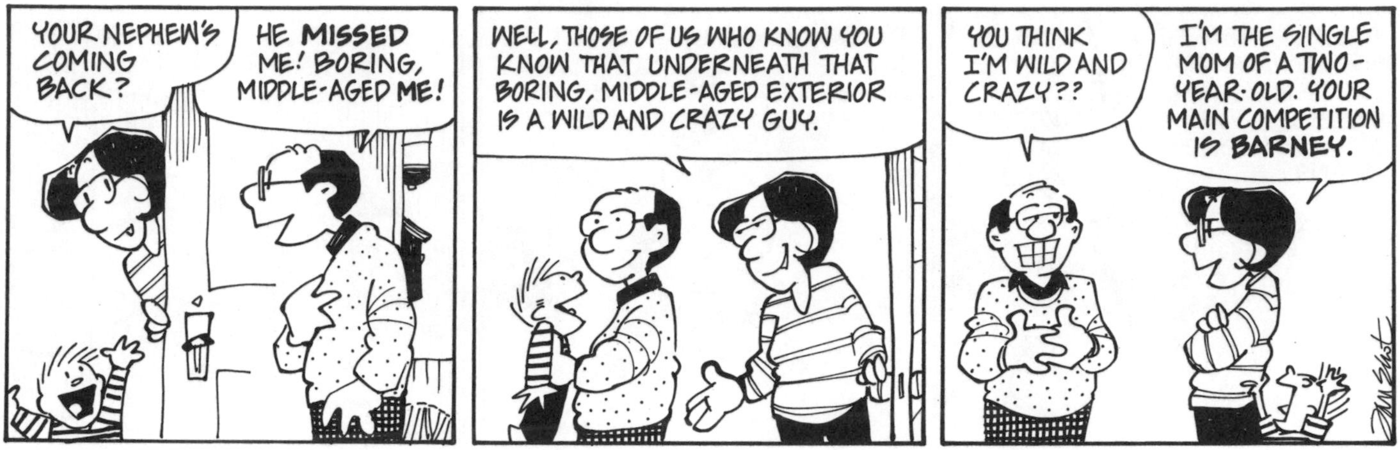
YOUR NEPHEW'S COMING BACK?
HE MISSED ME! BORING, MIDDLE-AGED ME!
WELL, THOSE OF US WHO KNOW YOU KNOW THAT UNDERNEATH THAT BORING, MIDDLE-AGED EXTERIOR IS A WILD AND CRAZY GUY.
YOU THINK I'M WILD AND CRAZY??
I'M THE SINGLE MOM OF A TWO-YEAR-OLD. YOUR MAIN COMPETITION IS BARNEY.

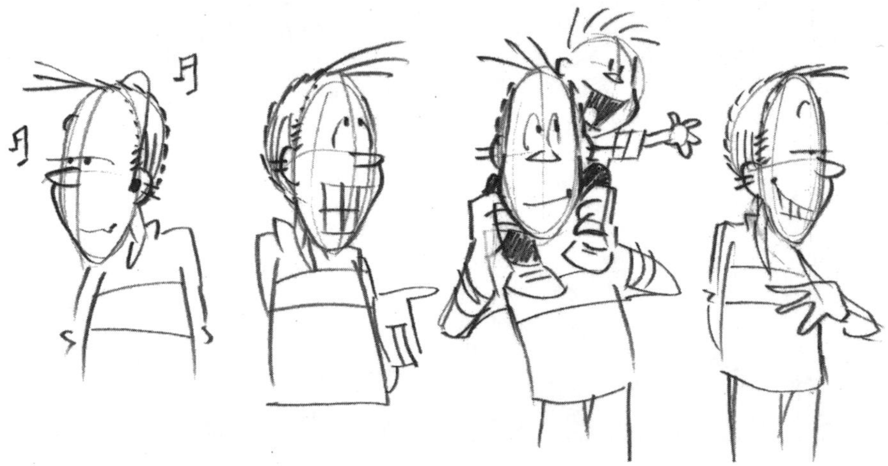

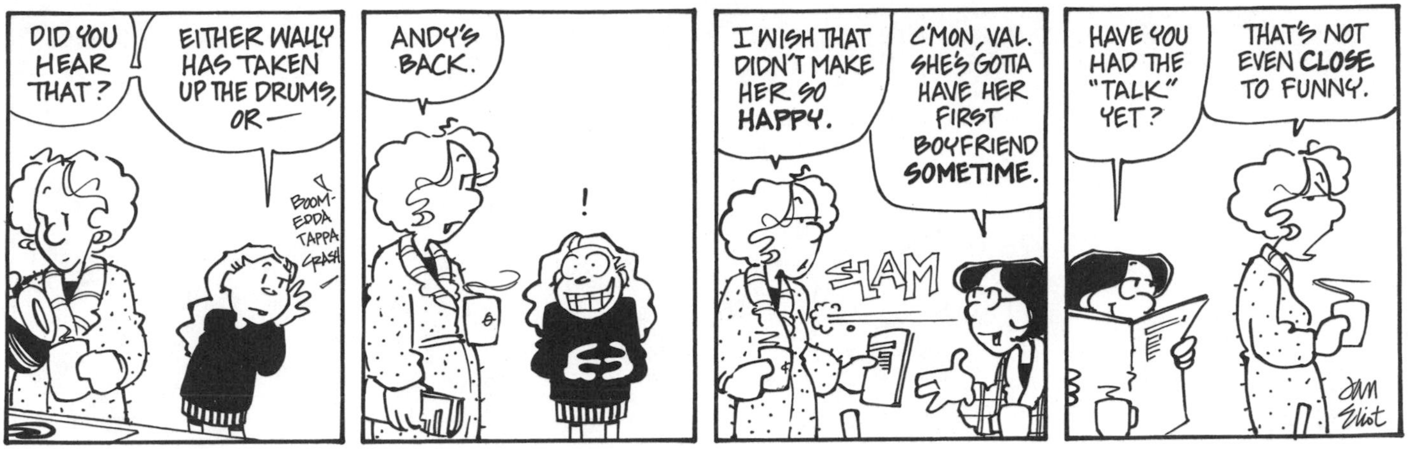
DID YOU HEAR THAT?
EITHER WALLY HAS TAKEN UP THE DRUMS, OR—
BOOM-EDDA TAPPA CRASH
ANDY'S BACK.
!
I WISH THAT DIDN'T MAKE HER SO **HAPPY**.
SLAM
C'MON, VAL. SHE'S GOTTA HAVE HER FIRST BOYFRIEND **SOMETIME**.
HAVE YOU HAD THE "TALK" YET?
THAT'S NOT EVEN **CLOSE** TO FUNNY.
JAN Eliot

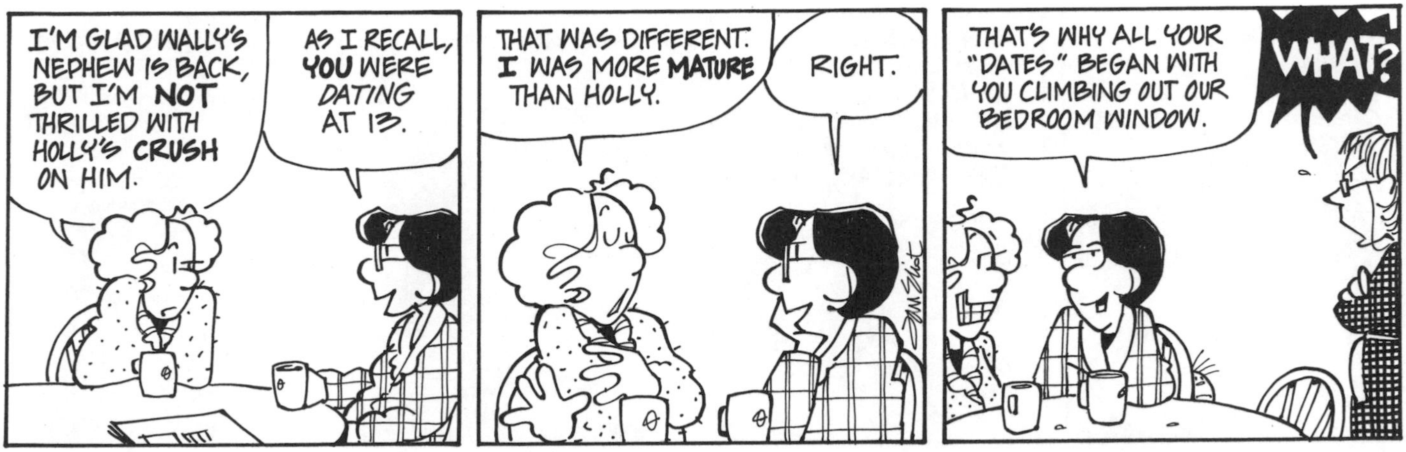
I'M GLAD WALLY'S NEPHEW IS BACK, BUT I'M **NOT** THRILLED WITH HOLLY'S **CRUSH** ON HIM.
AS I RECALL, **YOU** WERE *DATING* AT 13.
THAT WAS DIFFERENT. **I** WAS MORE **MATURE** THAN HOLLY.
RIGHT.
JAN Eliot
THAT'S WHY ALL YOUR "DATES" BEGAN WITH YOU CLIMBING OUT OUR BEDROOM WINDOW.
WHAT?

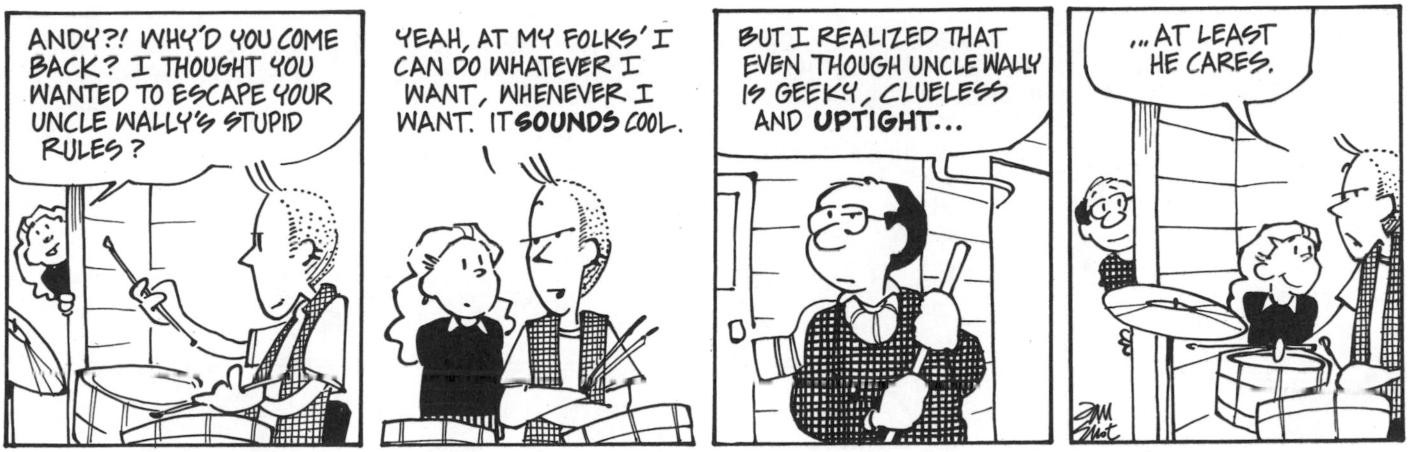
ANDY?! WHY'D YOU COME BACK? I THOUGHT YOU WANTED TO ESCAPE YOUR UNCLE WALLY'S STUPID RULES?
YEAH, AT MY FOLKS' I CAN DO WHATEVER I WANT, WHENEVER I WANT. IT **SOUNDS** COOL.
BUT I REALIZED THAT EVEN THOUGH UNCLE WALLY IS GEEKY, CLUELESS AND **UPTIGHT**...
...AT LEAST HE CARES.
JAN Eliot

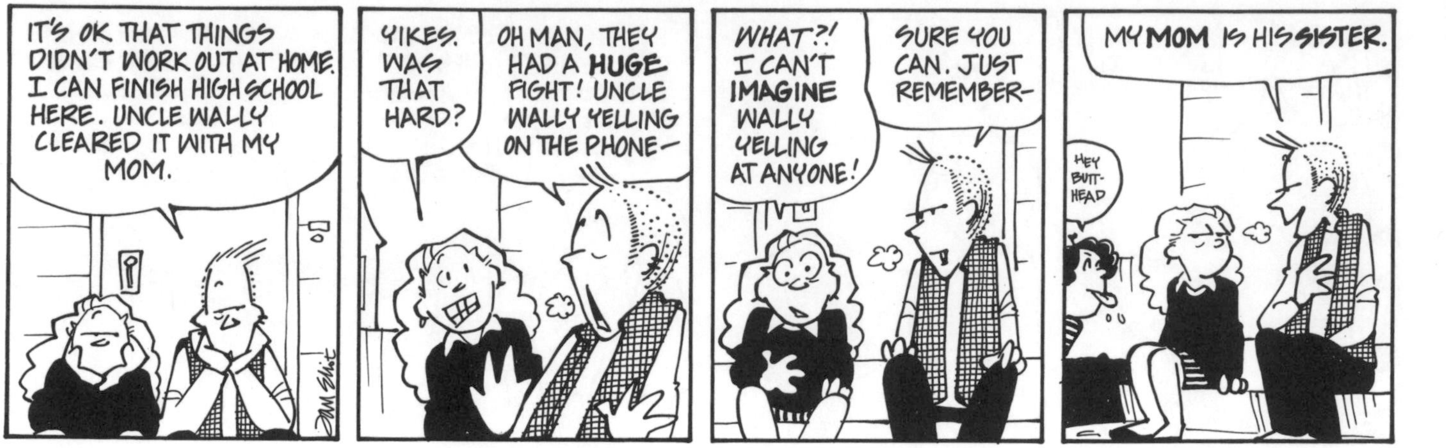
IT'S OK THAT THINGS DIDN'T WORK OUT AT HOME. I CAN FINISH HIGH SCHOOL HERE. UNCLE WALLY CLEARED IT WITH MY MOM.
YIKES. WAS THAT HARD?
OH MAN, THEY HAD A **HUGE** FIGHT! UNCLE WALLY YELLING ON THE PHONE—
WHAT?! I CAN'T **IMAGINE** WALLY YELLING AT ANYONE!
SURE YOU CAN. JUST REMEMBER—
MY **MOM** IS HIS **SISTER**.
HEY BUTT-HEAD

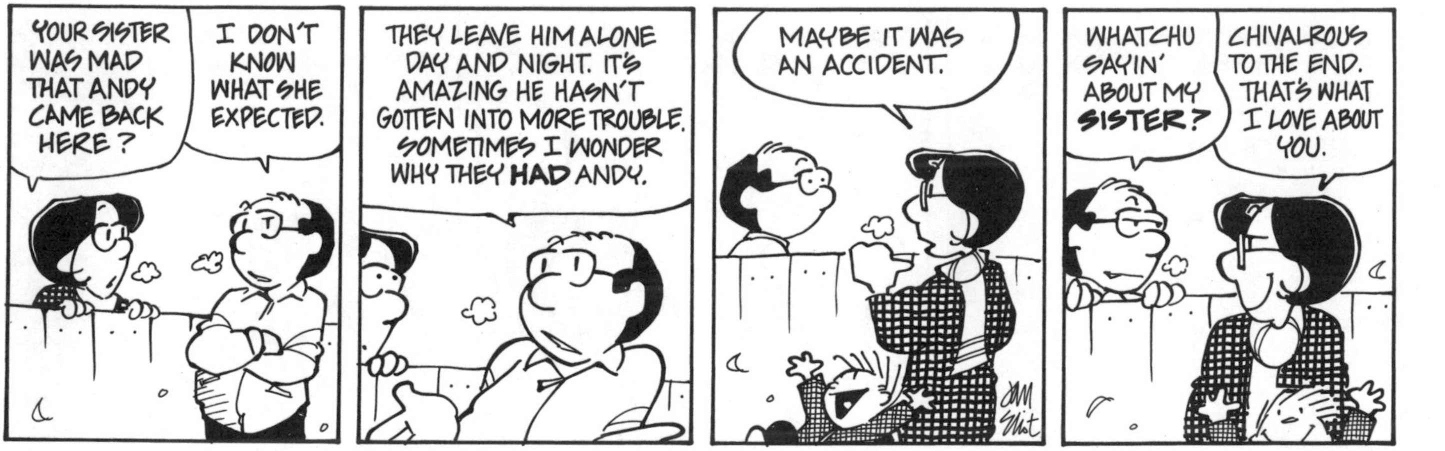
YOUR SISTER WAS MAD THAT ANDY CAME BACK HERE?
I DON'T KNOW WHAT SHE EXPECTED.
THEY LEAVE HIM ALONE DAY AND NIGHT. IT'S AMAZING HE HASN'T GOTTEN INTO MORE TROUBLE. SOMETIMES I WONDER WHY THEY **HAD** ANDY.
MAYBE IT WAS AN ACCIDENT.
WHATCHU SAYIN' ABOUT MY **SISTER?**
CHIVALROUS TO THE END. THAT'S WHAT I LOVE ABOUT YOU.

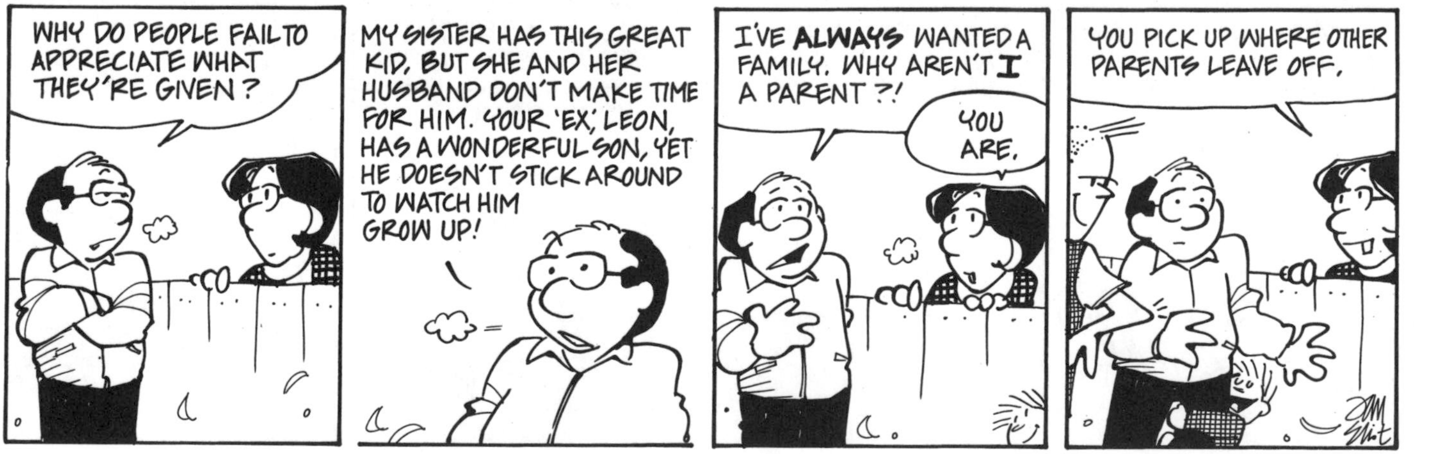
WHY DO PEOPLE FAIL TO APPRECIATE WHAT THEY'RE GIVEN?
MY SISTER HAS THIS GREAT KID, BUT SHE AND HER HUSBAND DON'T MAKE TIME FOR HIM. YOUR 'EX,' LEON, HAS A WONDERFUL SON, YET HE DOESN'T STICK AROUND TO WATCH HIM GROW UP!
I'VE **ALWAYS** WANTED A FAMILY. WHY AREN'T **I** A PARENT?!
YOU ARE.
YOU PICK UP WHERE OTHER PARENTS LEAVE OFF.

Stone Soup

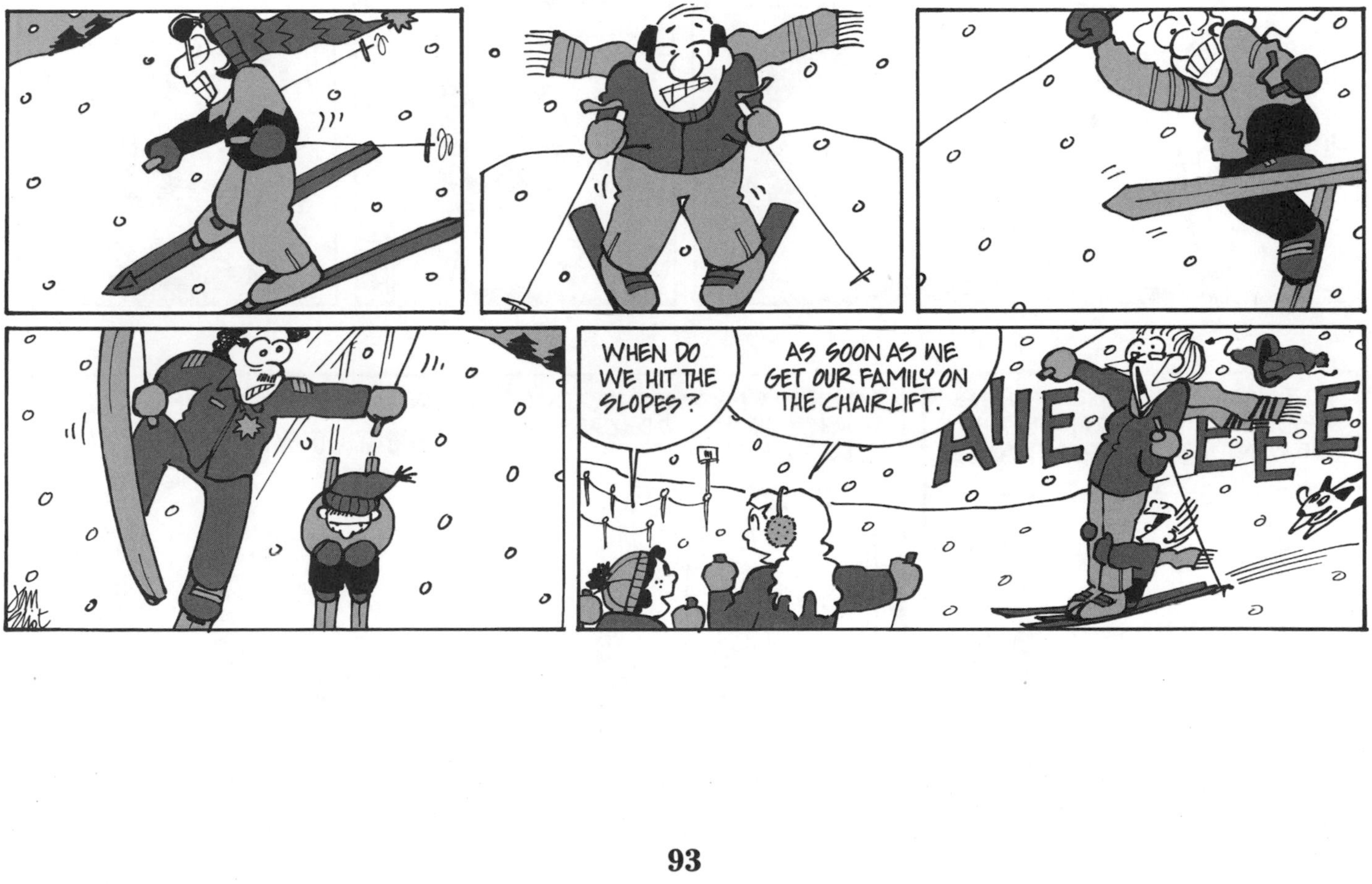

WHEN DO WE HIT THE SLOPES?
AS SOON AS WE GET OUR FAMILY ON THE CHAIRLIFT.
AIIEEEE

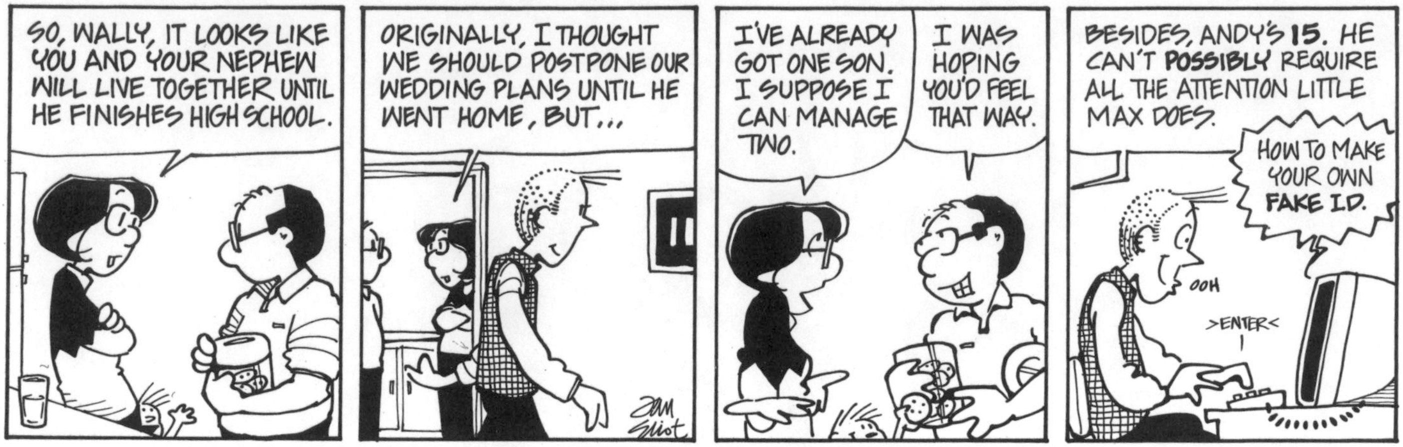
SO, WALLY, IT LOOKS LIKE YOU AND YOUR NEPHEW WILL LIVE TOGETHER UNTIL HE FINISHES HIGH SCHOOL.
ORIGINALLY, I THOUGHT WE SHOULD POSTPONE OUR WEDDING PLANS UNTIL HE WENT HOME, BUT...
I'VE ALREADY GOT ONE SON. I SUPPOSE I CAN MANAGE TWO.
I WAS HOPING YOU'D FEEL THAT WAY.
BESIDES, ANDY'S **15**. HE CAN'T **POSSIBLY** REQUIRE ALL THE ATTENTION LITTLE MAX DOES.
HOW TO MAKE YOUR OWN **FAKE I.D.**
OOH
>ENTER<

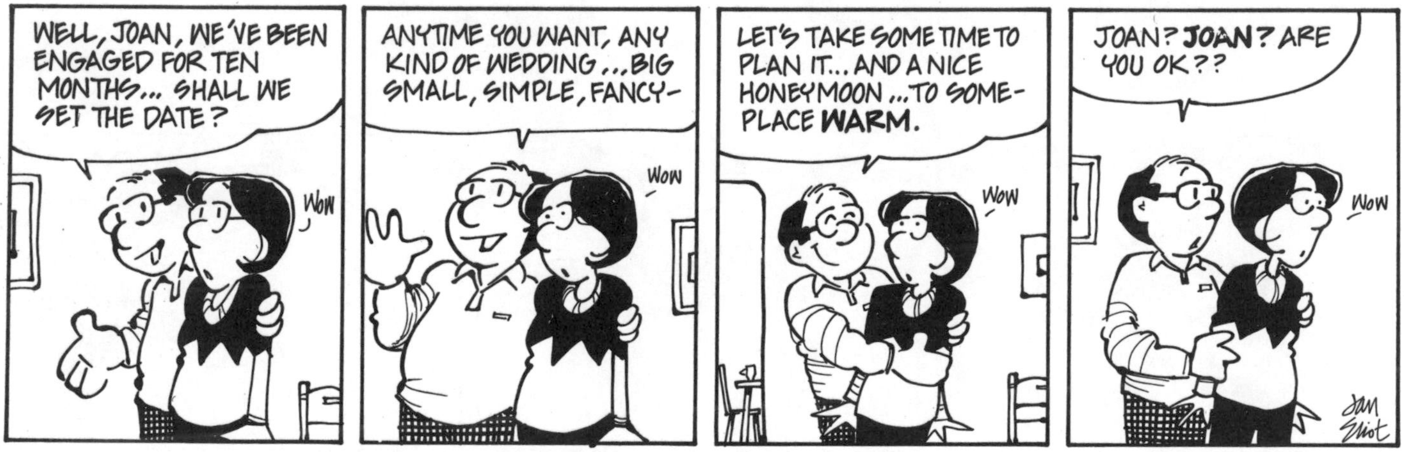
WELL, JOAN, WE'VE BEEN ENGAGED FOR TEN MONTHS... SHALL WE SET THE DATE?
WOW
ANYTIME YOU WANT, ANY KIND OF WEDDING...BIG SMALL, SIMPLE, FANCY-
WOW
LET'S TAKE SOME TIME TO PLAN IT... AND A NICE HONEYMOON...TO SOMEPLACE **WARM**.
WOW
JOAN? **JOAN?** ARE YOU OK??
WOW

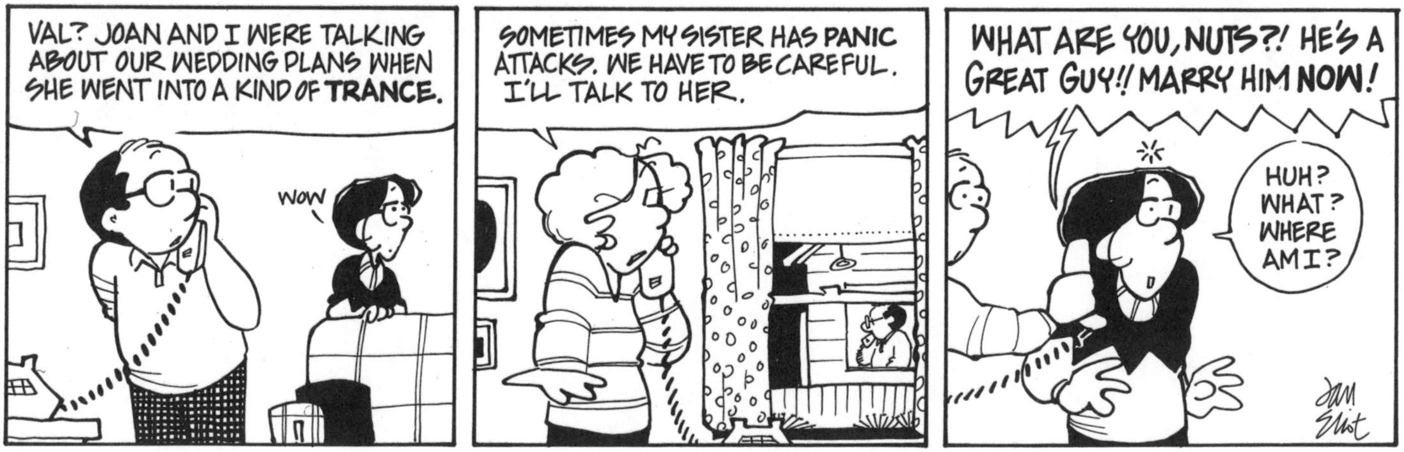
VAL? JOAN AND I WERE TALKING ABOUT OUR WEDDING PLANS WHEN SHE WENT INTO A KIND OF **TRANCE**.
WOW
SOMETIMES MY SISTER HAS **PANIC** ATTACKS. WE HAVE TO BE CAREFUL. I'LL TALK TO HER.
WHAT ARE YOU, **NUTS?!** HE'S A GREAT GUY!! MARRY HIM **NOW**!
HUH? WHAT? WHERE AM I?

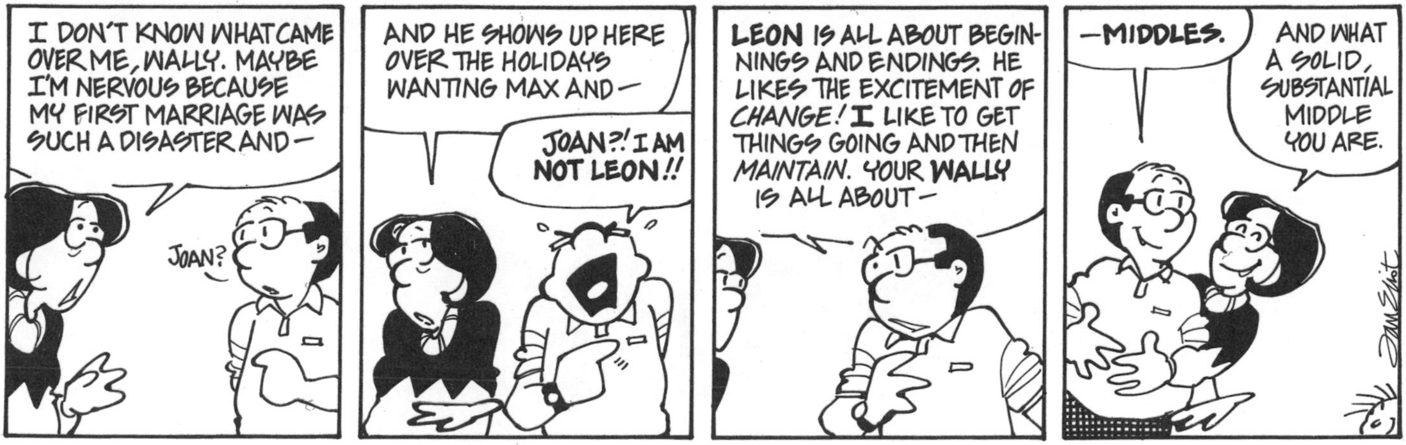
I DON'T KNOW WHAT CAME OVER ME, WALLY. MAYBE I'M NERVOUS BECAUSE MY FIRST MARRIAGE WAS SUCH A DISASTER AND —
JOAN?
AND HE SHOWS UP HERE OVER THE HOLIDAYS WANTING MAX AND —
JOAN?! I AM NOT LEON!!
LEON IS ALL ABOUT BEGINNINGS AND ENDINGS. HE LIKES THE EXCITEMENT OF CHANGE! I LIKE TO GET THINGS GOING AND THEN MAINTAIN. YOUR WALLY IS ALL ABOUT —
— MIDDLES.
AND WHAT A SOLID, SUBSTANTIAL MIDDLE YOU ARE.

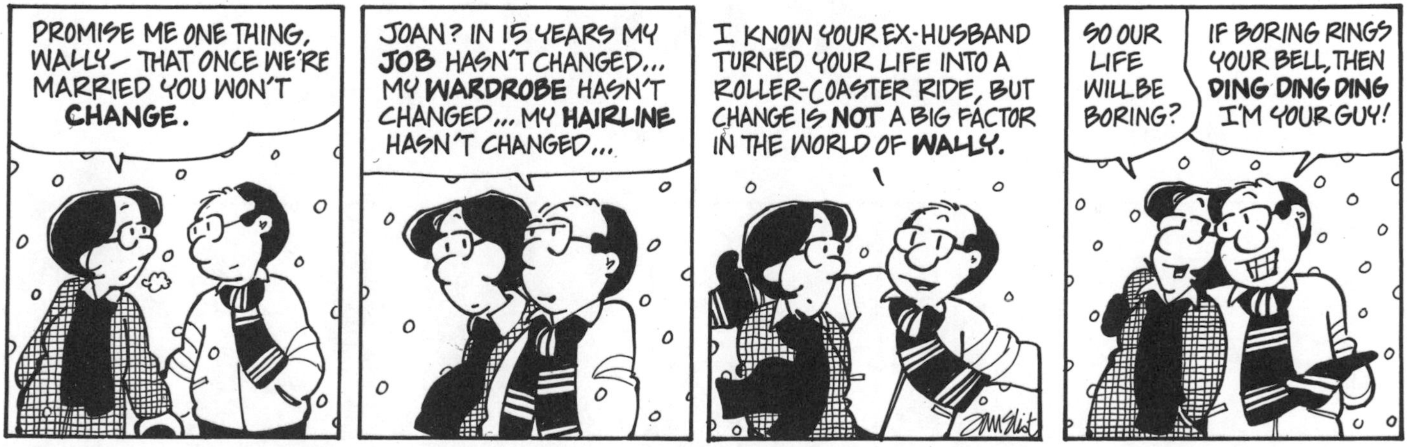
PROMISE ME ONE THING, WALLY — THAT ONCE WE'RE MARRIED YOU WON'T CHANGE.
JOAN? IN 15 YEARS MY JOB HASN'T CHANGED... MY WARDROBE HASN'T CHANGED... MY HAIRLINE HASN'T CHANGED...
I KNOW YOUR EX-HUSBAND TURNED YOUR LIFE INTO A ROLLER-COASTER RIDE, BUT CHANGE IS NOT A BIG FACTOR IN THE WORLD OF WALLY.
SO OUR LIFE WILL BE BORING?
IF BORING RINGS YOUR BELL, THEN DING DING DING I'M YOUR GUY!

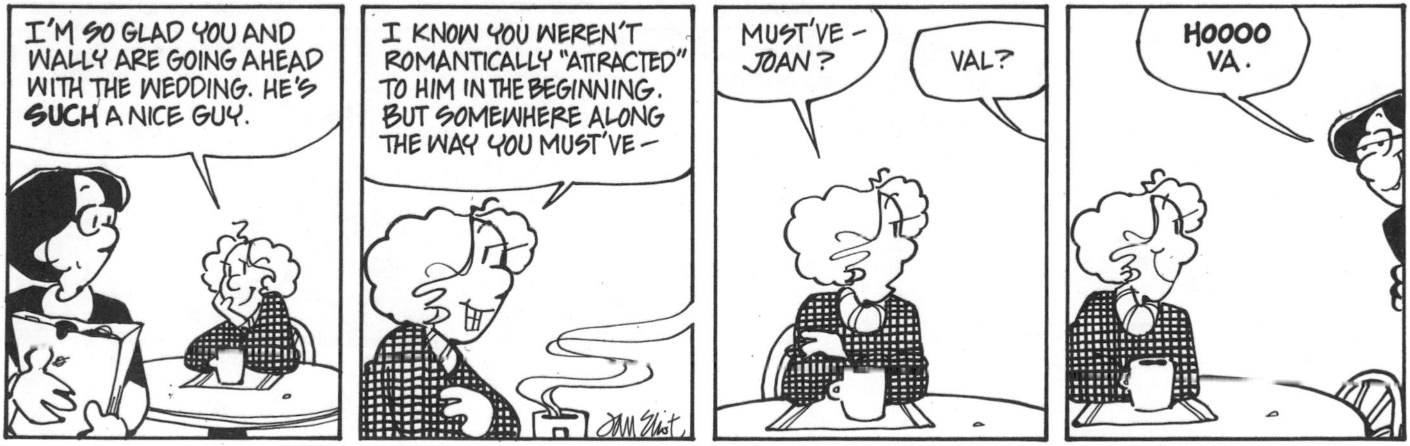
I'M SO GLAD YOU AND WALLY ARE GOING AHEAD WITH THE WEDDING. HE'S SUCH A NICE GUY.
I KNOW YOU WEREN'T ROMANTICALLY "ATTRACTED" TO HIM IN THE BEGINNING. BUT SOMEWHERE ALONG THE WAY YOU MUST'VE —
MUST'VE — JOAN?
VAL?
HOOOO VA.

Stone Soup

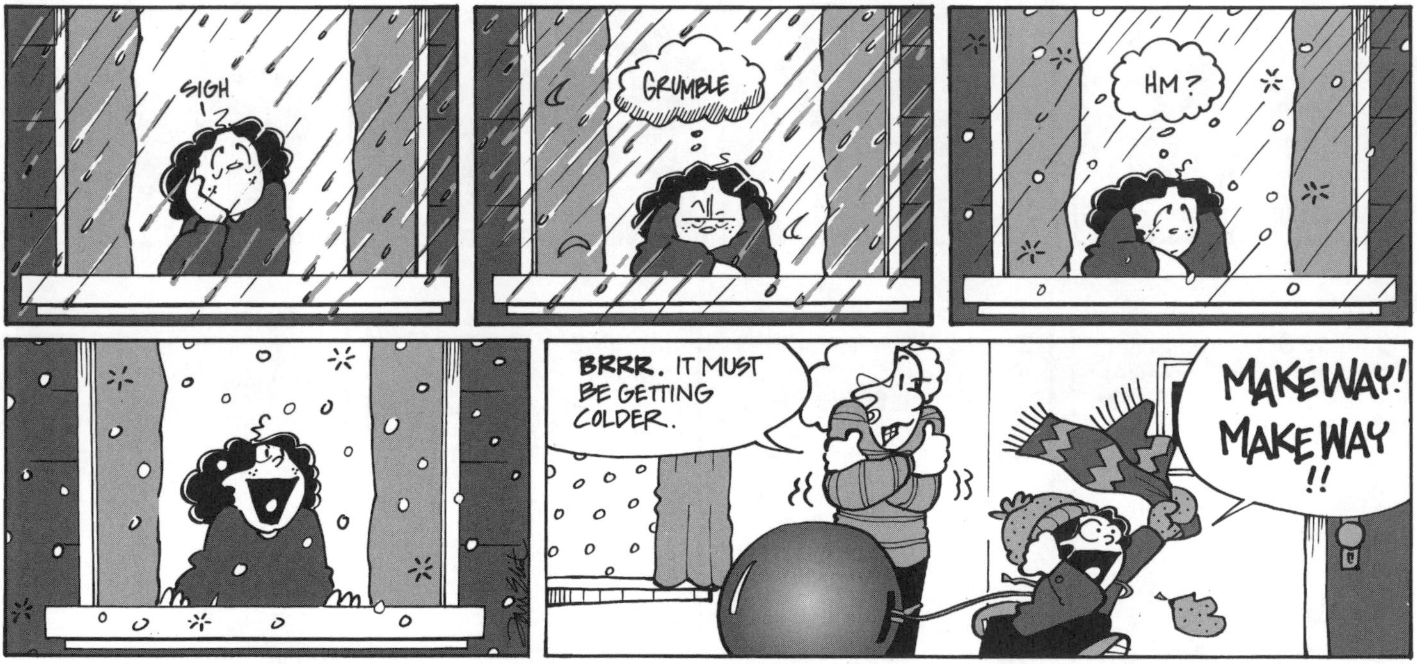
SIGH
GRUMBLE
HM?
BRRR. IT MUST BE GETTING COLDER.
MAKE WAY! MAKE WAY!!

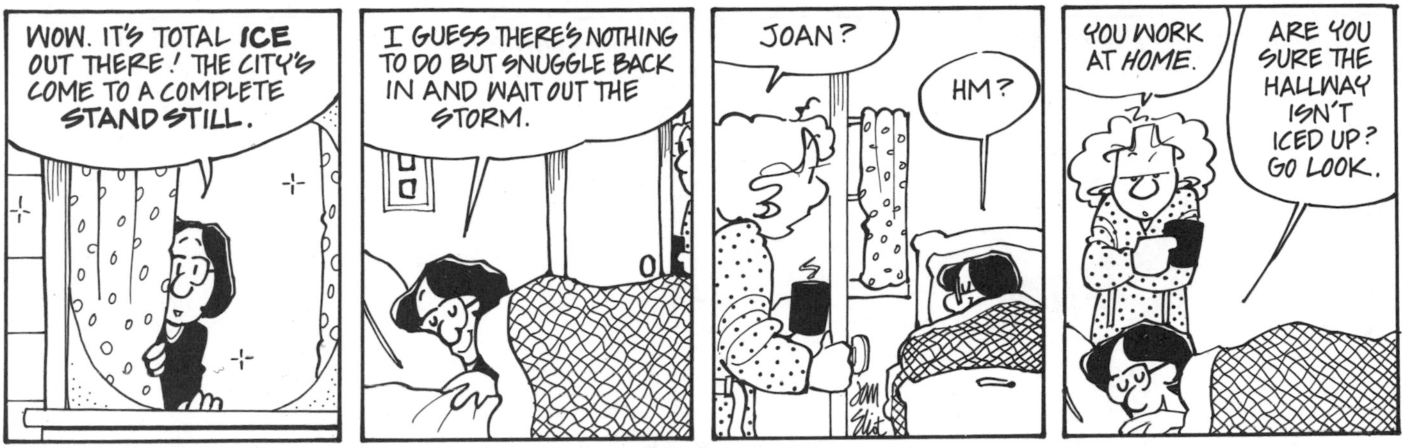
WOW. IT'S TOTAL ICE OUT THERE! THE CITY'S COME TO A COMPLETE STANDSTILL.
I GUESS THERE'S NOTHING TO DO BUT SNUGGLE BACK IN AND WAIT OUT THE STORM.
JOAN?
HM?
YOU WORK AT HOME.
ARE YOU SURE THE HALLWAY ISN'T ICED UP? GO LOOK.

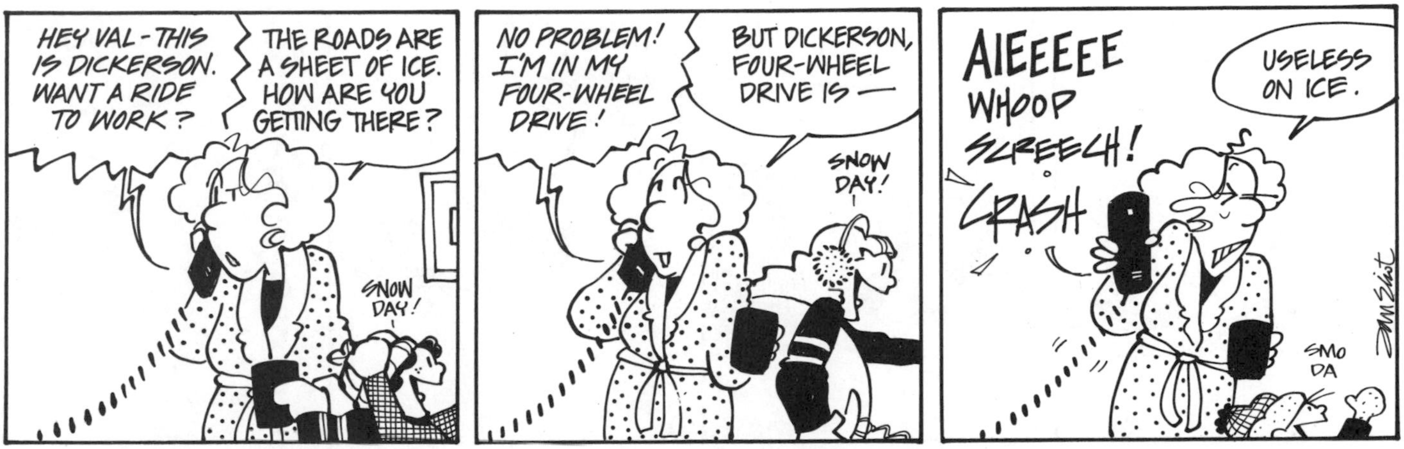
HEY VAL - THIS IS DICKERSON. WANT A RIDE TO WORK?
THE ROADS ARE A SHEET OF ICE. HOW ARE YOU GETTING THERE?
SNOW DAY!
NO PROBLEM! I'M IN MY FOUR-WHEEL DRIVE!
BUT DICKERSON, FOUR-WHEEL DRIVE IS —
SNOW DAY!
AIEEEEE
WHOOP
SCREECH!
CRASH
USELESS ON ICE.
SMO DA

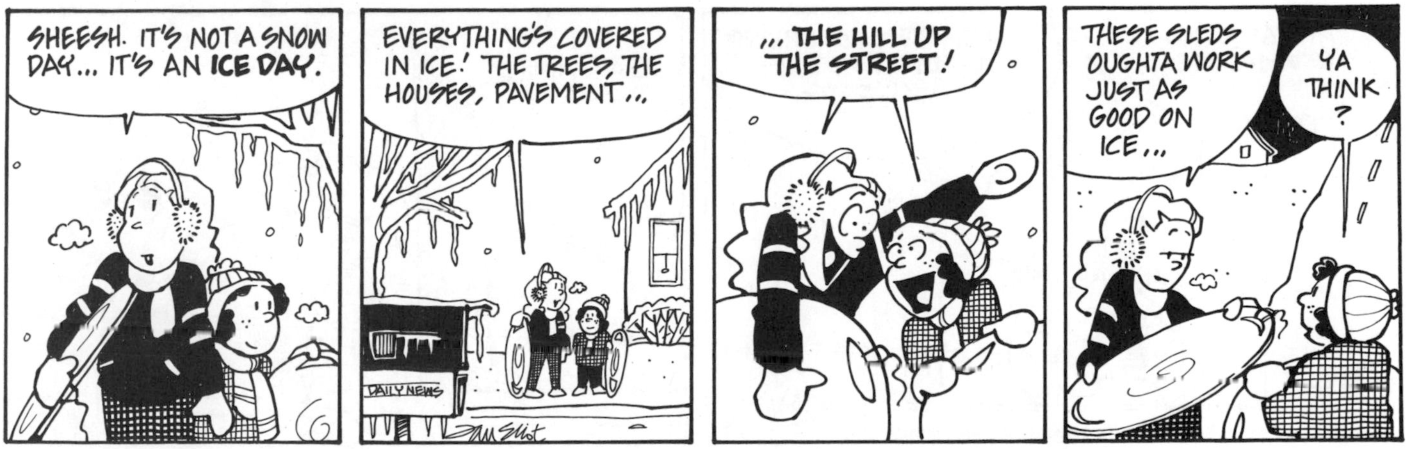
SHEESH. IT'S NOT A SNOW DAY... IT'S AN ICE DAY.
EVERYTHING'S COVERED IN ICE! THE TREES, THE HOUSES, PAVEMENT...
DAILY NEWS
... THE HILL UP THE STREET!
THESE SLEDS OUGHTA WORK JUST AS GOOD ON ICE...
YA THINK?

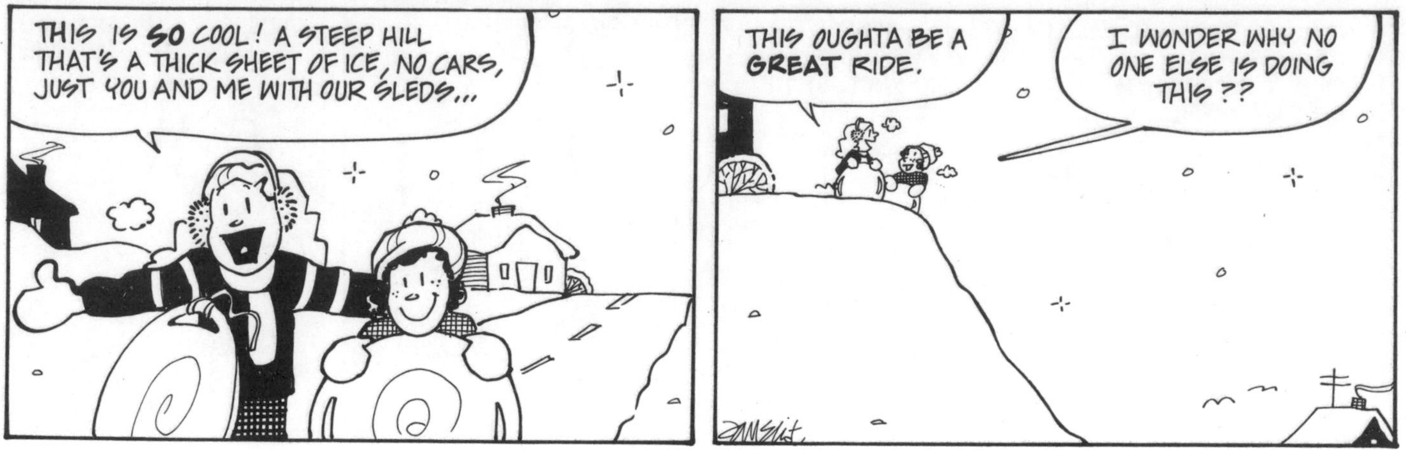
THIS IS SO COOL! A STEEP HILL THAT'S A THICK SHEET OF ICE, NO CARS, JUST YOU AND ME WITH OUR SLEDS...
THIS OUGHTA BE A GREAT RIDE.
I WONDER WHY NO ONE ELSE IS DOING THIS??

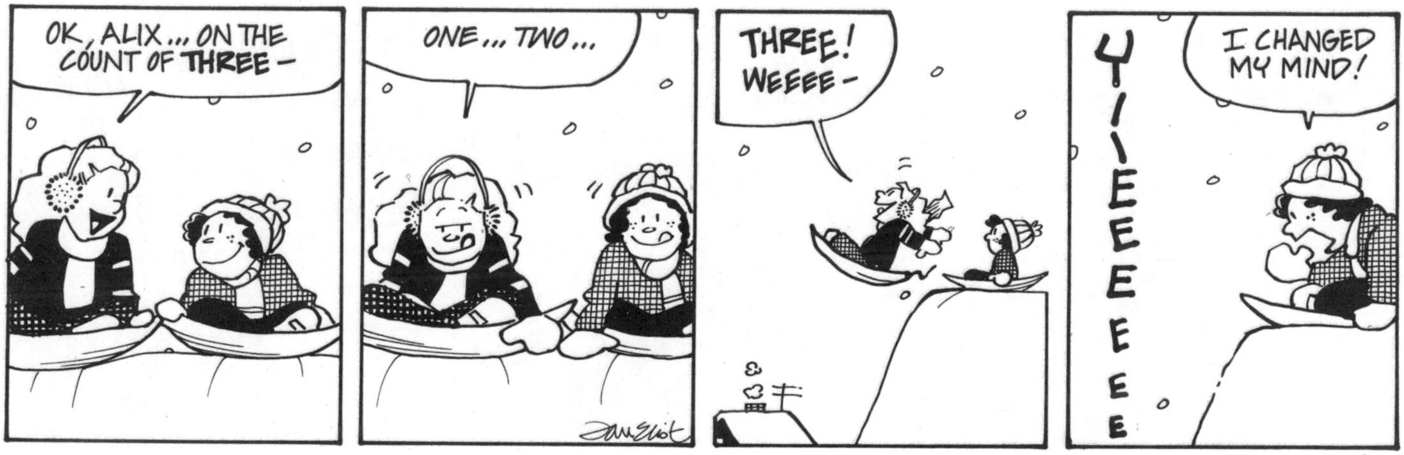
OK, ALIX... ON THE COUNT OF THREE –
ONE... TWO...
THREE! WEEEE –
YIIEEEEEE
I CHANGED MY MIND!

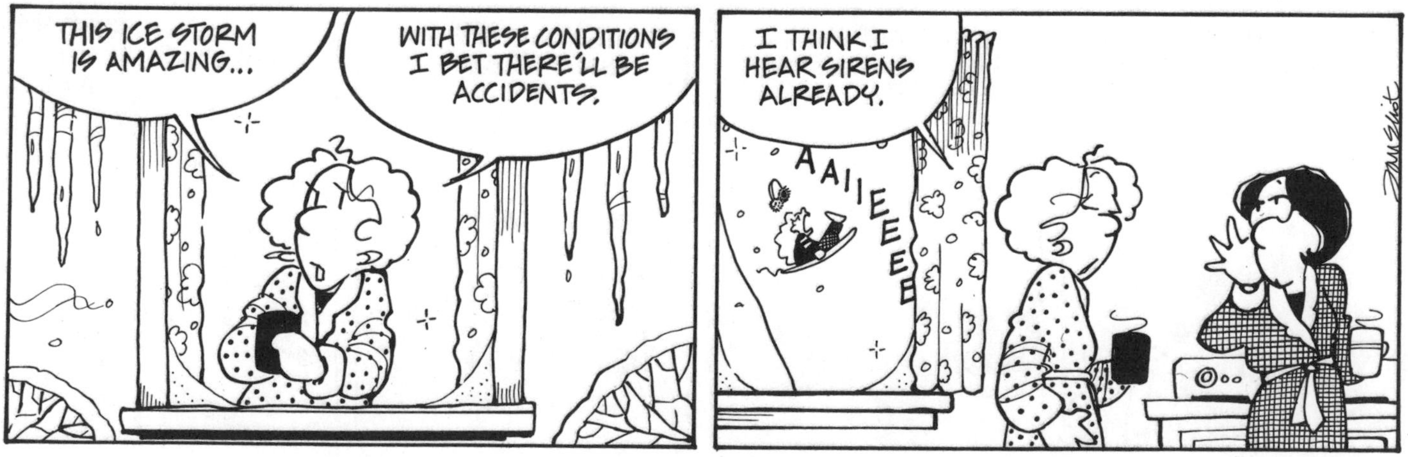
THIS ICE STORM IS AMAZING...
WITH THESE CONDITIONS I BET THERE'LL BE ACCIDENTS.
I THINK I HEAR SIRENS ALREADY.
AAIIEEEE

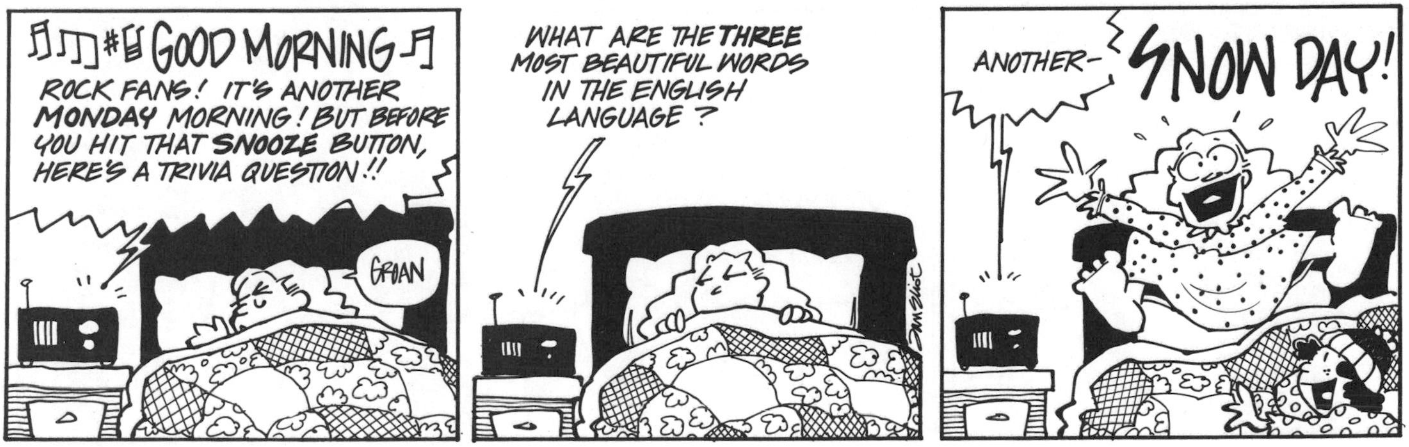
GOOD MORNING
ROCK FANS! IT'S ANOTHER MONDAY MORNING! BUT BEFORE YOU HIT THAT SNOOZE BUTTON, HERE'S A TRIVIA QUESTION!!
GROAN
WHAT ARE THE THREE MOST BEAUTIFUL WORDS IN THE ENGLISH LANGUAGE ?
ANOTHER-
SNOW DAY!

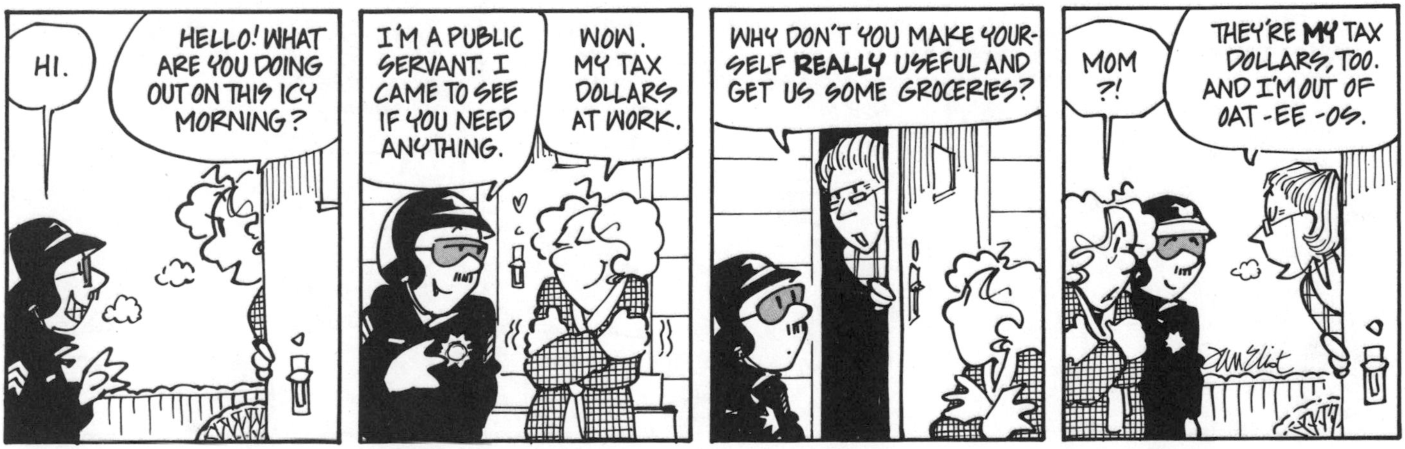
HI.
HELLO! WHAT ARE YOU DOING OUT ON THIS ICY MORNING?
I'M A PUBLIC SERVANT. I CAME TO SEE IF YOU NEED ANYTHING.
WOW. MY TAX DOLLARS AT WORK.
WHY DON'T YOU MAKE YOURSELF REALLY USEFUL AND GET US SOME GROCERIES?
MOM ?!
THEY'RE MY TAX DOLLARS, TOO. AND I'M OUT OF OAT-EE-OS.

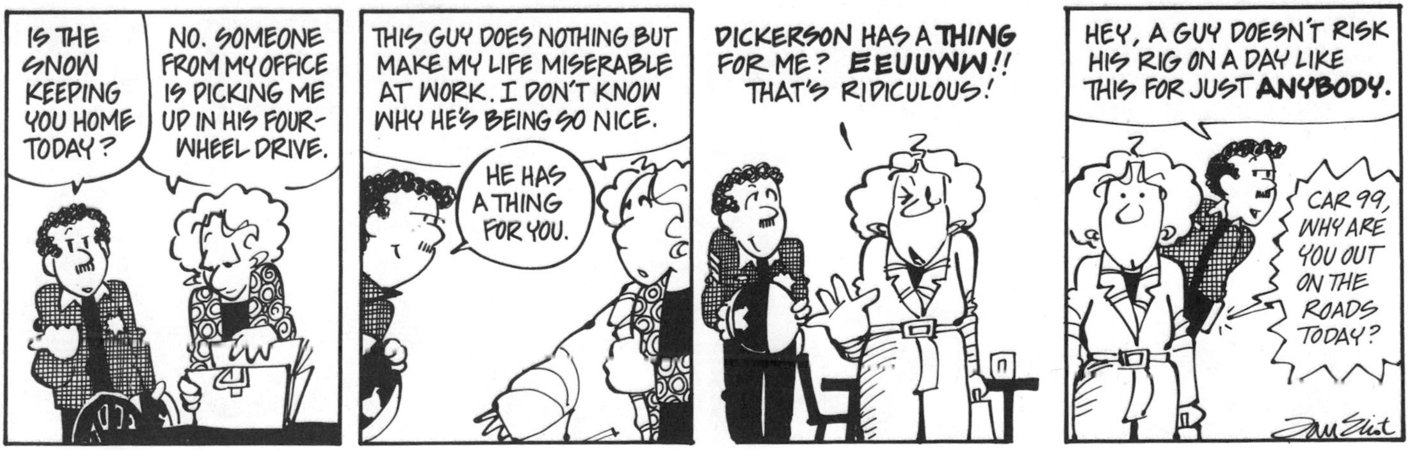
IS THE SNOW KEEPING YOU HOME TODAY?
NO. SOMEONE FROM MY OFFICE IS PICKING ME UP IN HIS FOUR-WHEEL DRIVE.
THIS GUY DOES NOTHING BUT MAKE MY LIFE MISERABLE AT WORK. I DON'T KNOW WHY HE'S BEING SO NICE.
HE HAS A THING FOR YOU.
DICKERSON HAS A THING FOR ME? EEUUWW!! THAT'S RIDICULOUS!
HEY, A GUY DOESN'T RISK HIS RIG ON A DAY LIKE THIS FOR JUST ANYBODY.
CAR 99, WHY ARE YOU OUT ON THE ROADS TODAY?

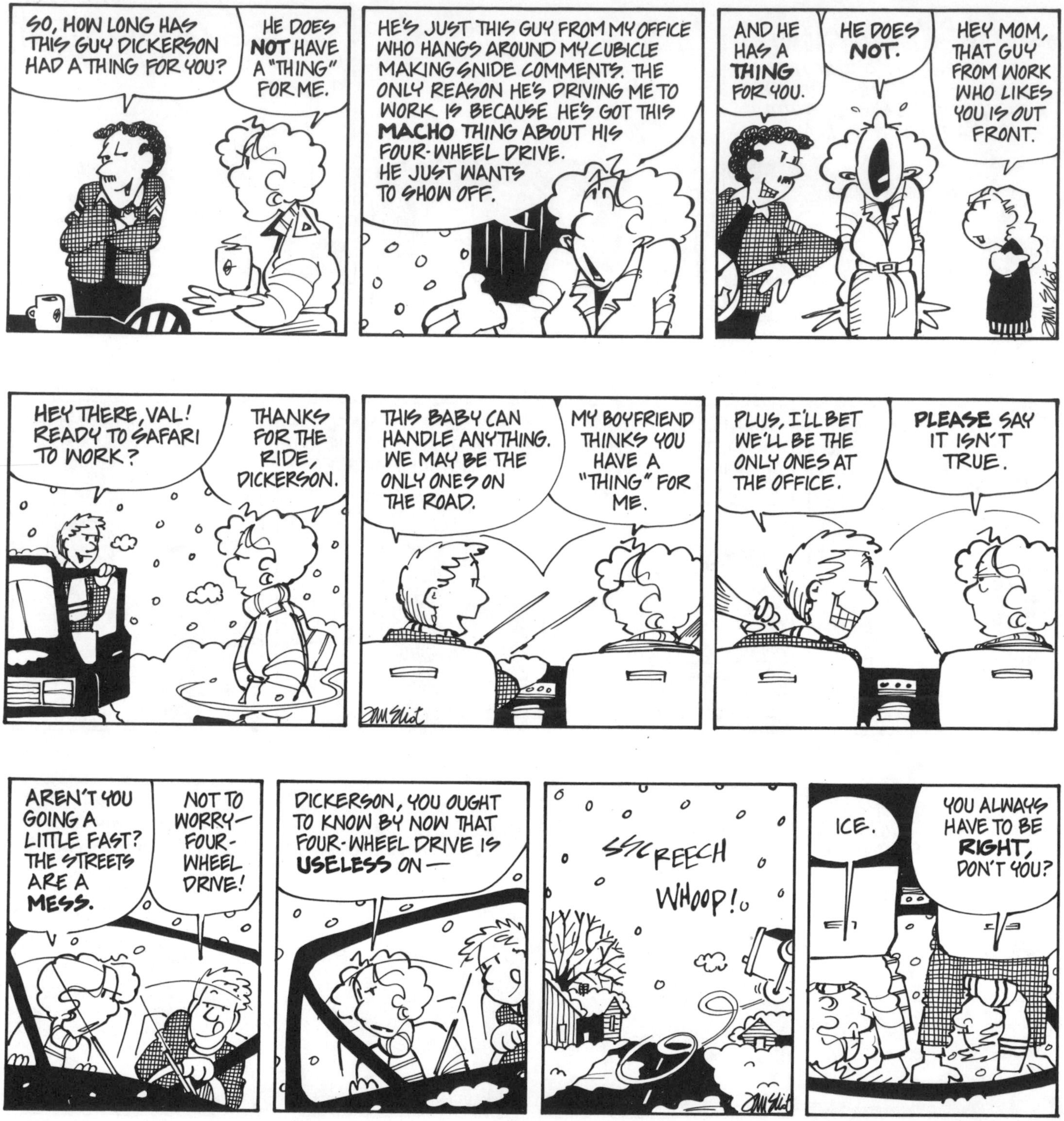

SO, HOW LONG HAS THIS GUY DICKERSON HAD A THING FOR YOU?
HE DOES **NOT** HAVE A "THING" FOR ME.
HE'S JUST THIS GUY FROM MY OFFICE WHO HANGS AROUND MY CUBICLE MAKING SNIDE COMMENTS. THE ONLY REASON HE'S DRIVING ME TO WORK IS BECAUSE HE'S GOT THIS **MACHO** THING ABOUT HIS FOUR-WHEEL DRIVE. HE JUST WANTS TO SHOW OFF.
AND HE HAS A **THING** FOR YOU.
HE DOES **NOT**.
HEY MOM, THAT GUY FROM WORK WHO LIKES YOU IS OUT FRONT.
HEY THERE, VAL! READY TO SAFARI TO WORK?
THANKS FOR THE RIDE, DICKERSON.
THIS BABY CAN HANDLE ANYTHING. WE MAY BE THE ONLY ONES ON THE ROAD.
MY BOYFRIEND THINKS YOU HAVE A "THING" FOR ME.
PLUS, I'LL BET WE'LL BE THE ONLY ONES AT THE OFFICE.
PLEASE SAY IT ISN'T TRUE.
AREN'T YOU GOING A LITTLE FAST? THE STREETS ARE A **MESS**.
NOT TO WORRY— FOUR-WHEEL DRIVE!
DICKERSON, YOU OUGHT TO KNOW BY NOW THAT FOUR-WHEEL DRIVE IS **USELESS** ON—
SSCREECH
WHOOP!
ICE.
YOU ALWAYS HAVE TO BE **RIGHT**, DON'T YOU?

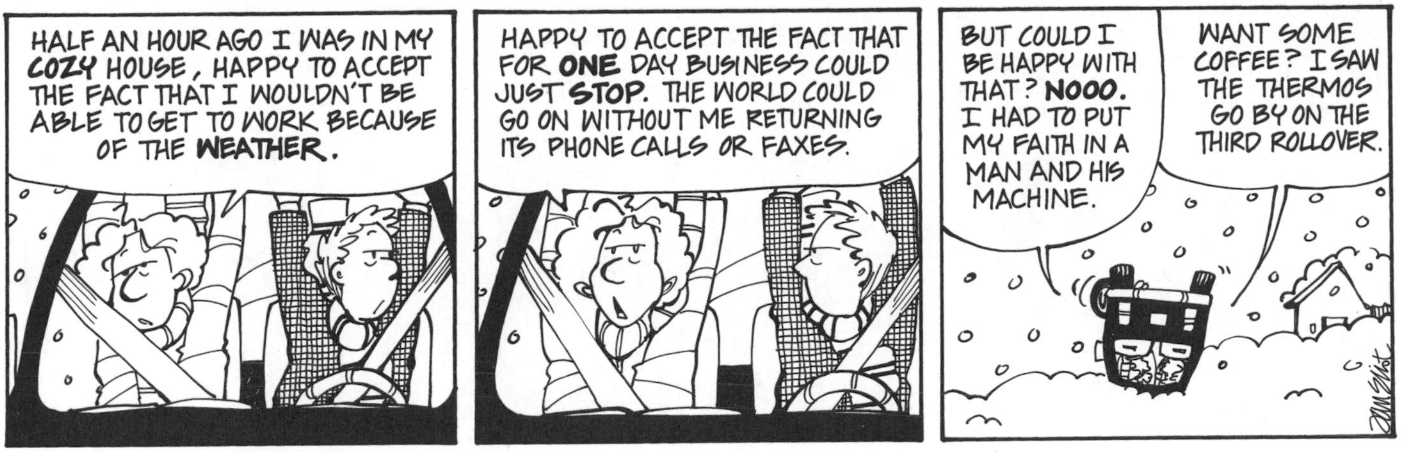
HALF AN HOUR AGO I WAS IN MY **COZY** HOUSE, HAPPY TO ACCEPT THE FACT THAT I WOULDN'T BE ABLE TO GET TO WORK BECAUSE OF THE **WEATHER**.
HAPPY TO ACCEPT THE FACT THAT FOR **ONE** DAY BUSINESS COULD JUST **STOP**. THE WORLD COULD GO ON WITHOUT ME RETURNING ITS PHONE CALLS OR FAXES.
BUT COULD I BE HAPPY WITH THAT? **NOOO.** I HAD TO PUT MY FAITH IN A MAN AND HIS MACHINE.
WANT SOME COFFEE? I SAW THE THERMOS GO BY ON THE THIRD ROLLOVER.

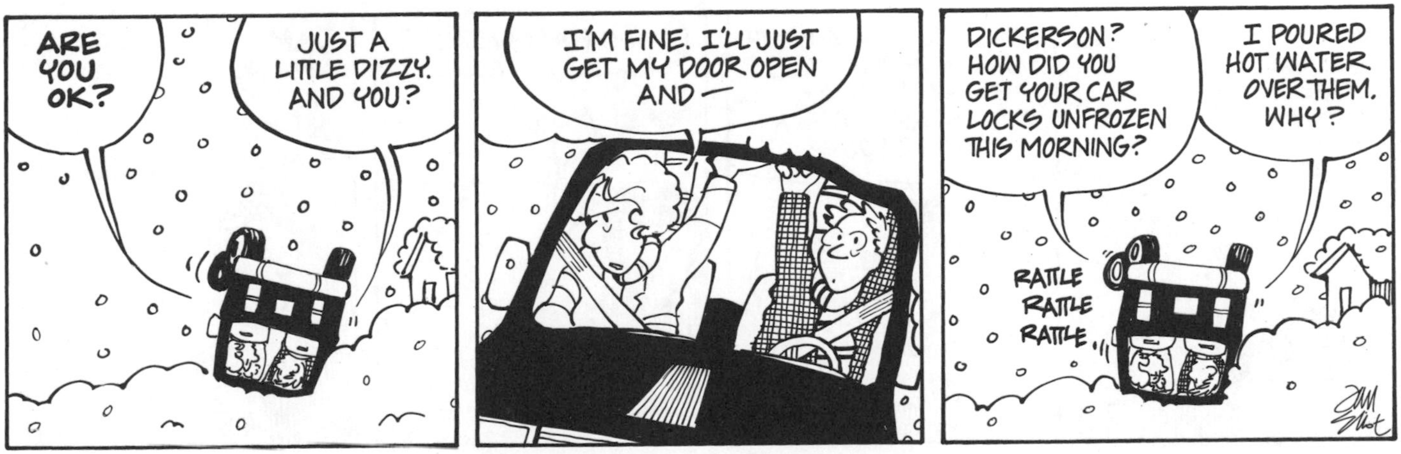
ARE YOU OK?
JUST A LITTLE DIZZY. AND YOU?
I'M FINE. I'LL JUST GET MY DOOR OPEN AND—
DICKERSON? HOW DID YOU GET YOUR CAR LOCKS UNFROZEN THIS MORNING?
I POURED HOT WATER OVER THEM. WHY?
RATTLE RATTLE RATTLE

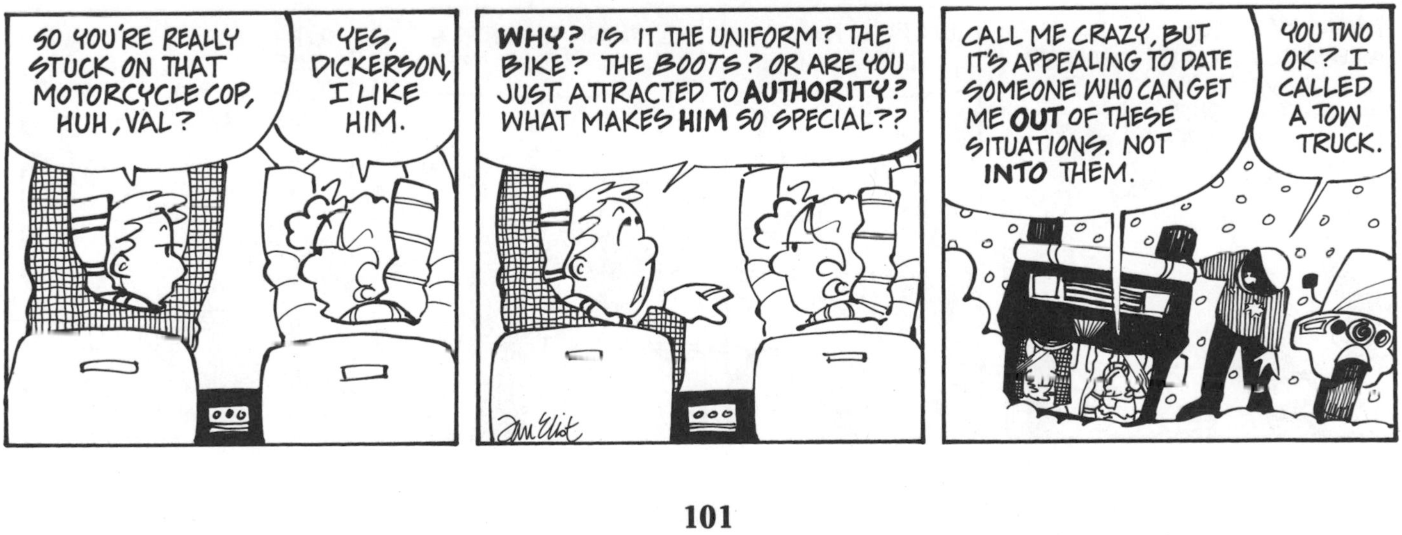
SO YOU'RE REALLY STUCK ON THAT MOTORCYCLE COP, HUH, VAL?
YES, DICKERSON, I LIKE HIM.
WHY? IS IT THE UNIFORM? THE BIKE? THE *BOOTS*? OR ARE YOU JUST ATTRACTED TO **AUTHORITY**? WHAT MAKES **HIM** SO SPECIAL??
CALL ME CRAZY, BUT IT'S APPEALING TO DATE SOMEONE WHO CAN GET ME **OUT** OF THESE SITUATIONS. NOT **INTO** THEM.
YOU TWO OK? I CALLED A TOW TRUCK.

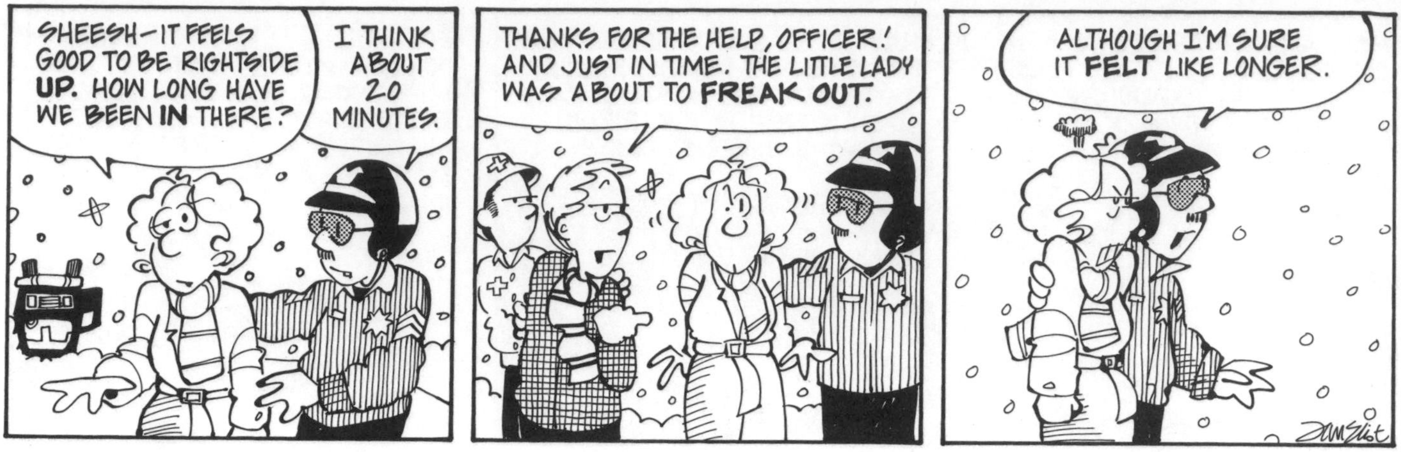
SHEESH—IT FEELS GOOD TO BE RIGHTSIDE UP. HOW LONG HAVE WE BEEN IN THERE?
I THINK ABOUT 20 MINUTES.
THANKS FOR THE HELP, OFFICER! AND JUST IN TIME. THE LITTLE LADY WAS ABOUT TO FREAK OUT.
ALTHOUGH I'M SURE IT FELT LIKE LONGER.

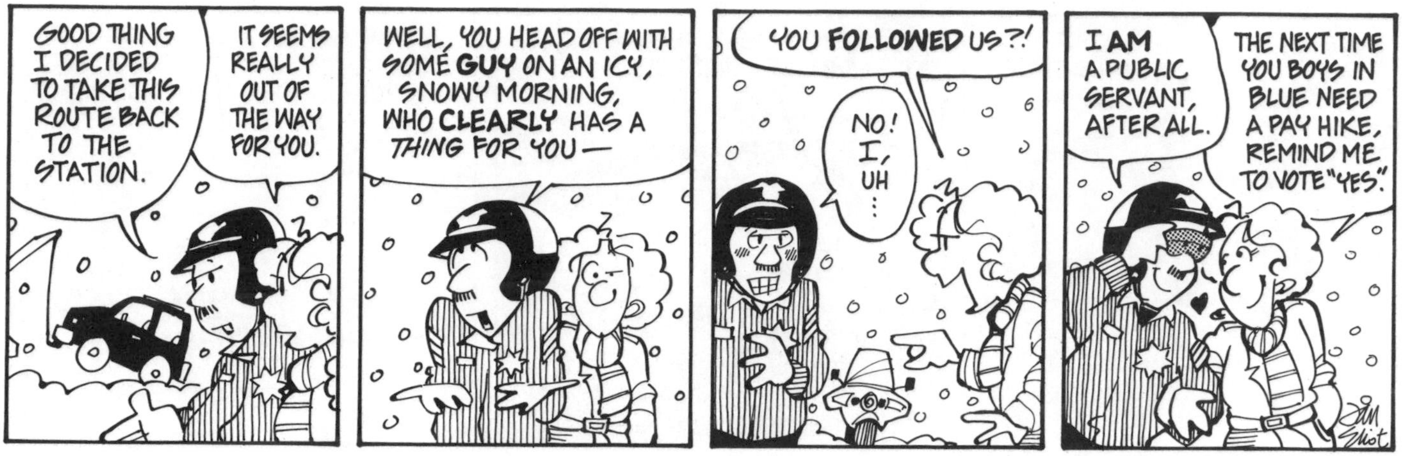
GOOD THING I DECIDED TO TAKE THIS ROUTE BACK TO THE STATION.
IT SEEMS REALLY OUT OF THE WAY FOR YOU.
WELL, YOU HEAD OFF WITH SOME GUY ON AN ICY, SNOWY MORNING, WHO CLEARLY HAS A THING FOR YOU—
YOU FOLLOWED US?!
NO! I, UH...
I AM A PUBLIC SERVANT, AFTER ALL.
THE NEXT TIME YOU BOYS IN BLUE NEED A PAY HIKE, REMIND ME TO VOTE "YES."

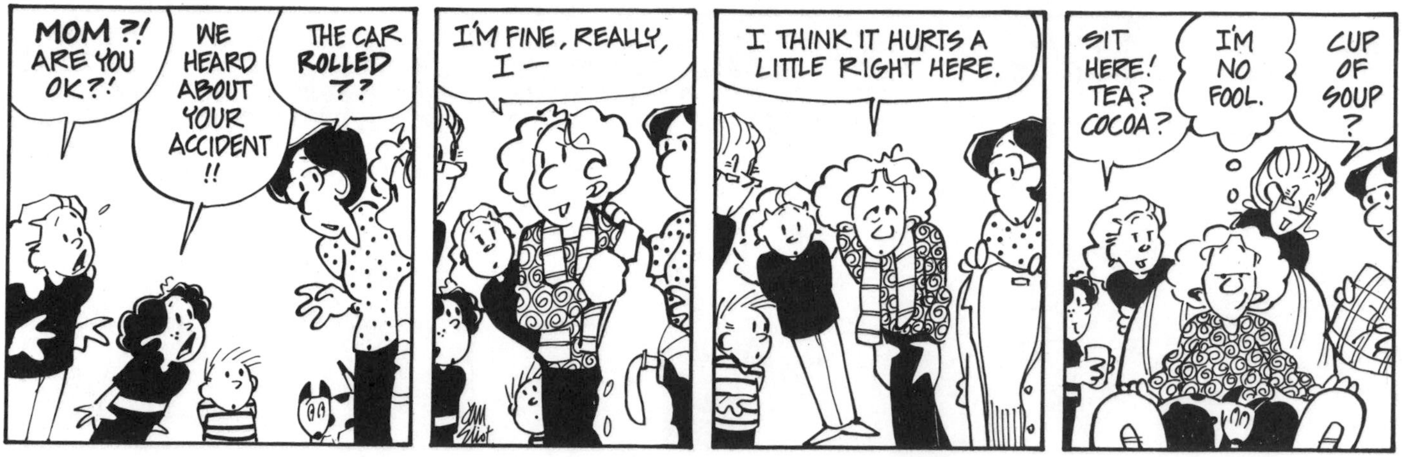
MOM?! ARE YOU OK?!
WE HEARD ABOUT YOUR ACCIDENT!!
THE CAR ROLLED??
I'M FINE, REALLY, I—
I THINK IT HURTS A LITTLE RIGHT HERE.
SIT HERE! TEA? COCOA?
I'M NO FOOL.
CUP OF SOUP?

Stone Soup

Panel 1:
WHAT MAKES YOU HAPPY, PHIL?

OHH... FRESH WAX ON MY CRUISER... A GOOD STEREO ... ALMOND CROISSANTS AND FLEECE-LINED SLIPPERS.

Panel 2:
AND "RAINDROPS ON ROSES AND WHISKERS ON KITTENS..."

FINE. MAKE FUN OF ME. WHAT MAKES **YOU** HAPPY?

Panel 3:
A DRIVE IN THE COUNTRY?

WASTE OF FOSSIL FUELS. DESTROYS OZONE LAYER...

Panel 4:
SHOPPING?

OH, PLEASE. PROMOTES NEEDLESS CONSUMPTION, AND POOR LABOR PRACTICES OVERSEAS.

Panel 5:
FIRE IN THE FIREPLACE?

INEFFICIENT HEAT, AIR POLLUTION!!

Panel 6:
REMIND ME—**WHY** DO I LIKE YOU SO MUCH?

BECAUSE I BRING SO MUCH **JOY** TO YOUR LIFE.

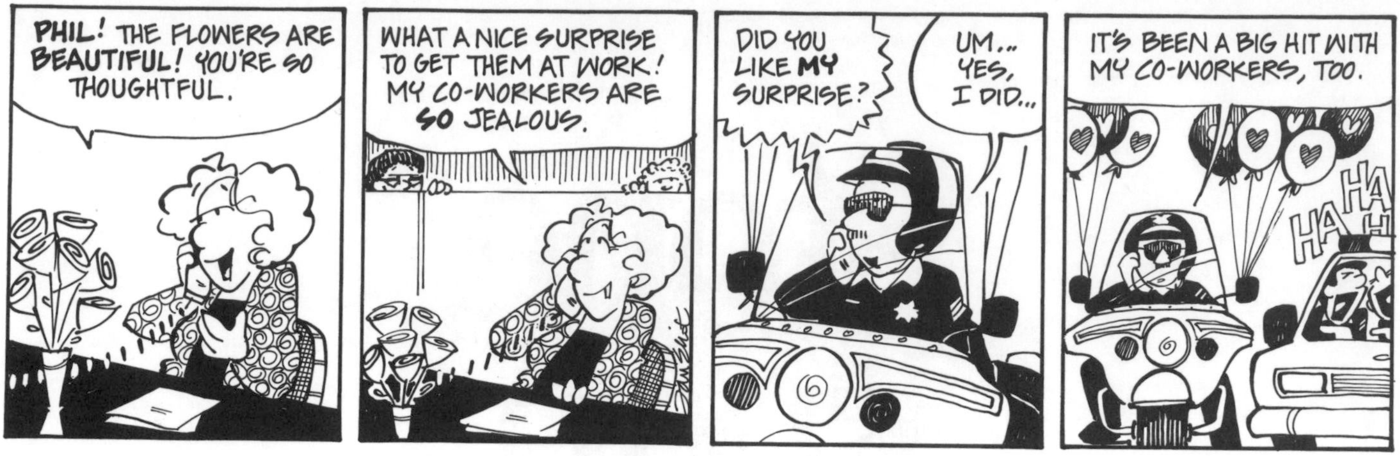
PHIL! THE FLOWERS ARE BEAUTIFUL! YOU'RE SO THOUGHTFUL.
WHAT A NICE SURPRISE TO GET THEM AT WORK! MY CO-WORKERS ARE SO JEALOUS.
DID YOU LIKE MY SURPRISE?
UM... YES, I DID...
IT'S BEEN A BIG HIT WITH MY CO-WORKERS, TOO.
HA HA HA

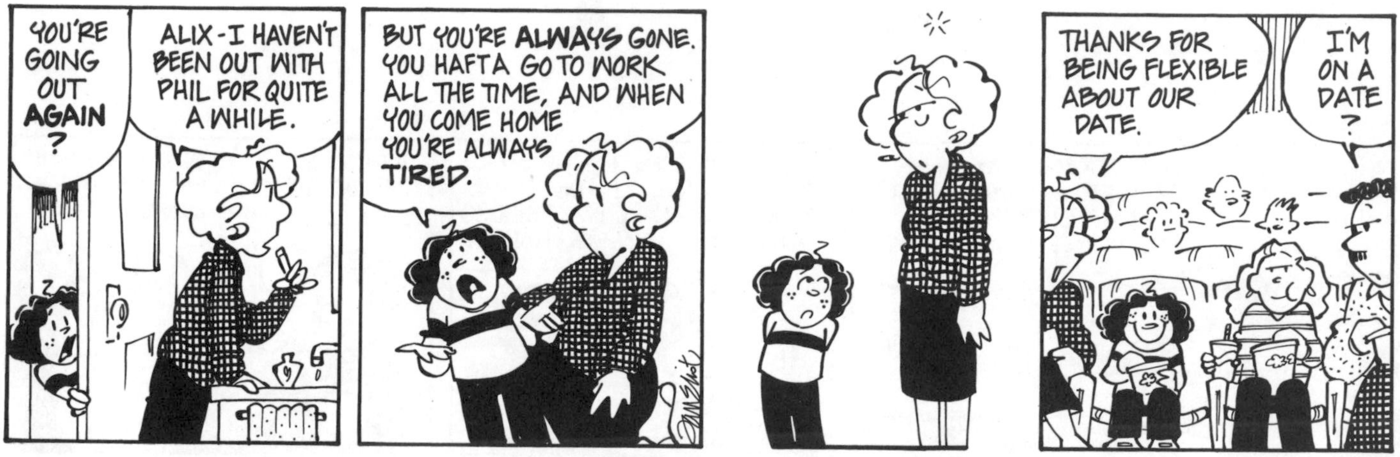
YOU'RE GOING OUT AGAIN?
ALIX - I HAVEN'T BEEN OUT WITH PHIL FOR QUITE A WHILE.
BUT YOU'RE ALWAYS GONE. YOU HAFTA GO TO WORK ALL THE TIME, AND WHEN YOU COME HOME YOU'RE ALWAYS TIRED.
THANKS FOR BEING FLEXIBLE ABOUT OUR DATE.
I'M ON A DATE?

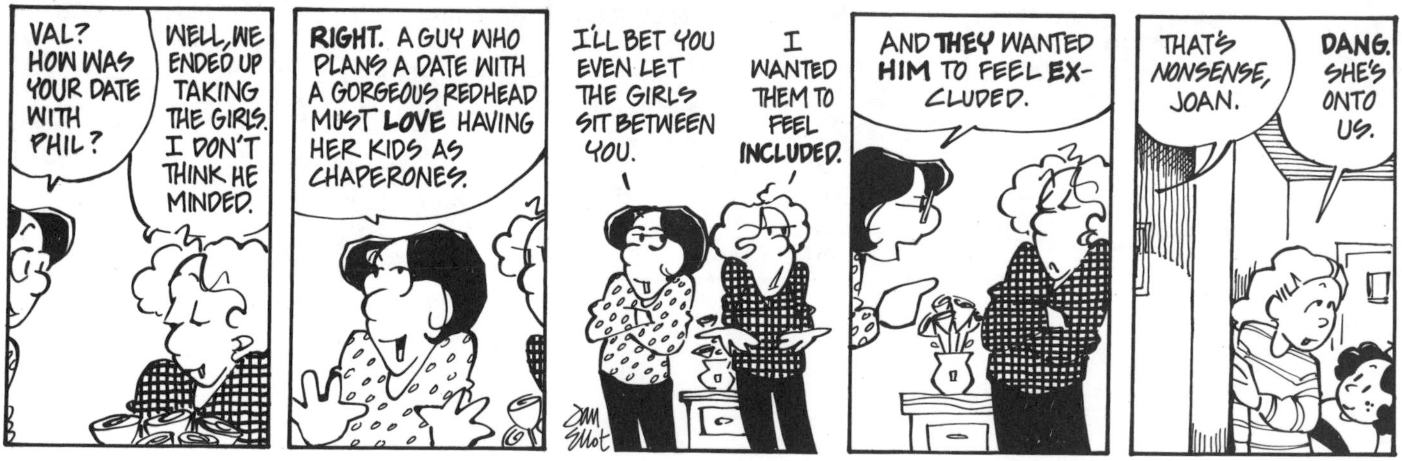
VAL? HOW WAS YOUR DATE WITH PHIL?
WELL, WE ENDED UP TAKING THE GIRLS. I DON'T THINK HE MINDED.
RIGHT. A GUY WHO PLANS A DATE WITH A GORGEOUS REDHEAD MUST LOVE HAVING HER KIDS AS CHAPERONES.
I'LL BET YOU EVEN LET THE GIRLS SIT BETWEEN YOU.
I WANTED THEM TO FEEL INCLUDED.
AND THEY WANTED HIM TO FEEL EX-CLUDED.
THAT'S NONSENSE, JOAN.
DANG. SHE'S ONTO US.

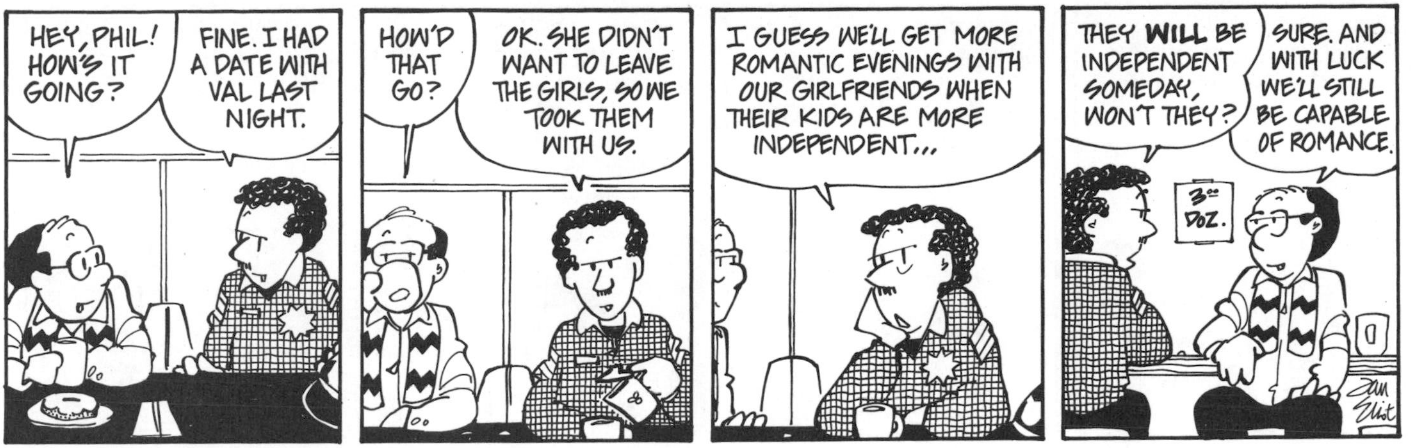
HEY, PHIL! HOW'S IT GOING?
FINE. I HAD A DATE WITH VAL LAST NIGHT.
HOW'D THAT GO?
OK. SHE DIDN'T WANT TO LEAVE THE GIRLS, SO WE TOOK THEM WITH US.
I GUESS WE'LL GET MORE ROMANTIC EVENINGS WITH OUR GIRLFRIENDS WHEN THEIR KIDS ARE MORE INDEPENDENT...
THEY **WILL** BE INDEPENDENT SOMEDAY, WON'T THEY?
SURE. AND WITH LUCK WE'LL STILL BE CAPABLE OF ROMANCE.

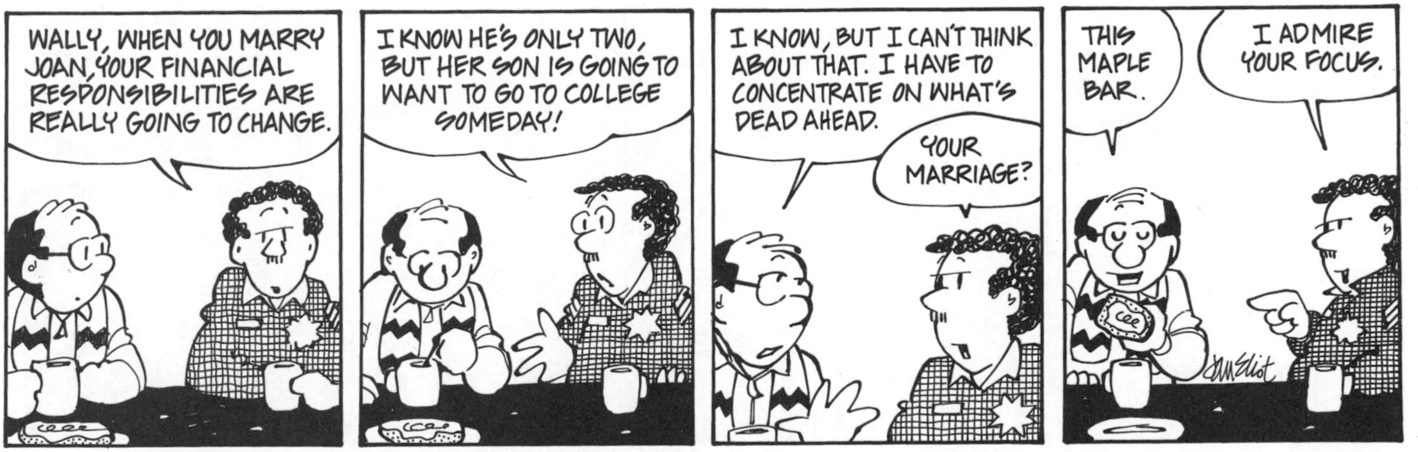
WALLY, WHEN YOU MARRY JOAN, YOUR FINANCIAL RESPONSIBILITIES ARE REALLY GOING TO CHANGE.
I KNOW HE'S ONLY TWO, BUT HER SON IS GOING TO WANT TO GO TO COLLEGE SOMEDAY!
I KNOW, BUT I CAN'T THINK ABOUT THAT. I HAVE TO CONCENTRATE ON WHAT'S DEAD AHEAD.
YOUR MARRIAGE?
THIS MAPLE BAR.
I ADMIRE YOUR FOCUS.

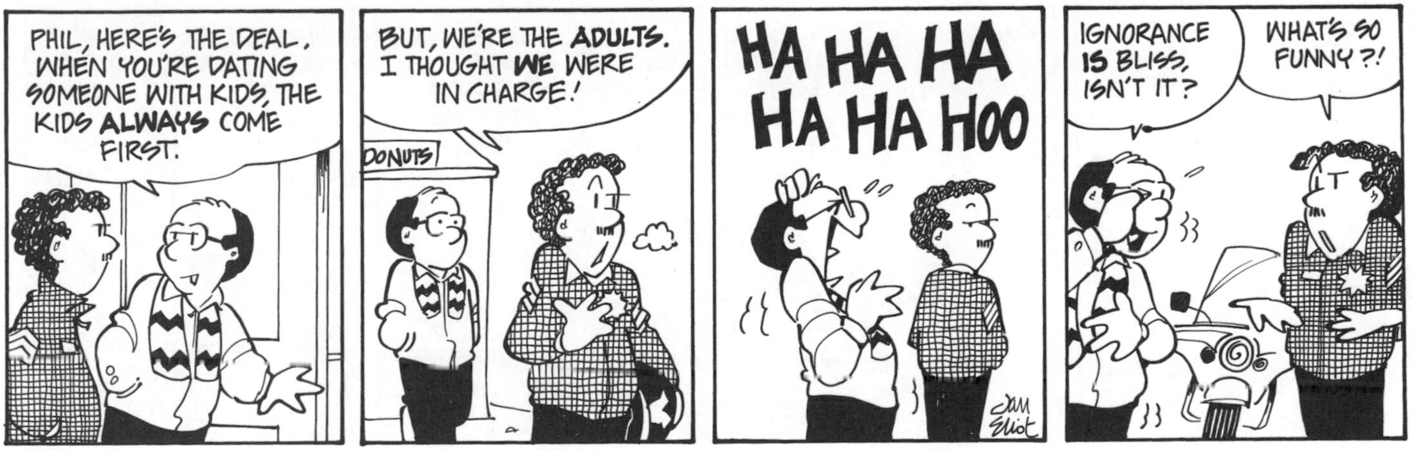
PHIL, HERE'S THE DEAL. WHEN YOU'RE DATING SOMEONE WITH KIDS, THE KIDS **ALWAYS** COME FIRST.
DONUTS
BUT, WE'RE THE **ADULTS.** I THOUGHT **WE** WERE IN CHARGE!
HA HA HA HA HA HOO
IGNORANCE **IS** BLISS, ISN'T IT?
WHAT'S SO FUNNY?!

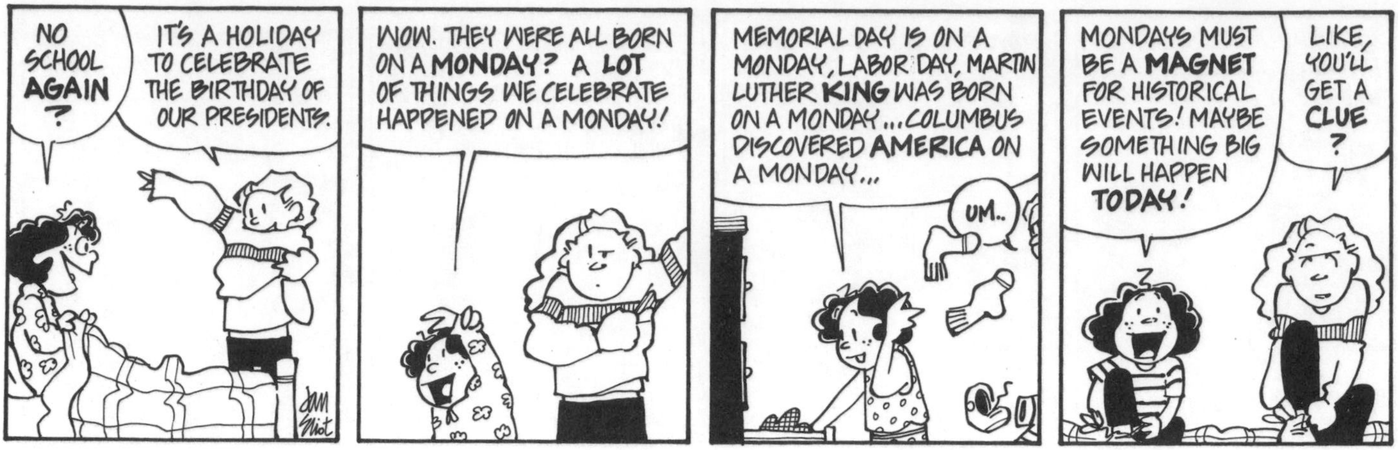
NO SCHOOL AGAIN ?
IT'S A HOLIDAY TO CELEBRATE THE BIRTHDAY OF OUR PRESIDENTS.
WOW. THEY WERE ALL BORN ON A MONDAY? A LOT OF THINGS WE CELEBRATE HAPPENED ON A MONDAY!
MEMORIAL DAY IS ON A MONDAY, LABOR DAY, MARTIN LUTHER KING WAS BORN ON A MONDAY... COLUMBUS DISCOVERED AMERICA ON A MONDAY...
UM..
MONDAYS MUST BE A MAGNET FOR HISTORICAL EVENTS! MAYBE SOMETHING BIG WILL HAPPEN TODAY!
LIKE, YOU'LL GET A CLUE ?

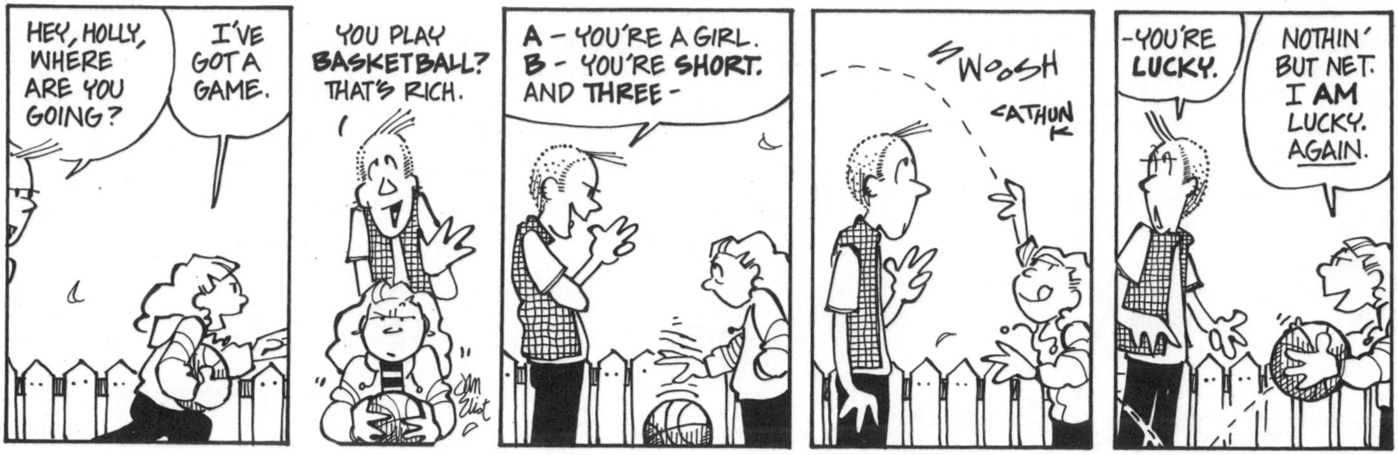
HEY, HOLLY, WHERE ARE YOU GOING?
I'VE GOT A GAME.
YOU PLAY BASKETBALL? THAT'S RICH.
A - YOU'RE A GIRL. B - YOU'RE SHORT. AND THREE -
SWOOSH
CATHUNK
-YOU'RE LUCKY.
NOTHIN' BUT NET. I AM LUCKY. AGAIN.

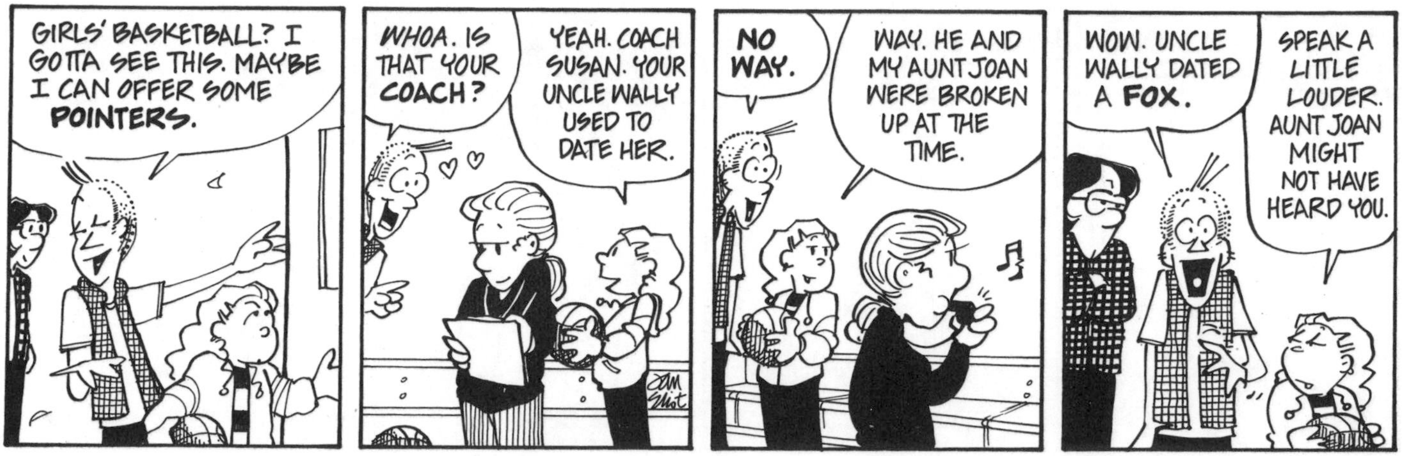
GIRLS' BASKETBALL? I GOTTA SEE THIS. MAYBE I CAN OFFER SOME POINTERS.
WHOA. IS THAT YOUR COACH?
YEAH. COACH SUSAN. YOUR UNCLE WALLY USED TO DATE HER.
NO WAY.
WAY. HE AND MY AUNT JOAN WERE BROKEN UP AT THE TIME.
WOW. UNCLE WALLY DATED A FOX.
SPEAK A LITTLE LOUDER. AUNT JOAN MIGHT NOT HAVE HEARD YOU.

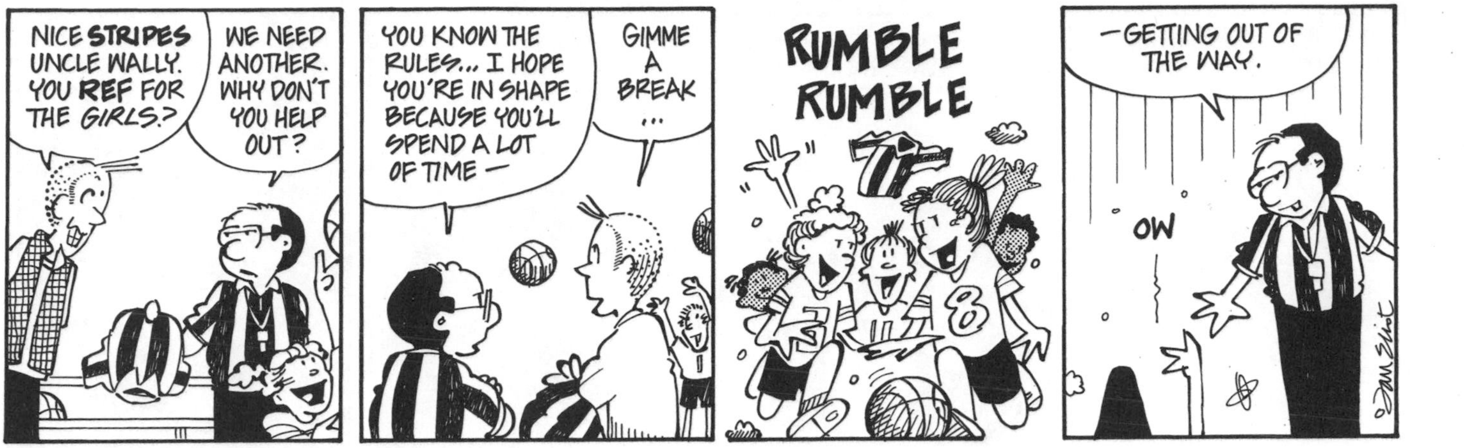
NICE STRIPES UNCLE WALLY. YOU REF FOR THE GIRLS?
WE NEED ANOTHER. WHY DON'T YOU HELP OUT?
YOU KNOW THE RULES... I HOPE YOU'RE IN SHAPE BECAUSE YOU'LL SPEND A LOT OF TIME —
GIMME A BREAK ...
RUMBLE RUMBLE
— GETTING OUT OF THE WAY.
OW

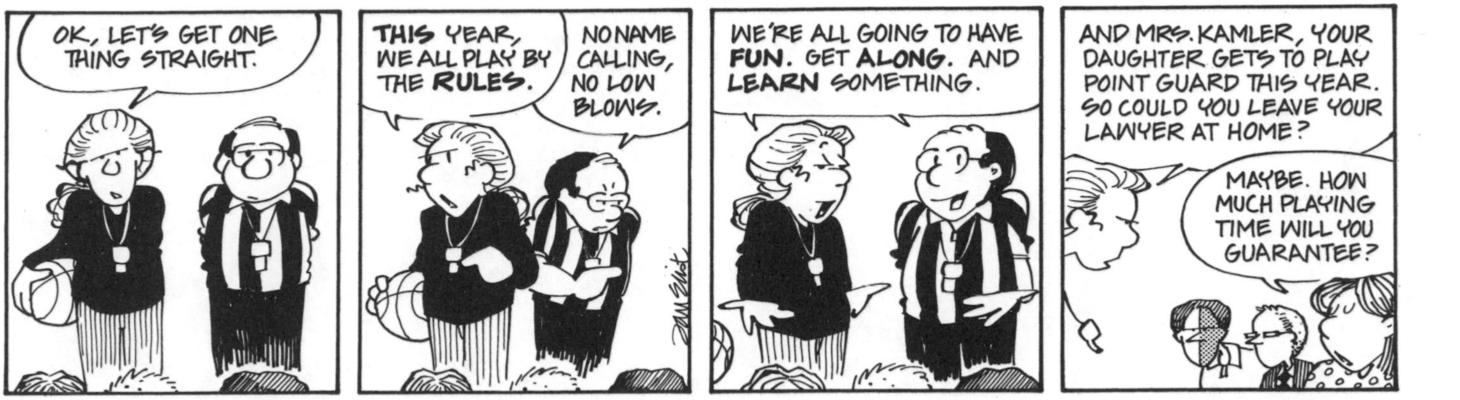
OK, LET'S GET ONE THING STRAIGHT.
THIS YEAR, WE ALL PLAY BY THE RULES.
NO NAME CALLING, NO LOW BLOWS.
WE'RE ALL GOING TO HAVE FUN. GET ALONG. AND LEARN SOMETHING.
AND MRS. KAMLER, YOUR DAUGHTER GETS TO PLAY POINT GUARD THIS YEAR. SO COULD YOU LEAVE YOUR LAWYER AT HOME?
MAYBE. HOW MUCH PLAYING TIME WILL YOU GUARANTEE?

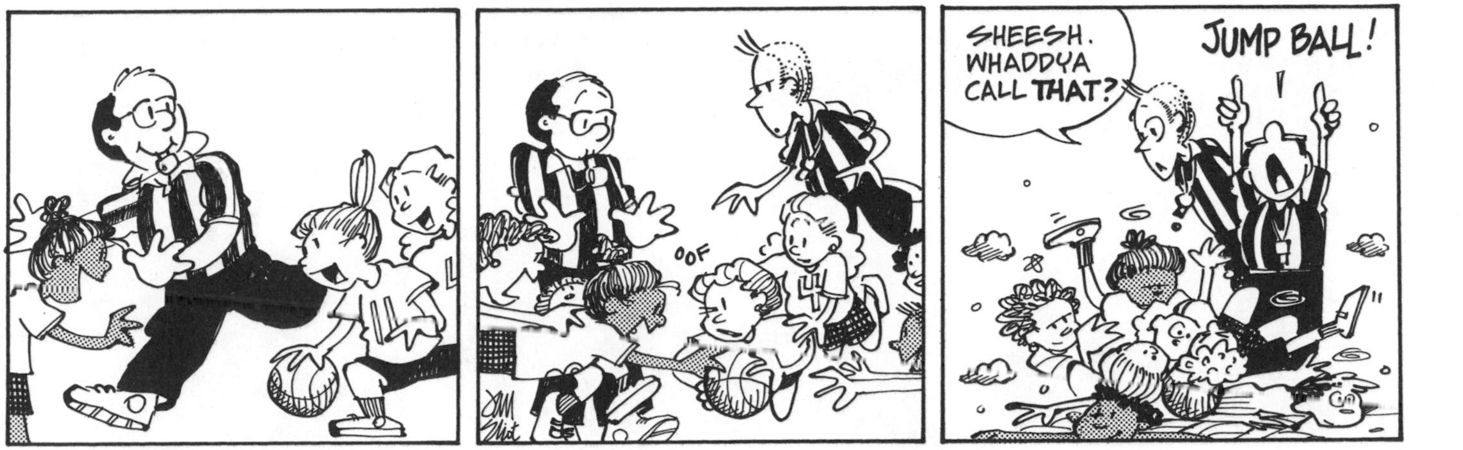
OOF
SHEESH. WHADDYA CALL THAT?
JUMP BALL!

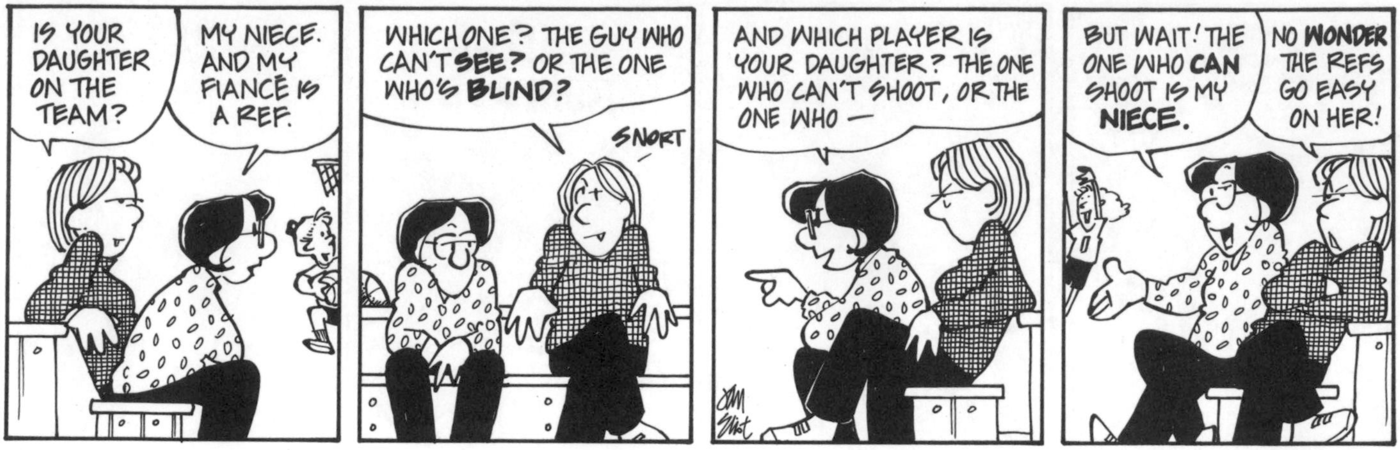
IS YOUR DAUGHTER ON THE TEAM?
MY NIECE. AND MY FIANCÉ IS A REF.
WHICH ONE? THE GUY WHO CAN'T SEE? OR THE ONE WHO'S BLIND?
SNORT
AND WHICH PLAYER IS YOUR DAUGHTER? THE ONE WHO CAN'T SHOOT, OR THE ONE WHO —
BUT WAIT! THE ONE WHO CAN SHOOT IS MY NIECE.
NO WONDER THE REFS GO EASY ON HER!

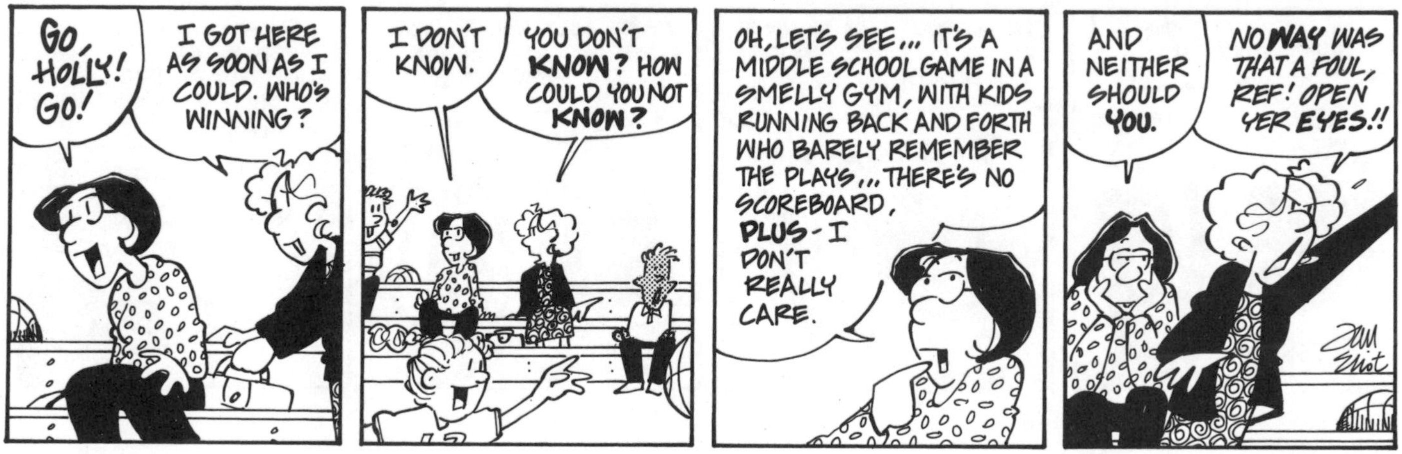
GO, HOLLY! GO!
I GOT HERE AS SOON AS I COULD. WHO'S WINNING?
I DON'T KNOW.
YOU DON'T KNOW? HOW COULD YOU NOT KNOW?
OH, LET'S SEE... IT'S A MIDDLE SCHOOL GAME IN A SMELLY GYM, WITH KIDS RUNNING BACK AND FORTH WHO BARELY REMEMBER THE PLAYS... THERE'S NO SCOREBOARD, PLUS - I DON'T REALLY CARE.
AND NEITHER SHOULD YOU.
NO WAY WAS THAT A FOUL, REF! OPEN YER EYES!!

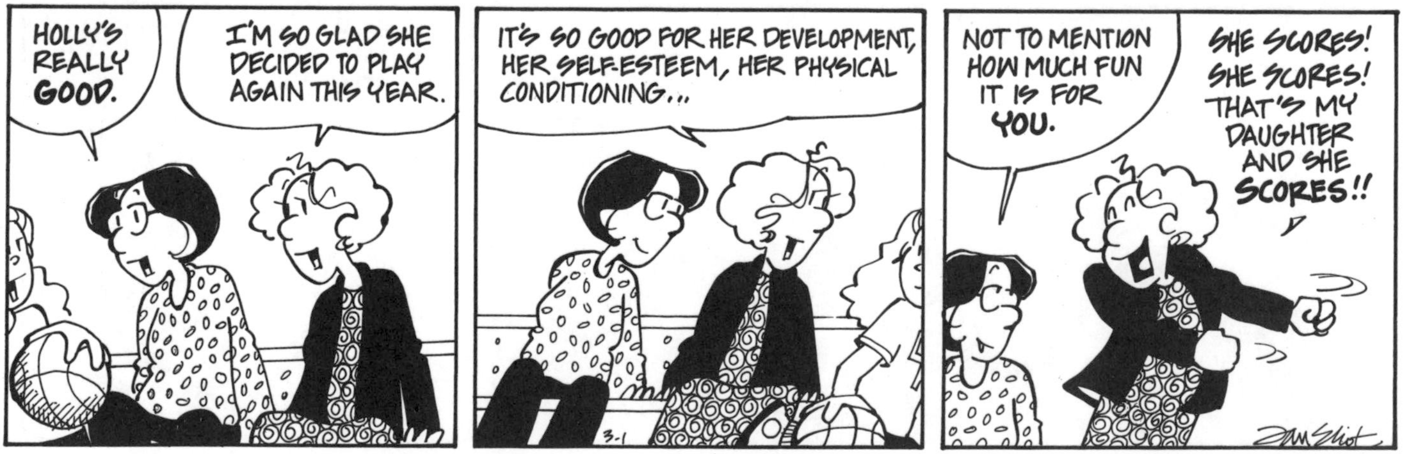
HOLLY'S REALLY GOOD.
I'M SO GLAD SHE DECIDED TO PLAY AGAIN THIS YEAR.
IT'S SO GOOD FOR HER DEVELOPMENT, HER SELF-ESTEEM, HER PHYSICAL CONDITIONING...
NOT TO MENTION HOW MUCH FUN IT IS FOR YOU.
SHE SCORES! SHE SCORES! THAT'S MY DAUGHTER AND SHE SCORES!!

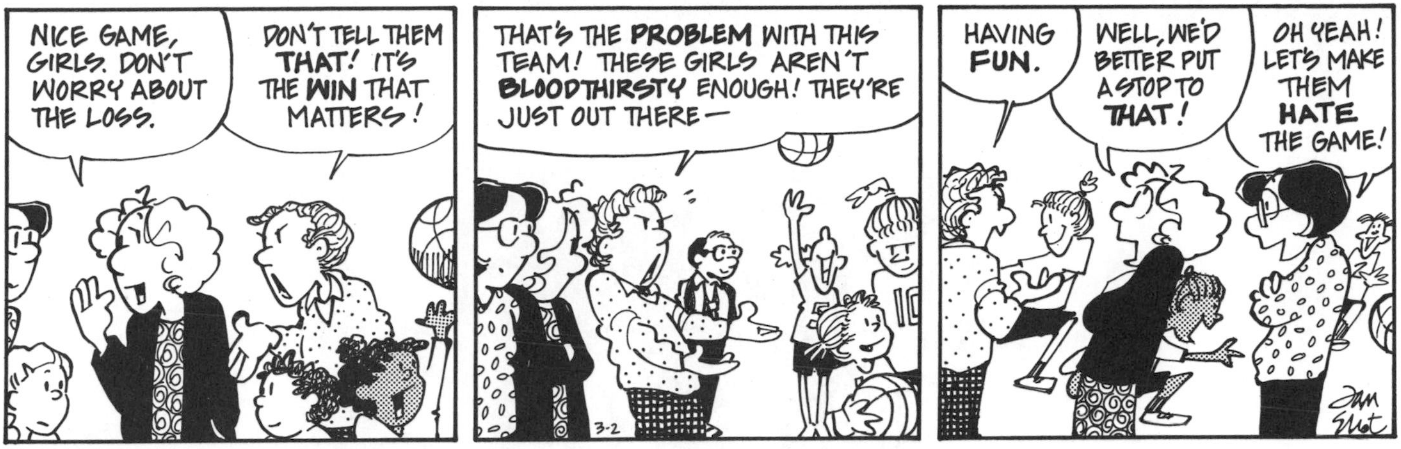
NICE GAME, GIRLS. DON'T WORRY ABOUT THE LOSS.
DON'T TELL THEM **THAT!** IT'S THE **WIN** THAT MATTERS!
THAT'S THE **PROBLEM** WITH THIS TEAM! THESE GIRLS AREN'T **BLOODTHIRSTY** ENOUGH! THEY'RE JUST OUT THERE—
HAVING **FUN.**
WELL, WE'D BETTER PUT A STOP TO **THAT!**
OH YEAH! LET'S MAKE THEM **HATE** THE GAME!

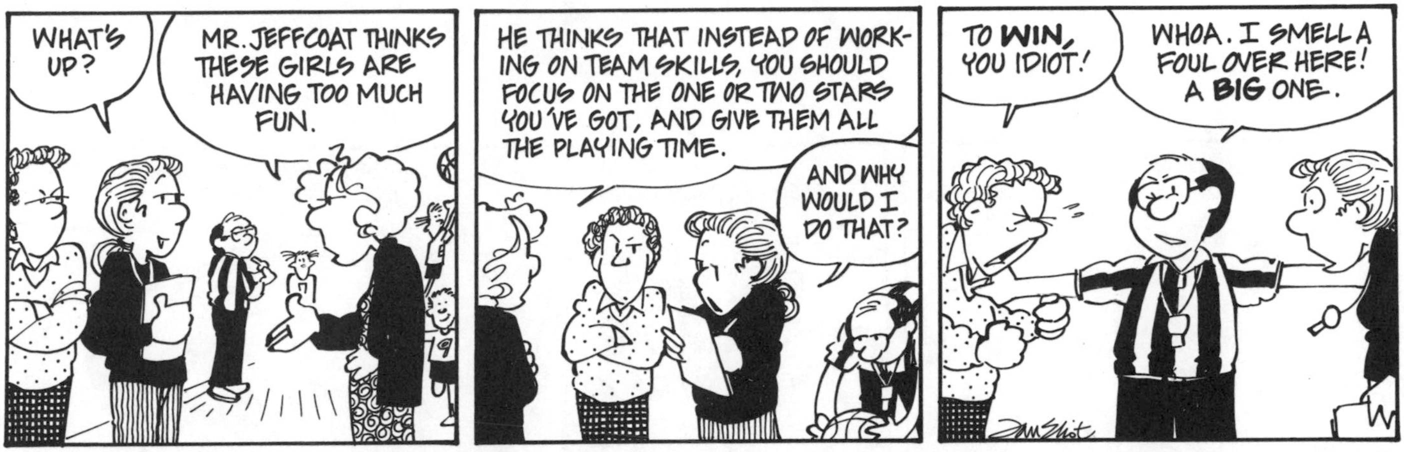
WHAT'S UP?
MR. JEFFCOAT THINKS THESE GIRLS ARE HAVING TOO MUCH FUN.
HE THINKS THAT INSTEAD OF WORKING ON TEAM SKILLS, YOU SHOULD FOCUS ON THE ONE OR TWO STARS YOU'VE GOT, AND GIVE THEM ALL THE PLAYING TIME.
AND WHY WOULD I DO THAT?
TO **WIN,** YOU IDIOT!
WHOA. I SMELL A FOUL OVER HERE! A **BIG** ONE.

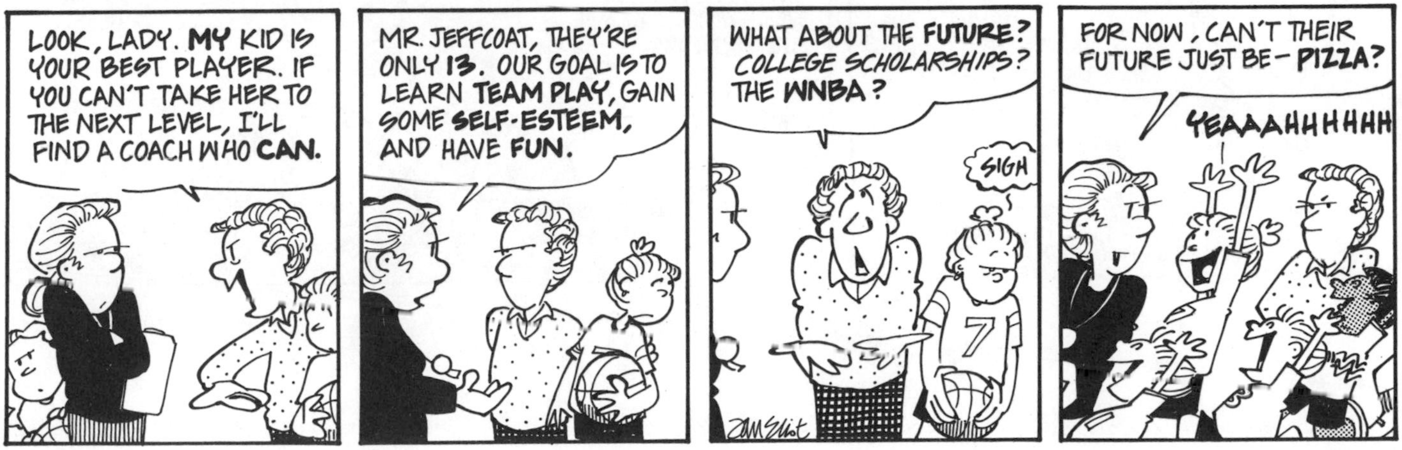
LOOK, LADY. **MY** KID IS YOUR BEST PLAYER. IF YOU CAN'T TAKE HER TO THE NEXT LEVEL, I'LL FIND A COACH WHO **CAN.**
MR. JEFFCOAT, THEY'RE ONLY **13**. OUR GOAL IS TO LEARN **TEAM PLAY**, GAIN SOME **SELF-ESTEEM,** AND HAVE **FUN.**
WHAT ABOUT THE **FUTURE?** *COLLEGE SCHOLARSHIPS?* THE **WNBA?**
SIGH
FOR NOW, CAN'T THEIR FUTURE JUST BE—**PIZZA?**
YEAAAHHHHHH

Stone Soup

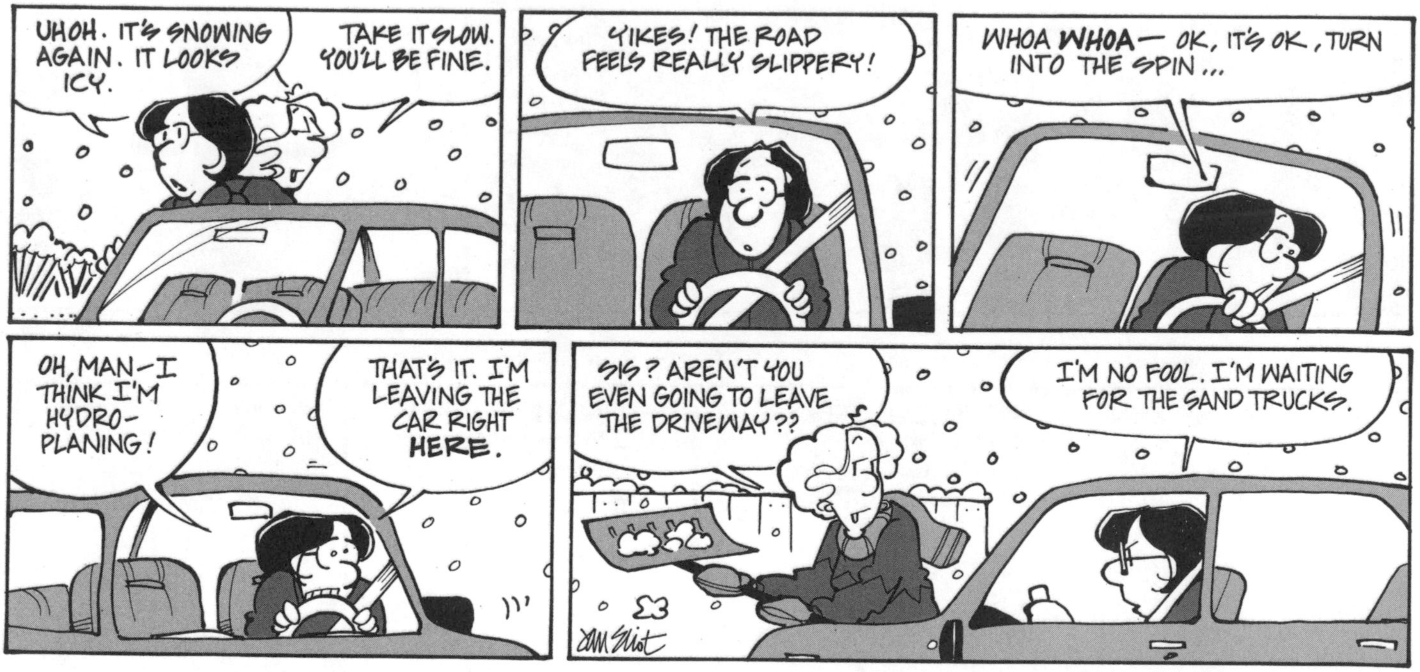

UHOH. IT'S SNOWING AGAIN. IT LOOKS ICY.
TAKE IT SLOW. YOU'LL BE FINE.
YIKES! THE ROAD FEELS REALLY SLIPPERY!
WHOA WHOA— OK, IT'S OK, TURN INTO THE SPIN...
OH, MAN—I THINK I'M HYDRO-PLANING!
THAT'S IT. I'M LEAVING THE CAR RIGHT HERE.
SIS? AREN'T YOU EVEN GOING TO LEAVE THE DRIVEWAY??
I'M NO FOOL. I'M WAITING FOR THE SAND TRUCKS.

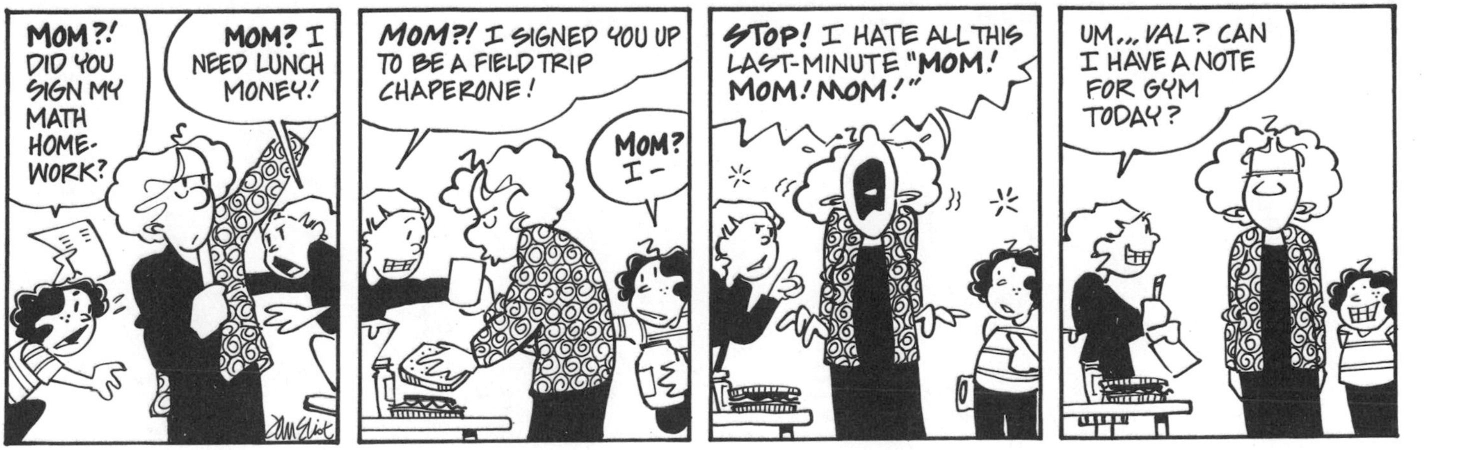
MOM?! DID YOU SIGN MY MATH HOME-WORK?
MOM? I NEED LUNCH MONEY!
MOM?! I SIGNED YOU UP TO BE A FIELD TRIP CHAPERONE!
MOM? I -
STOP! I HATE ALL THIS LAST-MINUTE "MOM! MOM! MOM!"
UM... VAL? CAN I HAVE A NOTE FOR GYM TODAY?

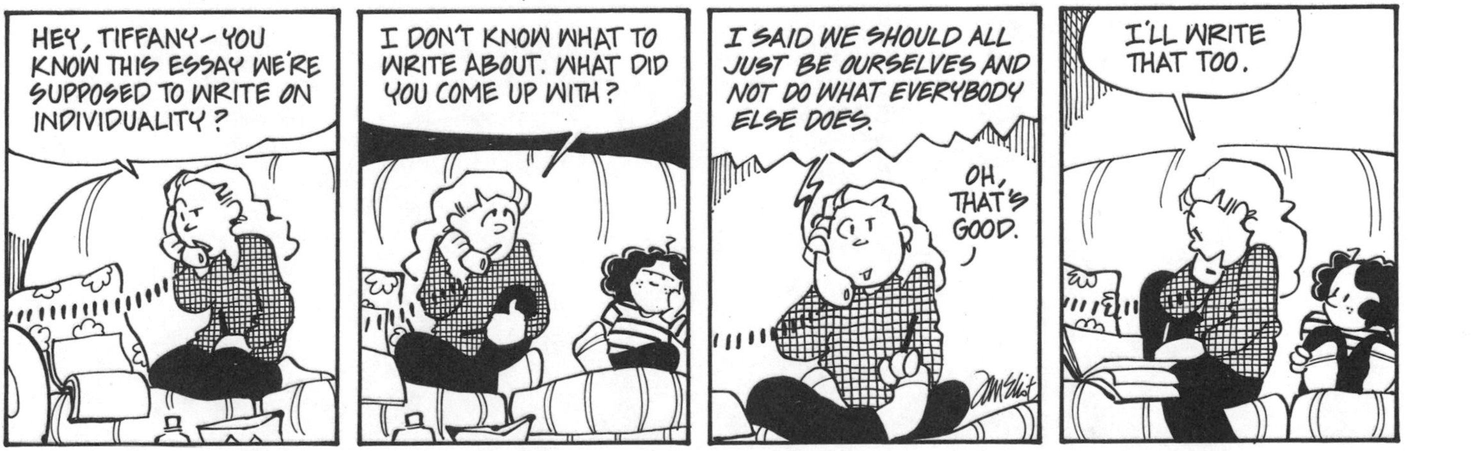
HEY, TIFFANY- YOU KNOW THIS ESSAY WE'RE SUPPOSED TO WRITE ON INDIVIDUALITY?
I DON'T KNOW WHAT TO WRITE ABOUT. WHAT DID YOU COME UP WITH?
I SAID WE SHOULD ALL JUST BE OURSELVES AND NOT DO WHAT EVERYBODY ELSE DOES.
OH, THAT'S GOOD.
I'LL WRITE THAT TOO.

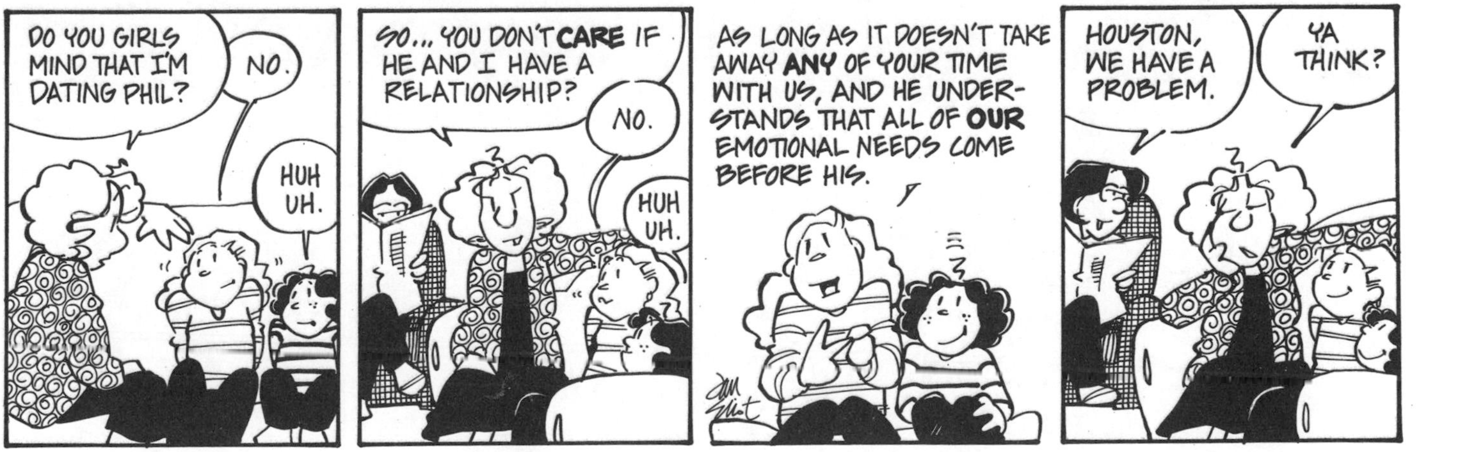
DO YOU GIRLS MIND THAT I'M DATING PHIL?
NO.
HUH UH.
SO... YOU DON'T CARE IF HE AND I HAVE A RELATIONSHIP?
NO.
HUH UH.
AS LONG AS IT DOESN'T TAKE AWAY ANY OF YOUR TIME WITH US, AND HE UNDER-STANDS THAT ALL OF OUR EMOTIONAL NEEDS COME BEFORE HIS.
HOUSTON, WE HAVE A PROBLEM.
YA THINK?

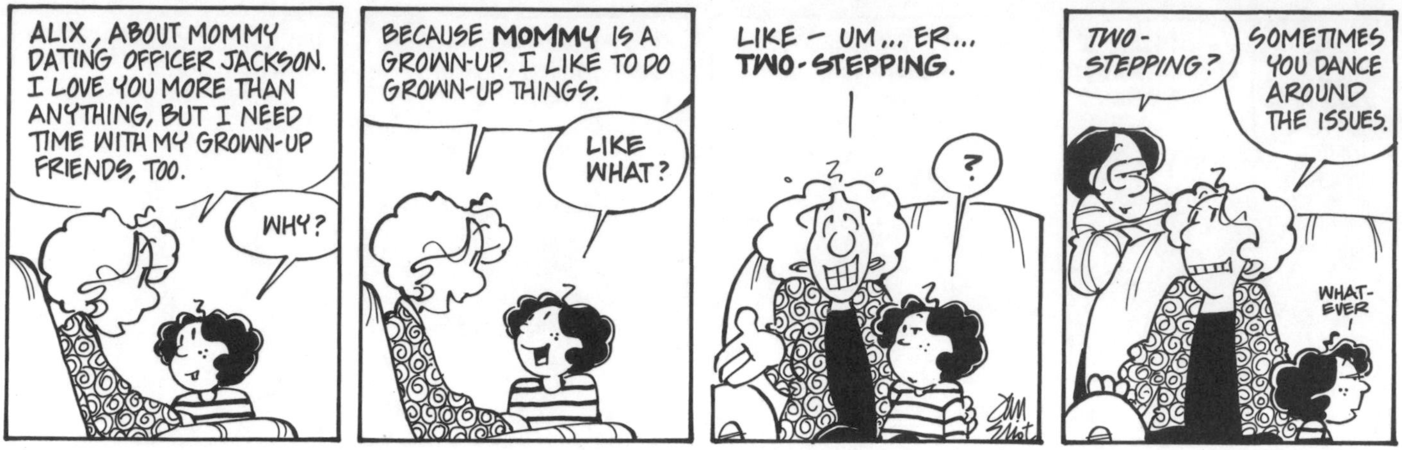
ALIX, ABOUT MOMMY DATING OFFICER JACKSON. I LOVE YOU MORE THAN ANYTHING, BUT I NEED TIME WITH MY GROWN-UP FRIENDS, TOO.
WHY?
BECAUSE MOMMY IS A GROWN-UP. I LIKE TO DO GROWN-UP THINGS.
LIKE WHAT?
LIKE – UM... ER... TWO-STEPPING.
?
TWO-STEPPING?
SOMETIMES YOU DANCE AROUND THE ISSUES.
WHAT-EVER!

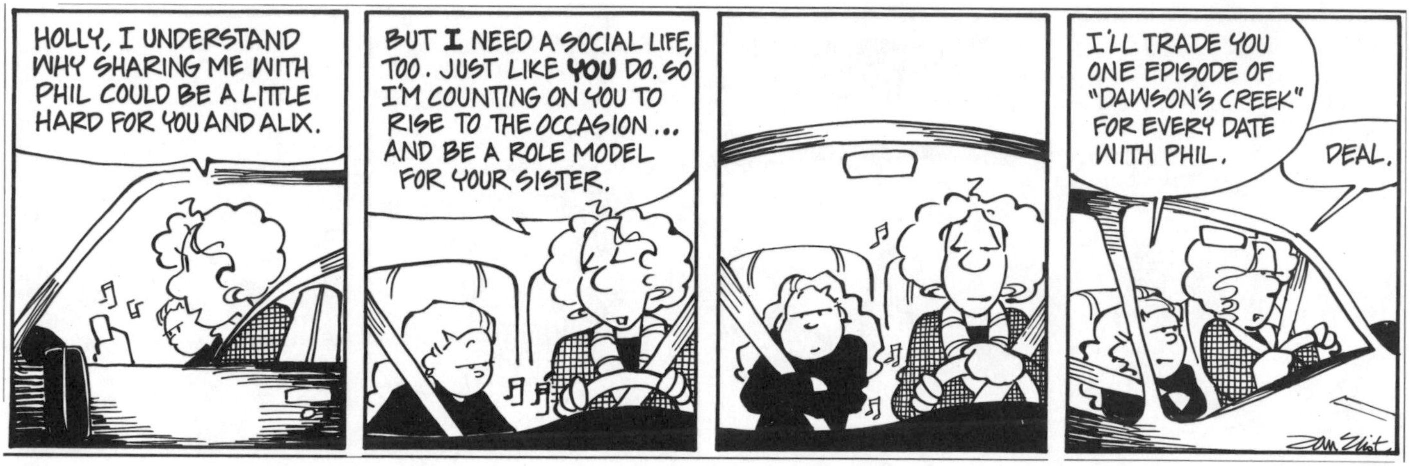
HOLLY, I UNDERSTAND WHY SHARING ME WITH PHIL COULD BE A LITTLE HARD FOR YOU AND ALIX.
BUT I NEED A SOCIAL LIFE, TOO. JUST LIKE YOU DO. SO I'M COUNTING ON YOU TO RISE TO THE OCCASION... AND BE A ROLE MODEL FOR YOUR SISTER.
I'LL TRADE YOU ONE EPISODE OF "DAWSON'S CREEK" FOR EVERY DATE WITH PHIL.
DEAL.

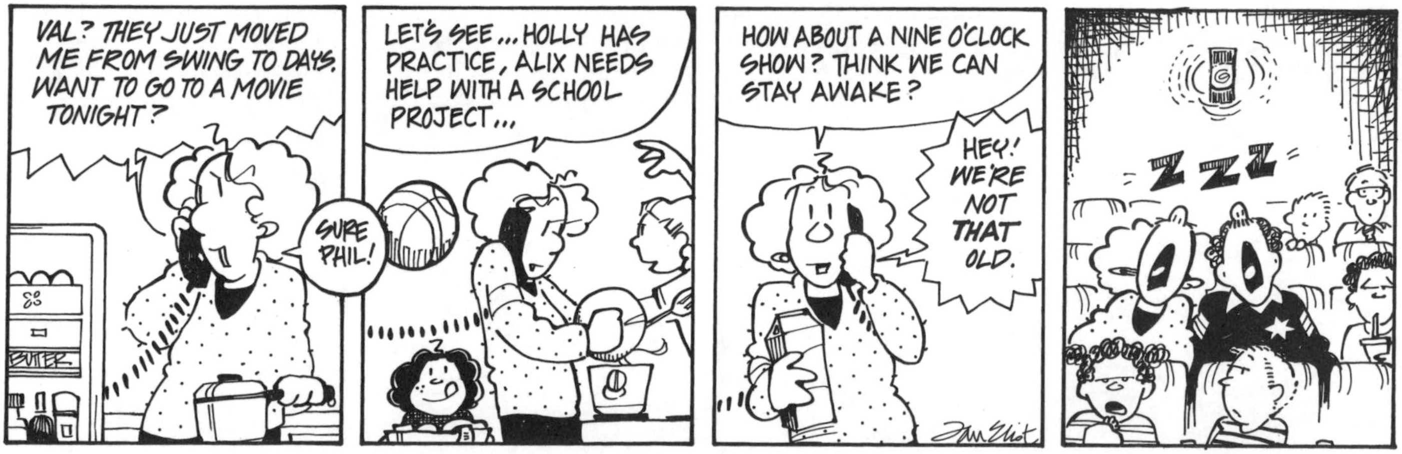
VAL? THEY JUST MOVED ME FROM SWING TO DAYS. WANT TO GO TO A MOVIE TONIGHT?
SURE PHIL!
BUTTER
LET'S SEE... HOLLY HAS PRACTICE, ALIX NEEDS HELP WITH A SCHOOL PROJECT...
HOW ABOUT A NINE O'CLOCK SHOW? THINK WE CAN STAY AWAKE?
HEY! WE'RE NOT THAT OLD.
ZZZ

Stone Soup

Panel 1: OKAY— GOSH! NINE O'CLOCK! I AM SO **TIRED!** BEDTIME!

Panel 2: ONCE UPON A TIME THEY WENT TO A BALL AND LIVED HAPPILY EVER AFTER **THE END.**

SEE YOU IN THE MORNING!

Panel 3: YOU KNOW, WE ALL LOOK SO TIRED! IF WE GO TO BED RIGHT **NOW** WE'LL GET A COUPLE EXTRA HOURS SLEEP.

Panel 4: I PARKED DOWN THE BLOCK SO THEY WOULDN'T HEAR MY CYCLE.

I PRETENDED TO BE TIRED AND GOT THEM TO GO TO BED EARLY.

Panel 5: **SHEESH** IT'S A LOT OF WORK TO GET PRIVACY WHEN YOU DATE SOMEONE WITH A FAMILY!

SHH

WELL, IT'S AN **ILLUSION** OF PRIVACY, BUT WE'LL GO WITH IT.

SHHH

SHH

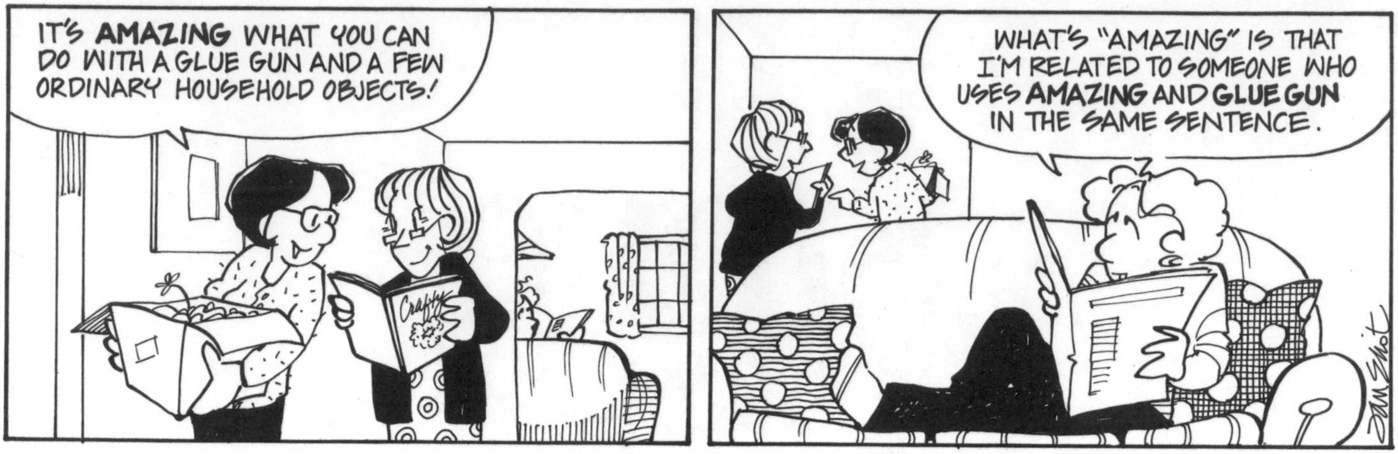
IT'S **AMAZING** WHAT YOU CAN DO WITH A GLUE GUN AND A FEW ORDINARY HOUSEHOLD OBJECTS!
WHAT'S "AMAZING" IS THAT I'M RELATED TO SOMEONE WHO USES **AMAZING** AND **GLUE GUN** IN THE SAME SENTENCE.

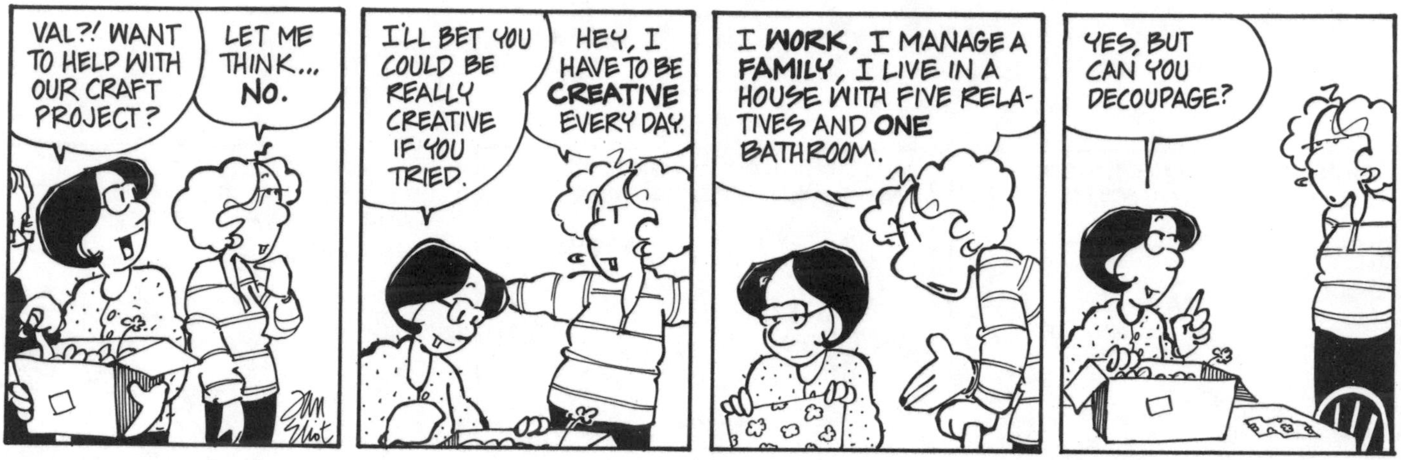
VAL?! WANT TO HELP WITH OUR CRAFT PROJECT?
LET ME THINK... **NO.**
I'LL BET YOU COULD BE REALLY CREATIVE IF YOU TRIED.
HEY, I HAVE TO BE **CREATIVE** EVERY DAY.
I **WORK**, I MANAGE A **FAMILY**, I LIVE IN A HOUSE WITH FIVE RELATIVES AND **ONE** BATHROOM.
YES, BUT CAN YOU DECOUPAGE?

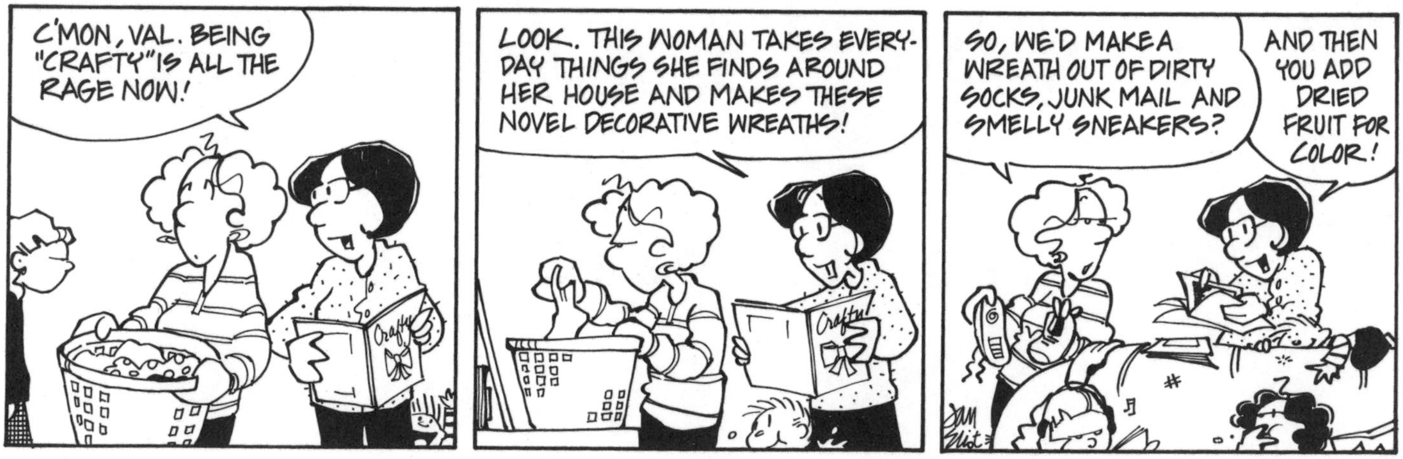
C'MON, VAL. BEING "CRAFTY" IS ALL THE RAGE NOW!
LOOK. THIS WOMAN TAKES EVERYDAY THINGS SHE FINDS AROUND HER HOUSE AND MAKES THESE NOVEL DECORATIVE WREATHS!
SO, WE'D MAKE A WREATH OUT OF DIRTY SOCKS, JUNK MAIL AND SMELLY SNEAKERS?
AND THEN YOU ADD DRIED FRUIT FOR COLOR!

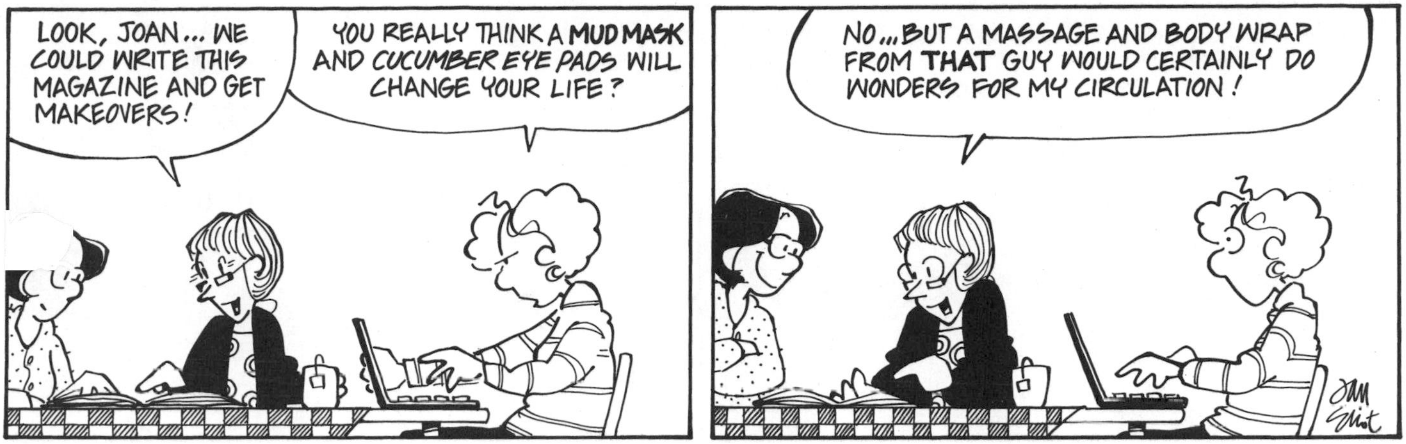
LOOK, JOAN... WE COULD WRITE THIS MAGAZINE AND GET MAKEOVERS!
YOU REALLY THINK A MUD MASK AND CUCUMBER EYE PADS WILL CHANGE YOUR LIFE?
NO... BUT A MASSAGE AND BODY WRAP FROM THAT GUY WOULD CERTAINLY DO WONDERS FOR MY CIRCULATION!

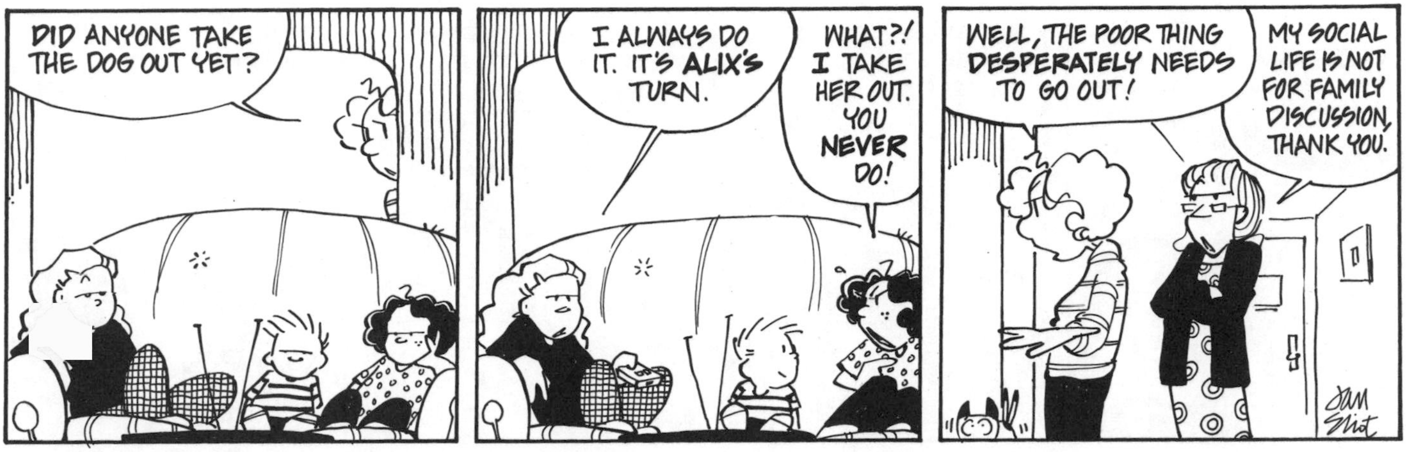
DID ANYONE TAKE THE DOG OUT YET?
I ALWAYS DO IT. IT'S ALIX'S TURN.
WHAT?! I TAKE HER OUT. YOU NEVER DO!
WELL, THE POOR THING DESPERATELY NEEDS TO GO OUT!
MY SOCIAL LIFE IS NOT FOR FAMILY DISCUSSION, THANK YOU.

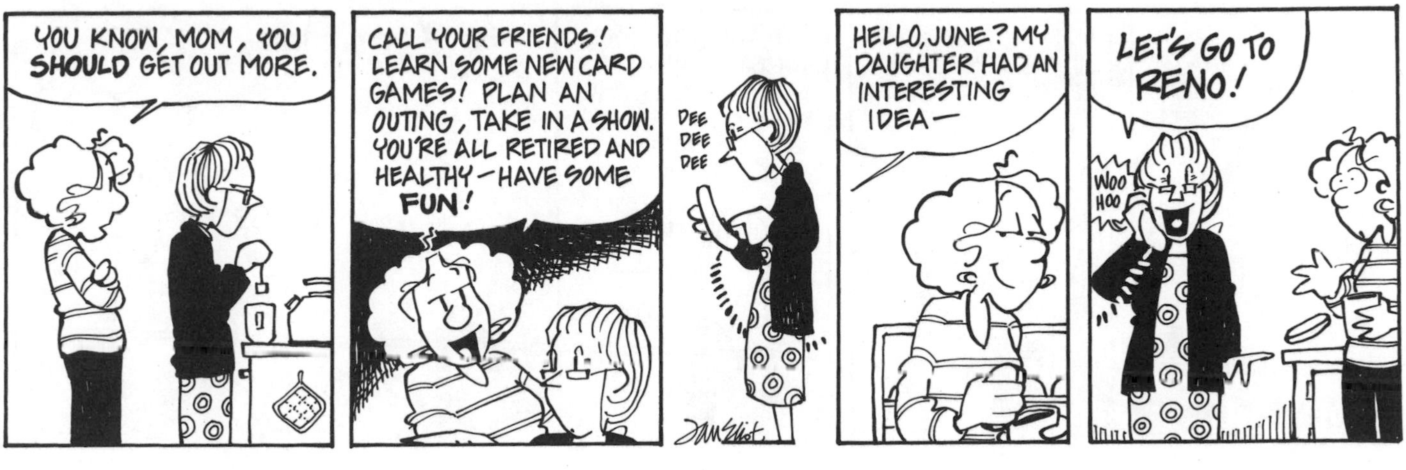
YOU KNOW, MOM, YOU SHOULD GET OUT MORE.
CALL YOUR FRIENDS! LEARN SOME NEW CARD GAMES! PLAN AN OUTING, TAKE IN A SHOW. YOU'RE ALL RETIRED AND HEALTHY — HAVE SOME FUN!
DEE DEE DEE
HELLO, JUNE? MY DAUGHTER HAD AN INTERESTING IDEA —
LET'S GO TO RENO!
WOO HOO

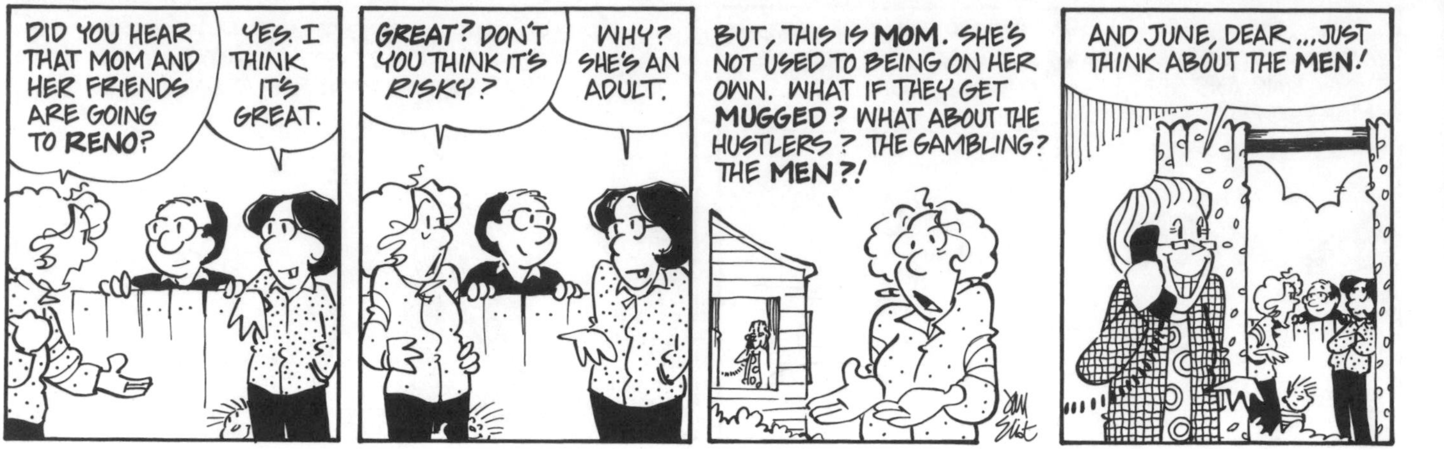
DID YOU HEAR THAT MOM AND HER FRIENDS ARE GOING TO RENO?
YES. I THINK IT'S GREAT.
GREAT? DON'T YOU THINK IT'S RISKY?
WHY? SHE'S AN ADULT.
BUT, THIS IS MOM. SHE'S NOT USED TO BEING ON HER OWN. WHAT IF THEY GET MUGGED? WHAT ABOUT THE HUSTLERS? THE GAMBLING? THE MEN?!
AND JUNE, DEAR ... JUST THINK ABOUT THE MEN!

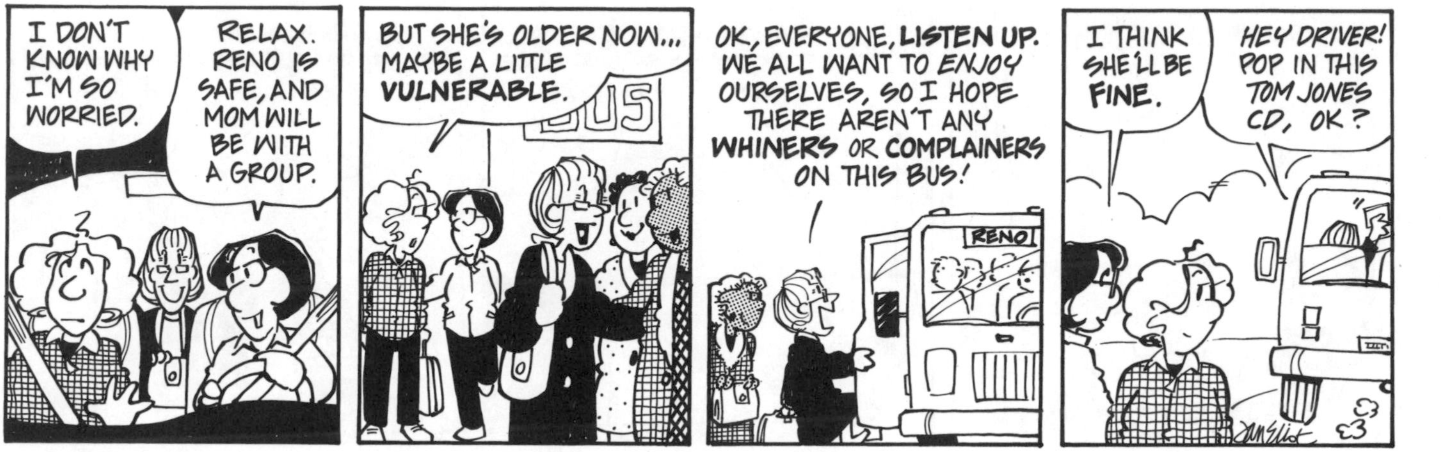
I DON'T KNOW WHY I'M SO WORRIED.
RELAX. RENO IS SAFE, AND MOM WILL BE WITH A GROUP.
BUT SHE'S OLDER NOW... MAYBE A LITTLE VULNERABLE.
BUS
OK, EVERYONE, LISTEN UP. WE ALL WANT TO ENJOY OURSELVES, SO I HOPE THERE AREN'T ANY WHINERS OR COMPLAINERS ON THIS BUS!
RENO
I THINK SHE'LL BE FINE.
HEY DRIVER! POP IN THIS TOM JONES CD, OK?

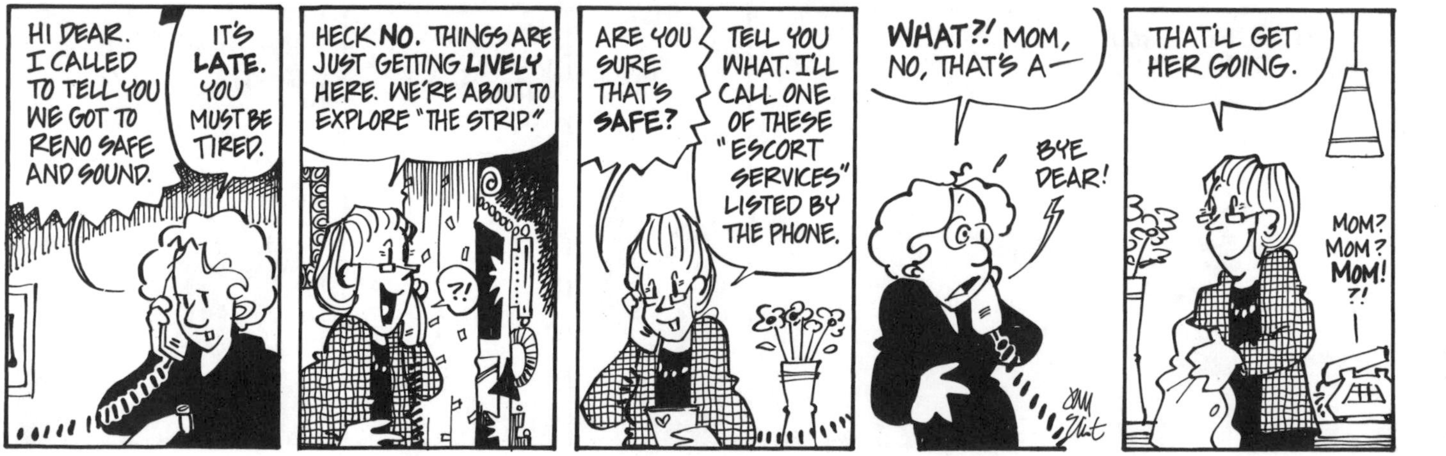
HI DEAR. I CALLED TO TELL YOU WE GOT TO RENO SAFE AND SOUND.
IT'S LATE. YOU MUST BE TIRED.
HECK NO. THINGS ARE JUST GETTING LIVELY HERE. WE'RE ABOUT TO EXPLORE "THE STRIP."
?!
ARE YOU SURE THAT'S SAFE?
TELL YOU WHAT. I'LL CALL ONE OF THESE "ESCORT SERVICES" LISTED BY THE PHONE.
WHAT?! MOM, NO, THAT'S A—
BYE DEAR!
THAT'LL GET HER GOING.
MOM? MOM? MOM! ?!

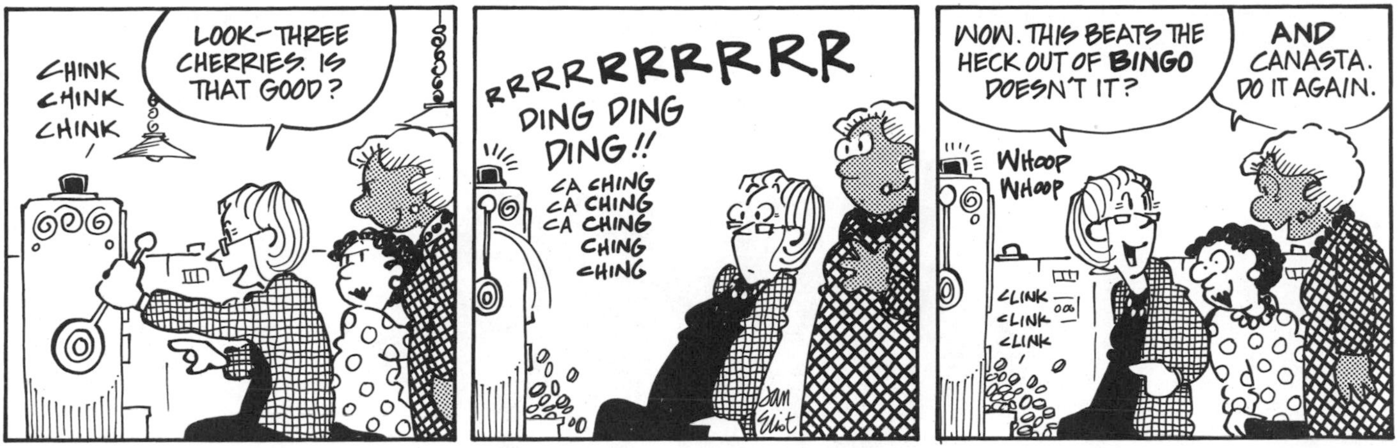
CHINK
CHINK
CHINK
LOOK—THREE CHERRIES. IS THAT GOOD?
RRRRRRRRRRR
DING DING DING!!
CA CHING
CA CHING
CA CHING
CHING
CHING
WOW. THIS BEATS THE HECK OUT OF BINGO DOESN'T IT?
AND CANASTA. DO IT AGAIN.
WHOOP
WHOOP
CLINK
CLINK
CLINK

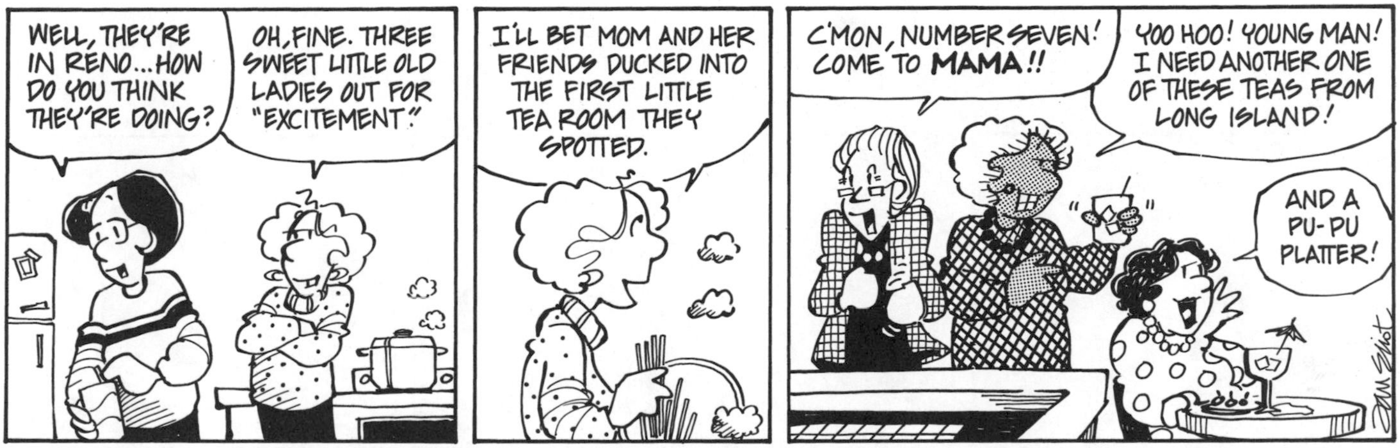
WELL, THEY'RE IN RENO... HOW DO YOU THINK THEY'RE DOING?
OH, FINE. THREE SWEET LITTLE OLD LADIES OUT FOR "EXCITEMENT."
I'LL BET MOM AND HER FRIENDS DUCKED INTO THE FIRST LITTLE TEA ROOM THEY SPOTTED.
C'MON, NUMBER SEVEN! COME TO MAMA!!
YOO HOO! YOUNG MAN! I NEED ANOTHER ONE OF THESE TEAS FROM LONG ISLAND!
AND A PU-PU PLATTER!

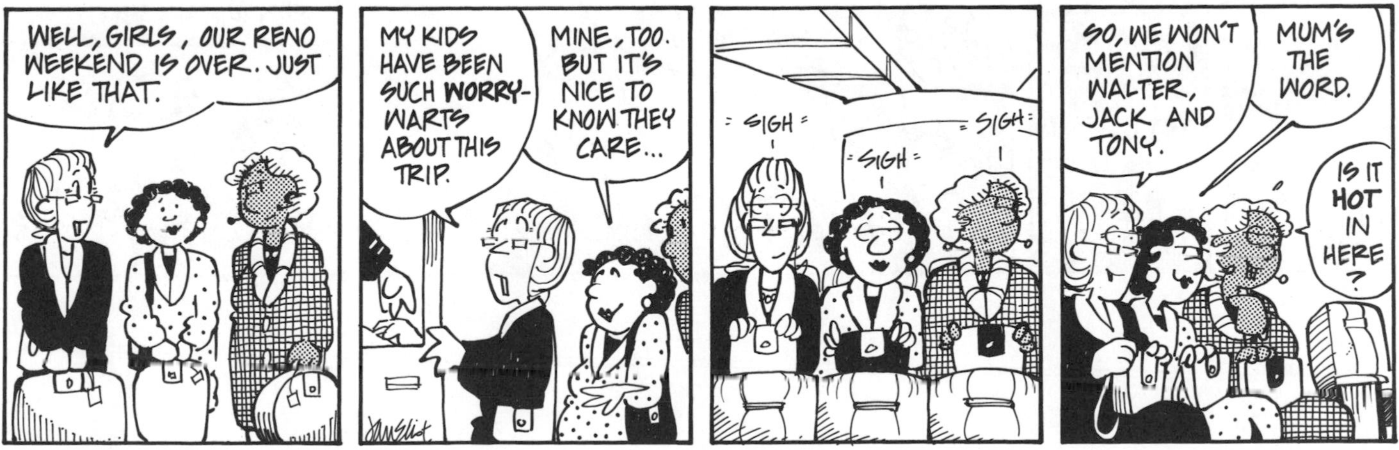
WELL, GIRLS, OUR RENO WEEKEND IS OVER. JUST LIKE THAT.
MY KIDS HAVE BEEN SUCH WORRY-WARTS ABOUT THIS TRIP.
MINE, TOO. BUT IT'S NICE TO KNOW THEY CARE...
= SIGH =
= SIGH =
= SIGH =
SO, WE WON'T MENTION WALTER, JACK AND TONY.
MUM'S THE WORD.
IS IT HOT IN HERE?

Stone Soup

ZZZ
ZZZ
TIP
TIP
CREAK
SHHH
AHHH
?
BARK
BARK
BARK
BARK
MOM ?! WHAT'S FOR BREAKFAST? WE'RE STARVED !!
RRRR
I SURE HOPE YOU KNOW HOW TO MAKE **WAFFLES**.
WOOF?

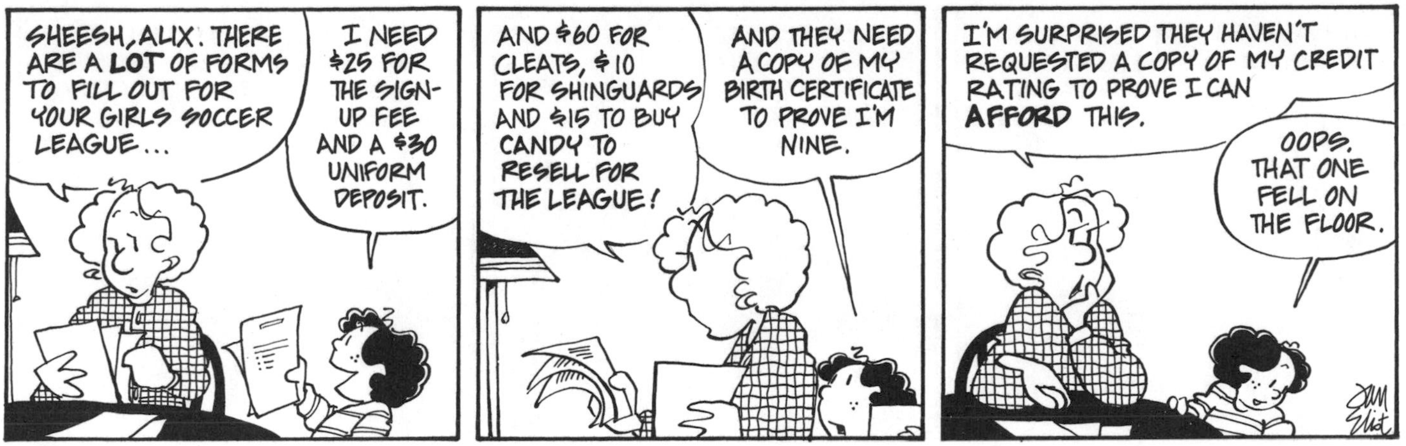
SHEESH, ALIX. THERE ARE A LOT OF FORMS TO FILL OUT FOR YOUR GIRLS SOCCER LEAGUE...
I NEED $25 FOR THE SIGN-UP FEE AND A $30 UNIFORM DEPOSIT.
AND $60 FOR CLEATS, $10 FOR SHINGUARDS AND $15 TO BUY CANDY TO RESELL FOR THE LEAGUE!
AND THEY NEED A COPY OF MY BIRTH CERTIFICATE TO PROVE I'M NINE.
I'M SURPRISED THEY HAVEN'T REQUESTED A COPY OF MY CREDIT RATING TO PROVE I CAN AFFORD THIS.
OOPS. THAT ONE FELL ON THE FLOOR.

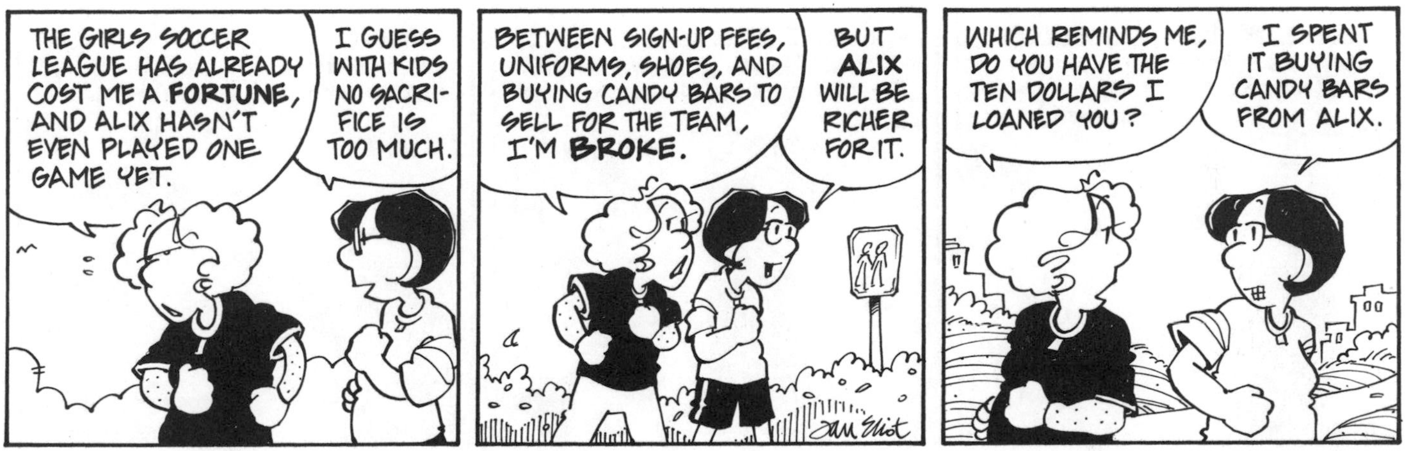
THE GIRLS SOCCER LEAGUE HAS ALREADY COST ME A FORTUNE, AND ALIX HASN'T EVEN PLAYED ONE GAME YET.
I GUESS WITH KIDS NO SACRIFICE IS TOO MUCH.
BETWEEN SIGN-UP FEES, UNIFORMS, SHOES, AND BUYING CANDY BARS TO SELL FOR THE TEAM, I'M BROKE.
BUT ALIX WILL BE RICHER FOR IT.
WHICH REMINDS ME, DO YOU HAVE THE TEN DOLLARS I LOANED YOU?
I SPENT IT BUYING CANDY BARS FROM ALIX.

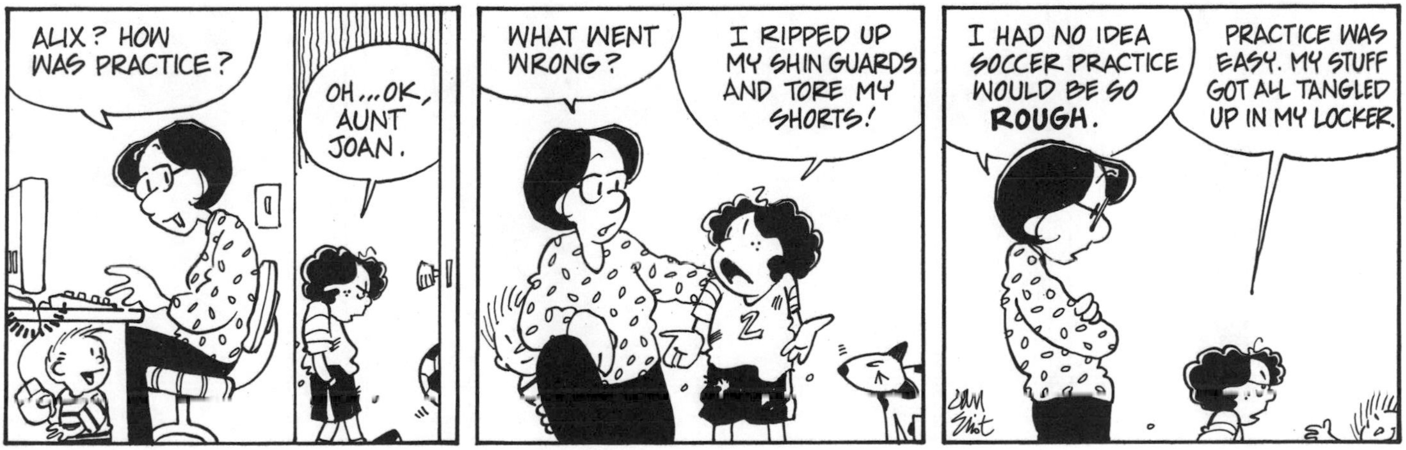
ALIX? HOW WAS PRACTICE?
OH...OK, AUNT JOAN.
WHAT WENT WRONG?
I RIPPED UP MY SHIN GUARDS AND TORE MY SHORTS!
I HAD NO IDEA SOCCER PRACTICE WOULD BE SO ROUGH.
PRACTICE WAS EASY. MY STUFF GOT ALL TANGLED UP IN MY LOCKER.

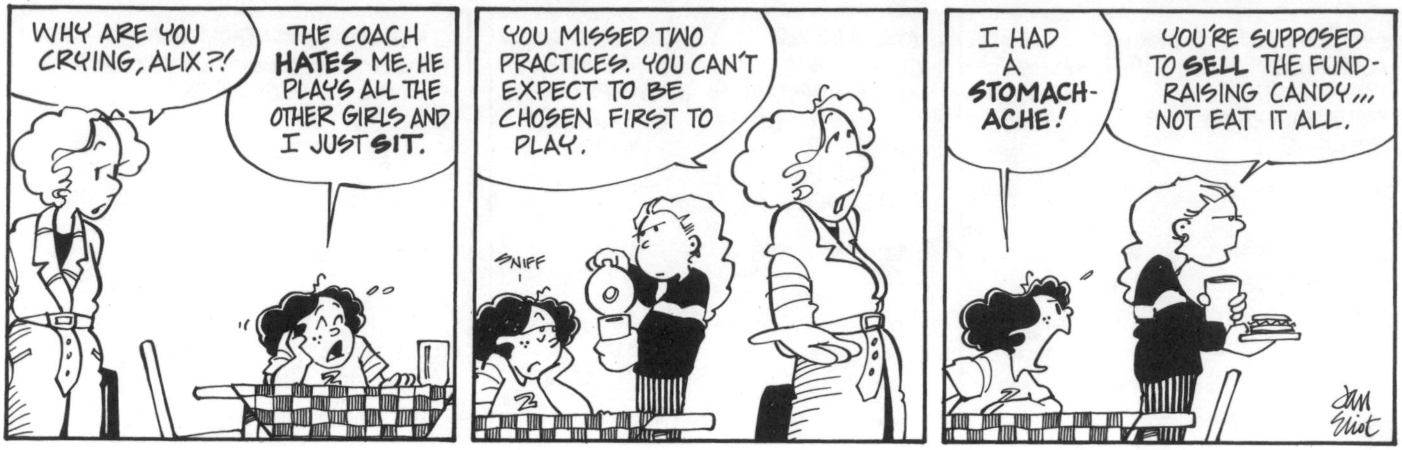
WHY ARE YOU CRYING, ALIX ?!
THE COACH **HATES** ME. HE PLAYS ALL THE OTHER GIRLS AND I JUST **SIT**.
YOU MISSED TWO PRACTICES. YOU CAN'T EXPECT TO BE CHOSEN FIRST TO PLAY.
SNIFF
I HAD A **STOMACH-ACHE**!
YOU'RE SUPPOSED TO **SELL** THE FUND-RAISING CANDY,,, NOT EAT IT ALL.

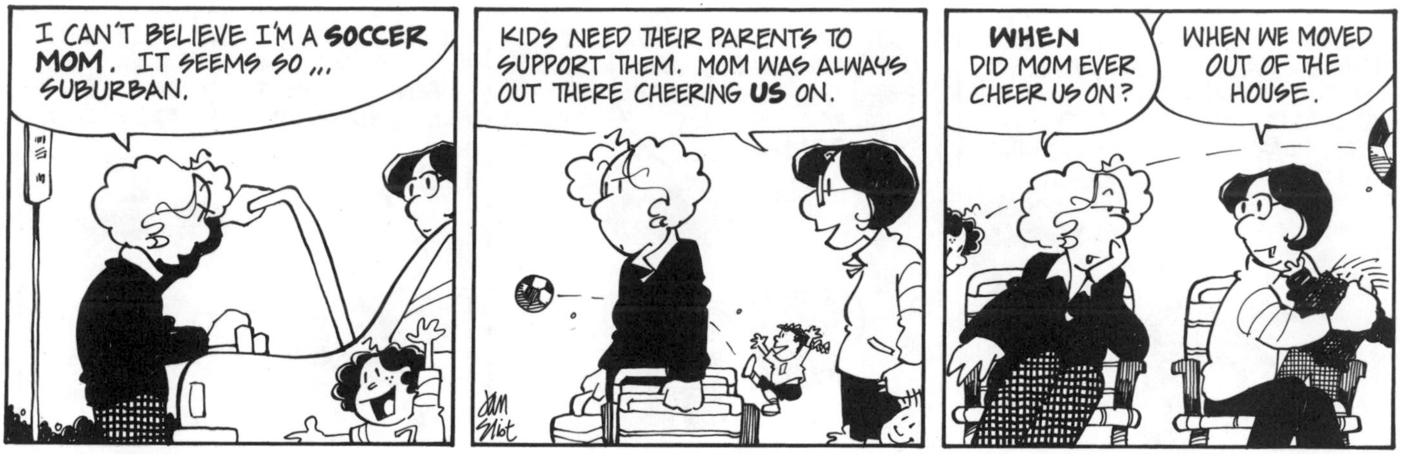
I CAN'T BELIEVE I'M A **SOCCER MOM**. IT SEEMS SO ,,, SUBURBAN.
KIDS NEED THEIR PARENTS TO SUPPORT THEM. MOM WAS ALWAYS OUT THERE CHEERING **US** ON.
WHEN DID MOM EVER CHEER US ON?
WHEN WE MOVED OUT OF THE HOUSE.

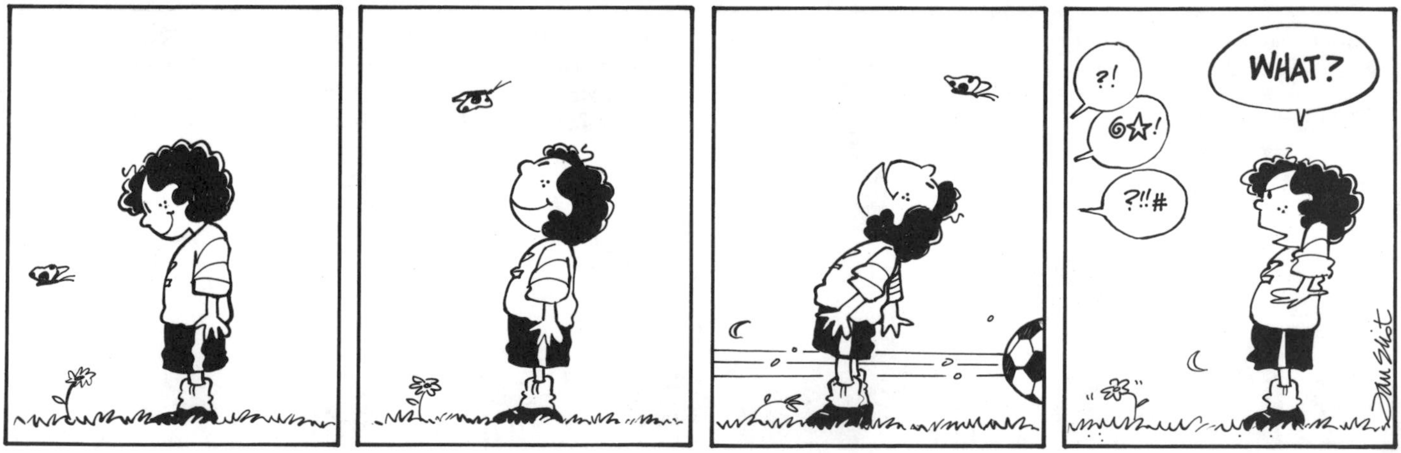
?!
?!!#
WHAT?

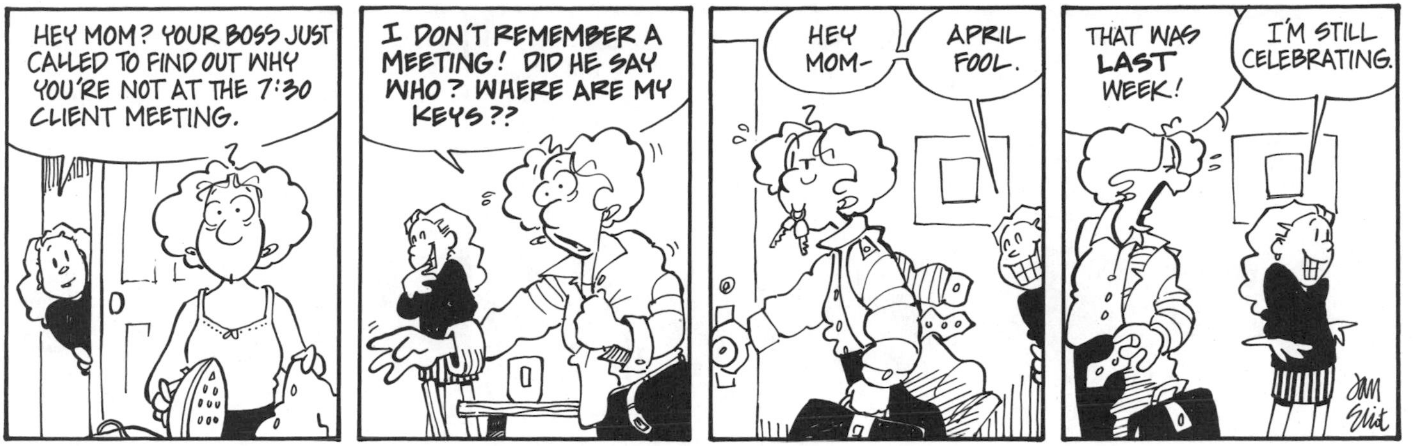
HEY MOM? YOUR BOSS JUST CALLED TO FIND OUT WHY YOU'RE NOT AT THE 7:30 CLIENT MEETING.
I DON'T REMEMBER A MEETING! DID HE SAY WHO? WHERE ARE MY KEYS??
HEY MOM-
APRIL FOOL.
THAT WAS LAST WEEK!
I'M STILL CELEBRATING.

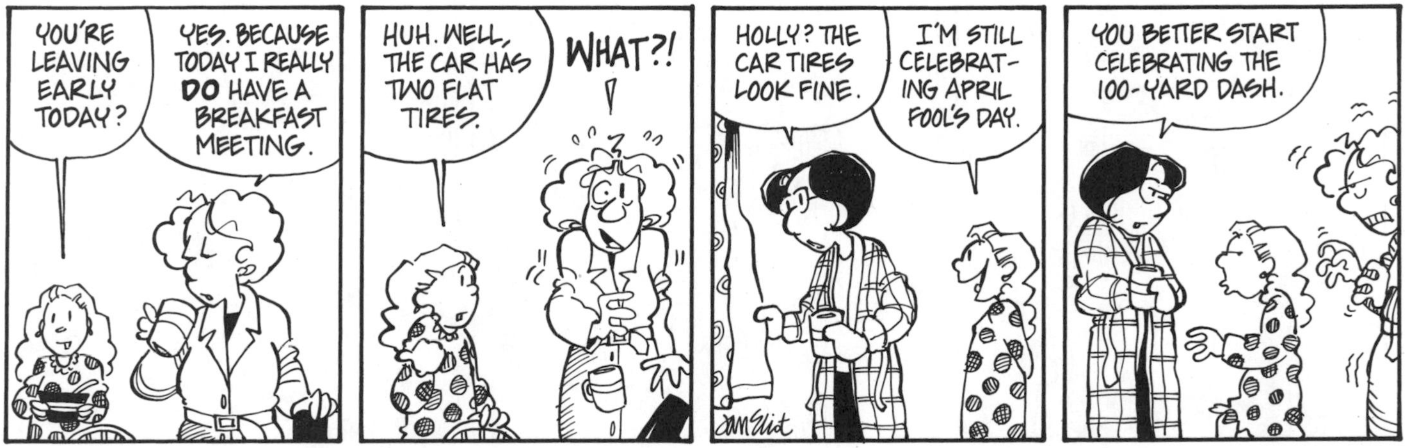
YOU'RE LEAVING EARLY TODAY?
YES. BECAUSE TODAY I REALLY DO HAVE A BREAKFAST MEETING.
HUH. WELL, THE CAR HAS TWO FLAT TIRES.
WHAT?!
HOLLY? THE CAR TIRES LOOK FINE.
I'M STILL CELEBRATING APRIL FOOL'S DAY.
YOU BETTER START CELEBRATING THE 100-YARD DASH.

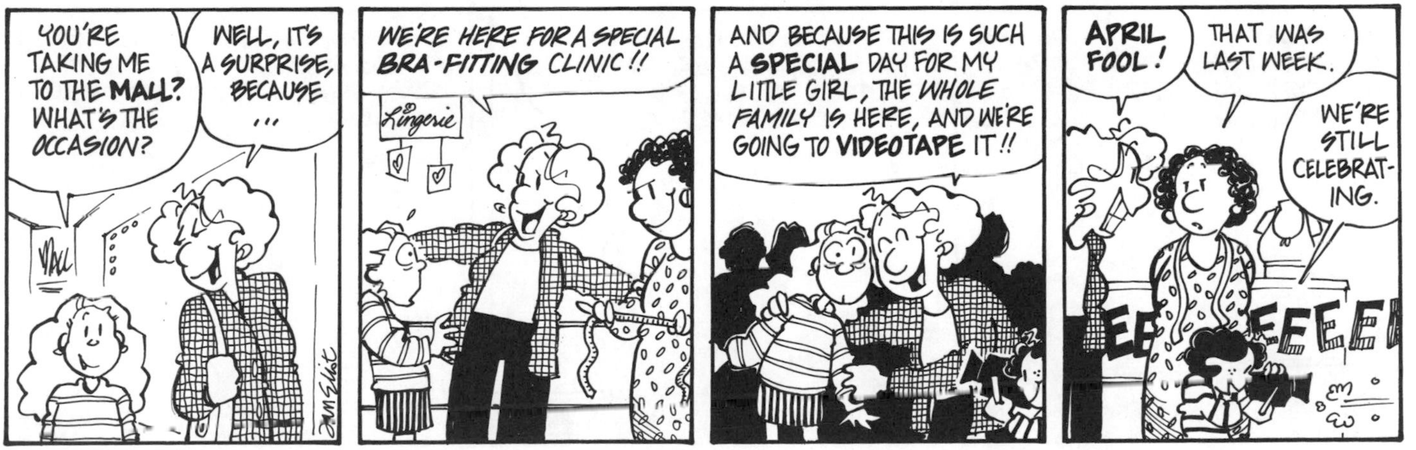
YOU'RE TAKING ME TO THE MALL? WHAT'S THE OCCASION?
WELL, IT'S A SURPRISE, BECAUSE ...
MALL
Lingerie
WE'RE HERE FOR A SPECIAL BRA-FITTING CLINIC!!
AND BECAUSE THIS IS SUCH A SPECIAL DAY FOR MY LITTLE GIRL, THE WHOLE FAMILY IS HERE, AND WE'RE GOING TO VIDEOTAPE IT!!
APRIL FOOL!
THAT WAS LAST WEEK.
WE'RE STILL CELEBRATING.

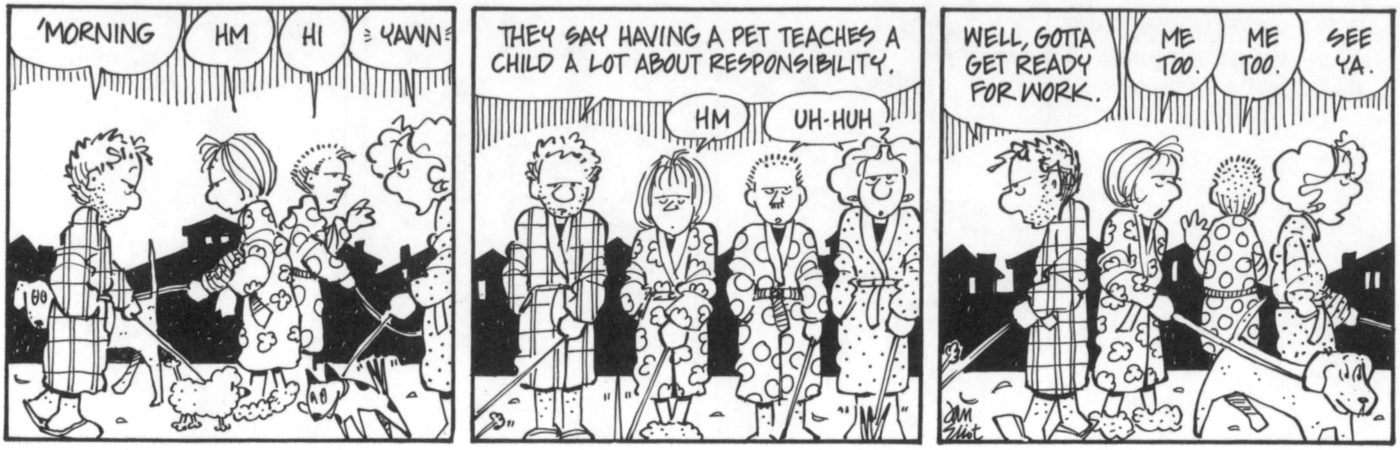
'MORNING
HM
HI
YAWN
THEY SAY HAVING A PET TEACHES A CHILD A LOT ABOUT RESPONSIBILITY.
HM
UH-HUH
WELL, GOTTA GET READY FOR WORK.
ME TOO.
ME TOO.
SEE YA.

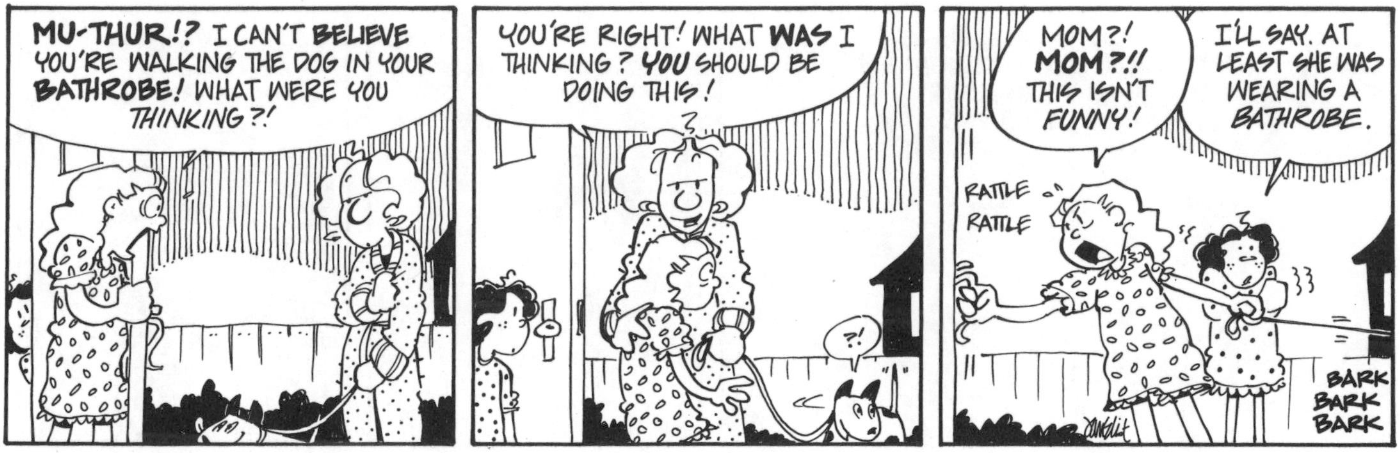
MU-THUR!? I CAN'T BELIEVE YOU'RE WALKING THE DOG IN YOUR BATHROBE! WHAT WERE YOU THINKING?!
YOU'RE RIGHT! WHAT WAS I THINKING? YOU SHOULD BE DOING THIS!
?!
MOM?! MOM?!! THIS ISN'T FUNNY!
I'LL SAY. AT LEAST SHE WAS WEARING A BATHROBE.
RATTLE
RATTLE
BARK
BARK
BARK

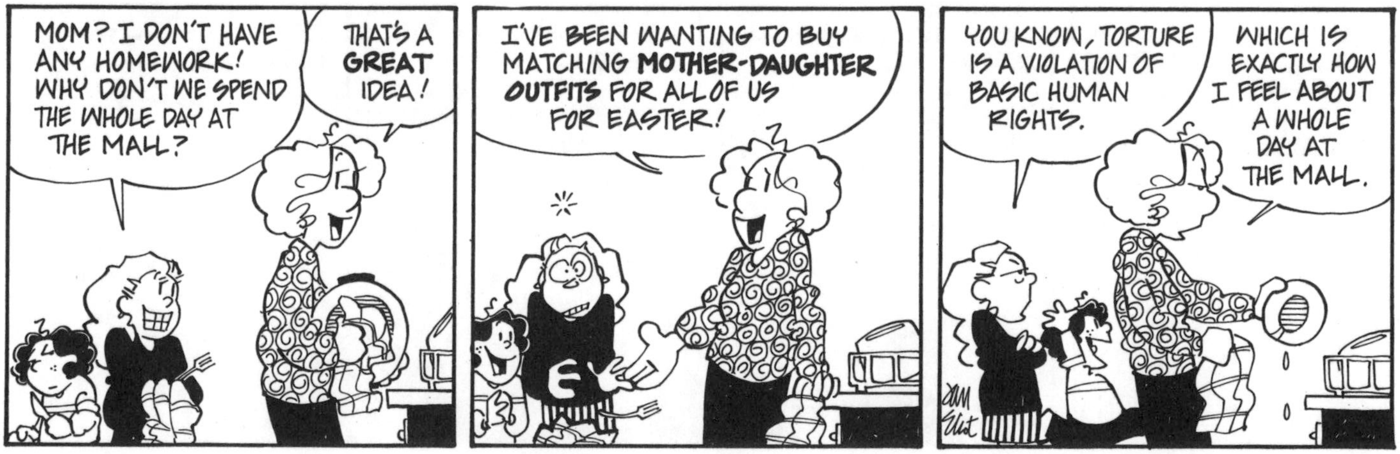
MOM? I DON'T HAVE ANY HOMEWORK! WHY DON'T WE SPEND THE WHOLE DAY AT THE MALL?
THAT'S A GREAT IDEA!
I'VE BEEN WANTING TO BUY MATCHING MOTHER-DAUGHTER OUTFITS FOR ALL OF US FOR EASTER!
YOU KNOW, TORTURE IS A VIOLATION OF BASIC HUMAN RIGHTS.
WHICH IS EXACTLY HOW I FEEL ABOUT A WHOLE DAY AT THE MALL.

Stone Soup

WHAT'RE YOU HAVING FOR BREAKFAST?

TOAST WITH PEANUT BUTTER, HONEY AND BANANA.

HAND ME THE FRONT PAGE. YOU KNOW, PEANUT BUTTER'S NOT GOOD FOR YOU. IT'S FULL OF FAT.

SOOO...WHAT'S PASSING FOR NEWS TODAY?

IT SAYS HERE THAT 20% OF ADULTS IN THE U.S. SUFFER FROM DEPRESSION!

AND 25% OF THOSE ARE ON ANTI-DEPRESSANTS.

HUH.

WHY DO YOU SUPPOSE THAT IS?

BECAUSE PEOPLE KEEP TELLING THEM THEY CAN'T EAT PEANUT BUTTER!!

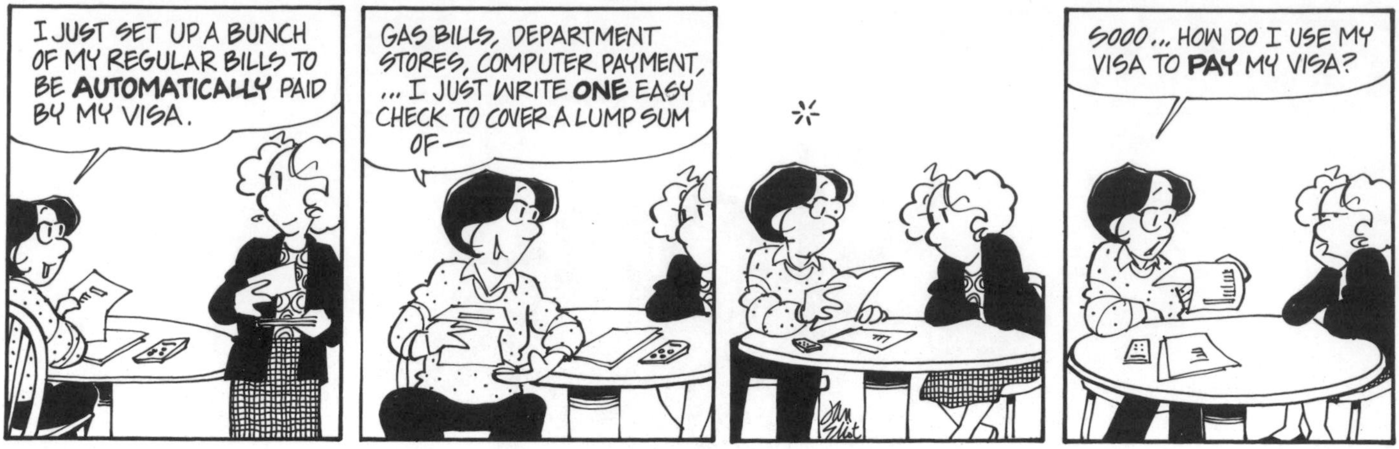
I JUST SET UP A BUNCH OF MY REGULAR BILLS TO BE **AUTOMATICALLY** PAID BY MY VISA.
GAS BILLS, DEPARTMENT STORES, COMPUTER PAYMENT, ... I JUST WRITE **ONE** EASY CHECK TO COVER A LUMP SUM OF—
SOOO... HOW DO I USE MY VISA TO **PAY** MY VISA?

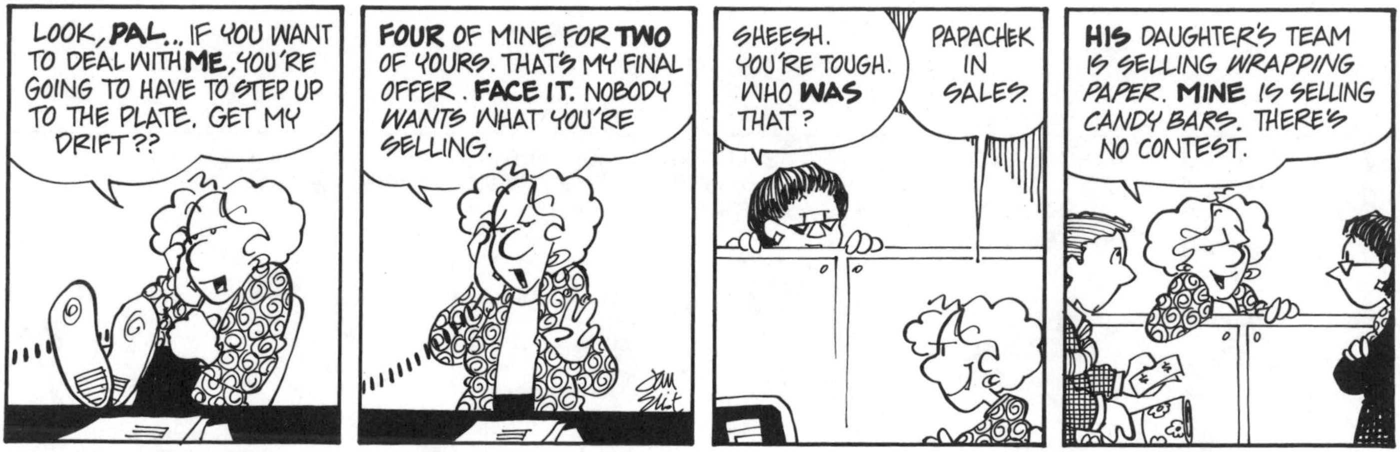
LOOK, **PAL**... IF YOU WANT TO DEAL WITH **ME**, YOU'RE GOING TO HAVE TO STEP UP TO THE PLATE. GET MY DRIFT??
FOUR OF MINE FOR **TWO** OF YOURS. THAT'S MY FINAL OFFER. **FACE IT.** NOBODY *WANTS* WHAT YOU'RE SELLING.
SHEESH. YOU'RE TOUGH. WHO **WAS** THAT?
PAPACHEK IN SALES.
HIS DAUGHTER'S TEAM IS SELLING *WRAPPING PAPER*. **MINE** IS SELLING *CANDY BARS*. THERE'S NO CONTEST.

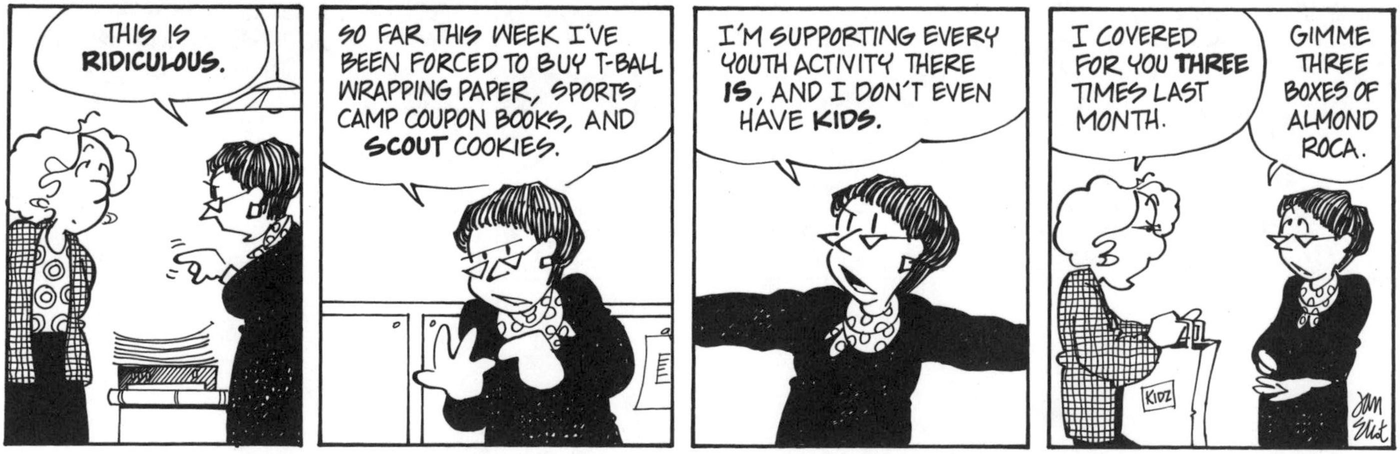
THIS IS **RIDICULOUS.**
SO FAR THIS WEEK I'VE BEEN FORCED TO BUY T-BALL WRAPPING PAPER, SPORTS CAMP COUPON BOOKS, AND **SCOUT** COOKIES.
I'M SUPPORTING EVERY YOUTH ACTIVITY THERE **IS**, AND I DON'T EVEN HAVE **KIDS**.
I COVERED FOR YOU **THREE** TIMES LAST MONTH.
GIMME THREE BOXES OF ALMOND ROCA.
KIDZ

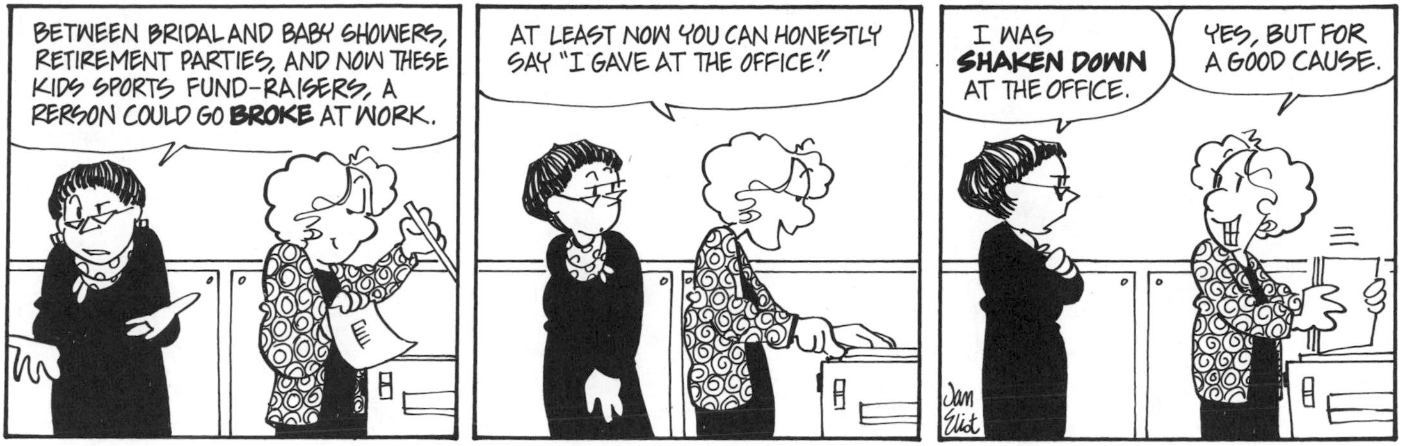
BETWEEN BRIDAL AND BABY SHOWERS, RETIREMENT PARTIES, AND NOW THESE KIDS SPORTS FUND-RAISERS, A PERSON COULD GO **BROKE** AT WORK.
AT LEAST NOW YOU CAN HONESTLY SAY "I GAVE AT THE OFFICE."
I WAS **SHAKEN DOWN** AT THE OFFICE.
YES, BUT FOR A GOOD CAUSE.

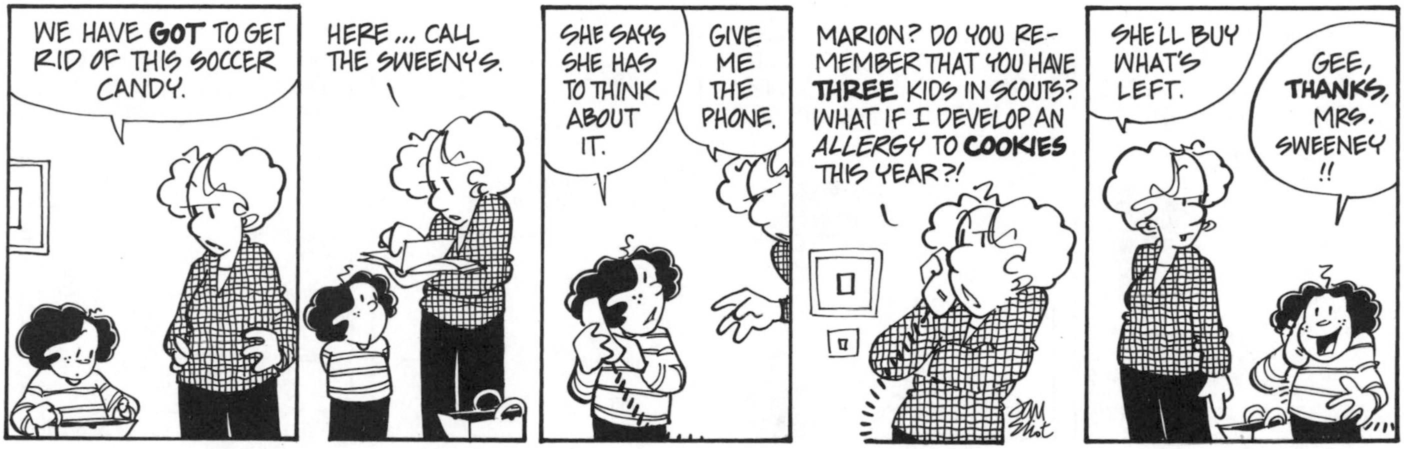
WE HAVE **GOT** TO GET RID OF THIS SOCCER CANDY.
HERE... CALL THE SWEENYS.
SHE SAYS SHE HAS TO THINK ABOUT IT.
GIVE ME THE PHONE.
MARION? DO YOU RE-MEMBER THAT YOU HAVE **THREE** KIDS IN SCOUTS? WHAT IF I DEVELOP AN *ALLERGY* TO **COOKIES** THIS YEAR?!
SHE'LL BUY WHAT'S LEFT.
GEE, **THANKS**, MRS. SWEENEY!!

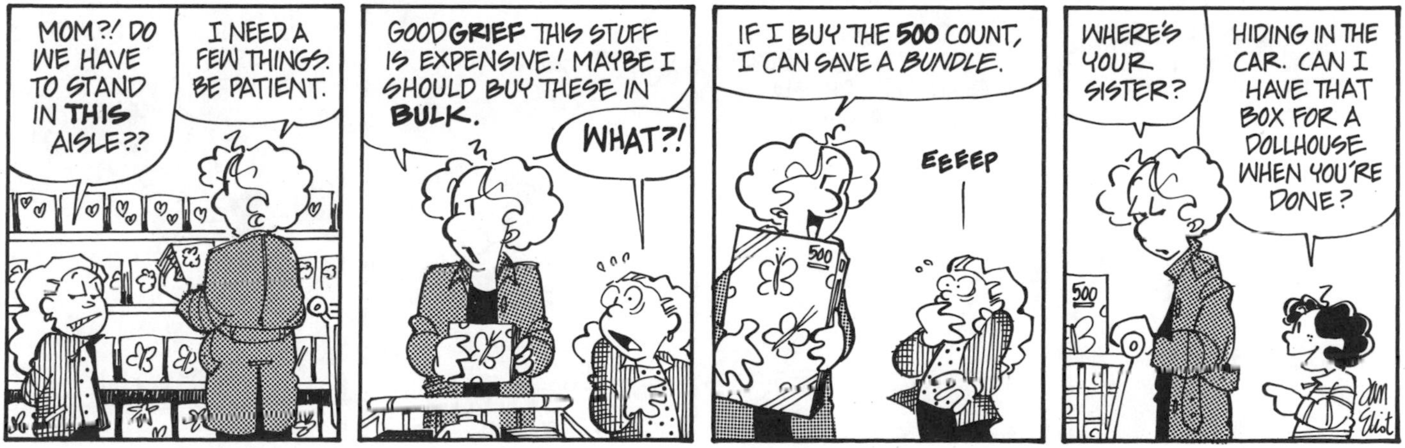
MOM?! DO WE HAVE TO STAND IN **THIS** AISLE??
I NEED A FEW THINGS. BE PATIENT.
GOOD **GRIEF** THIS STUFF IS EXPENSIVE! MAYBE I SHOULD BUY THESE IN **BULK**.
WHAT?!
IF I BUY THE **500** COUNT, I CAN SAVE A *BUNDLE*.
EEEEP
WHERE'S YOUR SISTER?
HIDING IN THE CAR. CAN I HAVE THAT BOX FOR A DOLLHOUSE WHEN YOU'RE DONE?

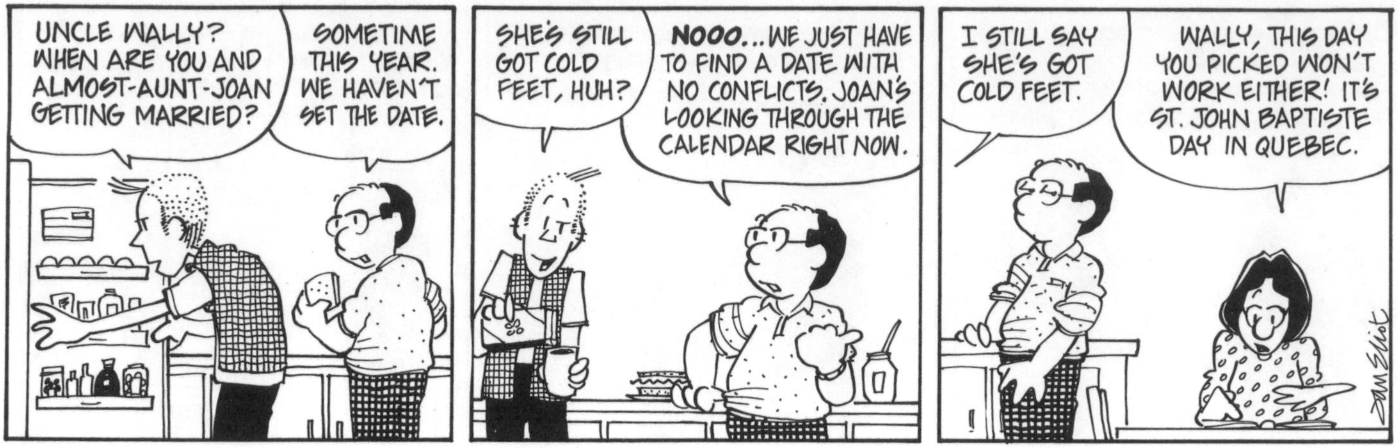
UNCLE WALLY? WHEN ARE YOU AND ALMOST-AUNT-JOAN GETTING MARRIED?
SOMETIME THIS YEAR. WE HAVEN'T SET THE DATE.
SHE'S STILL GOT COLD FEET, HUH?
NOOO... WE JUST HAVE TO FIND A DATE WITH NO CONFLICTS. JOAN'S LOOKING THROUGH THE CALENDAR RIGHT NOW.
I STILL SAY SHE'S GOT COLD FEET.
WALLY, THIS DAY YOU PICKED WON'T WORK EITHER! IT'S ST. JOHN BAPTISTE DAY IN QUEBEC.

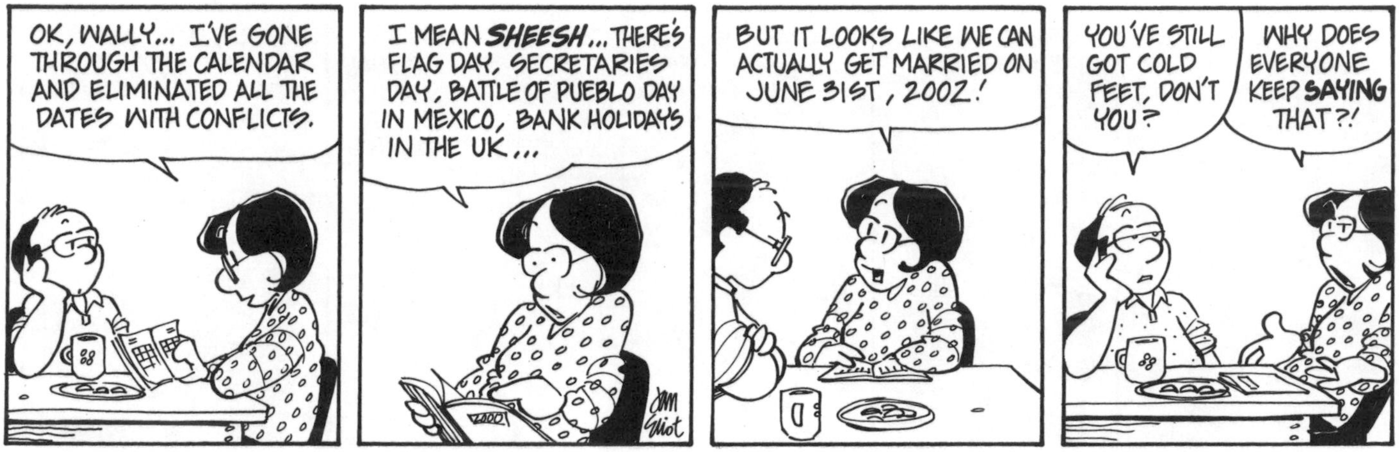
OK, WALLY... I'VE GONE THROUGH THE CALENDAR AND ELIMINATED ALL THE DATES WITH CONFLICTS.
I MEAN SHEESH... THERE'S FLAG DAY, SECRETARIES DAY, BATTLE OF PUEBLO DAY IN MEXICO, BANK HOLIDAYS IN THE UK...
BUT IT LOOKS LIKE WE CAN ACTUALLY GET MARRIED ON JUNE 31ST, 2002!
YOU'VE STILL GOT COLD FEET, DON'T YOU?
WHY DOES EVERYONE KEEP SAYING THAT?!

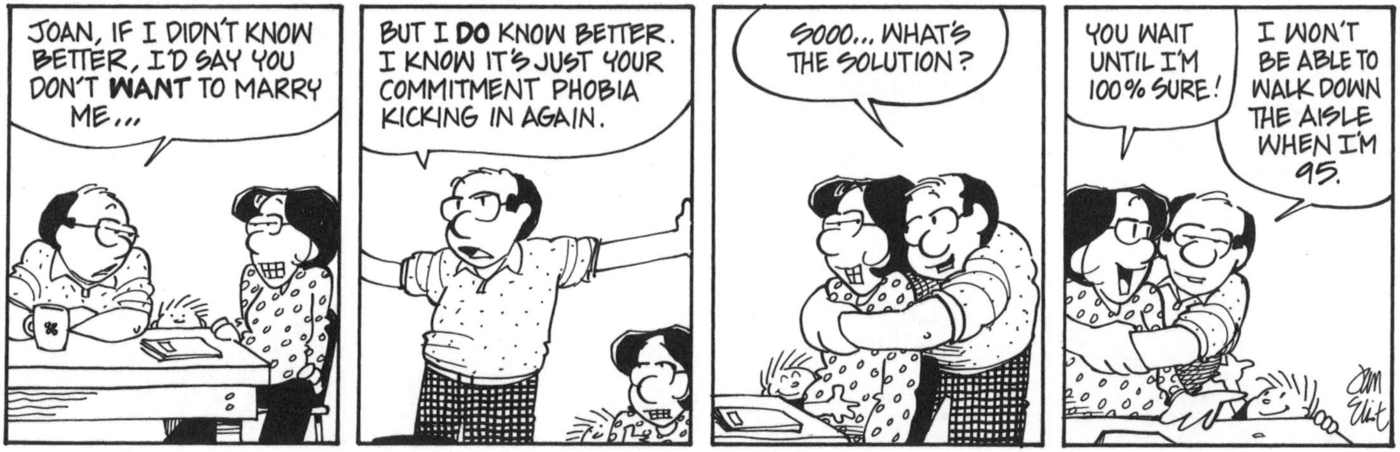
JOAN, IF I DIDN'T KNOW BETTER, I'D SAY YOU DON'T WANT TO MARRY ME...
BUT I DO KNOW BETTER. I KNOW IT'S JUST YOUR COMMITMENT PHOBIA KICKING IN AGAIN.
SOOO... WHAT'S THE SOLUTION?
YOU WAIT UNTIL I'M 100% SURE!
I WON'T BE ABLE TO WALK DOWN THE AISLE WHEN I'M 95.

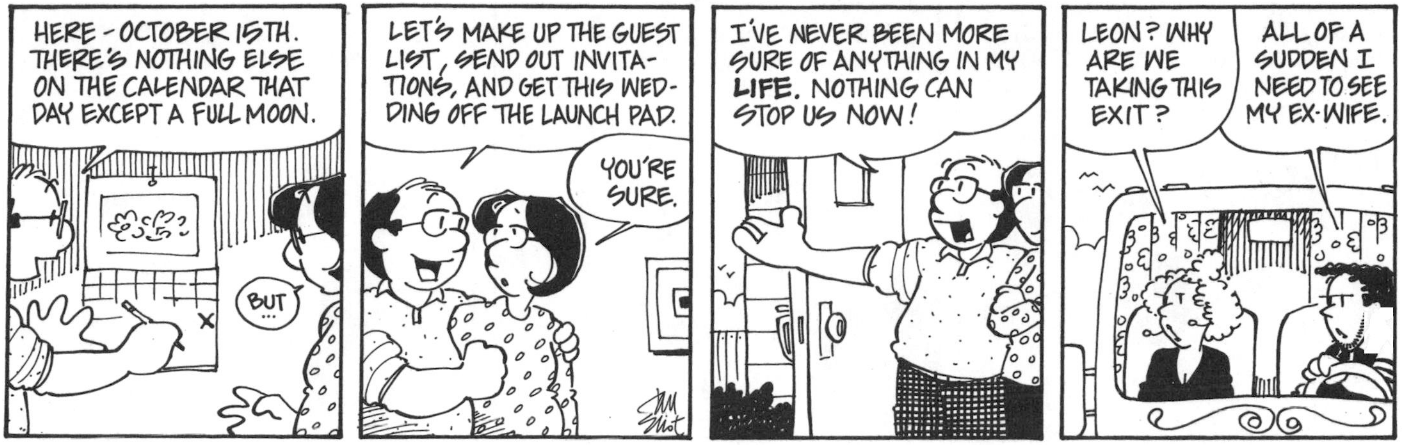
HERE - OCTOBER 15TH. THERE'S NOTHING ELSE ON THE CALENDAR THAT DAY EXCEPT A FULL MOON.
BUT ...
LET'S MAKE UP THE GUEST LIST, SEND OUT INVITATIONS, AND GET THIS WEDDING OFF THE LAUNCH PAD.
YOU'RE SURE.
I'VE NEVER BEEN MORE SURE OF ANYTHING IN MY **LIFE.** NOTHING CAN STOP US NOW!
LEON? WHY ARE WE TAKING THIS EXIT?
ALL OF A SUDDEN I NEED TO SEE MY EX-WIFE.

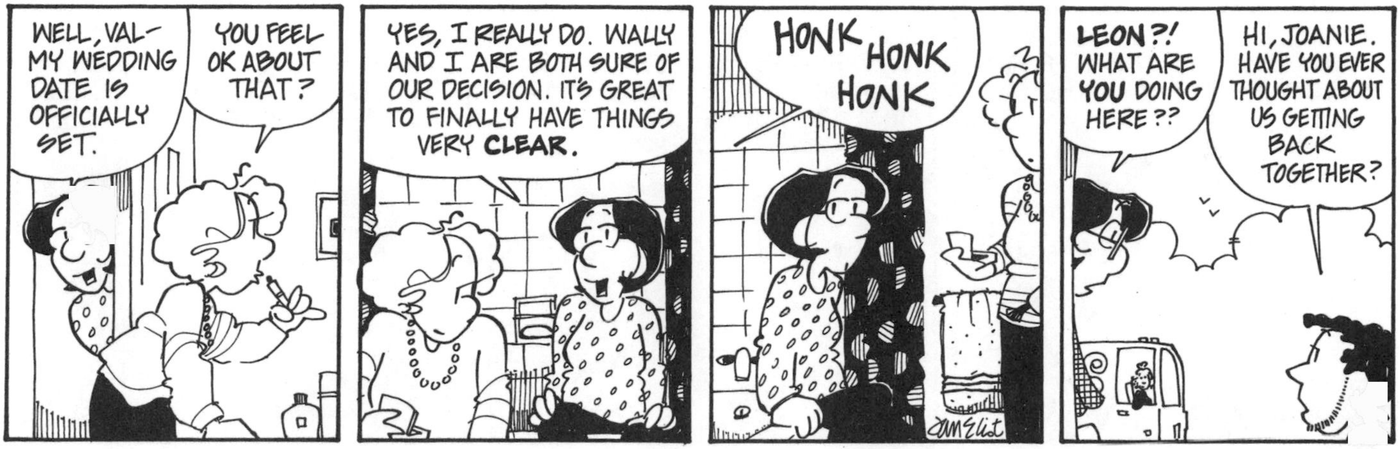
WELL, VAL- MY WEDDING DATE IS OFFICIALLY SET.
YOU FEEL OK ABOUT THAT?
YES, I REALLY DO. WALLY AND I ARE BOTH SURE OF OUR DECISION. IT'S GREAT TO FINALLY HAVE THINGS VERY **CLEAR.**
HONK HONK HONK
LEON?! WHAT ARE **YOU** DOING HERE??
HI, JOANIE. HAVE YOU EVER THOUGHT ABOUT US GETTING BACK TOGETHER?

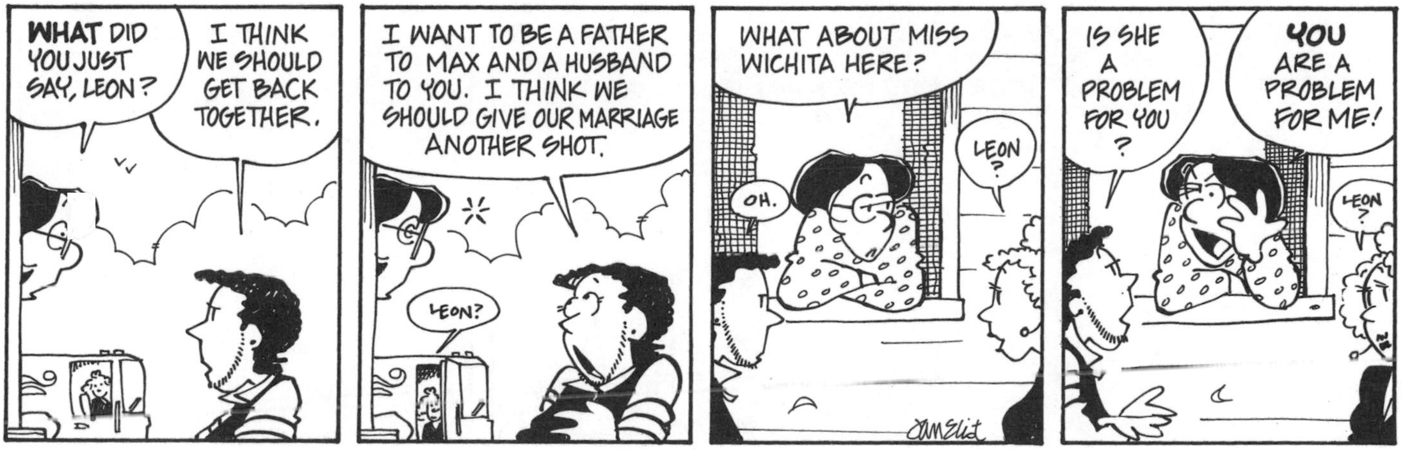
WHAT DID YOU JUST SAY, LEON?
I THINK WE SHOULD GET BACK TOGETHER.
I WANT TO BE A FATHER TO MAX AND A HUSBAND TO YOU. I THINK WE SHOULD GIVE OUR MARRIAGE ANOTHER SHOT.
LEON?
WHAT ABOUT MISS WICHITA HERE?
OH.
LEON?
IS SHE A PROBLEM FOR YOU?
YOU ARE A PROBLEM FOR ME!
LEON?

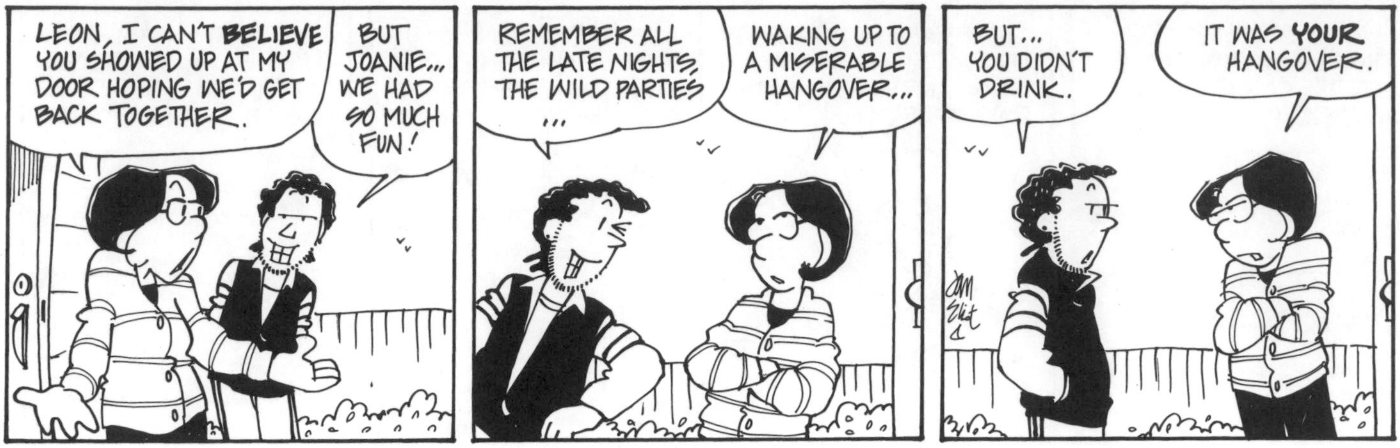
LEON, I CAN'T **BELIEVE** YOU SHOWED UP AT MY DOOR HOPING WE'D GET BACK TOGETHER.
BUT JOANIE... WE HAD SO MUCH FUN!
REMEMBER ALL THE LATE NIGHTS, THE WILD PARTIES ...
WAKING UP TO A MISERABLE HANGOVER...
BUT... YOU DIDN'T DRINK.
IT WAS **YOUR** HANGOVER.

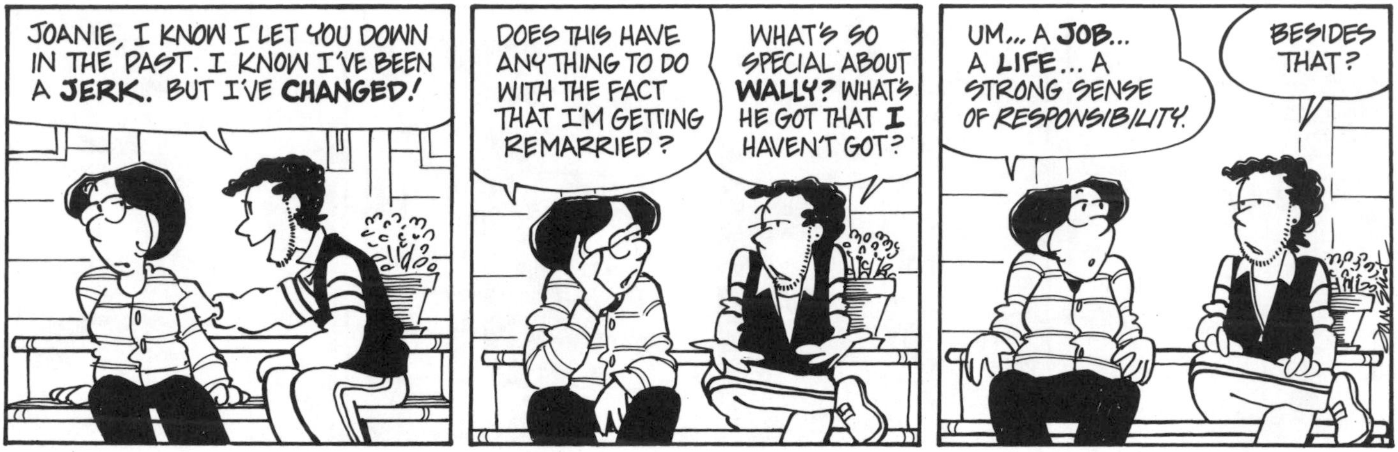
JOANIE, I KNOW I LET YOU DOWN IN THE PAST. I KNOW I'VE BEEN A **JERK**. BUT I'VE **CHANGED**!
DOES THIS HAVE ANYTHING TO DO WITH THE FACT THAT I'M GETTING REMARRIED?
WHAT'S SO SPECIAL ABOUT **WALLY?** WHAT'S HE GOT THAT **I** HAVEN'T GOT?
UM... A **JOB**... A **LIFE**... A STRONG SENSE OF *RESPONSIBILITY*.
BESIDES THAT?

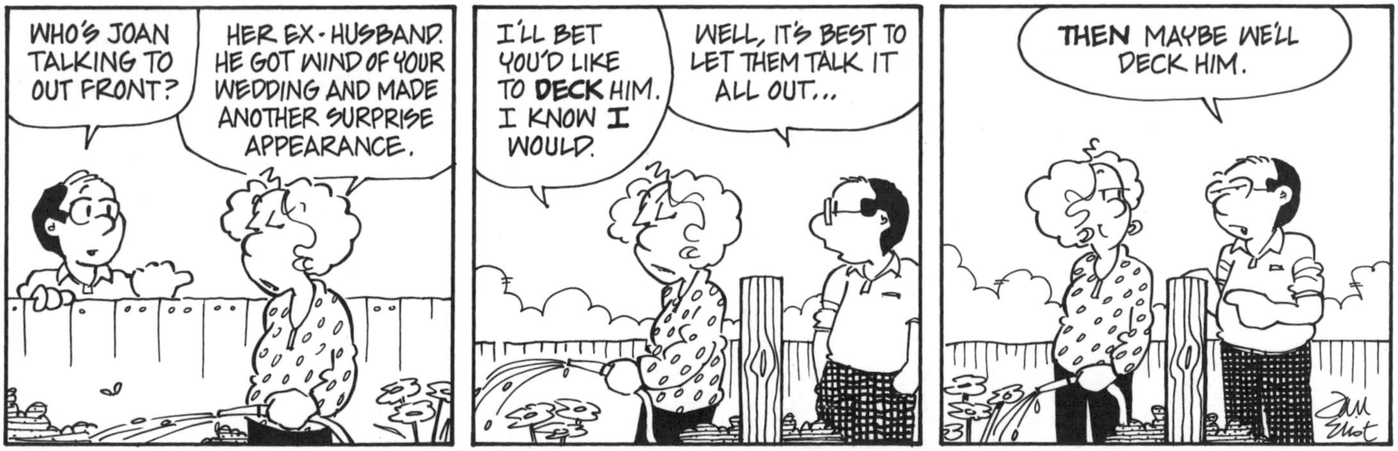
WHO'S JOAN TALKING TO OUT FRONT?
HER EX-HUSBAND. HE GOT WIND OF YOUR WEDDING AND MADE ANOTHER SURPRISE APPEARANCE.
I'LL BET YOU'D LIKE TO **DECK** HIM. I KNOW **I** WOULD.
WELL, IT'S BEST TO LET THEM TALK IT ALL OUT...
THEN MAYBE WE'LL DECK HIM.

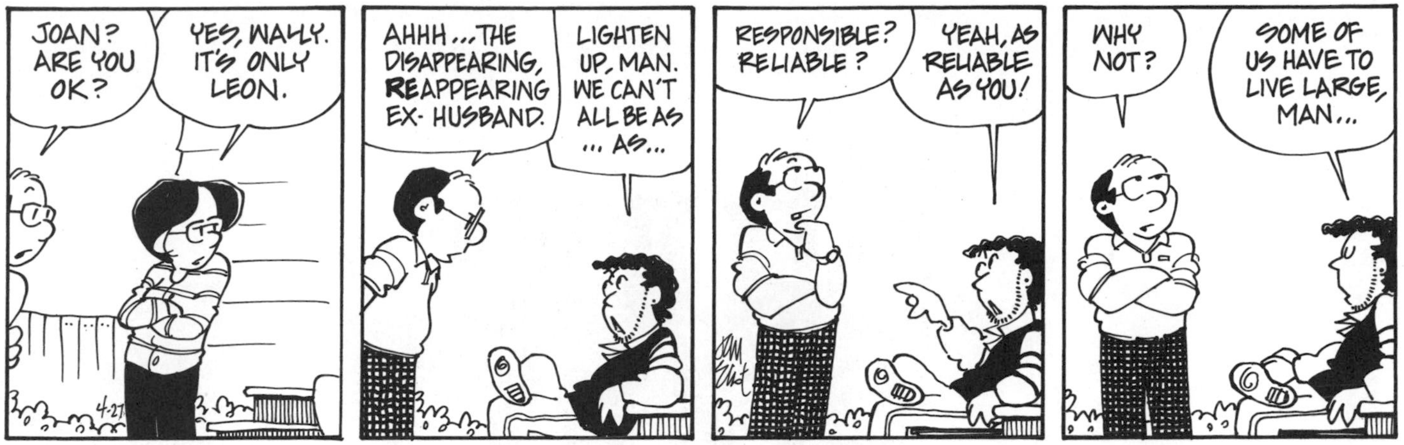
JOAN? ARE YOU OK?
YES, WALLY. IT'S ONLY LEON.
AHHH ... THE DISAPPEARING, REAPPEARING EX- HUSBAND.
LIGHTEN UP, MAN. WE CAN'T ALL BE AS ... AS...
RESPONSIBLE? RELIABLE?
YEAH, AS RELIABLE AS YOU!
WHY NOT?
SOME OF US HAVE TO LIVE LARGE, MAN...

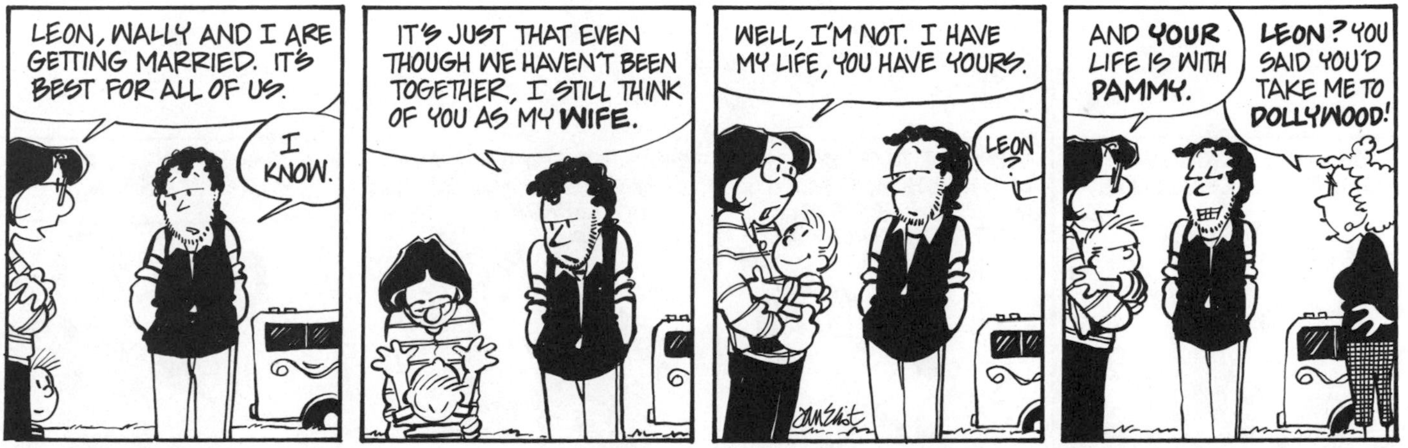
LEON, WALLY AND I ARE GETTING MARRIED. IT'S BEST FOR ALL OF US.
I KNOW.
IT'S JUST THAT EVEN THOUGH WE HAVEN'T BEEN TOGETHER, I STILL THINK OF YOU AS MY WIFE.
WELL, I'M NOT. I HAVE MY LIFE, YOU HAVE YOURS.
LEON?
AND YOUR LIFE IS WITH PAMMY.
LEON? YOU SAID YOU'D TAKE ME TO DOLLYWOOD!

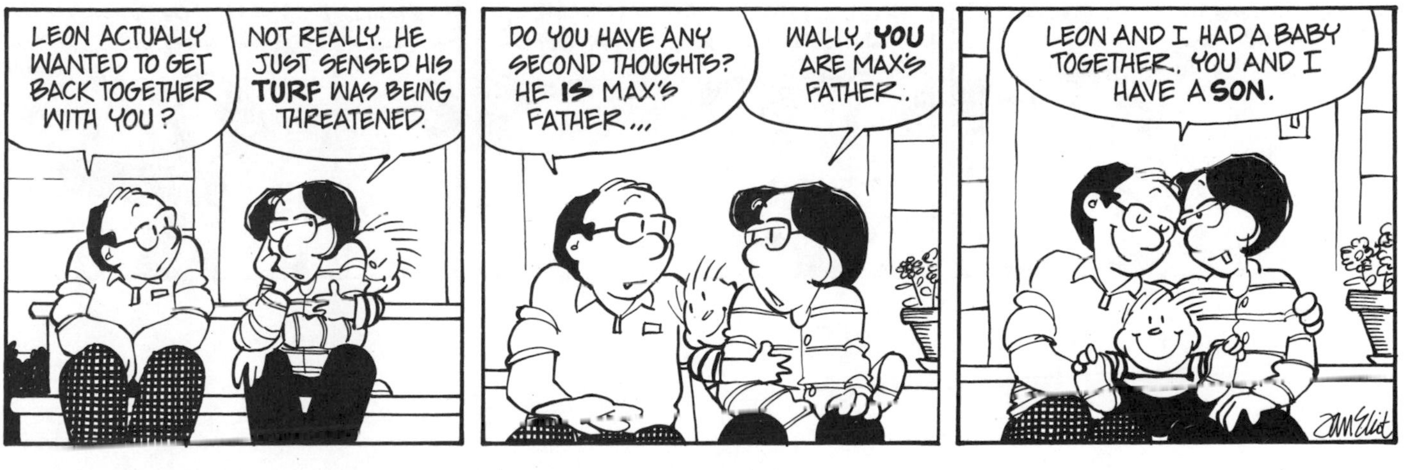
LEON ACTUALLY WANTED TO GET BACK TOGETHER WITH YOU?
NOT REALLY. HE JUST SENSED HIS TURF WAS BEING THREATENED.
DO YOU HAVE ANY SECOND THOUGHTS? HE IS MAX'S FATHER...
WALLY, YOU ARE MAX'S FATHER.
LEON AND I HAD A BABY TOGETHER. YOU AND I HAVE A SON.

Stone Soup

YOU KNOW, DATING VAL IS SOMETIMES A **CHALLENGE**.

SHE'S GOT TWO **KIDS**. SHE LIVES WITH HER **MOM**... AS WELL AS HER SISTER AND THE TWO-YEAR OLD.

SHE'S BUSY WITH HER OWN CAREER. SHE WILL **NEVER** DO MY LAUNDRY.

AND SHE PREFERS **WOMEN'S** SPORTS TO **MEN'S**!

BUT SHE'S SMART, FUNNY, GORGEOUS, AND SHE SAYS THE MOST **EXCITING** THINGS TO ME.

LIKE WHAT?

HEY VAL— WANNA GO DO A LITTLE ANTIQUING?

ARE YOU **NUTS?** IT'S THE **PLAYOFFS!**

WHAT A WOMAN.

PINCH ME SO I KNOW I'M NOT DREAMING.

ARE YOU COMING?

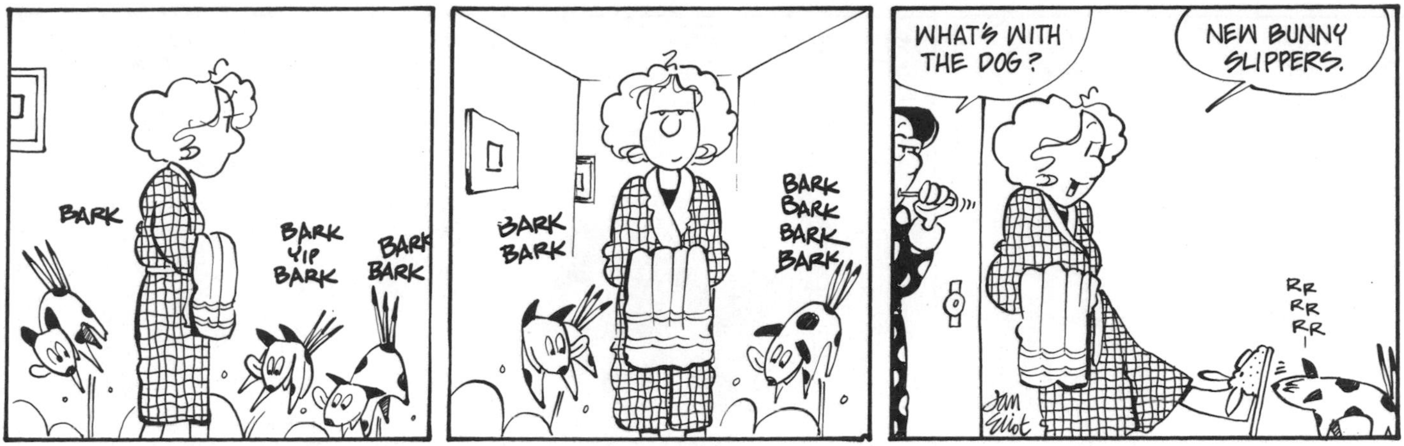
BARK
BARK YIP BARK
BARK BARK
BARK BARK
BARK BARK BARK BARK
WHAT'S WITH THE DOG?
NEW BUNNY SLIPPERS.
RR RR RR

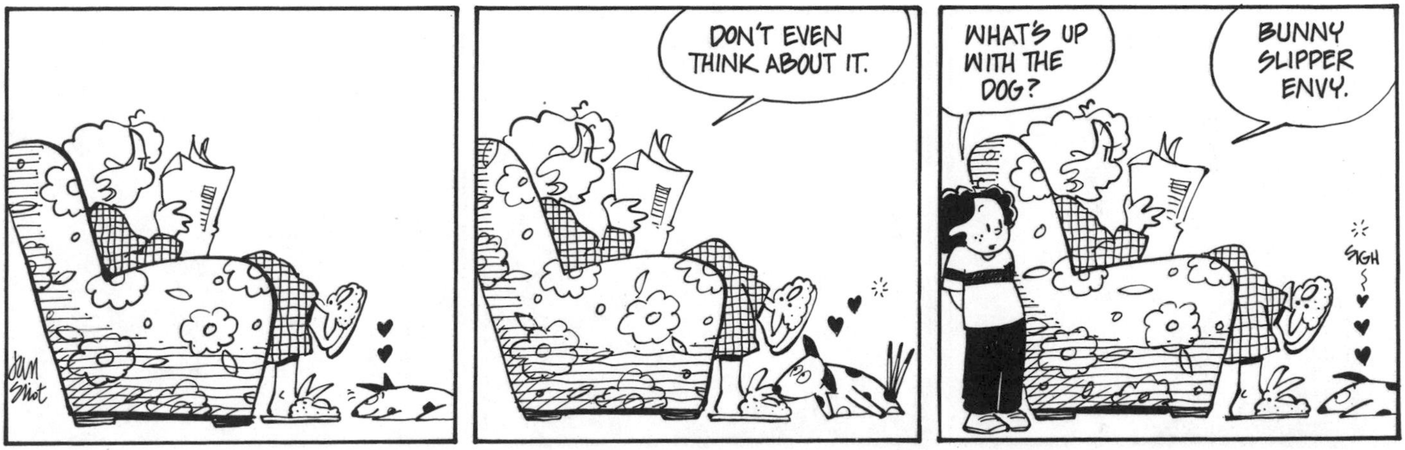
DON'T EVEN THINK ABOUT IT.
WHAT'S UP WITH THE DOG?
BUNNY SLIPPER ENVY.
SIGH

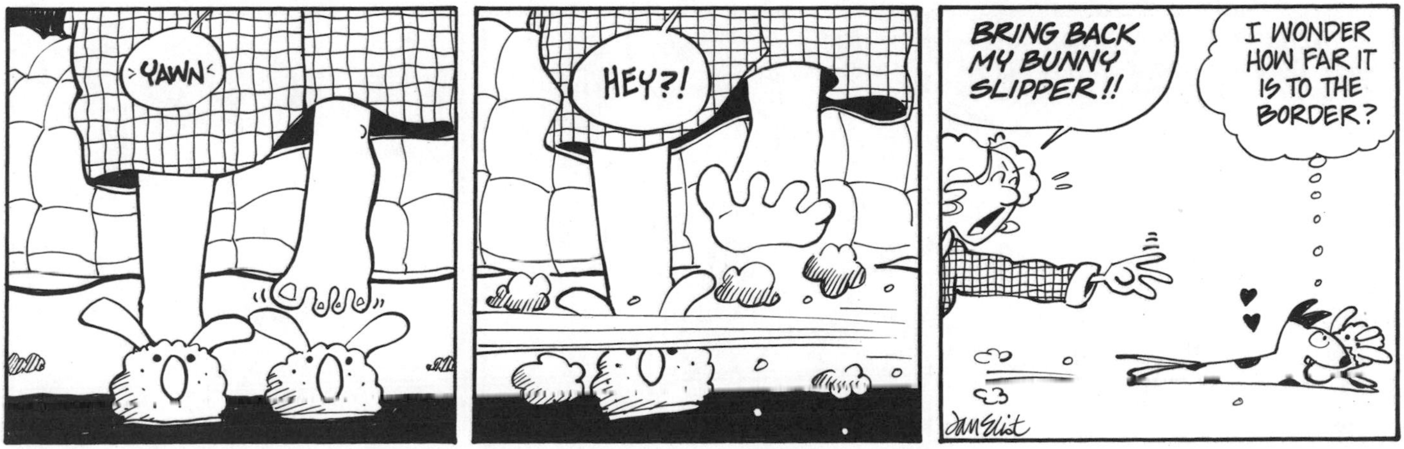
YAWN
HEY?!
BRING BACK MY BUNNY SLIPPER!!
I WONDER HOW FAR IT IS TO THE BORDER?

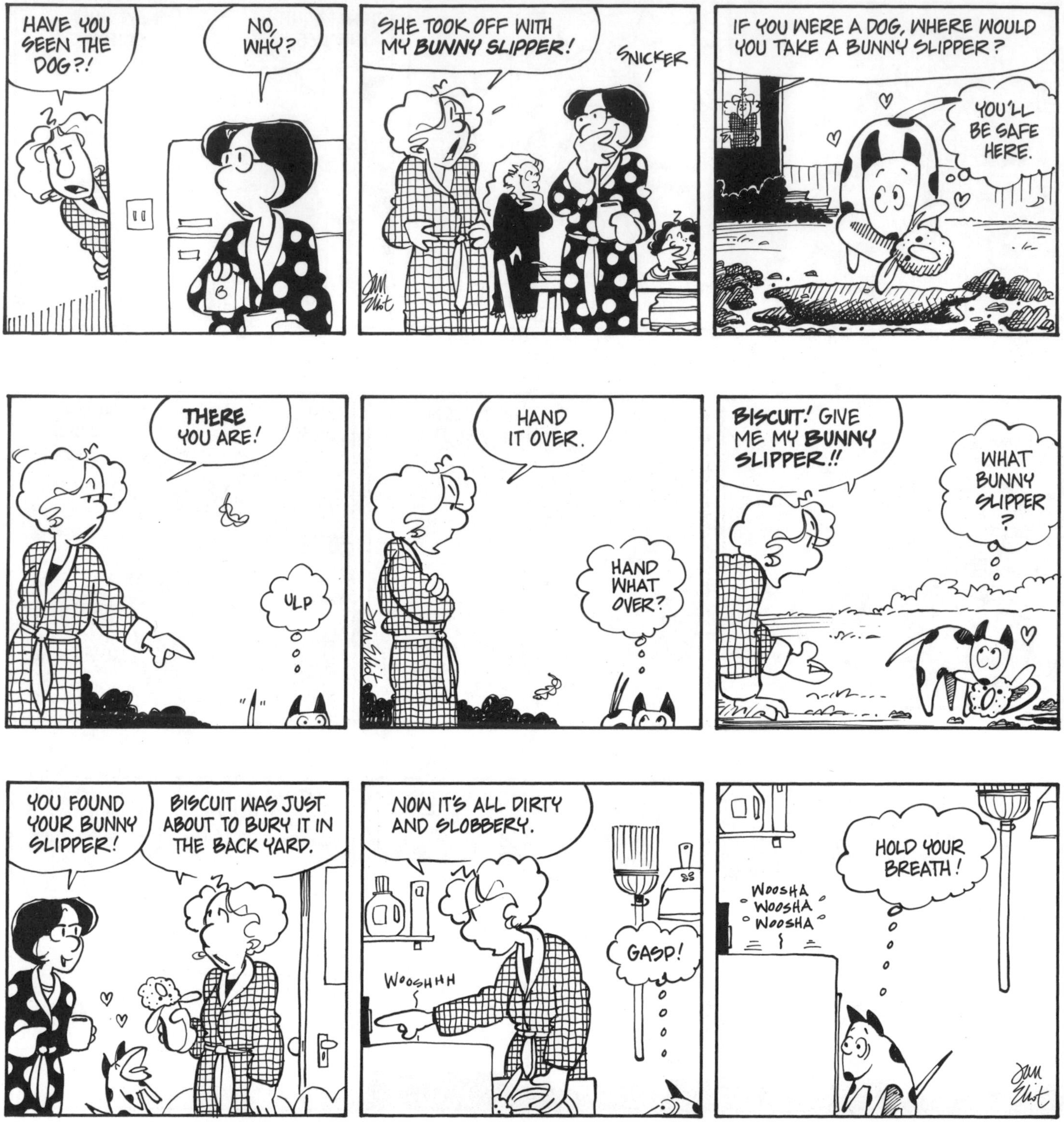
HAVE YOU SEEN THE DOG?!
NO, WHY?
SHE TOOK OFF WITH MY BUNNY SLIPPER!
SNICKER
IF YOU WERE A DOG, WHERE WOULD YOU TAKE A BUNNY SLIPPER?
YOU'LL BE SAFE HERE.
THERE YOU ARE!
ULP
HAND IT OVER.
HAND WHAT OVER?
BISCUIT! GIVE ME MY BUNNY SLIPPER!!
WHAT BUNNY SLIPPER?
YOU FOUND YOUR BUNNY SLIPPER!
BISCUIT WAS JUST ABOUT TO BURY IT IN THE BACK YARD.
NOW IT'S ALL DIRTY AND SLOBBERY.
WOOSHHH
GASP!
HOLD YOUR BREATH!
WOOSHA WOOSHA WOOSHA

Stone Soup

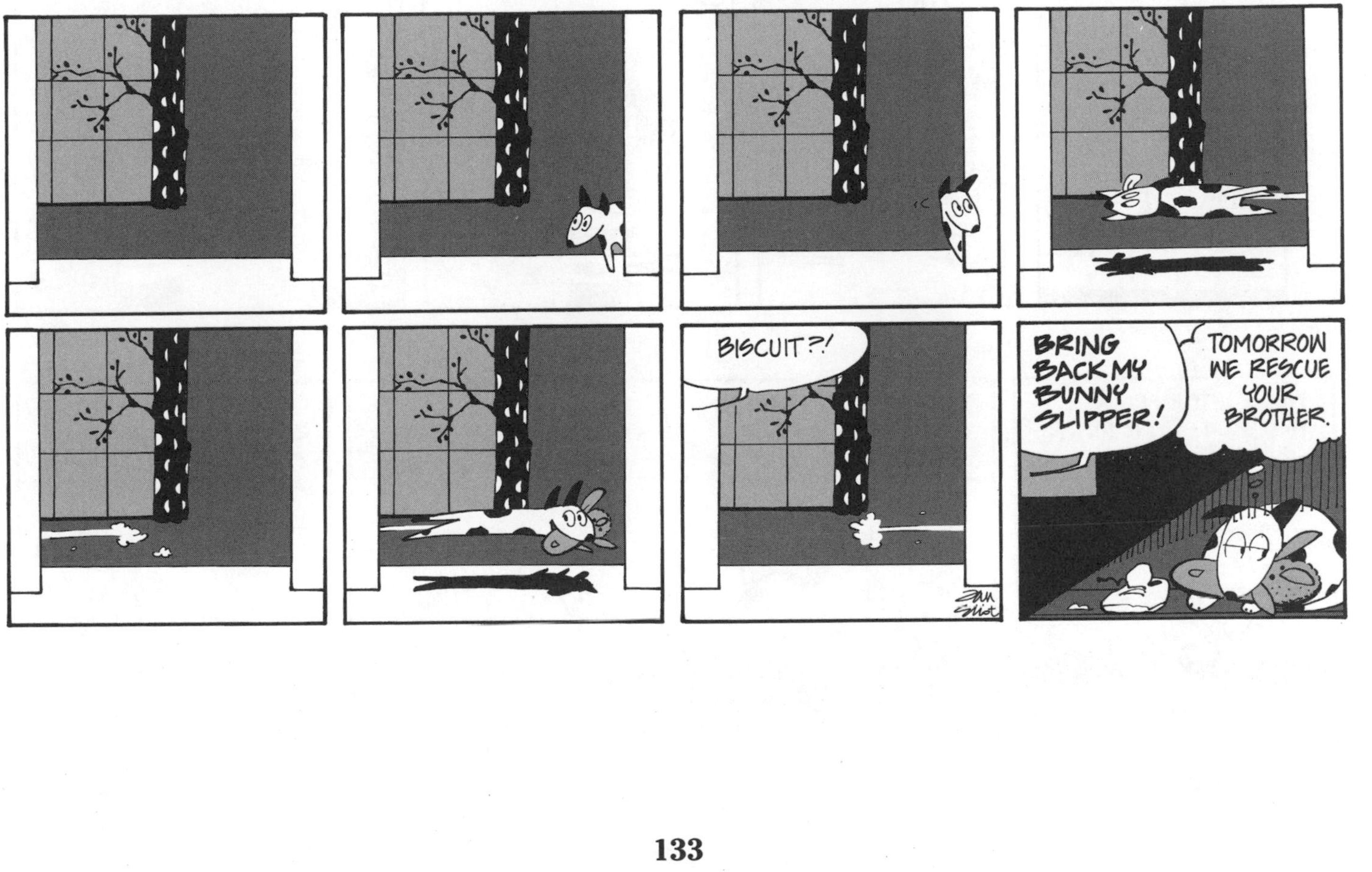
BISCUIT?!
BRING BACK MY BUNNY SLIPPER!
TOMORROW WE RESCUE YOUR BROTHER.

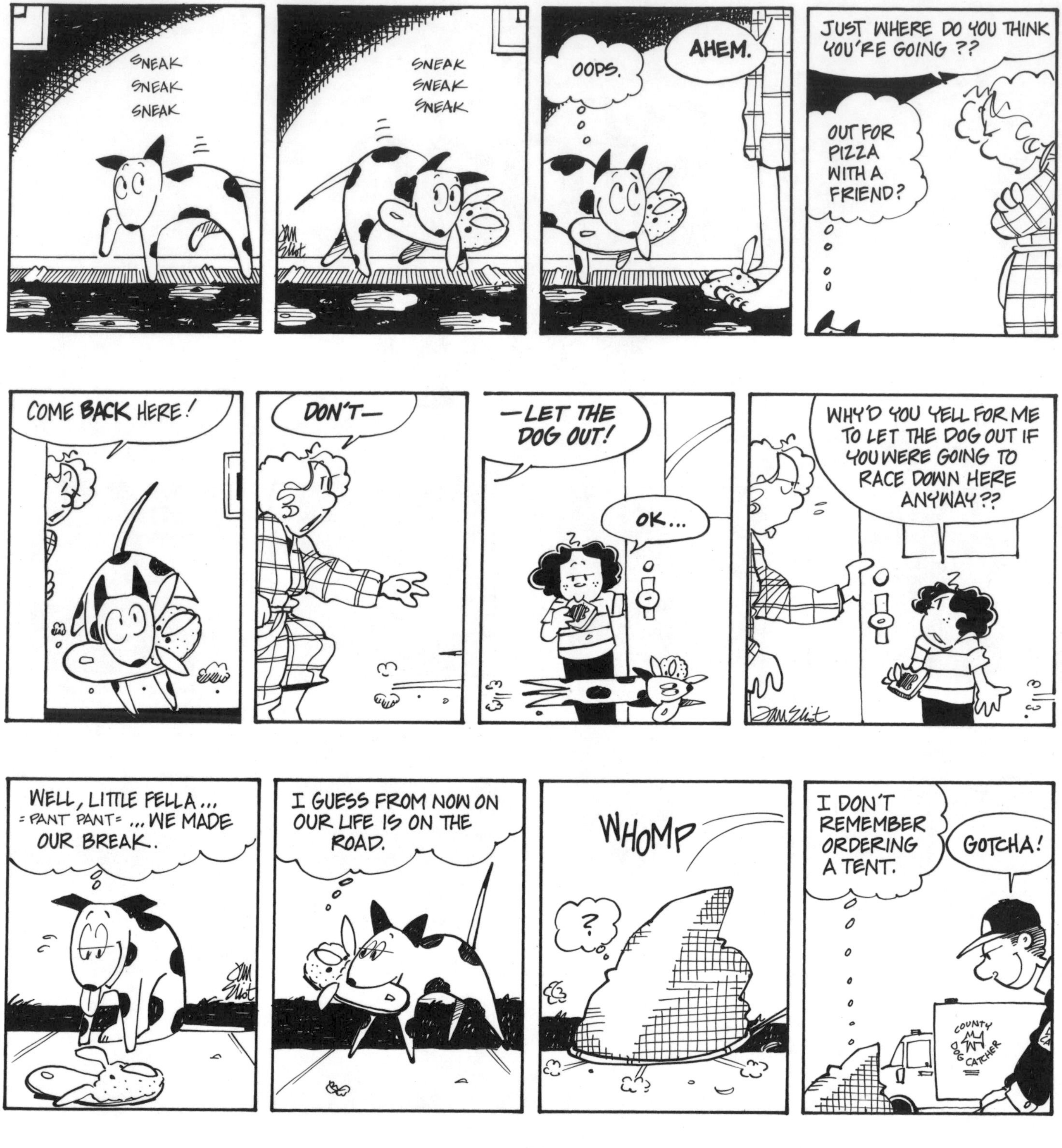
SNEAK
SNEAK
SNEAK
SNEAK
SNEAK
SNEAK
OOPS.
AHEM.
JUST WHERE DO YOU THINK YOU'RE GOING ??
OUT FOR PIZZA WITH A FRIEND?
COME BACK HERE!
DON'T—
—LET THE DOG OUT!
OK...
WHY'D YOU YELL FOR ME TO LET THE DOG OUT IF YOU WERE GOING TO RACE DOWN HERE ANYWAY??
WELL, LITTLE FELLA... =PANT PANT= ...WE MADE OUR BREAK.
I GUESS FROM NOW ON OUR LIFE IS ON THE ROAD.
WHOMP
?
I DON'T REMEMBER ORDERING A TENT.
GOTCHA!
COUNTY DOG CATCHER

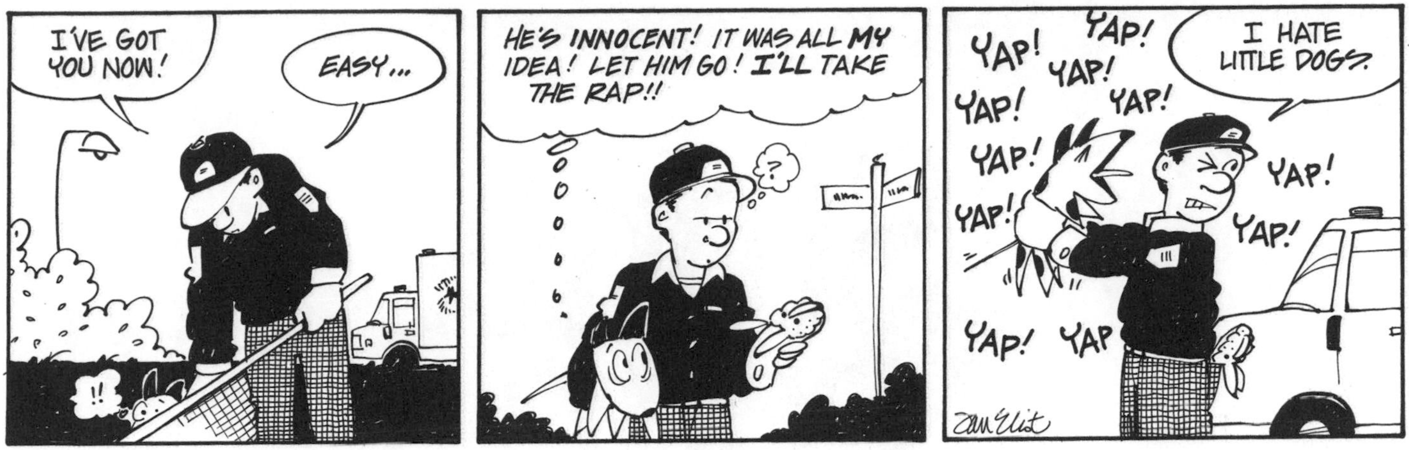
I'VE GOT YOU NOW!
EASY...
HE'S **INNOCENT**! IT WAS ALL **MY** IDEA! LET HIM GO! **I'LL** TAKE THE RAP!!
YAP! YAP! YAP! YAP! YAP! YAP! YAP! YAP! YAP! YAP! YAP
I HATE LITTLE DOGS.

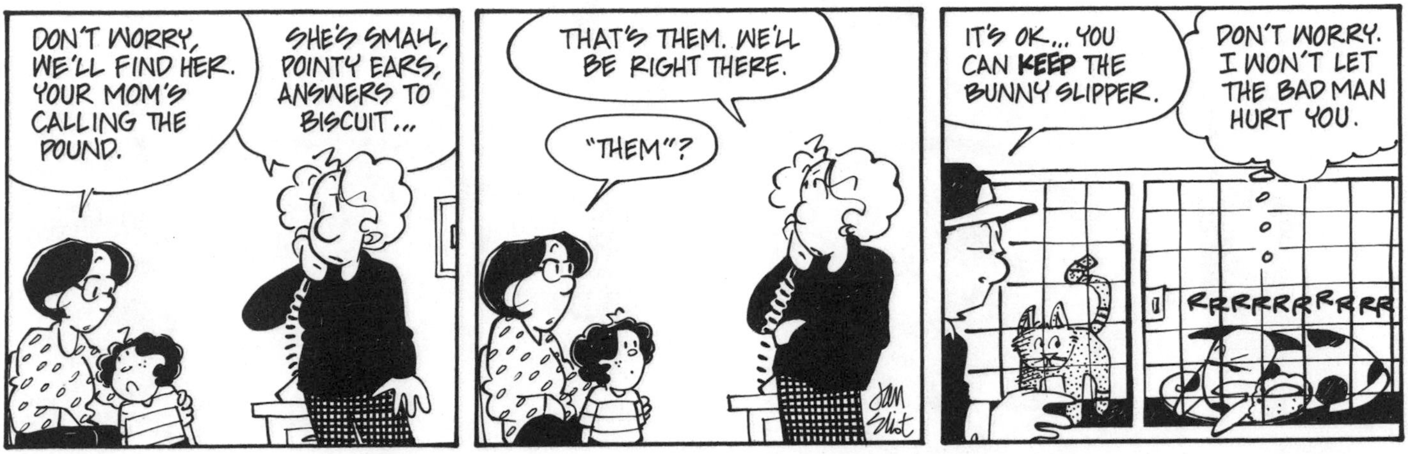
DON'T WORRY, WE'LL FIND HER. YOUR MOM'S CALLING THE POUND.
SHE'S SMALL, POINTY EARS, ANSWERS TO BISCUIT...
THAT'S THEM. WE'LL BE RIGHT THERE.
"THEM"?
IT'S OK... YOU CAN **KEEP** THE BUNNY SLIPPER.
DON'T WORRY. I WON'T LET THE BAD MAN HURT YOU.
RRRRRRRRRRR

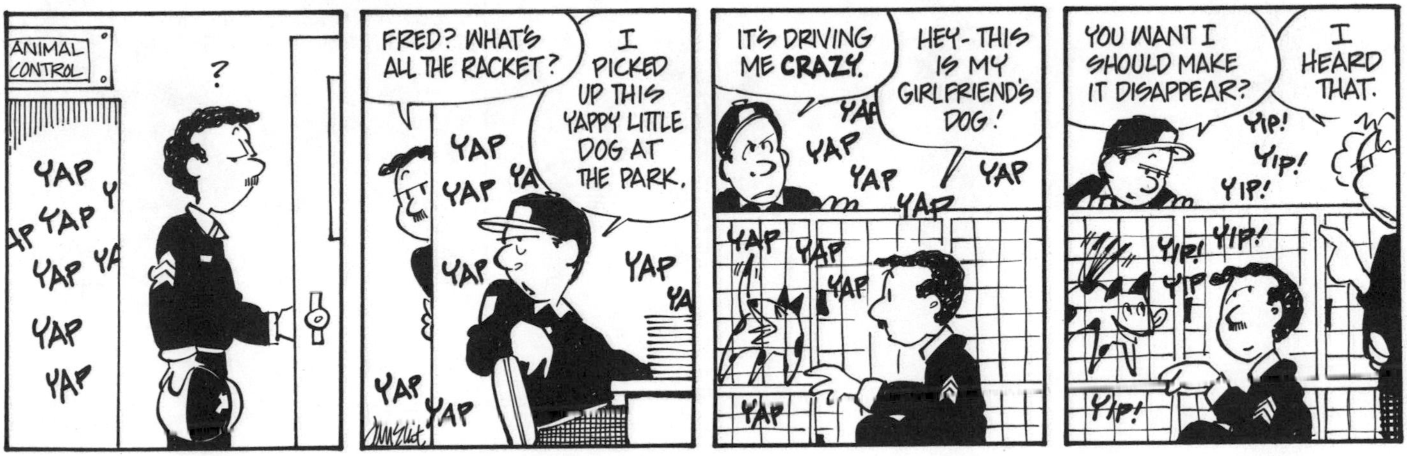
ANIMAL CONTROL
?
YAP YAP YAP YAP YAP YAP
FRED? WHAT'S ALL THE RACKET?
I PICKED UP THIS YAPPY LITTLE DOG AT THE PARK.
YAP YAP YAP YAP YAP YAP
IT'S DRIVING ME **CRAZY**.
HEY- THIS IS MY GIRLFRIEND'S DOG!
YAP YAP YAP YAP YAP YAP YAP
YOU WANT I SHOULD MAKE IT DISAPPEAR?
I HEARD THAT.
YIP! YIP! YIP! YIP! YIP! YIP!

Stone Soup

TUCK TUCK
APPARENTLY I SPENT $100 ON SHOES AND CLEATS SO SHE COULD OUTRUN HER OWN TEAM.
GO ALIX!

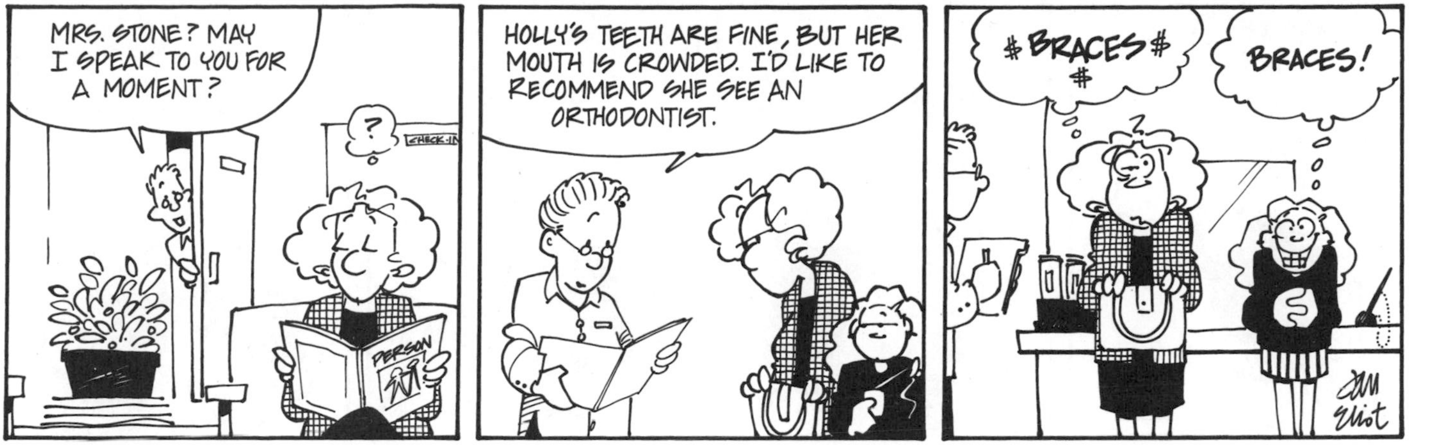
MRS. STONE? MAY I SPEAK TO YOU FOR A MOMENT?
?
PERSON
HOLLY'S TEETH ARE FINE, BUT HER MOUTH IS CROWDED. I'D LIKE TO RECOMMEND SHE SEE AN ORTHODONTIST.
$ BRACES $ $
BRACES!

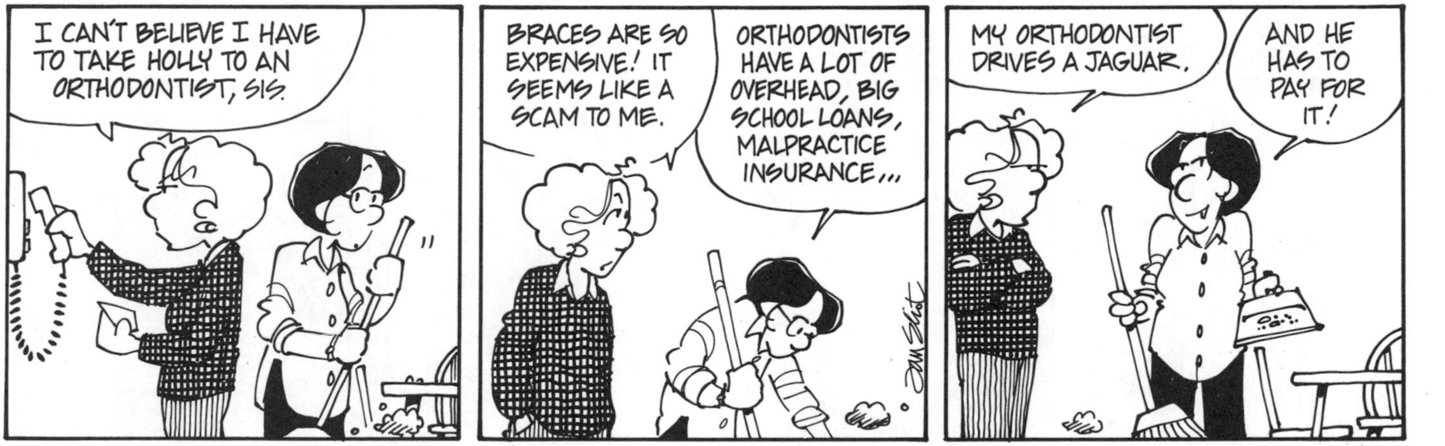
I CAN'T BELIEVE I HAVE TO TAKE HOLLY TO AN ORTHODONTIST, SIS.
BRACES ARE SO EXPENSIVE! IT SEEMS LIKE A SCAM TO ME.
ORTHODONTISTS HAVE A LOT OF OVERHEAD, BIG SCHOOL LOANS, MALPRACTICE INSURANCE...
MY ORTHODONTIST DRIVES A JAGUAR.
AND HE HAS TO PAY FOR IT!

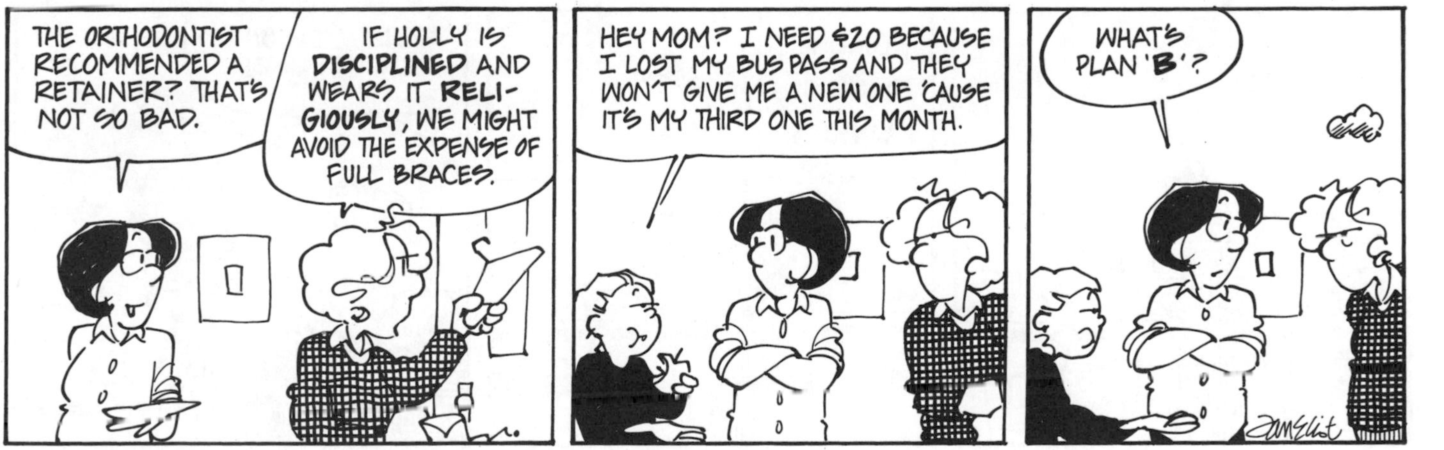
THE ORTHODONTIST RECOMMENDED A RETAINER? THAT'S NOT SO BAD.
IF HOLLY IS DISCIPLINED AND WEARS IT RELIGIOUSLY, WE MIGHT AVOID THE EXPENSE OF FULL BRACES.
HEY MOM? I NEED $20 BECAUSE I LOST MY BUS PASS AND THEY WON'T GIVE ME A NEW ONE 'CAUSE IT'S MY THIRD ONE THIS MONTH.
WHAT'S PLAN 'B'?

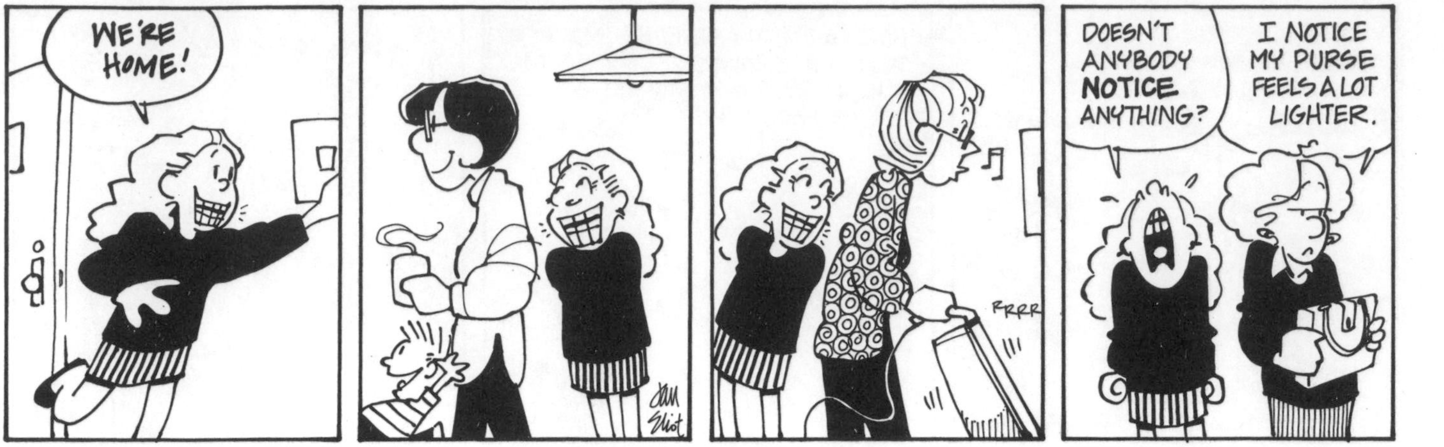
WE'RE HOME!
RRRR
DOESN'T ANYBODY **NOTICE** ANYTHING?
I NOTICE MY PURSE FEELS A LOT LIGHTER.

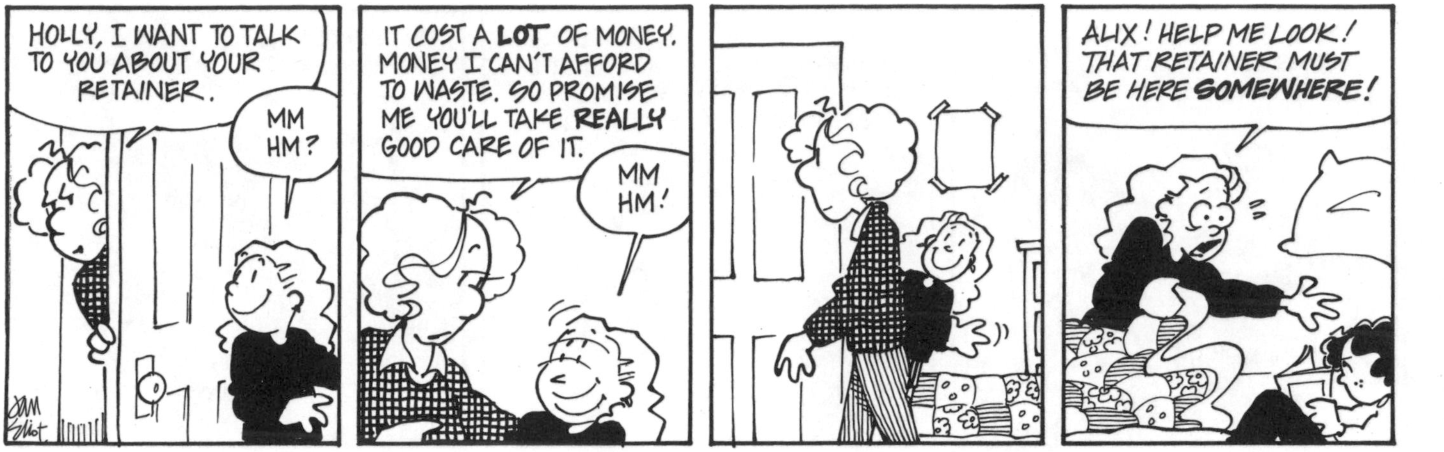
HOLLY, I WANT TO TALK TO YOU ABOUT YOUR RETAINER.
MM HM?
IT COST A **LOT** OF MONEY. MONEY I CAN'T AFFORD TO WASTE. SO PROMISE ME YOU'LL TAKE **REALLY** GOOD CARE OF IT.
MM HM!
ALIX! HELP ME LOOK! THAT RETAINER MUST BE HERE **SOMEWHERE**!

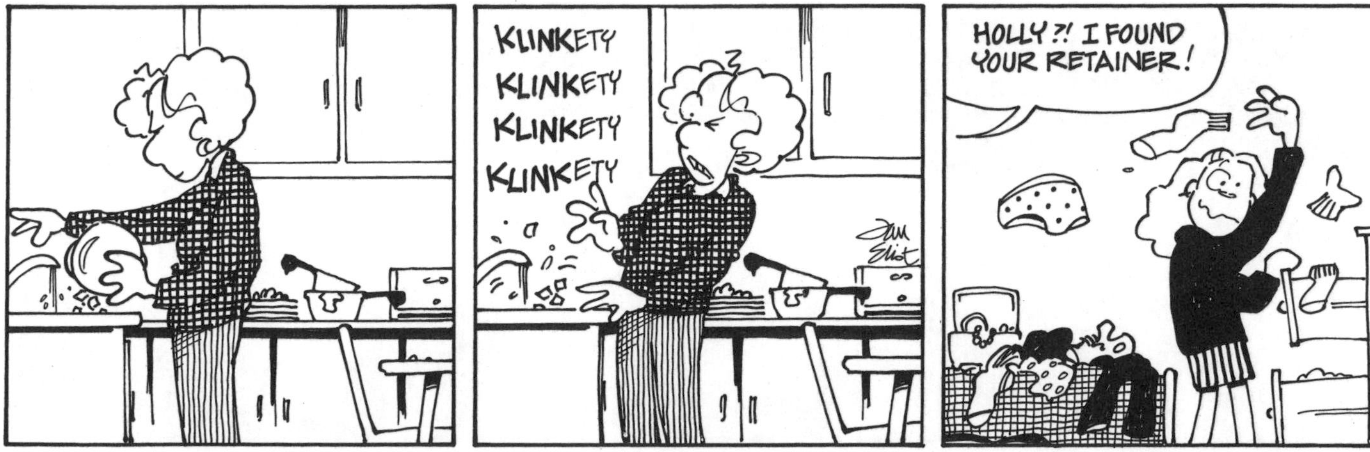
KLINKETY
KLINKETY
KLINKETY
KLINKETY
HOLLY?! I FOUND YOUR RETAINER!

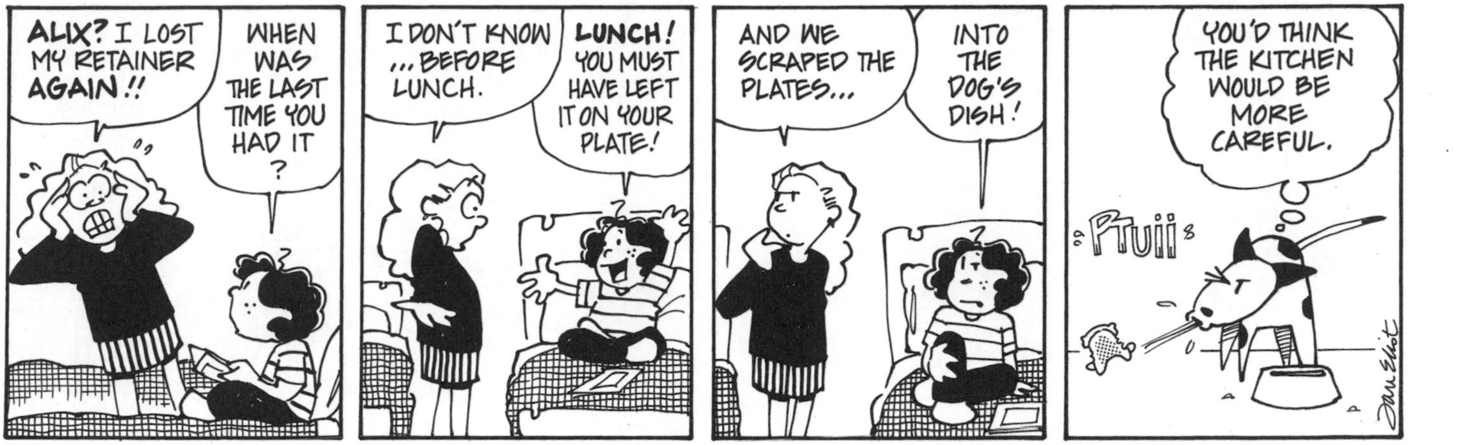
ALIX? I LOST MY RETAINER AGAIN!!
WHEN WAS THE LAST TIME YOU HAD IT?
I DON'T KNOW ... BEFORE LUNCH.
LUNCH! YOU MUST HAVE LEFT IT ON YOUR PLATE!
AND WE SCRAPED THE PLATES...
INTO THE DOG'S DISH!
YOU'D THINK THE KITCHEN WOULD BE MORE CAREFUL.
PTUII

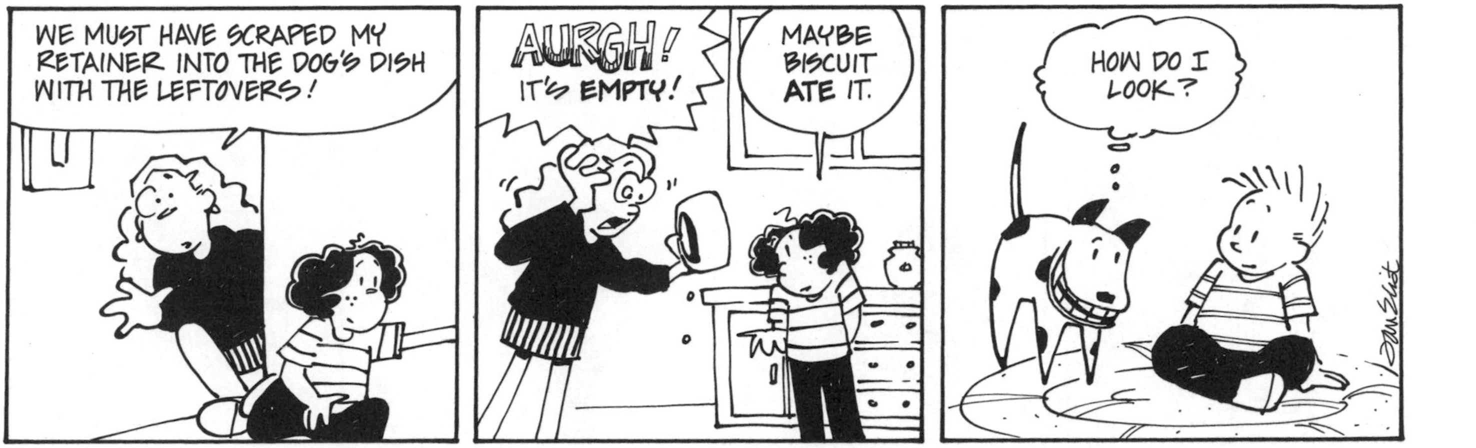
WE MUST HAVE SCRAPED MY RETAINER INTO THE DOG'S DISH WITH THE LEFTOVERS!
AURGH! IT'S EMPTY!
MAYBE BISCUIT ATE IT.
HOW DO I LOOK?

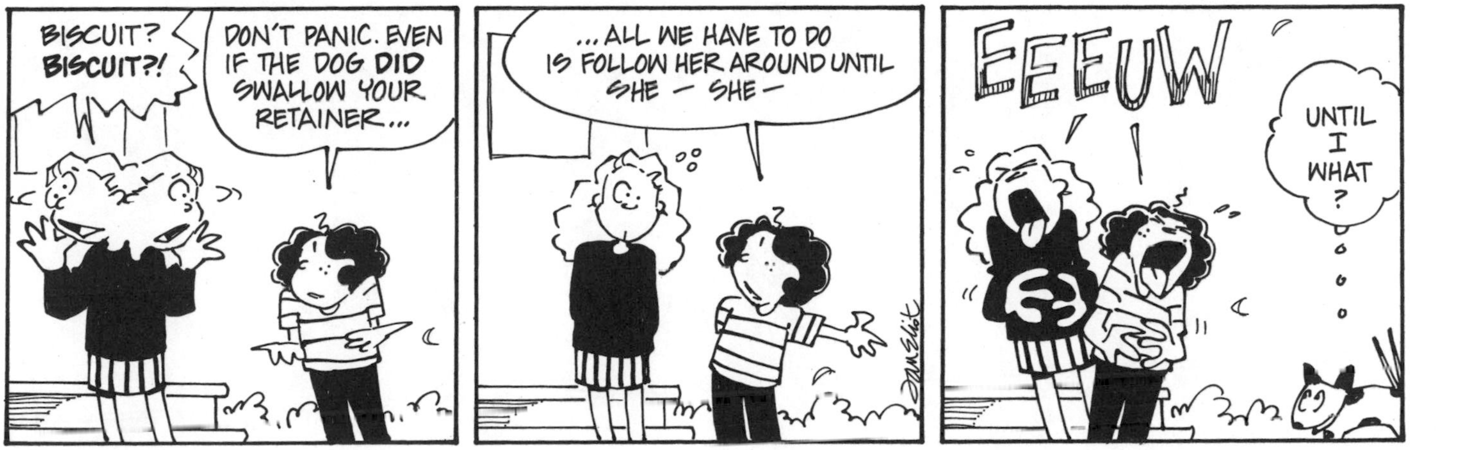
BISCUIT? BISCUIT?!
DON'T PANIC. EVEN IF THE DOG DID SWALLOW YOUR RETAINER...
...ALL WE HAVE TO DO IS FOLLOW HER AROUND UNTIL SHE — SHE —
EEEUW
UNTIL I WHAT?

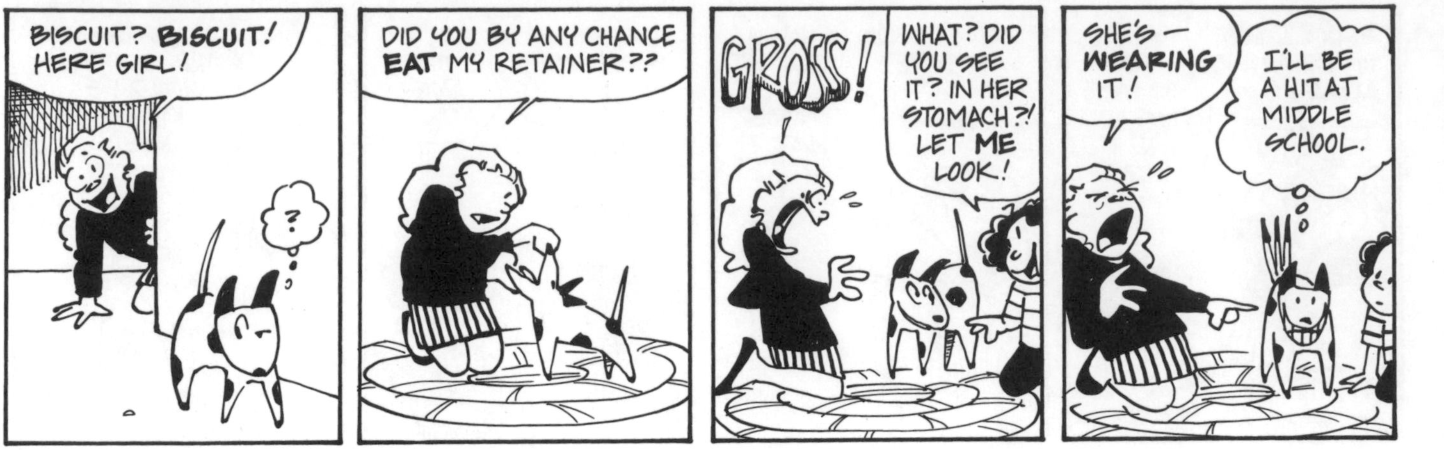
BISCUIT? BISCUIT! HERE GIRL!
?
DID YOU BY ANY CHANCE EAT MY RETAINER??
GROSS!
WHAT? DID YOU SEE IT? IN HER STOMACH?! LET ME LOOK!
SHE'S — WEARING IT!
I'LL BE A HIT AT MIDDLE SCHOOL.

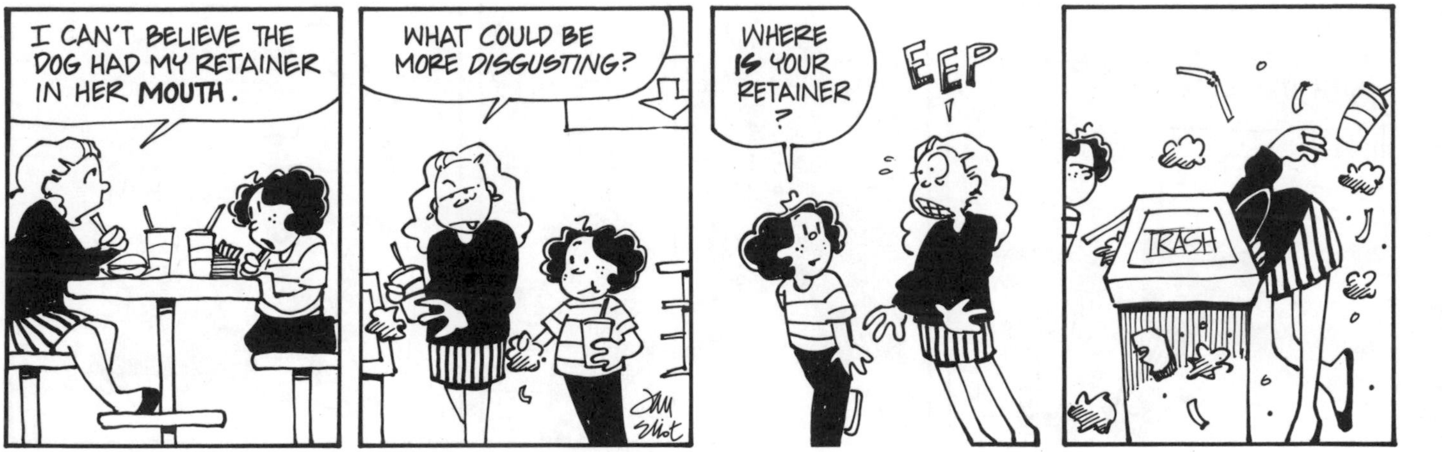
I CAN'T BELIEVE THE DOG HAD MY RETAINER IN HER MOUTH.
WHAT COULD BE MORE DISGUSTING?
WHERE IS YOUR RETAINER?
EEP
TRASH

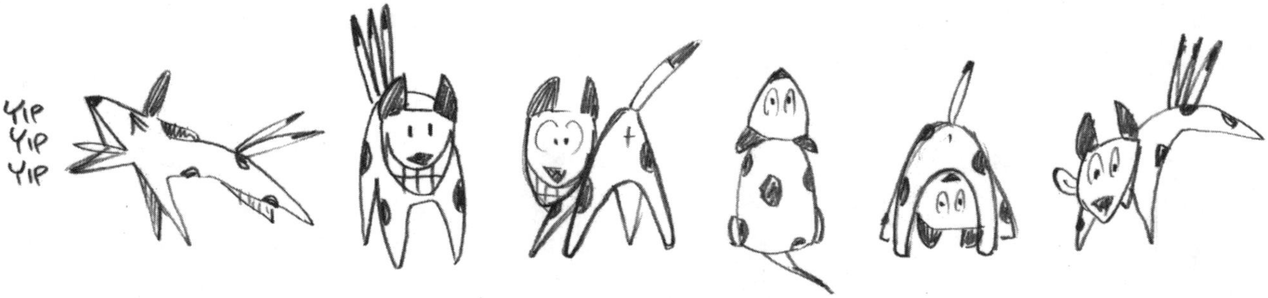
YIP
YIP
YIP

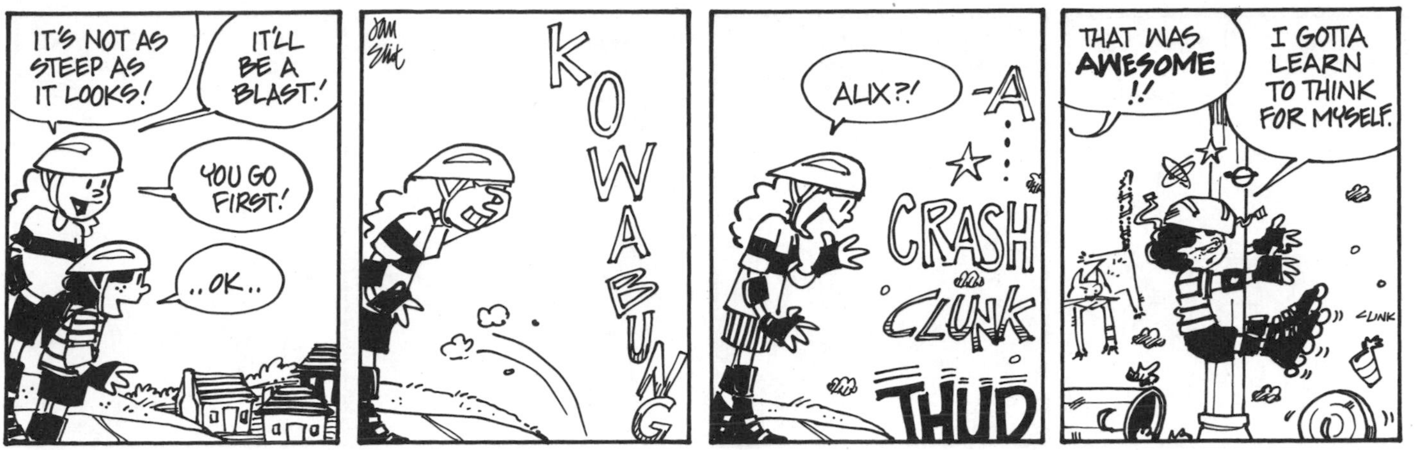
IT'S NOT AS STEEP AS IT LOOKS!
IT'LL BE A BLAST!
YOU GO FIRST!
..OK..
KOWABUNG
ALIX?!
-A
CRASH
CLUNK
THUD
THAT WAS AWESOME!!
I GOTTA LEARN TO THINK FOR MYSELF.
CLUNK

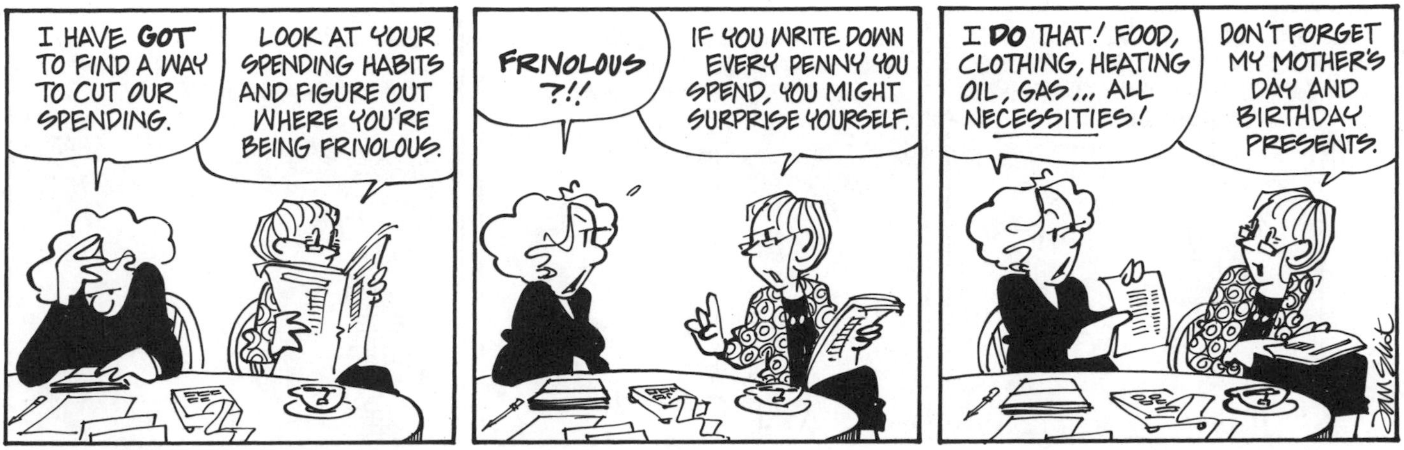
I HAVE GOT TO FIND A WAY TO CUT OUR SPENDING.
LOOK AT YOUR SPENDING HABITS AND FIGURE OUT WHERE YOU'RE BEING FRIVOLOUS.
FRIVOLOUS?!!
IF YOU WRITE DOWN EVERY PENNY YOU SPEND, YOU MIGHT SURPRISE YOURSELF.
I DO THAT! FOOD, CLOTHING, HEATING OIL, GAS... ALL NECESSITIES!
DON'T FORGET MY MOTHER'S DAY AND BIRTHDAY PRESENTS.

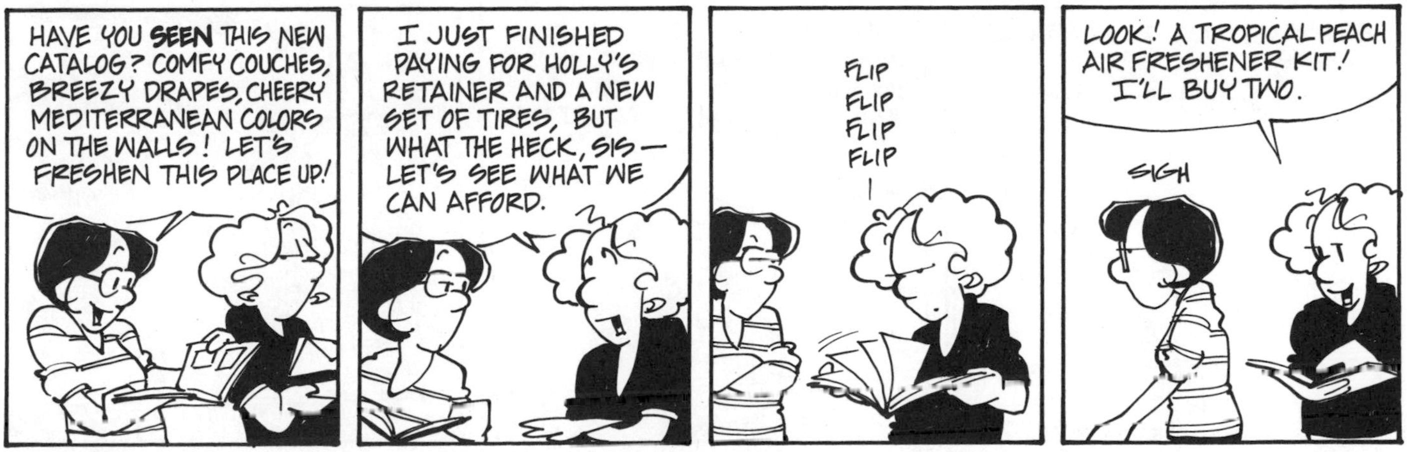
HAVE YOU SEEN THIS NEW CATALOG? COMFY COUCHES, BREEZY DRAPES, CHEERY MEDITERRANEAN COLORS ON THE WALLS! LET'S FRESHEN THIS PLACE UP!
I JUST FINISHED PAYING FOR HOLLY'S RETAINER AND A NEW SET OF TIRES, BUT WHAT THE HECK, SIS— LET'S SEE WHAT WE CAN AFFORD.
FLIP FLIP FLIP FLIP
LOOK! A TROPICAL PEACH AIR FRESHENER KIT! I'LL BUY TWO.
SIGH

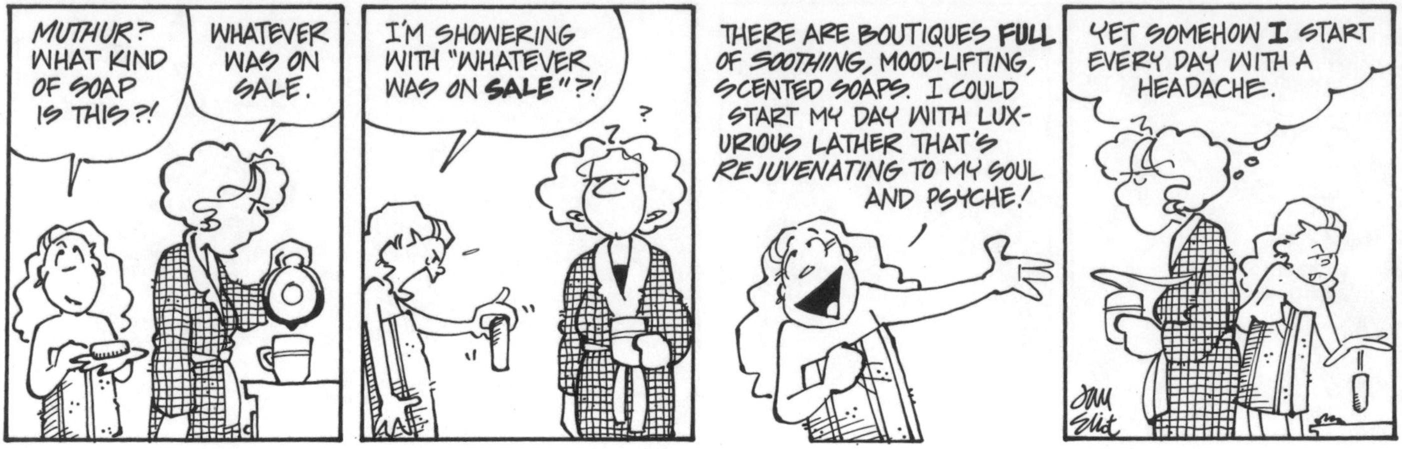
MUTHUR? WHAT KIND OF SOAP IS THIS?!
WHATEVER WAS ON SALE.
I'M SHOWERING WITH "WHATEVER WAS ON SALE"?!
? ?
THERE ARE BOUTIQUES FULL OF SOOTHING, MOOD-LIFTING, SCENTED SOAPS. I COULD START MY DAY WITH LUXURIOUS LATHER THAT'S REJUVENATING TO MY SOUL AND PSYCHE!
YET SOMEHOW I START EVERY DAY WITH A HEADACHE.

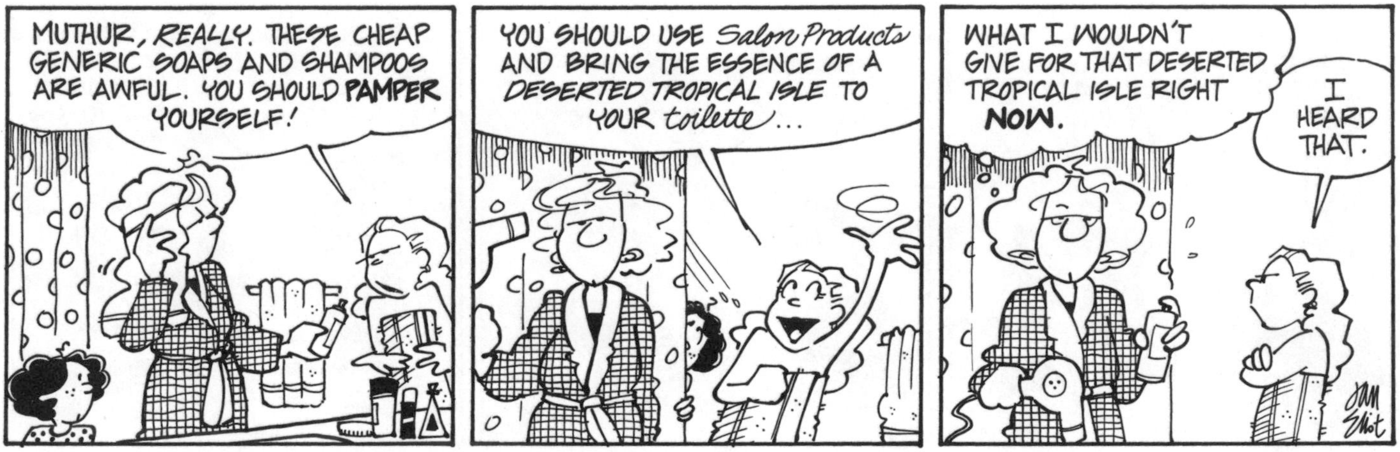
MUTHUR, REALLY. THESE CHEAP GENERIC SOAPS AND SHAMPOOS ARE AWFUL. YOU SHOULD PAMPER YOURSELF!
YOU SHOULD USE Salon Products AND BRING THE ESSENCE OF A DESERTED TROPICAL ISLE TO YOUR toilette...
WHAT I WOULDN'T GIVE FOR THAT DESERTED TROPICAL ISLE RIGHT NOW.
I HEARD THAT.

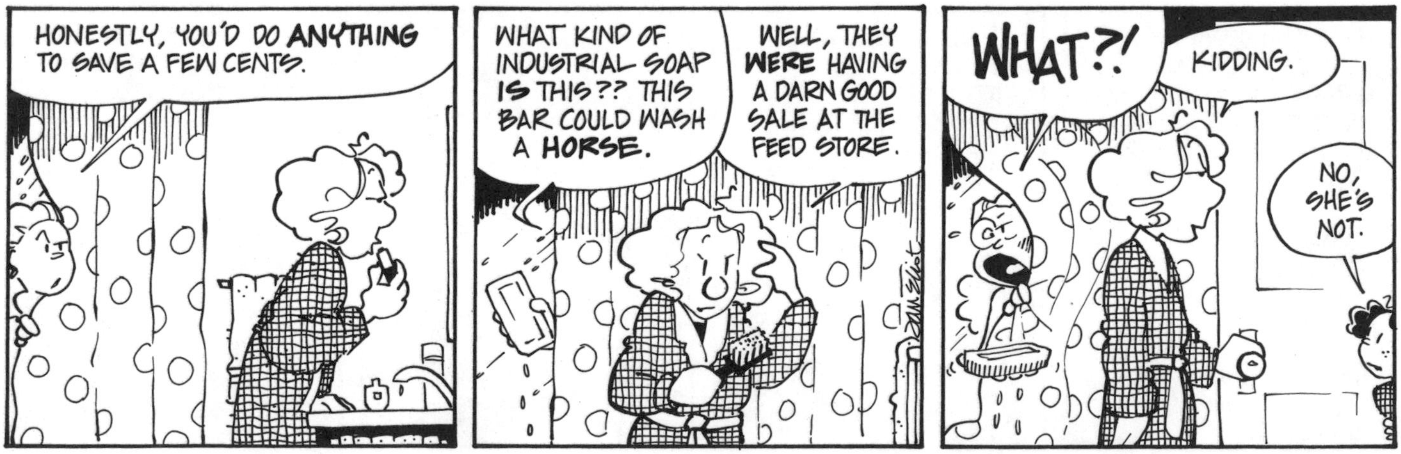
HONESTLY, YOU'D DO ANYTHING TO SAVE A FEW CENTS.
WHAT KIND OF INDUSTRIAL SOAP IS THIS?? THIS BAR COULD WASH A HORSE.
WELL, THEY WERE HAVING A DARN GOOD SALE AT THE FEED STORE.
WHAT?!
KIDDING.
NO, SHE'S NOT.

Stone Soup

HOW AM I GOING TO SELL ALL THIS CANDY FOR THE SOCCER TEAM?
GROCERY
KIDS
ZZZ
KID SPORT
GUESS WHAT, EVERYBODY! I SOLD ALL MY CANDY!!

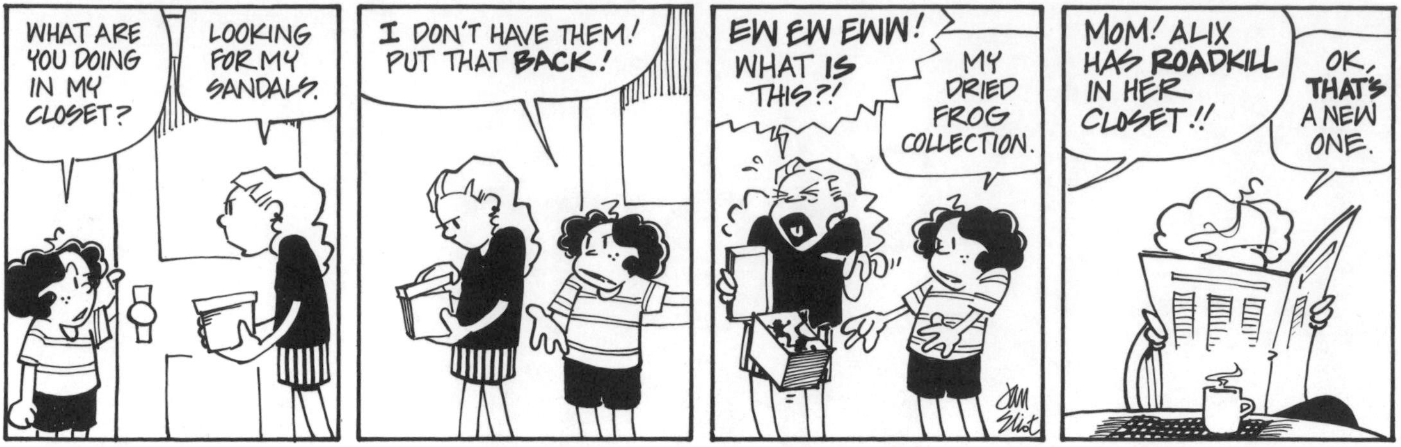
WHAT ARE YOU DOING IN MY CLOSET?
LOOKING FOR MY SANDALS.
I DON'T HAVE THEM! PUT THAT **BACK**!
EW EW EWW! WHAT **IS** THIS?!
MY DRIED FROG COLLECTION.
MOM! ALIX HAS **ROADKILL** IN HER CLOSET!!
OK, **THAT'S** A NEW ONE.

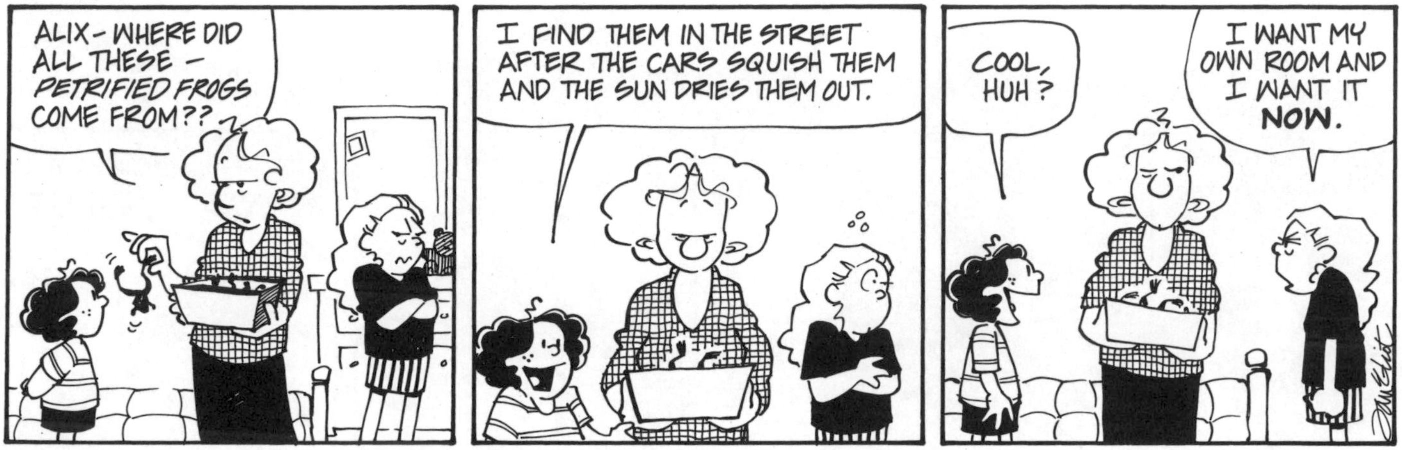
ALIX- WHERE DID ALL THESE - *PETRIFIED FROGS* COME FROM??
I FIND THEM IN THE STREET AFTER THE CARS SQUISH THEM AND THE SUN DRIES THEM OUT.
COOL, HUH?
I WANT MY OWN ROOM AND I WANT IT **NOW**.

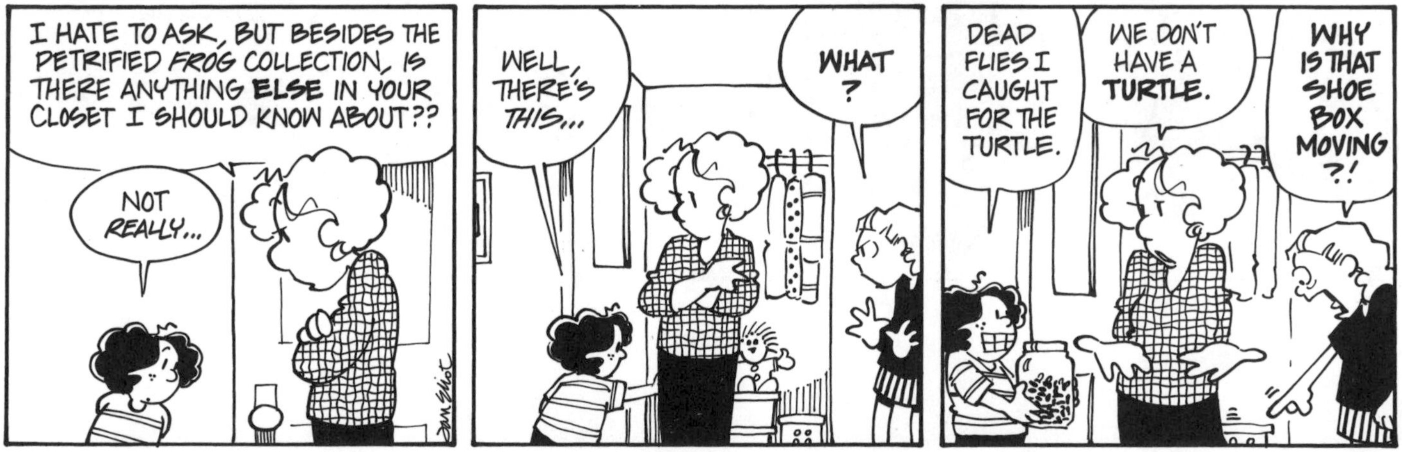
I HATE TO ASK, BUT BESIDES THE PETRIFIED *FROG* COLLECTION, IS THERE ANYTHING **ELSE** IN YOUR CLOSET I SHOULD KNOW ABOUT??
NOT *REALLY*...
WELL, THERE'S *THIS*...
WHAT ?
DEAD FLIES I CAUGHT FOR THE TURTLE.
WE DON'T HAVE A **TURTLE**.
WHY IS THAT SHOE BOX MOVING ?!

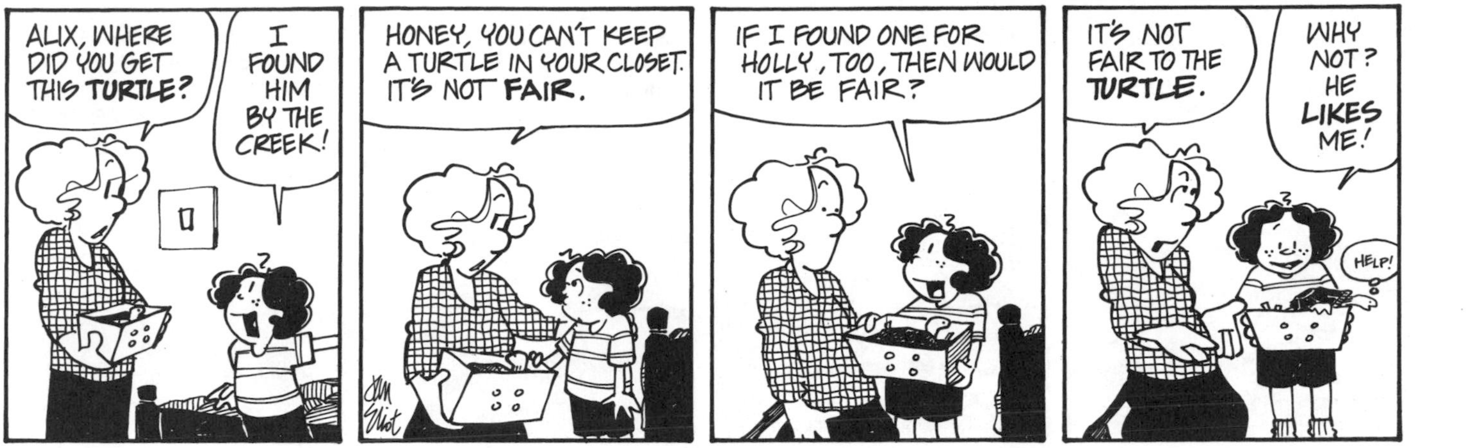
ALIX, WHERE DID YOU GET THIS **TURTLE?**
I FOUND HIM BY THE CREEK!
HONEY, YOU CAN'T KEEP A TURTLE IN YOUR CLOSET. IT'S NOT **FAIR.**
IF I FOUND ONE FOR HOLLY, TOO, THEN WOULD IT BE FAIR?
IT'S NOT FAIR TO THE **TURTLE.**
WHY NOT? HE **LIKES** ME!
HELP!

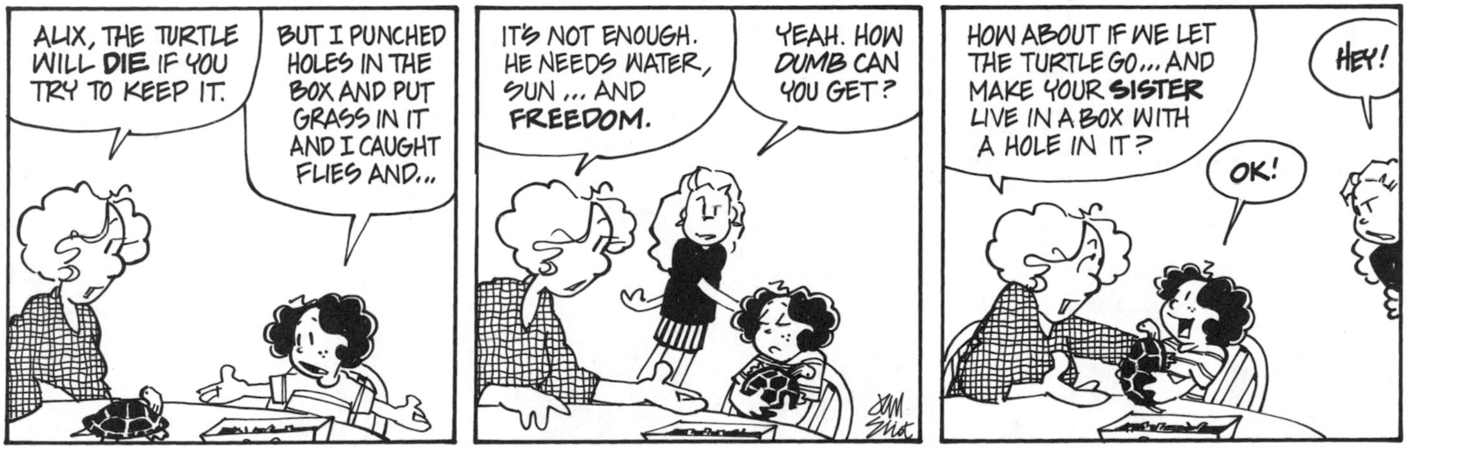
ALIX, THE TURTLE WILL **DIE** IF YOU TRY TO KEEP IT.
BUT I PUNCHED HOLES IN THE BOX AND PUT GRASS IN IT AND I CAUGHT FLIES AND...
IT'S NOT ENOUGH. HE NEEDS WATER, SUN ... AND **FREEDOM.**
YEAH. HOW *DUMB* CAN YOU GET?
HOW ABOUT IF WE LET THE TURTLE GO... AND MAKE YOUR **SISTER** LIVE IN A BOX WITH A HOLE IN IT?
OK!
HEY!

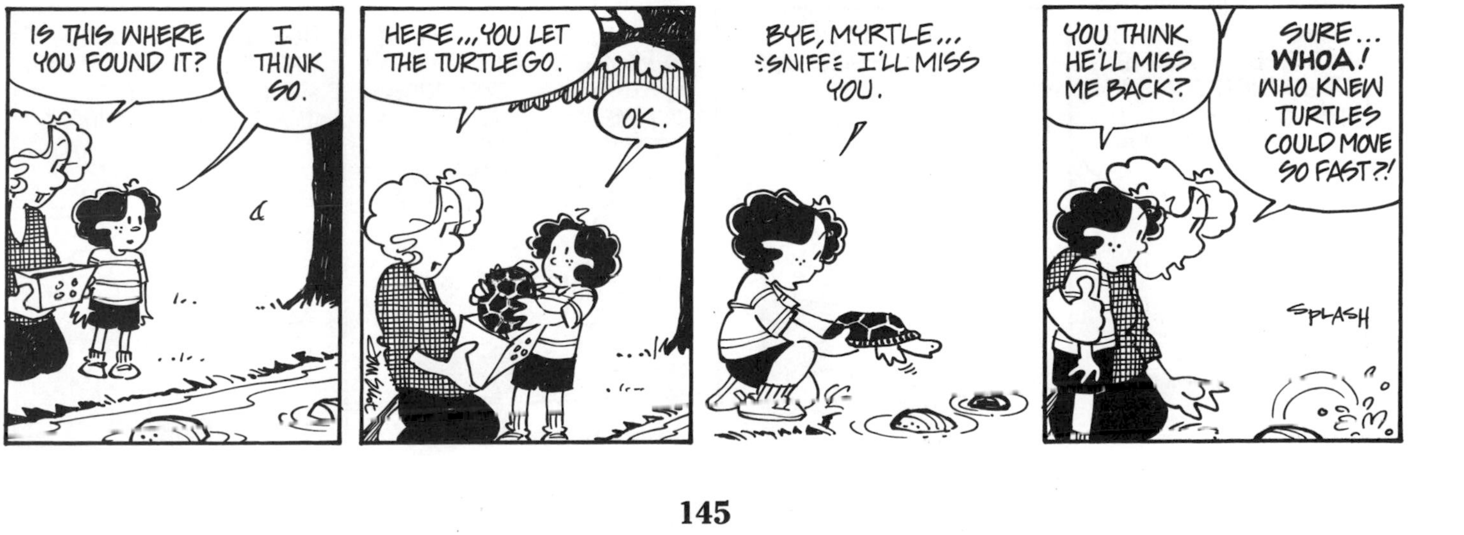
IS THIS WHERE YOU FOUND IT?
I THINK SO.
HERE... YOU LET THE TURTLE GO.
OK.
BYE, MYRTLE... SNIFF I'LL MISS YOU.
YOU THINK HE'LL MISS ME BACK?
SURE... **WHOA!** WHO KNEW TURTLES COULD MOVE SO FAST?!
SPLASH

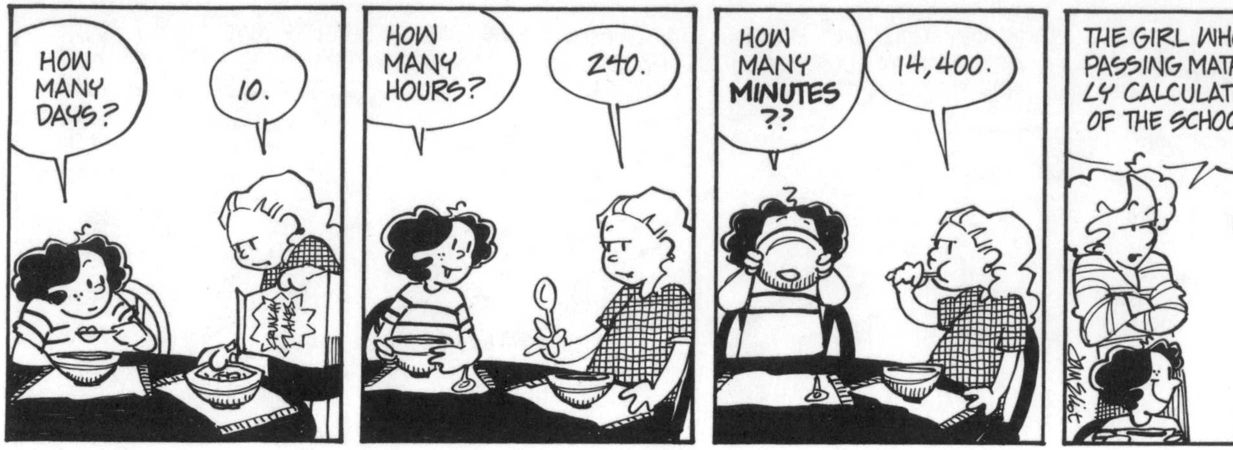
HOW MANY DAYS?
10.
HOW MANY HOURS?
240.
HOW MANY **MINUTES** ??
14,400.
THE GIRL WHO'S **BARELY** PASSING MATH CAN *MENTALLY* CALCULATE WHAT'S LEFT OF THE SCHOOL YEAR DOWN TO—?
864,000 SECONDS!

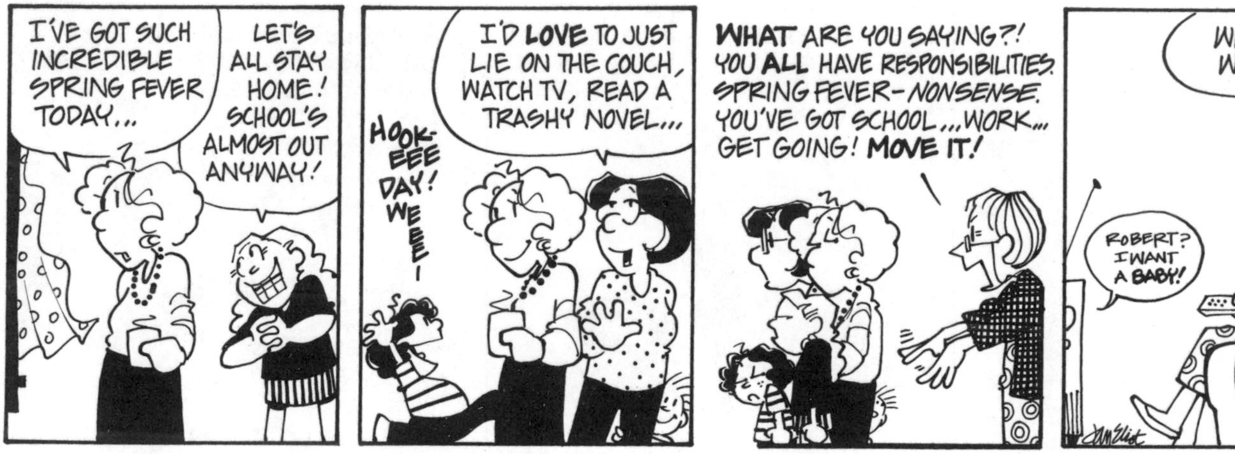
I'VE GOT SUCH INCREDIBLE SPRING FEVER TODAY...
LET'S ALL STAY HOME! SCHOOL'S ALMOST OUT ANYWAY!
HOOK-EEE DAY! WEEEE!
I'D **LOVE** TO JUST LIE ON THE COUCH, WATCH TV, READ A TRASHY NOVEL...
WHAT ARE YOU SAYING?! YOU **ALL** HAVE RESPONSIBILITIES. SPRING FEVER—*NONSENSE*. YOU'VE GOT SCHOOL... WORK... GET GOING! **MOVE IT**!
ROBERT? I WANT A **BABY**!
WHEW. THAT WAS **CLOSE**.

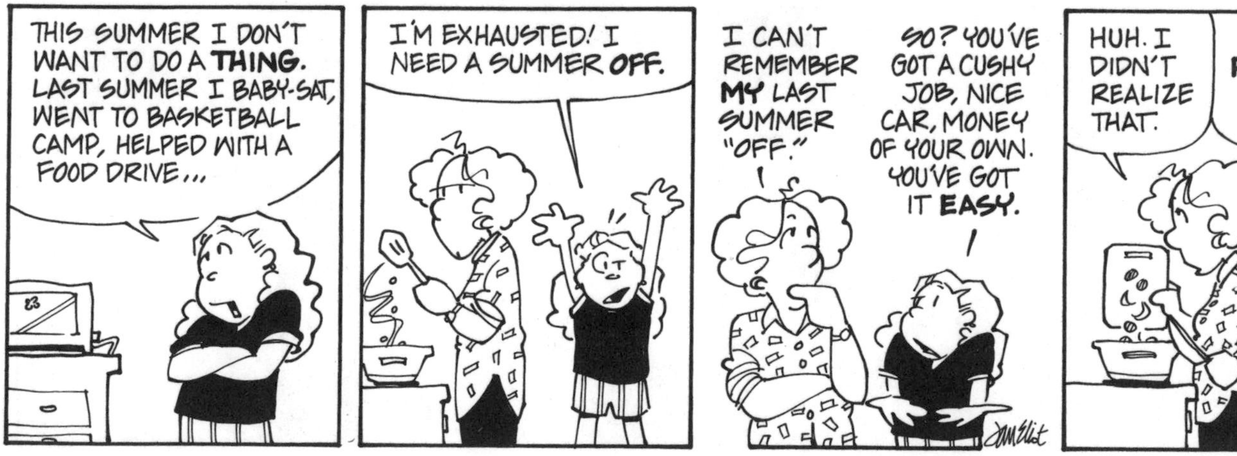
THIS SUMMER I DON'T WANT TO DO A **THING**. LAST SUMMER I BABY-SAT, WENT TO BASKETBALL CAMP, HELPED WITH A FOOD DRIVE...
I'M EXHAUSTED! I NEED A SUMMER **OFF**.
I CAN'T REMEMBER **MY** LAST SUMMER "OFF."
SO? YOU'VE GOT A CUSHY JOB, NICE CAR, MONEY OF YOUR OWN. YOU'VE GOT IT **EASY**.
HUH. I DIDN'T REALIZE THAT.
IF YOU WANT **REAL** STRESS, TRY MIDDLE SCHOOL.

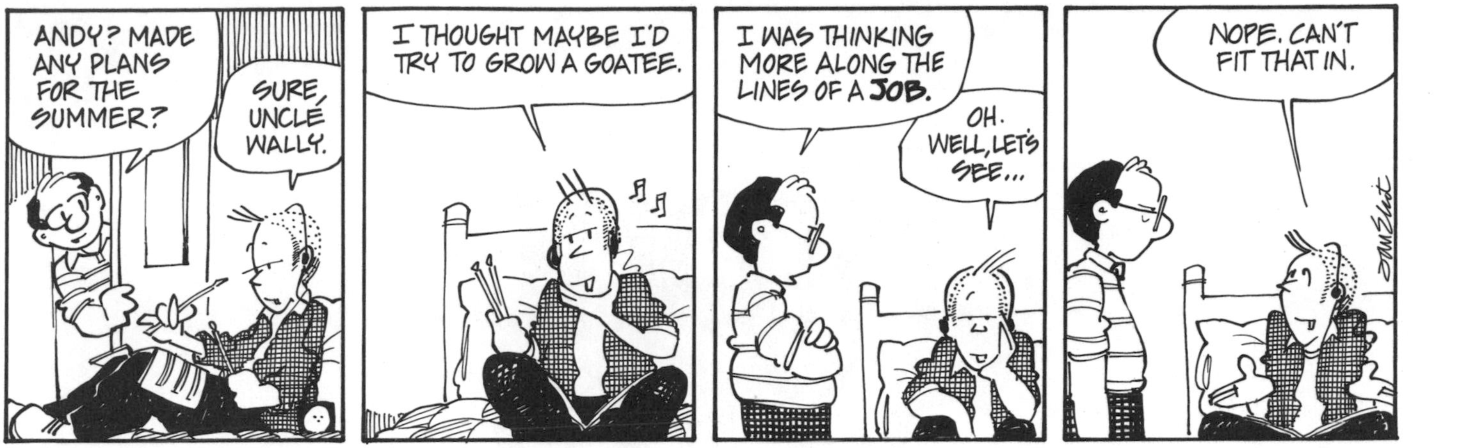
ANDY? MADE ANY PLANS FOR THE SUMMER?
SURE, UNCLE WALLY.
I THOUGHT MAYBE I'D TRY TO GROW A GOATEE.
I WAS THINKING MORE ALONG THE LINES OF A **JOB**.
OH. WELL, LET'S SEE...
NOPE. CAN'T FIT THAT IN.

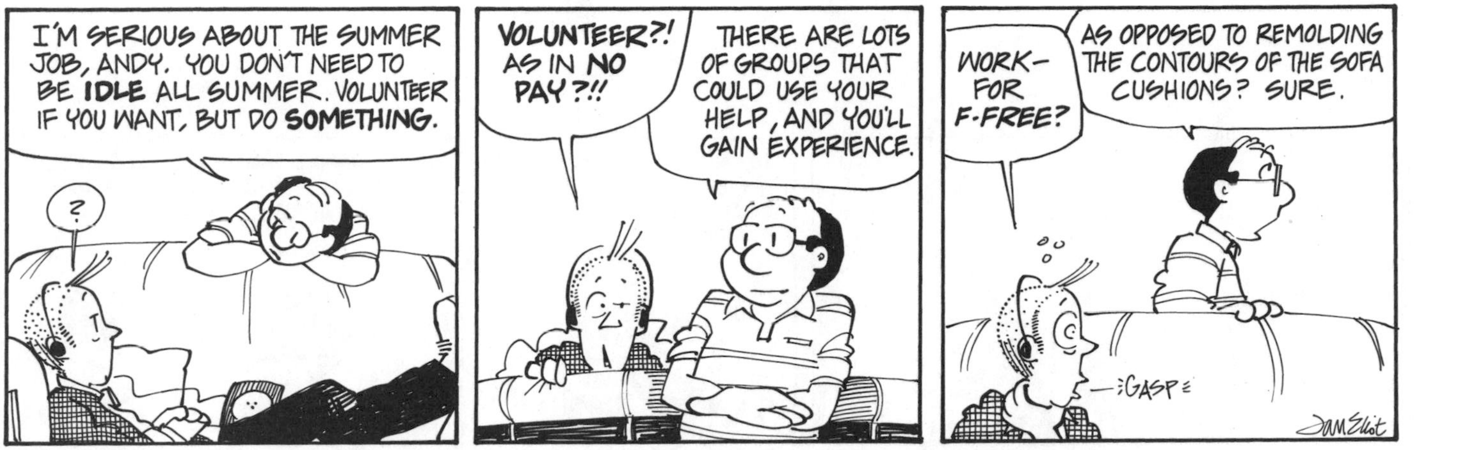
I'M SERIOUS ABOUT THE SUMMER JOB, ANDY. YOU DON'T NEED TO BE **IDLE** ALL SUMMER. VOLUNTEER IF YOU WANT, BUT DO **SOMETHING**.
?
THERE ARE LOTS OF GROUPS THAT COULD USE YOUR HELP, AND YOU'LL GAIN EXPERIENCE.
VOLUNTEER?! AS IN **NO PAY?!!**
WORK-FOR F-FREE?
AS OPPOSED TO REMOLDING THE CONTOURS OF THE SOFA CUSHIONS? SURE.
GASP

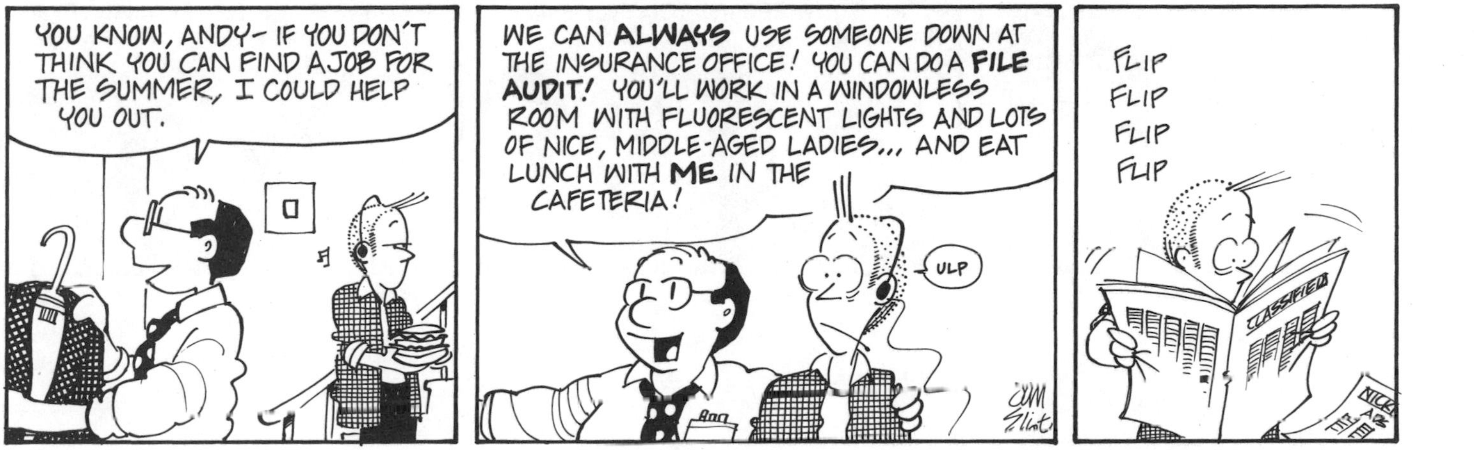
YOU KNOW, ANDY- IF YOU DON'T THINK YOU CAN FIND A JOB FOR THE SUMMER, I COULD HELP YOU OUT.
WE CAN **ALWAYS** USE SOMEONE DOWN AT THE INSURANCE OFFICE! YOU CAN DO A **FILE AUDIT**! YOU'LL WORK IN A WINDOWLESS ROOM WITH FLUORESCENT LIGHTS AND LOTS OF NICE, MIDDLE-AGED LADIES... AND EAT LUNCH WITH **ME** IN THE CAFETERIA!
ULP
FLIP
FLIP
FLIP
FLIP
CLASSIFIED

Stone Soup

IT'S MOTHER'S DAY?!
OOPS
WE BETTER MAKE A REALLY BIG CARD.
MAX SCRIBBLED ON ALL THE PAPER!
THE MARKERS ARE DRY!
HERE'S AN OLD PARTY INVITATION! MAYBE WE COULD ADAPT IT.
"LOOK WHO'S GOING TO BE 5"?
THE PICTURE'S CUTE. WE'LL JUST RIP OFF THE WORDS.
HERE'S A FLOWER FROM ONE OF MOM'S PLANTS.
MOM?! UM- HAPP-
IT'S 10 O'CLOCK? YOU LET US SLEEP IN! WHAT A WONDERFUL MOTHER'S DAY GIFT!
SHOULD WE MAKE HER BREAKFAST WHILE SHE'S IN THE SHOWER?
I SAY WE QUIT WHILE WE'RE AHEAD.

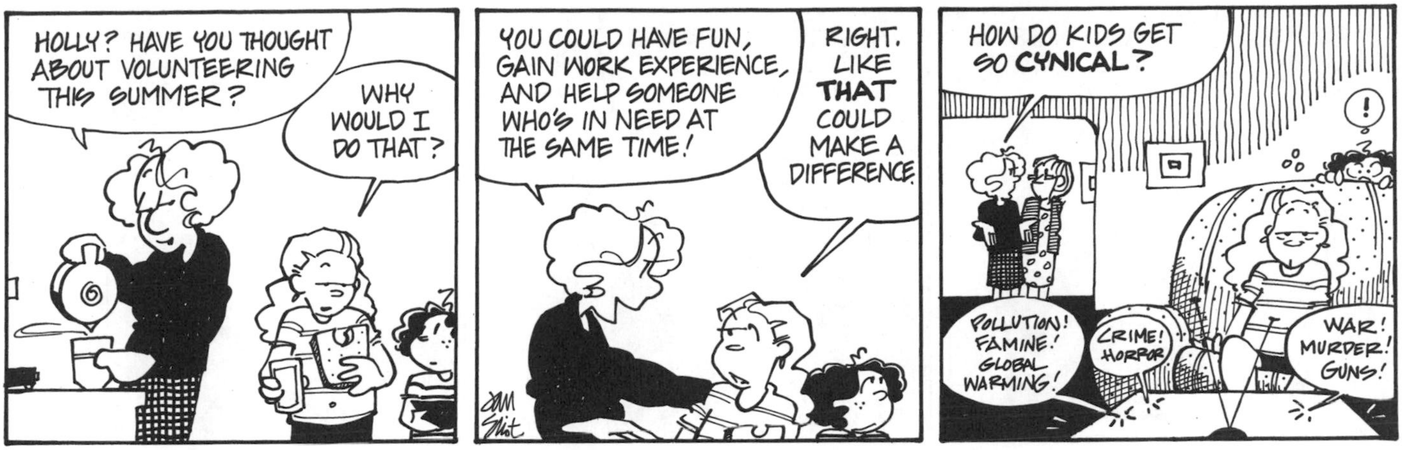

HOLLY? HAVE YOU THOUGHT ABOUT VOLUNTEERING THIS SUMMER?
WHY WOULD I DO THAT?
YOU COULD HAVE FUN, GAIN WORK EXPERIENCE, AND HELP SOMEONE WHO'S IN NEED AT THE SAME TIME!
RIGHT. LIKE THAT COULD MAKE A DIFFERENCE.
HOW DO KIDS GET SO CYNICAL?
!
POLLUTION! FAMINE! GLOBAL WARMING!
CRIME! HORROR
WAR! MURDER! GUNS!

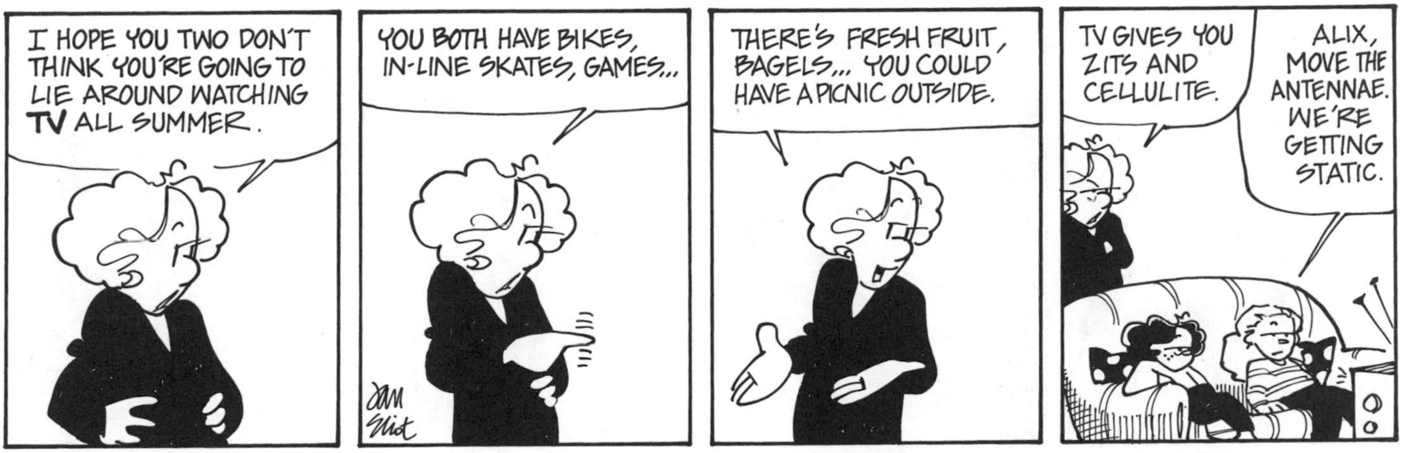

I HOPE YOU TWO DON'T THINK YOU'RE GOING TO LIE AROUND WATCHING TV ALL SUMMER.
YOU BOTH HAVE BIKES, IN-LINE SKATES, GAMES...
THERE'S FRESH FRUIT, BAGELS... YOU COULD HAVE A PICNIC OUTSIDE.
TV GIVES YOU ZITS AND CELLULITE.
ALIX, MOVE THE ANTENNAE. WE'RE GETTING STATIC.

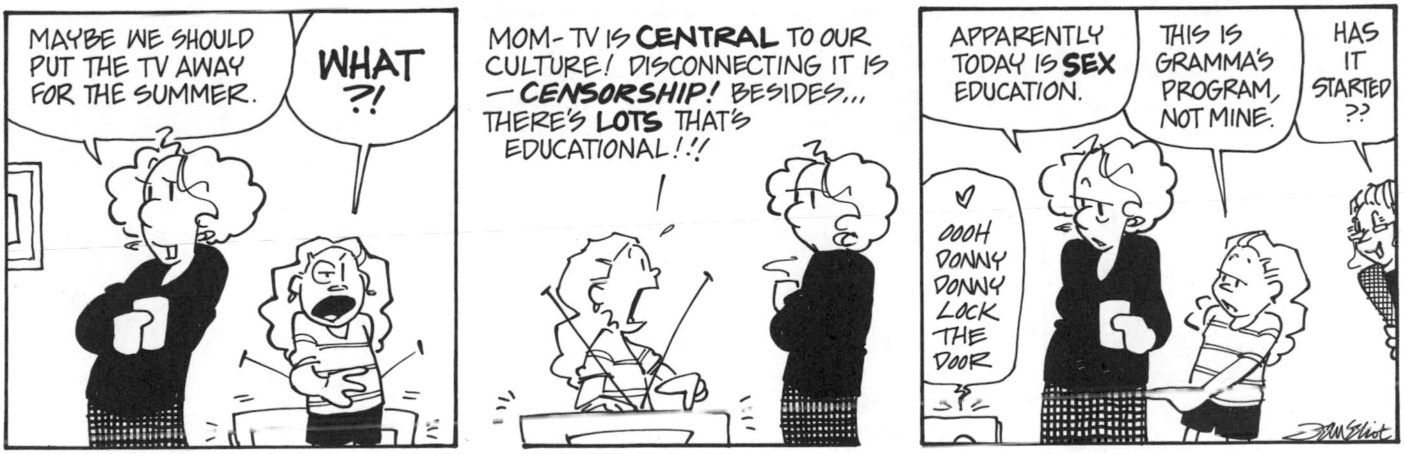

MAYBE WE SHOULD PUT THE TV AWAY FOR THE SUMMER.
WHAT ?!
MOM - TV IS CENTRAL TO OUR CULTURE! DISCONNECTING IT IS — CENSORSHIP! BESIDES... THERE'S LOTS THAT'S EDUCATIONAL!!!
APPARENTLY TODAY IS SEX EDUCATION.
THIS IS GRAMMA'S PROGRAM, NOT MINE.
HAS IT STARTED ??
OOOH DONNY DONNY LOCK THE DOOR

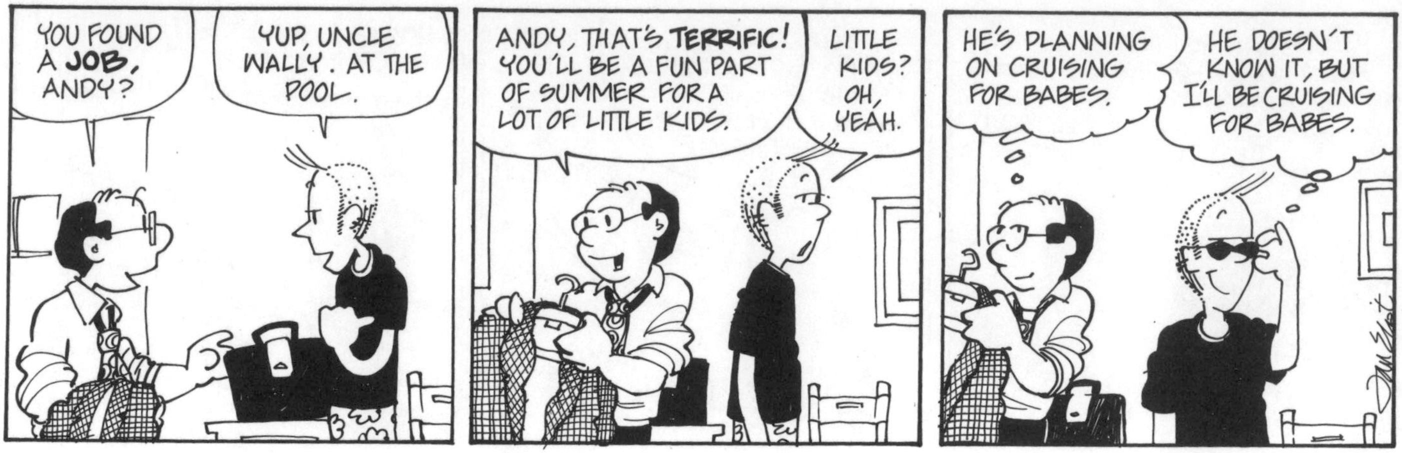
YOU FOUND A JOB, ANDY?
YUP, UNCLE WALLY. AT THE POOL.
ANDY, THAT'S TERRIFIC! YOU'LL BE A FUN PART OF SUMMER FOR A LOT OF LITTLE KIDS.
LITTLE KIDS? OH, YEAH.
HE'S PLANNING ON CRUISING FOR BABES.
HE DOESN'T KNOW IT, BUT I'LL BE CRUISING FOR BABES.

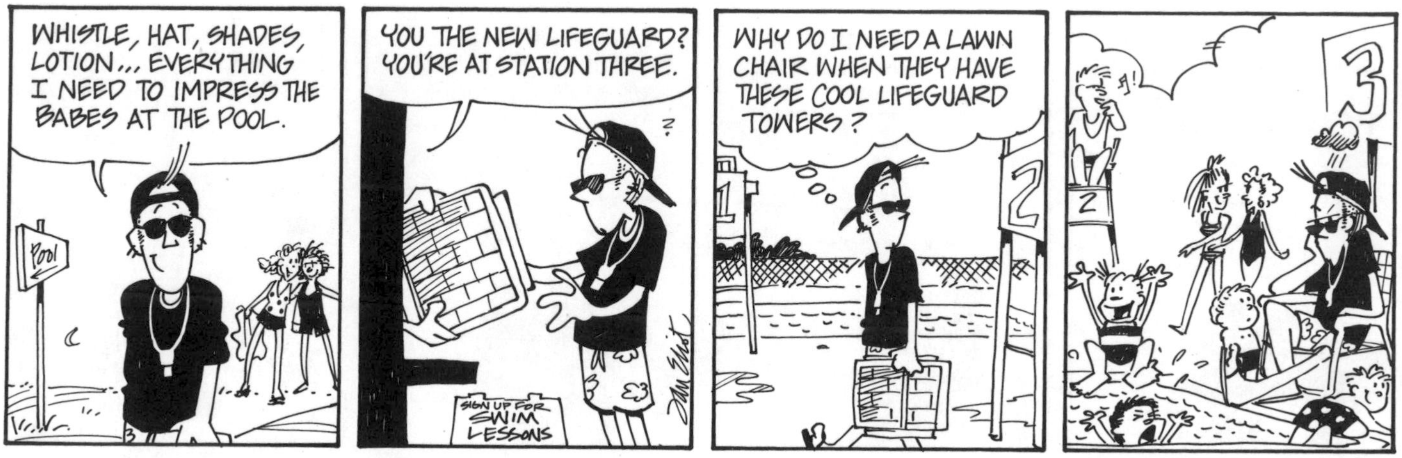
WHISTLE, HAT, SHADES, LOTION... EVERYTHING I NEED TO IMPRESS THE BABES AT THE POOL.
POOL
YOU THE NEW LIFEGUARD? YOU'RE AT STATION THREE.
SIGN UP FOR SWIM LESSONS
WHY DO I NEED A LAWN CHAIR WHEN THEY HAVE THESE COOL LIFEGUARD TOWERS?
1
2
3

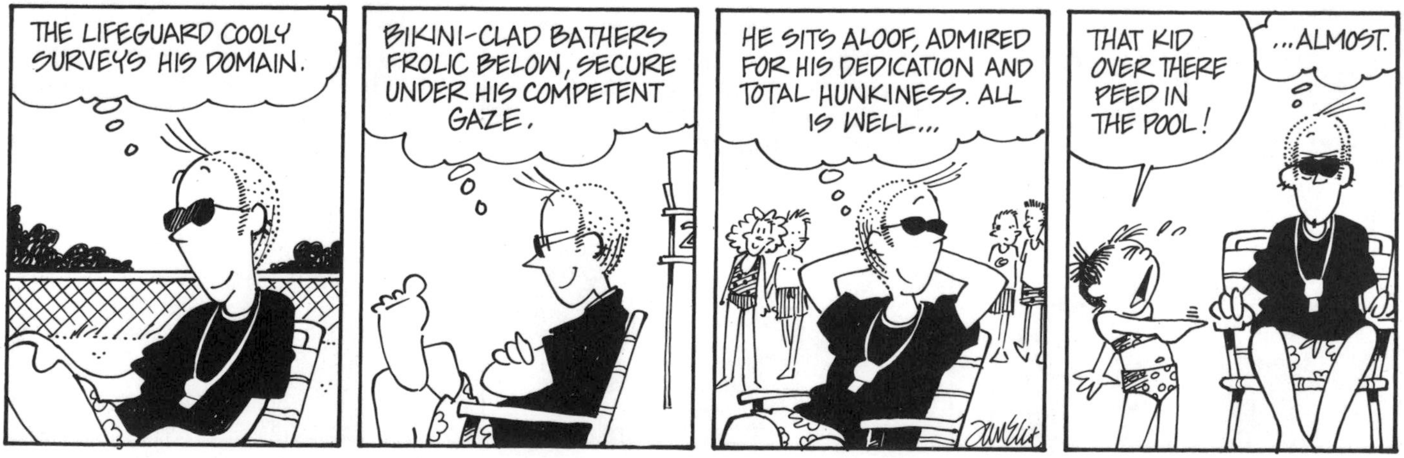
THE LIFEGUARD COOLY SURVEYS HIS DOMAIN.
BIKINI-CLAD BATHERS FROLIC BELOW, SECURE UNDER HIS COMPETENT GAZE.
HE SITS ALOOF, ADMIRED FOR HIS DEDICATION AND TOTAL HUNKINESS. ALL IS WELL...
THAT KID OVER THERE PEED IN THE POOL!
...ALMOST.

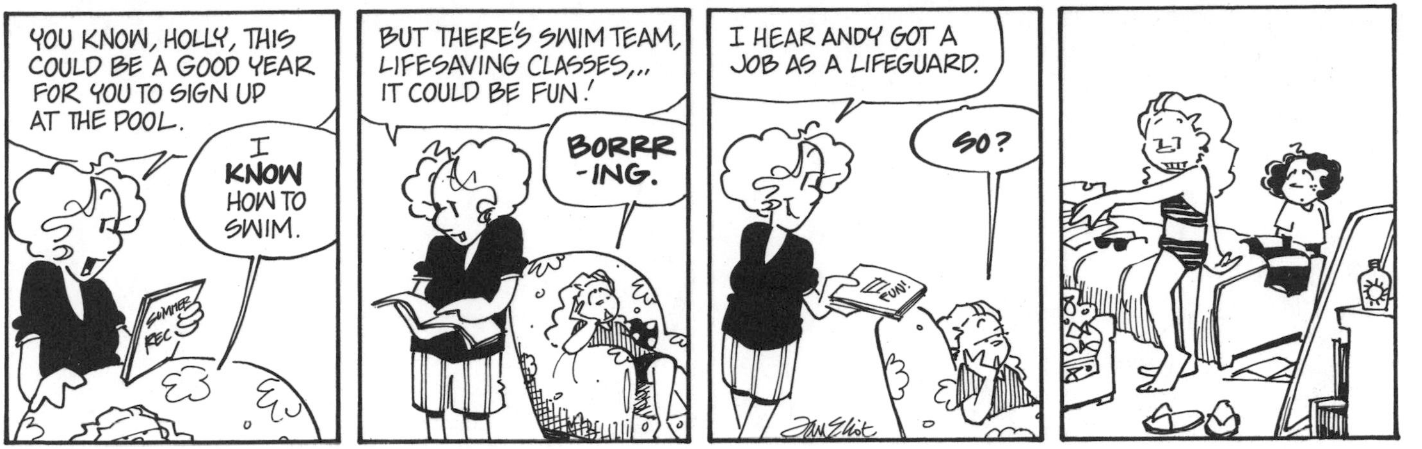
YOU KNOW, HOLLY, THIS COULD BE A GOOD YEAR FOR YOU TO SIGN UP AT THE POOL.
I **KNOW** HOW TO SWIM.
SUMMER REC
BUT THERE'S SWIM TEAM, LIFESAVING CLASSES,... IT COULD BE FUN!
BORRR -ING.
I HEAR ANDY GOT A JOB AS A LIFEGUARD.
SO?
FUN!

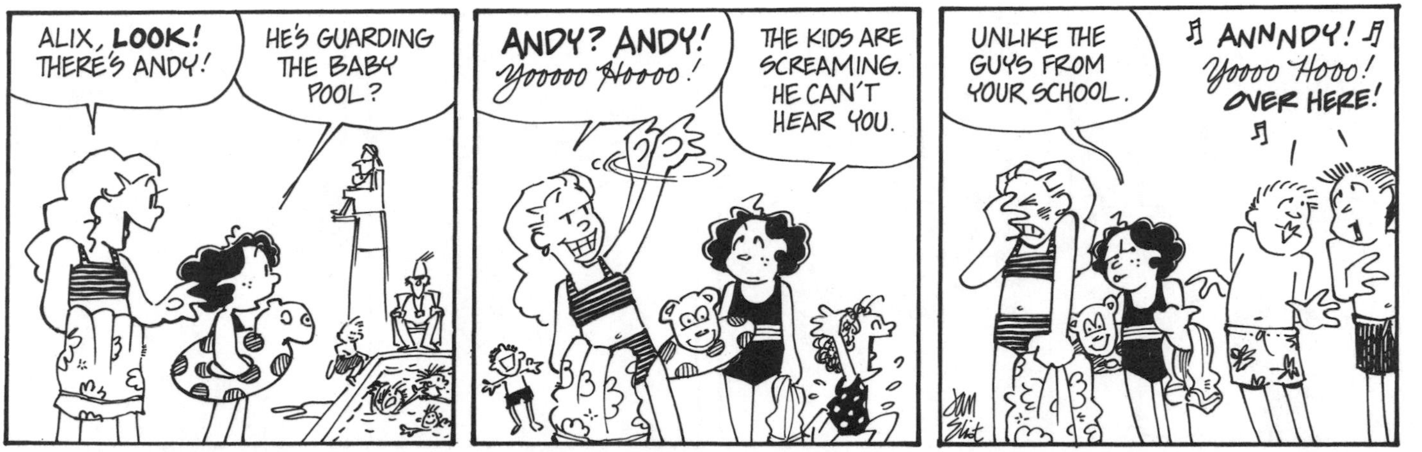
ALIX, **LOOK!** THERE'S ANDY!
HE'S GUARDING THE BABY POOL?
ANDY? ANDY! Yooooo Hoooo!
THE KIDS ARE SCREAMING. HE CAN'T HEAR YOU.
UNLIKE THE GUYS FROM YOUR SCHOOL.
ANNNDY! Yoooo Hooo! **OVER HERE!**

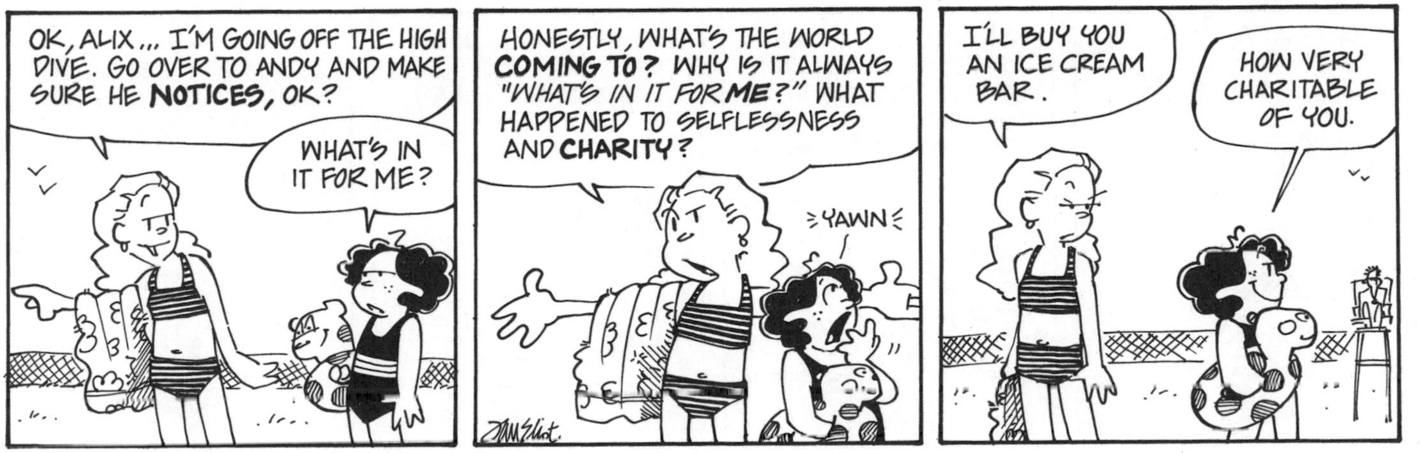
OK, ALIX... I'M GOING OFF THE HIGH DIVE. GO OVER TO ANDY AND MAKE SURE HE **NOTICES,** OK?
WHAT'S IN IT FOR ME?
HONESTLY, WHAT'S THE WORLD **COMING TO?** WHY IS IT ALWAYS "*WHAT'S IN IT FOR* **ME**?" WHAT HAPPENED TO SELFLESSNESS AND **CHARITY**?
YAWN
I'LL BUY YOU AN ICE CREAM BAR.
HOW VERY CHARITABLE OF YOU.

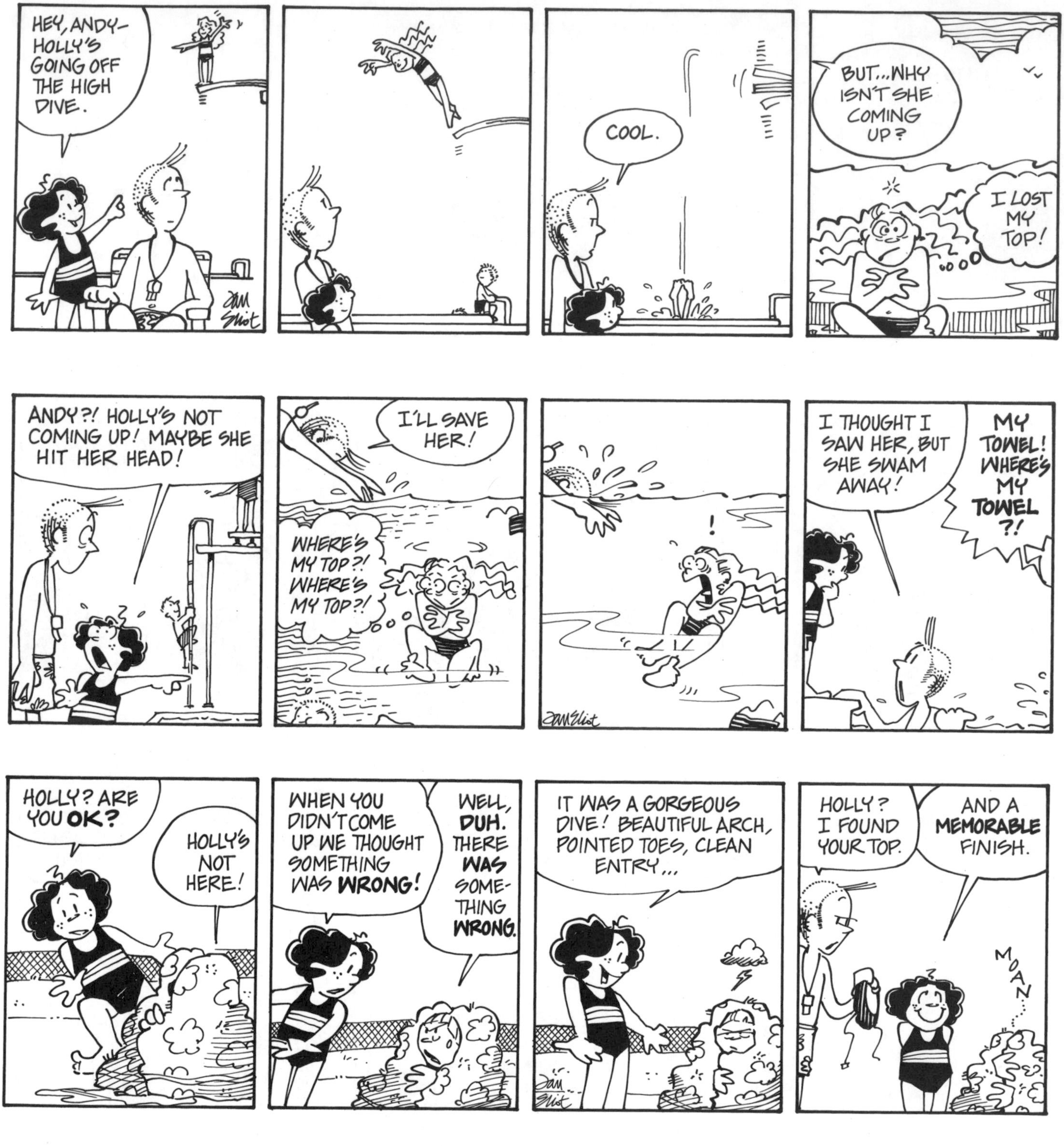
HEY, ANDY— HOLLY'S GOING OFF THE HIGH DIVE.
COOL.
BUT...WHY ISN'T SHE COMING UP?
I LOST MY TOP!
ANDY?! HOLLY'S NOT COMING UP! MAYBE SHE HIT HER HEAD!
I'LL SAVE HER!
WHERE'S MY TOP?! WHERE'S MY TOP?!
I THOUGHT I SAW HER, BUT SHE SWAM AWAY!
MY TOWEL! WHERE'S MY TOWEL?!
HOLLY? ARE YOU OK?
HOLLY'S NOT HERE!
WHEN YOU DIDN'T COME UP WE THOUGHT SOMETHING WAS WRONG!
WELL, DUH. THERE WAS SOME-THING WRONG.
IT WAS A GORGEOUS DIVE! BEAUTIFUL ARCH, POINTED TOES, CLEAN ENTRY...
HOLLY? I FOUND YOUR TOP.
AND A MEMORABLE FINISH.
MOAN...

Stone Soup

ENOUGH TV! GO MAKE YOUR OWN FUN!
RIGHT. WHAT'S FUN AROUND HERE?
GLUE GUN
HOLLY'S BARBIES
OW!
!
!!!
EXCEPT FOR THE FIRE, HOW'D I DO AT MAKING MY OWN FUN?
WHY DOES MY BARBIE HAVE THREE LEGS?!?

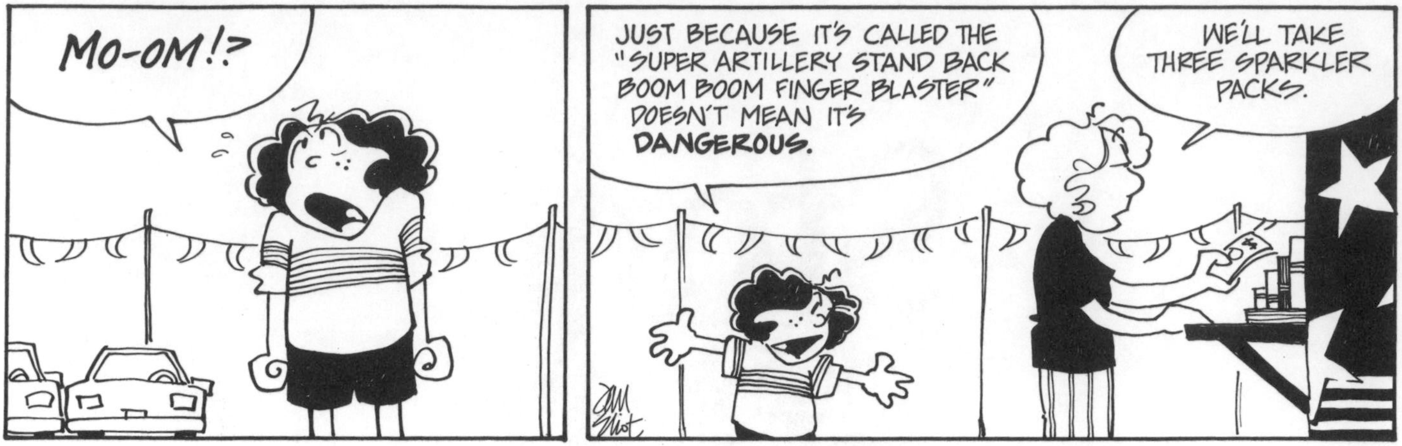
MO-OM!?
JUST BECAUSE IT'S CALLED THE "SUPER ARTILLERY STAND BACK BOOM BOOM FINGER BLASTER" DOESN'T MEAN IT'S **DANGEROUS.**
WE'LL TAKE THREE SPARKLER PACKS.

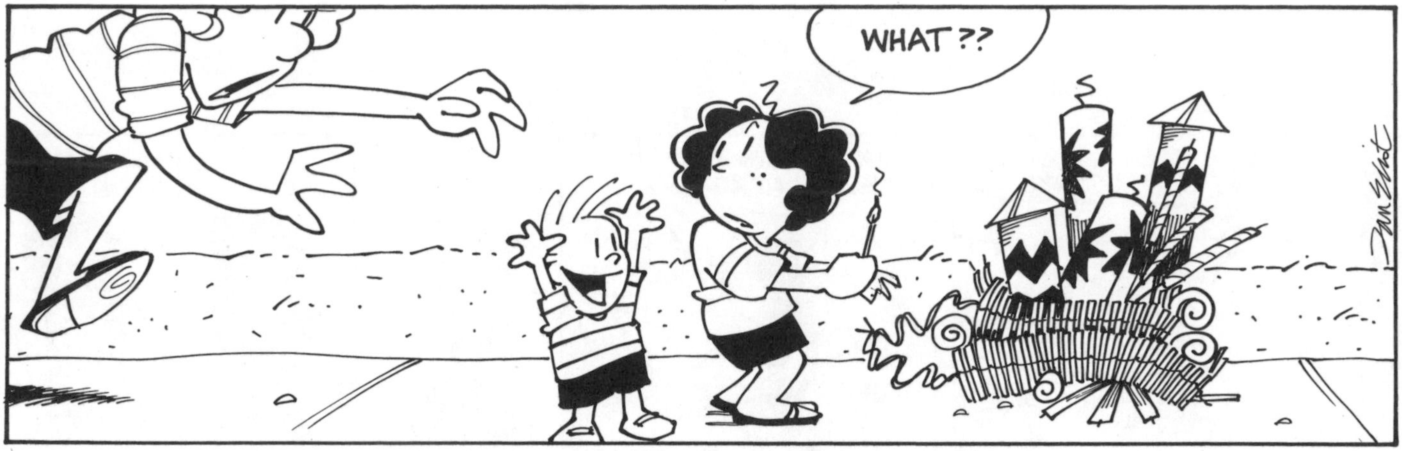
WHAT ??

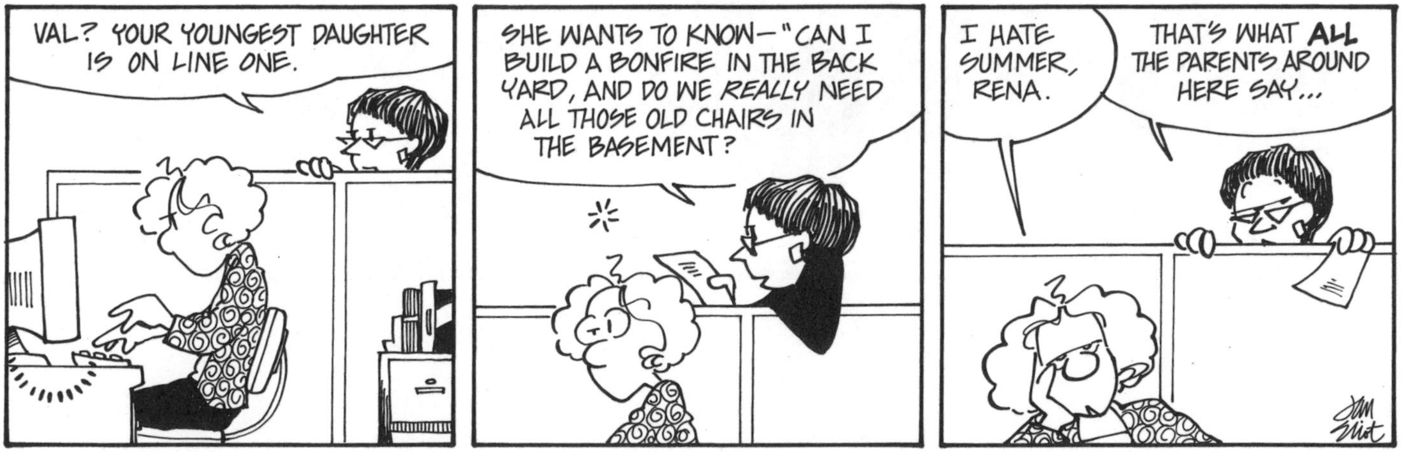
VAL? YOUR YOUNGEST DAUGHTER IS ON LINE ONE.
SHE WANTS TO KNOW—"CAN I BUILD A BONFIRE IN THE BACK YARD, AND DO WE *REALLY* NEED ALL THOSE OLD CHAIRS IN THE BASEMENT?
I HATE SUMMER, RENA.
THAT'S WHAT **ALL** THE PARENTS AROUND HERE SAY...

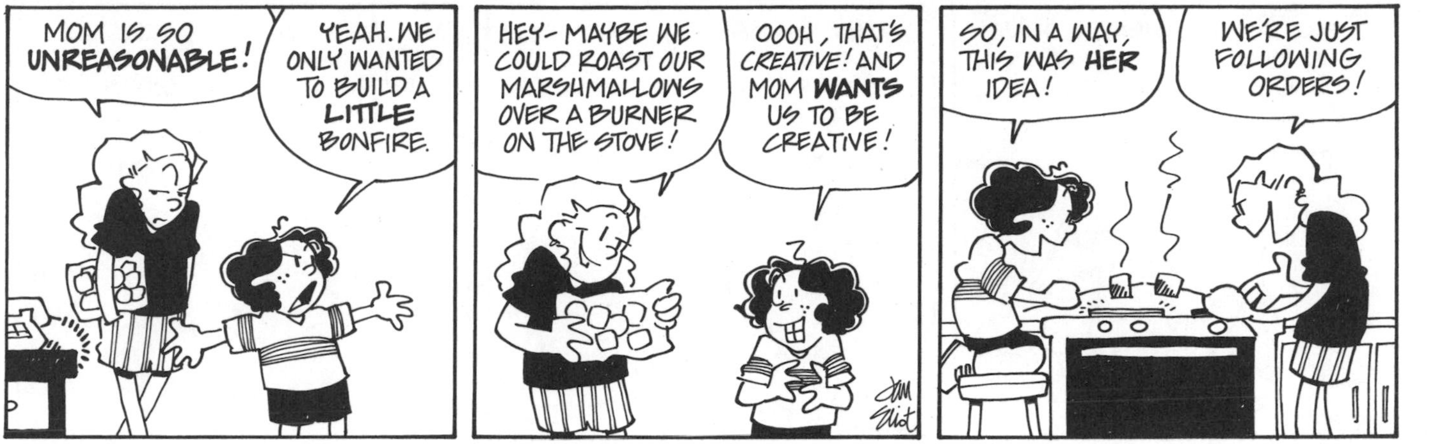
MOM IS SO UNREASONABLE!
YEAH. WE ONLY WANTED TO BUILD A LITTLE BONFIRE.
HEY- MAYBE WE COULD ROAST OUR MARSHMALLOWS OVER A BURNER ON THE STOVE!
OOOH, THAT'S CREATIVE! AND MOM WANTS US TO BE CREATIVE!
SO, IN A WAY, THIS WAS HER IDEA!
WE'RE JUST FOLLOWING ORDERS!

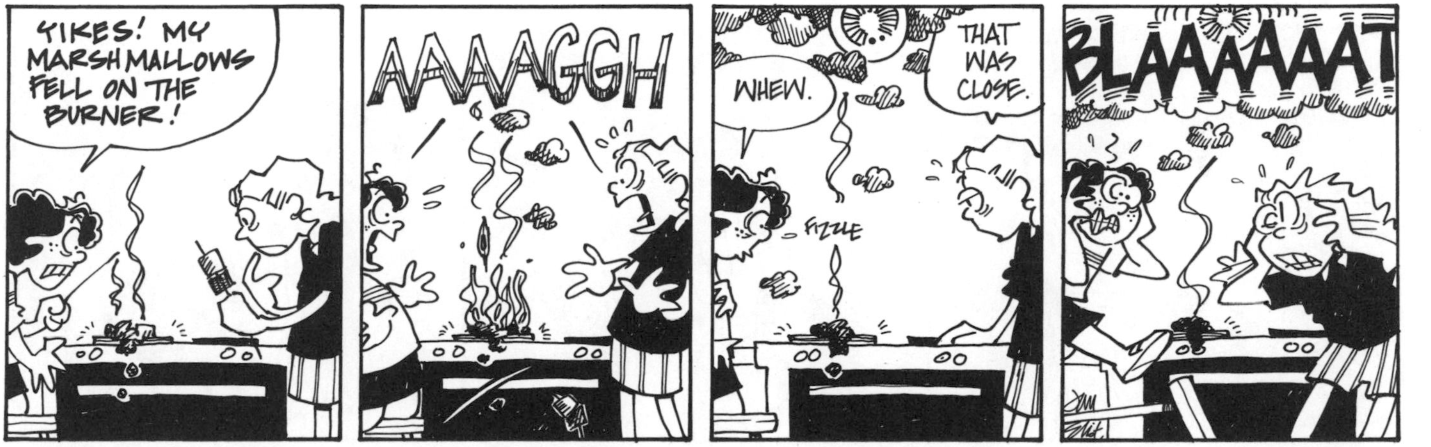
YIKES! MY MARSHMALLOWS FELL ON THE BURNER!
AAAAAGGH
WHEW.
THAT WAS CLOSE.
FIZZLE
BLAAAAAAT

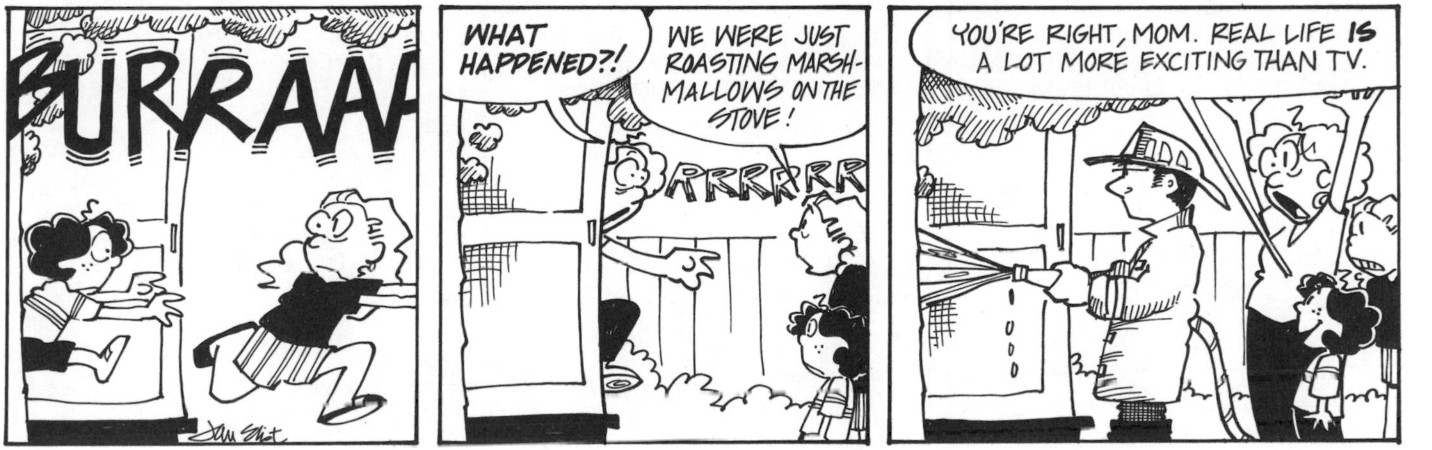
BURRAAA
WHAT HAPPENED?!
WE WERE JUST ROASTING MARSH-MALLOWS ON THE STOVE!
RRRRRRR
YOU'RE RIGHT, MOM. REAL LIFE IS A LOT MORE EXCITING THAN TV.

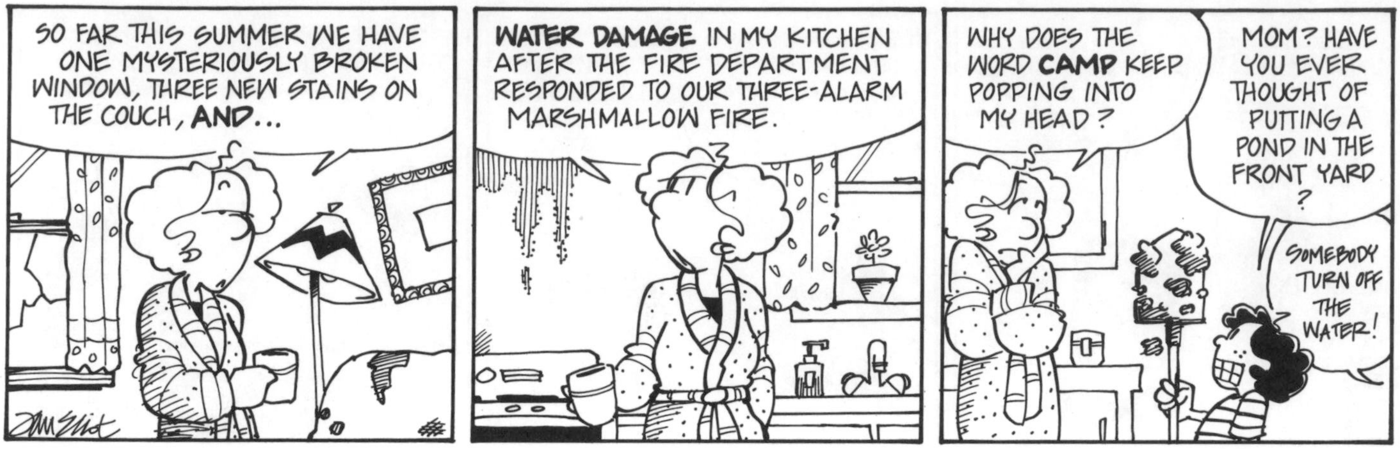
SO FAR THIS SUMMER WE HAVE ONE MYSTERIOUSLY BROKEN WINDOW, THREE NEW STAINS ON THE COUCH, AND...
WATER DAMAGE IN MY KITCHEN AFTER THE FIRE DEPARTMENT RESPONDED TO OUR THREE-ALARM MARSHMALLOW FIRE.
WHY DOES THE WORD CAMP KEEP POPPING INTO MY HEAD?
MOM? HAVE YOU EVER THOUGHT OF PUTTING A POND IN THE FRONT YARD?
SOMEBODY TURN OFF THE WATER!

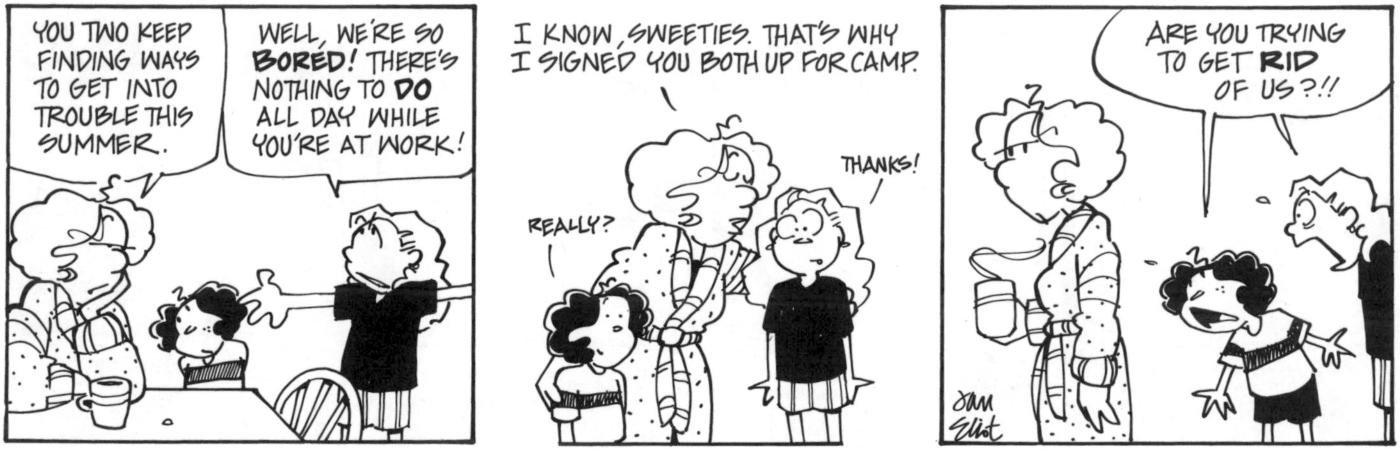
YOU TWO KEEP FINDING WAYS TO GET INTO TROUBLE THIS SUMMER.
WELL, WE'RE SO BORED! THERE'S NOTHING TO DO ALL DAY WHILE YOU'RE AT WORK!
I KNOW, SWEETIES. THAT'S WHY I SIGNED YOU BOTH UP FOR CAMP.
REALLY?
THANKS!
ARE YOU TRYING TO GET RID OF US?!!

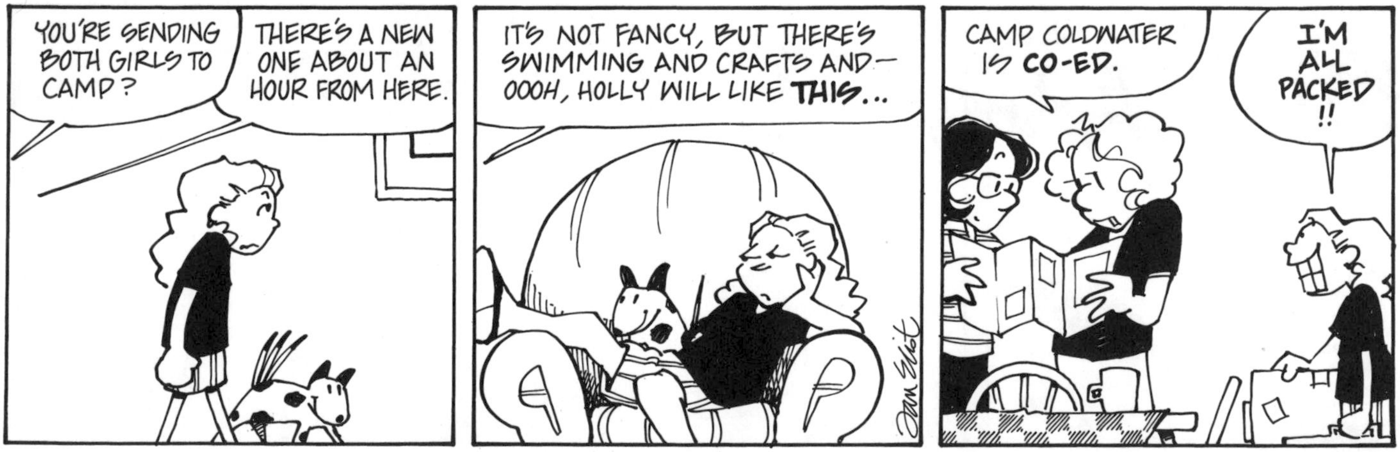
YOU'RE SENDING BOTH GIRLS TO CAMP?
THERE'S A NEW ONE ABOUT AN HOUR FROM HERE.
IT'S NOT FANCY, BUT THERE'S SWIMMING AND CRAFTS AND— OOOH, HOLLY WILL LIKE THIS...
CAMP COLDWATER IS CO-ED.
I'M ALL PACKED!!

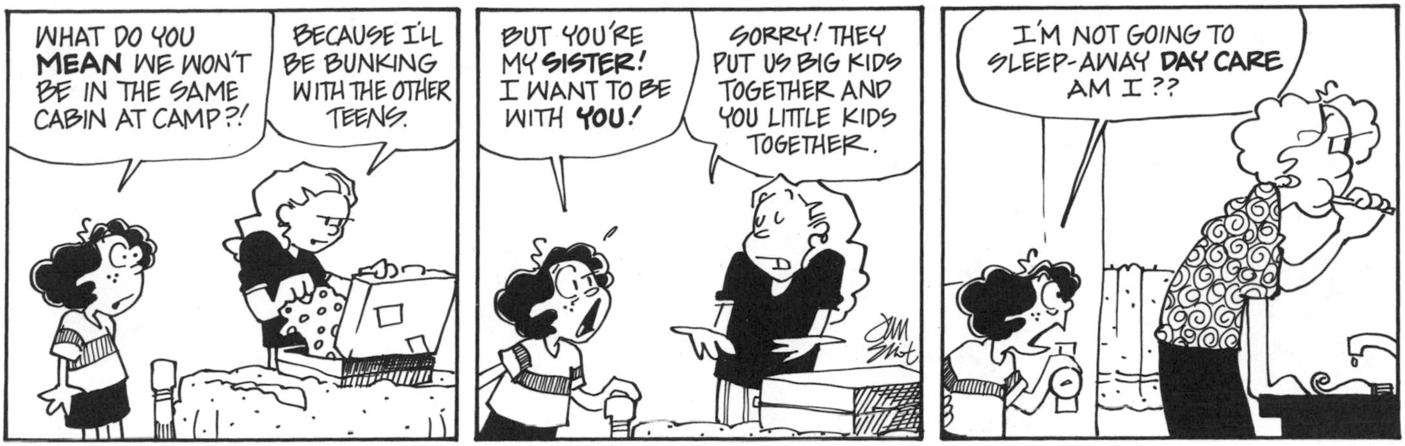
WHAT DO YOU MEAN WE WON'T BE IN THE SAME CABIN AT CAMP?!
BECAUSE I'LL BE BUNKING WITH THE OTHER TEENS.
BUT YOU'RE MY SISTER! I WANT TO BE WITH YOU!
SORRY! THEY PUT US BIG KIDS TOGETHER AND YOU LITTLE KIDS TOGETHER.
I'M NOT GOING TO SLEEP-AWAY DAY CARE AM I??

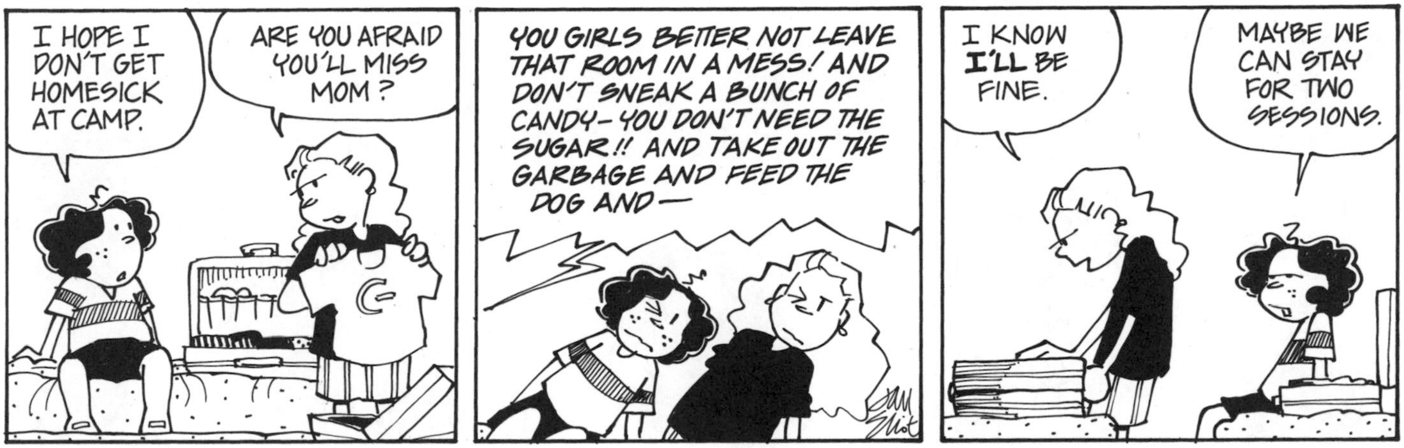
I HOPE I DON'T GET HOMESICK AT CAMP.
ARE YOU AFRAID YOU'LL MISS MOM?
YOU GIRLS BETTER NOT LEAVE THAT ROOM IN A MESS! AND DON'T SNEAK A BUNCH OF CANDY– YOU DON'T NEED THE SUGAR!! AND TAKE OUT THE GARBAGE AND FEED THE DOG AND—
I KNOW I'LL BE FINE.
MAYBE WE CAN STAY FOR TWO SESSIONS.

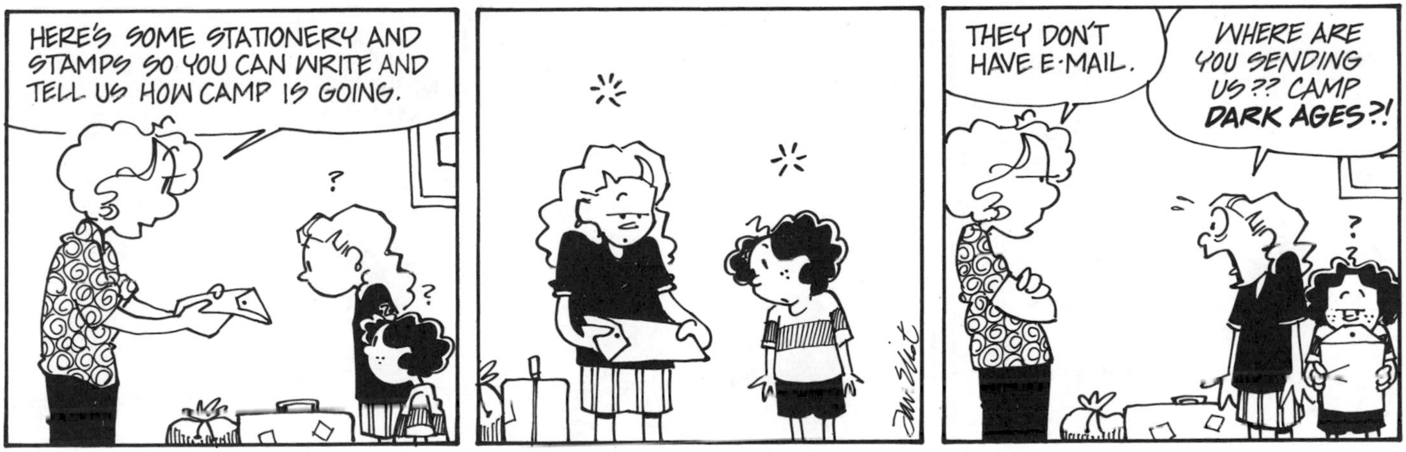
HERE'S SOME STATIONERY AND STAMPS SO YOU CAN WRITE AND TELL US HOW CAMP IS GOING.
THEY DON'T HAVE E-MAIL.
WHERE ARE YOU SENDING US?? CAMP DARK AGES?!

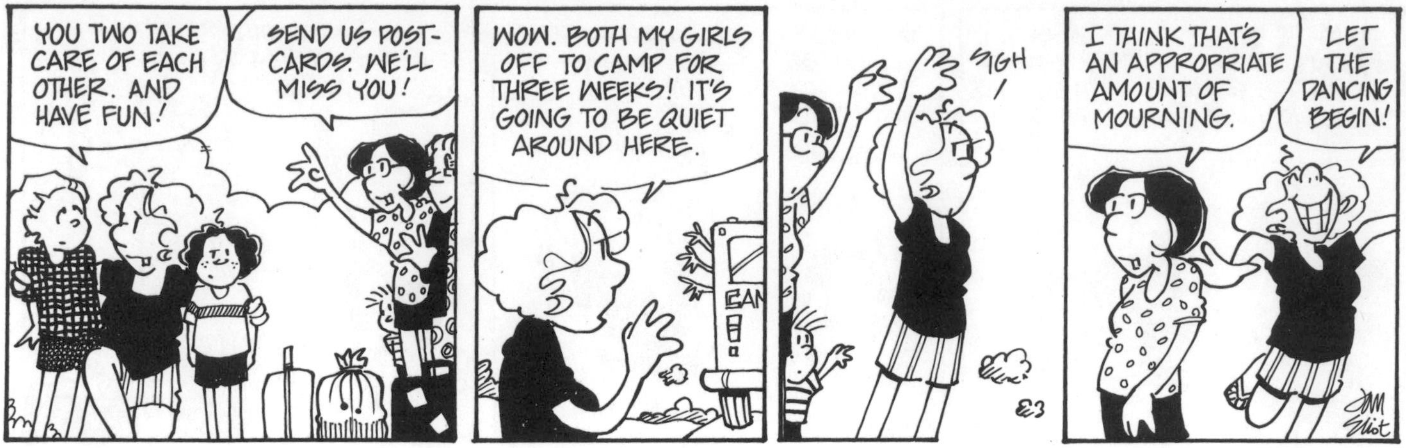
YOU TWO TAKE CARE OF EACH OTHER. AND HAVE FUN!
SEND US POST-CARDS. WE'LL MISS YOU!
WOW. BOTH MY GIRLS OFF TO CAMP FOR THREE WEEKS! IT'S GOING TO BE QUIET AROUND HERE.
SIGH!
I THINK THAT'S AN APPROPRIATE AMOUNT OF MOURNING.
LET THE DANCING BEGIN!

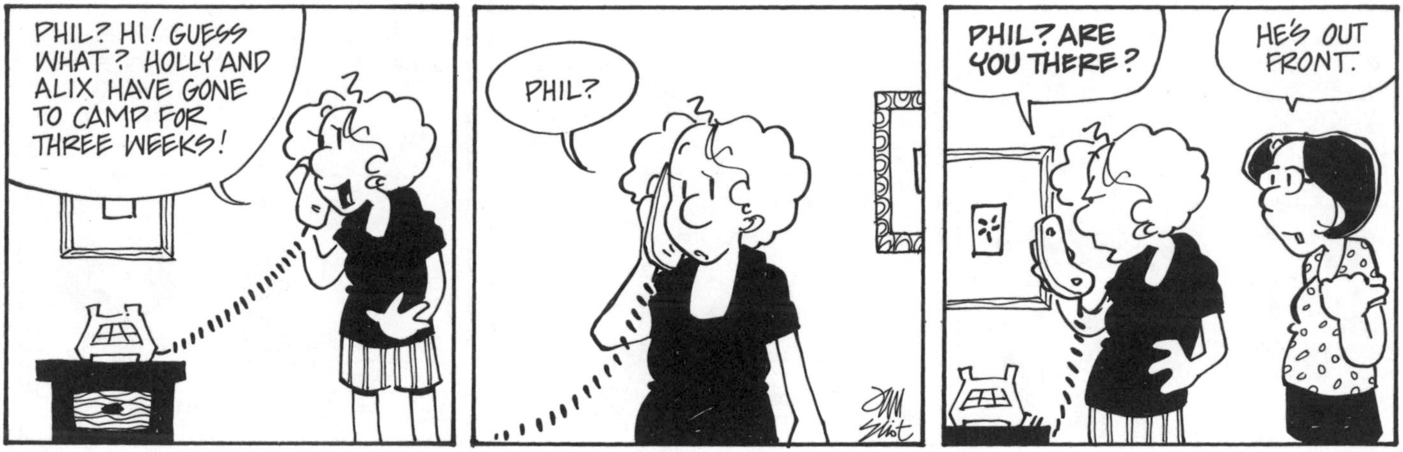
PHIL? HI! GUESS WHAT? HOLLY AND ALIX HAVE GONE TO CAMP FOR THREE WEEKS!
PHIL?
PHIL? ARE YOU THERE?
HE'S OUT FRONT.

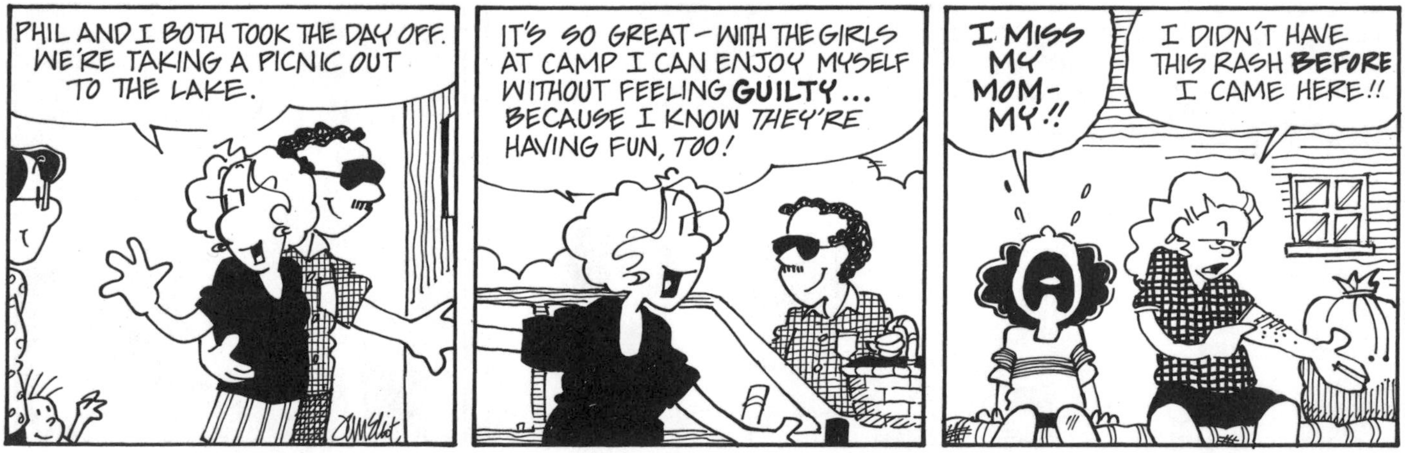
PHIL AND I BOTH TOOK THE DAY OFF. WE'RE TAKING A PICNIC OUT TO THE LAKE.
IT'S SO GREAT – WITH THE GIRLS AT CAMP I CAN ENJOY MYSELF WITHOUT FEELING GUILTY... BECAUSE I KNOW THEY'RE HAVING FUN, TOO!
I MISS MY MOM-MY!!
I DIDN'T HAVE THIS RASH BEFORE I CAME HERE!!

Stone Soup

PSST PSSST CRINKLE
CRUNCH CRINKLE POP FZZZZ
HEY!
PSST RUSTLE
WHY DON'T YOU TAKE YOUR GROCERY BAG FULL OF HOMEMADE SNACKS...
AND THIS PERSON YOU HAVE TO EXPLAIN THE MOVIE TO...
SHH
...BACK HOME FOR A NICE VIDEO WHERE YOU WON'T BOTHER ANYONE?
SHH
MA'AM ?
THEY KEEP TALKING AND THEY SNUCK IN THEIR OWN FOOD!! DON'T YOU CARE ABOUT IT?
HEY?! I'M NOT THE ONE DISRUPTING THINGS!
PSST PSST
I PAID FOR MY POPCORN! I WAS QUIET!
SLAM
I'VE NEVER BEEN THROWN OUT OF A MOVIE BEFORE. I'M GLAD I WASN'T IN UNIFORM.
THEY WERE DISTURBING MY PEACE! ARREST SOMEONE!!

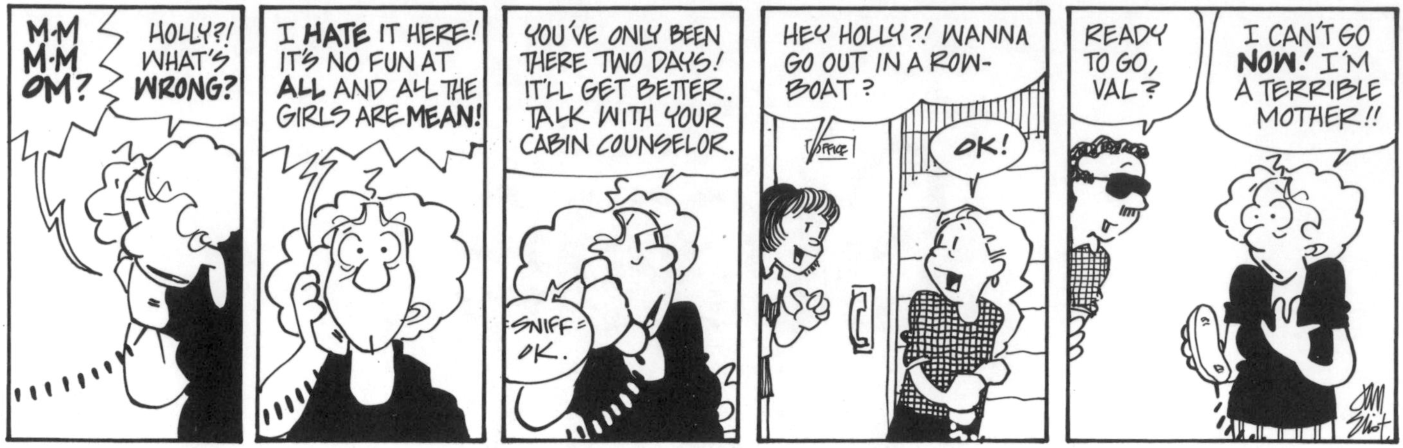
M-M M-M OM?
HOLLY?! WHAT'S WRONG?
I HATE IT HERE! IT'S NO FUN AT ALL AND ALL THE GIRLS ARE MEAN!
YOU'VE ONLY BEEN THERE TWO DAYS! IT'LL GET BETTER. TALK WITH YOUR CABIN COUNSELOR.
SNIFF OK.
HEY HOLLY?! WANNA GO OUT IN A ROW-BOAT?
OFFICE
OK!
READY TO GO, VAL?
I CAN'T GO NOW! I'M A TERRIBLE MOTHER!!

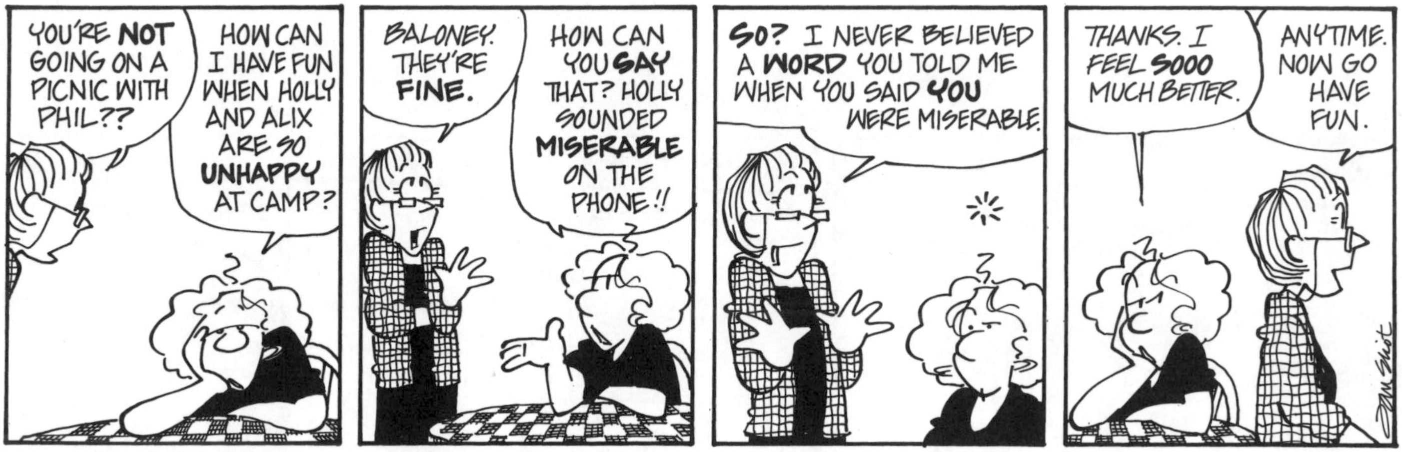
YOU'RE NOT GOING ON A PICNIC WITH PHIL??
HOW CAN I HAVE FUN WHEN HOLLY AND ALIX ARE SO UNHAPPY AT CAMP?
BALONEY. THEY'RE FINE.
HOW CAN YOU SAY THAT? HOLLY SOUNDED MISERABLE ON THE PHONE!!
SO? I NEVER BELIEVED A WORD YOU TOLD ME WHEN YOU SAID YOU WERE MISERABLE.
THANKS. I FEEL SOOO MUCH BETTER.
ANYTIME. NOW GO HAVE FUN.

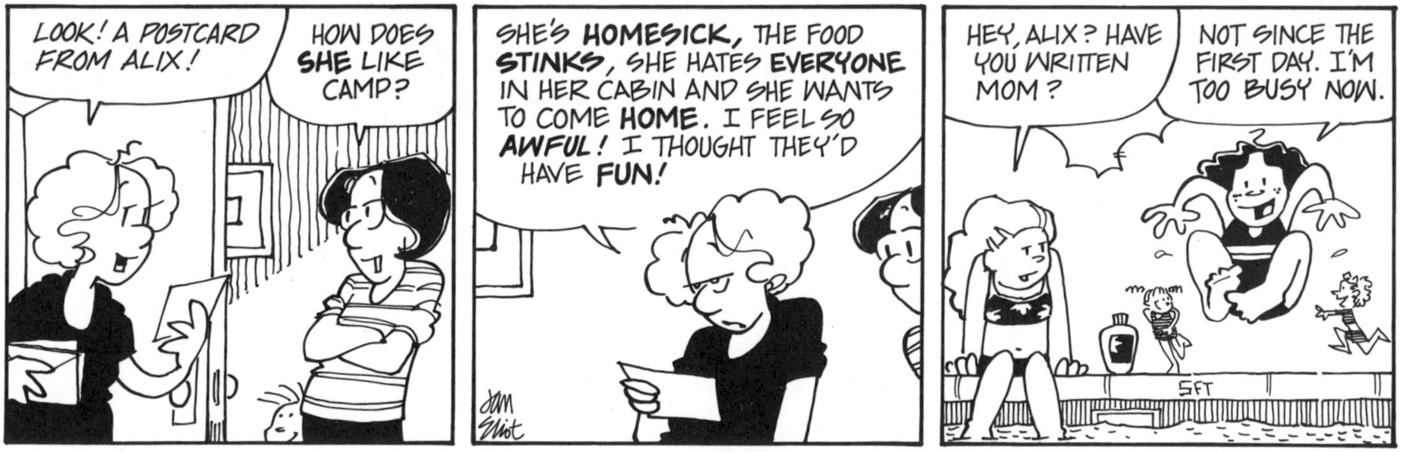
LOOK! A POSTCARD FROM ALIX!
HOW DOES SHE LIKE CAMP?
SHE'S HOMESICK, THE FOOD STINKS, SHE HATES EVERYONE IN HER CABIN AND SHE WANTS TO COME HOME. I FEEL SO AWFUL! I THOUGHT THEY'D HAVE FUN!
HEY, ALIX? HAVE YOU WRITTEN MOM?
NOT SINCE THE FIRST DAY. I'M TOO BUSY NOW.
5FT

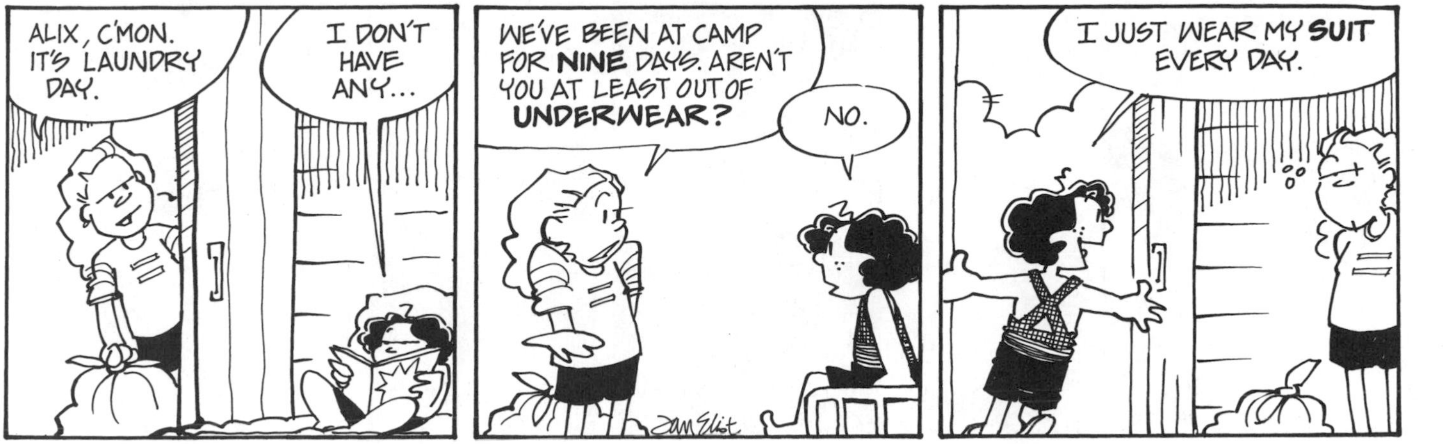
ALIX, C'MON. IT'S LAUNDRY DAY.
I DON'T HAVE ANY...
WE'VE BEEN AT CAMP FOR NINE DAYS. AREN'T YOU AT LEAST OUT OF UNDERWEAR?
NO.
I JUST WEAR MY SUIT EVERY DAY.

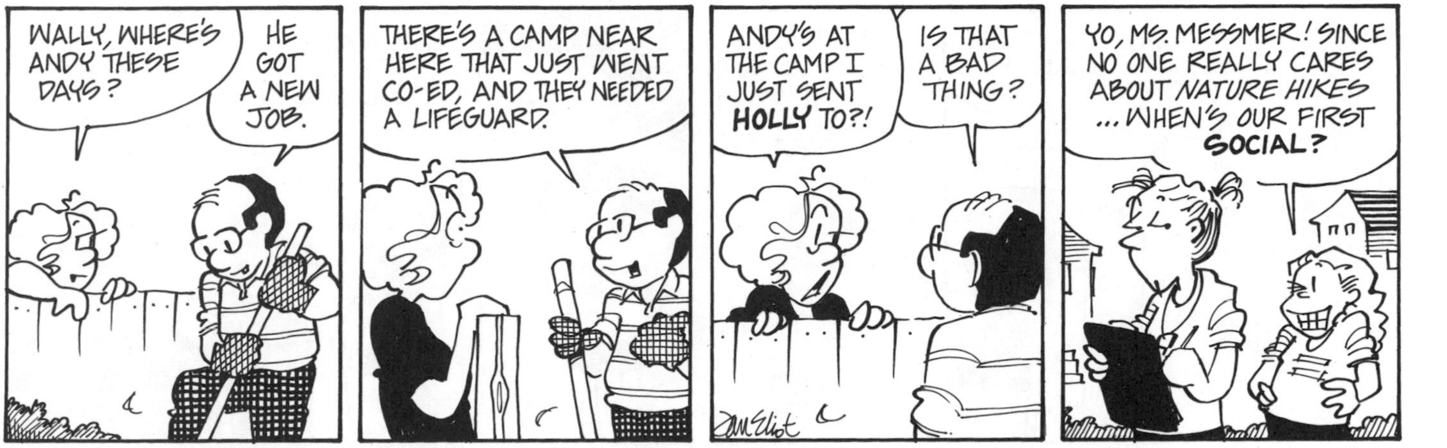
WALLY, WHERE'S ANDY THESE DAYS?
HE GOT A NEW JOB.
THERE'S A CAMP NEAR HERE THAT JUST WENT CO-ED, AND THEY NEEDED A LIFEGUARD.
ANDY'S AT THE CAMP I JUST SENT HOLLY TO?!
IS THAT A BAD THING?
YO, MS. MESSMER! SINCE NO ONE REALLY CARES ABOUT NATURE HIKES ...WHEN'S OUR FIRST SOCIAL?

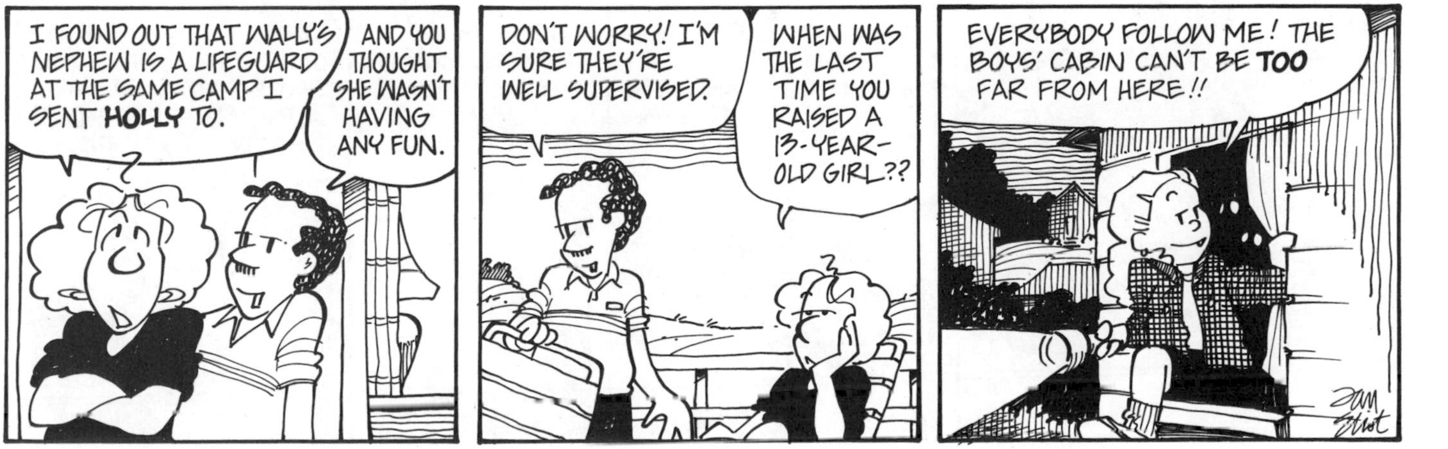
I FOUND OUT THAT WALLY'S NEPHEW IS A LIFEGUARD AT THE SAME CAMP I SENT HOLLY TO.
AND YOU THOUGHT SHE WASN'T HAVING ANY FUN.
DON'T WORRY! I'M SURE THEY'RE WELL SUPERVISED.
WHEN WAS THE LAST TIME YOU RAISED A 13-YEAR-OLD GIRL??
EVERYBODY FOLLOW ME! THE BOYS' CABIN CAN'T BE TOO FAR FROM HERE!!

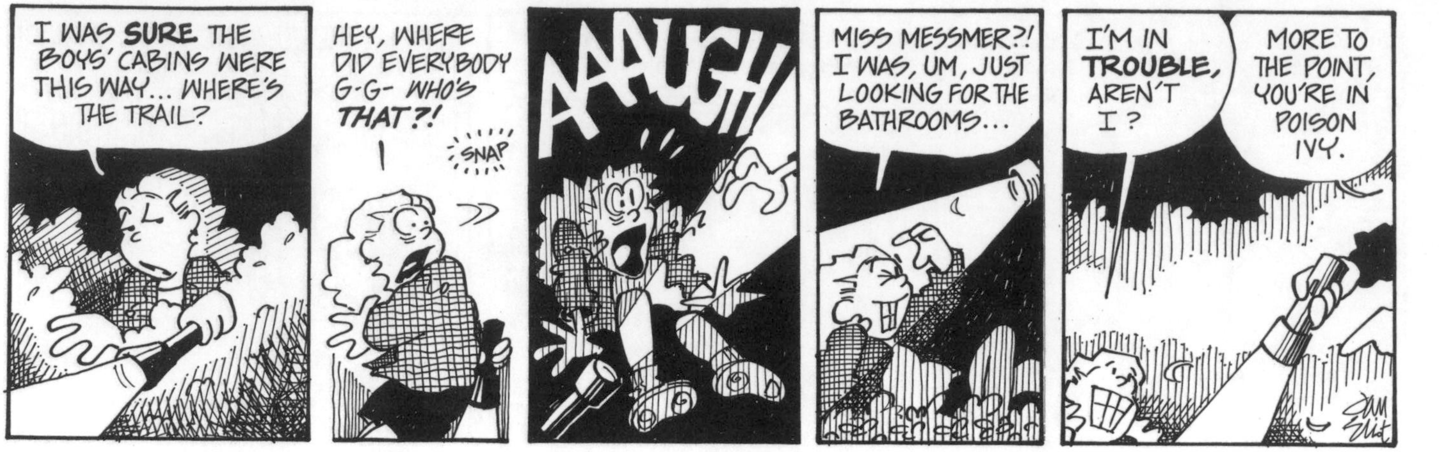
I WAS SURE THE BOYS' CABINS WERE THIS WAY... WHERE'S THE TRAIL?
HEY, WHERE DID EVERYBODY G-G- WHO'S THAT?!
SNAP
AAAUGH!!
MISS MESSMER?! I WAS, UM, JUST LOOKING FOR THE BATHROOMS...
I'M IN TROUBLE, AREN'T I ?
MORE TO THE POINT, YOU'RE IN POISON IVY.

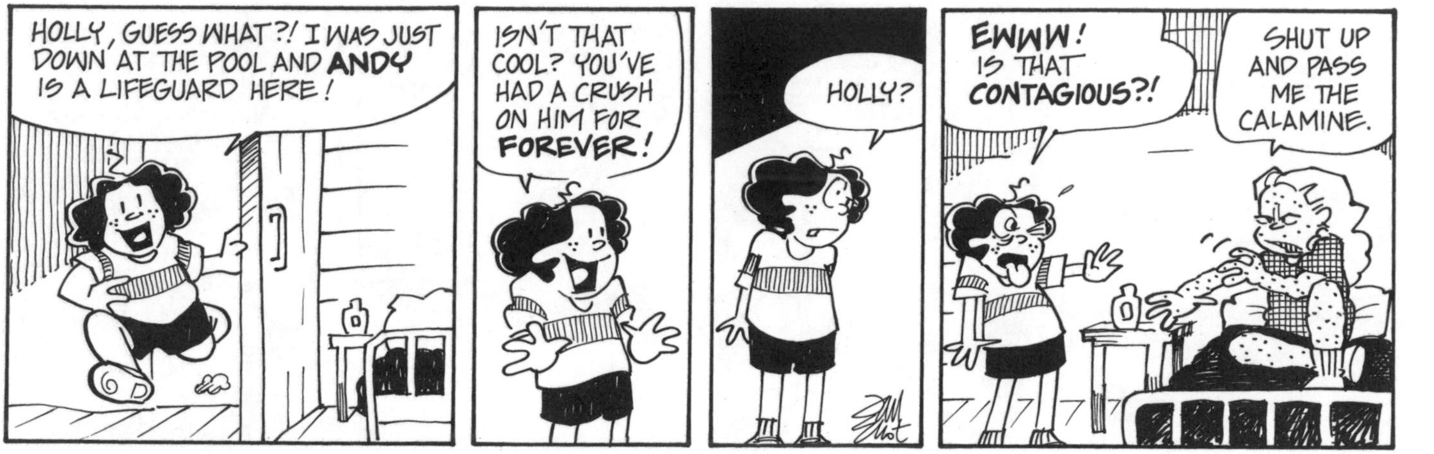
HOLLY, GUESS WHAT?! I WAS JUST DOWN AT THE POOL AND ANDY IS A LIFEGUARD HERE!
ISN'T THAT COOL? YOU'VE HAD A CRUSH ON HIM FOR FOREVER!
HOLLY?
EWWW! IS THAT CONTAGIOUS?!
SHUT UP AND PASS ME THE CALAMINE.

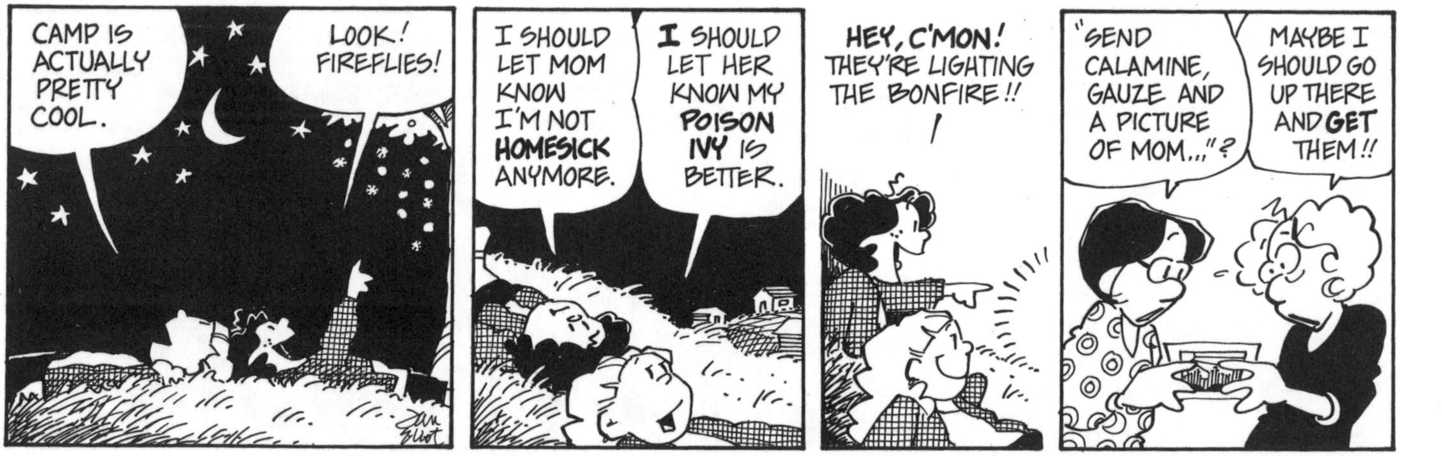
CAMP IS ACTUALLY PRETTY COOL.
LOOK! FIREFLIES!
I SHOULD LET MOM KNOW I'M NOT HOMESICK ANYMORE.
I SHOULD LET HER KNOW MY POISON IVY IS BETTER.
HEY, C'MON! THEY'RE LIGHTING THE BONFIRE!!
"SEND CALAMINE, GAUZE AND A PICTURE OF MOM..."?
MAYBE I SHOULD GO UP THERE AND GET THEM!!

Stone Soup

WHY ARE YOU WEARING YOUR TOWEL?

'CAUSE I HATE HOW I LOOK IN MY SUIT.

HOW CAN YOU HAVE ANY **FUN** LIKE THAT?! YOU LOOK FINE.

A LOT **YOU** KNOW.

WHAT'S THE BIG DEAL? I MEAN, LOOK AT THE **BOYS**...

SKINNY LEGS, KNOBBY KNEES, DORKY SHORTS...

WHAT DO YOU SUPPOSE **THEY'RE** THINKING?

LOOKIN' **GOOD!**

Hiiiii andy- ISN'T IT AMAZING THAT WE ENDED UP AT THE SAME CAMP?
YEAH, IT'S A GREAT GIG.
WHEN THEY ASKED ME TO BE A LIFEGUARD HERE, I THOUGHT "WHOA! THINK OF THE BABE POTENTIAL AT THAT PLACE!!"
REALLY?!
SHOWERS
MAIN HALL
OH, AND YOU LITTLE KIDS ARE OK, TOO.
PAT PAT PAT PAT

ANDY IS NEVER GOING TO NOTICE ME...
HEY HOLLY! WATCH ME!
WOOHOO
COUGH
CHOKE
SPUTTER
TAKE IT EASY, LITTLE BUDDY! YOU OK?
COUGH
SHE'S FINE. YOU CAN THROW HER BACK IN NOW.

ALIX? ARE YOU IN THERE?
HUH? WHAT'S GOING ON?
OUR CABIN COUNSELOR THOUGHT WE WERE ALL ASLEEP, AND LEFT!
OURS, TOO!
I HEARD THE COUNSELORS PLANNING AN END-OF-CAMP PARTY. LET'S GO SPY ON THEM!
THERE THEY ARE! AND THERE'S ANDY! AND HE'S-
KISSING MY CABIN COUNSELOR!!!

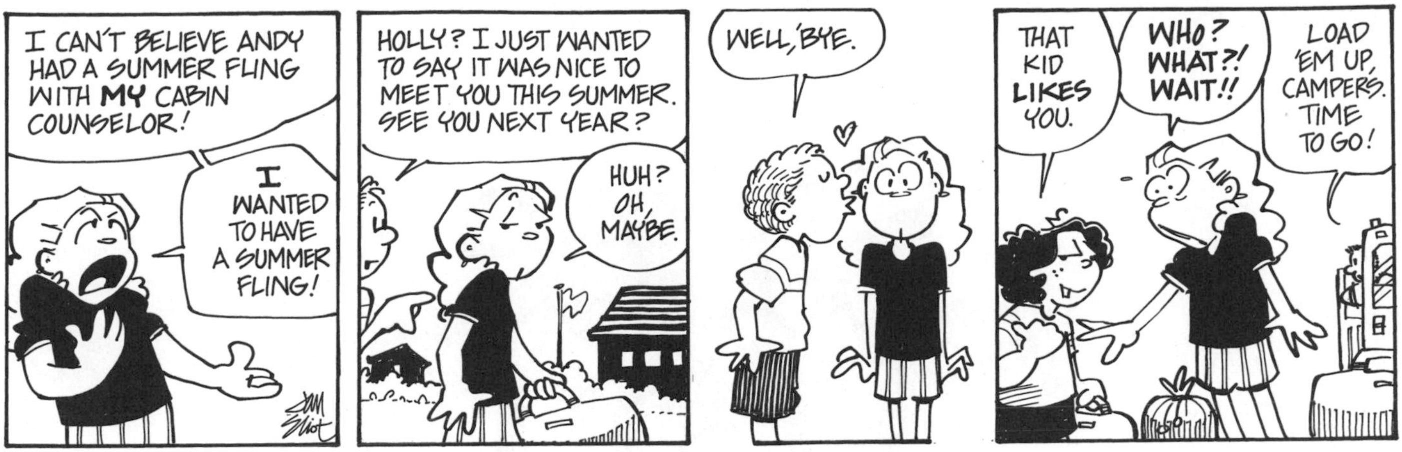
I CAN'T BELIEVE ANDY HAD A SUMMER FLING WITH **MY** CABIN COUNSELOR!
I WANTED TO HAVE A SUMMER FLING!
HOLLY? I JUST WANTED TO SAY IT WAS NICE TO MEET YOU THIS SUMMER. SEE YOU NEXT YEAR?
HUH? OH, MAYBE.
WELL, 'BYE.
THAT KID **LIKES** YOU.
WHO? WHAT?! WAIT!!
LOAD 'EM UP, CAMPERS. TIME TO GO!

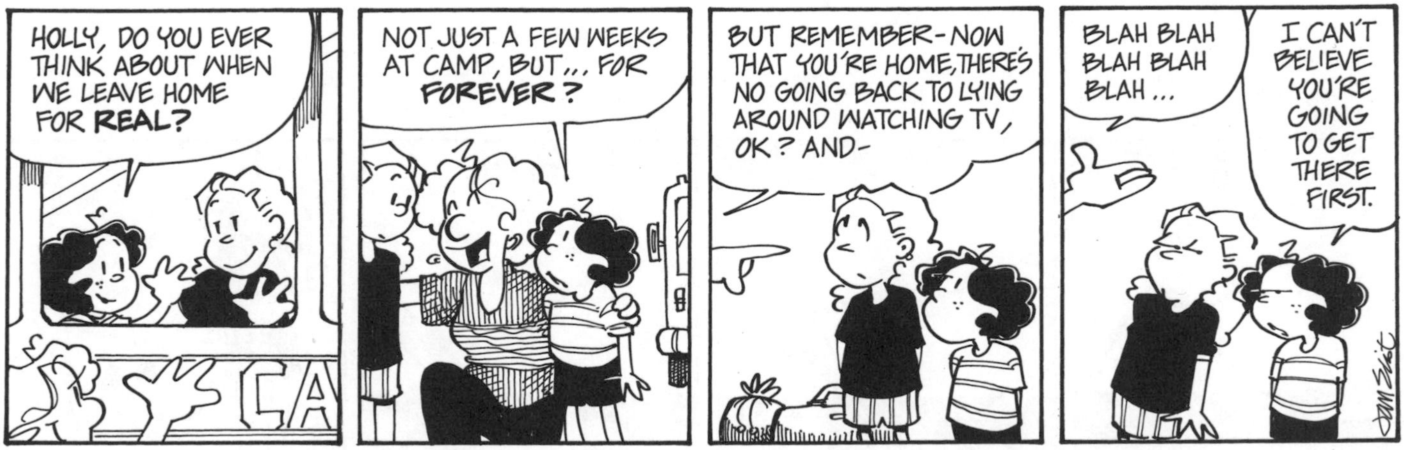
HOLLY, DO YOU EVER THINK ABOUT WHEN WE LEAVE HOME FOR **REAL?**
CA
NOT JUST A FEW WEEKS AT CAMP, BUT... FOR **FOREVER?**
BUT REMEMBER- NOW THAT YOU'RE HOME, THERE'S NO GOING BACK TO LYING AROUND WATCHING TV, OK? AND-
BLAH BLAH BLAH BLAH BLAH ...
I CAN'T BELIEVE YOU'RE GOING TO GET THERE FIRST.

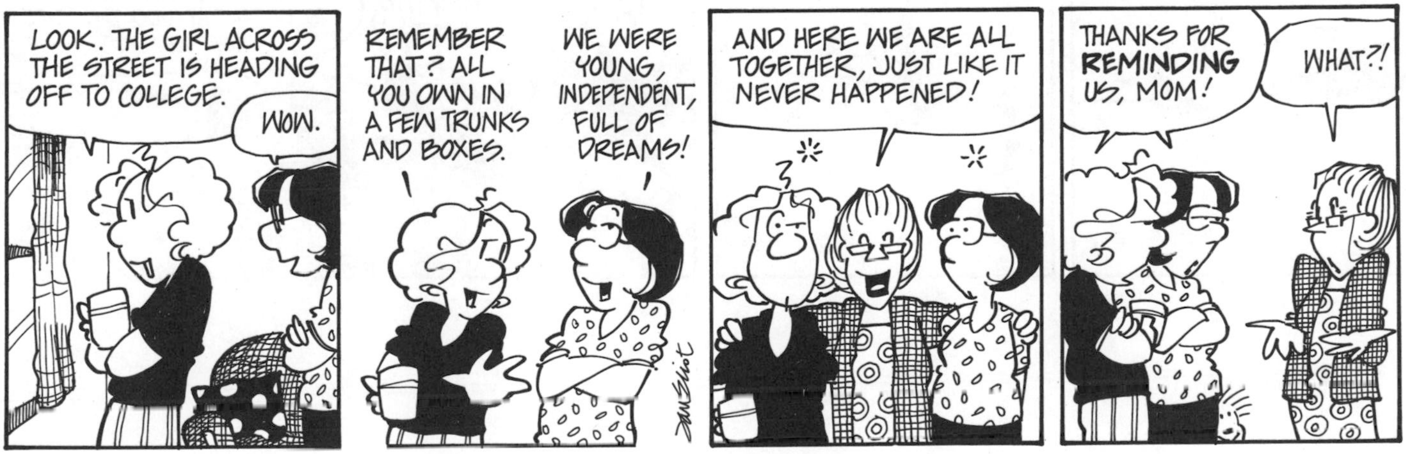
LOOK. THE GIRL ACROSS THE STREET IS HEADING OFF TO COLLEGE.
WOW.
REMEMBER THAT? ALL YOU OWN IN A FEW TRUNKS AND BOXES.
WE WERE YOUNG, INDEPENDENT, FULL OF DREAMS!
AND HERE WE ARE ALL TOGETHER, JUST LIKE IT NEVER HAPPENED!
THANKS FOR **REMINDING** US, MOM!
WHAT?!

Stone Soup

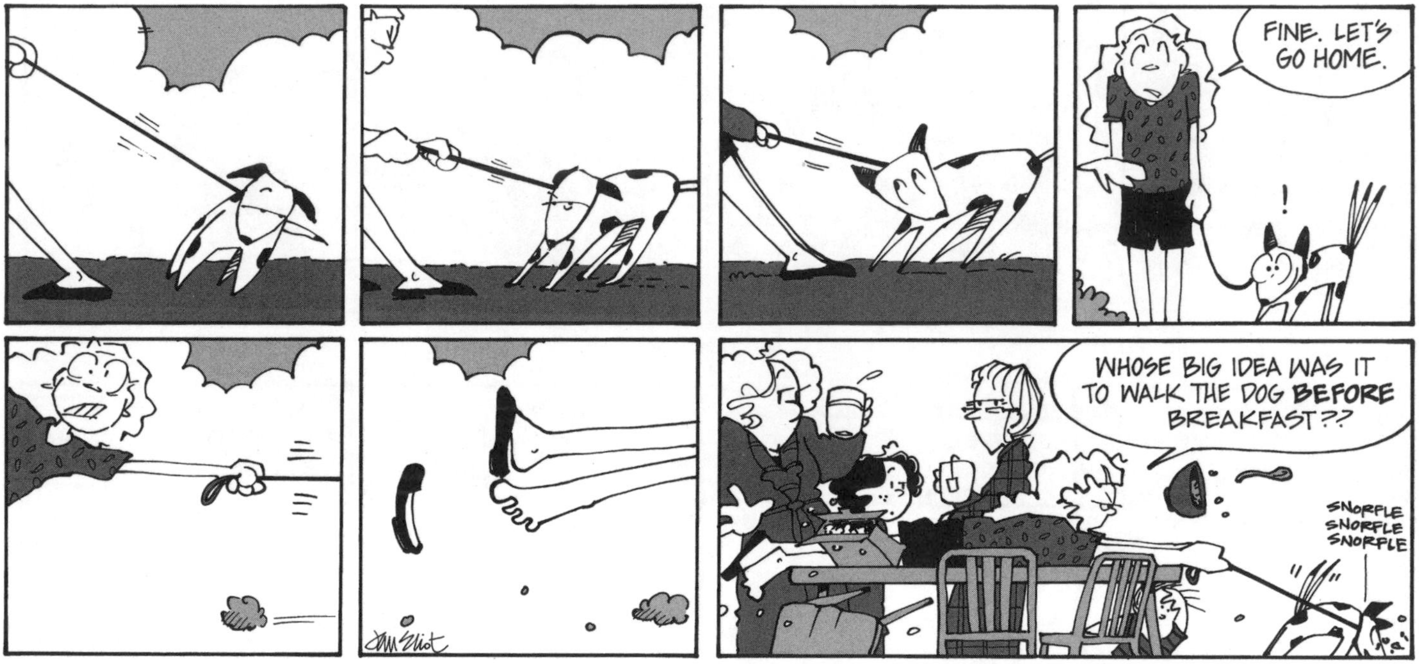
FINE. LET'S GO HOME.
!
WHOSE BIG IDEA WAS IT TO WALK THE DOG **BEFORE** BREAKFAST??
SNORFLE SNORFLE SNORFLE

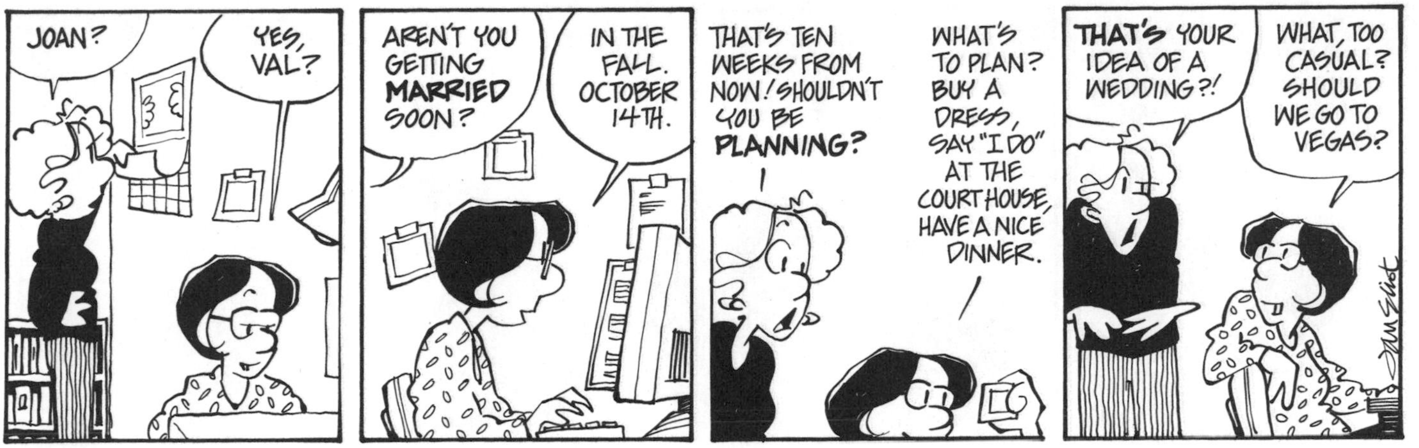
JOAN?
YES, VAL?
AREN'T YOU GETTING **MARRIED** SOON?
IN THE FALL. OCTOBER 14TH.
THAT'S TEN WEEKS FROM NOW! SHOULDN'T YOU BE **PLANNING?**
WHAT'S TO PLAN? BUY A DRESS, SAY "I DO" AT THE COURT HOUSE, HAVE A NICE DINNER.
THAT'S YOUR IDEA OF A WEDDING?!
WHAT, TOO CASUAL? SHOULD WE GO TO VEGAS?

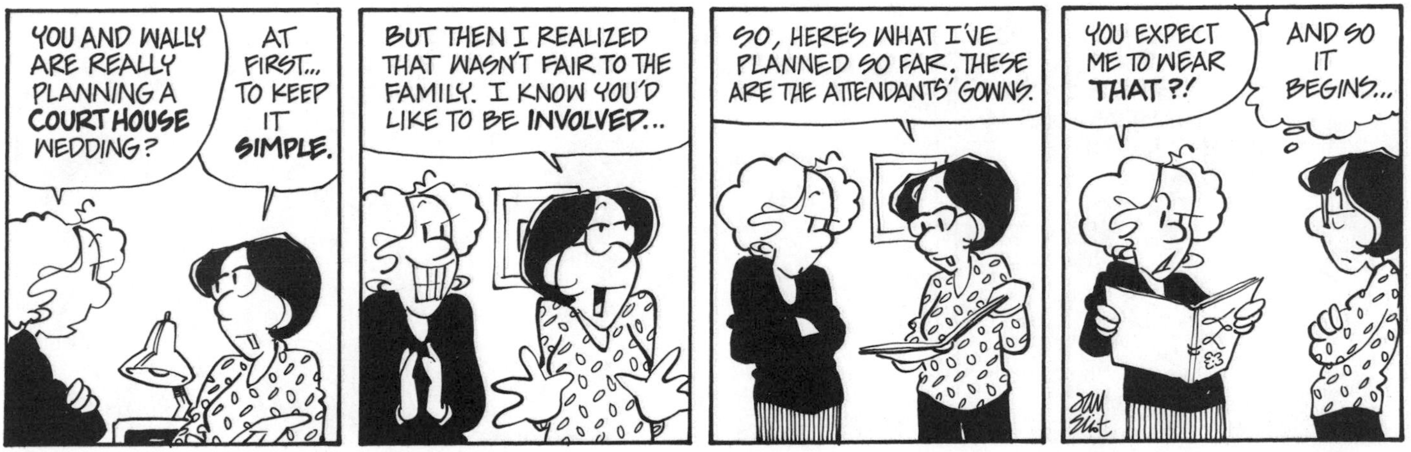
YOU AND WALLY ARE REALLY PLANNING A **COURTHOUSE** WEDDING?
AT FIRST... TO KEEP IT **SIMPLE.**
BUT THEN I REALIZED THAT WASN'T FAIR TO THE FAMILY. I KNOW YOU'D LIKE TO BE **INVOLVED**...
SO, HERE'S WHAT I'VE PLANNED SO FAR. THESE ARE THE ATTENDANTS' GOWNS.
YOU EXPECT ME TO WEAR **THAT**?!
AND SO IT BEGINS...

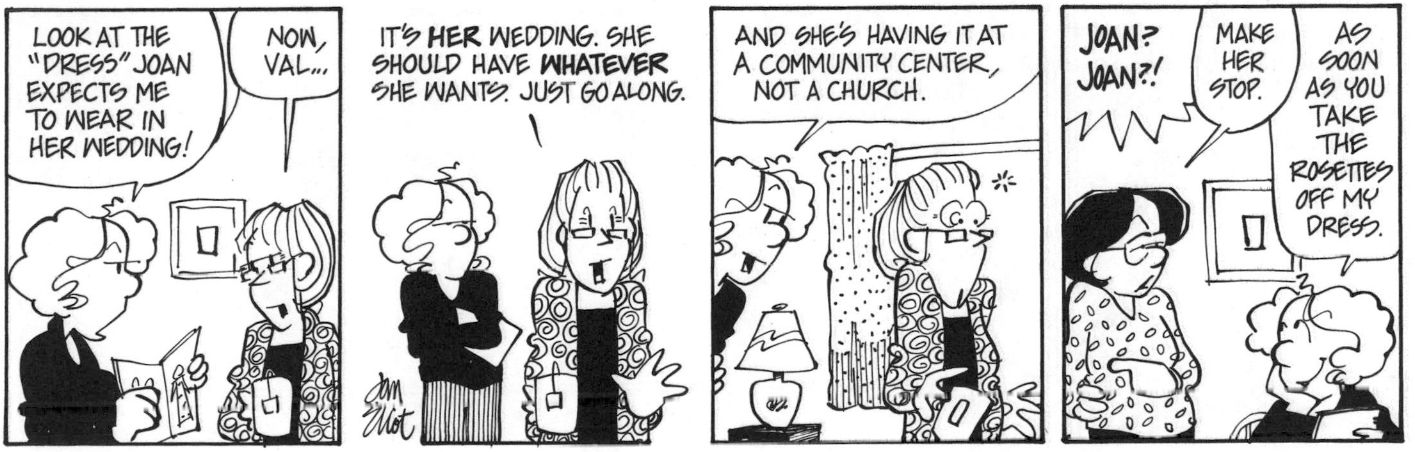
LOOK AT THE "DRESS" JOAN EXPECTS ME TO WEAR IN HER WEDDING!
NOW, VAL...
IT'S **HER** WEDDING. SHE SHOULD HAVE **WHATEVER** SHE WANTS. JUST GO ALONG.
AND SHE'S HAVING IT AT A COMMUNITY CENTER, NOT A CHURCH.
JOAN? JOAN?!
MAKE HER STOP.
AS SOON AS YOU TAKE THE ROSETTES OFF MY DRESS.

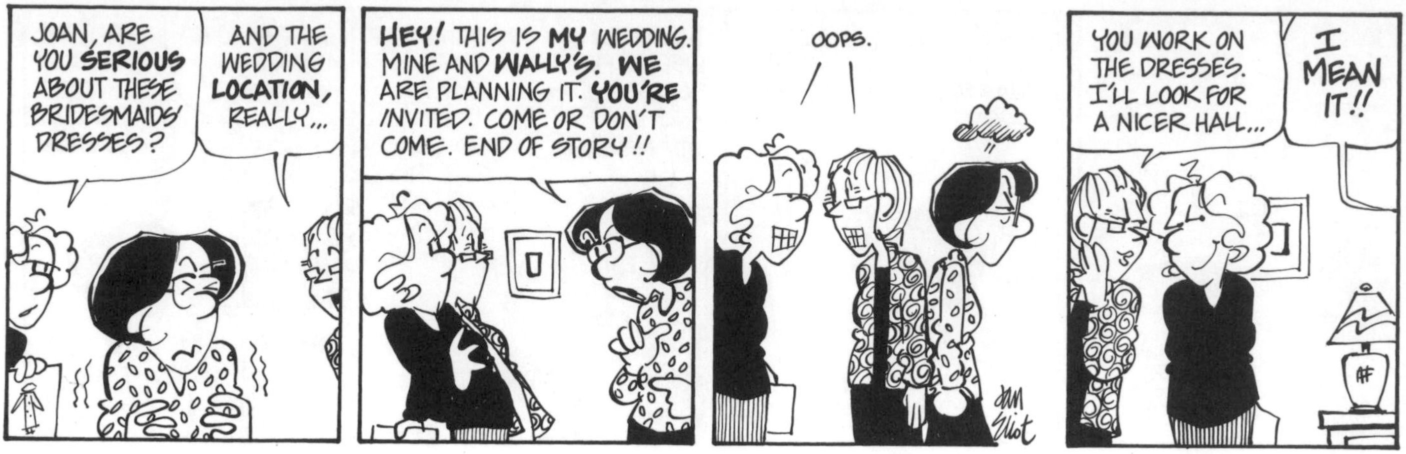
JOAN, ARE YOU **SERIOUS** ABOUT THESE BRIDESMAIDS' DRESSES?
AND THE WEDDING **LOCATION**, REALLY...
HEY! THIS IS **MY** WEDDING. MINE AND **WALLY'S. WE** ARE PLANNING IT. **YOU'RE** INVITED. COME OR DON'T COME. END OF STORY!!
OOPS.
YOU WORK ON THE DRESSES. I'LL LOOK FOR A NICER HALL...
I MEAN IT!!

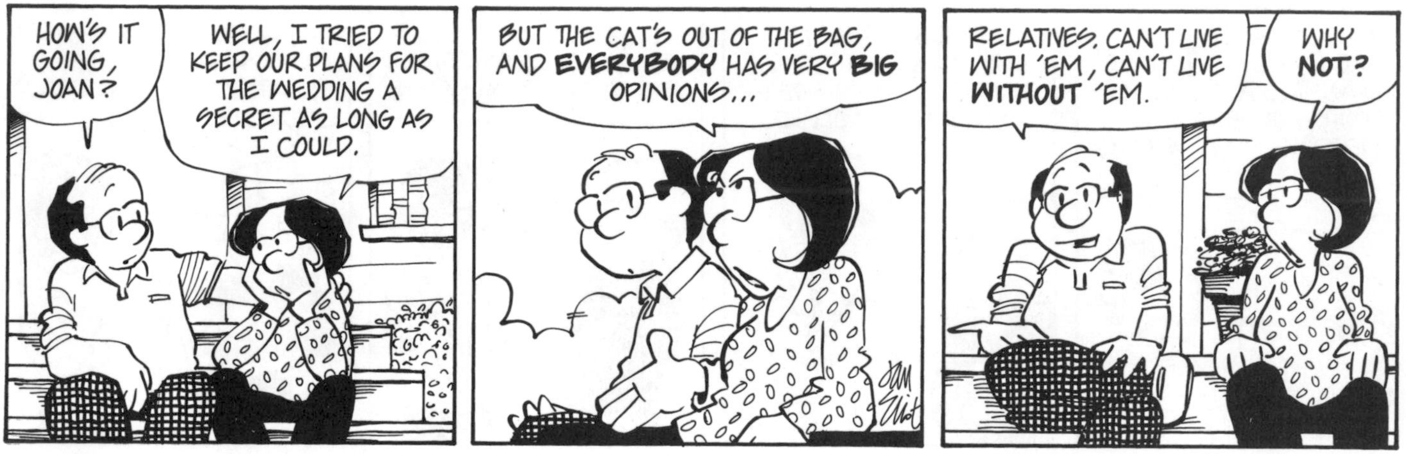
HOW'S IT GOING, JOAN?
WELL, I TRIED TO KEEP OUR PLANS FOR THE WEDDING A SECRET AS LONG AS I COULD.
BUT THE CAT'S OUT OF THE BAG, AND **EVERYBODY** HAS VERY **BIG** OPINIONS...
RELATIVES. CAN'T LIVE WITH 'EM, CAN'T LIVE **WITHOUT** 'EM.
WHY **NOT?**

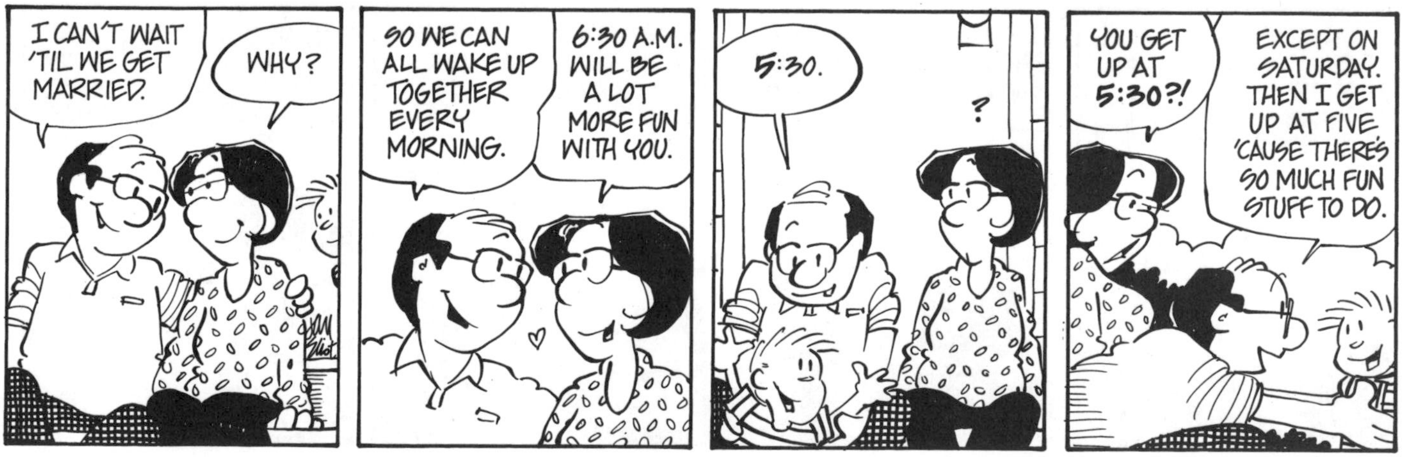
I CAN'T WAIT 'TIL WE GET MARRIED.
WHY?
SO WE CAN ALL WAKE UP TOGETHER EVERY MORNING.
6:30 A.M. WILL BE A LOT MORE FUN WITH YOU.
5:30.
?
YOU GET UP AT **5:30?!**
EXCEPT ON SATURDAY. THEN I GET UP AT FIVE. 'CAUSE THERE'S SO MUCH FUN STUFF TO DO.

Stone Soup

Father's Day Picnic
WALLY? WALLY?!
WHAT?
MAYBE YOU SHOULDN'T PLAY SO ROUGH WITH MAX RIGHT AFTER—
burrrack
—HE'S HAD THREE HOT DOGS AND A GRAPE SODA.
LOOK... NO HARM DONE.
EASY FOR YOU TO SAY.

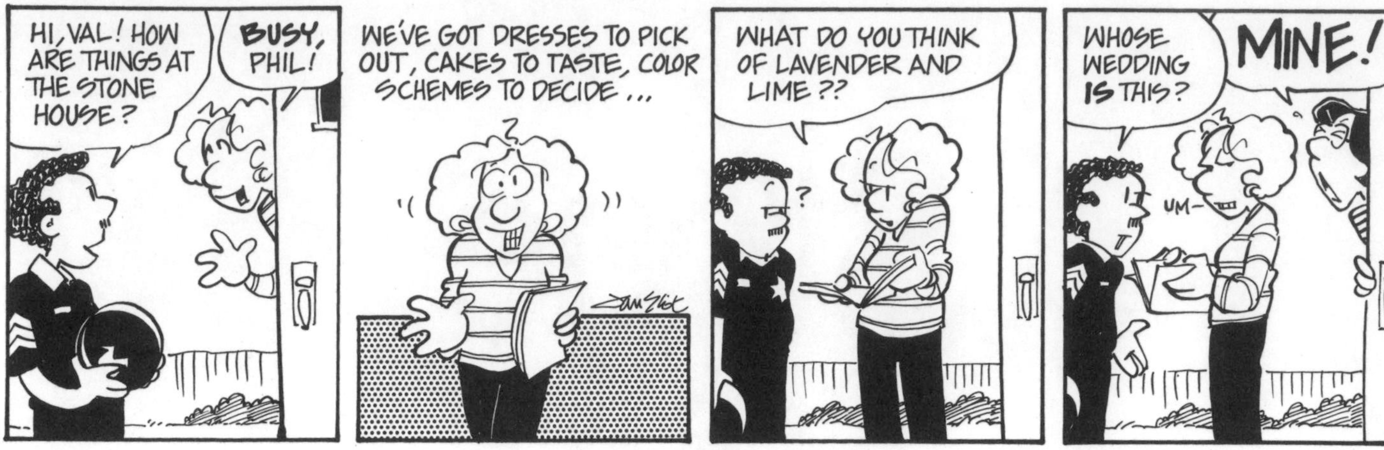
HI, VAL! HOW ARE THINGS AT THE STONE HOUSE?
BUSY, PHIL!
WE'VE GOT DRESSES TO PICK OUT, CAKES TO TASTE, COLOR SCHEMES TO DECIDE...
WHAT DO YOU THINK OF LAVENDER AND LIME??
WHOSE WEDDING IS THIS?
UM-
MINE!

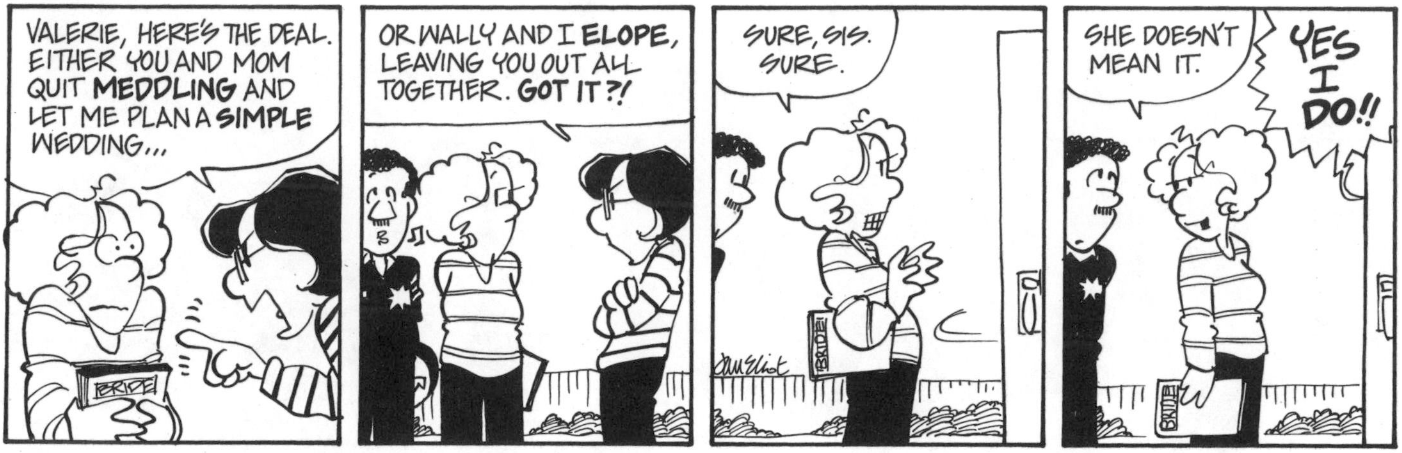
VALERIE, HERE'S THE DEAL. EITHER YOU AND MOM QUIT MEDDLING AND LET ME PLAN A SIMPLE WEDDING...
OR WALLY AND I ELOPE, LEAVING YOU OUT ALL TOGETHER. GOT IT?!
SURE, SIS. SURE.
SHE DOESN'T MEAN IT.
YES I DO!!

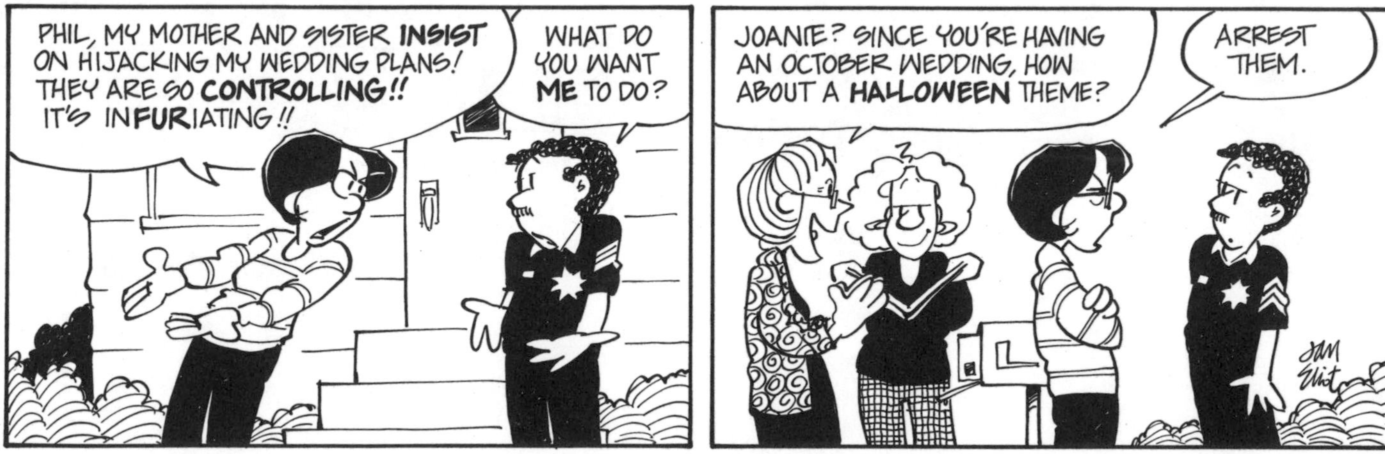
PHIL, MY MOTHER AND SISTER INSIST ON HIJACKING MY WEDDING PLANS! THEY ARE SO CONTROLLING!! IT'S INFURIATING!!
WHAT DO YOU WANT ME TO DO?
JOANIE? SINCE YOU'RE HAVING AN OCTOBER WEDDING, HOW ABOUT A HALLOWEEN THEME?
ARREST THEM.

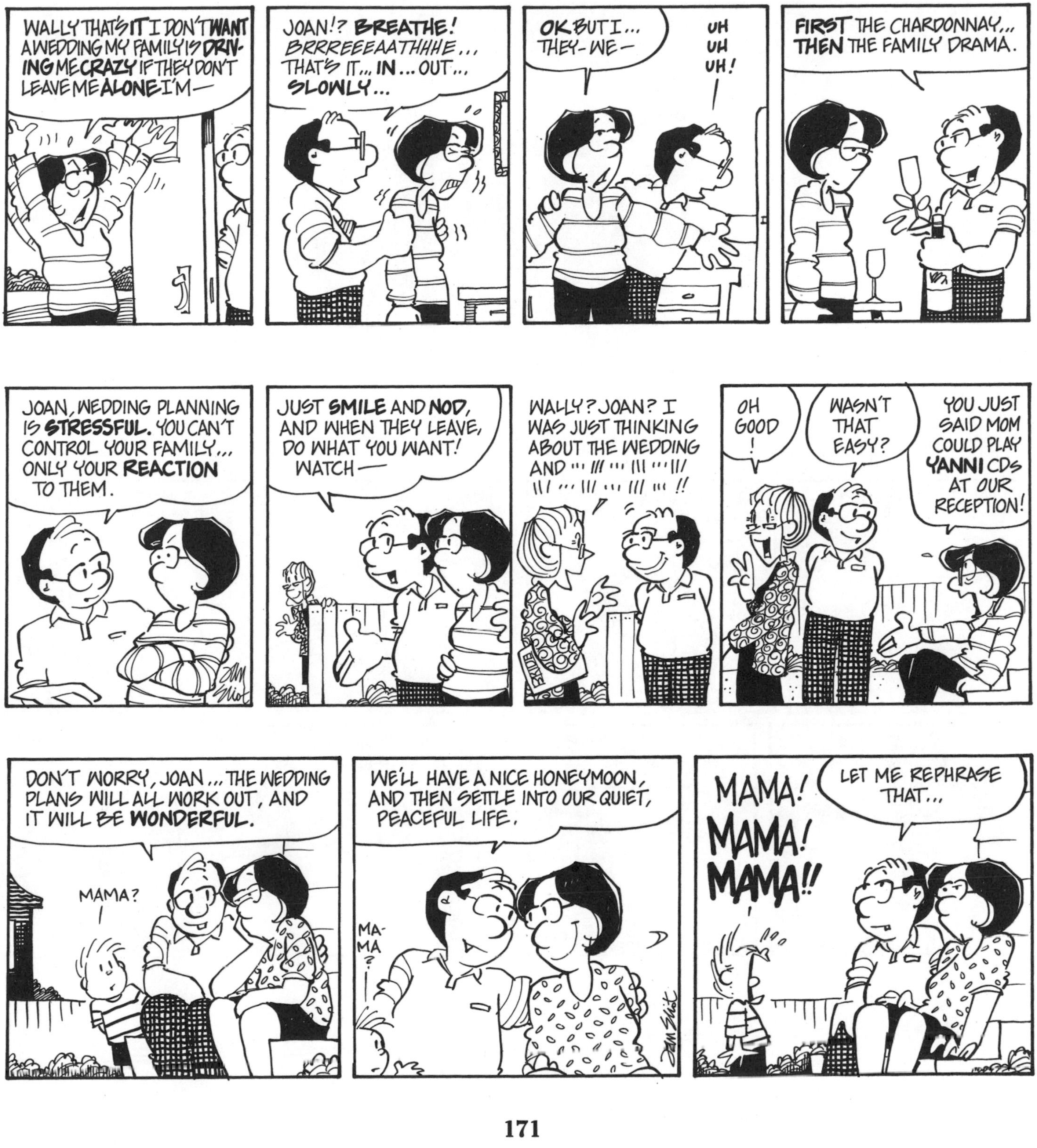
WALLY THAT'S IT I DON'T WANT A WEDDING MY FAMILY IS DRIVING ME CRAZY IF THEY DON'T LEAVE ME ALONE I'M—
JOAN!? BREATHE! BRRREEEAATHHHE... THAT'S IT... IN... OUT... SLOWLY...
OK BUT I... THEY- WE-
UH UH UH!
FIRST THE CHARDONNAY... THEN THE FAMILY DRAMA.
JOAN, WEDDING PLANNING IS STRESSFUL. YOU CAN'T CONTROL YOUR FAMILY... ONLY YOUR REACTION TO THEM.
JUST SMILE AND NOD, AND WHEN THEY LEAVE, DO WHAT YOU WANT! WATCH—
WALLY? JOAN? I WAS JUST THINKING ABOUT THE WEDDING AND ... !!
OH GOOD!
WASN'T THAT EASY?
YOU JUST SAID MOM COULD PLAY YANNI CDs AT OUR RECEPTION!
DON'T WORRY, JOAN... THE WEDDING PLANS WILL ALL WORK OUT, AND IT WILL BE WONDERFUL.
MAMA?
WE'LL HAVE A NICE HONEYMOON, AND THEN SETTLE INTO OUR QUIET, PEACEFUL LIFE.
MA-MA?
MAMA! MAMA! MAMA!!
LET ME REPHRASE THAT...

Stone Soup

HI, VAL! I-
HI, PHIL! HOLD ON A SEC-
NO, YOU CAN NOT PUT A PILLOW ON YOUR SISTER'S FACE AND SIT ON IT!
NOW, YOU WERE SAYING...
I-
HOLD ON-
DON'T WORRY! I CALLED THE PLUMBER!!
WHAT? OH- THE FIRE EXTINGUISHER IS UNDER THE SINK!
VAL? ARE YOU SURE THIS IS A GOOD TIME TO TALK??
SURE!
IT'S PRETTY QUIET AROUND HERE TODAY.

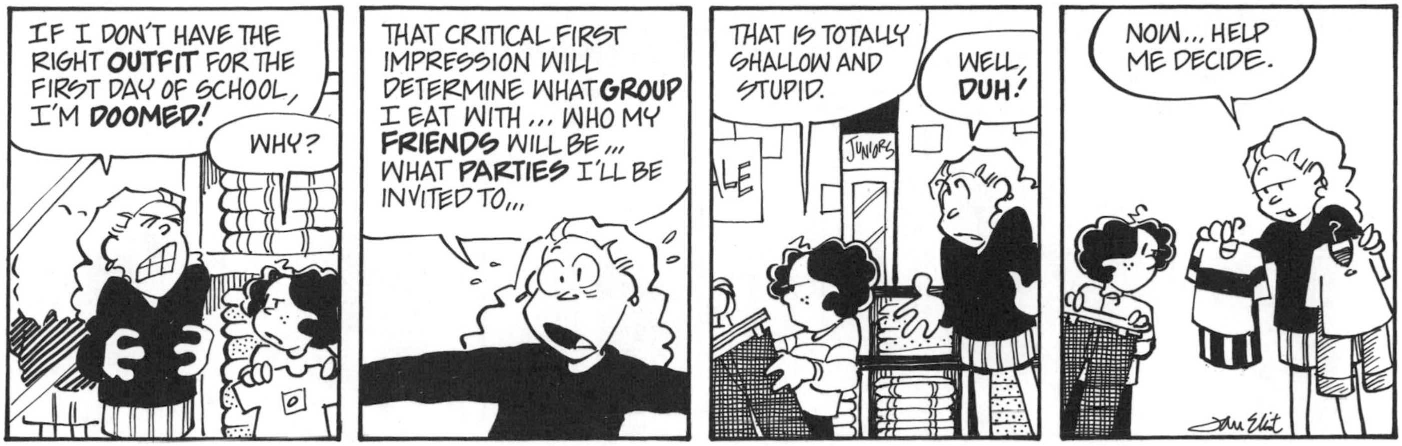
IF I DON'T HAVE THE RIGHT OUTFIT FOR THE FIRST DAY OF SCHOOL, I'M DOOMED!
WHY?
THAT CRITICAL FIRST IMPRESSION WILL DETERMINE WHAT GROUP I EAT WITH ... WHO MY FRIENDS WILL BE ... WHAT PARTIES I'LL BE INVITED TO...
THAT IS TOTALLY SHALLOW AND STUPID.
WELL, DUH!
JUNIORS
NOW... HELP ME DECIDE.

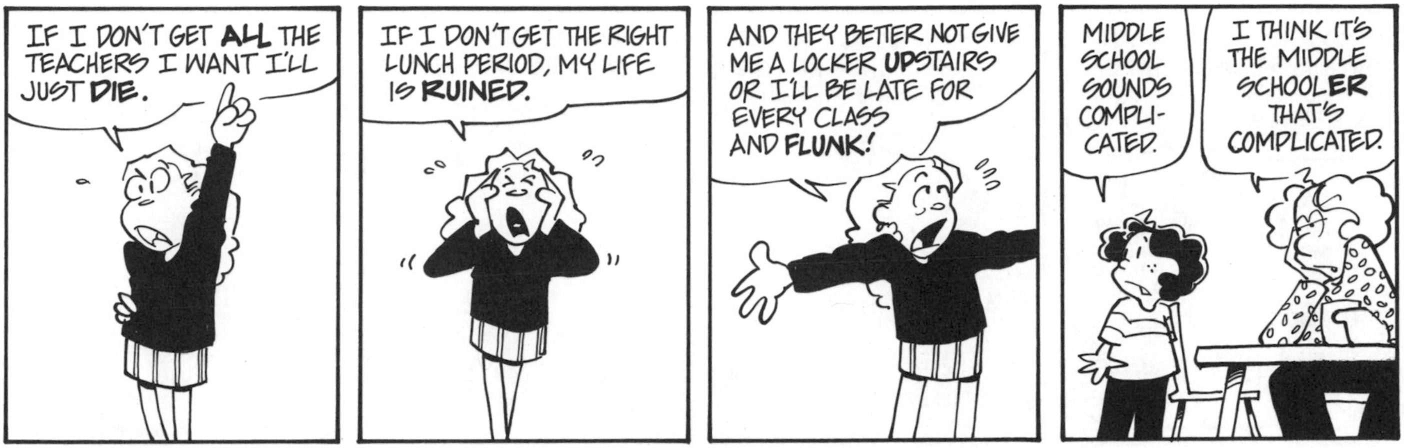
IF I DON'T GET ALL THE TEACHERS I WANT I'LL JUST DIE.
IF I DON'T GET THE RIGHT LUNCH PERIOD, MY LIFE IS RUINED.
AND THEY BETTER NOT GIVE ME A LOCKER UPSTAIRS OR I'LL BE LATE FOR EVERY CLASS AND FLUNK!
MIDDLE SCHOOL SOUNDS COMPLI-CATED.
I THINK IT'S THE MIDDLE SCHOOLER THAT'S COMPLICATED.

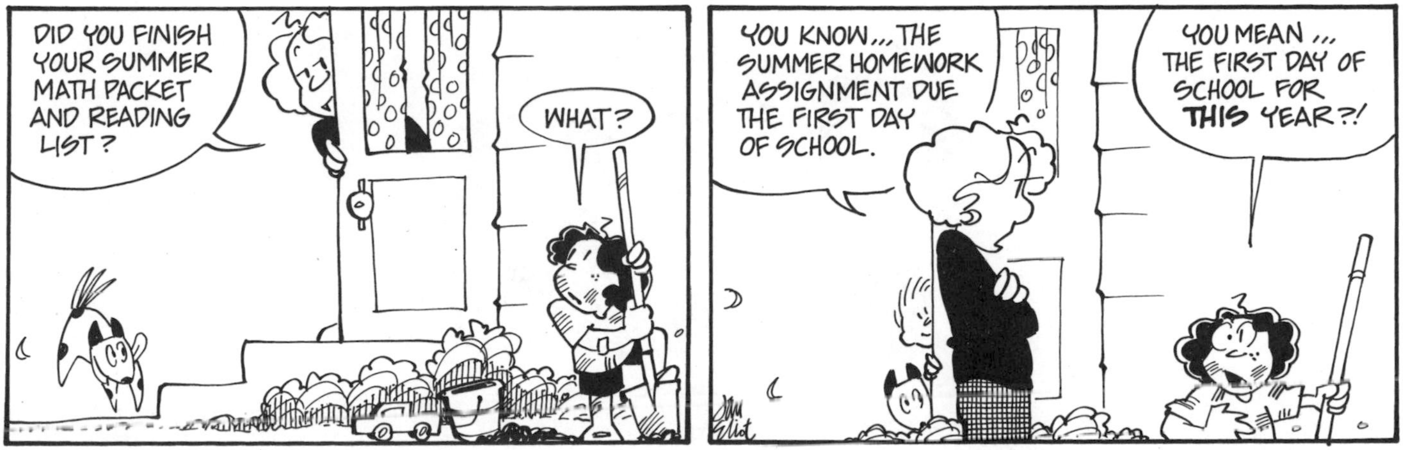
DID YOU FINISH YOUR SUMMER MATH PACKET AND READING LIST?
WHAT?
YOU KNOW... THE SUMMER HOMEWORK ASSIGNMENT DUE THE FIRST DAY OF SCHOOL.
YOU MEAN ... THE FIRST DAY OF SCHOOL FOR THIS YEAR?!

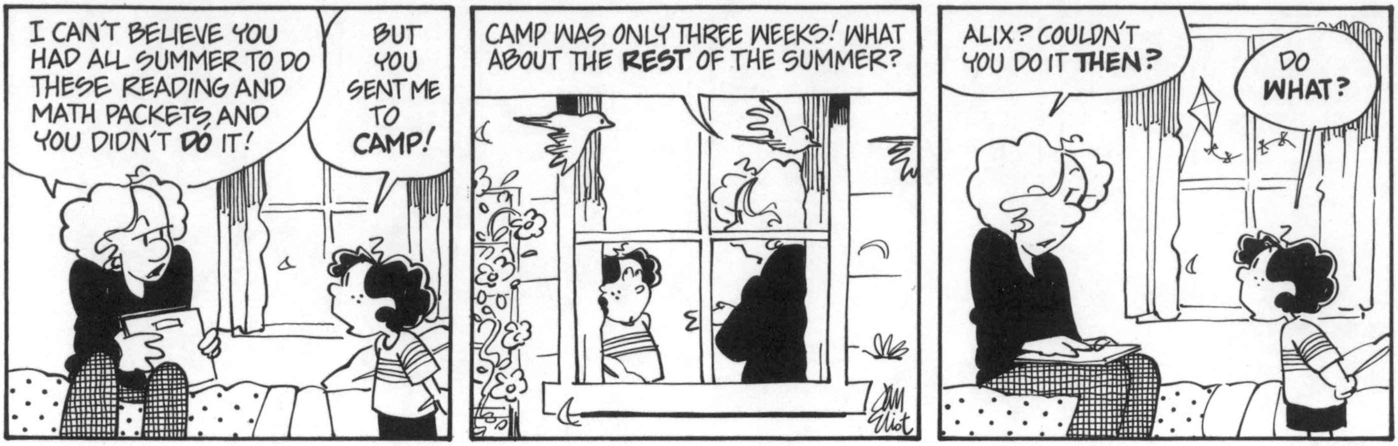
I CAN'T BELIEVE YOU HAD ALL SUMMER TO DO THESE READING AND MATH PACKETS, AND YOU DIDN'T **DO** IT!
BUT YOU SENT ME TO **CAMP**!
CAMP WAS ONLY THREE WEEKS! WHAT ABOUT THE **REST** OF THE SUMMER?
ALIX? COULDN'T YOU DO IT **THEN**?
DO **WHAT**?

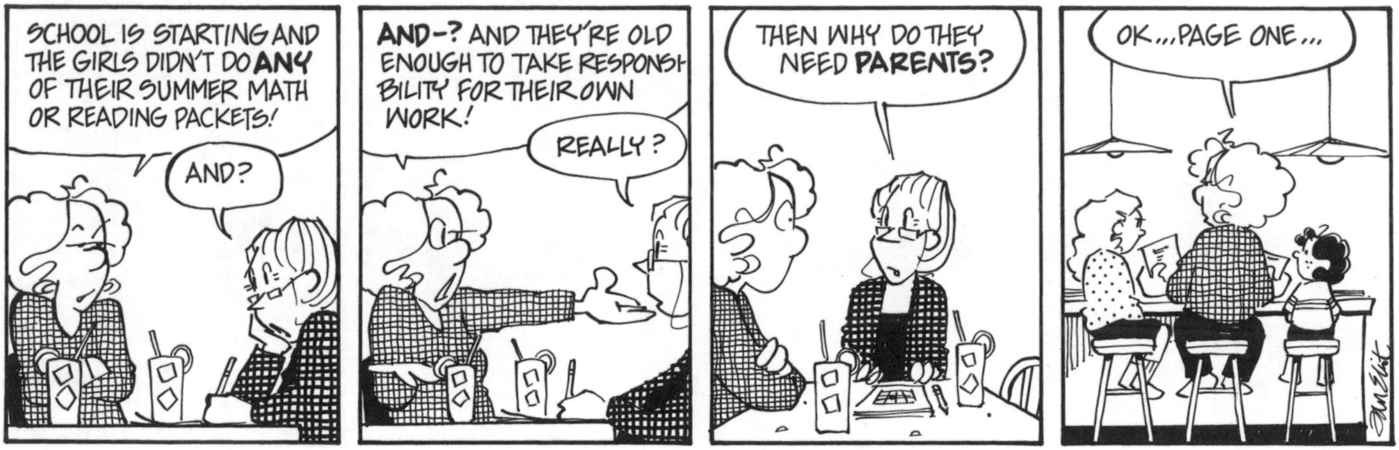
SCHOOL IS STARTING AND THE GIRLS DIDN'T DO **ANY** OF THEIR SUMMER MATH OR READING PACKETS!
AND?
AND-? AND THEY'RE OLD ENOUGH TO TAKE RESPONSI-BILITY FOR THEIR OWN WORK!
REALLY?
THEN WHY DO THEY NEED **PARENTS**?
OK...PAGE ONE...

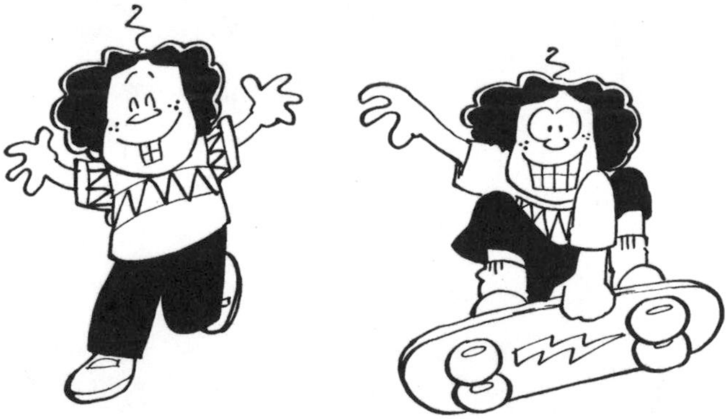

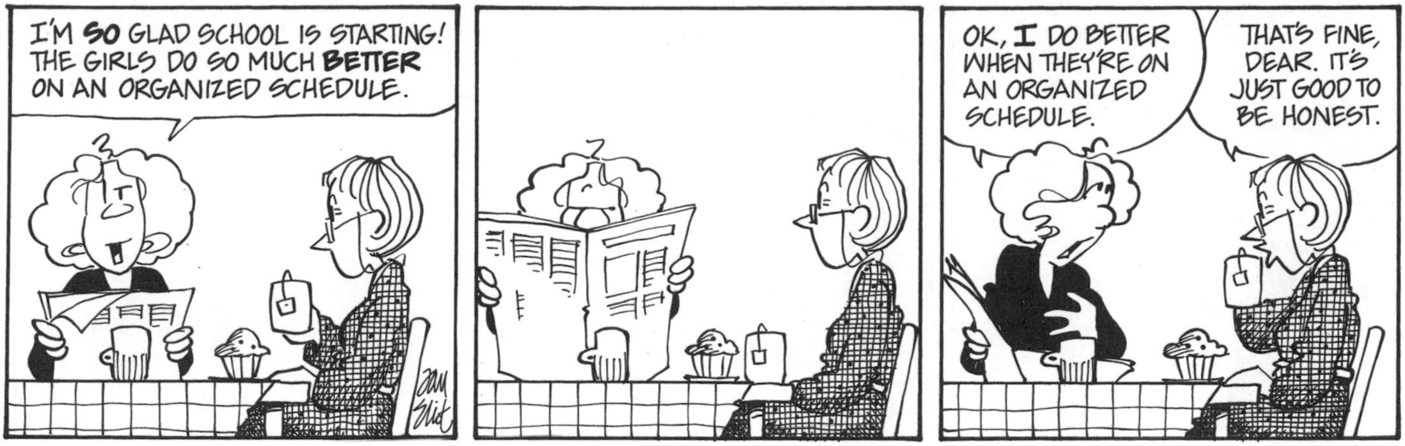
I'M SO GLAD SCHOOL IS STARTING! THE GIRLS DO SO MUCH BETTER ON AN ORGANIZED SCHEDULE.
OK, I DO BETTER WHEN THEY'RE ON AN ORGANIZED SCHEDULE.
THAT'S FINE, DEAR. IT'S JUST GOOD TO BE HONEST.

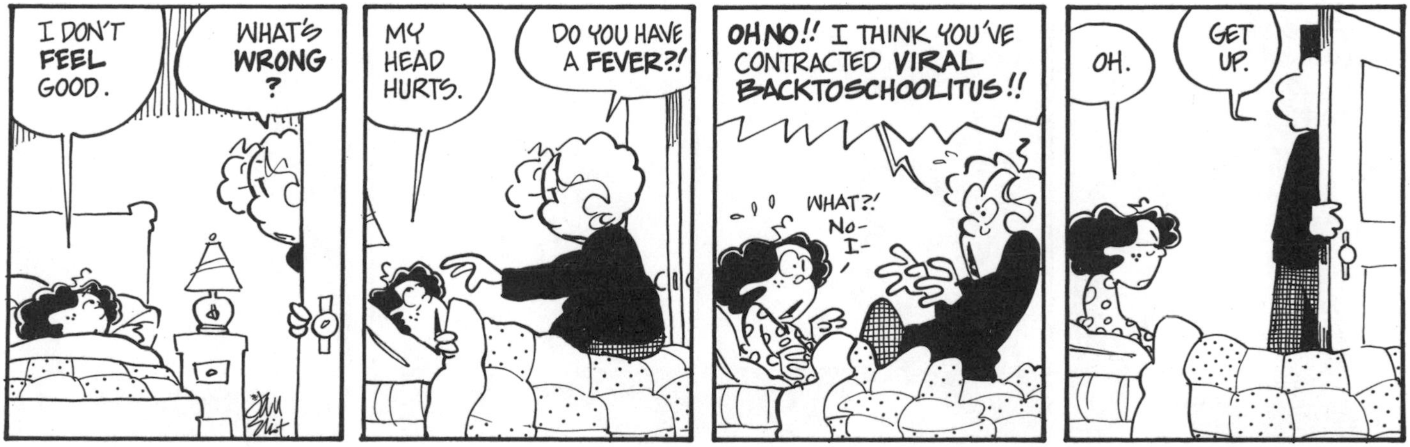
I DON'T FEEL GOOD.
WHAT'S WRONG?
MY HEAD HURTS.
DO YOU HAVE A FEVER?!
OH NO!! I THINK YOU'VE CONTRACTED VIRAL BACKTOSCHOOLITUS!!
WHAT?! NO- I-
OH.
GET UP.

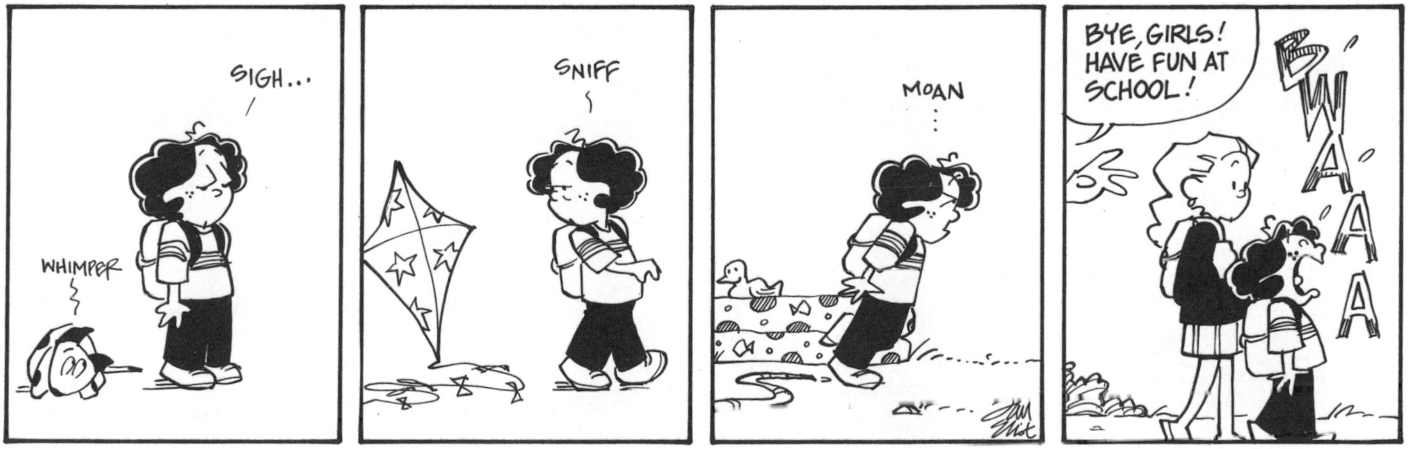
SIGH...
WHIMPER
SNIFF
MOAN
BYE, GIRLS! HAVE FUN AT SCHOOL!
BWAAAA

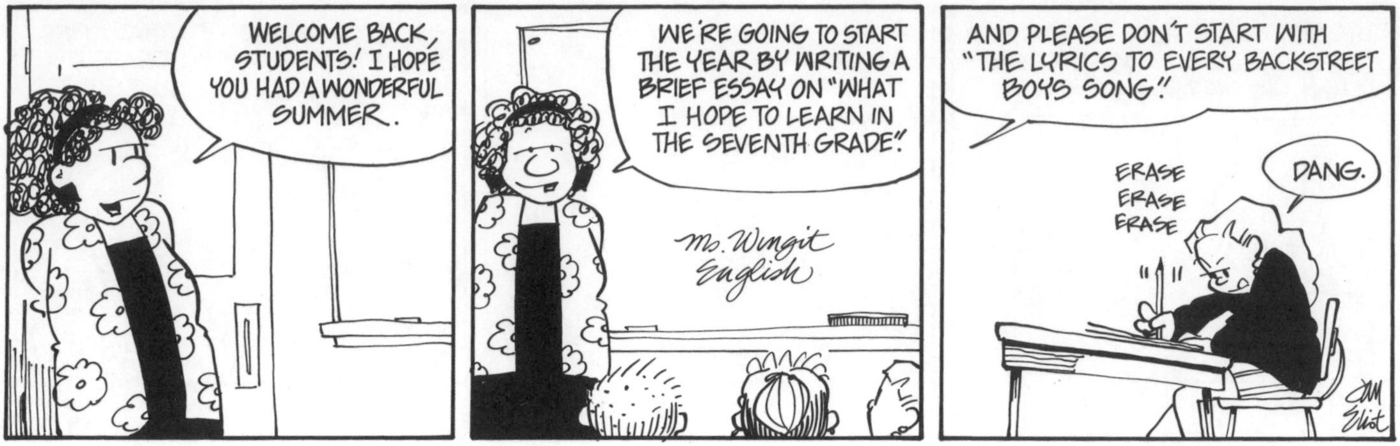
WELCOME BACK, STUDENTS! I HOPE YOU HAD A WONDERFUL SUMMER.
WE'RE GOING TO START THE YEAR BY WRITING A BRIEF ESSAY ON "WHAT I HOPE TO LEARN IN THE SEVENTH GRADE."
Ms. Wingit
English
AND PLEASE DON'T START WITH "THE LYRICS TO EVERY BACKSTREET BOYS SONG."
ERASE
ERASE
ERASE
DANG.

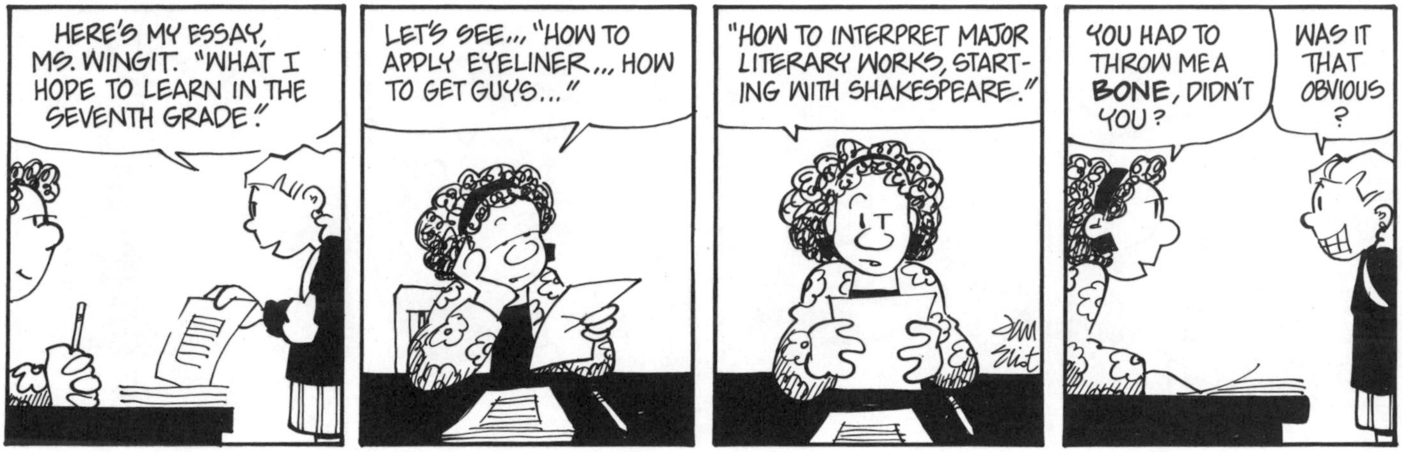
HERE'S MY ESSAY, MS. WINGIT. "WHAT I HOPE TO LEARN IN THE SEVENTH GRADE."
LET'S SEE... "HOW TO APPLY EYELINER... HOW TO GET GUYS..."
"HOW TO INTERPRET MAJOR LITERARY WORKS, STARTING WITH SHAKESPEARE."
YOU HAD TO THROW ME A **BONE**, DIDN'T YOU?
WAS IT THAT OBVIOUS?

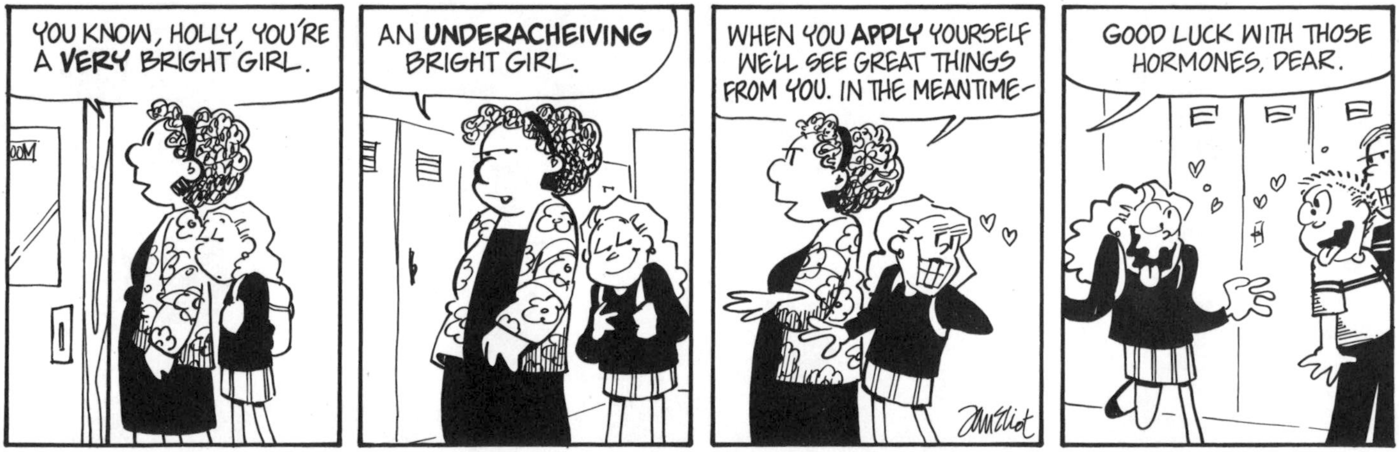
YOU KNOW, HOLLY, YOU'RE A **VERY** BRIGHT GIRL.
AN **UNDERACHEIVING** BRIGHT GIRL.
WHEN YOU **APPLY** YOURSELF WE'LL SEE GREAT THINGS FROM YOU. IN THE MEANTIME-
GOOD LUCK WITH THOSE HORMONES, DEAR.

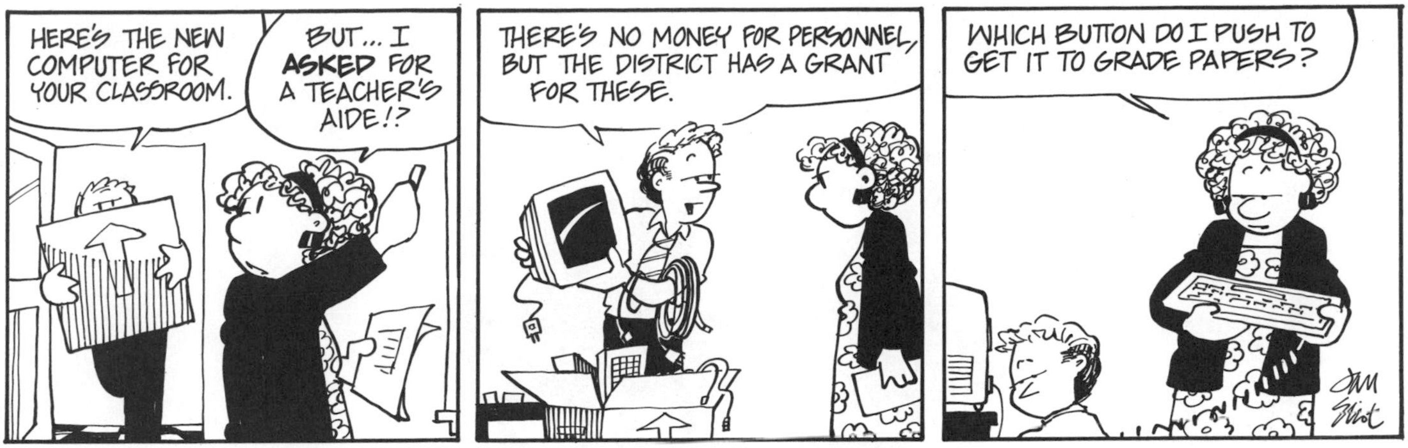
HERE'S THE NEW COMPUTER FOR YOUR CLASSROOM.
BUT... I **ASKED** FOR A TEACHER'S AIDE!?
THERE'S NO MONEY FOR PERSONNEL, BUT THE DISTRICT HAS A GRANT FOR THESE.
WHICH BUTTON DO I PUSH TO GET IT TO GRADE PAPERS?

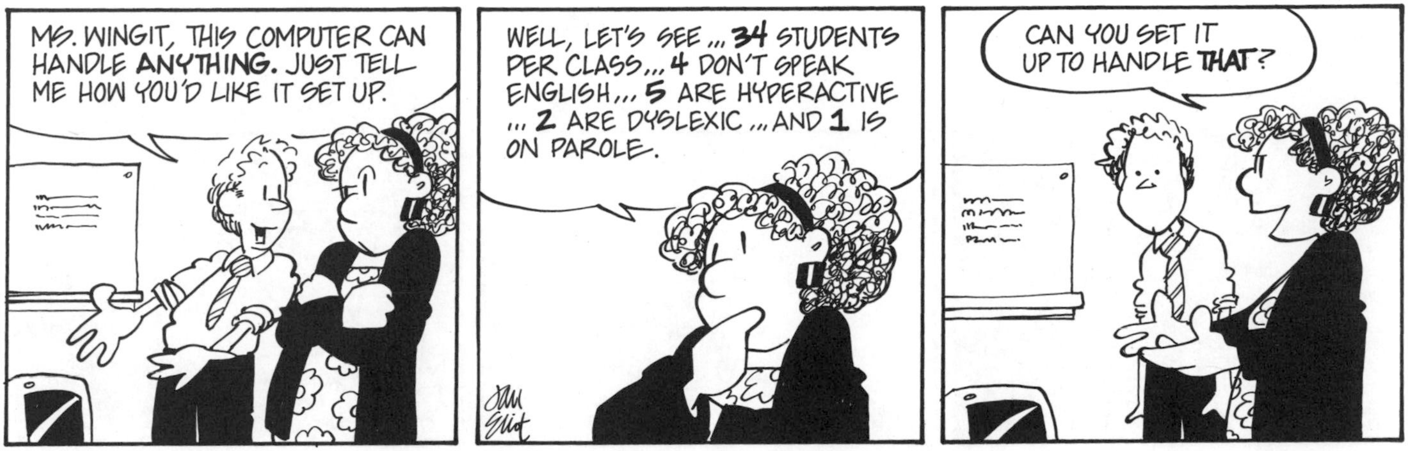
MS. WINGIT, THIS COMPUTER CAN HANDLE **ANYTHING.** JUST TELL ME HOW YOU'D LIKE IT SET UP.
WELL, LET'S SEE ... **34** STUDENTS PER CLASS... **4** DON'T SPEAK ENGLISH... **5** ARE HYPERACTIVE ... **2** ARE DYSLEXIC ... AND **1** IS ON PAROLE.
CAN YOU SET IT UP TO HANDLE **THAT**?

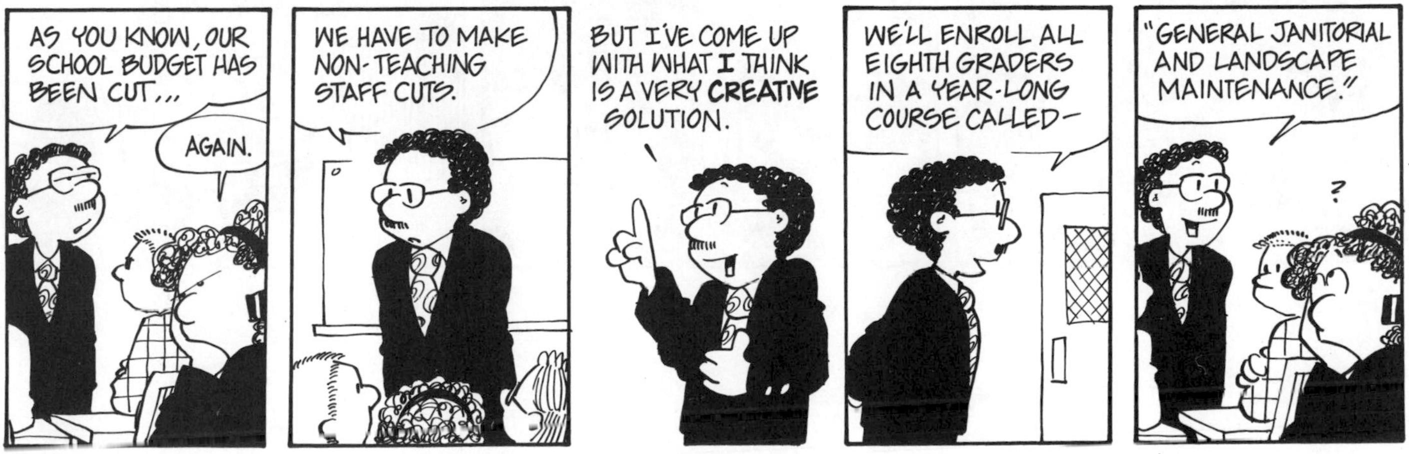
AS YOU KNOW, OUR SCHOOL BUDGET HAS BEEN CUT...
AGAIN.
WE HAVE TO MAKE NON-TEACHING STAFF CUTS.
BUT I'VE COME UP WITH WHAT **I** THINK IS A VERY **CREATIVE** SOLUTION.
WE'LL ENROLL ALL EIGHTH GRADERS IN A YEAR-LONG COURSE CALLED–
"GENERAL JANITORIAL AND LANDSCAPE MAINTENANCE."

Stone Soup

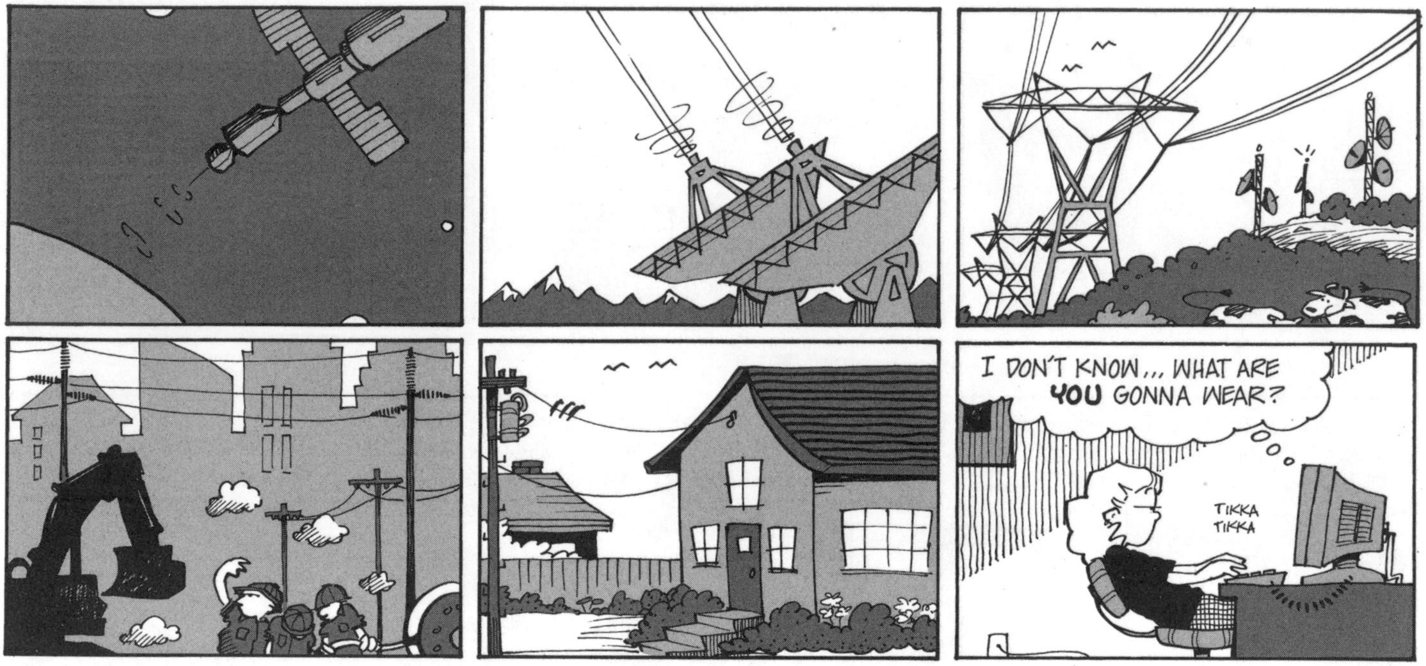
I DON'T KNOW... WHAT ARE YOU GONNA WEAR?
TIKKA TIKKA

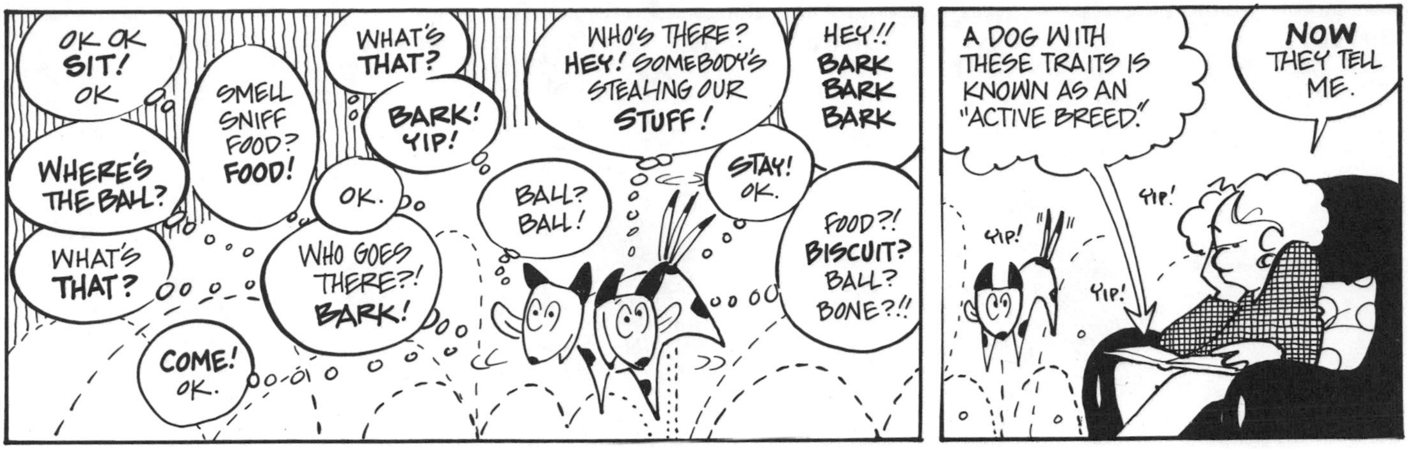
OK OK SIT! OK
WHERE'S THE BALL?
WHAT'S THAT?
COME! OK.
SMELL SNIFF FOOD? FOOD!
OK.
WHO GOES THERE?! BARK!
WHAT'S THAT?
BARK! YIP!
BALL? BALL!
WHO'S THERE? HEY! SOMEBODY'S STEALING OUR STUFF!
STAY! OK.
HEY!! BARK BARK BARK
FOOD?! BISCUIT? BALL? BONE?!!
A DOG WITH THESE TRAITS IS KNOWN AS AN "ACTIVE BREED."
NOW THEY TELL ME.
YIP!
YIP!
YIP!

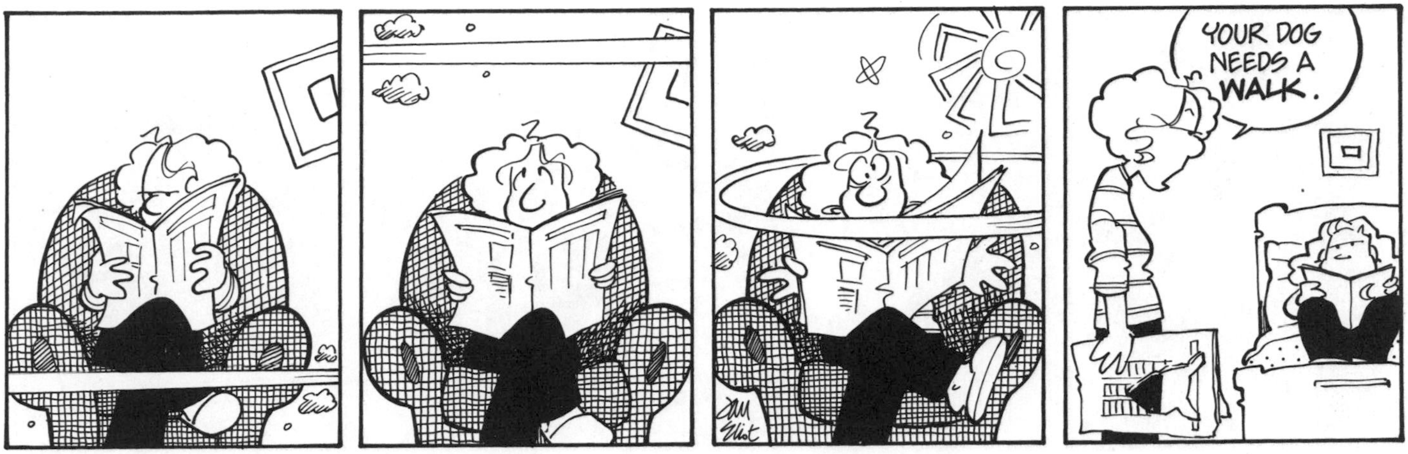
YOUR DOG NEEDS A WALK.

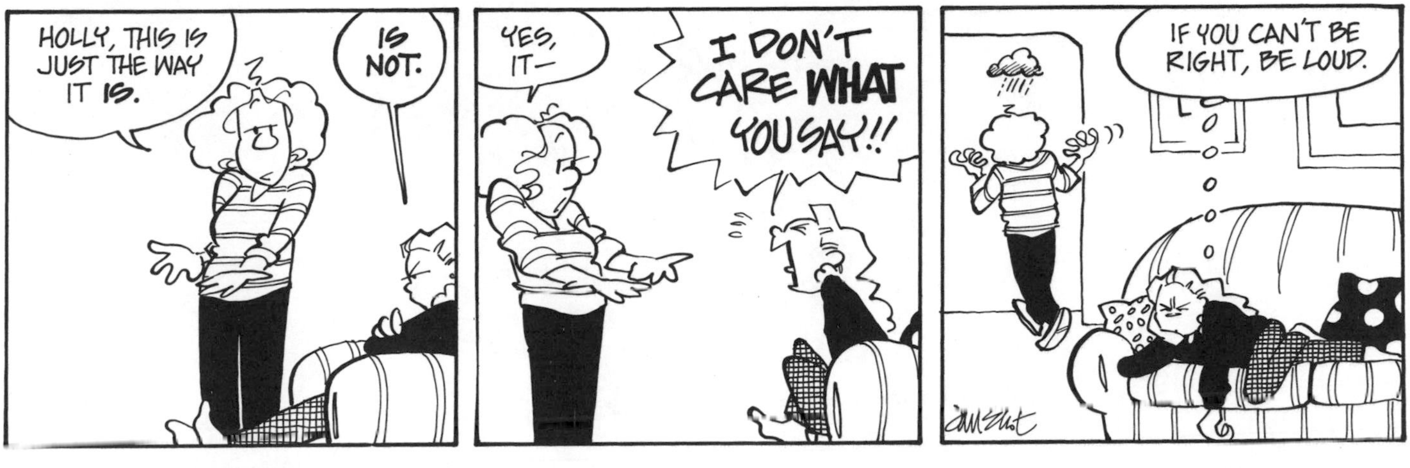
HOLLY, THIS IS JUST THE WAY IT IS.
IS NOT.
YES, IT—
I DON'T CARE WHAT YOU SAY!!
IF YOU CAN'T BE RIGHT, BE LOUD.

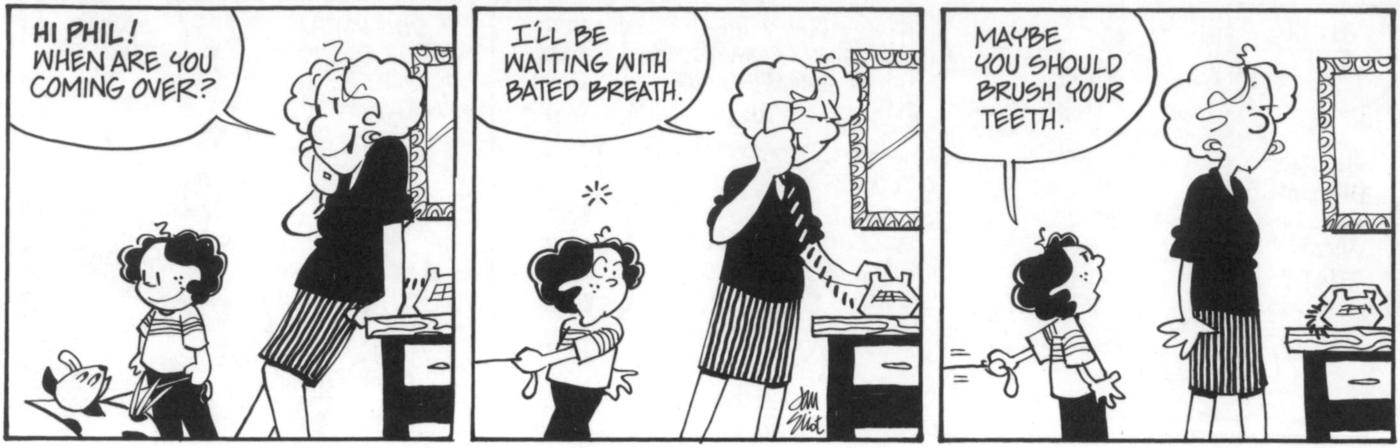
HI PHIL! WHEN ARE YOU COMING OVER?
I'LL BE WAITING WITH BATED BREATH.
MAYBE YOU SHOULD BRUSH YOUR TEETH.

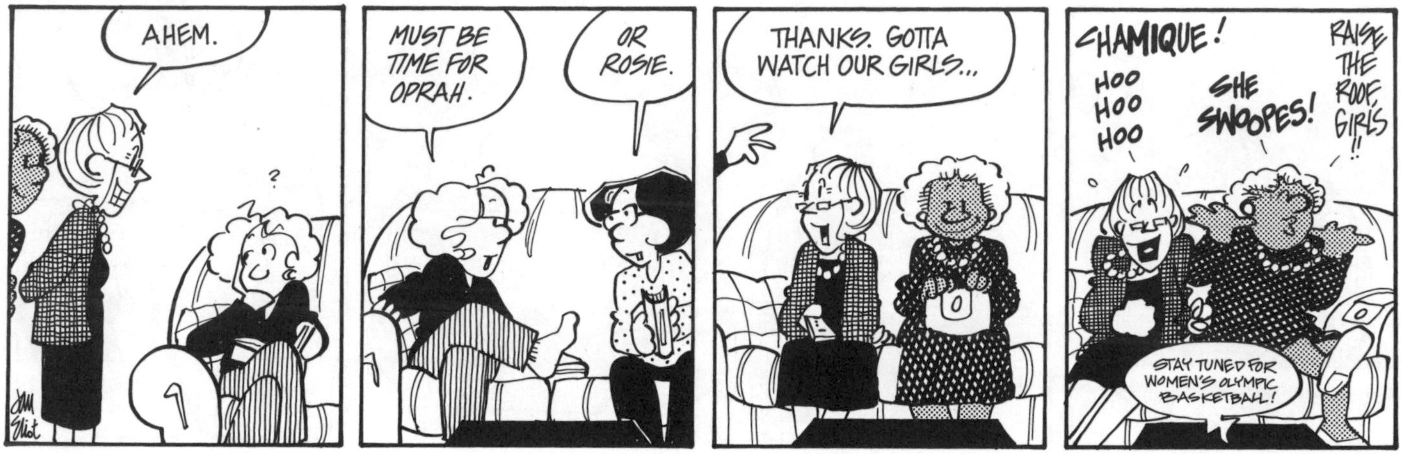
AHEM.
MUST BE TIME FOR OPRAH.
OR ROSIE.
THANKS. GOTTA WATCH OUR GIRLS...
SHAMIQUE!
HOO HOO HOO
SHE SWOOPES!
RAISE THE ROOF, GIRLS!!
STAY TUNED FOR WOMEN'S OLYMPIC BASKETBALL!

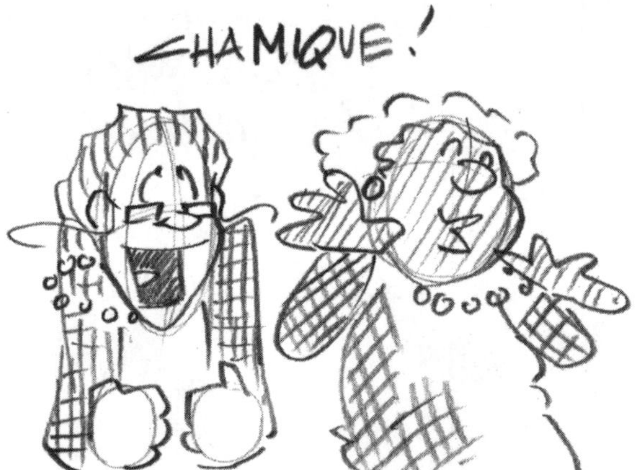
SHAMIQUE!

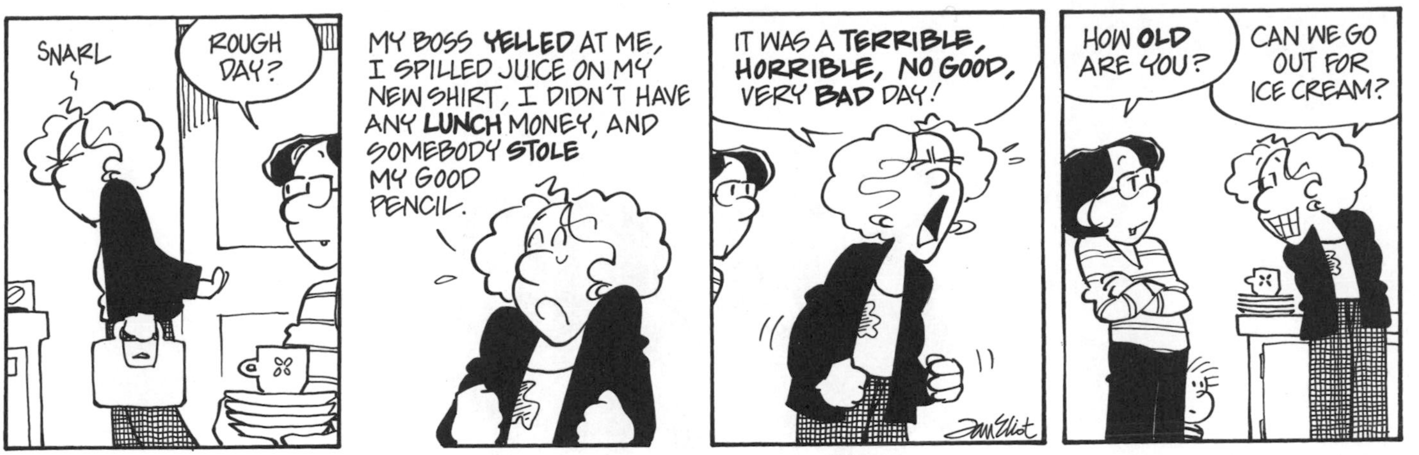
SNARL
ROUGH DAY?
MY BOSS YELLED AT ME, I SPILLED JUICE ON MY NEW SHIRT, I DIDN'T HAVE ANY LUNCH MONEY, AND SOMEBODY STOLE MY GOOD PENCIL.
IT WAS A TERRIBLE, HORRIBLE, NO GOOD, VERY BAD DAY!
HOW OLD ARE YOU?
CAN WE GO OUT FOR ICE CREAM?

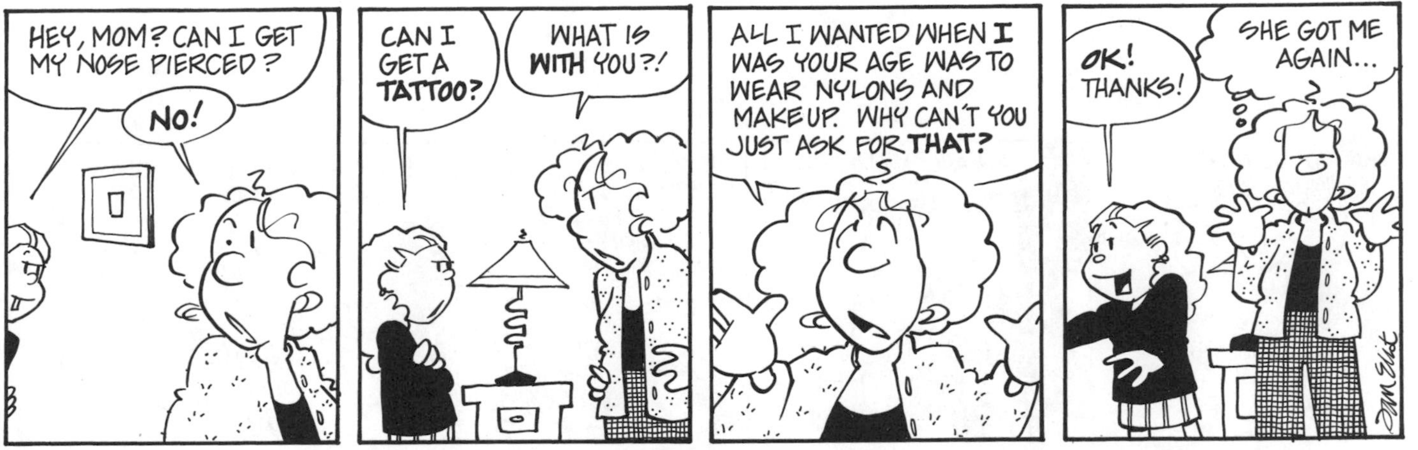
HEY, MOM? CAN I GET MY NOSE PIERCED?
NO!
CAN I GET A TATTOO?
WHAT IS WITH YOU?!
ALL I WANTED WHEN I WAS YOUR AGE WAS TO WEAR NYLONS AND MAKEUP. WHY CAN'T YOU JUST ASK FOR THAT?
OK! THANKS!
SHE GOT ME AGAIN...

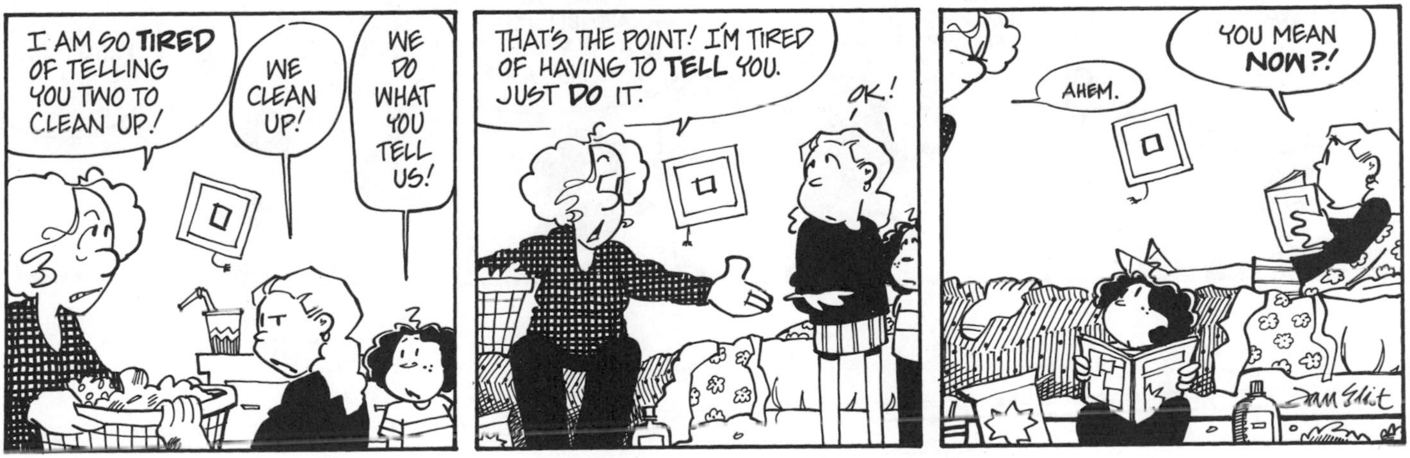
I AM SO TIRED OF TELLING YOU TWO TO CLEAN UP!
WE CLEAN UP!
WE DO WHAT YOU TELL US!
THAT'S THE POINT! I'M TIRED OF HAVING TO TELL YOU. JUST DO IT.
OK!
AHEM.
YOU MEAN NOW?!

Stone Soup

WHAT DO YOU WANT TO BE WHEN YOU GROW UP?

AN ARCHAEOLOGIST.

WE READ ABOUT IT IN SCHOOL TODAY! THEY DEVOTE THEIR LIVES TO DISCOVERING LOST CIVILIZATIONS!

THEY FIND TREASURE..., MUMMIES..., WHOLE CITIES SOMETIMES!!

WOW.

THE WORLD IS HUGE, ALIX. I CAN'T **WAIT** TO EXPLORE IT!

HI, GIRLS! HOW WAS SCHOOL?

MOM, **PUHLEASE** I'M **EXHAUSTED** JUST WANT TO **VEG OUT** LEAVE ME **ALONE**.

SIGHHH... THAT GIRL...

SOMETIMES I WONDER **WHAT** WILL BECOME OF HER.

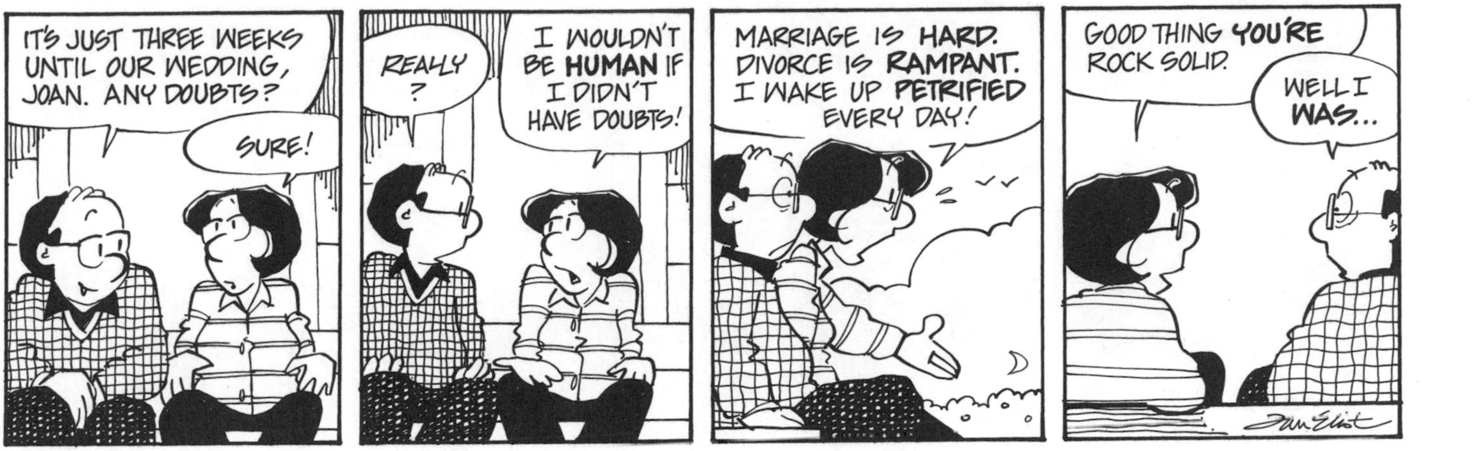
IT'S JUST THREE WEEKS UNTIL OUR WEDDING, JOAN. ANY DOUBTS?
SURE!
REALLY?
I WOULDN'T BE **HUMAN** IF I DIDN'T HAVE DOUBTS!
MARRIAGE IS **HARD.** DIVORCE IS **RAMPANT.** I WAKE UP **PETRIFIED** EVERY DAY!
GOOD THING **YOU'RE** ROCK SOLID.
WELL I **WAS...**

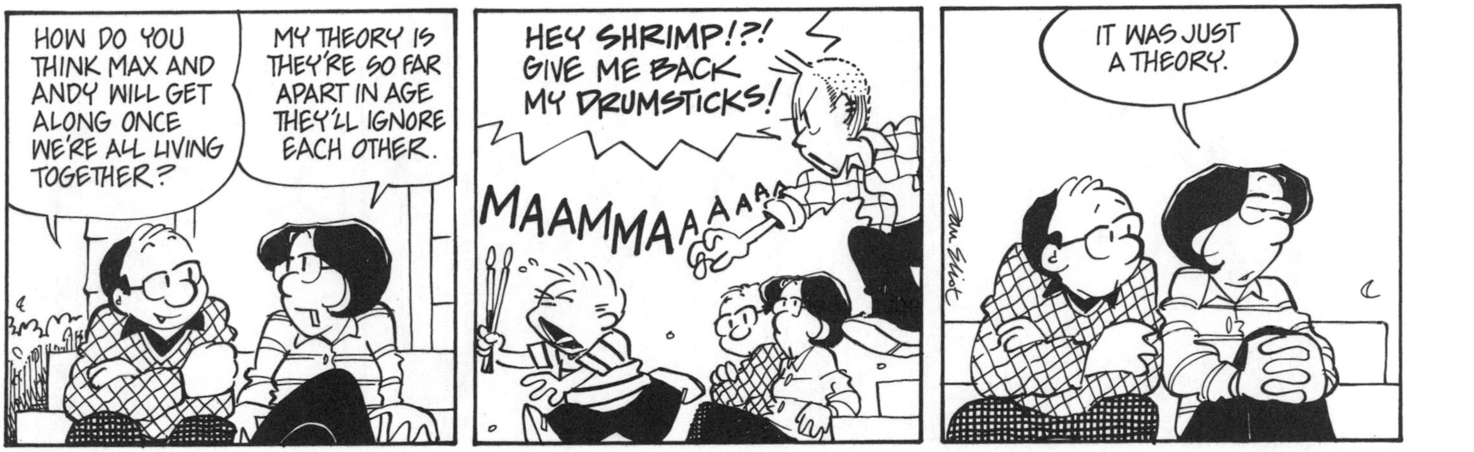
HOW DO YOU THINK MAX AND ANDY WILL GET ALONG ONCE WE'RE ALL LIVING TOGETHER?
MY THEORY IS THEY'RE SO FAR APART IN AGE THEY'LL IGNORE EACH OTHER.
HEY **SHRIMP!?!** GIVE ME BACK MY **DRUMSTICKS!**
MAAMMAAAAAA
IT WAS JUST A THEORY.

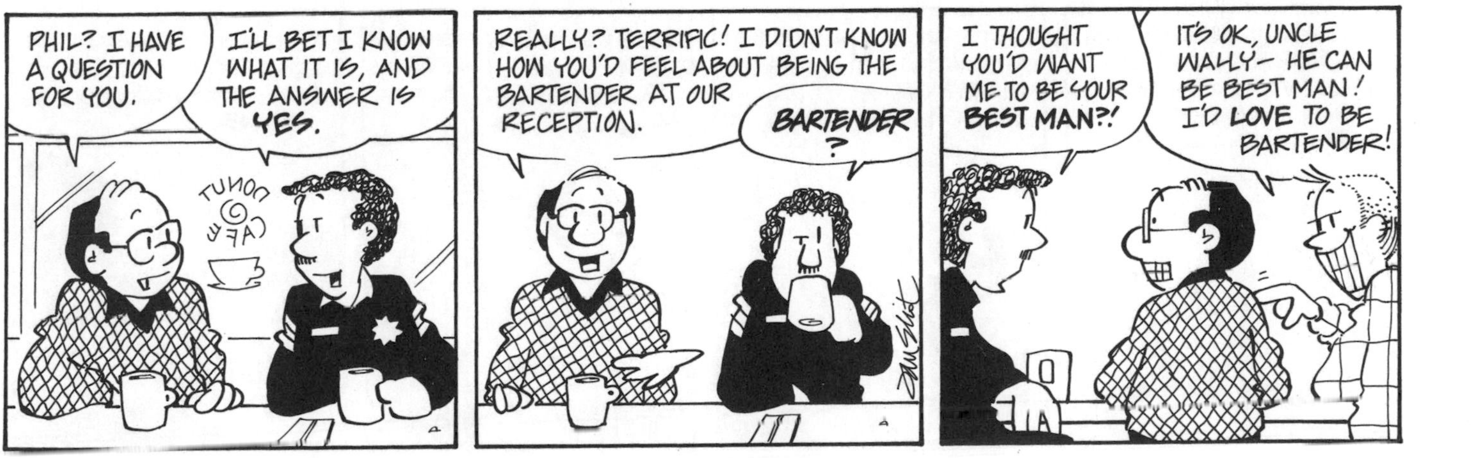
PHIL? I HAVE A QUESTION FOR YOU.
I'LL BET I KNOW WHAT IT IS, AND THE ANSWER IS **YES.**
REALLY? TERRIFIC! I DIDN'T KNOW HOW YOU'D FEEL ABOUT BEING THE BARTENDER AT OUR RECEPTION.
BARTENDER?
I THOUGHT YOU'D WANT ME TO BE YOUR **BEST MAN?!**
IT'S OK, UNCLE WALLY— HE CAN BE BEST MAN! I'D **LOVE** TO BE BARTENDER!

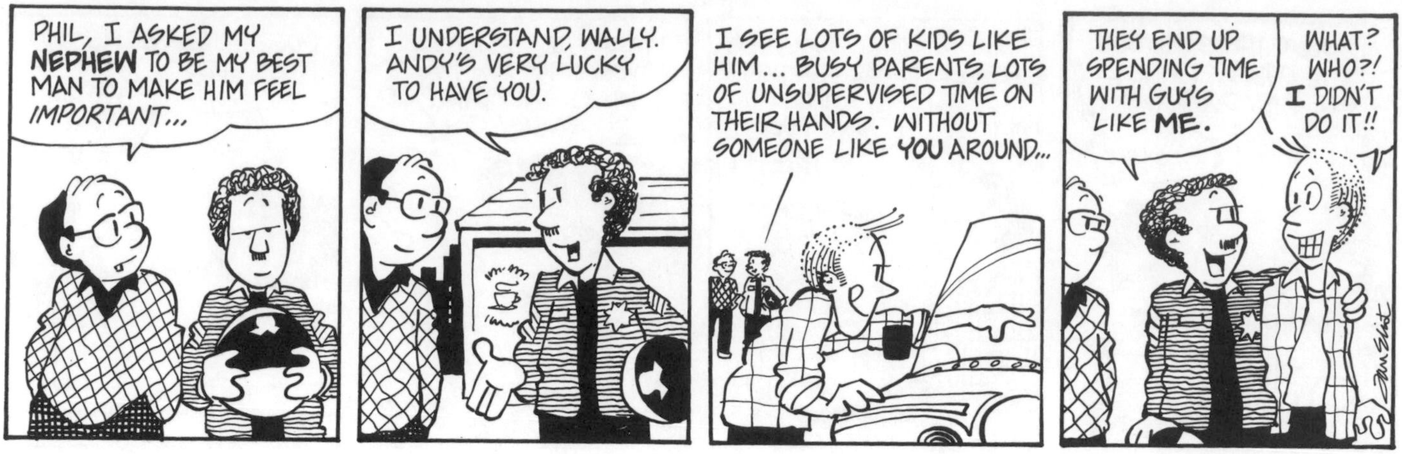
PHIL, I ASKED MY **NEPHEW** TO BE MY BEST MAN TO MAKE HIM FEEL *IMPORTANT...*
I UNDERSTAND, WALLY. ANDY'S VERY LUCKY TO HAVE YOU.
I SEE LOTS OF KIDS LIKE HIM... BUSY PARENTS, LOTS OF UNSUPERVISED TIME ON THEIR HANDS. WITHOUT SOMEONE LIKE **YOU** AROUND...
THEY END UP SPENDING TIME WITH GUYS LIKE **ME.**
WHAT? WHO?! **I** DIDN'T DO IT!!

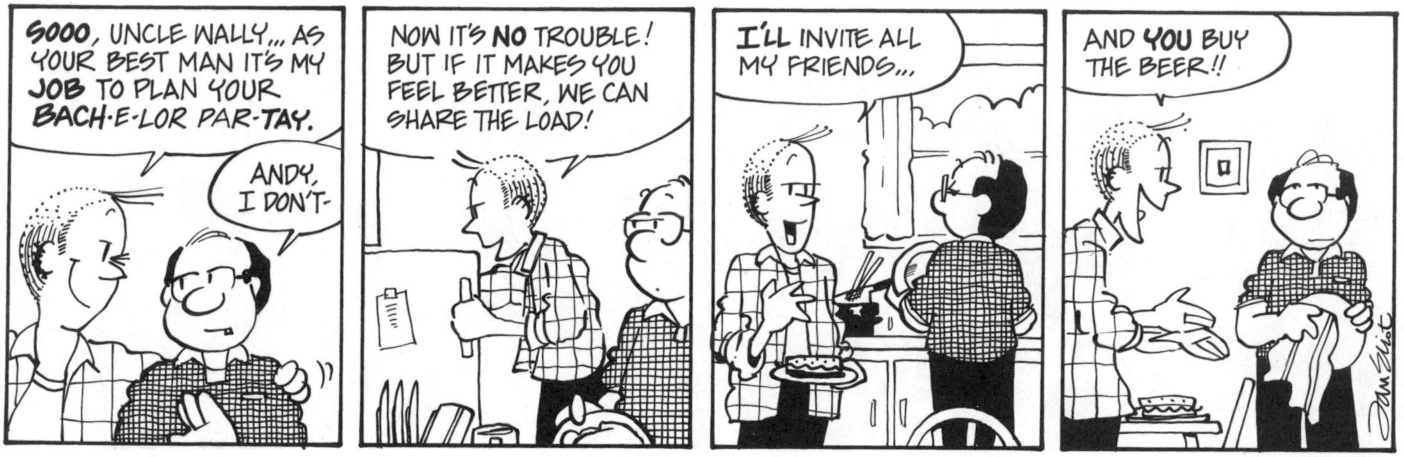
SOOO, UNCLE WALLY... AS YOUR BEST MAN IT'S MY **JOB** TO PLAN YOUR **BACH**-E-LOR PAR-**TAY.**
ANDY, I DON'T-
NOW IT'S **NO** TROUBLE! BUT IF IT MAKES YOU FEEL BETTER, WE CAN SHARE THE LOAD!
I'LL INVITE ALL MY FRIENDS...
AND **YOU** BUY THE BEER!!

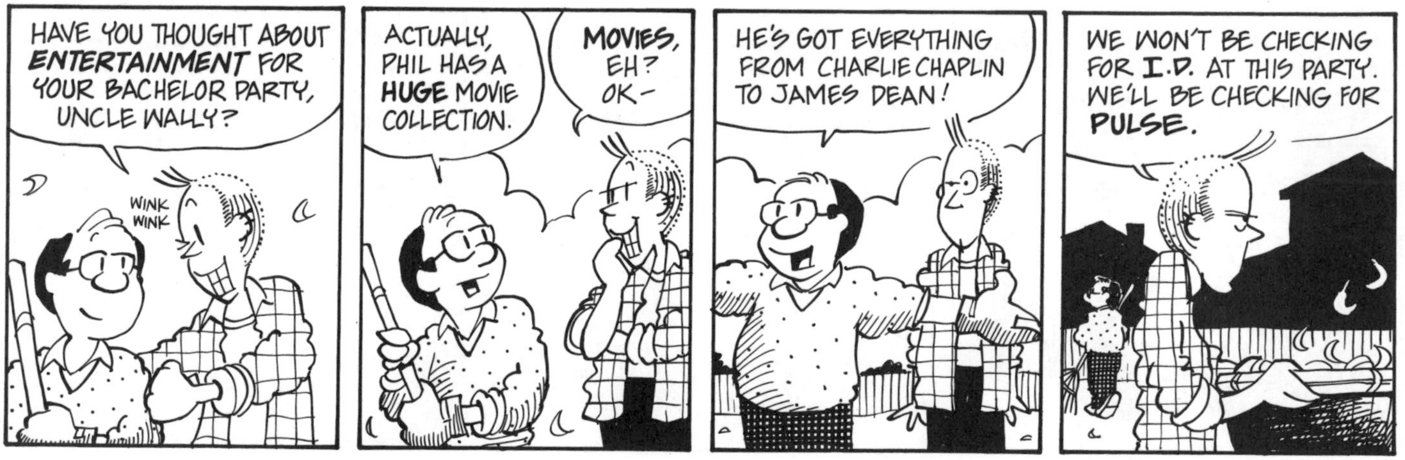
HAVE YOU THOUGHT ABOUT ***ENTERTAINMENT*** FOR YOUR BACHELOR PARTY, UNCLE WALLY?
WINK WINK
ACTUALLY, PHIL HAS A **HUGE** MOVIE COLLECTION.
MOVIES, EH? OK-
HE'S GOT EVERYTHING FROM CHARLIE CHAPLIN TO JAMES DEAN!
WE WON'T BE CHECKING FOR **I.D.** AT THIS PARTY. WE'LL BE CHECKING FOR **PULSE.**

Stone Soup

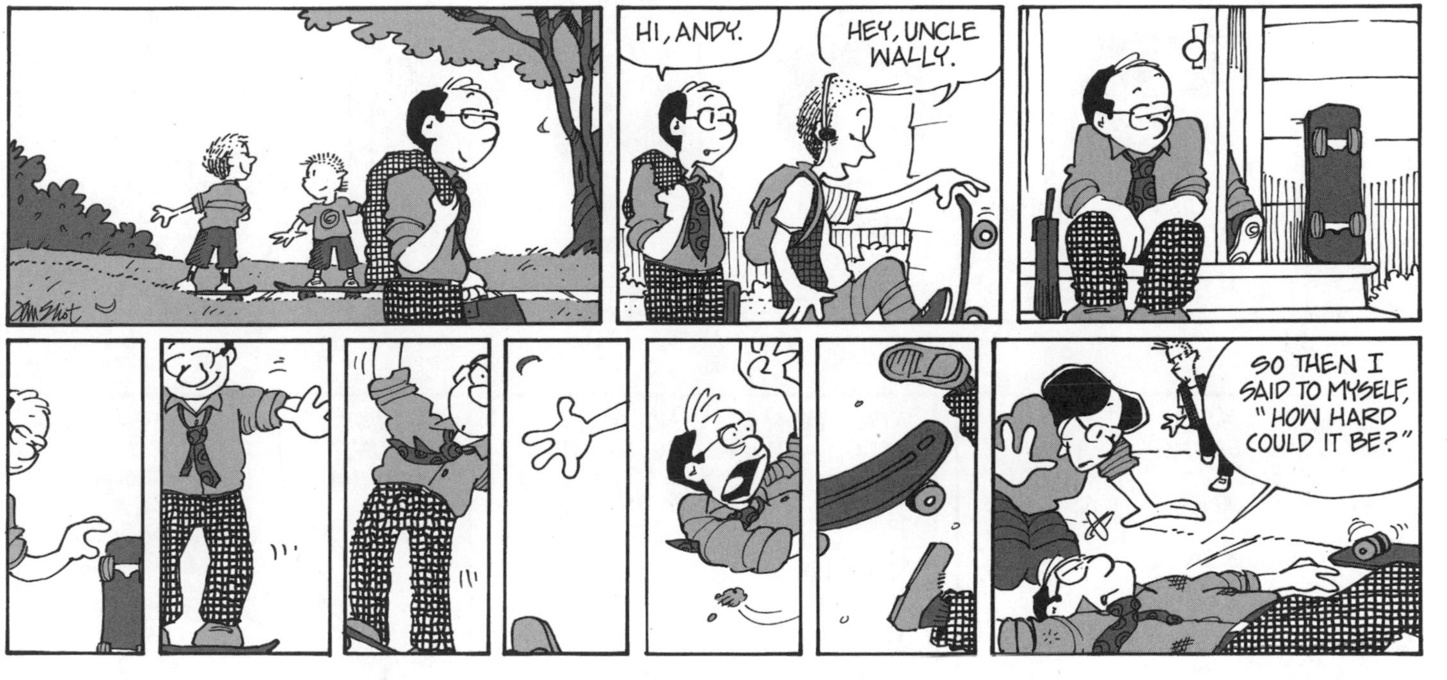
HI, ANDY.
HEY, UNCLE WALLY.
SO THEN I SAID TO MYSELF, "HOW HARD COULD IT BE?"

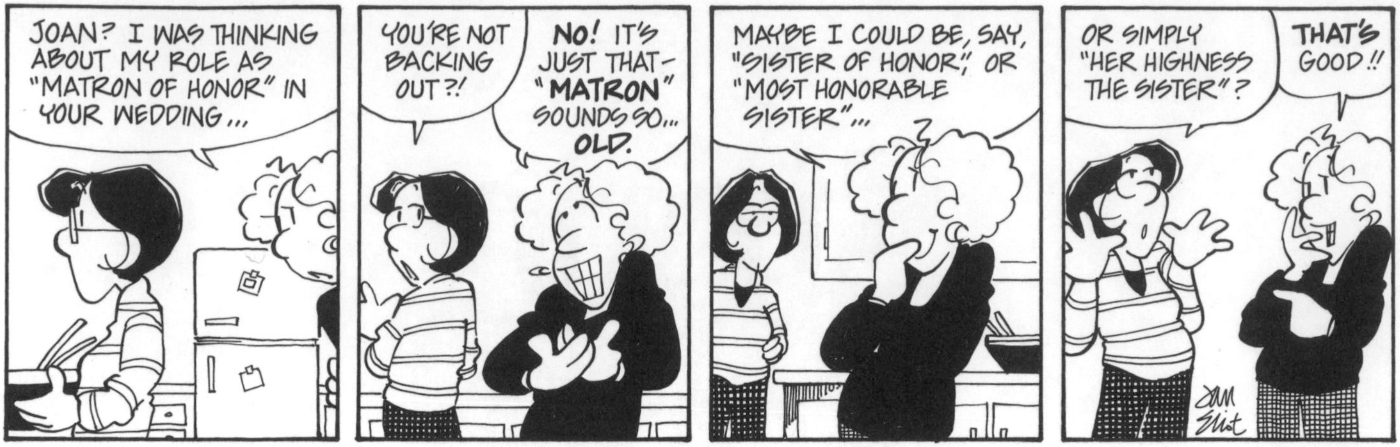
JOAN? I WAS THINKING ABOUT MY ROLE AS "MATRON OF HONOR" IN YOUR WEDDING...
YOU'RE NOT BACKING OUT?!
NO! IT'S JUST THAT- "MATRON" SOUNDS SO... OLD.
MAYBE I COULD BE, SAY, "SISTER OF HONOR," OR "MOST HONORABLE SISTER"...
OR SIMPLY "HER HIGHNESS THE SISTER"?
THAT'S GOOD!!

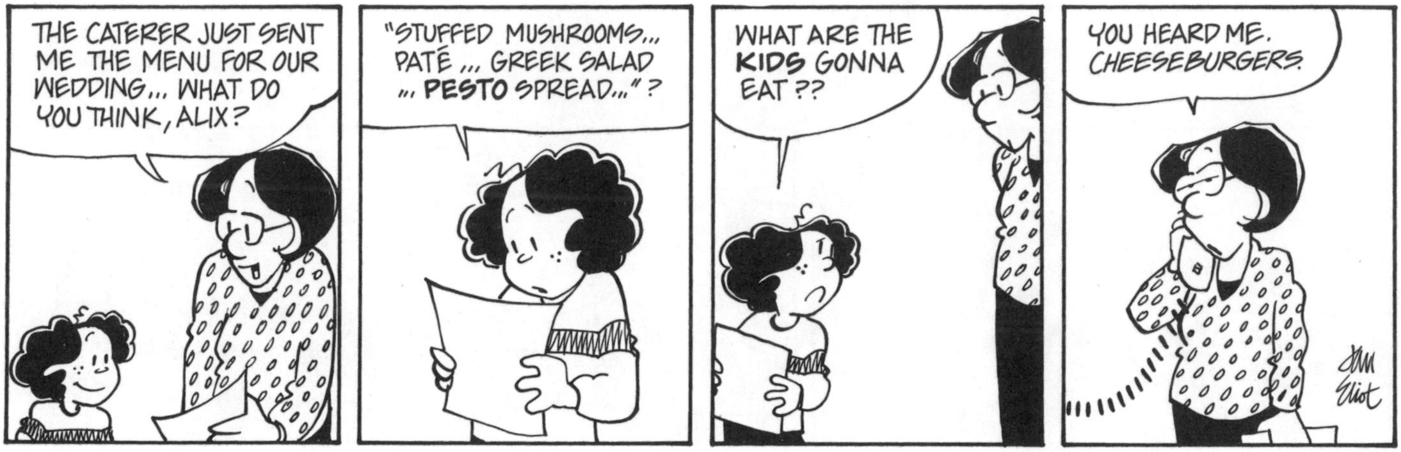
THE CATERER JUST SENT ME THE MENU FOR OUR WEDDING... WHAT DO YOU THINK, ALIX?
"STUFFED MUSHROOMS... PATÉ ... GREEK SALAD ... PESTO SPREAD..."?
WHAT ARE THE KIDS GONNA EAT??
YOU HEARD ME. CHEESEBURGERS.

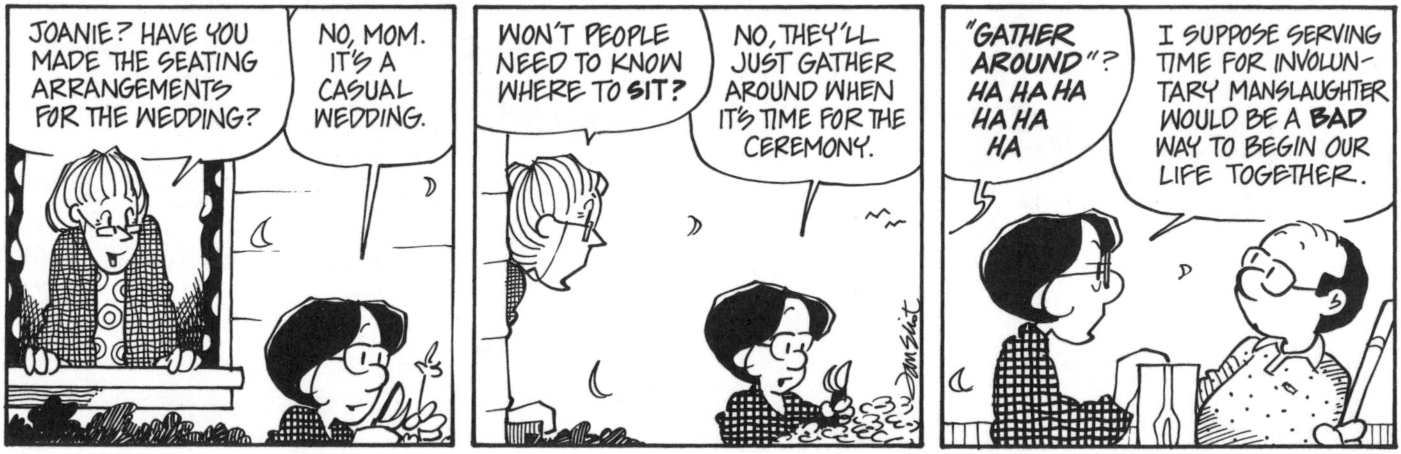
JOANIE? HAVE YOU MADE THE SEATING ARRANGEMENTS FOR THE WEDDING?
NO, MOM. IT'S A CASUAL WEDDING.
WON'T PEOPLE NEED TO KNOW WHERE TO SIT?
NO, THEY'LL JUST GATHER AROUND WHEN IT'S TIME FOR THE CEREMONY.
"GATHER AROUND"? HA HA HA HA HA HA
I SUPPOSE SERVING TIME FOR INVOLUNTARY MANSLAUGHTER WOULD BE A BAD WAY TO BEGIN OUR LIFE TOGETHER.

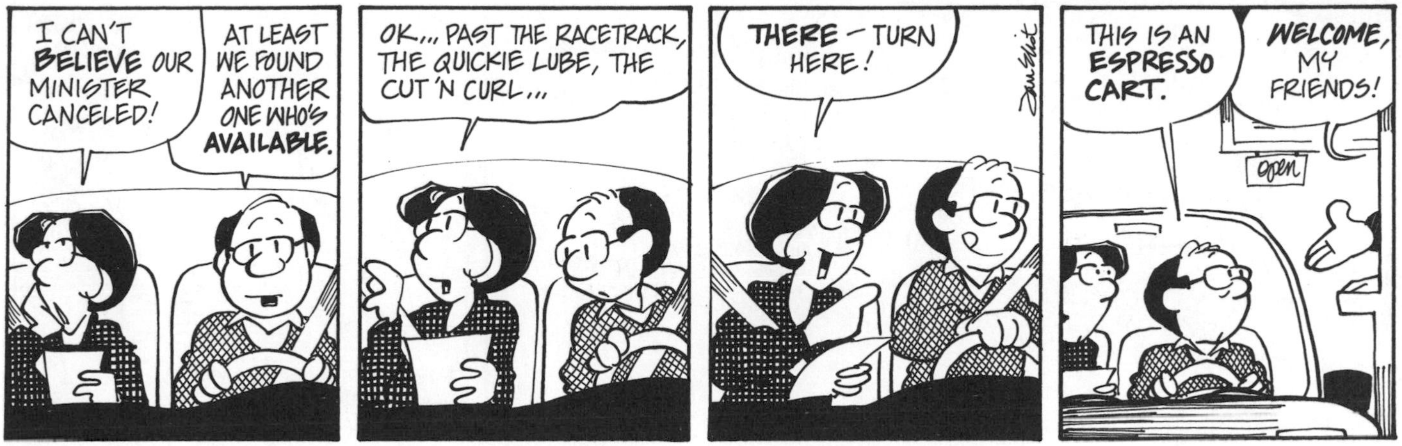
I CAN'T **BELIEVE** OUR MINISTER CANCELED!
AT LEAST WE FOUND ANOTHER ONE WHO'S **AVAILABLE**.
OK,,, PAST THE RACETRACK, THE QUICKIE LUBE, THE CUT 'N CURL,,,
THERE – TURN HERE!
THIS IS AN **ESPRESSO CART.**
WELCOME, MY FRIENDS!

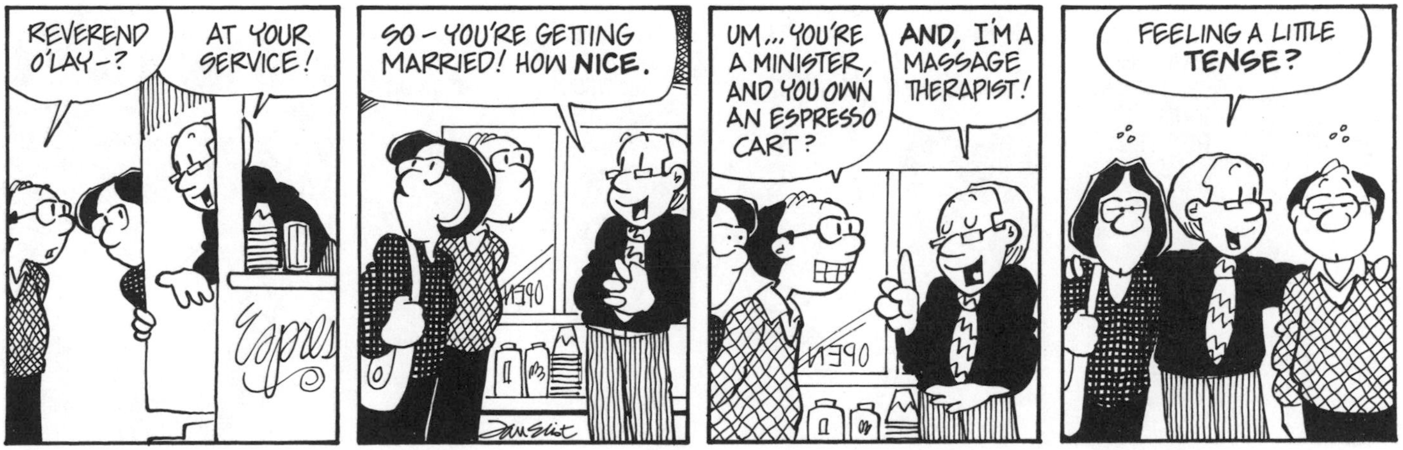
REVEREND O'LAY – ?
AT YOUR SERVICE!
SO – YOU'RE GETTING MARRIED! HOW **NICE**.
UM... YOU'RE A MINISTER, AND YOU OWN AN ESPRESSO CART?
AND, I'M A MASSAGE THERAPIST!
FEELING A LITTLE **TENSE**?

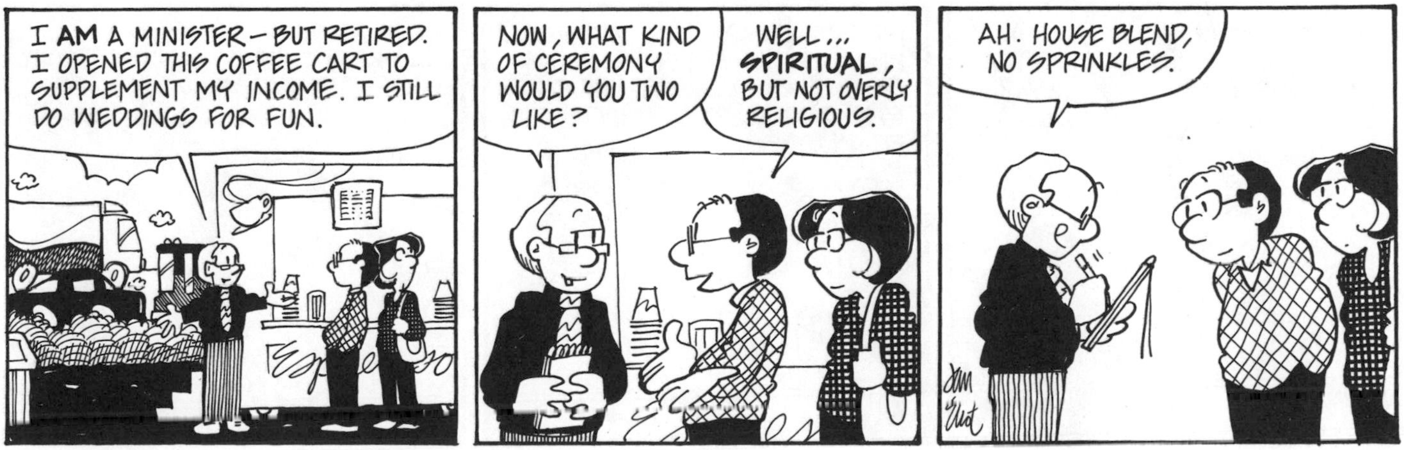
I **AM** A MINISTER – BUT RETIRED. I OPENED THIS COFFEE CART TO SUPPLEMENT MY INCOME. I STILL DO WEDDINGS FOR FUN.
NOW, WHAT KIND OF CEREMONY WOULD YOU TWO LIKE?
WELL... **SPIRITUAL**, BUT NOT OVERLY RELIGIOUS.
AH. HOUSE BLEND, NO SPRINKLES.

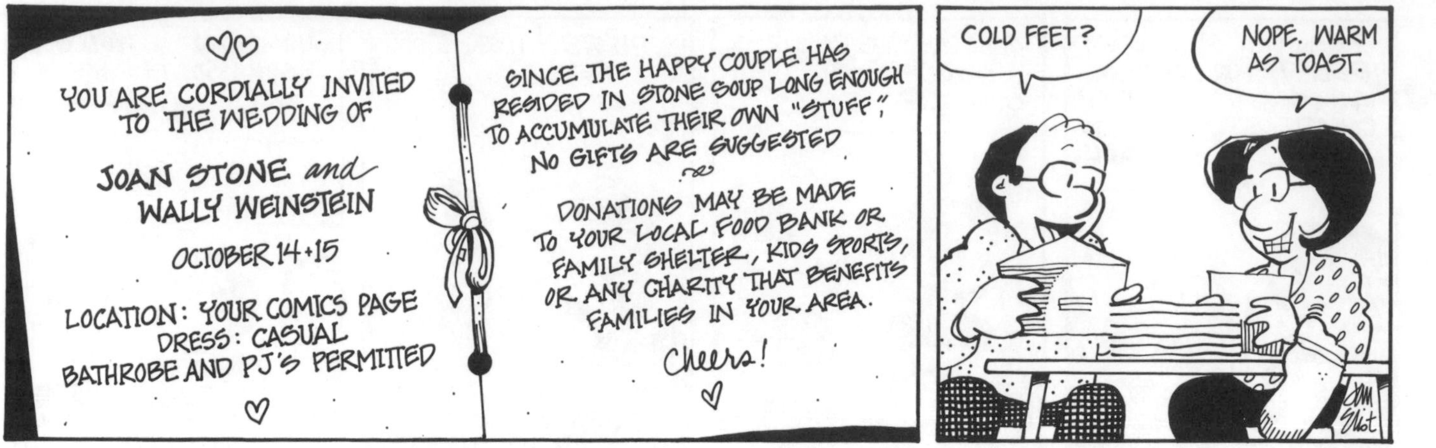
YOU ARE CORDIALLY INVITED TO THE WEDDING OF
JOAN STONE and WALLY WEINSTEIN
OCTOBER 14+15
LOCATION: YOUR COMICS PAGE
DRESS: CASUAL
BATHROBE AND PJ'S PERMITTED
SINCE THE HAPPY COUPLE HAS RESIDED IN STONE SOUP LONG ENOUGH TO ACCUMULATE THEIR OWN "STUFF," NO GIFTS ARE SUGGESTED
DONATIONS MAY BE MADE TO YOUR LOCAL FOOD BANK OR FAMILY SHELTER, KIDS SPORTS, OR ANY CHARITY THAT BENEFITS FAMILIES IN YOUR AREA.
Cheers!
COLD FEET?
NOPE. WARM AS TOAST.

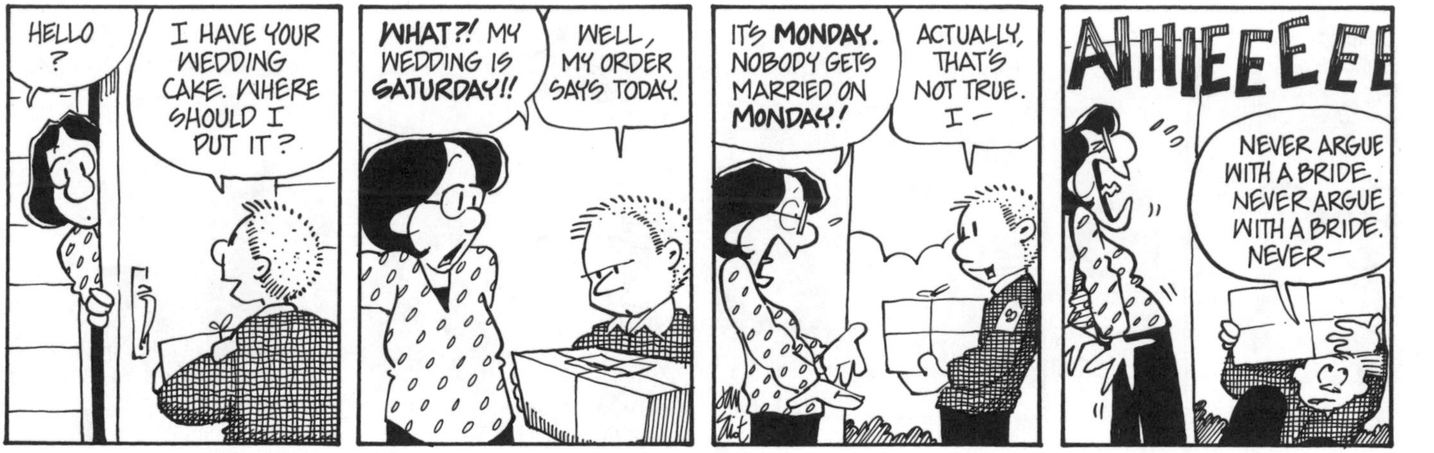
HELLO ?
I HAVE YOUR WEDDING CAKE. WHERE SHOULD I PUT IT?
WHAT?! MY WEDDING IS SATURDAY!!
WELL, MY ORDER SAYS TODAY.
IT'S MONDAY. NOBODY GETS MARRIED ON MONDAY!
ACTUALLY, THAT'S NOT TRUE. I—
AIIIEEEEE
NEVER ARGUE WITH A BRIDE. NEVER ARGUE WITH A BRIDE. NEVER—

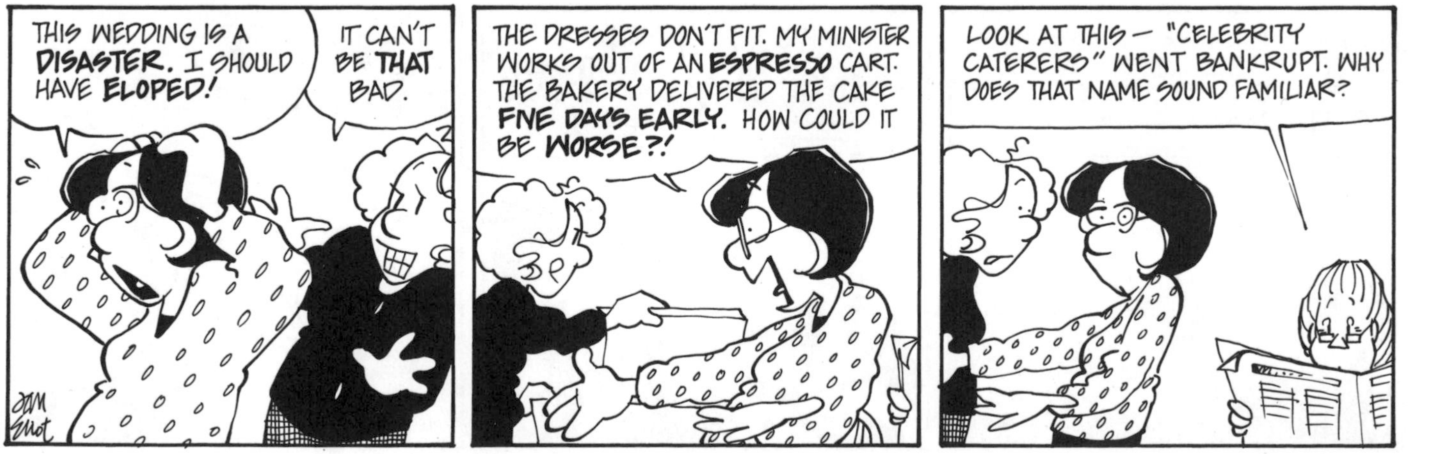
THIS WEDDING IS A DISASTER. I SHOULD HAVE ELOPED!
IT CAN'T BE THAT BAD.
THE DRESSES DON'T FIT. MY MINISTER WORKS OUT OF AN ESPRESSO CART. THE BAKERY DELIVERED THE CAKE FIVE DAYS EARLY. HOW COULD IT BE WORSE?!
LOOK AT THIS — "CELEBRITY CATERERS" WENT BANKRUPT. WHY DOES THAT NAME SOUND FAMILIAR?

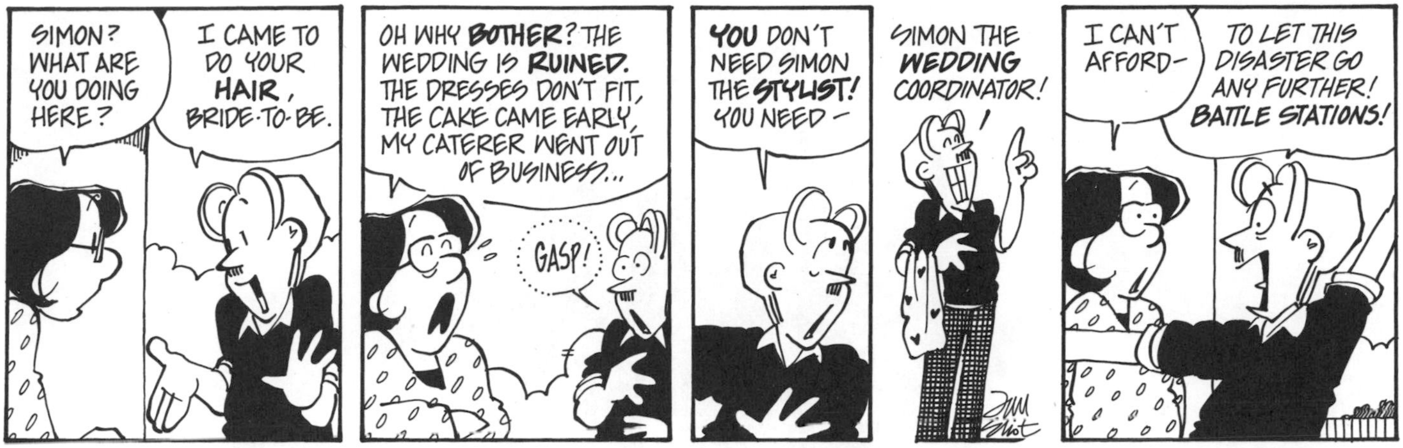
SIMON? WHAT ARE YOU DOING HERE?
I CAME TO DO YOUR HAIR, BRIDE-TO-BE.
OH WHY BOTHER? THE WEDDING IS RUINED. THE DRESSES DON'T FIT, THE CAKE CAME EARLY, MY CATERER WENT OUT OF BUSINESS...
GASP!
YOU DON'T NEED SIMON THE STYLIST! YOU NEED –
SIMON THE WEDDING COORDINATOR!
I CAN'T AFFORD–
TO LET THIS DISASTER GO ANY FURTHER! BATTLE STATIONS!

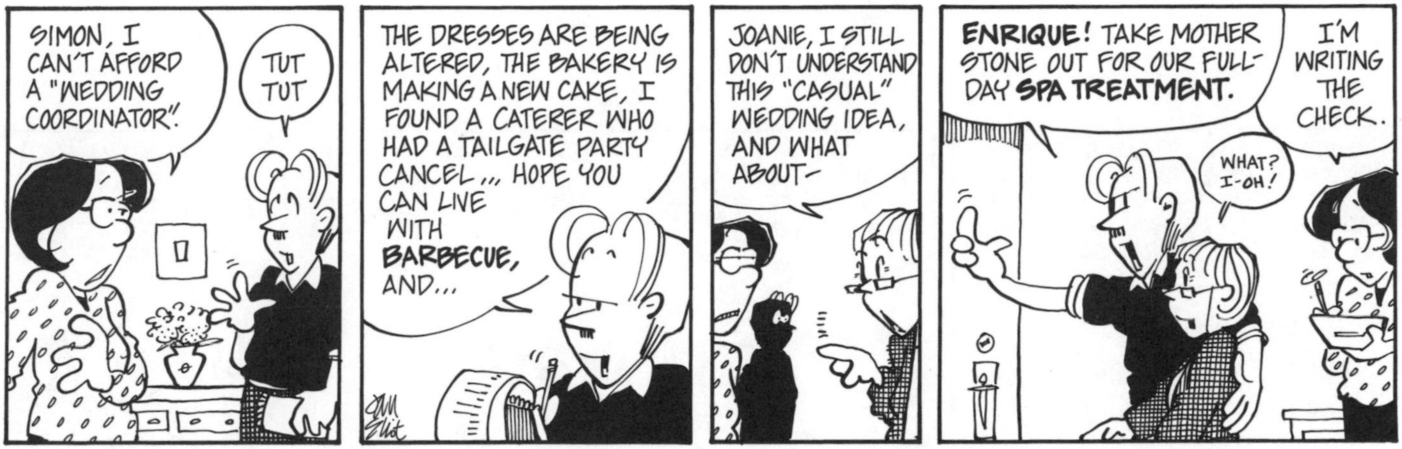
SIMON, I CAN'T AFFORD A "WEDDING COORDINATOR".
TUT TUT
THE DRESSES ARE BEING ALTERED, THE BAKERY IS MAKING A NEW CAKE, I FOUND A CATERER WHO HAD A TAILGATE PARTY CANCEL... HOPE YOU CAN LIVE WITH BARBECUE, AND...
JOANIE, I STILL DON'T UNDERSTAND THIS "CASUAL" WEDDING IDEA, AND WHAT ABOUT–
ENRIQUE! TAKE MOTHER STONE OUT FOR OUR FULL-DAY SPA TREATMENT.
WHAT? I–OH!
I'M WRITING THE CHECK.

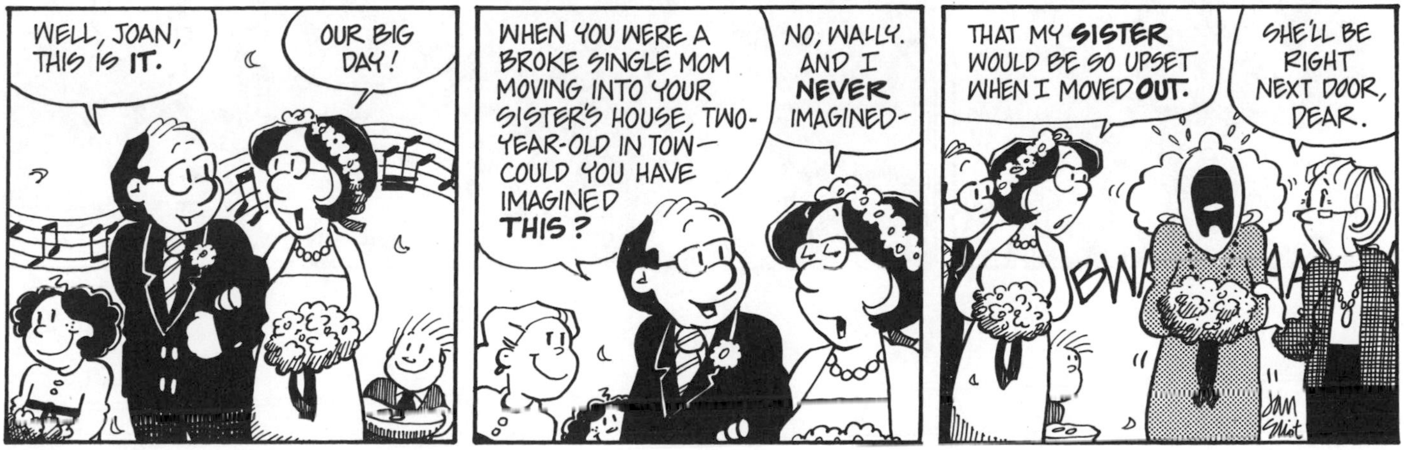
WELL, JOAN, THIS IS IT.
OUR BIG DAY!
WHEN YOU WERE A BROKE SINGLE MOM MOVING INTO YOUR SISTER'S HOUSE, TWO-YEAR-OLD IN TOW– COULD YOU HAVE IMAGINED THIS?
NO, WALLY. AND I NEVER IMAGINED–
THAT MY SISTER WOULD BE SO UPSET WHEN I MOVED OUT.
BWA AA
SHE'LL BE RIGHT NEXT DOOR, DEAR.

Stone Soup

"JUST AS TWO DIFFERENT THREADS WOVEN IN OPPOSITE DIRECTIONS CAN FORM A BEAUTIFUL TAPESTRY, SO CAN TWO LIVES BE WOVEN TOGETHER TO FORM A BEAUTIFUL—"
DO YOU TWO REALLY KNOW WHAT YOU'RE GETTING INTO?
WE DO.
IF PEOPLE REALLY KNEW WHAT THEY WERE GETTING INTO, THEY'D NEVER DO ANYTHING.

To follow the continuing adventures of the *Stone Soup* clan, follow the strip in your daily paper or online at **www.ucomics.com**.

Also by Jan Eliot:

Stone Soup *The First Collection of the Syndicated Cartoon* from Andrews McMeel Publishing

You Can't Say Boobs On Sunday *The Second Collection of the Syndicated Cartoon Stone Soup* from Four Panel Press

Stone Soup the Comic Strip *The Third Collection of the Syndicated Cartoon* from Four Panel Press

Stone Soup books are available through your local or online bookstore, and at www.stonesoupcartoons.com.

Stone Soup merchandise can be purchased at **www.cafepress.com**.